ACCURIZING THE FACTORY RIFLE

by M.L. McPherson

Published by Precision Shooting, Inc.

© Copyright 1999 by Precision Shooting, Inc.

Second printing, November 2001

Published by: Precision Shooting, Inc.
222 McKee Street
Manchester, CT 06040

DISCLAIMER NOTICE
Throughout these pages appear discussions by the author regarding such topics as handloads and firearms alterations…which have obviously proven to be safe in the author's own experiences. Neither the writer nor the publication make any representation or warranty as to the safeness of loading information or firearms alterations when applied to other rifles. There are a myriad of circumstances that may make your firearm different than the ones discussed in these pages. Proceed with caution, and seek a professional gunsmith if you have any uncertainty with regard to altering your firearm.

(Photo courtesy of Joe Rychetnik)

The author, M.L. (Mic) McPherson, at the 1997 Shot Show.

Table of Contents

Dedication vi

Editor's Introduction vii

Part I:

Author's Introduction 3
Section 1:   The Trouble With Barrels, Part I 9
Section 2:   The Trouble With Stocks, Part I 57
Section 3:   The Trouble With Receivers, Part I 109
Section 4:   The Trouble With Triggers, Part I 119
Section 5:   The Trouble With Bolts, Part I 131
Section 6:   The Trouble With Box Magazine (Clips), Part I 143
Section 7:   The Trouble With Receiver-Mounted Sights, Part I 145
Section 8:   Miscellaneous, Part I 161

Part II:

Section 9:   Acknowledgments and Introduction, Parts II & III 167
Section 10:   The Trouble With Barrels, Part II 177
Section 11:   The Trouble With Bolts, Part II 183
Section 12:   The Trouble With Sights, Part II 189
Section 13:   The Trouble With Lever-Action and Single-Shot Rifle Stocks, Part II 201
Section 14:   The Trouble With Lever-Action and Single-Shot Receivers, Part II 241
Section 15:   More Troubles With Two-Piece Stocks, Single-Shot Rifles, Part II 281
Section 16:   The Trouble With Single-Shot Rifle Receivers, Part II 293
Section 17:   The (Lack Of!) Trouble With The New England Firearms Handi-Rifle
                          (H&R Ultra), Part II 301
Section 18:   Miscellaneous Considerations, Single-Shot (And Other) Rifles, Part II 309

Part III:

Section 19:   Gunsmith Specific Alterations, Part III 319

Dedication

As with all such endeavors, completion of this project required the help of many persons and companies. The following list highlights only a few by name. . . .

To Bob and Joyce McPherson, my parents — for their unending support of my childhood tinkering
To Winse Meyer, my friend and mentor — who sparked my interest in guns and handloading
To Bob Hodgdon (Hodgdon Powder Company), Norm Nelson (outdoor writer), Bob Bell (Author and Editor, *Handloader's Digest*) — all of whom encouraged my pursuit of this career
To Dave Brennan, Editor, *Precision Shooting*, for his confidence and support
To Peggy Widegren McPherson, my wife, whose continued support and proofreading skills make my writing possible and comprehensible
To those companies and individuals interested in the pursuit of extreme rifle accuracy, without whom such tinkering would not be possible
To our antecedents in the benchrest fraternity and those carrying on the tradition, without whom the truly accurate rifle, as we now know it, would never have been developed

My sincerest thanks,

M. L. (Mic) McPherson

Editor's Introduction

The good M.L. (Mic) McPherson casually remarked to us one day that he was "between projects," and did we have any ideas in mind to sort of point-him-at.

We mentioned that we saw a need for a book on accurizing factory rifles that was midway between real basic content (*How To Mount Scope Blocks For Fun and Profit*)...and the real advanced stuff (*Mounting A Norden Bomb Sight On Your Ruger 10/22 In 64 Easy Steps*).

When Mic advanced the opinion that "There's a lot of those already in existence," we mildly suggested that he take an hour or so out of his day, make a list of the book titles that the hour of research in to this genre turned up, and perhaps favor us with a call back.

A while later a puzzled McPherson called back, and conceded that the field was seemingly, at best, "sparsely populated."

Since that time, a certain amount of water has flowed over the dam. Since writers and editors have the same general relationship as cobras and mongooses anyway, a few harsh words, a few hysterics, and a few "We'll meet at dawn; choose your seconds" have been exchanged here and there in the ensuing months. Not to worry...par for the course for a new book around here. Finally...here it is...*Accurizing the Factory Rifle*...with several hundred pages, several hundred photos. The book fills a unique middle ground...it deals with a level of knowledge that is somewhere between that of the full-time gunsmith with a well equipped shop, and yet it far transcends the knowledge level of the shooter who approaches a scope mounting job with much (justifiable) trepidation. Furthermore, not only does the book deal with the accurizing of the ubiquitous bolt action rifle, but it also covers, in considerable depth, the poor country cousins of the bolt action...the pump, the lever action, and the single shot rifle.

An executive with one of the largest rifle manufacturers in the United States recently remarked to a *Precision Shooting* writer that it costs them approximately $15.00 to make a rifle barrel. So it should come as no particular surprise that a bore-scope study of such a barrel is not going to reveal a barrel that might be mistaken for one of Harry Pope's better efforts. Still, all things considered, today's factory rifle, as delivered to you "NIB" (New In Box) is not really bad. But then again...it's not really good, either. There is a type of shooter who, after purchasing a nice, new bolt-action .308 (or .243, or whatever) and finding on initial testing that it shoots 2.5 inch five shot groups at 100 yards, accepts that fact that he has a 2.5 minute of angle rifle. Such shooters do not subscribe to *Precision Shooting* magazine. Neither would they be particularly interested in the McPherson tome that you, good reader, are currently perusing. After all, the fellow has a 2.5 minute of angle rifle, and that's that.

There is another type of shooter who, if his initial testing revealed his new bolt-action .308 was turning in half-inch five shot groups, would feel: a) quite pleased indeed; after all, half-inch factory rifles do not exactly grow on trees these days...and b) mildly frustrated...because while the gun is shooting well...*darn it, he didn't have anything to do with that accomplishment.*

There is a lot of satisfaction to be had with taking a new bolt-action rifle that is shooting two inch groups as it came from the factory...and transforming it into a half-minute of angle rifle, using the relatively simple techniques advanced and explained here in these pages by the redoubtable Mic McPherson. And it can indeed be done...presuming that you have been blessed with a reasonably good barrel from that factory. The chapter on Fire Lapping™ is of particular importance...the writer has seen this step bring remarkable improvements to a multitude of those $15.00-to-make factory barrels...many of which arrive with bores as rough as the proverbial cob.

If you're one who likes to tinker with rifles, and who derives personal satisfaction from a tack-driving rifle that you personally worked on (as opposed to a custom-built rifle with which you had no involvement more complex than writing a four-figure check at the time of delivery to you)...then you're going to both enjoy and benefit from this book. It's a good one, and with the benefit of hindsight (admittedly always 20/20)...Mic McPherson was just the right guy to author it.

Dave Brennan
Editor
Precision Shooting magazine

Part I

Author's Introduction

Acknowledgments:

My heartfelt appreciation and thanks to all those individuals and companies who provided assistance, including but not limited to: my wife (Peggy McPherson) and Randolph Constantine, grammatical and editorial assistance and proofreading; Karl Bosselman; Brownells, Frank Brownell *et al*; Bushnell, Bill Cross and Barbara Mellman; C&H Research; Counter Coil, Jerry Danuser; Kick-Eez, Bob Pierce; Lyman, Ed Schmidt; Marble Arms (CRL Incorporated); Pachmayr, Carl Cupp; Reinhart Fajen®, Incorporated and Midway Arms, Incorporated, Larry Potterfield; Sinclair International, Bill Gravatt; William's Gun Sight Company.

Introduction and Explanation of the Purpose of this Book:

In this book, it is my goal to explore many of the principles and techniques involved in accurizing and improving the functioning of various types of rifles. In *Part I*, I will specifically consider both typical turn-bolt rifles and Remington's pump-action, which I will often refer to simply as *The Pump*. I will also cover Savage's Model-170 Pump-Action Rifle, long discontinued. Also note, in many instances, similar or identical modifications are fully applicable to certain semi-automatic rifles, especially Remington's Model-740 and its various descendants. Also, some of the noted modifications apply to various lever-action and falling-block single-shot rifles but I will cover those separately, in *Part II*. Finally, many of the modifications listed here are germane to various shotguns, rimfire rifles and air rifles, but those are not the topic of this work.

Since this is a generic tome (volume one of a planned series of similar books) I cannot make any significant inroads toward discussing every bolt-action rifle design in particular. There are simply too many variations on the same basic theme. I will, however, try to cover specific areas that are of general interest in such a way as to suggest what modifications you might consider for your turn-bolt rifle. I will specifically discuss Remington's Model-700 and related actions, Savage's Model-110 series, and typical military and commercial Mausers and their myriad descendants. Many of the specific discussions herein will relate directly to all other rifles sharing basic design features with any of these turn-bolt guns.

(In some instances, I will include instructions that might not seem appropriate for a specific rifle. For example, I ignore that new Savage bolt-action rifles have an indexing tab on the recoil lug. I try to look at the worst-case scenario: some early Savage bolt-actions might not have this tab! Ignore instructions that are clearly inappropriate for your specific rifle.)

Remington's Pump-Action High-Power Rifle uses an articulated turn-bolt action, sharing many of the characteristics of the standard bolt-action rifle. The Pump does, however, feature unique barrel attachment and trigger systems. On older models, three main pieces compose the barrel assembly. These are the barrel, the piece that allows connection of the barrel and the receiver, and a piece containing the recesses that the bolt's locking lugs engage and which assembles the other two pieces. Newer model Pumps dispense with the separate nut, combining the latter two parts in a single, more robust piece.

The Pump's trigger and hammer assembly comprises a unique removable unit that resembles those found on Remington's pump-action shotguns. This mechanism represents the sole weakness in The Pump's design. Excepting the earliest models, all Remington pumps have free-floated barrels. On The Pump, a through-bolt in the buttstock connects it to the receiver. Each of these areas, and several others, represent opportunities for unique improvement in The Pump's functioning.

Savage's Model-170 shares a somewhat similar trigger mechanism with Remington's pump but is otherwise quite distinct. This action features a lifting bolt, which functions similarly to the bolt on Savage's Model-99 lever-action rifle. The Model-170 has a tubular magazine and a very handy tang-mounted safety lever. Although the Model-170 is a somewhat rare rifle, it is capable of quite impressive accuracy. It is, therefore, certainly worthy of discussion here. For these reasons, I will include it in this text.

Several systems on these pump-action rifles require discussions separately from the general comments on bolt-action guns. Similarly, many models of bolt-action rifles have unique characteristics that also deserve separate consideration (for example, the barrel attachment system of the Savage 110 series). Finally, many of the techniques discussed herein are also wholly applicable to various similar shotgun actions.

I will attempt to gear this text and the associated photographs and diagrams toward explaining general concepts and techniques so that the reader can apply these ideas more generally. However, the reader will have to discern when modifications are applicable to other action makes, designs and types. Also note, *Part II* will specifically address the various falling block, breech break and rolling-block style single-shot and lever-action repeating rifles. Finally, at the end of *Part I* and again in *Part III* I will address certain gunsmith specific topics.

Specifically, I will address those areas where the serious tinker can improve fit, function and accuracy of turn-bolt and pump-action rifles. I will also consider more difficult or involved modifications and alterations, those where you might choose to have a gunsmith undertake the work. If the job is reasonably achievable in the home workshop by a competent tinker using ordinary or reasonably obtainable tools, I will pursue the discussion to its completion. I will also explore those jobs that are strictly gunsmith oriented but only to the extent necessary to inform the reader about the work required and why that modification might improve the gun's functioning or performance.

Where significant, I will also mention handloading techniques you might consider for improving your rifle's functioning. While I will limit this discussion, it is of general interest since, in many cases, it will help point out weaknesses in various designs. Further, I cannot ignore that many millions of shooters are also avid handloaders — an especially high percentage, no doubt, among those interested in home gunsmithing.

A partial listing of subjects we will explore together in *Part I* includes:

- Barrel-To-Fore-end Bedding
- Barrel-To-Receiver Engagement
- Barrel Crowning
- Barrel Rechambering
- Chamber Polishing
- Bore Lapping
- Fixed Sight Modifications (Barrel-mounted)
- Receiver Deburring
- Receiver-To-Stock Bedding
- Receiver-To-Magazine Floor-Plate Bedding
- Bolt Deburring
- Bolt Cocking-Ramp Modification And Polishing
- Bolt Lug(s)-To-Receiver Lapping
- Striker Modifications & Replacement
- Striker Centering And Striker-Hole Fitting
- Striker-Spring Replacement
- Trigger-Spring Adjustment
- Trigger-To-Sear Engagement Adjustment
- Trigger Sear Modification
- Trigger Mechanism Replacement
- Trigger-Lever Modification
- Stock-Length Modification
- Stock-Drop Modification
- Stock Checkering
- Stock Refinishing
- Recoil-Pad Attachment
- Kinetic Recoil "Absorber" Device Functioning And Installation
- Hydraulic Recoil "Absorber" Functioning And Installation
- Cold Bluing
- Cryogenic Treating Of Gun Parts
- Electro-Chemical Barrel Treatments
- Mounting Scopes And Receiver Sight Bases
- Mounting Scopes
- Adjusting Scope-Sight Eye-Relief
- Leveling Scope Reticle
- Spirit-Level Installation
- Action Type Specific Handloading Considerations

No doubt we will explore other areas but this is a relatively complete listing.

My goal will be to educate the reader regarding why any particular modification might be beneficial and in how to go about determining if that modification might be worthwhile on any particular gun. From there I will go directly into a step-by-step discussion of how to perform that modification. I will liberally lace the text with explanative photographs and occasional sketches. In all instances, I will discuss commonly available workshop tools necessary to perform the work and those, not so common, tools that would ease the task. Where the job is beyond workshop status I will explain what a professional gunsmith should do. Often, I will offer an opinion (based upon information kindly

Author's Introduction

provided by Brownells Incorporated) of what a reasonable charge for that service should be.

I will also include typical sources for the more esoteric of tools discussed herein. Generally, however, most of the tools will be available through your local hardware store, the local gun store or Brownells Incorporated — the premier worldwide source for gunsmithing tools, supplies and accessories. Also note that *Gun Digest* and *Handloader's Digest*, from DBI Books, Incorporated (now Krause Publications, Inc.), list many of the companies offering tools and custom parts and accessories mentioned in this text.

I will assume a rather advanced degree of expertise in the use of hand tools and standard workbench equipment. Also note: no amount of discussion can steady one's hand. Those with limited dexterity and tinkering skills should proceed with caution and knowledge of the risks they are taking. Botching some of these jobs can ruin a gun part — quick as a wink!

Regretfully, I have to make the following precautionary statements. First, many of the jobs discussed herein have the potential to lead to an unsafe condition in the gun and its functioning. If you do not fully understand how any work might affect the gun's safety characteristics, do not attempt it! I cannot stress this point too strongly. It is much better to pay a professional than create an unsafe condition! Second (I am sure this seems foolishly obvious to all of us, but I must state it nonetheless), never work on any gun until you have safely verified the unloaded condition of both chamber and any magazine! The number of so-called "accidental discharges" resulting from manipulation of a gun that someone thought was empty is a continuing source of profound amazement for this author. Obviously, any unintentional firing is a potential tragedy. None of us want that. Rest assured, whenever that happens we all suffer — sooner or later, directly or indirectly, but inevitably.

A final note: this text is intended to offer advice and suggestions to those who are seriously interested in improving the fit, function and intrinsic accuracy of a particular rifle; while this tome might be interesting reading for some, it is chiefly intended for those ready, willing and able to spend the time, effort and money to make a good rifle better! Also note that, as with many similar activities, the amateur gunsmith should pursue any home gunsmithing task only after a thorough examination of the problem and after taking plenty of time to ponder the possible solutions, and then taking more time to consider and ponder his options. For the most part, if you are in a hurry, do not do it!

For the close inspection tasks, of which this book is replete, I highly recommend the Opti-Visor, available from Brownells. The magnification provided is very helpful in crowning and many other operations — those jobs where one is often looking for variations in the sub-one-thousandth of an inch range. The Opti-Visor allows one to examine such things with both hands free, a big advantage.

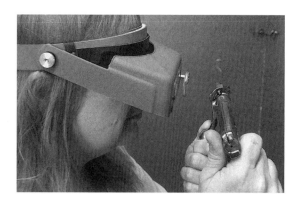

For almost any tinker, the Opti-Visor equipped with the Opti-Loupe is, perhaps, the finest vision-enhancing tool on the market! The Opti-Visor is available with various interchangeable primary lenses. The #3 provides significant magnification and a good field of view for finish work. The #5 is, likely, more valuable for close examination of precision parts. The Opti-Loupe attaches easily and articulates into and out of the field of view, as needed. Brownells stocks the entire line of Opti-Visor products. Here the Opti-Visor and Opti-Loupe greatly facilitate examination of a critical surface while functioning the part. Try making such an examination using a hand loupe!

One other comment I should make somewhere. We are likely all guilty of using the wrong tool. I have certainly done so. However, when you are working on a valuable gun it just makes sense to use the proper tool. Please, try not to "make do". Using the proper tool for the job at hand will always pay big dividends.

One more safety concern to mention here: most solvents are both extremely flammable and biologically active. Always use adequate ventilation whenever you are working with any solvent. Use particular caution when working with acetone. Never leave the container open. Finally, do not attempt to use common acetone-

based fingernail remover as a degreaser — this product contains hydrocarbons (oil).

Also note, in many places I discuss using alcohol as a degreaser. For most applications common rubbing alcohol will suffice. However, residue-free isopropyl alcohol, which is available at many pharmacies, is a better choice. The home tinker can use other products, such as the older types of carburetor or brake system cleaners (if he can locate those). The important point is to degrease the surface and leave no residue behind.

(Note, regrettably, there is no good grammatical construction in English indicating "he or she". Since this author abhors the incorrect usage of "they" and since "one" can become stilted I have chosen to sometimes use "he" in the general sense, as applied to whomever might be performing the action in question, regardless of sex. No sexism intended, if I expected that more ladies than gentlemen would buy this book I would certainly have chosen to use "she".)

With that, my best wishes in your endeavors to make your rifle the best it can be. Meanwhile, never forget that you are solely responsible for your actions: any consequences of any action you choose to take are ultimately your responsibility. Your safety, and that of others, depends upon your undertaking any such task only with the proper understanding, abilities and due caution.

Partial listing of companies referred to in this text with addresses and phone numbers:

BlackStar, 800-433-5782, ext. 21
Brownells Inc., 200 S. Front St. Montezuma, IA 50171, 515-623-5401
Loctite Corp., 1001 Trout Brook Crossing, Rocky Hill, CT 06067, 860-571-5465
Midway Arms Inc., 5875 W. Van Horn Tavern Rd., Columbia, MO 65203, 800-243-3220
NECO, 536-C Stone Rd. PO Box 427, Benicia, CA 94510
Segway Industries, Dept. PS-PO Box 783, Suffern, NY 10901-0783, 914-357-5510
Sentry Solutions Ltd, 111 Sugar Hill Rd., Contoocook, NH 03229-0130
Sinclair Int., 2330 Wayne Haven St., Fort Wayne, IN 46803, 219-493-2530
300 Below, Inc. (Cryo-Treating), 1160 S. Monroe, Decatur, IL 62521, 217-423-3070

Selected catalogue sources, reference sources and texts:

Brownells Inc., 200 S. Front St. Montezuma, IA 50171, 515-623-5401
Gun Digest, DBI Books Inc., 4092 Commercial Ave., Northbrook, IL 60062, 847-272-2051
Handloader's Digest, DBI Books Inc., 4092 Commercial Ave., Northbrook, IL 60062,
Loctite Corp., 1001 Trout Brook Crossing, Rocky Hill, CT 06067, 860-571-5465
Metallic Cartridge Reloading, DBI Books Inc., 4092 Commercial Ave., Northbrook, IL 60062
Midway Arms Inc., 5875 W. Van Horn Tavern Rd., Columbia, MO 65203, 800-243-3220
Sinclair Int., 2330 Wayne Haven St., Fort Wayne, IN 46803, 219-493-2530

Gunsmith services, pricing guide, courtesy of Brownells Inc., Catalogue # 48, Circa 1996. (Rounded up to the nearest dollar, costs for labor only, price of parts and material not included.)

SERVICES CHARGES	Surveyed Price Range	
Per Man Hour	$25	$55
Per Man & Machine Hour	30	75
Minimum Charge Per Job	20	40
Written Appraisals, Cost Estimates	25	50
CLEAN & OIL CUSTOMER GUN	25	40
METAL FINISHING		
Rebluing	25	95
Hunter Finish Handgun	40	85
Hunter Finish Rifle	50	125
Deluxe Finish Handgun	60	110
Deluxe Finish Rifle/Shotgun	65	130
Master Finish Handgun	70	150
Master Finish Rifle/Shotgun	75	200
Belgian Bluing Handgun	40	165
Belgian Bluing Rifle/Shotgun	75	180
Slow Rust Bluing	125	250
Bluing of Stainless and Cast Steel, add to basic cost above	25	75
NitreBlue Bluing	40	150
Baking Lacquer Finish	25	60
Bead Sandblast or Wire Brush Stainless Steel	20	50
Browning	50	115
Electroless Nickel Plating, handguns and small parts only	50	125
Electroless Nickel Plating, rifles/shotguns	70	185
Duplex Selective Plating/Bluing	70	175

Author's Introduction

Task	Low	High
Stripping Nickel	15	45
Parkerizing	45	85
Metal Checkering	25	100
Engine Turning Bolt	25	55
Engine Turning Small Parts	15	40
Draw Filing	25	63

SIGHT WORK

Task	Low	High
Sight-in Customer Gun, less targets, ammo, etc.	10	30
Bore Sight Customer Gun	10	20
Pattern Shotgun, less targets, ammo, etc.	10	40
Drill & Tap Barrel or Receiver for Sights, per hole	15	25
Cut Dovetail in Barrel	15	35
Install Front Sight Ramp, sweat-on type	20	46
Install Front Sight Ramp, screw-on type	15	30
Install Front Sight Ramp, band type	35	70
Install Insert in Front Pistol Sight	15	30
Buildup or Construct Extra High Front Pistol Sight	30	75
Install Target Rib Sight on Handgun	25	45
Install Front or Mid-Rib Bead on Shotgun	15	35
Install Front or Mid-Rib Bead on Shotgun, plug hole and redrill	25	65
Install Receiver Sights, gun drilled and tapped	10	30
Scope Mounting, basic job	15	30
Scope Mounting, Drilling and tapping holes	30	65

GENERAL BARREL, ACTION AND RIFLE WORK

Task	Low	High
Test-Fire Customer Gun, ammo not included	8	30
Check Headspace	10	30
Check Firing Pin Protrusion	10	23
Make Chamber Cast	13	25
Remove Fired Case From Chamber	13	38
Remove Live Round From Chamber	25	50
Remove Obstruction From Bore	25	90
Remove Fouling From Barrel	15	25
Lap Barrel	20	50
Straighten/Adjust Barrel	30	60
Install Liner in Barrel (labor only)	40	150
Cut & Crown Barrel	25	45
Chamber and Fit Barrel to Action (labor only)	70	150
Install Pre-Threaded and Chambered Barrel (labor only)	40	112
Lap In Bolt Lugs	25	50
Weld On New Bolt Handle	30	75
Forge Bolt Handle	30	55
Make and Install Spring, flat	30	85
Make and Install Spring, "V"	35	85
Make and Install Spring, coil	30	70
Install Mark II Type Safety	20	35
Install Model 70 Type Safety	45	125
Trigger Installation or Adjustment, Timney, Dayton-Traister type	25	40
Trigger Installation or Adjustment, Double-Set, Single Set	43	125
Trigger Installation or Adjustment, Shilen Match Type	25	65
Install Muzzle Brake	50	100

STOCK WORK

Task	Low	High
Hunter Finish, simple stock	35	100
Hunter Finish, complicated stock	50	135
Gunsmith Finish, simple stock	55	150
Gunsmith Finish, complicated stock	78	200
Gunsmith Finish, spray finish, lacquer or polyurethane	45	150
Recutting Checkering, average simple pattern	40	100
Recutting Checkering, complicated pattern	60	150
Glass Bedding Barrel & Action, hunting rifle	35	75
Glass Bedding Barrel & Action, Match Rifles	50	150
Glass Bedding Barrel & Action, pillar bed	60	150
Install Recoil Pad	25	60
Install Sling Swivels, standard & quick detachable	10	25
Install Cross Bolt in Stock, to strengthen	20	50
Install Recoil Reducer, simple installation in buttstock	15	35
Install and Finish Semi-Inletted Stock, Fajen, basic	70	240
Fit, Bed and Finish Fiberglass Stock Blank	80	200
Install Prefinished Synthetic Stock	35	90
Camo Paint Stock	35	100

Section 1: The Trouble With Barrels, *Part I*

Separation of the barreled-action from the stock is either necessary or helpful in several of the jobs discussed in this section. For a detailed discussion of the process see *Section 2*, The Troubles With Stocks.

Crowning Problems and Effects:

There are several areas where the home gunsmith can improve the performance of a typical rifle barrel. For convenience sake, we will start at the front and work our way toward the chamber end. See Photograph # 1-1.

For several reasons, barrel crowning is a particularly critical consideration in most high-powered rifle calibers. First, the recessed barrel crown provides protection for the end of the rifle's bore, which is critical to accuracy. A damaged barrel crown is certain to result in decreased accuracy. Second, a proper barrel crown provides a clean, concentric end for the barrel, one that is perpendicular (normal) to the axis of the gun's bore — an important feature.

If the crown is not normal to the gun's bore, or if it incurs damage from use or handling, one area of a fired bullet's base clears the confines of the bore before any other area. Further, the bullet's base might also incur damage as it exits a damaged barrel crown. The greater the imperfection or damage at the crown, the more that imperfection is liable to disrupt the bullet's down-range flight — accuracy. See Photograph #s 1-2/3.

Photograph 1-1: Savage Model-170 pump-action rifle, barrel crown before recrowning operation. Note wear line and scars on the existing crown. Examination with the Opti-Loupe revealed damage, which is not visible in this photograph. This gun shot okay as it was but it definitely shot better after repairing the crown.

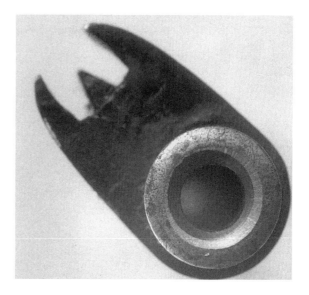

Photograph 1-2: Here we are just beginning a 79° crowning cut on a semi-sporterized 7mm Mauser Military rifle. In shortening the barrel, the sporterizing practitioner has clearly failed to cut the barrel squarely to the axis of the bore. Note that the 79° recrowning cut is much wider near the bottom and is just beginning to touch at the top of the barrel.

Consider a barrel where one portion of the bullet exits the bore before any other, as happens when the end of the barrel is not perpendicular to the axis of the bore. As the bullet passes from the barrel, one portion of the base would clear the barrel first. The more clearance any one area of the bullet's base has with the bore, before the entire bullet's base is free of the bore, the worse the effects on accuracy. To a considerable extent, the accuracy-spoiling effects are a function of muzzle gas pressure and total powder gas volume for the specific load you are using. For example, a .22 rimfire rifle would be much less sensitive to a poor crown compared to a 7mm Remington Magnum. Muzzle pressure in the 7mm Rem. Mag. is several orders of magnitude (hundreds of times) higher than a .22 RF. Total powder volume in the former is about one one-hundredth of the latter.

There are two significant consequences of an imperfectly square crown. The first relates to bullet confinement. As the bullet travels down the bore, the barrel compresses it through lateral confinement. The bullet swells in the bore as a result of the high pressure gasses confined behind (and accelerating) it. The bullet swells because its internal strength is insufficient to withstand the induced stress of acceleration. It presses against the sides of the bore. In response, the barrel swells. How much the barrel swells depends upon how hard the bullet swells. These forces balance when barrel-stretching stress equals bullet-swelling stress. At that point, the barrel's resistance prevents further bullet swelling.

When one portion of the bullet's base escapes the bore before any other portion, the result is an asymmetric release of the stored elastic energy contained in the bullet, which results from the barrel's confining pressure and the forces accelerating the bullet. The result is an expansion of the bullet's base toward the side of the bore where the bullet base first clears the barrel. Similarly (for every action there is an equal and opposite reaction), the barrel reacts by moving away from the side where the bullet is still pushing against it.

This almost instantaneous shift of mass toward one side of the bullet's base induces a wobble, technically called yaw, in the bullet. This induced bullet wobble will eventually (after the bullet has traveled a few dozen to perhaps a few hundred yards) gyroscopically stabilize — a process known among serious target shooters as "going to sleep". This explains why the relative size of groups fired from some guns will decrease at longer ranges. It is not uncommon to find a rifle that shoots no better than one-inch groups at one hundred yards but will manage two-inch groups at three hundred yards. Nevertheless, until the bullet stabilizes, the induced wobble will increase the bullet's wind resistance and, therefore, the rate of velocity loss. Also, obviously, this condition cannot contribute to overall accuracy!

Second, any gas pressure existing behind the bullet as it exits the bore (which is always significant in high-powered guns, even those that feature ported barrels) will vent first from the initial opening, the area where one portion of the bullet's base is first to clear the bore. Initial venting gas velocities often exceed six thousand (6000) fps. This high-velocity venting creates a venturi effect — it creates a low pressure zone where the velocity is the greatest. This low-pressure zone pulls that side of the bullet's base toward the jetting gas. However, conflicting high pressure created by the surplus of gas on that side of the bullet counteracts this effect, pushing on the bullet. The net result, as the bullet continues to come free from the bore, is unpredictable.

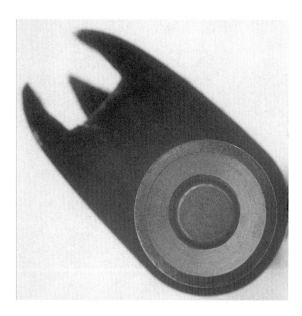

Photograph 1-3: Here we have almost completed a 79° crowning cut on a semi-sporterized 7mm Mauser Military rifle. Again, note clear evidence of unsquare barrel cut-off (the dark area between the bore and the inside of the new cut is much wider near the top of the barrel). For a complete discussion of the recrowning process, see the associated text and other photographs.

Section 1: The Trouble With Barrels, Part I

Most likely the influence will vary from one shot to the next. Regardless, as the bullet fully clears the bore these high velocity gases will almost certainly push the bullet base to one side and, likely, the bullet's nose to the opposite side, therefore pushing the bullet out of alignment with the bore. Once asymmetric gas flow begins it will continue until the bullet is well free of the gun's bore.

(Bad barrel crowning is a notorious problem; I have seen barrel crowns that looked as if a monkey with a bad hangover using a dull twist drill bit or perhaps a hammer and a chisel had produced the job!)

Recrowning by Lapping:

The simplest (and least expensive) method of fixing <u>minor</u> crowning imperfections and blemishes involves nothing more complicated than a common glass marble or ball bearing of slightly more than bore diameter with a dab of valve grinding or lapping compound. See Photograph #s 1-4 through 1-7.

The tinker simply applies the lapping compound to the hard sphere, places that in the end of the vertically affixed (and unloaded) gun barrel and, while applying moderate pressure, rolls the ball using one's finger or the palm of his hand. Often, several minutes of this treatment will remove any small imperfections from the end of the bore, leaving a splendidly refinished crown. Cost of a can of fine-grit valve grinding compound is a few dollars. This product is available at any automotive parts store.

A big step toward perfection in barrel crowning involves either a hand-driven or power-driven brass muzzle lap. To finish a barrel crown you use either of these tools in conjunction with six hundred (600) grit silicon carbide lapping compound. This combination can very quickly provide the ultimate in crowning perfection — assuming only that the initial crowning is square and centered to the bore. This process will also

Photograph 1-4: This is a low-tech and old but effective method of crowning a barrel. Here we have placed a simple glass marble on the muzzle. Application of a dab of 600 grit lapping compound at the contact, followed by a few minutes of rolling the marble by hand (sometimes one can do this using the palm of the hand), gets the job done nicely. See associated photographs and text.

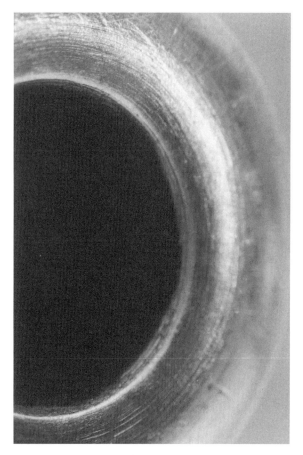

Photograph 1-5: Close-up-view of Savage Model-170 pump-action rifle muzzle before lapping. Perhaps you can see imperfections and scars in this crown. Any blemishes here are highly detrimental to accuracy.

remove <u>minor</u> damage from the crown. Cost for this tool is under twenty dollars ($20) and results are worthwhile. These tools are available from Brownells Incorporated. See Photograph # 1-8.

Before using the brass lap to refinish the barrel crown, verify the unloaded condition of both chamber and magazine. (This is good advice before undertaking any gunsmithing chore!) Mount the gun in a padded vise — Midway's handy shooter's gun vise is an excellent tool for this and many of the other jobs I will discuss throughout this text. With the gun stabilized, apply a dab of lapping compound to the rounded face of the lapping tool. Begin working the end of the bore by applying mild pressure between the tool and the bore and while twisting the tool back and forth randomly and while moving the free end of the tool in an ever-changing random orientation, generally slightly out of alignment with the axis of the bore. See Photograph # 1-9.

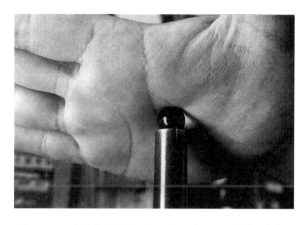

Photograph 1-7: When lapping burrs or blemishes out of a crown one can use a marble and a dab of 600 grit lapping compound. Sometimes one can roll the marble under the palm of the hand. However, usually, one must spin the marble between thumb and finger. See text and associated photograph captions for a complete discussion.

Photograph 1-8: Pictured is Brownells' brass lapping jig. This is their .27-35 caliber version. Three other sizes cover all calibers from .17 through .50. This is the power drill version, highly recommended since it eases the burden of maintaining proper pressure and geometry. Simply apply lapping compound (for this job use 600 grit or finer) and lap until you have removed all burrs. See associated photographs and text.

Photograph 1-6: Close-up-view after lapping with a glass marble and 600 grit lapping compound. While this might not be a perfect recrowning job it was certainly an improvement, as was verified by the results of subsequent accuracy testing.

Photograph 1-9: The (almost) final touch to a properly crowned bore. Here we are using a brass lap to hone the juncture of the cut edge and the bore with 600 grit grinding compound. This process removes any burrs from this critical area.

This procedure is perhaps easiest to explain for application to the power-driven version of this tool. Chuck the lapping tool into a variable speed hand drill. Lock the drill's trigger on and adjust the speed control until the drill runs at a very slow speed — several hundred rpm is sufficient. Black & Decker power drills facilitate this "locked-on-slow" mode very well. With the gun solidly mounted and with the drill running at a slow speed, apply a dab, perhaps a BB sized glob, of six hundred (600) grit silicon carbide lapping compound to the tip of the tool. Spread this over the entire radiused tip of the tool using very light finger pressure.

Bring the tool into contact with the end of the bore. Gently apply end pressure to the brass tool — you are not drilling a hole here, gently means <u>gently</u> — press only hard enough to keep the tool solidly against the bore, without chattering.

With the drill running slowly and with lapping compound between the brass bit and the bore, maintain application of gentle pressure. Begin wobbling the handle end of the drill in a random spiral-like pattern extending to, perhaps, a six-inch circle. In this manner, you ensure that the contact area between the lapping tool and the end of the bore is always changing — this prevents any one area of the brass tip from wearing more than any other, which keeps the tip properly shaped and ensures a consistently lapped radius on the bore. Be careful not to wobble the end of the drill too far; the cylindrical portion of the brass tool shaft should never touch the barrel. Also, do not allow the end of the tool to wander from proper centering in the bore — maintain sufficient pressure. See Photograph # 1-10.

A very poorly made or seriously damaged crown will require significant lapping. In this instance, it might be necessary to periodically recharge the tool with lapping compound. However, you should be careful not to lap away too much material using such a tool. Proper crowning requires only that the lapped area represents a concentric ring around the entire bore and that the lapped area extends slightly past the bottom of all rifling grooves. See Photograph # 1-11.

Photograph 1-11: Oblique-view of finished crown, after cutting with 79° tool and lapping with brass lapping jig (both available from Brownells). Note that this lapped surface extends equally to the bottom of all grooves. Here we used 800 grit lapping compound to achieve an almost mirror finish in the lapped area. Although we could make a final pass using 1200 grit (or finer) compound to achieve a higher level of finish, there seems little real advantage to such an approach.

Photograph 1-10: Pictured is Brownells' brass lap after use. Note the darkened area where the lapping action has distributed the compound and impregnated it into the brass. Also note the unused surfaces (perimeter and center). This suggests use of the proper amount of wobble on the drill during the lapping process. Wobbling the drill changes the axis of the lap. This brings new areas of the radiused tip into play and prevents uneven tip wear.

Recrowning by Recutting:

On barrels with a badly formed or a badly damaged crown, the best course is to recut the crown with a seventy-nine degree (79°) tool, available from Brownells Incorporated. Use of this tool involves a bit more expertise and significant costs, about fifty dollars ($50). Also, to finish the job you should still use the brass crowning lap, as described above. This brings the total investment to about seventy dollars ($70). However, if you have several rifles of the same caliber, these tools can be well worthwhile. This is especially true considering that poor crowning is among the most common of accuracy-destroying gun problems. Also note, adding other calibers requires only purchase of the proper caliber pilots for the seventy-nine degree (79°) tool, at about fifteen dollars ($15) each. See Photograph # 1-12.

If you only have one or two guns that require this advanced crowning process you might consider the services of a gunsmith. Typical charge for recrowning is about twenty-five dollars ($25). However, as noted, if you have many guns in the rack you might want to have these tools in your inventory. Crowns do become damaged....

Again, start by ensuring you have unloaded both the rifle's chamber and its magazine. Then properly affix the gun so that it will not move around, Midway's gun vise is sufficient for this job. It is best to affix the gun so the bore is pointing down, at least slightly. This limits migration of metal cuttings into the bore. Ensure that there is no abrasive material in the bore or on the crown. Assemble the crowning tool handle to the cutter and install the bore pilot into the cutter.

Lubricate the bore and the cutter with a quality cutting oil; for example, Do-Drill, available from Brownells. (Standard sulfur impregnated type cutting oils, available at any good hardware store, work very well.) See Photograph # 1-13.

This is a good place to emphasize the following point: the home hobbyist should always use cutting oil for all drilling, tapping and reaming operations in steel of all kinds; religious adherence to this protocol will extend cutting tool life by many times. Further, it will ultimately reduce the opportunity for a failed tool — you have not lived until you have suffered the hassle of trying to remove a tiny broken tap from a delicate piece! Also, special cutting oils intended for use with stainless steels are particularly valuable whenever you are working with those materials. See Photograph # 1-14.

Another note is in order here. On rifles featuring special shallow rifling, such as Marlin's Micro-Groove, the nominal pilot will generally not work correctly. However, in the .30 caliber bore a .303 caliber pilot will usually fit quite properly. In the .44 and .45 caliber bores, you can wrap one layer of cellophane tape around the nominal diameter pilot for a good fit. Since Brownells makes these pilots from hardened steel it is not feasible to buy a next size larger and turn it to fit. Until Brownells gets sufficient demand for these odd-sized pilots, cellophane tape will have to do!

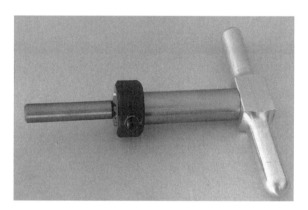

Photograph 1-12: Brownells' 79° crowning tool with handle, 7mm (28 caliber) pilot and homemade travel-limiting sleeve installed. Pilots are available for all standard calibers up to .45. A larger unit allows work on even bigger bores. For non-standard rifling types, such as Marlin's Micro-Groove, a special diameter pilot is necessary. Currently, however, these are not commercially available. The .303 pilot works in .30-30 chambered Micro-Groove barrels. For the .44 and .45 caliber Marlins one must use a cellophane tape-wrap on the corresponding pilot.

Note the depth of cut limiting sleeve. We made this piece from a grade #2-1/2" NC nut and a set screw. We clamped the nut, centered under the spindle on a drill press, and drilled through the threads using a 1/2" bit. This centered and square hole fits the 1/2" shank of the cutter. We then drilled and tapped the modified nut for an 8x24 set screw. Finally, we reversed the drill bit in the drill press. We then secured the nut to the lower (solid) end of the bit with the set screw, leaving the bottom of the nut extending below the bottom of the bit. In this manner, with the drill press running at a high speed, we polished the working face of the nut and squared that to the axis of the hole. Here we have adjusted the sleeve for the final cutting process. This both limits the depth of the cut and allows one to produce a very smooth final cut. However, it prevents resulting chips from falling out of the cutting flutes — use this adjustment only for the final cut!

Section 1: The Trouble With Barrels, Part I

Introduce the crowning tool pilot into the bore. This should be a very close fit with no more than about one-thousandths of an inch (0.001") clearance. Advance the tool until the seventy-nine degree (79°) cutting flutes contact the end of the barrel. While applying moderate pressure, slowly twist the handle to turn the tool clockwise. For best results, twist the handle only as far as is comfortable with one grip, slightly more than one-half turn for most of us, before changing grip and adding another one-half turn. Do not pull the tool back between cuts! After several turns, withdraw the tool. Clean all cuttings from the tool and the cutter. It is critically important to thoroughly clean all cuttings from the bore before reinserting the tool. See Photograph # 1-15.

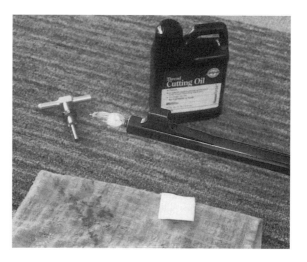

Photograph 1-14: We have partially completed this cut, removed the cutter tool and driven a clean patch from the breech completely out of the muzzle. We will next remove the patch and wipe the rod clean before withdrawing it. Upon checking progress of the cut, and before continuing, we will clean the barrel and cutter of <u>all</u> cutting debris then re-oil the bore and barrel face. See text and associated photographs.

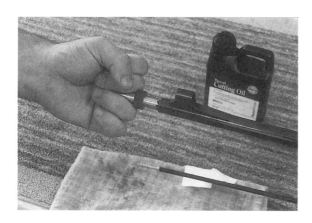

Photograph 1-13: Here we are cutting the crown on a left-hand Model 700 Remington bolt-action rifle chambered in 7mm Remington Magnum. We are using Brownells' 79° reamer fitted with a 7mm pilot, a hand-drive handle and a homemade travel-limiting sleeve. To do a proper job cutting oil and barrel cleaning components are critical, otherwise damage to the bore or tool are likely. Also note, the muzzle should slope downhill. This will limit cutting chip migration into the bore. Also, one should push a patched jag through the bore from the chamber end at regular intervals — certainly every time one checks the progress of the cut. Note the sleeve installed on the cutter shank (here adjusted clear of the cutter flutes to allow cuttings to freely fall from the tool during the initial phase of the crowning process). When we have finished the cut to the proper depth we will adjust this sleeve to almost touch the front of the barrel. Then a clean-up cut will eliminate chatter marks on the new crown. See text and associated photographs.

Photograph 1-15: In this oblique-view one can clearly see how Brownells' 79° crowning tool has just started cutting at the end of the barrel.

A soft cotton patch and a near bore-fitting hardwood dowel or cleaning rod section are good tools for removing any such cuttings. Ideally, insert the patch from the breech end, push it through the bore and remove it from the dowel after it exits the muzzle. Then wipe the end of the dowel (or cleaning rod section) clean before pulling it out of the muzzle end of the barrel. Repeat this process using new patches until the bore is <u>completely</u> free of cutting debris. See Photograph # 1-16.

Relubricate both tool and bore and make another series of one-half-turn cuts. When this procedure has resulted in sufficient cutting, typically when the cut area extends about three-fourths (3/4) of the way from the bore toward the barrel's perimeter, make one final cut, or series of cuts, as necessary. All the while apply a constant, albeit slight, end pressure to the tool.

The preliminary cutting brings the end of the bore to a smooth shallow funneled contour. However, it will leave chatter marks. The idea with this final, light pressure, cutting operation is to trim those chatter marks away. Realistically it is almost impossible to achieve a smoothly finished cut without installing something that positively limits the cutter's travel into the bore in some manner. You can achieve this limit in several ways.

One way of achieving this goal, on guns that have front sights or where you can clamp some similar block onto the barrel near the muzzle, is to install a bushing over the cutter shank and a sleeve that fits over the outside of the muzzle over that bushing. PVC pipe works very well for such a sleeve, providing only that you have a means of cutting the end perfectly square.

Photograph 1-16: Close-up-view, patch showing cuttings from recrowning operation. If one were to continue such a cutting operation without removing these cuttings from the bore, bore damage could occur. Here we have partially completed the cut. Upon checking our progress, and before continuing, we will clean the barrel of all cutting debris then re-oil the bore and tool.

You can easily accomplish attachment of the bushing, perhaps made of hardwood, to the cutter shank using either epoxy or hot glue. You can make such a bushing quite easily by drilling a one-half inch (1/2") hole through a piece of hardwood. (The standard 79° cutter shank from Brownells is 1/2" in diameter). After drilling the hole, run a one-half inch (1/2") bolt through the hole and snug a nut to lock the bushing between the bolt head and the nut.

Chuck the threaded end of the bolt in a vised one-half inch (1/2") electric drill or a drill press and proceed to rasp away the perimeter until it is round and of the proper size to fit a PVC pipe with about a one-inch (1.0") inside diameter. This bushing will not interfere with the tool's function. Once attached to the shank with epoxy, you can leave it in place for future use.

Attachment of the cylindrical PVC sleeve is a simple matter. Using a hacksaw, produce a centered slot extending down the sleeve for several inches. Slide the sleeve over the bushing, then an automotive hose clamp over the sleeve and position over the bushing. Position the clamp and snug the clamp to lock it in place on the bushing.

This square-ended cylindrical PVC sleeve should fit over the barrel and abut, with a true end, against the front sight-base or some object clamped to the bore near the muzzle. Simply insert the cutter fully into the nearly finished crown and adjust the sleeve until it almost abuts the sight or affixed stop on the barrel. A clearance of a few thousandths of an inch is sufficient to allow the additional cutting, necessary to eliminate any differential cutting depth or chatter marks in the seventy-nine degree (79°) crown.

Then it remains only to make final finishing cuts until the tool will no longer advance. Assuming a good pilot-to-bore fit, this method will leave the end of the bore as perfectly true as is feasible.

A simpler method of limiting the cutter's travel is to cut a hardwood dowel to the proper length to fit in the bore between the closed bolt and the end of the pilot. Cut this piece slightly long, then grind it incrementally shorter until the pilot is just clear of touching the dowel when you have completed the crowning cut. Continuing the cut until the pilot touches the dowel solidly will result in a true finish on the cut, just as the aforementioned method. The disadvantage is that the dowel is strictly application specific — the bushing and sleeve system, once built, will work for any rifle barrel, excepting perhaps the .577 Tyrannosaur from A-Square.

Section 1: The Trouble With Barrels, Part I

Another method, pictured here, involves an adjustable stop-bushing on the shank of the cutter. You can easily make this tool out of a one-half inch (1/2") grade-2 nut. (I have to wonder why Brownells has not offered such a logical attachment.) See the associated photographs for a complete explanation of construction and use. Photograph #s 1-17 through 1-20.

Photograph 1-17: Brownells' 79° crowning tool with homemade travel-limiting sleeve installed. Here we have adjusted the sleeve for the preliminary cutting process. This adjustment allows clearance for cuttings to freely fall from the tool. This also facilitates cleaning cutting debris (chips) from the tool between passes — a toothbrush facilitates chip removal. See associated photograph captions for a discussion of how we made this sleeve.

Photograph 1-18: Transverse-view of working end of Brownells' 79° crowning tool with homemade travel-limiting sleeve installed. Here we have adjusted the sleeve as we should for the final cutting process. This adjustment both limits the depth of the cut and allows one to produce a very smooth (chatter mark free) final cut.

Photograph 1-19: End-view of barrel with semi-completed 79° cut via Brownells' crowning tool. Note obvious chatter marks on cut surface. One can eliminate, or greatly reduce, these marks through proper adjustment and use of a travel-limiting sleeve. See photograph 1-20.

Photograph 1-20: End-view of barrel with completed 79° cut via Brownells' crowning tool. Note that we have almost completely removed the chatter marks, noted in photograph 1-19. Any remaining chatter marks are not obvious to the naked eye. After we achieved the desired cutting depth, we adjusted the travel-limiting sleeve. Then we made the final cuts using modest and constant end pressure on the tool. See associated photographs.

I recommend final lapping with the aforementioned brass tool. This removes the inevitable burs formed in the bore during the recrowning process. These burs are especially likely to have formed and remain at the bottoms of the rifling grooves. Such burs will eventually shoot out of the bore. However, that expeditious method leaves imperfections where the burs break off; a problem you can easily eliminate by lapping the finished cut. The cut-then-lap process, outlined above, will provide an attractive and functional barrel crown. This process is applicable to <u>any</u> type of rifled barrel. See Photograph # 1-21 through 1-24.

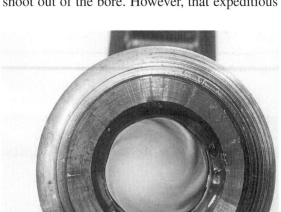

Photograph 1-21: Here we have partially completed the recrowning cut. Note that the width of the cut face is not equal around the perimeter. This fact might anticipate a poor crowning job. Note cutting oil in the bore and on the crown and cutting debris (steel chips) on the bore face. We will clean and re-oil the bore before proceeding.

Photograph 1-23: End-view of finished crown, after cutting with 79° tool and lapping with brass lapping jig (both available from Brownells). Note that the lapped surface extends equally to the bottom of all grooves. Here we used 800 grit lapping compound to achieve an almost mirror finish in the lapped area. Although we could make a final pass with 1200 grit (or finer) compound to achieve an ever higher level of finish, there seems little real advantage to such an approach.

Photograph 1-22: Here we have completed the recrowning cut. We have also adjusted the sleeve to limit cutter penetration. This has allowed us to produce a sufficiently smooth finished cut.

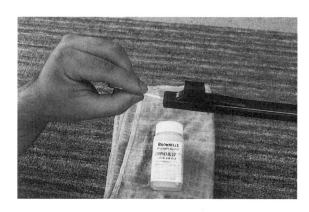

Photograph 1-24: Here we are applying Brownells' excellent "Oxpho-Blue" to the freshly cut surfaces on this new barrel crown. Cold bluing on freshly cut surfaces just makes good sense. Application of this, or a similar product, to any scarred area on blued steel limits corrosion.

Section 1: The Trouble With Barrels, Part I

Barrel Bore Lapping:

Moving on, we imagine scaling ourselves small enough to move right down into the barrel. At this scale, we would easily identify another common problem: the rough bore. Custom barrel makers, and there are plenty of good ones out there these days, routinely polish, via hand-lapping, their barrels to about a three-hundred and twenty (320) grit finish. Because of the labor-intensive nature of this process, commercial manufacturers seldom perform any bore lapping, except in .17 and .22 caliber barrels. In this respect, regardless of the barrel type and quality, the serious shooter can do much better. Even in woodworking, experts do not consider three-hundred twenty (320) grit a polish-grade compound. When you are working with steel, much finer grits are beneficial.

You can make lead barrel lapping slugs and hand-lap the bore using appropriate grades of lapping agent. However, this process is replete with pitfalls, probably takes more time than the following described process and is unlikely to provide equal results. Therefore, I will exclusively recommend and describe the Fire Lapping™ process, a superior method.

NECO, Benicia, CA, offers fire lapping kits that allow any shooter to polish the bore of almost any gun to a twelve hundred (1200) grit, "metallic mirror" finish. The process is reasonably straight-forward. It involves the firing of treated bullets through the bore with standard (or slightly reduced) handloads. One normally begins with bullets treated with two hundred twenty (220) grit and progresses to four hundred (400) grit, then eight hundred (800) grit and finally twelve hundred (1200) grit. In custom barrels and most factory .17 and .22 bored guns one should omit the two hundred twenty (220) grit stage and in top of the line barrels omit the four hundred (400) grit stage.

In recent years, *Precision Shooting* magazine and many other gun-trade publications have documented fire lapping but I will repeat the basic procedure here, nonetheless. The idea is conceptually simple: polish any rough high spots out of the bore using bullets that have had abrasive particles impregnated into the surface. Since all bullets (lead, gilding metal jacketed, copper clad steel jacketed, copper alloy solids or any other type) are much softer than barrel steel, the bullet acts as a perfect carrier for the abrasive.

NECO offers loaded ammunition with instructions for the non-handloader. This process is a little more expensive but is extremely easy to follow. We will return to a discussion of the firing procedure after discussing the handloader method of preparing bullets.

The handloader initially impregnates the appropriate grade abrasive particles into typical bullets by rolling the bullet between two hardened steel plates in the presence of the appropriate grit (lapping compound), which is a laboratory grade of special high-quality material. Unlike many abrasive compounds, NECO's lapping agent uses extremely well sorted abrasives. Well sorted means the particles are all of very similar size. NECO's abrasive particles are robust enough to easily withstand the forces associated with firing a bullet through a gun's barrel.

The shooter loads these treated bullets into standard handloads (but not hot top-of-the-line handloads!) then fires those through the bore. He must thoroughly clean the bore before the initial firing and after every third shot, or so and, especially, every time he changes grit size. Otherwise he is simply lapping the barrel fouling, which is not very productive! See Photograph # 1-25.

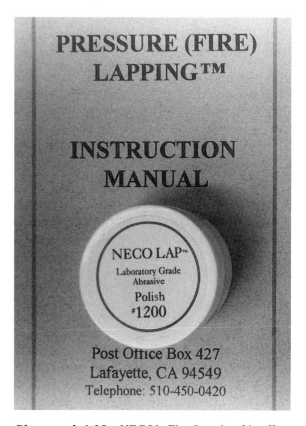

Photograph 1-25: NECO's Fire Lapping kit offers the handloader a truly superior method of polishing burrs from a gun's bore. This process works on all manner of firearms. Loaded ammunition is also available for the non-handloader. See text for a description of this process.

The typical protocol involves firing about eight 220 grit bullets, about ten 400 grit bullets, about twelve 800 grit bullets and about fifteen 1200 grit bullets. This process typically takes about two hours at the range.

For those with the logical and typical concern, which shooters often voice thus: "You want me to do WHAT to my barrel?!", I can offer this truth: when properly done, fire lapping will remove no more than one-half of one ten-thousandth to one ten-thousandth of an inch (0.00005"–0.0001") of material from the bore's interior.

However, if you use cast lead bullets for the work, fire lapping can remove the beginning of the rifling measurably forward — in some instances as much as ten-thousandths of an inch (0.010"). If throat length is a critical concern, do not use cast lead bullets for fire lapping. When you use jacketed bullets this throat progression does not happen unless there is something wrong with the barrel steel — certain impurities can create soft areas that are prone to rapid wear. This has happened, but is rare, and since there was a serious problem with any such barrel to begin with, this does little harm!

Also note, the increase in measured bore diameter is more a function of the lapping process removing all the high spots than it is a matter of the process actually increasing bore diameter throughout the length of the bore.

NECO includes pure lead slugs and instructions in how to properly slug a bore with their handloader-specific Fire Lapping kits. The idea is to slug the bore before beginning the lapping operation and at reasonable intervals during the process. Almost all novice barrel lappers will want to do this because this will assuage any concerns that they might be harming the bore. Slugging is also very beneficial as an educational experience, feeling the lubricated slug skip and hang as it passes through a typical bore can open your eyes to the level of imperfection involved in boring holes and forming rifling — believe me, that process is far from perfected.

After the lapping process is complete you will always see a significant reduction in the variation in internal bore diameter and surface finish quality. The lubricated slug will pass through the bore much more smoothly and with less variation in resistance. Through slugging, you can also identify a problematical barrel. For example, a barrel where bore diameter increases significantly as you measure closer to the muzzle — such a barrel is unlikely to produce match accuracy!

Fire lapping can do little to improve a reverse-tapered bore. Other than that limitation, you can expect fire lapping to improve almost any bore. Fouling reductions of about ninety percent (90%) are not at all uncommon — and, by the way, fouling reduction is the reason NECO invented and markets this system! Cost can be as low as a few dollars per barrel, if you have many guns to lap. The kit will allow lapping of more than a dozen barrels and retails for about seventy-five dollars ($75). See Photograph #s 1-26 through 1-32.

Photograph 1-26: NECO's Pressure (Fire) Lapping kit comes with four grades of lapping compound, slugging-bullets and two hardened-steel plates. The kit's cost reflects the quality of the lapping agents supplied. With careful use one can lap many barrels with this one kit. Here we are preparing to impregnate lapping agent into four .45 caliber lead slugs. We intend these bullets for use in Ruger's New Army cap & ball revolver. Typically we would use at least 15 bullets for the 1200 grit lapping stage. See text and associated photographs.

Photograph 1-27: Here we have prepared to impregnate three jacketed .45-70 bullets in one step.

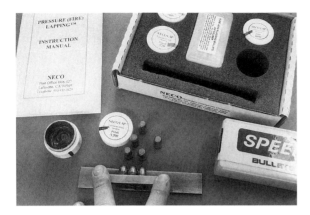

Photograph 1-28: Here we are impregnating three of a group of jacketed .45-70 bullets with 1200 grit lapping agent.

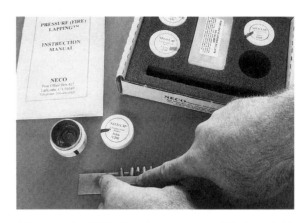

Photograph 1-31: Treating a group of jacketed .30 caliber bullets with 1200 grit lapping agent.

Photograph 1-29: Jacketed .45-70 bullets after we have impregnated the shanks with lapping agent.

Photograph 1-32: Five jacketed .30 caliber bullets after treating with 1200 grit lapping agent. The next step is to clean off the excess lapping agent. One handloads treated bullets with a standard load recipe then fires those through the gun's barrel. A typical scenario involves about 8 shots with 220 grit treated bullets; followed by about 10 shots with 400 grit treated bullets; followed by about 12 shots with 800 grit treated bullets; followed by about 15 shots with 1200 grit treated bullets. To avoid the useless result of polishing fouling instead of steel, one must clean the bore often during this shooting sequence.

Photograph 1-30: Here we have prepared to impregnate five jacketed .30 caliber bullets in one operation. The smaller the bullet the more we can treat in one step.

NECO also sells prepared color-coded bullets and loading instruction for the handloader who only wants to fire lap one gun and wants to do it easily. Also available are ammunition kits for those who want to fire lap a bore and do not have access to handloading or choose not to use that method. Simply follow NECO's excellent instructions and you will have no troubles gleaning the benefits fire lapping offers.

Electro-Chemical Barrel Treatments:

Similarly, but at a higher cost, electro-chemical barrel treating processes are available. BlackStar is a leader in this field. Application of this process is best with factory new (unfired!) barrels, or at least a barrel with its throat in good condition, and you must send the barrel to BlackStar. Cost is higher than the fire lapping process and turn-around is subject to the workload at BlackStar at the time. However, if you simply must have the best, this might be the way to go. Expect to spend somewhere around $150.00 (as this book goes to press).

Cryogenic Barrel Treatment:

Another step that will add to the barrel's accuracy and possibly to its life is cryogenic treating (deep freezing). Manufacturers perfected this process many decades back, as a means of significantly extending the life of tool-steel cutting instruments. The simple expedient of slowly cooling steel, in a controlled environment, to the lowest temperature economically feasible (about -320°F, *via* liquid nitrogen) can dramatically increase useful life of cutting tools — typically ten times.

The surprising thing is that until quite recently no one seems to have thought to try this process on gun barrels. When you understand why cryo-treating improves cutting steels, you can see why it might improve a barrel's accuracy.

Loosely, what happens during the production of any typical steel is that the alloy is first heated and then cooled in some process involving a more-or-less controlled environment. This heating and cooling cycle facilitates a precipitation process whereby alloying agents (which strengthen the iron and add corrosion resistance), and which manufacturers add to the iron, are first distributed more evenly throughout the crystalline structure and then spontaneously accumulate into differential zones of concentration. These zones follow a regular pattern, related to the crystalline structure of the steel. This precipitation continues until the piece stops cooling....

This latter point is critical. Obviously, you can figure out that the thermodynamic properties of the alloy are driving the aforementioned precipitation. Further, the alloying agent's natural tendency is to locate in an evenly spaced ordered manner within the crystalline structure — technically, despite the regular pattern involved, this distribution maximizes the system's overall entropy, or total disorder. Since Mother Nature prevents the alloy from ever cooling to absolute zero, these alloying agents cannot reach this state of perfect harmony, or disorder. (There is a lesson in this regarding Murphy's Law: nature defines perfect harmony as a total mess!)

This failure to reach absolute zero results in a situation where the alloying agents are not thermodynamically stable in the crystalline structure. This means that the internal structure of the alloy contains a considerable amount of self-induced stress. This stress contributes to zones of weakness, areas where wear and corrosion will occur more rapidly. Further, it induces zones of differential response to stress and vibratory stimulus. In a rifle barrel, the result is a loss of accuracy potential and accurate life. That seems simple enough.

There is very little you can do about this in the home workshop. You could place your rifle in the handy chest-type freezer (about -20°F) or take it on an arctic safari in the winter (-80°F); however, since these temperatures are vastly removed from absolute zero (-459.67°F) you cannot properly cryo-treat a gun at home. The commercial process is affordable and results seem to be ubiquitously good. By the way, it seems completely reasonable to consider application of this process to the receiver, the bolt and all other steel pieces having wear or stress surfaces. *(I am unaware if this process can be beneficial for other types of heat treated alloys but the potential seems reasonable and it cannot hurt....)*

If I fail to mention that the home gunsmith cannot do cryo-treating at home some tyro is bound to obtain a jug of liquid Nitrogen and try it! Since the stuff costs no more than milk, this might seem feasible. However, to achieve a proper cryo-treatment one must precisely control both the cool-down and warm-up stages of the process. Those in the business use computer control to achieve very precise rates of temperature change. Simply immersing a piece of steel in liquid nitrogen will introduce monumental thermal stress into the steel. Do not do it!

Since cryo-treating can marginally increase the effective hardness of the steel you might consider putting this step off until you complete all machining and lapping operations. However, since cryo-treating might result in minor stress-relief related changes in surface contour on large pieces, areas such as the front of the receiver, you might choose to do this operation before performing any other work on the gun. Take your pick! Cost of this process, including shipping and handling, should be well under one-hundred dollars ($100).

Section 1: The Trouble With Barrels, Part I

Chamber Polishing:

Having considered barrel crowning, bore polishing and cryo-treating — the combination of which can dramatically improve any barrel — we are ready to move to the big end of the tube. Here we will look first at the interior finish of the chamber.

There is precious little the home hobbyist can do here other than a bit of fine polishing to improve the existing surface finish. You can best accomplish chamber polishing in action designs providing open access to the chamber from the rear and with a straight shot from the back of the gun. However, given sufficient patience, you can do this job using a long dowel inserted from the muzzle end, as is necessary on Remington's Pump-Action Rifle and similar guns.

Ideally, the home gunsmith should do this job while he or she has the barrel and receiver separated; a process discussed later in this text.

In a typical bolt-action rifle, you begin by removing the bolt. Locate a hardwood dowel that is at least one size bigger than bore diameter but is small enough to allow a few wraps of corundum (aluminum oxide) paper and still be smaller than the body portion of the chamber.

On straight, slightly tapered or slightly bottle-necked chambers (for example, the .44 Magnum, .38-55 Winchester and .35 Whelen), you must use a dowel that is smaller than bore diameter — the chamber is not significantly larger than the bore and you must have room for the abrasive paper. In these instances, you must be very careful to avoid moving the dowel forward far enough so that the corundum paper can touch the rifling — a genuine no-no. See Photograph # 1-33.

Cut the dowel long enough to reach through the action, fully into the chamber and a hand drill's chuck with a few inches to spare. Chuck the dowel in a vised drill or a drill press. With the drill locked on and running at a slow speed, rasp the end of the dowel until you have tapered it to approximately match the taper in the rifle's chamber. Typically this requires tapering about two-inches (2") of the end of the dowel by about thirty-thousandths of an inch (about 1/32").

Then, using a standard hacksaw, cut a lengthwise slot. Center this slot down the tapered end of the dowel and extending about two inches. Cut a similar width strip of six hundred (600) grit or eight hundred (800) grit corundum paper that is long enough to allow wrapping around the dowel until it creates a near fit in the rifle's chamber. See Photograph # 1-34.

Run the end of the corundum paper into the slot so that it just extends to the other side of the slot. Make a sharp bend at the slot's edge so that the cutting surface is to the outside. Then wrap the sandpaper around the dowel until the diameter is similar to the body of the cartridge for which the gun is chambered.

Affix the gun in a vise and insert the paper-wrapped dowel into a variable speed hand drill. Lock the drill on at a moderate speed. Run the wrapped dowel into the chamber until it abuts to the chamber shoulder and until the paper is visibly polishing at the extreme rear of the chamber then slightly withdraw the dowel. Repeat this process. Also, move the drill body in a small circle so the paper eventually polishes against all sides of the chamber and equally so.

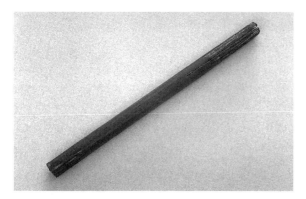

Photograph 1-33: Hardwood dowel for chamber polishing operation. Note slight taper on upper end and slot cut for corundum paper. With proper usage, this simple tool does a splendid job. See text and associated photographs.

Photograph 1-34: Note 660 grit corundum paper wrapped on end of dowel. This unit is ready for use in polishing a .30-30 chamber.

Unless the chamber is entirely too rough, in which case you should consider having it redone by a competent gunsmith, a minute or so of this polishing will remove all burs and render the inside of the chamber to a near mirror finish, sufficient for all purposes. Refer to photographs in the final sub-section of this text.

Barrel-to-Receiver Contact:

The next area of concern is the barrel shoulder, where it abuts to the receiver or recoil lug. Commonly, contact of these mating surfaces is not adequately precise. The fault can either be in the barrel, the receiver or in the recoil lug, which interposes the two in some rifle designs (Remington and Savage Bolt-Action Rifles). Most typically, the receiver face is out of square with the threaded hole. If any of these surfaces are not square with the axis of the threads on the barrel or in the receiver, there is a problem. As you tighten the barrel the barrel shoulder will contact one area of the receiver first.

In this all-too-common situation as you continue to tighten the barrel, the uneven contact at the front of the receiver induces differential stress into both barrel and receiver. The resulting accumulated stress (force) will result in strain (bending): something has to, and will, give. This will change the alignment of barrel and receiver. Typically, both the barrel and the receiver will flex appreciably to accommodate the mismatch. This result cannot contribute to accuracy. Regardless of whether the barrel or the receiver is at fault, correction of this problem involves the same steps; this begins with separation of barrel and receiver. See Photograph # 1-35.

Barrel Removal: Typical Bolt-Action, Savage Model-170 Pump & Many Other Rifle Types:

Before you consider separating a screwed-in barrel from a receiver, consider that your actions can change the rifle's headspace. Since proper headspace is fundamental to a gun's safety, consider purchase of a "GO" gauge, before you attempt any job requiring this action. If you do not understand how your rifle headspaces, and how to measure that quantity, please, forego any such alteration. Also note that rosin (as available from Brownells) is practically a prerequisite to successful barrel clamping.

First let us review a home workshop method that will facilitate removal of most barrels from actions. This will work on any gun where the previous assembler did not screw the barrel into the receiver too tightly. The first step is to reduce the gun to the basic barreled-action. Remove everything you can easily separate from the barreled-action. Include barrel-mounted sights attached with screws or cross pins, the bolt, the magazine assembly, the trigger mechanism and the stock.

Next, locate a normally hidden area of the barrel-to-receiver juncture and produce a set of aligned witness marks, one in the barrel and one in the receiver. Use a small, well-sharpened prick-punch and a solid tap from an 8- or 12-ounce ball-peen hammer. To form a deep enduring witness mark, the punch tip should taper at

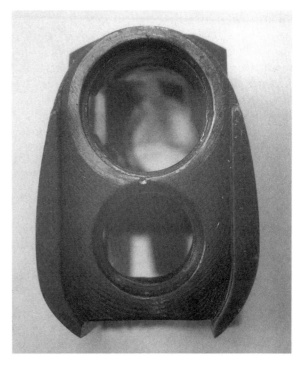

Photograph 1-35: Marlin Model-336, front-view of stripped receiver. Here we have partially lapped the barrel shoulder mating surface by installation of the barrel with 240 grit Brownells' lapping compound interposing receiver and barrel shoulder. With the receiver secured and vertically oriented in a vise we repeatedly snugged and loosened the barrel in the receiver. Note that factory bluing is still in place at the lower right while we have lapped the top left area fully past the factory machine marks. Before we were able to achieve solid and even contact around the entire circumference we had lapped about 0.01" more material away from the upper left area. Note indexing dimple at the bottom of the barrel threaded bore, near the center of the receiver. See text and associated text for a full discussion, including headspace concerns.

Section 1: The Trouble With Barrels, Part I

about thirty degrees (30°) to create a sharp sixty-degree (30° + 30° = 60°) point. A center-punch is not a good choice, the one-hundred and eighteen degree (118° point), which matches the point on a standard drill bit, is too flat. You should make the mark deep enough that you can easily see it and so that it will survive despite removal of several thousandths of an inch of material — about fifteen-thousandths of an inch (0.015") deep is generally sufficient. Also, locate this mark properly so that material removal does not hide it. If the action utilizes a recoil lug located between barrel and receiver, two separate sets of witness marks are necessary, one on either side of the recoil lug. In this case, it is also best to scribe the front of the recoil lug to indicate correct installation. See Photograph # 1-36.

Sharpening dulled center-punches is quite easy. Use a Dremel tool with a one-half inch (0.5") sanding disk or a bench-mounted vise. However, if the center-punch has a small enough shank, the best method is to chuck it into a drill press or a vised hand drill. Lock the drill on and file a very precise point using a small bastard- or smooth-cut file and forward strokes over the spinning tip. This action will take only a few seconds.

Regardless of the method used to sharpen cutting tools and chisels, use caution and restraint. Avoid overheating the steel during the sharpening operation; keep a water bath handy and use it often. Discoloration of steel is a sure sign of overheating, which will usually ruin the piece's temper.

Note that on Remington's Model-700, Savage's Model-110 and many other bolt action rifles the recoil lug is a separate piece fitting over the threaded portion of the barrel and interposing the barrel and receiver. Regarding lapping the barrel shoulder and receiver face, action designs that sandwich any such piece between the barrel and the receiver also introduce several new problems. First, as noted above, you will have to establish aligned sets of witness marks on both sides of the recoil lug and on both the barrel and receiver. Second, the recoil lug must be perfectly flat with parallel sides or it will introduce exactly the problem we are hoping to correct! We will visit each of these points in the continuing discussion. See Photograph # 1-37.

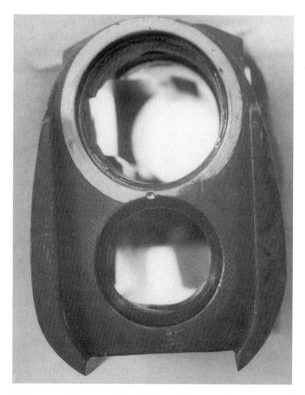

Photograph 1-36: Marlin Model-336, front-view of stripped receiver. Here we have finished lapping the barrel shoulder mating surface. See associated photograph showing partially completed job. In this instance, we will not proceed further owing to headspacing and barrel tightening limitations. However, this 98%+ contact zone is sufficient. Note that the indexing dimple, near bottom center of the lapped area is still clearly visible. This mark aligns to a similar dimple on the barrel. We produced both indentations before the gunsmith removed the barrel. This process is representative of that used on a typical bolt-action rifle.

Photograph 1-37: Left-hand Remington Model-700 bolt-action barreled-action. This view shows bottom of barrel at location of recoil lug. Remington has designed this lug to transfer recoil from the barreled-action to the stock. Use of this separate piece, interposing barrel and receiver, at once eases the task of lapping the abutting surfaces and makes the process a bit more complex! It is this lug that one glass beds into a hole in the stock, as described later in the text. (For that operation we suggest taping over the front, sides and bottom surfaces of this lug before bedding it in epoxy.)

Also note that Savage's method of using a nut to secure the barrel to the receiver mitigates but does not eliminate misalignment problems: the nut, recoil lug and receiver face should still mate squarely. The trouble here is that you have to loosen the nut to remove the barrel. This is a job best done with a wrench especially designed to fit the contours of the nut. Brownells offers such a tool but cost is rather high. Also, in this instance, you must make several witness marks to ensure proper alignment of the barrel, recoil lug and receiver during reassembly. See Photograph #s 1-38/39/40.

This is similar to making the above noted witness marks on a standard barrel-to-receiver-juncture with a separate recoil lug. However, it also involves scribing a line along the underside of the nut that aligns to the axis of the bore, you can use the edge of an existing channel in the nut as a factory-made reference line. Locate a normally hidden area (under the barrel), then after producing or choosing a reference line, produce center-punched witness marks in the barrel, the recoil lug and the receiver. These indentations should all align on the reference line on the nut. Finally, scribe a front indicator ("F") on the front side of the recoil lug. See Photograph # 1-41.

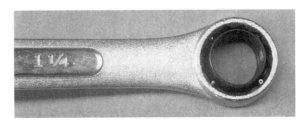

Photograph 1-40: Savage barrel nut assembled to a 1¼" box-end wrench. The four brazing-rod pins are each 3/32" in diameter. These pins transfer the load from the 12 point wrench to the nut while isolating the wrench from the nut — the brass pins cannot mar the steel!

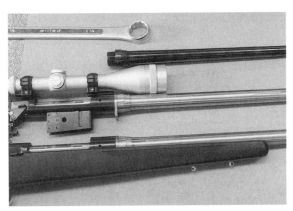

Photograph 1-38: Various Savage rifles in various states of assembly. Note 1¼" end wrench above barrel and nut. Such a wrench with four 3/32" brass pins allows one to easily remove the barrel nut from the action without fear of gun damage. One only has to properly vise the receiver. See text and associated photographs.

Photograph 1-39: Close-up-view of Savage barrel nut. Note recoil lug interposed between nut and receiver, alignment mechanism on recoil lug and eight longitudinal grooves on nut. These features add a twist or two to one's tuning of a Savage bolt-action rifle. See text.

Photograph 1-41: Alignment marks on a Marlin rifle. This witness mark indents both barrel and receiver. See text and associated photographs.

Section 1: The Trouble With Barrels, Part I

However, with the purchase of a "GO" gauge, available through Brownells or Sinclair International, you can set the headspace precisely on the Savage and certain other bolt-action rifles. Counterexamples include those rifles with any barrel-mounted fixtures, barrel projections extending into the chamber, or extractor slots cut into the rear of the barrel. Also, if you do not want any barrel markings to change alignment you must rule out any modification that would require turning the barrel further into the receiver. If your rifle lacks these restricting characteristics and you have the proper "GO" gauge, you will not need to make any witness marks and you can set the headspace perfectly with a bit of work and attention to detail. See Photograph # 1-42.

In many instances, home workshop barrel removal is no simple task. Truth is, this operation typically ranges from downright tough to impossible. We will discuss special homemade tools as well as tools the home gunsmith can purchase to accomplish barrel and receiver separation. The reason barrel removal often requires special tools? Commonly, manufacturers install barrels into the receiver very tightly (often too tightly); also, thread-locking agents are sometimes used. I will return to this latter point several times throughout this discussion.

Now, finally, about separating barrel and receiver. I once removed a barrel from a Marlin Model-1936 using a bench-mounted vise, a block of hardwood and a rubber mallet! I clamped the barrel in a 2½ x 2½ inch oak block that I had drilled a barrel-diameter hole through and then sawed a one-eighth inch (1/8") wide slot through and about two inches past the hole. See sketch. This basic mechanism is very useful for clamping any tubular piece without damage.

Note, before beginning any such work on any rifle featuring a tubular magazine, remove the magazine and any other barrel attachments that might be damaged if the barrel turned in the clamping blocks. Similarly, always remove the bolt from any rifle before attempting to remove the barrel. On various lever-actions and Savage's pump-action, protrusions from the front of the bolt's body enter ramps in the barrel. Turning the barrel in the receiver without opening the bolt will destroy something!

BASIC CONCEPT OF WOOD CLAMP FOR RIFLE BARRELS

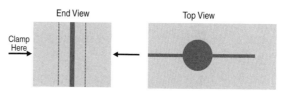

Hole is diameter of clamped piece
(often tapered)
Cut slot with standard wood saw
(1/8" wide cut).

To make this wood block, measure the diameter of the largest portion of the barrel, as close to the chamber as possible; where the barrel has a straight or only slightly tapered contour; and where the sights will not interfere. The best course involves sight removal. See the sub-section on barrel-mounted sight repair. Use the largest drill bit that is just smaller than the measured barrel diameter. If you have an adjustable wood drill bit (available at any good hardware store) you can easily adjust the drill bit to bore the exact diameter hole you need. See Photograph # 1-43.

After drilling the hole, you might choose to use a large round file to bring the hole's shape closer to matching the barrel's exterior. Slightly rasp at one end of the hole, holding the file at a slight angle to the centerline of the hole. The idea is to taper the hole to match the barrel's

Photograph 1-42: If you are doing any job that might alter the gun's headspace you should invest in a set of headspace gauges. If the action will close normally on this Forster "GO" gauge, the chamber is long enough to chamber standard cartridges. If it will close normally on Forster's similar "NO GO" gauge the gun has excessive (potentially dangerous) headspace. Many of the receiver-related gunsmithing measures discussed in the text can either increase or decrease headspace. Use extreme caution in any such operation. Verify that the finished chamber is within specification length. Excessive headspace is, perhaps, the single most dangerous condition a gun can exhibit! See text and associated photograph for a full discussion.

taper, if necessary. A little wood removal goes a long way here. Try to visualize the angle formed by the surface of the barrel and the axis of the bore. Hold the file at that angle, which will always be almost no angle at all! Often the taper in the file's shank is sufficient — the file's taper is similar in degree to the barrel's taper. In that case, you can hold the center-line of the file aligned to the centerline of the hole. When the file is cutting full length of the hole, around the entire circumference of the hole, the hole's taper will match the barrel's. See Photograph # 1-44.

Should the front sight interfere with slipping the finished block over the barrel, either remove the front sight or continue the saw cut slot all the way through the block. Of course this latter approach creates two pieces, which is not as handy.

As a superior alternative, the home gunsmith can exactly fit the channel to the barrel by using Acraglas to fill the voids in the channel. The process is quite simple. Apply Acra-release to the barrel. If the blocks are not fully separated, cut the slot full-width to achieve separation. Clean the channel in the blocks with alcohol or acetone and let that dry. Mix up an appropriate batch of Acraglas or other high-strength epoxy.

Apply a sufficient layer of the mix into the channels in the wood blocks. Apply the wood blocks over the proper section of the barrel. Wrap a layer or two of vinyl electrical tape around both ends of the blocks.

After the epoxy cures, use a plastic mallet to break the epoxy free from the barrel. Slide the assembly off the front of the barrel. Use a standard hacksaw to resaw the block apart following the same cut. Owing to the barrel-contour matching epoxy, these blocks can clamp the barrel with significantly more force than the plain-wood blocks.

The next important step is to degrease the area of the barrel where you will clamp it in the hardwood blocks. Alcohol and water are the minimum requirement here. It is better to use a heavy duty degreaser; the cleaner the steel the better the chances of successful bonding with the rosined wood clamp. (Acetone is the best readily available solvent for this purpose.) See Photograph # 1-45.

Apply rosin (available from Brownells Incorporated) to the barrel and the hole in the hardwood block. Then slip the block over the barrel until it fits snugly but with a gap along both sides at the cut. Position the blocks so that

Photograph 1-43: The makings of a hardwood barrel clamp. Note the cracks on both blocks. We added backing blocks to support these. We attached the oak backing blocks with glue and screws and with the grain running across these cracks, the finished modified units held-up to our most severe testing — we could not tighten our vise sufficiently to damage the blocks when we clamped on a solid steel rod of approximately barrel-diameter.

Photograph 1-44: Rough finished hardwood blocks. Note hole drilled endwise through center of each block — we clamped the blocks together then drilled down the seam with a barrel diameter bit. We used a round bastard file to taper the resulting hole. When we mate these blocks, the drilled and filed hole forms a barrel-fitting clamping channel. Rosin, available through Brownells, is a tremendous asset in any clamping operation. Never use such a clamping device on any thin-walled barrel, such as a shotgun barrel — one can easily crush or deform any such thin-walled tube.

Section 1: The Trouble With Barrels, Part I

this gap is about forty-thousandths of an inch (0.040", the width of a hacksaw cut) wide. Vise the block in a heavy duty bench-mounted vise and clamp with enough force to deform the wood, as evidenced by minor cracking noises. These noises result from crushing of high spots on the wood. Do not clamp any thin-walled (shotgun-like) barrel in this manner — the potential to damage the barrel is entirely too great! See Photograph # 1-46.

Never forget, along the grain or across a typical knot the compressive strength of wood is much higher than steel. Compressive strength across the grain in dense hardwoods can be comparable to steel; therefore, do not over-tighten any such clamp. If you try hard enough you can (read will!) damage any barrel!

Now we have the barrel affixed in the vise. Remember, we have also created witness marks, as necessary, on some normally hidden area where the barrel abuts the receiver. Apply a dab of high-quality penetrating oil, available at any good automotive products store, at both the barrel-to-receiver joint and at the rear of the barrel threads inside the receiver. Wait several minutes to allow that product an opportunity to achieve full penetration. Be careful not to get any oil of any kind into the clamped area. Oil will compromise the tenuous bond between the rosin and the clean, polished steel. See Photograph # 1-47.

Photograph 1-46: Rifle barrel with rosin and clamping blocks. This did not work. We later modified the blocks, as explained in the associated photograph captions. Nevertheless, without special (gunsmith) tools we were unable to break the barrel loose from the receiver — Remington Model-700. (We tried using a hardwood pry lever in the action, penetrating oil and impacts to the receiver at the barrel ring using a one-pound hard-plastic mallet.) We ended up taking the gun to a gunsmith! Cost of that service should not exceed $30, if you take in a stripped barreled-action and request only barrel removal. In this case, after we completed the necessary work, reassembly using only these home-workshop tools was a snap. See associated text. Also note, before attempting to disassemble any barreled-action ensure that the gun does not use a retaining or alignment pin and that you have properly indexed the barrel and receiver to facilitate accurate reassembly. See text for details.

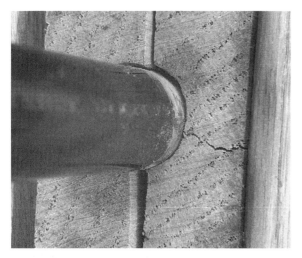

Photograph 1-45: Barrel clamped between blocks with backing boards attached. Note crack in right-hand block. When the barrel was torqued, this block failed. As noted in the associated photograph caption, subsequent (successful) repair involved gluing and screwing these blocks to backing boards (with the grain running across the grain in these clamping blocks).

Photograph 1-47: Here we are applying penetrating oil to the barrel-to-receiver threads. A plastic extension nozzle guides the penetrant into the proper area. See text and associated photograph captions for a complete discussion. In this instance, we later discovered the manufacturer had bonded the receiver and barrel with an epoxy-like substance applied to the threads. We were forced to refer to a gunsmith's services.

Before proceeding, make absolutely certain a cross pin does not retain the barrel in place! If you are in doubt about possible pinning, you should have a gunsmith look the barreled-action over or at least call an expert who might know if that particular gun uses a pinned barrel (this practice is common in some revolver types). If a cross-pin does retain the barrel, remove that by tapping against its end with a properly fitting pin punch and a light weight ball-peen hammer. Also note, remove the bolt before attempting to unscrew the barrel, on some action designs the extractor or other action extensions protrude into slots at the back of the barrel. Where such conditions occur, unless you first remove or withdraw the bolt, turning the receiver on the barrel will damage or destroy something.

Practically all rifles use right-hand threads. If you can see the threads, you should be able to ascertain if they are right-hand or left-hand. Obviously, turn the receiver the correct way.

As a first effort, which will work if the barrel is not too tight, try tapping on the receiver in an area near the front and below the barrel with a hard rubber or plastic mallet. On many action types you can insert an oak block, sized properly to fit through the magazine well, and pass out the top of the action. Such a block that is perhaps two feet long allows significant torque. If the wood is of sufficient quality, it will withstand just about all the force the home gunsmith can apply and almost certainly more than the previously described barrel clamp will hold. See Photograph #s 1-48/49.

If this will not get the job done, consider purchasing the proper receiver wrench from Brownells. Take no chances with damaging the receiver!

An alternative method involves a one-half inch (0.5") thick three-inch (3") wide mild steel bar that is about twenty-four inches (24") long. Place several layers of paperboard along both sides of this bar until it is as tight a fit as possible as it passes through the magazine well and out the top of the action. This will easily provide more strength and leverage than the barrel clamp can hold. However, one must provide spacers and padding to prevent any portion of this bar from touching against the receiver. Also, one has to use spacers to prevent any stress on delicate interior features of the receiver. For example, the protrusions that form the top of the magazine well on a Remington Model-700 and other rifles. Remember, manufacturers necessarily make the receiver from very soft steel, be careful not to dent, bend, ding or otherwise damage it.

If you cannot manage to loosen the barrel using either the wood or steel bar, you will almost certainly have to increase the clamping

Photograph 1-48: Tools for pulling a barrel from an action in the home workshop. A substantial and rigidly mounted bench vise is a basic minimum. Here we have clamped the barrel in a fitted channel between two blocks of oak. We have liberally applied Brownells' rosin into this channel. We tighten the vise until the wood exhibits cracking noises (but never on any thin-walled barrel). Here we have fitted the end of an oak board to pass through the action's feed rails. Note the Liquid Wrench. Application of such a product to the barrel threads several hours ahead of time can help. See text and associated photograph captions for a complete discussion.

Photograph 1-49: Hammering on the front receiver ring with a plastic mallet, while applying steady pressure to the board, might help free recalcitrant threads. However, in this instance, the threads were factory epoxied. Despite our best efforts, separation required a gunsmith's services. See text and associated photograph captions for a complete discussion.

Section 1: The Trouble With Barrels, Part I

force on the barrel before proceeding to other methods. Often, one can apply more torque with a hardwood bar than the hardwood barrel clamp will withstand.

Remember, almost all barrel threads are right-handed. The receiver will screw off just like a nut from a right-hand threaded bolt.

Often the above described method and tools will not do the job. If not, try the following modification. Apply about all the force you can to one end of the pry bar, but without breaking the rosin free in the barrel clamp. Then, while holding this steady torque on the threaded joint, hammer on the free end of the bar using a one-pound hard-rubber or plastic mallet. Often the shock this hammering generates will do the job when nothing else will.

However, do not hammer too vigorously, especially if the receiver is in any way flimsy, and watch for failure of any paper or wood spacers alongside the pry bar inside the action. Such failure could result in damage to the receiver. One final technique to try: apply pressure to the end of the pry bar and use a hard-plastic (nylon) mallet to hammer on the receiver ring — over the barrel threads. This method generates significant shock and will often get the job done.

If the barrel clamp will not hold sufficiently for any of the above methods to result in loosening of the barrel, consider fashioning a barrel clamp that is perhaps six-inches (6") wide so that it clamps over a larger area of the barrel; doubling the clamp's length can double the clamping friction. Many bench vises have a six-inch (6") wide jaw. If your vise jaws are six-inches (6") wide it is advantageous to use a six- to eight-inch (6"-8") wide wood clamp. Also, consider fashioning the inside of the wood clamp to more correctly fit the barrel, if possible.

Finally, reapply a quality penetrating oil and allow the piece to sit for several hours or days. Often time will make the difference.

As noted above, the most likely expedient is to hammer on the receiver adjacent to the barrel using a hard-plastic (nylon) mallet. Repeated blows, while applying unscrewing torque on the receiver will sometimes do the job.

You might consider application of heat using a portable hair dryer. If you wrap the barrel with a wet rag placed adjacent to the receiver and apply the heated air to the rear of the receiver there is a chance the differential heating might loosen the bond, especially if the factory installation included a thread locking agent — which is quite common on Remington bolt-action rifles. I have little confidence in this approach and application of more heat is not advisable. Nevertheless, this is worth a try.

If even your best efforts will not free the barrel from the receiver, it is time to talk to a professional. Likely, if he does not already have these units, your local gunsmith will have to make a set of mild steel blocks that will clamp the barrel perfectly. He will use these and other special tools to free the offending joint. This service should cost a modest amount, perhaps twenty-five dollars ($25). Often, after you have completed the alterations described below, you can reinstall the barrel at home quite easily using only the above-mentioned methods. See Photograph # 1-50.

Photograph 1-50: These are the tools a gunsmith uses to separate a barreled action into barrel and receiver. At lower center is the barrel clamp. A set of barrel shims are standing to the upper right of the clamping fixture. Our gunsmith has located the receiver in a special action wrench. Note that he hand tightens the wrench to the action. Wrench tightening such a tool can, and will, crush the receiver! See text and associated photographs.

Also as noted above, Brownells, Inc. sells action wrenches designed to fit specific types of rifles. These are a reasonable investment for those who want to do any of several alterations that require barrel removal on several similar rifles. These tools minimize the risk of damage. However, these are quite expensive and it seems more reasonable to support your local gunsmith through contracting this specialized job, when necessary. See Photograph # 1-51.

For use with any slab-sided receiver, a very good wrench system involves two three-eighths inch (3/8") mild steel strips that are about two and one-half inches (2½") wide and about twenty-four inches (24") long. Line these strips up and clamp tightly in a vise. Center-punch two locations where you will drill bolt holes. Center one hole from side-to-side and about one-inch (1") from one end of the straps. The second hole is about four-inches (4") from the first, also centered from side-to-side. Bore three-thirty-seconds inch (3/32") diameter pilot holes through both straps at both locations. Then bore both holes to thirteen-thirty-seconds inch (13/32") (most 3/8"-rated hand drills will accept a 13/32" drill bit). Use plenty of cutting oil for all hole drilling in steel.

Remove these straps from the vise. Using nylon reinforced tape (electrician's or duct tape will do), attach a two-inch by three-inch (2"x3") piece of one-quarter inch (1/4") plywood between the holes on one side of each strap. Install three-eighth inch (3/8"), grade-6 bolts that are at least two-inches (2") longer than the receiver is wide through each hole of one of the straps. The bolt heads should be on the side of the strap opposite the wood inserts. Install a piece of five-eighth inch (5/8") automotive heater hose over each bolt shank. These pieces of hose should be about the same length as the receiver is wide. Finally, reverse the second strap, end to end, and assemble it to the first so that it extends from the bolts the opposite way with the wood inserts also inside the straps. Screw standard nuts onto the bolts to bring the opening to about the width of the receiver.

Slip this assembly over the receiver until it achieves a good purchase. Preferably, you should locate this clamp as close to the front of the receiver as feasible. Snug the nuts until the wood begins to crunch in response. However, use no more clamping force than necessary. Remember, manufacturers necessarily make receivers of comparatively soft steel; you can easily deform the receiver by using too much clamping force. On some receivers, the top is wider than the bottom; adjust this clamp accordingly. No harm done, as long as only wood and the rubber hose touch the receiver.

This clamping system might also work on receivers that are essentially round, as in the Remington action. In this instance, locate one side of the clamp over the ejection port or against the bottom of the receiver where the magazine inserts. Never clamp against any weak area.

With the barrel rosined in the hardwood barrel clamp, that clamp vised tightly and the receiver clamped in this manner, you should be able to apply sufficient torque to separate the receiver from the barrel. As noted above, if the barrel-to-receiver joint is so tight that this procedure does not work, consider using the epoxy-

Photograph 1-51: This is how a gunsmith separates a barreled action into barrel and receiver. This wrench locks into special keying pieces, which fit in the rails and lock the wrench and receiver together, while preventing damage. A great deal of variation exists in barrel attachment. Some are extremely tight, others more reasonably snug.

matching method noted above. You can also use a wood clamp that is wider so that the wood clamps a greater length of the barrel, as noted above.

Never use excessive force in tightening any clamp on the receiver or when trying to unscrew the receiver. It is extremely easy to crush or otherwise deform a receiver. As noted, manufacturers must use comparatively soft steel for receivers. Keep this in mind. Slightly more than finger tight on clamping screws is generally both sufficient and all the clamping force one should apply. See Photograph # 1-52.

When the joint does begin to loosen, make a shallow witness mark on the barrel where the receiver witness mark aligns when the joint has fully loosened — that is, when the abutting faces just touch. The distance between the original barrel witness mark and this mark indicates the amount of interference fit induced by tightening the barrel.

After determining this distance, the home gunsmith can calculate the amount of material he can remove from the abutting faces and threads before he could no longer tighten the barrel properly — without turning it past the point of witness mark alignment. Begin by measuring the distance around the barrel at the breech. A fiber seamstress's tape will give a close-enough measure. For a more accurate measurement: wrap a piece of paper around the breech end of the barrel, mark the point of overlap, then measure the distance between the marks. However you get this measurement, record this number for reference.

Second, measure the distance between the centers of the witness marks on the barrel. Divide the latter by the former. This gives the portion of one turn represented by the interference fit created at the factory during barrel tightening. This is an important number. Therefore, for reference, record it also.

The next step is to count the number of threads per inch on the barrel. Over the threaded section of the barrel, measure one-half of an inch along the axis of the bore. Mark the ends of this section. Count the number of complete and partial threads in that one-half inch section. Multiply that number by two to get threads per inch. Divide the number of threads per inch into one. The resulting number represents the distance the barrel advances in one turn. Record this metered number.

For a significant listing of barrel thread pitch, refer to the *NRA Gunsmithing Guide*, pages 65-71. Nevertheless, measure your rifle's threads to be sure.

You now know the distance the barrel advances with each complete turn and the portion of one turn represented by the existing interference fit between the barrel and the receiver. Multiplication of those two numbers gives a very close measure of the distance the barrel would advance in response to turning the amount represented by the interference fit; that is, the total thickness of material the home gunsmith would have to remove from the mating surfaces to eliminate one-hundred percent (100%) of the interference fit.

An example is in order. Assume a typical barrel with a breech diameter of about one and one-quarter inch (1¼") that tightens with about two-tenths of an inch (2/10") of rotation creating interference fit, as measured at the circumference of the breech. Assume a barrel threaded at twenty (20) turns per inch:

Measurement will show that the breech is about 4" in circumference

Portion of one turn represented by the interference fit is 0.2" ÷ 4" = 0.05

Each turn of the barrel represents 1÷20 = 0.050" of barrel advance 0.05 of one turn of the barrel equals 0.050" ÷ 0.05 = 0.0025"

Therefore, removal of about 0.0025" of material from the barrel shoulder or receiver face would eliminate the interference fit.

Referring to the above example: removal of two and one-half thousandths of an inch of material between the mating surfaces would eliminate

Photograph 1-52: Close-up-view of clamping fixture. At center is the barrel clamp. One-half of a typical barrel shim lies under the barrel.

one-hundred percent (100%) of the interference fit. Actual interference fit on rifles usually ranges from about three-thousandths of an inch (0.003") to about six-thousandths of an inch (0.006"). Typically, an interference fit representing no more than one- to two-thousandths of an inch will provide sufficient tightening for maximum accuracy. On a typical barrel this suggests that if the original mark and the "just touching" mark are more than about one-eighth of an inch apart the barrel-to-receiver joint is almost certainly too tight for maximum accuracy.

Proper interference fit is no more than the amount required to prevent the barrel shoulder from pulling away from the receiver face in response to the stress of the cartridge's firing. Any tightening beyond this level introduces unnecessary, and almost certainly detrimental, stress into the system.

As I will discuss below, it is a simple matter to file away a few thousandths of an inch at this contact face. You can follow this with the lapping process to provide a square fit. However, before filing on anything, remember that lapping alone can remove a few thousandths of an inch, and rather quickly. Read this entire sub-section before proceeding with either filing or lapping.

Lapping to True the Barrel-to-Receiver Contact Area:

As observed in the above discussion of barrel removal, I must note that barrel removal brings up questions of proper reinstallation. Indexing is necessary and desirable on any barrel that has any attached fixtures, such as sights, or where the rear of the barrel has any extension or cuts that accommodate the extractor or other action parts. Also, lapping the barrel-to-receiver contact area will likely result in two consequences: first, the barrel will not be as tight when reinstalled to the same index mark after the lapping operation, which is generally a good thing; second, lapping will usually reduce headspace, also generally a good thing.

I will address both points later in this sub-section. Here I want to discuss the lapping process to give a general idea of the steps involved.

To lap the barrel-to-receiver contact area, mount the receiver in a padded bench-mounted vise so that the barrel screws into it vertically (ideally from below). In this arrangement, lapping proceeds with the barrel hanging against the threads and without any sideways load that would tend to bend the barrel against one side of the receiver — that is, the barrel threads are centered and balanced in the receiver threads and the barrel is not lying against one side of the receiver hole or bent out of alignment by gravity. See Photograph # 1-53.

The Remington-style recoil lug presents a significant variation here. We want all lapped surfaces to make square and solid contact. With the existence of an interposed recoil lug we have to modify this basic procedure.

Perhaps the easiest way to lap between the barrel and receiver on a rifle using an interposing recoil lug is as described hereafter. Begin by positioning the receiver as noted above. Then apply lapping compound (use a relatively coarse-grit lapping agent; 220 grit silicon carbide is perfectly acceptable) to both the receiver face and the barrel shoulder. Use caution to avoid contaminating the threads. Then install the lug over the barrel threads. Screw the barrel into the receiver until it just begins to lock the recoil lug in place.

Rotate the recoil lug, first one way, then the other. Repeat this rotation several times in a random pattern — a bit this way and more that way but never in a constant pattern. Soon the lug should turn noticeably freer. When the recoil lug turns free, first turn the barrel slightly looser, then slightly tighter (this will redistribute the abrasive) until the recoil lug turns hard.

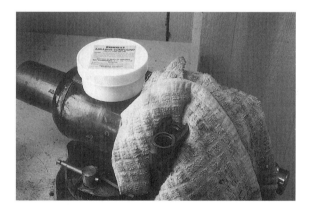

Photograph 1-53: Vised Marlin 336 lever-action receiver. Axis of the threads is vertical. This orientation limited differential stress during lapping. Brownells' lapping compound (240 grit) did that job in a hurry! See text and associated photograph captions for a complete discussion, including headspace concerns. We would use a very similar approach for any action type using screw threaded barrel-to-receiver attachment.

Section 1: The Trouble With Barrels, Part I

Repeat the above rotations of the recoil lug. After, perhaps, three minutes of this process, remove the barrel from the receiver. Separate the recoil lug from the barrel.

Clean all lapped surfaces; reassemble the recoil lug on the barrel; and screw the barrel into the receiver. Hand tighten the assembly and observe the distance between the index marks. If this distance exceeds, perhaps, fifty-thousandths of an inch (a bit less than 1/16") you still have room to work. In this case, additional lapping, if necessary, is possible.

Photograph 1-54: Partially lapped Remington Model-700 receiver. Note bright area, top left of photograph. Lapping has already removed the factory bluing and most of the machining tool marks in that area, yet the lower right area is almost pristine! This is not an unusual degree of misalignment. Tightening a barrel with such misalignment imparts stress to both barrel and receiver — accuracy suffers. In this instance, we will proceed with additional lapping to achieve a more accurate mating (see photograph 1-55). However, we will proceed carefully, fully cognizant of headspace control considerations. This lapping process typically shortens headspace; however, lug lapping (also beneficial) typically similarly lengthens headspace! Owing to barrel tightening considerations, installation of iron sights on this barrel limits our work here — we have to keep the sights aligned at the top of the gun! As it turned out, on the finished product, we were able to tighten the barrel in place using only hand tools and a plastic mallet, an ideal condition. We used Loctite Product #609 (a mounting agent) in the shoulder area and Loctite Product #222 (a low-strength thread locking agent) on the threads. This ensures the barrel will stay put and will not vibrate. Nevertheless, these products facilitate disassembly and provide corrosion protection.

Again, disassemble the barrel and recoil lug. Observe the lapping pattern. If the lapped areas show similar contact over both sides of the lug, the face of the receiver and the shoulder of the barrel you have finished this job. If not, repeat the above steps until all surfaces show lapped contact. However, observe the index mark separation at first contact, never lap away too much material, even if the surfaces do not come into full simultaneous contact. Better a bit of unlapped surface than a barrel you cannot properly tighten! See Photograph #s 1-54/55.

On the Savage Model-110 the procedure is similar. Here, screw the nut onto the barrel sufficiently to expose about five-eighths of an inch (5/8") of barrel threads. Then apply the lapping compound to the receiver-contacting face of the nut. Install the recoil lug (oriented properly front to back) over the threads. Screw the barrel into the receiver until the recoil lug contacts the receiver. Release the barrel to let it hang freely. Then work the recoil lug as noted above. Repeat this operation for several minutes. Here, on the Savage rifle, you cannot hurt anything by lapping

Photograph 1-55: Finished-lapped Remington Model-700 receiver. Note bright ring around entire perimeter. Also note extant machine marks on lower right area. While we would prefer to proceed further, barrel tightening considerations limit us at this point. Note that in this alignment enhancing procedure we also lapped the barrel and receiver threads, both sides of the recoil lug and the abutting shoulder of the barrel. See text and associated photograph captions for a complete discussion. Finally, note that we have lapped the locking lug working faces; a separate operation best done with the barrel removed using Brownells' special tool. See associated photographs.

too much. Therefore, make certain the contact is complete and solid around the entire circumference of the nut, on both sides of the recoil lug and of the receiver recoil lug abutting shoulder. To reiterate, the above comment (cannot lap too much) applies only to rifles using Savage's system with a separate barrel-locking nut.

Also note, new Savage 110s incorporate an alignment tab on the recoil lug — this makes it impossible to lap the lug-to-receiver contact joint. On these rifles consider filling any irregularities in this joint using steel reinforced glass bedding agent to semi-permanently bond the lug to the barrel.

On a gun lacking the interposed recoil lug or a separate barrel nut the procedure is conceptually simpler but harder to accomplish. Apply the lapping agent to the shoulder of the barrel and wipe it so that it covers the entire shoulder area. Use caution to avoid contaminating the barrel threads.

Screw the barrel into the receiver until the barrel shoulder touches the receiver. Apply as much hand tightening force as possible until the barrel stops turning. Then repeatedly loosen and hand tighten the barrel slightly. Periodically, loosen the barrel a few turns and reapply or redistribute the lapping agent, as necessary to maintain the lapping action, which you should be able to feel as you tighten and loosen the barrel. Make certain the lapping agent does not infiltrate the threads appreciably in this process. Lapping compound can jam or lap a portion of the threads. The latter condition leads to differential loading along the barrel threads as a result of tightening the barrel; a condition that is counter to best accuracy. See the associated sub-section on barrel thread lapping.

After perhaps twenty (20) cycles of loose and tight hand turning, remove the barrel and clean the barrel shoulder contact areas on both receiver and barrel. Look for a dull roughed-up area around the entire perimeter of both surfaces; the appearance of lapped areas is markedly distinct from that of machine cut, polished or blued unlapped areas. When your lapping effort has removed all high spots from both barrel and receiver contact areas, so that the entire barrel shoulder contacts the receiver simultaneously, you have finished this job. No additional lapping is necessary.

One can, however, use a very fine, preferably twelve hundred (1200) grit but certainly eight hundred (800) grit or finer, lapping agent to polish the contact surfaces to a nearly perfect mating. This added step cannot hurt anything.

Finish this job by applying a cold bluing agent to all lapped bluable steel surfaces. Brownells' formula 44-40 seems to work particularly fast and does not require immaculate degreasing of the part.

Too-Tight or Imperfect Barrel Threads:

An additional barrel related problem that is rare in rifles but rather common in certain revolvers is a too-tight barrel-to-receiver thread fit. One can easily detect a too-tight thread fit. As you turn the barrel free of the receiver observe indications of continued friction after turning the tube well beyond the point where the barrel shoulder contacts the receiver. Excepting the presence of a thread locking agent, any tightness indicates a too-tight thread. Where a prior assembler had used a thread locking compound, clean that substance from both barrel and receiver and retest the fit. Acetone is about the only common solvent that will work here. In combination with a brass bristle brush it will do the job quite well. Use plenty of ventilation.

Should you discover a tight thread, the best course is to have a gunsmith correct the problem. Typically the solution is to recut the barrel threads to a slightly smaller diameter. There is no good method for doing this at home. Lapping the threads together using compound in the twelve hundred (1200) grit range will theoretically do this job but you must be very careful not to overdo this process. Further, if the barrel is excessively tight in the receiver it will be unfeasible to use this approach; as the lapping compound infiltrates the threads it can lock the two pieces together. This could prevent you from turning the barrel in the receiver. However, for a slightly tight fit or where only a limited portion of the threads interfere, lapping might be feasible and is certainly worth a try. See the following sub-section.

Barrel Thread Lapping:

The home tinker can use a very fine lapping agent, eight hundred (800) grit or finer, to polish the threads to achieve a nearly perfect mating. Thread lapping with a sufficiently fine abrasive — to prevent thread jamming — is highly beneficial. For manufacturing expedience and other reasons manufacturers typically (always?) use cut threads, rather than the generally superior rolled threads, on the barrel and in the receiver.

Section 1: The Trouble With Barrels, Part I

Cut threads have several disadvantages. First, all cut threads have surface imperfections, such as high spots that concentrate the tightening load. Second, thread cutting induces stresses and fractures into the surface of the steel. These fractures and induced stress weakens the thread and, again, leads to concentrations of stress as you tighten the joint. Finally, cut threads always have some degree of surface irregularity; imperfections in pitch result in some portions of the threaded barrel shank taking more than a fair share of the tightening load. This latter problem is particularly common and detrimental.

For example, consider what happens when only the threads near the barrel shoulder touch the receiver threads. In this instance, which is common, barrel tightening stretches the chamber at the front of the threaded shank. This stretching results in localized stress. Conversely, in this situation, the extreme rear of the chamber is unstressed. Such differential loadings cannot contribute to accuracy.

Lapping removes high spots and relieves cutting-induced stress at the surface of the threads. However, the home gunsmith must practice moderation in the application of thread lapping. When you can first see that lapping has reached most of the working surface of the barrel threads, STOP! Additional lapping will only weaken the threads.

Also note, thread lapping will very quickly reduce the interference fit necessary for barrel tightening with proper headspace. Overdo this and you can render the barrel untightenable (while maintaining proper headspace and barrel alignment)! Refer to the above sub-sections to determine how much room you have to work with and when to stop.

Thread lapping is very simple. Clamp the receiver in a padded vise so the barrel will hang vertically below it. Apply a thin coating of an appropriately fine abrasive (600 grit or finer silicon carbide is preferable) evenly on the barrel threads. Screw the two pieces fully together then back apart several turns. Repeat the latter action until most of the threaded surface appears uniformly abraded, or polished (depending upon your definition).

For obvious reasons, the home gunsmith should make a serious effort to clean all lapping agent from every surface of the barrel and receiver after completion of this step. Again, finish this operation by cold bluing the lapped surfaces on any bluable alloy. See Photograph # 1-56.

Steps to Mitigate Excessive Barrel Tightening:

Mitigation of excessive barrel tightening is another area where we can improve many guns, some dramatically. Many factory barrel installations are unnecessarily tight, in the extreme. For maximum accuracy the barrel on most guns, excepting perhaps certain machine guns, should only be tight enough to prevent it from working loose under the stresses of normal use. Even what might seem to be a very loose barrel lockup can be adequate. Hand tight is often completely sufficient! Where the possibility of the barrel

Photograph 1-56: Here we have lapped the threads and receiver-mating shoulder on a Marlin Model-336 barrel. Note the dulled threads at rear of the barrel and dulled shoulder area. On this particular rifle, as shipped, two threads sustained 100% of the tightening load! Here the entire length of the threads mate to the corresponding threads in the receiver. One can now almost tighten this barrel by hand to the original (indexed) location, a few judicious blows with a plastic hammer do the job. With a dab of Loctite Product #222 on the threads and Loctite Product #609 on the shoulder area, this barrel will not vibrate or inadvertently come loose. Most importantly, tightening differentially stresses neither the barrel nor the receiver — this will improve intrinsic accuracy. See associated photograph captions and text for a complete discussion, including headspace concerns.

coming loose concerns a shooter, application of a dab of low-strength thread locking compound (Loctite Product # 222) will adequately bond the barrel to the receiver for all practical purposes. See Photograph # 1-57.

Proper tightness for accuracy is most typically only tight enough to prevent the two pieces from vibrating in separate modes or loosening under the stresses of firing. Chamber pressure pushes the barrel forward and the bolt back, in turn the bolt pushes the receiver back; if the barrel is not tight enough this can create a temporary separation between the mating surfaces — at the barrel-to-receiver shoulder.

Tightening any barrel tighter than "necessary" is bound to detract from accuracy; it strains both barrel and receiver out of shape and introduces uneven and unpredictable stresses into the steel. These stresses will result in temperature-sensitive strain responses, i.e., as the steel changes temperature it will bend differently! A rifle that occasionally throws an unexplained flier in any shot string might very well have a too-tight barrel-to-receiver abutment.

One can use additional lapping at the barrel receiver juncture to remove a few thousandths of an inch of material from the shoulder of the barrel and the front of the receiver. As noted in the above discussion, this loosens the lockup when the barrel is retightened and properly indexed. Before we proceed with this discussion we need to consider the effect this work has on headspace. Do not attempt this modification until you understand what it will do to the gun's headspace. . . .

Over tightening the barrel has two effects. First, it compresses the front of the receiver along the axis of the bore. In front-locking actions this has little effect on headspace. Second, it stretches the chambered portion of the barrel along the axis of the bore. This directly affects headspace.

Obviously, reducing the interference fit between the barrel and the receiver will tend to reduce headspace — barrel tightening stretches the chamber less. In extreme instances, this alteration could measurably shorten headspace.

Lapping the juncture of the barrel shoulder and receiver, to allow the barrel to tighten with less torque, also allows the back end of the barrel to move further into the receiver, perhaps a few thousandths of an inch, without stretching. Therefore, this operation will result in a commensurate headspace shortening. Since most factory-chambered rifles have about two-thousandths of an inch excess headspace, this chamber shortening is normally harmless, and perhaps beneficial.

However, this headspace shortening might cause problems in certain instances. Examples include guns where headspace was minimal and those where a handloader or handload user already has a supply of custom-fitted handloaded ammunition — where a slight shortening of chamber headspace length can render the ammunition unchamberable.

You can avoid the former problem by using a "GO" gauge as you proceed with the lapping. These gauges are available through Brownells Incorporated, Sinclair Int., Forster, Midway and others. As long as the action will close normally on the "GO" gauge, without application of any excessive pressure, the chamber is long enough to work with any specification ammunition. In the latter instance, custom fitted loads, the best approach is to first shoot up any such ammunition and then proceed to fix this problem — the potential benefit is worth the effort.

The "GO" gauge is also useful for testing how much headspace room is available. You can apply layers of transparent cellophane tape to the head of the gauge until the action will not close normally. Since each layer is about two-

Photograph 1-57: Here we are applying Loctite Product #222 to the degreased threads before reassembly of barrel and receiver. This low-strength thread-locking compound will prevent inadvertent loosening of the barrel. This product will also protect hidden surfaces against corrosion. It is important to clean and degrease both barrel and receiver threads. Note also application of Loctite Product #609 at shoulder area. This mounting agent provides vibration-free adhesion and corrosion protection. See text and associated photograph captions for a complete discussion.

thousandths of an inch (0.002") thick you can adequately judge how far you can shorten the chamber while maintaining adequate headspace. (Different brands and types will differ in thickness, use a ten-thousandths micrometer to measure ten layers, then divide by ten for a very precise determination of the thickness of one layer.)

However, if intrinsic headspace is critical, as noted by the aforementioned "GO" gauge and tape procedure, do not lap away any more of the abutting shoulders than is necessary to achieve complete simultaneous contact, as noted in the sub-section on squaring the receiver-to-barrel contact surface.

In those common instances where the home gunsmith needs to remove several thousandths of an inch of material, to allow proper and reasonable interference fit between the barrel and receiver when the barrel is properly indexed, he might choose to remove a layer of material from the receiver face using a wide fine-toothed single-cut file (a smooth- or extra-smooth-cut). If so, he should proceed with caution. A little goes a long way here. Further, remating the surfaces with lapping compound will likely remove a few more thousandths of an inch of material. Remember, almost always, you can achieve the proper interference fit through minimal lapping of the threads and abutting shoulders without any filing.

Retightening the Barrel:

After completing all lapping and fitting operations, consider using cold bluing agents to refinish all lapped surfaces. This is well worthwhile as this limits the potential for corrosion in hidden areas. Brownells sells a selection of quality cold bluing agents that work well on most bluable iron alloys. I am partial to Oxpho-Blue and Birchwood Casey's cold blue paste.

In action designs where the rear of the barrel has extensions or slots for one or more extractors, such as the Savage Model-170 and some other action styles, one should do any necessary work on those features before reassembling the barrel to the receiver. See the appropriate sub-sections.

In those instances where the barrel is free of attachments, receiver slots or extensions that would otherwise require specific indexing, the best option is to use a "GO" gauge to limit maximum barrel torqueing.

We are getting ahead of ourselves here but this method is worth discussing now. To use the "GO" gauge to determine proper barrel-to-receiver torque, install the gauge and periodically check chamber length, by noting if the bolt closes freely, as you progressively tighten the barrel. When the closing bolt just begins to touch the gauge, the barrel is just slightly too tight. For the handloader, this condition is likely of no concern. Occasionally, factory ammunition might not chamber (though this would be most unlikely). For assurance, slightly loosen the barrel until the bolt will just freely close to the fully locked position. Application of one layer of standard cellophane tape (0.002" thick) to the base of the "GO" gauge will provide adequate excess headspace for any purpose.

On rifles featuring a separate barrel locking nut, such as the Savage 110 series, this is particularly simple. Note, never force the bolt closed on any steel headspace gauge. That action is almost certain to damage the receiver, the bolt or both.

In any case, before reassembling the barrel to the receiver, thoroughly clean all pieces involved of all contaminants. As noted above, you might consider application of a small dab of a low-strength thread locking agent (Loctite Product #222) to the clean threads. This will sufficiently bond the barrel against inadvertent loosening. Regardless of your decision on that, you should also use a retaining agent (Loctite Product #609) between all mating shoulders. See Photograph # 1-58.

Photograph 1-58: Here we are applying Loctite Product #609 to the barrel-shouldering area of the receiver before reassembly of barrel to receiver. See associated photograph and caption.

These products serve many useful purposes. Both prevent infiltration of corrosive agents and seal the mated surfaces against climatic evils; fill inevitable voids; bond the surfaces against vibration; aid in preventing unintentional barrel loosening; and lubricate the surfaces to substantially facilitate proper reassembly.

On systems where the barrel screws into the receiver with no interposing devices, simply vise the barrel in the hardwood clamp fashioned for barrel removal and reverse the removal procedure. Use caution to avoid tightening past the index marks, which can easily happen — you can typically tighten the barrel much easier than you can remove it! When the index marks line up you have completed the basic job.

On rifles where a recoil lug is interposed between the barrel and receiver, the procedure is similar. However, there is the complication that the recoil lug must end up pointing in the correct direction! This is not too difficult. Usually, unless the barrel is entirely too tight, you can tap it into proper alignment using a brass hammer as you bring the barrel into final alignment. Here the only requirement is sufficient alignment of all indexing marks.

On Savage Model-110 series bolt-action rifles the process is a little more complicated. Apply a dab of low-strength thread locker (Loctite Product #222) to the barrel threads, if desired. Screw the barrel nut all the way on the barrel. Then screw the barrel a few threads into the receiver. Chamber a dummy cartridge or (preferably) the "GO" gauge. Insert and close the bolt. Then screw the barrel into the receiver until the chambered dummy solidly stops it. Then screw the nut toward the receiver until it touches lightly. Back the nut off until the scribed line on the nut aligns with the witness mark on the receiver. Then turn the barrel, always back out of the receiver slightly (if more than a small portion of a turn something is wrong!), until the witness mark on the barrel lines up with the line on the nut.

We now have the barrel properly indexed and headspaced. It remains only to tighten the barrel locking nut sufficiently to lock the barrel in place without disrupting the barrel's alignment. Apply retaining agent (Loctite Product #609) to the abutting face of the nut before tightening it. Again, only tighten the nut sufficiently to lock the barrel in place against the stresses of firing a cartridge. Also note that you can easily verify proper barrel indexing by comparing the offset from the original scribed line on the nut with both index marks.

Turning the barrel slightly too far into the receiver is generally okay but it is possible that the rear of the barrel might touch the front of the bolt. This would be very unusual, except, perhaps, in the Savage design. It could happen in a rifle where the original assembly resulted in the front of the bolt almost touching the barrel's rear face. In that situation, if the barrel were turned slightly farther into the receiver the barrel could touch the closed bolt — this would also create a false headspace reading.

In unusual cases, this might also happen with standard barrel attachments. As you lapped the receiver face the assembled chamber length would shorten as the barrel was stretched less during tightening. At the same time, the rear face of the barrel would move closer to the bolt. Let us look at an example.

Assume you have a rifle with SAAMI maximum headspace, six-thousandths of an inch (0.006") but only one-thousandth of an inch (0.001") clearance between the front of the bolt and the rear of the barrel (which would be very unusual on bolt-action rifles). During disassembly you discover the barrel is extremely tight. You want to reduce the torque required to install it, since the barrel has no attachment you are unconcerned with where it ends up with regard to rotation. You start lapping the receiver face and barrel shoulder, as described above, and periodically check headspace with the "GO" gauge.

Everything seems to be going along properly until you lap one more time and hand-tighten the barrel into the action for another headspace check. Now the bolt will not lock up properly! To verify the situation you recheck without inserting the "GO" gauge. You discover that the bolt is still not locking up properly!

By lapping the abutment faces you have allowed the barrel to move back in the receiver. In this situation there is no harm done, since you can simply file a few thousandths of an inch off the rear face of the barrel. Nevertheless, this is something you have to watch out for, especially since it can result in a false headspace reading!

Normally, however, turning the barrel slightly too far into the receiver, compared to the original setting, only serves to slightly shorten headspace, which is usually no problem. Turning the barrel insufficiently (slightly) into the receiver will increase headspace slightly, which can be a safety problem. While differences in witness mark alignment of no more than about fifteen-thousandths of an inch (0.015") should pose no hazard, it is always better to minimize

Section 1: The Trouble With Barrels, Part I

headspace. Therefore, the best approach is to redo the assembly to ensure proper indexing of the barrel — as it was originally, or slightly tighter. To ensure correct installation of the barrel on the Savage Model-110, compare a line that is parallel to the scribed line on the nut and aligned with the witness marks on the receiver and the barrel. Again, a "GO" gauge is a useful tool. See the above discussion.

After allowing sufficient time for complete curing of any thread locking or retaining agents used, perhaps a day or longer, a thorough application of a quality penetrating rust preventive is a very good idea. There is no better product available for this purpose than TSI-301, available through NECO. See Photograph # 1-59.

Barrel Attachment on Remington's Pump:

(Again, before attempting any gunsmithing work ensure that the gun is empty and remove the magazine.)

Remington's Pump-Action Rifle has a unique barrel-to-receiver mounting system. Here, barrel-to-receiver attachment involves a barrel carrier. This piece, with the barrel threaded into it, slips into the front of the receiver. A separate nut, located under the barrel, affixes the barrel assembly to the receiver. The back end of the tube, upon which the rifle's articulating pump handle slides, contains the attachment nut. Hereafter, I will call this tube the action-tube. This action-tube threads onto a rigid bolt that extends through the receiver from the inside front of the magazine well. This bolt is parallel to the barrel, centered and about one-inch below the bottom of the barrel at the breech.

Separating the barrel from the receiver on these fine rifles is quite simple. The under-barrel tube has sets of opposed three-sixteenth inch (3/16") diameter holes drilled through it. You can locate these holes by closing the action and looking at the portion of the action-tube exposed between the back of the fore-end (pump handle) and the front of the receiver. See Photograph # 1-60.

Photograph 1-60: Here we have mounted a Remington pump-action rifle in Midway's handy Shooter's Vise. We have inserted the special takedown tool through the most vertically aligned holes in the action tube (One must close the action first). One should apply moderate pressure to the handle, here pushing it away. Then tap on the near side of the exposed steel shank using moderate force and an eight or twelve ounce ball-peen hammer. Normally this procedure quite easily loosens the action tube. Typically, after one has rotated the tube one-quarter turn or so, one can freely spin it by hand.

Photograph 1-59: TSI-301, a high-performance lubricant and protective agent. This aerosol product is particularly useful for application into intricate mechanisms. No product we know provides superior corrosion protection for steel. NECO distributes TSI-301.

Obtain a long-shanked screwdriver with a three-sixteenth inch (3/16") diameter shank; this is a quite common size. Cut the bit end off the shank. This leaves a three-sixteenth inch (3/16") diameter shank with a handle. Tape-wrap the shank of this tool so that only three-quarters of an inch (3/4") of the shank can pass through the action-tube. The correct amount is sufficient to fully penetrate both holes but not enough to allow the end of the tool to touch the barrel. See Photograph # 1-61.

Position the action in a padded vise, preferably with the bottom facing up and level. Insert the tool through one set of holes; typically the ones aligned most nearly vertically. Press on the handle to unscrew the right-hand threaded tube, using moderate force. Tap the shank of the tool, near the handle, with a plastic mallet. Application of moderate force on the handle and taps on the shank from a light hammer will soon loosen the action-tube. Normally, when the tube has turned only slightly it will loosen, whereupon you can unscrew it by hand. See Photograph # 1-62.

When you have fully unscrewed the action-tube from the retaining bolt, you can slide the entire assembly (bolt assembly, pump handle, barrel and ejection port cover) forward and out of the receiver. Be careful here; the action contains two hardened steel pins; these facilitate articulation of the turn-bolt. After separation of the barrel assembly and receiver the action does not contain these pins. Since these pins are double-ended (symmetrical) and of different diameters, there is no chance of a mix-up during reassembly. However, you do not want to lose one! Simply pull those out of the bolt carrier and store both appropriately until you are ready to reassemble the rifle. See Photograph # 1-63.

You can then remove all free action parts from the barrel and barrel extension assembly. This requires patient manipulation of the pump handle and action bars. To prevent damage to the bluing, tape-wrap the lower surfaces of the barrel extension. This will prevent damage to the finish when you spread the action bars and slide those down over the bottom of the barrel extension. This action will separate the pump handle assembly from the barrel assembly.

Separation of the barrel from the barrel extension requires special tools. I cannot recommend this procedure on any Remington pump

Photograph 1-61: Pictured is a "Special" tool for take down of Remington's Model-760 and Model-7600 pump-action rifles. We modified this well-used 3/16" shanked screw driver in the following manner: Cut bit off, polish rust and burs off shank, tape-wrap leaving 3/4" of shank exposed beyond tape. One uses this tool to loosen barrel-to-receiver assembly connecting bolt, which is also the tube the pump handle slides upon. See associated photographs and text.

Photograph 1-62: Light blows from a hammer, while pushing with moderate force on the screw driver handle, should loosen the barrel-to-action assembly nut on Remington's pump-action rifle. Be careful not to damage the fore stock. See associated photographs and text.

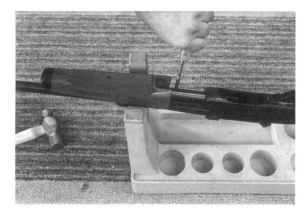

Photograph 1-63: You can free this nut through judicious taps with a hammer on the screw driver shank, just below the handle (see photograph 1-62). You might have to produce several quarter-turns of the screw before it comes finger loose. If it does not, thereafter, spin freely, likely something is binding it. To facilitate easy disassembly, slightly adjust slide and barrel positioning.

Section 1: The Trouble With Barrels, Part I

and I must strongly discourage any attempt on older pumps where a separate nut attaches the barrel extension; that nut also contains the bolt locking lug recesses — the home gunsmith could very easily break this thin-walled nut during any attempt to remove it! Very few professional gunsmiths will tackle that job!

Nevertheless, the home gunsmith can freely lap and true the contact area between the extension and the receiver. However, he must first remove the barrel-to-receiver attachment bolt.

Mount the receiver vertically in a padded vise; it is not necessary to tighten the vise very much. Screw the action-tube fully onto the attachment bolt and tap lightly on the end of the tube using a piece of hardwood similar to a hammer handle. Rapid light taps with a moderate-sized piece of hardwood will do the job best and with minimal risk of damaging the tube. See Photograph # 1-64.

When the bolt moves back into the magazine well, the splines that secure it against rotation and against pulling through the front of the receiver will come free. Unscrew the action-tube from the bolt and remove the bolt.

Apply a thin layer of two hundred twenty (220) (or finer) grit silicon carbide lapping compound to the front of the receiver and insert the barrel assembly in the normal orientation. With the attachment bolt removed from the receiver, you can twist the barrel about one-third of one turn. Rotate it back and forth about thirty degree (30°) each way ten times. Remove the barrel assembly and clean the contact surfaces. See Photograph # 1-65.

Observe the areas of contact where lapping has occurred. You will note that the area of the receiver face between the centerline of the barrel and the bottom of the receiver-to-barrel assembly attachment bolt is inletted and will not contact with the barrel assembly. This is as it should be. This design feature allows the barrel assembly and receiver to mate properly (rigidly). Repeat the lapping process until the contacting surfaces at the top and bottom of the receiver mate uniformly. This lapping should produce dull gray areas that cover most of the surface on both the barrel and the receiver. Small patches of bluing persisting in the lower lapped area are of no harm. The important thing is to get good flat contact across the contacting surfaces with all areas mating at once. See Photograph # 1-66.

Photograph 1-64: Bottom-view of receiver on Remington 760 pump-action rifle. Note barrel-to-receiver connecting bolt is partially removed into the action's magazine well. Note bolt's serrated head. Before reinstalling this bolt you must properly re-align these serrations to the original orientation. See text and associated photograph captions for a complete discussion.

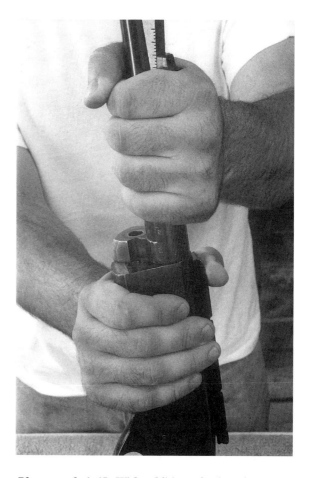

Photograph 1-65: With addition of a bit of 220 grit grinding compound on the joint, this twisting action of the disassembled barreled-action in the receiver quickly mates the shouldering surfaces to provide proper contact. See text and associated photographs.

Another step that might be beneficial is countersinking the area around the bolt hole on both the front and rear of the barrel extension. The correct twist drill size for this job is one-half inch (1/2"). You can do this by hand using only a sharp one-half inch (1/2") twist drill bit. This modification will hurt nothing and, since it might result in a more solid lockup, it is a good idea. Start by mounting the barrel in a padded vise. Align a sharp one-half inch (1/2") twist drill bit with the axis of the hole and turn it by hand while applying modest pressure. In a few seconds this procedure will produce a bevel around the entire circumference of the hole. Do not cut this bevel too deeply. A width of about fifty-thousandths of an inch (slightly less than 1/16") is more than sufficient. See Photograph # 1-67.

Use a cold bluing agent to reblue all abraded surfaces. Reinstall the action-to-barrel-extension connecting bolt. Observe the location of the serration cuts in the perimeter of the hole through the receiver. The flutes on the head of the receiver-to-barrel attachment bolt formed these cuts during the initial (factory original) installation. If the bolt does not begin to move into the receiver freely you do not have it correctly positioned! Try again until the fluted head easily slips at least part way into the hole in the receiver. Application of a low-strength thread locking agent (Loctite Product #222) to the fluted area of the bolt is a good idea.

Photograph 1-66: Receiver from a Remington 760 pump-action rifle with the bolt that connects the receiver to the barrel assembly removed. View of front end showing lapped surfaces at bottom and top only — these are the only areas where these two pieces touch. Degree of lapping shown here is sufficient to allow consistent mating without differential stressing.

Photograph 1-67: Left, Remington Model-7600 barrel assembly in unaltered factory condition. Right, Remington Model-760 with lapped under-lug, polished feed ramp, chamfered bolt hole and polished ejection port. Note lapped arc across the bottom of the under lug, just below slotted bolt hole. You might also be able to discern the dulled appearance of the exposed shoulder at the top of the barrel. These are the two areas that contact the receiver. Also note chamfering around rear of bolt hole (front side is equally chamfered). Modified and polished ejection port area does not show in this photograph (see separate photographs).

Note several minor, albeit significant, differences in these two actions, the Model-7600 does not use a slotted bolt hole in the barrel extension. It also features an alignment slot for the bolt carrier (located at the top of the barrel extension).

Section 1: The Trouble With Barrels, Part I

Slip the basic barrel assembly back into the receiver. Install and firmly tighten the action-tube. This will pull the action-to-barrel connecting bolt fully into place; the head of the bolt must pull past flush in the front of the magazine well.

Remove the action-tube and separate the barrel assembly. Thoroughly clean both surfaces of the contact area with alcohol or a more effective degreasing agent, such as acetone. (Ensure adequate ventilation.) Before reassembly, apply a retaining compound (Loctite Product #609) between the mating surfaces. A few drops distributed on the contact surfaces will harden to create a significantly improved and solid bonding between the two assemblies. This is a consequential and worthwhile step. Application of a small amount of low-strength thread locker (Loctite Product #222) on the threads of the action-to-barrel attachment bolt is also a good idea. However, use restraint here; very little goes a long way. The more thread locker you use, the harder it will be to separate the barrel from the action in the future. Also, before final reassembly, consider the following sub-section. See Photograph #s 1-68/69.

Other Barrel Modifications:

The final barrel-specific considerations I will address concerns the rear face of the barrel. Certain types of actions utilize extractor slots and other cuts at the rear end of the chamber. Where this occurs, these slots can often be deburred with a fine finish file or fine-grit corundum paper wrapped over an appropriate sanding block. As long as you only remove the burs and polish the surface you cannot harm anything.

During bolt lockup in some guns, particularly those chambering a rimmed cartridge, a portion of the receiver or the barrel (most likely the latter) lifts or pushes the extractor away from the cartridge case. Sometimes one can observe this action through the ejection port. If not, this is an easy condition for which to test. See Photograph # 1-70.

Paint the entire front end of the extractor with a thin coat of typist's Wite-Out® (the product used to cover mistakes and allow corrections). After allowing the Wite-Out® to dry, install a sized and deprimed case into the bolt by slipping it under the extractor. Then carefully close the bolt. After closing the bolt, unlock and relock the action several times without retracting the bolt. This will mark the whited surface of the extractor anywhere it touches anything.

Photographs 1-68 and 1-69: Here we are applying two useful Loctite Products, where appropriate.

Photograph 1-68: Product #609, a retaining compound, for shoulder area of the barrel extension on this Remington Pump — use caution here, do not use too much! Use just enough to fill gaps and prevent vibrations. See text and associated photographs.

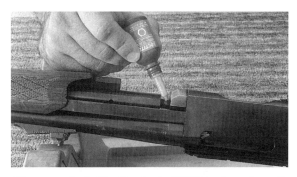

Photograph 1-69: Product #222, a low-strength thread locking compound, for the threads on the barrel-to-receiver attachment bolt on this Remington Pump. Use moderation here; do not use too much! Just enough to lock the tube against use-related loosening. See text and associated photographs.

Photograph 1-70: This view of a Marlin Model-1894 ejection port shows a polished area at the top of the ejector ramp at the back end of the barrel. On guns where the extractor touches the barrel (when one closes the action on a chambered round), one should modify either the extractor or the barrel slot, or both, to eliminate this undesirable condition. See text and associated photographs.

Extract the case and observe the extractor. If this action has worn or crushed the white paint on any portion of the extractor tip, other than where the extractor grasps the case, you need to remove material from the slot in the outside of the barrel, from the extractor or from both, as necessary, to allow clearance between the extractor and the slot. See Photograph # 1-71.

If you observe such a situation, it is generally best for purposes of maximum accuracy and action functionality to remove material from the slot in the barrel or receiver. However, advance slowly here. Remove no more material than is necessary to achieve a complete separation of the extractor tip and any other surface excepting the case. This simple modification improves repeatable chambering of cartridges and can significantly improve accuracy! See Photograph # 1-72.

The reason this is so? If the extractor is pushing against the head of the case it will always push the head of the case against the opposite side of the chamber. If nothing pushes against the side of the case head, the head of the case can settle anywhere in the chamber! Typically, case heads left to their own devices will fail to settle consistently in the chamber — inconsistency is anathema to accuracy. See Photograph # 1-73.

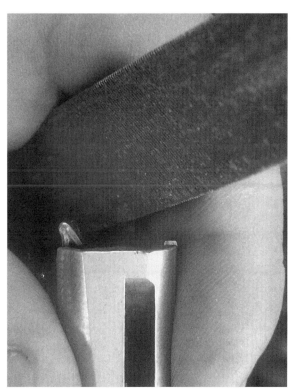

Photograph 1-72: A bit of judicious filing on the extractor is also a valuable modification toward preventing the extractor from pulling away from the head of a chambered cartridge. However, note that one must use care — avoid weakening the extractor. Here we are preparing to file a high spot near one side. See text and associated photograph captions for a complete discussion.

Photograph 1-71: Here we are slightly altering the ejector recess on a Marlin barrel. This alteration can improve accuracy of any rifle where the ejector protrudes forward, past the rear of the barrel, when one locks the action. The purpose of this alteration is to prevent the ramp from lifting the ejector away from the cartridge as one closes and locks the action. If the extractor is pushing firmly against the case head it will similarly locate all chambered cartridges. However, one must use caution here to avoid producing this slot deeper than the front of the solid web of the case or excessively thinning the slot's forward extent. A Dremel tool equipped with the proper stone is a better choice here. That set-up allows precisely controlled cutting, only where needed. See text and associated photograph captions for a complete discussion.

Photograph 1-73: Marlin Model-1894 bolt showing modified extractor. Filed along the top-front corner (in this view); to provide clearance from the barrel's extractor cut (see associated photograph). One must take care to avoid weakening or disabling the extractor. Similar modifications are useful on any gun where the extractor abuts against a ramp on the barrel when one locks the action on a chambered round. See text.

Section 1: The Trouble With Barrels, Part I

Remember never to cut any slot into the back of the barrel that extends past the location of the front of the solid web of the chambered case. For safety's sake, dissect a case by cutting it lengthwise into two pieces, using a hacksaw. Insert one side of the case into the chamber and thereby determine the maximum extent any slots can reach into the rear of the chamber without compromising the strength of the action (typically about 0.150"). Also, for safety's sake, no slot should extend much beyond the depth of the bottom of the primer pocket; since case web thickness is not SAAMI specified and can, therefore, vary from brand to brand and lot to lot of cases.

Most such slots are straight cuts that angle out and forward on the exterior of the barrel. These often extend considerably up the outside of the barrel while becoming shallower toward the front. Minimize any deepening of such slots since this thins the barrel over the chamber, thereby weakening it. Such thinning beyond the extreme rear of the barrel should not be necessary. Observe where extractor contact occurs. Remove material from that area, accordingly. There is no advantage in removing material from any area where the extractor cannot reach. In this regard, if you do not understand exactly what you are doing, do nothing!

Photograph 1-74: Remington Model-7600 pump-action rifle, view of feed ramp in barrel extension. Note here that we have polished the feed ramp and added a slight radius to the step in front of the feed ramp (barely visible in front of the ramp). These changes <u>greatly</u> ease chambering of exposed-lead cartridges. We used a Dremel tool for this job: First, a 1/4" fine sanding drum to remove the factory machining marks then a felt tip with jeweler's rouge to polish the sanded surfaces to a mirror-finish. A final touch with cold bluing, to limit corrosion, is a good idea.

Finally, many barrels or barrel extensions, such as both Remington's and Savage's Pump-Action Rifles have a feed ramp built into the barrel assembly. While the barrel is out of the gun, you can easily polish this ramp. This is also the best time to polish any feed ramp in the receiver. A Dremel tool with a small-diameter (1/4") sanding drum is the ideal tool for removing any rough machining marks. (You can do this job with other tools but not nearly so easily!) Follow this sanding with a polishing step. Use a jeweler's rouge-impregnated felt-tip or felt drum attachment in the Dremel tool. Just cleaning up any rough high spots or sharp edges will dramatically smooth cartridge feeding, which will reduce bullet tip deformation resulting from high feeding forces.

(For these and similar jobs, Brownells markets the Cratex line of abrasive and polishing tools. These tools fit a standard Dremel tool and are available in a wide variety of grades and shapes. These do a splendid job.) See Photograph # 1-74.

On many bolt-action rifles the feed ramp is part of the receiver. While you have the barrel removed from the receiver is also the best time to polish such a feed ramp. The procedure is the same: sand with a small-diameter sanding drum to remove any burs or roughness and improve the ramp's contour, where possible. Finish by polishing with a rouge-impregnated felt-tip attachment. See Photograph #s 1-75/76/77.

Dovetailed Front Sights:

Barrel-mounted fixed sights are not the best choice for most applications; often this is particularly true of such sights installed at the factory. This situation is certainly understandable. Since so many hunters add telescopic sights to their rifles it makes little sense for the factory to spend a great deal of money on a set of high-quality iron sights the gun's owner will just as likely never use.

Common deficits in typical factory iron sights include improper dovetail machining (too loose or not transverse to the bore axis), a too-short or too-long front sight post, inadequate or incorrect screw attachment and many other problems. The home gunsmith can correct many of these deficits. In some instances he can repair the existing parts with a bit of tinkering or adjustment. He can correct other problems through installation of after-market pieces.

Marble Arms (now CRL, Incorporated)

offers a wide selection of replacement dovetailed front sights. Marble offers replacement sights in various designs, styles and dovetail widths and post heights. As an example where replacing the front sight is beneficial, consider a hunting rifle where one has installed either a receiver-mounted or tang-mounted peep sight. Typically, assuming correct installation of the aperture sight, the factory front sight will work. However, installation of a somewhat taller front sight will often improve sight acquisition, speed proper sighting alignment and make the gun more pleasant to shoot. See Photograph # 1-78.

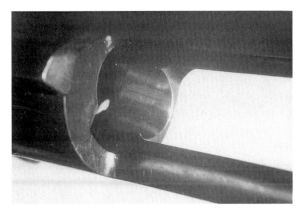

Photograph 1-77: Barreled-action from a Remington Model-700 left-hand bolt-action rifle. View looking down through receiver. Note polished feed ramp at front of magazine port. See associated photograph showing unpolished ramp. This simple modification can significantly improve smoothness of cartridge feeding. We accomplished this job by first sanding away the machining marks using a Dremel tool fitted with a fine 1/4" sanding drum. We then polished the sanded surface using a jeweler's rouge impregnated felt tip.

Photograph 1-75: Barreled-action from a Remington Model-700 left-hand bolt-action rifle. View looking down through receiver. Note unpolished feed ramp at front of magazine port. Note, also, evident machining marks running across ramp. See associated photograph showing polished ramp.

Photograph 1-76: Here we have fitted the Dremel tool with a jeweler's rouge impregnated felt tip. We are polishing the feed ramp to a mirror finish after doing similar work using a fine sanding drum and the same tool. The resulting feed ramp displays a mirror finish. As a result of this work even lead-tipped cartridges feed effortlessly and with minimal bullet-tip damage. Similar feed ramp work on other action makes and types is equally beneficial to ease of use.

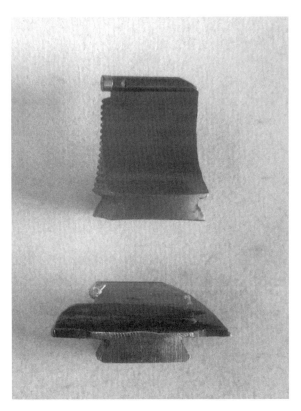

Photograph 1-78: As these examples suggest, dovetail front sights come in a wide variety of types and heights.

Section 1: The Trouble With Barrels, Part I

There are several reasons for this result. First, moving the front sight higher above the barrel reduces the amount of the barrel a shooter can see through the rear aperture. The more of the barrel the shooter can see when looking through the aperture the harder it is to center the front bead in the peep aperture. The harder it is to center the bead in the aperture the longer it will take and the less precision the shooter can achieve.

Visibility of any portion of the gun, other than the front sight bead, through the aperture distracts the brain from automatically centering the bead in the aperture. The greater the distraction the longer it takes the shooter's brain to put everything together properly for a correct sight picture.

Ideally, the perfect aperture-sight sight-picture is the following: looking through the aperture the shooter should see only one portion of the gun, a floating bead — the front sight. He should see this disembodied bead centered in the peep aperture. This picture should center on the target.

Of course, such an arrangement is practically impossible. However, a taller and narrower front post often dramatically improves matters. Often the post is so thin that it is practically invisible. The typical problem is that the front sight has a too-short front post, which leaves much of the barrel visible through the peep hole. Considering the modest price and typical simplicity of replacing a front sight, it makes sense to take this extra step whenever installing an aperture sight.

However, I do not recommend going to a front sight that is more than about one-eighth inch (1/8") taller than the original sight on any hunting rifle. Such sight blades are more prone to damage from mishandling and the inevitable accidents that will happen in the hunting field. Further, the higher the blade the greater the error introduced by any given degree of canting — failure to hold the gun correctly to orient the sights vertically above the centerline of the bore. Finally, there is no intrinsic sighting advantage to excessive blade height.

A second area where significant improvement in the typical front sight is possible is through the installation of a hooded post. With iron sights, lighting conditions can dramatically alter the apparent sight picture. Shifts in point of aim exceeding two minutes of angle are not at all uncommon. Depending upon lighting conditions and the type of front sight bead, sun glint on the front post tends to push the front sight away from or toward the direction of the sun. A hood over the post can eliminate this problem. See Photograph # 1-79.

One final improvement for any sighting system is installation of a spirit bubble level. These are affordably available for scope sight installation. Front sights featuring spirit levels are also available, albeit they are rather expensive. For consistent target or long-range shooting, it is critical that the shooter keeps the gun oriented vertically for every shot, canting will lower the bullet's impact and move it toward the direction the shooter tips the top of the gun. The amount of sighting error induced by canting can be quite significant, particularly at longer ranges.

A second reason to consider replacing the original front sight is simply to improve the quality of the bead. After-market blades featuring brass beads are often superior to the plain black posts found on many rifles — at least under most lighting conditions.

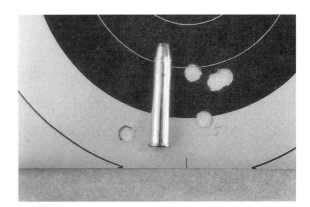

Photograph 1-79: When shooting with open sights sun angle and glare are important considerations. Here my son was working on a very good 100 yard group. He was shooting a Model-1895 (45-70) Marlin with cast-bullet loads. On the second shot, for the only time that (late) afternoon, clouds intervened. He commented on how much better the sight picture was. However, note that this also influenced his aim. That shot went low and to the left (the sun was low to our left and he was shooting north). Cartridge for comparison only, the test-load consisted of a 405 grain Bear Creek Bullets molybdenum-disulfide coated cast bullet (without any other lubrication) in front of 27.5 grains of Accurate Arms XMP-5744 using CCI-300 primers — yes, a lever-action rifle can shoot! With a scope mounted, this rifle routinely puts 5 shots inside one-inch (on centers) at 100 yards — when we do our part.

Dovetailed front sight replacement begins with marking the barrel to indicate the lateral location of the original front sight blade. This facilitates proper centering of the replacement blade. However, if the gun is equipped with a windage adjustable receiver-mounted or tang-mounted sight or if you intend to install one, you should center the new sight on the barrel — regardless of how off-center original sight installation was.

If you need to mark the barrel, a good method is to wrap the barrel just in front of the dovetail with masking tape. Then, with a fine tip pen, indicate the center of the existing sight bead through visual alignment. Locate the unloaded gun solidly in a padded bench-mounted vise, then look down over the front sight so that the top of the post hides the pedestal — this ensures you are looking straight down on the sight. A simple pen mark on the tape will locate the center of the post to an accuracy of a few thousandths of an inch — closer than you are likely to align the new sight by tapping it in place! See Photograph # 1-80.

To drive the old sight out, you will need a properly sized punch, preferably of brass, and a light (8- to 12-ounce) ball-peen hammer. Use of a cold steel punch will often damage the sight-base. This is of little concern if you are replacing the piece. However, if you intend to use the same tool to drive the new sight into the dovetail, brass is better; it will not damage the sight-base. The working end of the brass punch should be no larger than the diameter of a common pencil.

By observing the sides of the dovetail base on the original sight you should be able to determine from which side of the barrel factory installation had occurred. Remove the sight by tapping it toward the side from which it had been originally installed. Install the new sight from the same side of the dovetail from which you pushed the original sight. This protocol minimizes dovetail loosening.

An old adage goes, "In from the right, out from the left". This suggests that you should install a dovetail part from the right side and drive it back out by tapping on the left side.

Depending upon how tight the sight fits the dovetail, you might have to apply considerable energy to install the new sight. Be patient. Keep the hammer blows at a moderate energy level. If the piece is moving, just keep tapping. If it is not moving, pound a little harder. If it simply will not move to the center of the dovetail with hammer blows of reasonable energy, remove the piece. Gently file the dovetail base slightly narrower on the side that installs first. In this instance, "slightly" means no more than one- or two-thousandths of an inch.

For installation of dovetailed pieces, application of a retaining compound (Loctite Product #609) is most beneficial. First, clean both the new sight blade and the dovetail with alcohol (or acetone) and cotton swabs until the swabs come out clean. Apply the retaining compound into the dovetail. This product will positively lock the sight in place and prevent corrosion in the hidden joint. However, do not use this product if you might have to move the sight after the initial installation. As noted, if you intend to use this product, it is important to clean and degrease both the dovetail and the sight-base before reassembly. You can apply this product after sight installation, providing the area has remained clean. Simply wet the entire perimeter of the dovetail with the product. This agent will migrate sufficiently into the dovetail to seal it rather well.

Installation of the new sight is just the reverse of removal of the old sight. As noted above, start the new sight in the dovetail; install from the same side where you removed the old sight. It is often helpful to slightly radius the first-installed end of the new sight; this simplifies starting it into the dovetail and can ease proper positioning. Do not overdo this rounding. A slight taper with a fine triangular file will do the job and is all that is desirable.

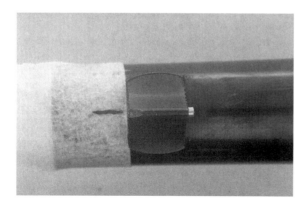

Photograph 1-80: This view shows a front sight almost properly centered with an alignment mark on a pre-applied piece of masking tape. Aligning this replacement sight with this mark locates it where the original sight was centered.

Section 1: The Trouble With Barrels, Part I

Semi-Permanent Dovetail Fixtures:

After installation and centering of the sight, allow the assembly to set for several hours. This will allow the retaining compound (Loctite Product #609) sufficient time to cure; thereby permanently affixing the sight in place. Remember, when the tinker has properly applied retaining compound, removal of the piece commonly requires either application of significant heat to the front sight blade (using a propane torch) or application of tremendous force. For practical purposes, such a product will render the front sight permanent and positively mounted, preventing its inadvertent movement, even in a somewhat loose dovetail.

A long soaking in acetone might help. Wrap the area in an acetone saturated rag and seal that with an air-tight plastic wrap — but note that many types of plastic will not withstand acetone.

Obviously this approach is useful for any dovetail fixture where it is desirable to increase the rigidity and permanence of the joint. This will do little to solve a problem where recoil forces are sufficient to bend the dovetail, such as in certain high recoiling magazine rifles where the magazine attachment is *via* a dovetail (Marlin's Model-1895). However, retaining compound will always strengthen the dovetail connection.

Loose Dovetail Joints:

If the dovetail is loose and your goal is only to tighten the sight, the following approach will suffice. Remove the sight and peen the top edges of the dovetail using <u>light</u> blows delivered with either an 8-ounce or a 12-ounce ball-peen hammer. Again, addition of a self-curing retaining product, such as Loctite Product #609, in the clean joint is a good idea and will tighten loose dovetails. This product will also provide a great deal of resistance against inadvertent movement. However, it will eliminate the potential of windage sight adjustment, characteristic of dovetail sight mounting systems. See Photograph #s 1-81/82.

These steps will do the job for almost any situation. If done carefully, the results of peening are almost invisible once the tinker has installed the sight. However, you can create a more permanent joint by carefully drilling a slight dimple at the center of the dovetail on the sight — the ramped edge that fits under the overhang on the dovetail cut. This requires a proper size drill bit

Photograph 1-81

Photograph 1-82

Photographs 1-81/82: Loctite's Product #609 (a mounting agent) is particularly useful for locking dovetail sights and other fixtures in place. However, do not apply this product until you are ready to set the fixture in its final location! When properly applied, this product will render the sight (or other fixture) practically unmovable! A small amount will do the job. This product also provides significant protection against corrosion.

and careful manipulation to avoid scarring the top of the sight-base or whatever fixture you might be modifying.

Install this dimpled piece and then use a round ended punch to peen the barrel material into the dimple. This modification will result in minor cosmetic damage to the barrel but will certainly render the fixture solid. When the home gunsmith combines this technique with application of a retaining agent the joint becomes virtually permanent.

Crooked Dovetails:

If the dovetail is not perpendicular to the bore you have a bit of a problem. On the front sight one possible cure is to heat the sight riser (that area between the dovetail base and the bead) and bend it, twisting the top of the post along the axis of the bore. Begin by vising the unloaded rifle. Then regulate a small adjustable wrench until it just fits the top of the sight blade. Remove the wrench for the next step.

Focus a fine flame from a small tipped propane torch on the sight riser. When the riser is hot enough to glow a moderate red in a dully lit room, quickly use the wrench to twist the top of the blade until it aligns with the axis of the bore. Note, such heating will likely destroy beads made of materials other than steel, brass or gold. Also, application of too much heat will damage the bluing of the adjacent barrel surface. Have a wet rag handy to douse the barrel after you finish bending the sight riser.

As noted, do this job as fast as possible. Rapid heating, bending and cooling is the safest method; that is, least apt to damage the barrel bluing. Typically, a little goes a long way here. Do not use too much force or too much heat and avoid repeated heatings without allowing the barrel time to fully cool. See Photograph # 1-83.

Normally, you cannot use the same basic method to align a crooked rear sight to the gun's bore. There, you should remove the sight and determine whether bending is possible without destroying the sight. If so, mount the sight in a vise, heat it carefully and attempt to adjust it, as necessary, to facilitate alignment with the bore. This seems a remote possibility for most types of sights. Fortunately, crooked dovetails are rather rare — in my modest collection I only have two rifles featuring this condition!

You can adjust the rear sight notch to provide a clean sight picture despite a crookedly mounted sight-base. Ideally, open sights should always feature the characteristic Patridge hallmark: the rear sight opening tapers, wider at the front; the front sight post and bead rail taper, thinner at the front. In this way, both surfaces provide a sharp-edge contrast in the field of view.

Screw Attached Front Sights:

Many rifles, such as Remington's Models-700 and Model-7600, use screw-attached sight assemblies. These particular sights are certainly acceptable for hunting use. However, improvement is possible in several areas; most significant are dependability and visibility. The first big step any serious shooter should consider concerns dependability.

You should remove the mounting screws, clean everything up and apply a thread locker (Loctite Product #222) before reassembly. Equally important, for fixture permanence, is application of a retaining agent (Loctite Product #609) between the barrel and the sight-base. If the tinker cleans all surfaces properly these products will go a long way toward remedying the attachment functionally permanent. This will also prevent corrosion in the hidden surfaces.

In a recent test, I used the aforementioned products while attaching the front sight-base on a Remington Model-7600 Pump-Action Rifle. Several days later, I removed the screws. The retaining agent bond was sufficient to render sight removal impossible without resorting to a brass hammer! That is the sort of adhesion we all want in the hunting field — screws do come

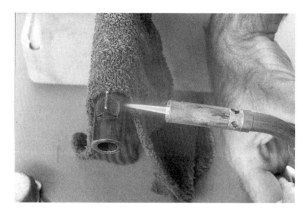

Photograph 1-83: A wet rag draped over the barrel will mitigate overheating of the barrel. Here we are heating a front sight riser. When we have heated the riser sufficiently we will use an adjustable end-wrench to realign the top of the sight to the gun's bore axis. See text for a discussion of this rarely necessary but useful technique.

loose! Note that I had properly degreased the surfaces; these chemicals cannot provide maximum effectiveness unless afforded properly degreased surfaces for adhesion.

Where location of the front sight dovetail is over the front attachment screw, as on typical Remington rifles and many others, one must remove the sight to achieve disassembly of the sight-base from the barrel. Dovetailed sights installed in separate screw mounted bases are sometimes an extremely tight fit. The reason such installations can be tighter than barrel dovetailed installations: manufacturers often use a much harder piece of steel to make the separate base, compared to the barrel. The harder steel will not bend as easily to accommodate the installation. It is sometimes impossible to remove the insert without using a clamping tool! (Williams offers this tool but, at $50, it seems a significant investment.) See Photograph # 1-84.

Do not remove the visible mounting screw before attempting to slide the dovetail free. You should be able to devise a clamp that will push the dovetailed insert out of the base. Use a bench-mounted vise and a properly shaped block that rests against the base of the sight and around the barrel. From the other side, push against the inset with a small brass dowel. With careful manipulation and a bit of thought, such an assembly should facilitate insert removal. There are several ways to go about this. One involves clamping with the vise to push the insert out of the base. Another involves use of a separate ("C") clamp to push the insert out of the base. You could also use a hammer and punch to do the job, once you have the rifle and sight-base properly supported in a vise.

Typically, however, the insert will not be so tight that the home gunsmith cannot remove it using only a brass punch and a small ball-peen hammer — as with typical barrel-mounted dovetails. As with sights dovetailed directly to the barrel, note the direction of the factory installation. Push the sight out the same side from which original installation occurred.

This effort would hardly be worthwhile just to place a thread locker on the one hidden screw. However, it also facilitates replacement of the existing sight insert with one of a different height and/or a better bead design. Installation of a sight featuring a better bead is an important way you can improve open sights.

Another advantage of screw-mounted sight removal is that this operation allows you to verify that the attachment screws are the correct length. Surprisingly often, screws in blind holes are either too long or are too short. These screws should reach almost to, but never impinge upon, the bottom of the hole.

You can easily determine this by comparing the number of complete and partial revolutions the screw will turn into the hole, first without the mounted fixture and then with the fixture in place. Too-short screws might not provide sufficient attachment. Too-long screws will not provide solid fixture attachment. Perhaps more importantly, too-long screws might damage the piece into which they screw. We discuss screw replacement and modification in the following sub-section, which see.

Also note that you might consider lapping to match the underside of the sight base to the barrel contour. While this will damage the finish on the barrel, it is worthwhile since it will eliminate the potential for tightening the sight base attachment screws to place stress on the barrel. You will have to decide if the cosmetic flaw is worthwhile.

If you want the ideal attachment, interpose a dab of 220 grit lapping agent under the sight base. Then slide the base fore and aft on the top of the barrel until the entire underside of the base touches the barrel. Clean off the lapping agent

Photograph 1-84: Remington front sight: Dovetailed blade removed to expose sight base mounting screw. Here we are reassembling the sight after degreasing sight base, sight blade, barrel and screws. We applied Loctite Product #609 (a mounting fixture) where the sight base rests on the barrel and Loctite Product #222 (a low-strength thread locker) onto the screw shoulders and threads. Note dull appearance of barrel under sight base. Proper degreasing results in a gray appearing finish on most blued surfaces (the blue color results from diffraction in a thin layer of oil). Before driving the sight blade back in place we will apply a dab of Loctite Product #609 in the edges of the dovetail grooves. We do not want to get this product on the head of the screw; that would complicate future screw removal.

and degrease the areas. Use a cold-bluing agent to touch up the lapped surfaces.

Barrel-mounted Rear Sight Modifications:

You should also disassemble, remove and thoroughly clean screw-mounted rear sight assemblies. Thoroughly clean all screws and threads and the mating surfaces on both the sight and the barrel. Application of Loctite Product #222, on the mounting screws, and Loctite Product #609, on any flat mating surfaces, is most advisable.

During reassembly of the rear sight, you should consider your options carefully. If your purposes require routine adjustment of the sight, you cannot lock everything in place with a high-strength thread locker! In this case, use a dab of Loctite Product #222, (a low-strength thread locking agent) on the degreased bolt threads and on the degreased pins. Be careful not to get any such product on surfaces designed to slide during sight adjustments.

Conversely, on a sight assembly system that you can attach and then affix in place with no further need of adjustment, you can do a better (more permanent) job. Once you have ascertained the final adjustment, you can apply the various locking agents to render the assembly practically bullet proof. In this case, affix all pins and sight-assembly screws by application of Loctite Product #222, a low-strength thread locking agent, and Loctite Product #609, a retaining agent, to the degreased pins and screws before reassembly. You should also apply the retaining agent to the joint between any sliding surfaces. Here Loctite Product # 290, a penetrating thread locker, is a good option. Simply assemble and adjust everything properly, to achieve the point of impact desired with the ammunition type of choice, then apply Product # 290 at every pin, screw and joint. Capillary action will wick the product into the joints, where it will harden and bond the parts. In this instance, it is particularly important that everything be immaculately clean.

The number of iron-sight failures related to loosening screws or pins that fall out would surprise many shooters. Such lost parts or loss of adjustments always seem to happen at the worst possible moment.

Barrel-mounted rear sight modifications are similar to front sight replacements and can include several other steps. First, as noted above, assuming the tinker prefers to retain the factory-mounted rear sight, he should ensure rigid connection of the sight-base to the barrel. If the design relies upon screws, he should verify those for correct length. On dovetail mounts, he should verify the dovetail for tightness and make corrections, as necessary — as explained in the previous sub-section.

Not uncommonly, screws used in bottomed holes are too long. This results in a situation where the screw tightens against the bottom of the hole rather than on the shoulder of the screw head. Obviously, such a situation will not result in a properly affixed sight body (or other attachment). It can also lead to bore damage — if the bottom of the hole is thin enough the end of the screw can drive that material into the bore. I have seen this happen!

In designs using screws, remove those one at a time and ensure the ends are not impinging upon the bottom of the screw hole. If a screw does show evidence of excessive length, as exhibited by contact between the end of the screw and the bottom of the hole, simply grind the end of the screw shorter by, perhaps, one-half thread and recheck the screw's fit in the hole. When you note no further interference between the end of the screw and the bottom of the hole (with the base in place), thoroughly clean both the hole and the screw with alcohol (or acetone).

Set the screw aside for reassembly. During reassembly, after the solvent has dried, apply a good thread locking compound and install the screw with adequate torque. When all screws have thus been shortened, as necessary, and secured with a thread locking compound applied to cleaned parts, you can be sure the sight will stay in place! Where sight attachment relies upon a dovetail, refer to the above sub-section on tightening dovetails.

Also check for screws that do not reach sufficiently close to the bottom of the hole. The easiest way to verify this is to compare the number of turns the screw advances into the hole; first, with the attachment removed, then with the attachment in place. If these results vary by more than about one-half turn, you should consider shortening a longer screw to fit. These screws are often available where scopes are sold and mounted.

See the above sub-section on matching the sight base tot he barrel contour. Be sure to clean all surfaces and use a mounting agent (Loctite #609) in the installation of the base to the barrel.

Section 1: The Trouble With Barrels, Part I

Replacement of Rear Sight:

Several manufacturers offer replacement barrel-mounted rear sights. A high quality barrel-mounted sight is a worthwhile improvement. However, these seem ill advised except for emergency backup use with a scope-sighted rifle or for very specialized applications.

When installing such a sight, follow the manufacturer's recommendations. Also, note the above discussion regarding ensuring a permanent attachment of rear-sight assemblies. See Photograph # 1-85.

Removal of Rear Sights:

Often hunters remove the factory rear sight for scope use, or for replacement with a receiver- or tang-mounted peep sight — a vastly superior iron sighting system. Other than to mention repairing the unsightly holes this process leaves behind, I will not address this further here — I will address receiver-mounted sights in the sub-section covering receiver modifications.

Marble's, Lyman and, perhaps, others offer inserts (blanks) to fill dovetails where someone has removed the barrel-mounted dovetailed sight. Installation is quite simple, the only advice I will offer is that the home gunsmith can often simplify this chore by slightly filing the inserted edge to allow proper alignment of the piece as he starts it into the slot. Also, application of a very heavy grease or Loctite #609 is beneficial. The former will prevent rusting, as long as it stays in place. The latter will lock the piece in place and indefinitely prevent rusting or other corrosion. A dovetail blank thus mounted will not come out spontaneously. Further, this product resists all common solvents and adheres tenaciously to unfinished or blued steel surfaces. See Photograph #s 1-86/87.

Plug, or blanking, screws are also commonly available to fill unused iron sight attachment screw hole locations. Typically, the blanking screws removed to attach the scope base are ideal for this application. Obviously the tinker should include application of a low-strength thread locking compound (Loctite Product #222) during installation of such screws; this will prevent both screw loss and hidden corrosion. See Photograph #s 1-88/89.

Photograph 1-86: Rear sight dovetail, after sight removal. Often one can determine which side of the barrel the factory had installed the sight from, by observing tool marks on one side of the sight base. Drive the sight out the same side from which it had been installed. See text.

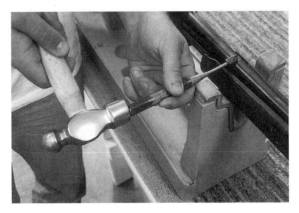

Photograph 1-87: Brass punches are most desirable for gunsmithing work. Here we are driving a dovetail sight mount blank into a dovetail on an early Model-760 Remington pump-action rifle. As is typical, the dovetail blank enters one side easier. One should install it from that side. See text and associated photograph captions for a complete discussion.

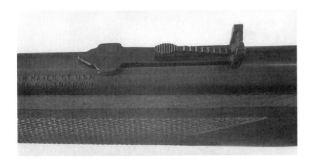

Photograph 1-85: Typical dovetail-mounted barrel sight. Both front and rear sights often use this system. Dovetails can be loose or off-axis. One can easily correct the former condition; repairing the latter is not so easy. See text. Often one can install a superior receiver or tang-mounted rear sight and eliminate the barrel-mounted rear sight. See associated photographs.

Photographs 1-88/89: Marble's Dovetail Sight Blank, driven partially into a dovetail (photograph 1-88). Then final installation (photograph 1-89). In this application a receiver-mounted peep sight will replace the barrel-mounted rear sight. The peep sight offers a significantly longer sight radius and superior sighting accuracy — for precision shooting, the best peep sight systems rival even the best scope sights (in practiced hands)! Note the slight brass discoloration on the barrel below the installed sight blank. We can easily remove these brass mars without harming the barrel finish! Also note that brass tools do not deform the sight blank.

Photograph 1-88

Photograph 1-89

Section 2: The Trouble With Stocks, Part I

The stock, as a means of connecting the barreled-action with the shooter, suffers many pitfalls. In the days before laminated and synthetic stocks were common, not the least of those pitfalls was the potential for temporary or permanent warpage and the reality of continual zero-destroying dimensional changes. The aforementioned modern materials and designs limit warpage but do not <u>completely</u> eliminate that concern, neither do those materials and designs eliminate inconsistencies in stock-to-barreled-action hook-up.

There are three basic areas where gunsmithing can improve the functioning of the stock. These are: fit, constancy, and rigidity. Fit concerns the individual shooter and that gun. Constancy concerns the structural relationship between the barreled-action and the stock. Rigidity regards how solidly the stock holds the receiver and whether the stock forces the receiver to fit it or vice versa — ideally, these two pieces mate naturally.

Stock checkering is a significant modification that can dramatically improve the handling qualities of the rifle. We shall discuss checkering in a separate sub-section.

Shooter Fit and Handling Function:

I will first cover the area of shooter fit. This topic involves several questions. First, is the stock the correct length? A too-short or too-long stock is not conducive to good shooting. The test is fairly simple. Before beginning, unload the gun. Then dress in your typical hunting (or otherwise) garb. Assume a typical shooting pose, close both eyes, bring the rifle into firing position and place your trigger finger through the trigger guard. Then open your eyes and look through the sights.

If any part of this process is in any way awkward, the buttstock might be improperly proportioned or positioned for you. Common problems include the rifle's heel catching on clothing as the gun is shouldered. In that instance, generally, the buttstock is too long, the heel of the butt is too sharp or the butt is too deep (too tall from top to bottom). If the finger guard does not naturally fall under your trigger finger or if you have to bend your arm excessively, the buttstock is likely too short. If the sights do not naturally line up in your field of view the stock's drop is likely not correct.

Repeat the above test many times while attempting to forget what gun you are handling — shooters can easily acquire a bad habit of stretching or scrunching when using an ill-fitting rifle. Here we want to find out if the rifle fits the shooter, not if the shooter can adjust to fit the rifle! Compare the gun in question to one that fits like the proverbial glove. Generally, once you have established the correct length of pull (the distance between the centerline of the butt and the trigger) using one particular rifle, you will find the measurement is very similar for almost all rifles.

Correcting length of pull is conceptually among the simplest of gunsmithing chores. In many instances, the home gunsmith can add more than one-inch to this fundamental measurement by simply installing a recoil pad in place of a stock recoil plate — few guns or shooters require a greater increase in length of pull. (I will return to the details of recoil pad installation later.) See Photograph #s 2-1/2.

Similarly, shortening a buttstock in conjunction with recoil pad installation is a routine matter. Assuming an otherwise correctly dimensioned stock, the home gunsmith can easily shorten the stock before installing the pad. We will discuss this modification here but I must note that you should verify all measurements first and verify that no other stock modifications are necessary before proceeding; other design changes can alter effective length of pull. See Photograph # 2-3.

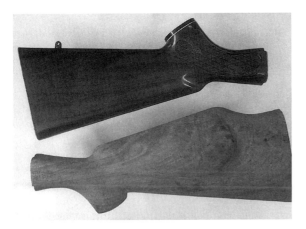

Photograph 2-1: Original Remington Gamemaster Model-760 buttstock, top, has epoxy finish and embossed "checkering". Fajen replacement, bottom, offers room to adjust for a longer length of pull, a built-in cheek piece and semi-fancy black walnut — this piece finished up into a very attractive stock. Besides finishing sanding, we drilled the butt to lighten the stock, shortened the stock for proper length of pull with a recoil pad installed, modified the drop-off at the top back of the cheek piece, fitted the front to the receiver, fitted and installed a Kick-Eez Sorbothane recoil pad, glass bedded the stock to the receiver, installed sling stud, and finished with Tung Oil. This work took about eight hours. Tools used included belt sander, sanding block, various grit sandpapers, four-ought steel wool, various drill bits (15/16", 5/8", 3/32", 5/64"), and hand drill.

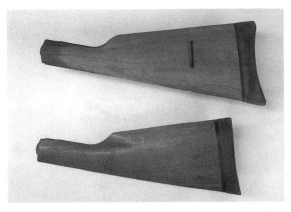

Photograph 2-2: By purchasing an inexpensive Fajen buttstock you can set up your two-piece stocked rifle to properly fit two shooters. This is an especially handy feature for a youth rifle, after your daughter grows up you can refit the gun. Semi-finished Marlin buttstocks are currently available for about $35. Buttstock swapping on Marlin or Winchester lever-action rifles is a one-screw simple job! Fitting and finishing takes about 4 hours. Stocks for Remington and Savage pumps are currently special order items but are not exorbitantly expensive.

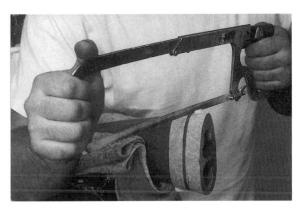

Photograph 2-3: Here we are set up to shorten the existing stock about 1.25". The tape-wrap acts as a guide. Use of a hack saw with a fine-toothed blade minimizes wood chipping and roughness. This pays off during the refinishing stages of this operation. Note the heavy cloth padding in the vise jaws — one does not want to damage the stock by skimping on padding! See text and associated photograph captions for a complete discussion.

Stock Removal:

Both the Savage and Remington Pump-Action Rifles are classic examples of tang-mounted buttstocks. These are similar to many non-bolt-action designs such as the typical lever-action rifle. It is very easy to separate these stocks from the action. Begin by affixing the unloaded gun in a padded vise; for this job it is best to clamp on the sides of the receiver. Remove the buttplate (or recoil pad, where used) by turning out the screws (typically Phillips head). Recoil pad installations also typically use Phillips head mounting screws.

On pads featuring hidden screws, the tinker can find the screw locations and the access holes through the face of the recoil pad (where each screw passed through) by pulling near the top and bottom edges of the pad to stretch it away from the center. Lubricate the bit and shank of a # 1 Phillips screwdriver with liquid soap; a # 1 bitted Phillips screwdriver generally has a smaller shank, this tool will generally loosen the screw and is less apt to damage the small hole in the face of the recoil pad. In this instance, you should loosen the attachment screws from the stock stepwise (without forcing the screws through the face of the recoil pad).

Push the bit through the first of these two holes. Loosen that screw only a few turns then move to the other screw. Turn one screw out until it begins to push against the inside of the face of

Section 2: The Trouble With Stocks, Part I

the recoil pad then loosen the other screw likewise. Switch back and forth, as necessary, until you have removed both screws.

Removal of the recoil plate or pad exposes a large diameter hole in the stock. (This hole runs from the rear several inches forward.) Located at the bottom of this hole is the slotted head of a long bolt. This bolt passes through the remainder of the buttstock and screws into a nut affixed at the back end of the receiver. Tightening this screw attaches the stock to the receiver. I will refer to this bolt as the "through-bolt". See Photograph # 2-4.

With a large-bitted long-shanked standard screwdriver one can loosen and remove this screw. This action completely frees the buttstock from the receiver. On Remington Pumps you will note a stamped-steel plate interposed between buttstock and receiver, do not lose this piece.

Photograph 2-4: Remington Model-760 pump-action rifle buttstock with recoil plate removed. The existing through-bolt hole (where the through-bolt inserts to connect the stock to the receiver) is correctly sized and shaped for installation C&H Research's recoil suppressor. See section on Inertial Recoil Mitigation Devices, later in this chapter. If you drill such a hole for any reason (either to lighten a stock or add a recoil suppressor device, as would be typical on a bolt-action rifle) make certain the hole follows the angle of the bottom of the stock, does not interfere with the bottom butt plate screw hole and does not produce through the side of the stock or come too close to the side or bottom of the stock. For installation of a typical mercury recoil suppresser tube this hole must be slightly more than 4" deep and 7/8" in diameter. Models 742, 7600, 7400 and the limited-release fancy versions of the pump-action and semi-automatic rifles are similar. Savage's Model-170 also has an existing hole.

Besides length of pull, several buttstock modifications are possible and potentially desirable on the Remington Pump. You might choose to adjust drop at the comb (essentially the distance from centerline of bore to the top of the cheek piece). This is a rather simple modification on these rifles. Recesses formed for the tang extensions on the buttstock of the Savage Pump limit the amount of drop adjustment that is feasible. However, sufficient adjustment is typically possible. You should also consider epoxy bedding this style buttstock to the receiver. I will consider each of these modifications later.

On typical bolt-action rifles, stock removal is slightly more complicated. Usually two or three screws pass through the stock from the bottom in the receiver area. Location of the first screw is near the front of the receiver, generally just behind the juncture of the barrel and receiver; location of a second screw (when used) is just in front of the trigger guard; location of the third screw is just behind the trigger guard. Removal of these screws often separates the action from the stock. However, in some designs this only works to separate the trigger guard assembly from the receiver. In this instance, removal of the trigger guard will expose one or more other screws that you will have to remove to complete separation of receiver and stock. Regardless, before working on the stock it is best to fully separate it from the receiver. See Photograph # 2-5.

Photograph 2-5: Front action screw on a Military Mauser showing locking screw. This is a useful design. It allows one to lock the action-mounting screw against unintentional adjustment without over-tightening it — one does not have to relay upon excessive screw torque to keep it tight! Original military Mausers featured a superior bedding system sharing many features with "modern" pillar bedding! Nevertheless, one can improve these fine rifles through glass bedding. See text and associated photographs, later in this chapter.

Begin by mounting the unloaded gun in a bench vise, such as Midway's handy unit. If so equipped, remove the scope, then invert the rifle in the vise. Remove all action-mounting screws. First, the trigger guard assembly will separate from its inletted channel in the bottom of the stock. Often you can then remove the magazine well through the bottom of the stock. If not, this piece might come loose when you separate the stock and the barreled-action. However, some designs use pins or welds to attach the magazine box to the receiver.

Separation of the stock and receiver might require a bit of judicious manipulation and, perhaps, light rapping in the right spot with a rubber mallet. This is often the case on actions that have been glass bedded. However, if the action refuses to move at all, and especially if it moves slightly only to refuse to fully separate, you have probably missed an action mounting screw, barrel band or other attachment device. Check carefully.

Shortening a Buttstock:

(For a discussion of how to determine correct length of pull, refer to the previous sub-section on recoil pad installation.)

First note, shortening of any stock assumes eventual reattachment of the original buttplate or recoil pad or addition of a recoil pad. In all instances, such work involves attachment to the stock, typically with wood screws.

As a rule, whenever installations use wood screws, the safest, strongest and easiest attachment results from predrilling the holes at least as deep as the screw is long with a drill bit that is just smaller than the minor diameter of the wood screw shank. To determine this visually, hold the screw behind the solid shank of the drill bit and aligned with the drill bit. If you can just see the sides of the solid shank of the screw the drill bit is the correct diameter. See Photograph # 2-6.

Forcing wood screws into solid wood adds nothing to the strength of the bond, requires undue force that can result in damage to the head of the screw, and this can also easily split the wood! Before drilling the hole, determine the correct location and mark that deeply with a center-punch. A deep center-punch mark helps prevent drill bit wander as you begin drilling the hole.

Assuming the home gunsmith has determined that in combination with installation of the recoil pad of choice (or none, as the case might be) he needs to shorten the stock some specific amount — we will assume one-inch for this discussion — the next step, after separating the stock from the barreled-action, is to properly mark the stock.

Remove the buttplate or existing recoil pad assembly. If the stock has an existing curve to the butt you can retain this feature if you like. Note, however, that dispensing with any slight curvature of the butt of the stock greatly simplifies recoil pad installation — it is easier to cut and

Photograph 2-6: Here we are drilling screw holes for recoil pad installation. We located the pad, centered over the buttstock, and marked the screw locations using an ice-pick passed through the holes in the pad. Pre-drilling holes for wood screws is critical. Forcing a wood screw into any dense wood without a substantial pilot hole is apt to split the wood. Even if the wood does not split, the screw will provide less hold, compared to installation into a properly sized pilot hole (screw-shank diameter and depth). Wood screws are not nails and are not designed to work like nails! See associated photographs and text.

Section 2: The Trouble With Stocks, Part I

finish to straight lines. However, if you intend to reuse the old buttplate you must, of course, match to the original contour.

Also note, the tinker can bend most quality recoil pads somewhat to match a curved buttstock. Simply heat the pad in boiling water and bend, as necessary. Hold the pad in the bent configuration until it cools.

One easy way to mark a specific and consistent amount of stock for removal is to locate masking tape of the proper width and carefully wrap that around the extreme rear of the stock. This tape-wrap should not contain gaps or overlap with the rear end of the stock. If you use short pieces of tape across the top and bottom and at least two pieces on each side, this process can very accurately map an outline for the general contour of the correct cut that will shorten the stock the required amount and leave it with a very close match to the existing shape.

Also note that you should save all saw dust created during the cut and any filing or sanding operations used to finish the cut surface to the correct contour. If necessary, you can mix the finest of these particles of wood with a clear hobby epoxy and use the resulting product as a filler. This filler will match the color of the wood very closely and, if used in small areas will be almost invisible. It is a good practice to use a thin layer of such a mix between the recoil pad and the stock. This will provide a good seal for the freshly cut wood surface and will also fill any voids created by minor contour mismatches.

To provide maximum protection for the stock, you can wrap the rear few inches with a smooth layer of vinyl electrical tape pulled tight. Make this wrap before applying the masking tape, which you will use to demarcate how much stock to remove and the correct cutting line. You can easily remove electrical tape later — if left in place on a clean surface for too long, masking tape can bond to the surface making removal problematical. Also, application of vinyl tape minimizes chipping or incidental damage to the stock's finish during the cutting operation.

Once you have marked the stock for the cut, mount it in a solidly affixed vise (be sure to use non-marring pads, tire sidewalls work wonderfully). Clamp across a solid portion of the stock with sufficient force to hold the piece solidly but not so tightly as to damage the stock!

I prefer a hacksaw fitted with either an eighteen (18) or twenty-four (24) tooth per inch (tpi) blade. Standard wood saws will easily do this job but those can also chip the wood or any epoxy-type finish. Further, standard wood saws will not allow you to cut along a rounded contour. Begin any wood cut with a few reverse strokes — pulling the saw toward yourself (correctly mounted, a hacksaw blades cut on the forward stroke, just like all other hand saws). During these back strokes the saw is less apt to chatter or jump and move away from the intended line of cut. Once you have established a good groove with back strokes, you can proceed with normal (two-directional) strokes. The fine toothed hacksaw blade will get this job done very rapidly and with a minimum of peripheral damage.

After you have completed the cut the next step is to true the cut to a smooth flat surface and to eliminate any high spots from the interior of the cut. To eliminate potential visible gaps you should ensure that the buttplate or recoil pad will rest solidly against the entire perimeter of the cut area. See Photograph # 2-7.

Where you have cut the stock off to create a straight-cut end, you can accomplish surface finishing very quickly using any type of power sander featuring a flat sanding surface. Use a fairly coarse-grit sandpaper, perhaps one-hundred twenty (120) grit. On concave cuts you can do part of the job using the idler wheel on many types of belt sanders, either bench-mounted or hand-held. However, use caution. It is very easy to cut too deeply, creating a real problem.

Photograph 2-7: Here we are filing off cut marks from the stock. This half-round bastard file does the job fairly quickly. Other methods are possible. For example, one could use a belt sander. However, use caution to avoid changing the angle of this cut surface from square to the bore axis (in either the vertical or horizontal sense). See associated photographs and text.

If the cut is concave, the best tool for finishing the surface is often the original buttplate. If this piece is sufficiently rigid and has a flat back it makes a good sanding block.. Otherwise you can use the block of wood you just cut from the stock. Regardless of which piece you use for a sanding block, you can simply interpose a sheet of sixty (60) grit or eighty (80) grit sandpaper between the sanding block and the stock. Then, with the cutting side of the paper toward the stock, work the sanding block and paper in small ellipses. Typically, move about two-inches in the long direction of the block and about one-half inch in the short direction. That is, move the block in small ellipses. These motions should be about one-half the height and width of the butt. Always keep the block pressed solidly against the stock — do not let it rock from side to side, which will rapidly round the edges.

If the saw cut was particularly crooked and you are using the wood scrap for a sanding block, it might be necessary to reverse the paper several times and sand enough material away from both surfaces to achieve a better match between the stock and the block. Eventually, this process will result in a smoothly contoured surface that should be sufficiently close to matching the original cut.

As noted, if you intend to reuse the original buttplate you can use that piece as a sanding block to achieve a final fitting shape (if it is solid on the back). However, when you use the original buttplate, you will have to fit the perimeter of that piece to the shortened stock; shortening the stock usually reduces both height and width at the butt — stocks taper from rear to front.

You can best accomplish reduction of the perimeter of the original buttplate to fit the stock by reattaching the plate to the tape-wrapped stock and sanding the edges at the original angle using a coarse belt on a fixed belt sander. See the discussion at the beginning of this sub-section on proper installation of wood screws. Once this process has proceeded to the point that the sanding belt is touching the tape everywhere, remove any sharp edges at the rear of the recoil plate by hand sanding a bevel, as necessary. Remove the plate to finish the sanded areas. Hand-sand using progressively finer papers until the appropriate surface quality is achieved.

On a straight cut stock you can use any good sanding block and 60 grit or 80 grit sandpaper. This will soon render the surface close to smooth and flat. I often continue the sanding process using incrementally finer grit sandpaper. You can proceed beyond one-hundred fifty (150) grit sandpaper just to smooth things up but this is not necessary.

What is necessary on this fresh cut surface is the thorough application of an effective sealant. You can use Tung Oil, Linseed Oil, an epoxy-based product or any other product of choice (some prefer a urethane varnish, especially in such hidden applications). If I do not use the aforementioned epoxy and wood filings mix, I prefer Tung Oil. It is so easy to apply, develops a beautiful finish and provides a varnished surface — simply rub it into the wood until it cures. The rubbing action works to drive the oil into the surface porosity of the wood. Frictional heating from this hand-rubbing process speeds curing (oxidation). Regardless of the material chosen to do this job, if the surface is wood or some other porous material, seal it and seal it well.

Also, whether you deepen and reuse the old screw holes or make new screw holes for buttplate or recoil pad mounting, you should ensure that you have properly sealed all such holes, whether used or not. One good way is to oil the hole and the screw with an oil-based sealant and install the screw. Then remove the screw and re-oil the hole a second time. Even if the hole will be unused, this is a good step as it helps to drive the sealing oil into the wood and thereby create a better seal.

I cannot overemphasize wood sealing. Changing moisture content changes the dimensions of any piece of wood — whether you can see this effect or not these changes occur, any such dimensional change is a warpage. Who is to say how far moisture might migrate into the stock? Warping wood is not conducive to consistent zeros or good groups.

As noted above, shortening the stock will typically change the butt dimensions enough so that the existing plate or pad will no longer fit. Resizing the original buttplate is possible. However, where the factory had equipped the stock with a plastic or metal recoil plate, you might prefer to spend the time and money required to fit a quality recoil pad to the stock. Consider this option before deciding how much you want to shorten the stock — the finished stock length with whatever plate or pad you end up choosing installed is the important measurement. Obviously if you intend to shorten the stock one-inch, then shorten the wood one-inch and later decide to add a one-inch thick recoil

Section 2: The Trouble With Stocks, Part I

pad you will have gained very little in the process!

I should note that installation of a quality recoil pad, such as Pachmayr's Decelerator or the Sorbothane from Kick-Eez, is a worthwhile improvement for most shooters, even when recoil is not punishing. Recoil pads are particularly beneficial when bench testing almost any rifle. Bench shooting sets the shooter in a position that results in a marked increase in felt recoil. Also, even when shooting offhand, less felt recoil is always more conducive to developing good shooting habits, compared to more felt recoil!

I highly recommend a flexible pad over hard materials, every time. There is no margin in being tough, your reflexive nervous system knows what the gun is doing to your body whether you admit it or not! Finally, while a good recoil pad might not help you shoot better it will, at the very least, reduce the risk of damage to the gun during handling and use.

I will return to the specific process of installing a recoil pad after reviewing other stock modifications you might choose to make.

Lengthening a Buttstock:

Often, the tinker will choose to lengthen the buttstock. Many long-armed shooters need more length of pull than factory stocks offer. If this is your situation you can do the job quite easily. As noted above, installation of a recoil pad of the appropriate thickness can add as much as one-inch to the length of pull. However, please note, adding a recoil pad without shortening the stock is ill-advised unless you actually need a longer stock! See the sub-section, which follows, on recoil pad installation.

Adjusting Cheek Piece Height (Drop at Comb):

Formerly, manufacturers often designed rifle stocks strictly for shooting with open sights. While this design characteristic does not disallow scoped rifle shooting, it does lead to a poor fit when using a scope sight. To a lesser extent, this is also true when using a front sight that is taller than the original sight. See Photograph #s 2-8/9.

Poor stock fit is no friend of accurate shooting. Often it is desirable to raise the cheek piece to allow the shooter's face to rest comfortably aligned with the sights. Equally, it is often desirable to alter the contour along the top of the cheek piece so that the stock's top surface moves away from the shooter's face as the gun recoils into the shooter's shoulder. Both cheek piece

Photographs 2-8/9: Not all stocks are properly shaped. A properly angled cheek piece of the correct height are critical. Both affect speed of sight acquisition and have a startling effect upon subjective recoil. Photograph 2-8: Since this is a .22 Rimfire-chambered rifle, this evidently poor cheek piece fit and shape are of little consequence, regarding recoil. However, imagine if this were a high recoiling rifle. During recoil such a gun typically moves back about 2" relative to one's face (as anyone who has fired such a gun set up with too-little eye relief on a scope can well attest). A surface in contact with the shooter's face on a stock shaped as this one would move up about 3/8" while moving back 2". That means the stock would move up 3/8" in less than 1/100 of one second. That is certainly fast enough to deliver trauma to us mere mortals. See text and associated photographs and captions for comparisons and a complete discussion.

Photograph 2-9: This sporterized Model-98 Mauser features a properly angled cheek piece, although it is a bit low for this shooter. The top of the stock is just about parallel with the axis of the bore. During recoil, as the rifle moves back, the cheek piece does not move up and into the shooter's face. Therefore, it cannot deliver trauma to one's cheek bone. See text and associated photographs and captions for comparison and discussion.

height and angle are important considerations. See Photograph # 2-10.

Basically, in relationship to the centerline of the bore, the cheek piece of the stock should slope down as the shooter's face moves toward the front of the stock during recoil. A straight-edge positioned along the cheek piece should show that the front of the comb is slightly lower than the back, when compared to the centerline of the bore. On bolt-action rifles the tinker can easily measure this relationship by inserting a bore-fitting dowel through the barrel (after removing the bolt) and extending the dowel over the stock. Clearance between the cheek piece and dowel should be slightly greater near the front than near the back. See Photograph # 2-11.

On high-recoil guns, cheek piece configuration is an especially important consideration. A reverse (incorrectly) sloped cheek piece will be moving into the shooter's face as the gun moves back and up during recoil. Such a design can easily deliver a sufficient blow to cause a concussion — this author speaks from personal bad experience in this regard! Conversely, a properly contoured stock will move away from the shooter's face and cannot directly cause cranial trauma.

An aside here: your brain is you. Why would anyone want to prove anything through some measure of how much abuse to their brain cage they can stand? This is not a contest, shooting should be fun, not grueling.

Should you think you would prefer to have your face absorb some of the gun's recoil, rather than allowing your shoulder to do the entire job, I have a test you are welcome to try (devised by my friend Norm Nelson). Using your left fist, reach up and pop yourself as hard as you can in the right shoulder (if you shoot right-handed). You will note very little discomfort, i.e., you can deliver a very hard blow and suffer little pain. Now, double up and hit yourself in the right cheek using the same force, if you have the nerve! To belabor the point, any shouldered gun should not recoil into your face at all, if you feel the gun slapping your face during recoil, stock configuration is improper. Correction of this deficit is most worthwhile.

On one-piece stocked guns, typical of the bolt-action fraternity, modification of the cheek piece is no simple matter. The tinker can change the slope of the top of the cheek piece by lowering the front slightly. He can also change the overall drop to the cheek piece slightly by either deepening the fore-end channel or lowering the top of the tang slightly, as required. In either case, he must modify the remainder of the stock's inletting to match the new configuration. While only small changes in geometry are typically possible, small changes can sometimes make a great deal of difference.

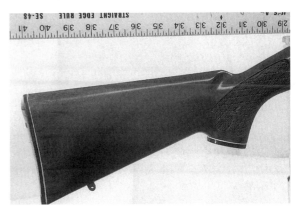

Photograph 2-10: Remington Model-760 pump-action rifle (1970s manufacture). Note straight-edge above top of stock. I have attached the rule along the top of the barrel and (approximately) parallel with the axis of the bore. Note that on this unmodified stock the front end of the cheek piece is slightly closer to the edge of the rule than the back end of the cheek piece (I have slightly exaggerated the condition in this pose). This situation is not conducive to good shooting. One should correct it, if possible. See associated photographs and text. During recoil this stock would move into one's face and, therefore, would transfer energy and create impact trauma in that sensitive area. See photograph 2-11 for comparison.

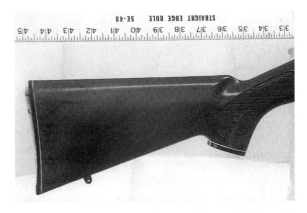

Photograph 2-11: Note that on this <u>modified</u> stock the front end of the cheek piece is slightly farther away from the edge of the rule than the back end of the cheek piece. This is as things should always be on any high-power rifle or shotgun. During recoil this stock will move away from one's face and, therefore, cannot create impact trauma in that sensitive area. See photograph 2-10 for comparison.

Section 2: The Trouble With Stocks, Part I

Generally, if the stock is oil finished the home tinker can successfully accomplish such modifications. This work requires careful attention to detail, especially during cutting or sanding on the wood. Also, you will have to refinish the affected area with a similar oil-based finish to match the original finish, which is often very difficult. Usually it is better to at least lightly sand the entire stock, with two hundred forty (240) grit (or finer) sandpaper, then refinish it. However, if the original finish incorporated a stain, this approach might not be satisfactory. Where the original finish included a wood stain, consider sanding the entire surface to substantially remove the original finish.

On stocks featuring epoxy, polyurethane or varnish type finishes, refinishing is a major hassle. Many home gunsmiths would consider the process to be too much trouble. The basic problem is that you have to entirely remove the old finish, which is nothing less than a major pain. You can do this but it seems to this tinker that it takes more time than it is worth!

Especially if the stock has an epoxy finish, or is checkered, it might be easier and cheaper to replace the stock with a properly-designed synthetic or wood unit! Fajen offer such replacement stocks that are readily available and modestly priced. Installation varies from a simple drop-in to final fitting and finishing versions. Since synthetic stocks are generally stronger and much less resistant to weather-induced dimensional changes, these are a good idea and a reasonable investment. However, many still prefer the beauty of natural wood grain despite its disadvantages — take your pick.

I will not visit all the details of such an installation here but I will note that you should not consider such a replacement a cure-all. The gunsmithing tinker should properly fit, bed and finish any replacement stock, as necessary. For discussions of those areas, refer to the appropriate information throughout this section.

Inertial Recoil Mitigation Devices (Mercury Recoil Suppressers):

One important area where we can modify a stock to improve a rifle's handling characteristics involves mitigation of recoil. An effective method involves installation of an inertial recoil absorber. These units work by spreading the recoil impulse over a longer period. See Photograph # 2-12.

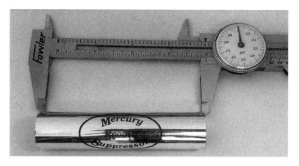

Photograph 2-12: This shiny foil-covered tube contains about 12 ounces of movable mercury. Physics and geometry work to allow the mercury to prolong the recoil impulse over a greater distance and thereby reduce the kick's "sharpness". See text for technical discussion of how this works. On a typical installation one removes a few, perhaps four, ounces of wood from the stock to install this 14 ounce device. Obviously the added weight also helps tame the gun's recoil. This quality unit is from C&H Research, available through Brownells.

As the gun moves back, in response to the bullet and powder moving forward (for every action there is an equal and opposite reaction), the mercury charge, located at the back end of the sealed tube, stays in place (inertia). When the gun has moved far enough so that the front of the mercury tube housing hits the front of this stationary column of mercury, the gun will be recoiling at nearly maximum recoil velocity (in high-recoil guns that is about 20 fps). When the front of the tube hits the mercury, the mercury will rebound at a very high velocity, as necessary to provide conservation of both energy and momentum — as required by the laws of physics.

An exact analysis is not feasible here. However, for a perfectly elastic collision between the mercury and the gun the following mathematical solution is correct. While this does not represent exactly what happens, it is conservative — our assumptions understate the actual recoil damping effects.

Assuming the moving portion of the gun weighs ten pounds and is initially recoiling at twenty feet per second (20 fps) and that the mercury weighs one-half pound, the following equations and units apply:

Before impact with mercury column:
Gun recoil energy = mass times velocity squared = $10 \times 20^2 = 4000$ units
Gun recoil momentum = mass times velocity = $10 \times 20 = 200$ units

After impact with mercury column:
Total system recoil energy = 4000 units
Total system recoil momentum = 200 units

(After the gun collides with the stationary mercury, total recoil energy must still equal 4000 units; also total recoil momentum must still equal 200 units. However, the new recoiling weight will be 10.5 pounds. Hereafter we will refer to gun mass units as "A" and mercury mass units as "B".)

$(10 \times A^2) + (0.5 \times B^2) = 4000$ (Recoil Energy Equation)
$(10 \times A) + (0.5 \times B) = 200$ (Recoil Velocity Equation)

Therefore:
$10 \times 20^2 = (10 \times A^2) + (0.5 \times B^2) = 4000$
$10 \times 20 = (10(A) + (0.5 \times B) = 200$ (With a bit of algebra)

$(100 \times A^2) + (5 \times B^2) = 40{,}000$ (Ten times the first equation)
$(100 \times A^2) + (0.25 B^2) + (10 \times A \times B) = 40{,}000$ (Squaring the second equation)

$(4.75 \times B^2) - (10 \times A \times B) = 0$ (Subtracting the second equation from the first)
$B((4.75 \times B) - (10 \times A)) = 0$ (Factoring out the common B)
$(4.75 \times B) - (10 \times A) = 0$ (Dividing both sides by B)
$4.75 \times B = 10 \times A$ (Adding $(10 \times A)$ to both sides)
$0.475 \times B = A$ (Dividing both sides by 10)
$B = A \div 0.475$ (Dividing both sides by 0.475)

(Finally, we can substitute back into the Recoil Energy Equation or the Recoil Velocity Equation to solve for, post impact, velocities of both gun and mercury.)

$(10 \times A) + (0.5 \times B) = 200$
$(10 \times (.475 \times B)) + (0.5 \times B) = 200$
$(4.75 \times B) + (0.5 \times B) = 200$
$5.25 \times B = 200$
$B = 200 \div 5.25$
$B \approx 38$ fps (Mercury velocity, about 38 fps)

$(10 \times A) + (0.5 \times B) = 200$
$(10 \times A) + (0.5(A \div 0.475)) = 200$
$(10 \times A) + (A \times (0.5 \div 0.475)) = 200$
$A \times (10 + (0.5 \div 0.475)) = 200$
$A = 200 \div (10 + (0.5 \div 0.475))$
$A \approx 200 \div 11.05$
$A \approx 18$ fps (Rifle Velocity, about 18 fps)

Recoil energy is a function of velocity squared. Therefore, at the instant the gun contacts the mercury, the gun exhibits a surprising twenty-three percent (23%) reduction in recoil energy! ($20 \times 20 = 400$ | $18 \times 18 = 324$ | $324 \div 400 = 81$ | 81 is $\approx 23\%$ less than 100) Of course the mercury will soon collide with the back of the tube and thereby accelerate the rifle but that all takes time and, in so doing, this system spreads the recoil impulse out over time.

Newton's laws take over with this system. As noted in the above mathematical discussion, conservation of momentum and energy requires that after the recoiling gun impacts the mercury, the mercury must recoil toward the rear of the tube at relatively high velocity. This action markedly slows both the gun's rearward velocity and its instantaneous recoil energy. The mercury then hits the back of the tube, accelerating it backward while reversing the mercury toward the front of the tube. The net result is a spreading out in time of the gun's rearward impulse — effectively, the gun recoils slower but further.

For this reason, the shooter feels a softer, albeit longer, push applied to the shoulder — the perception of recoil is substantially different, and more pleasant! Since it is mostly the overall velocity of recoil that inflicts trauma, installation of an inertial mercury tube offers a big advantage.

Most guns are lighter than ten pounds and the mercury column is slightly heavier than one-half pound. Therefore, results for the typical installation would be better than suggested by our mathematical dissertation, which is a conservative estimate of recoil mitigation. See Photograph #s 2-13/14.

Many rifles lack any hole in the base of the buttstock. Boring a hole of nearly one-inch diameter more than four-inches (4") into the base of a buttstock requires care to avoid hitting air or compromising the stock's integrity. Use the correct tools and get help, if necessary, to line things up correctly. See associated photographs for a technique that allows one person to safely do this job.

In stocks where a through-bolt attaches the buttstock to the receiver, generally you can simply insert the recoil absorber into the existing hole. Often installation of this device, which typically weighs the better part of one-pound, significantly alters the rifle's balance. For this reason, most shooters will want to experiment with positioning the device both toward front and toward the rear of the hole in the buttstock to determine which position feels best during field carrying, handling and shooting. However, often the existing hole is only marginally longer than the tube. In this instance, moving the tube front-to-rear will offer little variation in the gun's balance. See Photograph #s 2-15/16.

Section 2: The Trouble With Stocks, Part I

Photograph 2-13: Here we have marked the location for the center of a 15/16" hole we will drill in this buttstock. The goal is installation of a C&H Research Mercury recoil suppressor. This hole will have to be at least 4¼" deep and should follow the angle of the base of the stock. It should not produce through or too close to the side of the stock! See text and associated photograph captions for further discussion.

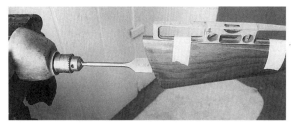

Photograph 2-14: Here we are prepared to drill the 15/16" hole. The hand drill is vised solidly with the bit producing level from the chuck — as verified by a spirit bubble level! We have inverted the stock and attached a spirit bubble level to the under surface. In this way one person can keep that surface parallel to the axis of the drill bit. By looking down on this assembly as drilling proceeds, one can keep the horizontal axis of both stock and bit lined up correctly. All that remains is to keep the sides of the stock vertically oriented as one drills the hole fully 4¼" deep....

Photograph 2-15: A bench-mounted grinder is handy for shaping hard wood. Here we are preparing an end of a dowel for backing a C&H Research mercury recoil absorber tube. We will have to grind the end at an angle to provide full support at the rear of the angled hole in the buttstock. See text and associated photograph captions for a complete discussion.

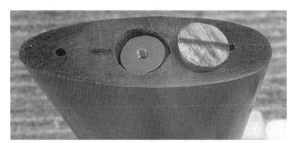

Photograph 2-16: After drilling the hole, we taped-wrapped both ends of the recoil suppresser to provide a snug fit; inserted it into the hole, in the final configuration; and cut a hardwood plug, of the proper shape to fill the hole (shown here beside the hole). This plug is critical; it keeps the tube in place thereby preventing damage to the tube, the stock or the butt plate. In this instance we used a Pachmayr Decelerator® recoil pad (which is slightly hollow at the center). Therefore, we left the plug slightly (about 1/16") long to insure the recoil suppresser stays put. Compressible rubber at the center of the base of the pad will push against this plug.

In either situation, the tinker can cut a hardwood dowel to fit either in front of or behind the mercury unit. This spacer must be designed to hold the tube rigidly in place during recoil — the buttplate or recoil pad prevents both the dowel and inertial recoil absorber from moving endwise in the hole. It is also necessary to wrap vinyl electrical tape around the tube to achieve a solid fit of the tube in the hole in the stock. See Photograph # 2-17.

One advantage of this type of recoil absorber is that it detracts nothing from the classic beauty of the gun's lines; the stock and recoil pad completely hide it.

I should note that since this unit works by moving mercury around, which induces heating in the mercury and the device, there is a commensurate reduction in recoil energy. This effect is real, albeit negligible. See Photograph # 2-18.

The Counter-Coil Hydraulic Recoil Absorber:

Another type of recoil control device, most appropriate for heavy caliber rifles, is the hydraulic recoil "absorber" system. In this system, the gunsmith installs a controlled collapsing unit at the rear of the buttstock. Adjustments control the rate of hydraulic bleed off, maximizing diffusion of the recoil impulse, regardless of the gun and load's recoil velocity. That is, the shooter adjusts this unit to match the gun's weight; the specific cartridge, bullet weight and muzzle velocity; and the shooter's physiology. When correctly adjusted, the Counter-Coil® unit should fully collapse before re-extending but without any slamming at the end of the collapsing cycle.

Owing to variations in shooter pose and resulting physiological resistance, on average the best adjustment will only come close to achieving this ideal. Regardless, the unit converts the recoil impulse from a sharp — almost instantaneous — hammering blow to a prolonged slower push. Typically, the bullet and all powder gasses exit the muzzle within less than two-thousandths of one second from the instant they start moving. At the end of that very short period of time, the gun is already moving back at maximum achieved velocity! See Photograph #s 2-19/20/21.

I should note that correct usage is also important; if the shooter collapses the spring by pulling the gun too tightly against his shoulder (before he fires the shot), he will have defeated the unit's functioning! See Photograph # 2-22.

I should also note that since this unit works by metered hydraulic displacement and spring

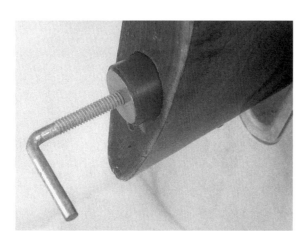

Photograph 2-17: C&H Research mercury recoil suppresser tape wrapped (vinyl electrical tape) to fit the existing 1" diameter hole in this Model-760 Remington Pump. Other installations are similar. Tape wraps at both ends of the 4" tube keep it snugly fitted in the hole. This 1/4" "L" bolt is installed to demonstrate tube-removal technique — tapped hole is only on back end of tube. Models 742, 7600, 7400 and the limited-release fancy versions of the pump-action rifle and semi-automatic and Savage's Model-170 are similar.

Photograph 2-18: Hardwood plug fitted for installation behind a recoil suppresser tube. One must angle the end of this plug to match the angle this hole makes to the rear face of the stock. This Remington Model-760 pump-action rifle installation is typical. This plug keeps the tube from shifting around in the stock. Shifting would limit its function and could lead to buttstock, recoil tube or recoil plate damage. Models 742, 7600, 7400 and the limited-release fancy versions of the pump-action rifle and semi-automatic and Savage's Model-170 are similar. However, refer to text for complete discussion of possible differences.

Section 2: The Trouble With Stocks, Part I

Photograph 2-19: The Counter Coil® system is an active recoil mitigation device. An adjustable pneumatic shock absorber and a spring (housed in the central column) combine to provide effective recoil control in a very lightweight package. Hogging out and shortening the average stock for installation renders a near-zero change in finished gun weight! Installation instructions provide all the information one needs to manage a quality installation in the home workshop. Photograph 2-20 shows the procedure for removing the butt pad portion to facilitate adjustment (see photograph 2-21). See text and associated photograph captions for a complete discussion.

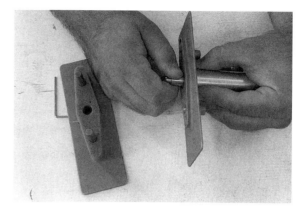

Photograph 2-21: Turning the central piston on the Counter Coil® unit is all that is required to change the unit from a soft hydraulic shock absorber, useful for very modestly recoiling rifles, to a very hard hydraulic shock absorber, useful on the most punishing of guns. Do not turn this piston forcefully past its tactually obvious adjustment end-points. Shooters often employ this device on .50 BMG chambered sporting rifles — guns where recoil is truly massive. The restoring spring is not particularly stiff. Therefore, do not pull the rifle hard into your shoulder, that will collapse this spring and defeat the system! See text and associated photograph captions for a complete discussion.

Photographs 2-20/21: One adjusts the Counter Coil® for guns of varying recoil by a simple hand adjustment of the central piston. Photograph 2-20: Separating main body from butt plate. One can and should tune the unit to the gun, shooter and load. If the setting is too-hard the unit will not function fully. This limits effectiveness. If the setting is too-soft the unit will collapse too easily and the gun will manage to deliver a sharp blow through the fully collapsed device. Any setting that is nearly perfect will provide substantially all the benefit possible. Therefore, achieving a precise setting is not critical. However, the closer the better! See text and associated photograph captions for a complete discussion.

Photograph 2-22: The Counter Coil® system features a return spring designed only to keep the unit extended between shots. Do not pull the gun rigidly against your shoulder — you can easily collapse this extending spring and render the unit functionless! Note the stainless-steel pins to either side. As the unit collapses these alignment pins protrude through the front plate. One must make room in the stock accordingly. See text and associated photograph captions for a complete discussion.

compression (which induces heating in the device) it, like the aforementioned mercury device, converts some inertial energy into heat energy — there is a commensurate reduction in recoil. This effect is real, albeit minor. See Photograph # 2-23.

With due regards to the Counter-Coil Company, this device, unlike the aforementioned recoil-impulse-slowing mercury suppresser, or energy dissipating recoil pads, discussed later, does detract from the classic beauty of a fine rifle. Counter-coil intends this device for installation on "working guns" — those rifles and shotguns where usefulness, not appearance, is the critical criterion. In that regard, the Counter-Coil does exactly what its designer intended — it reduces felt recoil substantially, making the gun easier to shoot properly, no mean feat! See Photograph #s 2-24/25.

Counter-Coil installation involves shortening the stock, drilling holes for the unit's guide rails, finishing the unit to fit the stock, attaching a recoil pad to the unit and attaching the assembly to the stock. As noted above, the finished piece has a bit of a futuristic appearance; however, recoil force mitigation on truly heavy caliber rifles or on the lightest of hunting sporters is sufficient to warrant any such sacrifice in appearance. The associated photographs should clarify what is required to properly install this device. Also, the supplied instructions are understandable. See Photograph #s 2-26/27.

Installation of Recoil Pads:

Installing a recoil pad is not as simple an operation as it might seem. This is a job that is well worth the few dollars most gunsmiths charge. However, you can do this at home. This procedure requires only a bit of time and any one of several special tools. A bench-mounted grinder with a coarse aluminum oxide (corundum) wheel of adequate diameter with open access to the side of the grinding wheel will do. Alternatively, you can use a belt or disk sander; this is a superior method. Perhaps you could use other tools. . . . See Photograph # 2-28.

If you intend to use a bench grinder, before beginning, remove the standard guards from the

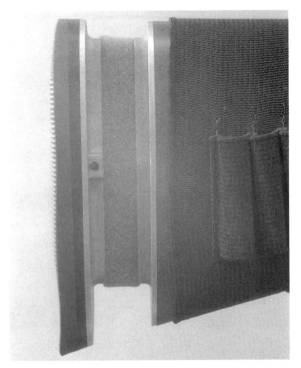

Photograph 2-24: While not the most beautiful adornment ever devised for a rifle, the Counter Coil® is one of the best! Properly adjusted, these units can tame the recoil of a monster rifle sufficiently to allow significant bench testing without undue shooter trauma. Further, this unit adds almost nothing to the weight of the average rifle — wood removed during installation is typically almost as heavy as this device, sometimes heavier! That is sometimes an important consideration such as this installation on a .30-06 chambered lightweight Ruger Model-77. Note the cartridge band and the lightweight recoil pad. This rifle belongs to the daughter of Mr. Danuser, owner of Counter Coil®. It has seen use in Africa with no complaints! See text and associated photograph captions for a complete discussion.

Photograph 2-23: Close-up-view of Counter Coil® equipped Model 77 Ruger Lightweight rifle chambered in .30-06. A light rifle that will deliver substantial energy without punishing recoil is no small matter. Note the handy cartridge band on the stock and the lightweight nylon sling. This rifle has seen service in Africa with no complaints.

Section 2: The Trouble With Stocks, Part I

end and front of the wheel. Ensure there is adequate access to the wheel to maneuver the stock, as necessary to grind away all excess material. However, since you have removed the safety guards, use caution to avoid inadvertent damage to the stock or your hide!

After shortening the stock as necessary, attach the pad to the stock. Follow the aforementioned advice for stock shortening, contouring, finishing and wood screw installation. It is a good idea to leave a few wraps of electrical tape around the rear of the stock. These will act as a warning marker to prevent damaging the stock by grinding the pad too deeply — when the grinding wheel begins to roughen the tape, the fit is very close. See Photograph #s 2-29/30.

Here a bit of an eye for contour is important. You should attempt to grind the pad until all edges match the contour of the stock — you should shape the finished pad just as if it were a natural extension of the stock. For this reason, ideally, you should do this job before completion of a stock's exterior contour and application of the finish. See Photograph #s 2-31/32.

Grind the material slowly and while turning the stock. In this way, remove only a modest amount of material from any area before grinding adjacent areas to a similar contour. It is best to work on each side in turn until both are close to the required finished contour. After you have nearly finished grinding the sides of the pad,

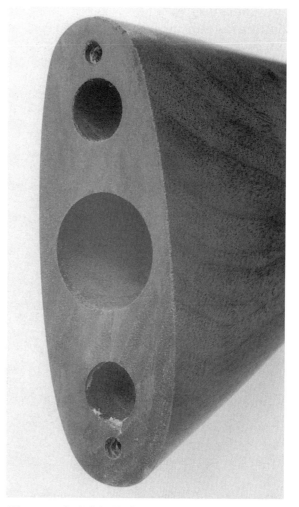

Photograph 2-26: End-on oblique-view of a rifle stock modified for Counter Coil® installation. Note that the screw-mounting holes are rather near the top and bottom edges of this stock (this could present a problem with shortened stocks on very petite rifles. However, one can locate attachment holes elsewhere. The bigger top and bottom holes provide clearance for the guide rods during the unit's collapse (in response to recoil forces). The middle hole provides clearance for the spring-loaded hydraulic unit, the heart of the device. See text and associated photograph captions for a complete discussion.

Photograph 2-25: While not the most beautiful adornment ever devised for a rifle, the Counter Coil® is one of the best! Properly adjusted these units can tame the recoil of a heavy recoil rifle. Mitigation is often sufficient to allow significant bench testing without undue shooter trauma. Further, this unit adds almost nothing to the weight of the average rifle — wood removed during installation is typically almost as heavy as the device, sometimes heavier! See text and associated photograph captions for a complete discussion.

contour first the top and finally the bottom edges to the approximate final shape.

After you have reached the point where all edges are close to the proper size and shape, proceed with due caution. Generally, you have almost finished the grinding portion of the job when the corundum (aluminum oxide) wheel first touches the electrical tape as you make a final pass and with the stock in the correct orientation, relative to the side of the grinding wheel. Finish the sizing and shaping job by carefully grinding only the solid base of the pad, near the juncture of the pad and stock. Use a slightly increased angle and carefully grind until the base of the pad is very close to matching the stock.

If you are working with an unfinished stock or an oil finished stock you can improve the fit to perfection by filing along the joint with a medium-sized bastard-cut file until the file is touching the wood everywhere as you bring the plastic base of the pad to final size and contour. Follow this filing by sanding using progressively finer sandpaper mounted on a good sanding block or strips of corundum paper as you would use a shoe polish rag. See the associated photographs. Continue the sanding process using progressively finer grades of sandpaper until you achieve the necessary level of finish. Generally, since you will be sanding across the grain, you will have to go one step finer than the finish on the rest of the stock, perhaps to three-hundred twenty (320) grit or even four hundred forty (440) grit, depending upon the hardness of the wood. See Photograph # 2-33.

Adjusting Cheek Piece Fit (Drop at Comb):

On Remington Pump-Action Rifles and many other two-piece stocked guns, modification of the buttstock to adjust the drop at the comb (height of cheek piece) is a simple matter.

Photograph 2-27: Oblique-view of Counter Coil® fitted rifle. Here we have removed the recoil plate assembly from a Counter Coil® device. Rotation of the exposed central piston affords shock absorber adjustment. One should match this characteristic to the rifle, load and shooter. The only way to do this is with shooting tests. A good way to test for proper adjustment is to install a tell-tale such as a small piece of Styrofoam between the stationary-mounted plate and the moving plate (remove the foam rubber insert). When the tell-tale just fully collapses one has the unit properly adjusted. See text and associated photograph captions for a complete discussion.

Photograph 2-28: One has several options in premium recoil pads. Here we picture Pachmayr Decelerator® and Kick-Eez Sorbothane® models. Both pads are about one inch thick and designed for installation on smaller buttstocks. The Kick-Eez features inserts to fill the visible screw holes. The Pachmayr relies upon the natural elasticity of the pad face to hide the pin holes one makes, through which the attachment screws pass. An ice-pick is the best tool for producing these holes. Insert the pick from the hidden face and force its tip out through the patterned face. Application of a bit of liquid soap to the ice pick and the screw threads and head facilitates installation. Soaped screws pass through the tiny holes easily and without damaging the visible face of the pad. See associated photographs and text.

Section 2: The Trouble With Stocks, Part I

Photograph 2-29: When adding a one-inch recoil pad and shortening the finished stock about one-half inch one has to remove a considerable piece of wood! The front of this tape-wrap indicates the required cut line. This rifle belongs to my wife who, like many folks, is a bit short of stature (she prefers "petite"!). Standard stocks do not correctly fit her. Proper fit is critical to good shooting; for best shooting results, <u>always fit the stock to the gun's owner</u>! Typical length of pull adjustments range from shortening the factory stock about $1/2''$ to lengthening it about $1''$. Such minor adjustments can have a profound influence on gun-to-shooter fit. See associated photographs and text.

Photograph 2-30: Cutting the stock off using a hack saw fitted with a 24 tpi blade. Here we have turned the blade sideways to achieve a complete cut. Note that we have not tape-wrapped the stock where we are cutting. Normally we would use a wrap of electrical tape to limit chipping on the cut-out side. Here for the sake of photographic clarity we have omitted that step. Also that step was not necessary; we intend to fit the stock with a recoil pad while somewhat reducing the size of the butt — our recontouring will remove any minor chipped spots. See associated photographs and text.

Photograph 2-31: After much debate we choose Pachmayr's Decelerator® pad over the Kick-Eez Sorbothane® model. The deciding factor was weight. After many hours of skeletonizing we managed to reduce this rifle's weight to only $4^{1}/_{2}$ pounds. Since the Kick-Eez pad is a few ounces heavier than the Pachmayr pad, we choose the latter. However, the Kick-Eez might have provided superior recoil mitigation. As I said, considerable debate. Note how much material we will have to remove to properly fit this pad to this stock. This is not unusual and explains our choice of the small model. Trimming much further would result in discovery of the steel support frame, which ruins the pad — choose the smallest pad that will shape down correctly for the installation at hand! We used a vised belt sander to trim this pad to stock size and contour. We used a tape-wrap on the stock adjacent to the pad to note approach to finished contour. See associated photographs and text.

On older Remington Pump-Action and Semi-Automatic-Action Rifles (generally those with the Model-760 and Model-742 or Model-740 designation), such a modification is both simple and necessary for proper scope-equipped rifle-to-shooter fit.

Remove the stock, as described above, and note the areas of contact between the stock and the receiver. At the extreme front end of the stock there is a ring of wood between the perimeter relief groove and the hole for the through-bolt. This flat area is the only portion of the stock that does and should contact the receiver! Should you modify the stock so that contact occurs at the perimeter, recoil-induced stress-splits and surface chipping are likely to occur. See Photograph # 2-34.

Properly, the raised flat area supports all recoil forces and controls the angle of attachment between the buttstock and the receiver. You should modify both the perimeter relief groove and the interior flat, as necessary, to allow the stock to attach at an angle that brings the butt slightly higher (reduces drop at comb) and to provide a slight clearance around the entire perimeter. This modification is very helpful on older guns where the owner has added a telescopic sight.

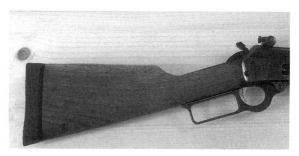

Photograph 2-33: The finished product. We shortened this stock about one-half inch to fit the gun's owner. We applied Tung oil to the 320 grit sanded stock. The installed Pachmayr Decelerator® recoil pad matches the stock and the stock matches the receiver. Finishing with Tung Oil seals and protects the wood. This also provides for simple repairs of use marks. See associated photographs and text.

Photograph 2-32: Here we have almost finished contouring this Pachmayr Decelerator® recoil pad to the stock. Note that the working area of the pad is slightly larger than the plastic backing and the stock. This results from the material's natural springiness, to minimize this effect apply very light sanding pressure and exercise patience! See associated photographs and text.

Photograph 2-34: Unmodified Remington Model-760 buttstock, receiver end. Note stress-relief channel, around perimeter; tang extension slot, bottom center; and hole for through-bolt, center. The flat area on the extreme front end separates the stock from the receiver and transfers the entire attachment load and all recoil forces from the receiver to the stock. If the stock touched the receiver anywhere around the perimeter, pieces might split off under these stresses. Various related pump-action and semi-automatic Remington models and Savage's Model-170 are similar. However, refer to text for complete discussion of possible differences.

However, any modification that raises the rear of the stock, by changing the attachment angle, also inappropriately alters the angle of the stock's butt. For this reason, the tinker should also remove a sliver of material from the rear bottom of the stock to compensate, thereby keeping the butt of the stock square to the bore's axis. See Photograph #s 2-35/36/37.

Drop height reduction also adds to the proper "dropping away" of the comb, as discussed above. This simple alteration can dramatically reduce the apparent recoil of these guns.

To calculate the amounts of material you should remove, it is first necessary to figure out how much you need to alter the stock's drop. To do this, mount the scope on the rifle, close your

Photograph 2-35: Butt-end of Remington Model-760 pump-action rifle stock. We have applied vinyl electrical tape to show approximately the angle of the necessary cut (about 0.125" at bottom tapered to zero at top) to keep the butt properly squared to the axis of the bore after modifying the stock to raise the cheek piece about 0.75". Models 742, 7600, 7400, the limited-release fancy versions of the pump-action rifle, various semi-automatic rifles and other two-piece buttstock rifles are similar. However, refer to text for complete discussion of possible differences.

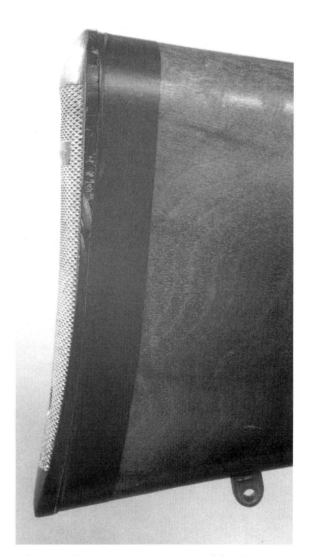

Photograph 2-36: Remington Model-760 pump-action rifle showing misfit of butt plate after slight modification of butt end of stock. We shortened the lower edge. See associated photographs and text for explanation. Note that butt plate now extends both slightly below and above the stock, at the bottom the sides also extend past the wood. The vinyl tape-wrap will protect the stock as we file at the excess plastic. This product will also provide a tell-tale to demonstrate approach to proper size. Other two-piece stocked rifles are similar. See associated photographs.

eyes and bring the gun to bear in a natural and comfortable position. Try to forget what you have had to do in the past to shoot the gun, just relax and allow the gun and your face to settle naturally.

Open your eyes. Note where you might have to move your head to obtain a full field of view through the scope. (This discussion assumes proper front-to-rear scope positioning.) If, as is most common, you have to cock your head, raising your eye, to achieve a full field of view, the stock has too much drop — the cheek piece is not high enough. See Photograph # 2-38.

If this is the case, do the following: interpose a taped-on layer of corrugated cardboard wrapped over the cheek piece. Then repeat the above test. Continue adding cardboard layers until your face comes to rest at the proper height to provide a natural full field of view through the scope while supported comfortably by the cardboard. Make sure that the cardboard does not wrap over the side of the cheek piece where it would interfere with your cheek coming to rest against the stock. The cardboard should only cover the top of the stock.

When everything is right you should feel comfortable with your head lying on the shimmed-up cheek piece — you should not have to force your face into the stock or hold it up above the stock, your face should rest naturally in the proper position. When everything is correct: you should be able to close your eyes and bring the gun to bear comfortably and naturally, then, upon opening your eyes, the scope's eyepiece should present you with a full field of view.

The point is: the shooter should not have to do anything other than bring the rifle to bear to have a full field of view through the scope. Anything less than this is less than ideal and will reduce the shooter's ability to fire the gun fast, comfortably and accurately. All are points that can make a dramatic difference either in the hunting field or at the shooting bench.

After you have determined the correct amount of cheek piece padding, things get slightly difficult! First, you have to measure the vertical thickness of the padding where your cheek rests. One easy way to do this is to insert a sharp needle into the stack of cardboard until it just touches the stock. While looking over the vised

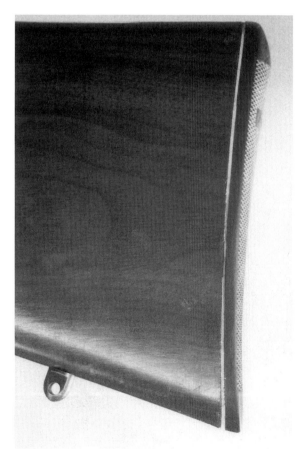

Photograph 2-37: Remington Model-760 pump-action rifle stock after fitting of butt plate to modified stock. See text and associated photographs for explanation of purpose and process. This modification would be necessary on any two-piece stocked rifle where one modified the buttstock to reduce drop at comb.

Photograph 2-38: This sporterized Model-98 Mauser features a properly designed cheek piece, although the cheek piece is a bit low for this shooter. The top of the stock is just about parallel with the axis of the bore. As the rifle moves back under recoil the stock does not move into the shooter's face. Therefore, it cannot deliver trauma to one's cheek bone. See text and associated photograph and captions for comparisons and additional discussion.

Section 2: The Trouble With Stocks, Part I

rifle from the rear, position the needle, centered over the stock and vertically aligned at about the location where your cheek rests. Then carefully shove the needle through the corrugated cardboard layers. Use of a thimble is certainly a good idea. When the needle touches the stock, paint the protruding portion with a permanent marker and mark the position of this hole in the cardboard for future reference.

Remove the marked needle. Measure the length of needle shank which you had inserted into the cardboard (the unpainted portion). Also, measure the distance from the receiver to the hole in the cardboard. Write down these numbers. Finally, measure the height of the raised pad where the buttstock abuts the rear of the receiver (on the Remington Pump this pad is about one and six-tenths inch (1.6") high). With these numbers in hand, you can do a bit of mathematical manipulation and come up with the amount of material that you have to trim from the top of the recoil pad at the front of the stock. See diagram.

Determining Proper "Drop At Comb" Adjustment

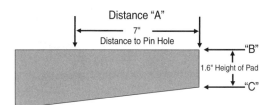

Assume you inserted the needle through the pad at "A". Assume you inserted one-quarter inch (1/4") of the needle before it touched the wood. In that case, removal of $1.6 \div 7 \times 0.25" \simeq 0.060"$ from the upper area at "B" would do the job. That is, removal of about sixty-thousandths of an inch (0.060") of material from the top of the pad at the front of the receiver is required. This trim should taper to zero cut at the bottom of the pad. Such a cut will result in a rotation of the attached stock enough to move the point at "A" up about one-quarter inch (1/4") — the necessary amount, as measured.

On older Remington Pumps and Semi-Autos this is a good average amount to change the stock. With the introduction of the newer models, generally with a four-lug locking bolt (Model-7400 and Model-7600 designations), Remington changed the stock design to more correctly fit with a scope; these stocks will require less, if any, modification. Note that the through-bolt will bend adequately to allow this reorientation of the stock with no problems. See Photograph #s 2-39 through 2-42.

Conveniently, the perimeter recess for stock clearance is about one-eighth inch (1/8"). This means that for the average shooter the tinker can simply grind away at the pad until the top edge of the stock is about one-half as thick (in relation to the perimeter groove) as it was and so that the

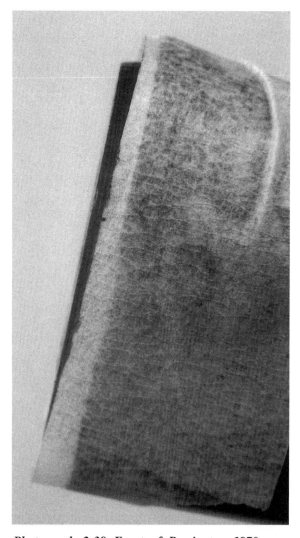

Photograph 2-39: Front of Remington 1970s era Model-760 pump-action rifle stock. Here a tape-wrap leaves exposed, approximately, the material one must remove to decrease drop at comb for proper shooter fit when shooting these rifles with a scope attached. See text and associated photographs. The amount of material one needs to remove depends upon the individual gun, shooter and scope mounting height. Models 742, 7600, 7400 and the limited-release fancy versions of the pump-action rifle and semi-automatic are similar. However, refer to text for complete discussion of possible differences — typically newer guns require less (if any) modification.

Photograph 2-40: With the stock rigidly vised in padded jaws we use a belt sander to bring the front of the stock to the angle indicated by the taped gauge. One could use a bench-mounted grinder, a file or a fixed sanding disk or belt for this operation. The method chosen is not critical but the care taken is! See text and associated photograph captions for a complete discussion.

Photograph 2-41: Close-up-view: We have rigidly vised the stock in padded jaws; we are using a belt sander to bring the front of the stock to the angle indicated by the taped gauge. See associated photograph and caption.

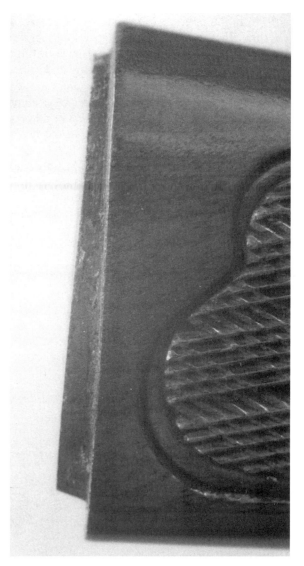

Photograph 2-42: Partially modified buttstock for Remington Model-760 Pump. Note that at the top the perimeter channel is only about one-half the depth it is at the bottom. We used a tape-wrap as a cutting guide, see associated photographs and captions. We now must cut the channel deeper to maintain proper perimeter channel-to-receiver clearance. We will use a tape wrap for that operation. We will leave that tape in place as an epoxy shield when we glass-bed the buttstock.

Section 2: The Trouble With Stocks, Part I

grinder just touches the finish on the bottom edge of the pad. Be careful here to keep the pad square to the axis of the through-bolt. If you fail to keep the pad square, in the horizontal sense, to the axis of the through-bolt, tightening the through-bolt will pull the horizontal axis of stock out of alignment with the bore! While such "cast offs" are a common feature of certain types of rifles, this is not generally a desirable feature. See Photograph # 2-43.

Finally, this modification requires a commensurate alteration of the perimeter relief channel, sufficient to prevent the edges of the stock from touching the receiver. This alteration represents an opportunity to bring the wood-to-metal fit very close, thereby enhancing the gun's appearance. See the following sub-section for a discussion of epoxy bedding necessary to achieve a particularly close fit.

However, as noted above, the wood at the perimeter should never touch the receiver. A good check for minimum clearance is to run a playing card or a six-thousandth inch thick (0.006") feeler gauge around the perimeter of the assembly. To alter the perimeter channel, clamp the buttstock in a vise and file the channel wider (front-to-rear) and to the correct depth at the top and along the sides of the buttstock, as necessary. A medium bastard file works well for this job.

Photograph 2-43: Straight-edge affixed to the top of a Remington Model-760 pump-action rifle and aligned with the axis of the bore. The Shooter's Vise from Midway is a big help in such an operation. Note the strip of masking tape at the rifle's butt end. Although the perspective is slightly wrong in this photograph, we have centered the visible edge of that tape on the stock. The centered straight-edge is almost exactly vertically above that; also, we have secured the gun in the vise with the receiver sides set vertically. This test demonstrates that our modifications have not resulted in significant "cast-off" to the buttstock. This is a necessary test after any modification to the tang area on this type of rifle. See text and associated photograph captions for a complete discussion. Models 742, 7600, 7400 and the limited-release fancy versions of the pump-action rifle and semi-automatic are similar. However, refer to text for complete discussion of possible differences.

This filing will proceed rather fast. Just keep checking the buttstock for the proper fit to the receiver. Then file at the high spots, as evidenced by the playing card test. See Photograph #2-44.

When you have properly shaped the wood to achieve a bit of clearance around the entire perimeter, remove the buttstock from the vise and connect it to the receiver with the through-bolt. If perimeter channel clearance is sufficient, the playing card or thin feeler gauge should still pass freely around the entire channel. See Photograph # 2-45.

As noted, this alteration will typically correct the fit on older Remington Pumps and Semi-Automatics, for those rifles mounted with a scope. To correctly finish this alteration, you should remove about one-eighth inch (1/8") from the bottom rear of the buttstock and taper that cut to zero at the top. This cut is necessary to keep the rear of the stock square to the axis of the bore, as it should be. See the above sub-section on shortening a stock. The same procedures apply to this alteration.

The same basic procedure is applicable to Savage's Model-170 Pump-Action Rifle (and many other types of rifles using two-piece stocks). However, existence of tang extensions (both upper and lower) complicates matters with the Model-170 and other rifles using a similar system. Nevertheless, modification to change the angle of the stock follows the same basic procedure. Just ensure that the reworking does not change the stock-to-receiver contact points and especially that the modified stock places no stress

Photograph 2-44: A half-round file is a handy tool for finishing flat cuts on wood. Here we are cutting to fresh wood (deeper than any oil penetration and through the old plastic finish) in preparation for glass-bedding the stock to the receiver. See text and associated photograph captions for a complete discussion. (This particular stock is from a Marlin lever-action rifle, the process is similar for any two-piece stocked rifle.)

on either tang — while the tangs can likely take the stress, very likely the stock will eventually split if it rests against either tang. For a discussion of epoxy bedding on this buttstock, see the following sub-section. See Photograph # 2-46.

As noted, the same procedure is generally applicable to any rifle with a two-piece stock. In applications using a vertical tang-mounting through-bolt, the tinker might need to do a little more work and include spacers in various areas. I will address other important modifications in detail in *Part II*.

Stock Bedding:

To achieve a very close stock-to-receiver fit on any rifle with a separate buttstock consider the appropriate modification of the following procedure. On the Remington Pump, separate the stock and clean the front surface of the wood, as necessary, with alcohol (or acetone). See representative photos in previous sub-section.

Mount the receiver with the base at the top and the buttstock abutment surface level.

Install the steel spacer into the receiver recess. Tape the perimeter of the opening at the back end of the receiver with one layer of masking tape. This tape should cover the entire perimeter but should not cover the inserted steel spacer, which interposes the stock and the receiver.

Apply a release agent to all surfaces of the back end of the receiver. Brownells' aerosol product works particularly well but Johnson's paste wax will do. Never use any oil or grease for a release agent, these products slowly soften epoxy. See Photograph # 2-47.

After the front surface of the buttstock is clean and dry, mix a small batch of slow-setting hobby epoxy or Brownells Acraglas-Gel®, perhaps a quarter teaspoonful. If you have saved wood sanding dust from a similar type of wood you can mix that in about a 50/50 ratio with the well-mixed hobby epoxy. This will improve the epoxy's color-match to the wood and add strength to the mix. Alternatively, you can add Brownells brown epoxy dye — a little goes a long, long way. Apply a good coating of this slow-setting hobby epoxy (or Acraglas-Gel) mix to all the freshly exposed wood and the cleaned original finish at the front of the stock, both in

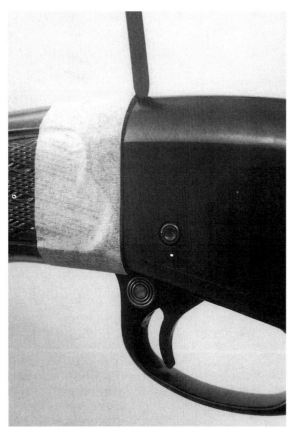

Photograph 2-45: Close-up-view of Remington Model-760 pump-action rifle at juncture of receiver and buttstock. We have prepared this rifle for epoxy bedding of the buttstock to the receiver. The feeler gauge verifies sufficient clearance around perimeter of stock.

Photograph 2-46: Close-up-view of front end of Savage Model-170 buttstock before preparation for glass bedding. Note depressions in various areas. These areas are where the stock had contacted the receiver. With glass bedding we will spread the contact surface, thereby strengthening and rigidifying the joint.

Section 2: The Trouble With Stocks, Part I

the perimeter channel and across the flat area. Wipe any excess from the perimeter area but ensure there is plenty to form a good solid cover over the raised central pad.

Finally, apply a wipe-on release agent both in the end of the through-bolt hole and to the exterior of the stock, adjacent to the epoxied end. Brownells' product works very well in this application. A cotton swab soaked with the rub-on agent is a good means of applying this material only where needed.

Install the buttstock to the receiver and lightly tighten the through-bolt. Ensure that the stock is square and properly centered at the joint between buttstock and receiver. If necessary, tap the stock into position using a rubber mallet. It is important to get the stock centered and square to the receiver in this step. Upon setting, the epoxy fixes the fit. When the orientation of the buttstock attachment is satisfactory, tighten the through-bolt sufficiently to pull the stock firmly against the receiver. See Photograph # 2-48.

Finally, turn over the assembly. Vise it with the stock at the bottom. This will limit epoxy migration into the action and, therefore, simplify clean-up. After allowing sufficient time for the epoxy to cure to the point of a hard but plastic consistency, remove the through-bolt and the stock.

You might find it necessary to file or cut epoxy from the perimeter of the front of the stock or other areas. For example, the recess the through-bolt nut enters. However, if epoxy in the through-bolt hole does not interfere with stock removal and replacement, you should leave it in place there; this will act to center and vertically align the stock during any subsequent disassembly and reassembly cycles. You can easily cut away excess epoxy on the exterior of the stock.

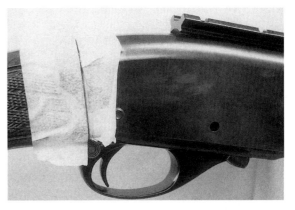

Photograph 2-48: Remington Model-760 pump-action rifle. Here we have mixed up a small batch of Brownell's Acraglas Gel; applied an even, thin coating of that product to the freshly surfaced front end of the stock; installed the treated stock to the receiver; and tightened the through-bolt. We got lucky on this installation. We used just enough epoxy. Note minor extrusion of epoxy at juncture. After the epoxy cured to a semi-solid putty-like consistency we used a razor knife to cut around the perimeter (the stock is slightly bigger than the receiver so we cut from the receiver side with the blade laying flat to the receiver). We then peeled away the protruding excess epoxy. Later, after the epoxy had fully cured, we disassembled the stock and removed the tape and release agent before final re-assembly. Note that the trigger mechanism's front retaining pin is not visible in this view; it is not missing, we only partially inserted it from the other side for this work. (We will soon have to remove this assembly for the clean-up phase.) Removal of the trigger housing assembly facilitates taping and cleanup. Models 742, 7600, 7400 and the limited-release fancy versions of the pump-action rifle and semi-automatic Remingtons are similar. However, refer to text for complete discussion of possible differences.

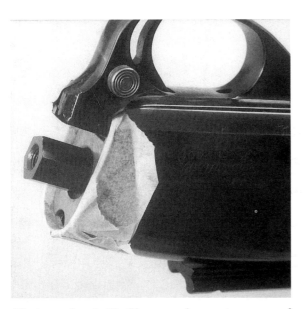

Photograph 2-47: Close-up-view at rear of Remington Model-760 pump-action rifle receiver. We have prepared this action for glass bedding. After cleaning the entire area we installed the stamped steel plate (visible around the hex nut) and applied tape to provide clearance between the receiver and the stock's perimeter channel. We used masking tape on the receiver and vinyl electrical tape on the trigger tang extension. After this taping we liberally applied Brownells' aerosol release agent (Acra-Release).

See the associated photographs and captions for a discussion of how to do this with the stock in place on the receiver. Finally, remove the tape from the receiver.

Epoxy bedding on the Savage Model-170 follows a similar approach to that described above for the Remington Pump. However, a particularly important consideration is to ensure that both tangs retain sufficient clearance with the stock. The associated photographs demonstrate this procedure quite well. See Photograph #s 2-49 through 2-53.

Assuming we have the buttstock correctly fitting the shooter, we need to look at areas of stock-to-barreled-action fit. Often we can trace wandering zero and poor intrinsic accuracy problems to several areas of connection between the stock and the barreled-action. Significantly, we can cure all such problems.

Strengthening Buttstock-To-Receiver Attachment, Remington or Savage Pump-Action Rifles:

Although touched upon elsewhere, I will visit this in detail here as a separate issue; it is a very worthwhile operation, whether or not you do any other buttstock modifications. On the Remington and Savage Pump-Action Rifles (and many other similarly stocked guns) bedding of the buttstock to the receiver is beneficial and is

Photograph 2-49

Photographs 2-49/50: Front end of buttstock from Savage Model-170 pump-action rifle before and after modification to seating angle, photographs 2-49 & 2-50, respectively. Masking tape shows alignment for modification to raise cheek piece. This modification will improve fit to shooter on guns fitted with a scope sight mounted in standard-height rings. This modification places the cheek piece a bit high for use with open sights. However, one can use those, nonetheless. I prefer to have a big game hunting rifle fit correctly for scope use. By removing about 0.075" of material from the top of the front of the stock's tang (and removing other material, as necessary to maintain clearances) we can raise the cheek piece about 0.75". We must also modify the rear of the stock (by shortening the base of the butt about 0.125"). This change will keep the butt square to the axis of the bore. Also, be careful to keep the stock axis aligned to the bore axis in the side-to-side sense. A similar modification is useful on Remington 760s. Remington has proportioned the buttstock on newer Remington Model-7600 and Model-7400 rifles for scope use. Nevertheless, one might benefit from raising those cheek pieces slightly. See text and associated photographs and captions.

Photograph 2-50: After modification. Note that we have ground the wood away to the edge of the masking tape (we used a bench-mounted grinder followed by a medium wood rasp). Other modifications are necessary to maintain proper wood-to-metal clearance in both the upper and lower tang areas and in the through-bolt recess. See text.

Section 2: The Trouble With Stocks, Part I

reasonably simple. Following on the design of pillar-bedding, you can bore the through hole to a larger diameter and install an aluminum or steel pillar. The procedure is basically the same as that for pillar-bedding on a bolt-action rifle, described earlier. The potential benefits are significant.

You should design the exterior of this through-bolt pillar to form an intimate rigid bond with the epoxy (perhaps by threading it). This pillar's interior diameter should be slightly larger than the shank of the through-bolt. Its interior end should support the head of the through-bolt. However, the other end should not protrude fully to the front end of the stock; this piece must end short enough to avoid interference with the nut

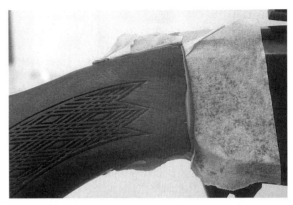

Photograph 2-52: Side-view of glass bedding operation on Savage Model-170 Pump. Here we have fully protected the rear of the receiver and all contacting surfaces of both tang extensions with masking tape. Also note, we have taped a double layer at the rear of both tang extensions. This will assure critical tang-to-stock clearance at those locations. Finally, we treated the taped areas of the receiver with Brownells' spray-on release agent and the outside of the stock with their wipe-on release agent (from the Acraglas kit). Believe me, if you fail to properly apply a release agent bad things can, and probably will) happen! I once had a thin hobby epoxy migrate three inches <u>uphill.</u> The tenacious stuff found its way into the front of the action on a Model-94 Winchester! I had repaired that rifle's badly shattered stock tang with epoxy and both steel and wooden dowels. To get the final shape and clearances correct I attached the epoxy impregnated stock to the rifle. Then, to retain the thin epoxy I tape-wrapped the entire tang area. Then I stood the rifle, muzzle up, in a corner. The epoxy defied gravity as it migrated up into the receiver! It bypassed several openings from which it could have escaped! Took me a week to get the action apart and clean up the resulting mess. A good lesson there, DO NOT SKIMP ON RELEASE AGENT!

Photograph 2-51: Top-view of buttstock from Savage Model-170. Note black marked area, barely visible in this photograph, at rear of top tang recess. One must remove this material to retain tang-to-stock clearance when reducing this stock's drop at comb, see associated photographs and text. A Dremel tool fitted with a $^1\!/_2$" sanding drum is ideal for this job. Distance one should lengthen this cut depends upon how much one raised the cheek piece. However, this 0.1" cut is typical — proper epoxy bedding techniques allow almost complete elimination of any gap, leaving only a bare margin of clearance, which is both necessary and proper.

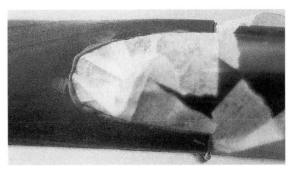

Photograph 2-53: Top-view of glass bedding operation on Savage Model-170 Pump. Here we have fully protected the rear of the receiver and all contacting surfaces of both tang extensions with a layer of masking tape. Also note, we have taped a double layer at the rear of both tang extensions. This provides critical epoxy to tang clearance at those locations. After the epoxy has set to a plastic consistency we will cut the excess free.

the through-bolt screws into, which protrudes significantly into a recess in the front of the buttstock — about one-half inch (1/2") on the Remington and one and one-quarter inch (1¼") on the Savage.

Here, portions of the stock should transfer the load (through an epoxy layer), provided by tightening the through-bolt, from the stock to the receiver. It is best if the pillar stops about one-quarter inch (1/4") short of touching the nut into which the through-bolt screws.

Install the pillar by drilling the through-bolt hole <u>just</u> large enough to allow the pillar to enter freely — this will keep it centered in the hole. Clean the hole and the pillar immaculately. Install a hardened steel, bolt-fitting washer on the through-bolt, grind the outside diameter of this washer until it is just <u>slightly</u> larger than the outside diameter of the pillar. Also, bevel the outside diameter of the washer slightly, making it smaller at the front edge. The idea is to leave the washer resting upon the pillar without touching the stock at all.

With the washer installed, tape wrap the shank of the through-bolt in two spots. First, adjacent to the head of the bolt. Second, at a location so the tape wrap will slightly protrude from the end of the pillar that is furthest removed from the bolt head when you fully install the pillar on the through-bolt. Slide the pillar onto the through-bolt until it rests solidly against the washer and until it pushes the washer solidly against the head of the bolt. Apply release agent to the bolt head, the washer and the entire exposed portion of the bolt's shank. Insert a plastic drinking straw over the exposed threaded portion of the shank. See Photograph # 2-54.

Mix a small batch of epoxy and apply that to the entire interior of the through-bolt hole making sure you have wetted all surfaces. Similarly, wet the exterior of the pillar with a layer of epoxy. Insert the bolt and pillar assembly, proceeding from the butt end of the stock. Ensure that the assembly fully enters the hole. The end of the pillar should stop about three-quarter of an inch (3/4") from the front end of the through-bolt hole on the Remington, about 1½" from the end of this hole on the Savage Model-170. As much as is feasible, remove any excess epoxy that has entered the front end of the through-bolt hole. Finally, remove the drinking straw from the end of the bolt.

Position the screwdriver, used to remove the through-bolt, in a vise with the shank pointing up vertically. Tape wrap the shank of the screwdriver to about the diameter of the hole in the buttstock in two places. One near the bit and the other several inches up the shank. (This will center the screwdriver and, thereby, ease the next task.)

Liberally apply release agent to the bit and the shank of the screwdriver. Then lower the buttstock over the screwdriver shank and manipulate the stock until the end of the screwdriver engages the slot in the through-bolt. This should

Photograph 2-54: Here we have set up to hollow the shank of a long ½" lag bolt. (Any ½" bolt will work and a grade-2 carriage bolt would have been a better choice since it would have been easier to drill!) Note that we have already sawed away most of the thickness of the hex head. We have clamped, centered and vertically aligned this bolt, below the drill-press-mounted 5/16" bit. Cutting oil is at hand. While drilling this hole almost 4" down the shank we kept the hole almost perfectly centered. Such precision requires attention to detail. See associated photographs and text for an explanation of the purpose and installation of this through-bolt bushing. One can use such a strengthening device on any through-bolt attached buttstock.

keep the pillar correctly positioned until the epoxy cures, as revealed by the condition of any excess epoxy from the mix.

Next, prepare the front end of the buttstock for epoxy bedding. You can achieve this in the following way. Thoroughly clean the stock and receiver. This area is a natural trap for all manner of grit, grime, oil and debris.

Make a slight bevel around the end of the through-bolt hole. Also, roughen the receiver-end of the stock, as necessary, to remove oil-soaked or damaged wood and to increase the area for the epoxy to bond with and to increase the thickness of the epoxy layer, at least in limited areas. It is also useful to bore shallow holes into the stock to create epoxy wells where more stock material can come into play in transferring the stress of recoil. Also, you can use a clean, stiff-bristled wire brush to abrade the front of the stock to improve epoxy bonding.

Remove the through-bolt from the stock and remove the tape wraps from the bolt. If the stock retains the washer, this is fine, that is just where the washer needs to be! Apply release agent to all areas of the back end of the receiver and the nut that the through-bolt screws into (also the tang extensions on the Savage).

In preparing the Remington stock, ensure that all perimeter areas of the stock clear the receiver. Those areas should not touch at all; that condition can lead to fracturing or splintering of the surface of the stock. On the Savage, ensure clearance along both the top tang and bottom tang extensions.

Further, you should round off any sharp corners in the stock, where the receiver might touch. This will limit stress concentrations that could induce cracking. You can make such reliefs using a Dremel tool and a small rotary rasp. Undercut any such areas, as necessary.

The idea is to increase the structural rigidity between these two pieces; nothing more, nothing less. If properly done, this process will also improve the sealing of the front of the stock. If you have modified the stock to change the drop, this epoxy application will seal the stock quite well. In that case, refer to the discussion in that sub-section regarding tape wrapping, a process that is necessary to provide perimeter and tang clearances. Here, we are not considering application of epoxy in the tang recesses or at the perimeter because on an unaltered stock those areas are already finished. However, should you want to achieve a better fit on those areas, refer to the (previous) sub-section on adjusting the drop on these stocks.

Apply release agent to the rear of the receiver and the tang extensions. Also apply release agent to the outside of the stock adjacent to the end and in the relief channel at the perimeter of the Remington pump and in the tang reliefs on the Savage and the Remington.

When you have fully prepared both stock and receiver, mix a batch of bedding epoxy and apply it liberally to ensure complete wetting of all contact areas of the front of the stock. Then remove any excess epoxy and install the buttstock.

Apply release agent to the through-bolt, install that and tighten it moderately. Ensure that the stock remains aligned properly with the action — on the Remington it will turn slightly to either side of center — center it! Position the gun in a padded vise with the stock down and the joint between buttstock and receiver horizontal. If you properly tightened the through-bolt the limited weight of the stock will not flex the joint sufficiently to open a gap. The idea here is to keep the epoxy in place in any existing wood-to-receiver gaps, as much as possible.

After the epoxy has fully cured, remove the buttstock. Clean any epoxy from the action; the exterior of the stock; the relief channel around the perimeter of the Remington stock; and the tang reliefs. Unless the epoxy that has infiltrated the through-bolt hole in the front end of the stock interferes with assembly and disassembly, leave it in place. Clean epoxy from any other places it has infiltrated where it should not be.

Some folks prefer to clean away excess, uncured, epoxy from exterior surfaces using a cotton-swab and the old-style carburetor cleaners (such as Gumout® brand). However, be careful what solvents you use for this, some might contaminate and thereby weaken the epoxy.

Remington and Savage Pump-Action Fore-end Modifications:

On these rifles, the fore-end runs on a tube located under the barrel. In many examples, careless or extreme manipulation of the fore-end can result in binding between the fore-end and the barrel. Any contact between these pieces as the marksman fires the gun is almost certain to change the bullet's point of impact. This problem is quite common on Remington Pumps.

On a well-used gun, examination of the bluing on the underside of the barrel along the length of the fore-end's travel will reveal any areas where these two parts have found occasion to meet — on well-used guns where the bluing is fully intact there is evidently no problem. Another test is to hold the gun normally and deliberately twist the fore-end when it is fully forward. If the fore-end touches the barrel when you apply only a modest twisting force, it is probably a good idea to increase the clearance between these two pieces. See Photograph # 2-55.

Removal of the fore-end on the Savage Pump involves practically a complete disassembly of the gun — you even have to separate the buttstock and receiver, but one can leave the sight mounted! This procedure is quite straight forward but there is an easier way to repair the problem, which I will return to shortly.

Removal of the fore-end on the Remington Pump is no problem, simply remove the screw from the front of the fore-end and slide it forward. However, as with the Savage, the barrel channel can easily and most accurately be enlarged without removing the fore-end.

Begin by fixing the unloaded gun in a padded vise — clamp on the flat sides of the receiver and assure access to the action release lever. Slide the fore-end fully to the rear to open the action. Wrap several layers of duct tape around the barrel. Begin at the front of the fore-end and extend the tape wrap to the extreme forward point of the fore-end's forward travel (about four-inches (4") forward of the tip of the open-action fore-end). Close and lock the action.

Next you have to do two things at once: one operation requires two hands, the other at least one hand. You can certainly figure a way around this little problem. For example, an elastic cord hooked in the front of the fore-end and attached to something else could provide the required torque on the fore-end. However, a willing helper seems a better solution!

Insert a sheet of sixty (60) grit sandpaper (rough side out) between the barrel and the front end of the fore-end, the only area where the potential for fore-end-to-barrel contact exists). Then <u>gently</u> torque the fore-end toward one side until it touches the paper. Sand away the offending portion of the fore-end. Then torque the fore-end the opposite way and repeat the sanding, as necessary. When you have sanded away a sufficient thickness of the fore-end to render barrel-to-fore-end contact unlikely during normal use, remove the tape-wrap from the barrel. See Photograph # 2-56.

You can also accomplish refinishing of the sanded areas in the fore-end channel without removing the fore-end. Slightly dampen a rag with Tung Oil and run that through the channel while manipulating the fore-end from side-to-side. Clean off any excess exposed Tung Oil. You have finished this task.

Bolt-Action Rifle Barrel-to-Fore-end Channel Pressure Bedding:

Our first consideration regards the barrel-to-fore-end channel. In days gone by, there was a heated argument regarding barrel floating versus pressure bedding. Happily, that argument has essentially ended. Certainly, I will consider it moot. (<u>Moot</u> means the point might be debatable

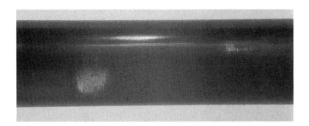

Photograph 2-55: Looking from below at a section of barrel on a well-used Remington Model-760 pump-action rifle (Model-7600 is the same). This is the area under the front end of fore-end when one closes the action. Note wear spots. These are zones, where significant use has worn the bluing off the barrel (this rifle has accounted for more than twenty elk). This pattern is typical. These are areas where the fore-end will or can contact the barrel. We will modify this rifle's fore-end to reduce any such contact. See associated photographs and text.

Photograph 2-56: Remington Model-760 pump-action rifle fore-end. (Model-7600 is practically the same.) Here we show the sanded area where we removed material. This modification prevents (or at least limits) potential barrel-to-fore-end contact during action manipulation or firing of the gun. Eliminating contact here can significantly improve accuracy of these fine rifles. See associated photographs and text.

Section 2: The Trouble With Stocks, Part I

but, for one reason or another, we will not proceed to debate it here.) Assuming you have a good barrel and a good barrel-to-receiver fit, the correct set-up is always a fully free-floated barrel. If that arrangement does not provide the best accuracy and consistency in zero, there is almost certainly something else wrong with the gun.

Free-floating is easy to achieve and for those with grave concerns that it might not be the right thing to do for some particular rifle, I will note that this action is extremely easy to reverse! Assuming a fully floated barrel, you only have to add a small dab of epoxy near the front bottom of the fore-end channel. To achieve a set degree of pressure bedding you will have to get a measurement. See Photograph #s 2-57/58.

First, ensure that you have unloaded the gun. Locate the gun in a vise with the barrel level. Carefully measure the separation between the barrel and the fore-end channel at the front of the channel. Layers of notebook paper are a good gauge. Slip as many layers of paper between the fore-end and the barrel as will fit without binding. Measure the thickness of this stack of paper with a dial caliper.

Tie fisherman's knots in both ends of a foot long piece of ten pound (10#) test (or heavier) fishing line. Wrap the line over the barrel about two-inches back from the front of the fore-end (assuming there is sufficient clearance, as there should be in a fully floated fore-end channel. Slip both ends of this line over a hook attached to a ten-pound weight. Those who argue for pressure bedding seem to agree that ten pounds is about right for most sporting-barreled high-powered rifles — of course you are free to choose some other weight. With the weight in place, remeasure the barrel-to-fore-end gap at the front of the barrel channel, as before. The difference in these two measurements indicates the amount that pressure bedding will increase the fore-end-to-barrel gap at the front of the channel. However, the important measurement here is simply the gap with the weight in place. For this example, assume the weighted gap is thirty-thousandths of an inch (just less than 1/32").

To achieve this gap, the following approach works very well. On the barrel, mark the location of the front of the fore-end. Separate the barreled-action from the stock. Then measure the barrel diameter just behind the mark indicating where the front of the fore-end aligns to the barrel.

Beginning with the tape at the top of the barrel and just behind the fore-end mark, tape-wrap sufficient layers of vinyl electrical tape to achieve a barrel plus tape diameter sixty-thousandths of an inch (just about 1/16") greater than the barrel diameter just measured. When this occurs you will have added thirty-thousandths of an inch (a short 1/32") to the underside of the barrel, the necessary spacing. Next, tape-wrap with one less layer of the same tape at a spot about one-inch behind the first tape-wrap. This will provide a dam to prevent epoxy from migrating back along the barrel channel.

Of course, if you want a longer section of epoxy contact, move the second tape wrap further

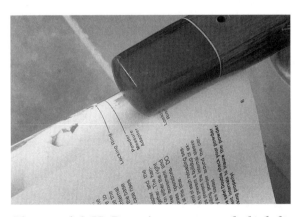

Photograph 2-57: Preparing to pressure-bed a bolt-action rifle. The barrel was previously free-floated. Note that 8 pages of this particular catalogue (4 sheets of paper) fit between fore-end channel and barrel. See photograph 2-58.

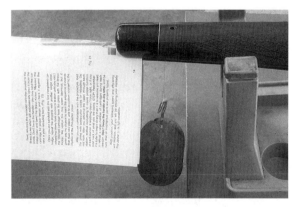

Photograph 2-58: After we hang a ten-pound weight (the weight one chooses to use is purely subjective) from the spot where we intend to pressure bed the barrel we note that 7 sheets of this paper fit between the fore-end and the barrel at the front, compare to photograph 2-57. By measuring the thickness of these sheets we can determine the amount of tape-wrap to use on the barrel when applying the epoxy pillar. See text for complete discussion.

back. However, if you choose to position the second tape-wrap further back, decrease the number of tape layers accordingly to keep that tape-wrap from holding the barrel away from the front tape-wrap. A slight gap between the fore-end channel and this rearmost tape-wrap will hurt nothing but this rearmost tape-wrap should not bind against the barrel.

Finally, apply one layer of the same tape to either side of the barrel in the gap between the tape-wraps. The gap between these strips will determine how wide the epoxy bed is.

You can also get fancy. For example, let us imagine one wanted to bed only along the lower sides but not across the bottom. To do this, you could cut a narrow strip of vinyl tape to fit between the tape-wraps and place that along the bottom of the barrel. You could then position side strips to limit the upper reach of the epoxy bed. You could be as creative as seemed worthwhile.

In any case, after application of this tape, as needed or desired, apply a coating of release agent to the tape and this entire section of the barrel. Then thoroughly clean the barrel channel with alcohol (or acetone) and allow that to dry. Mount the stock in a padded vise, providing access to the action-screws. Mix a sufficient batch of glass bedding material or a high-quality high-temperature hobby epoxy.

Apply the epoxy mix to the section of the fore-end channel located between the tape-wraps on the barrel. Apply release agent to the perimeter of the fore-end near the epoxy gob — in case epoxy overflows the channel when you install the barreled-action. Install the barreled-action and tighten the action screws normally but make sure the front of the receiver pulls against the stock. See Photograph # 2-59.

After the epoxy has cured to a hard plastic condition, as evidenced by the leftover epoxy on the mixing pad, separate the barreled-action from the stock. Clean up any epoxy overflow. Remove all tape from the barrel, or anywhere else it might have stuck. Clean the release agent from the barrel and the stock. Reassemble the rifle.

By this simple, albeit sophisticated, process you have added a precise measure of fore-end pressure to the barrel with a properly fitting, positioned and shaped epoxy bedding pad.

An alternative, and potentially more precise method is much simpler to execute but requires use of a putty-like epoxy. After determining the amount of preload wanted, mount the rifle stock in a vise with the barrel channel on the bottom.

Apply an adequate dollop of epoxy mix in the appropriate area of the cleaned fore-end channel. Apply release agent to the appropriate area of the barrel. Insert the barreled-action and start the action screws, several turns each. Hang the chosen weight from the barrel. Tighten the action screws. Wait for the epoxy to cure. To locate and shape the epoxy bed you can incorporate the damming tape as in the previously described method.

Bolt-Action Rifle Fore-end Free Floating:

Now, finally, back to free floating: on typical bolt-action rifles the following procedure works well. First, verify that you have unloaded the gun. Separate the stock from the barreled-action. Then wrap the portion of the barrel that is in the fore-end with a single layer of masking or vinyl tape. Slight gaps are okay, but do not overlap this tape wrap. See Photograph # 2-60.

Photograph 2-59: Epoxy bed at front of fore-end. Here the fore-end was fully free-floated first. Then we tested the rifle for accuracy. Then we installed an epoxy bed providing about 10# of upward force on the barrel. See text and associated photographs for explanation of method. Retesting the rifle showed no accuracy improvement. Therefore, owing to the potential for change of zero with this method of barrel bedding, we removed this epoxy pedestal, leaving the barrel fully free-floated. See text, associated photographs and captions.

Photograph 2-60: Early barrel channel work on a typical bolt-action rifle. (Here a left-hand Remington Model-700.) We used a round file to remove the epoxy finish and the factory barrel-bedding pedestal. See text and accompanying photographs.

Section 2: The Trouble With Stocks, Part I

Reinstall the barreled-action in the stock and loosely attach the action to the stock using only the front and rear action screws. Vise the stock so the barreled-action is hanging vertically and you have clear access to both the top of the gun and the action screws.

Cut a piece of sixty (60) grit sandpaper into a one-third sheet strip. Wrap this strip, paper side toward barrel, around the underside of the barrel in front of the fore-end. Using a sawing motion, pull this sanding paper back into the fore-end channel. Once the paper moves into the channel, work it end to end and from the front of the channel back almost to the receiver. If you note no friction, as you saw the paper back and forth, pause to slightly tighten the action-screws. Repeat the sawing motion. Continue to snug the action screws, as necessary, until the paper binds slightly. See Photograph # 2-61.

Unless the barrel was already properly floated, this procedure will eventually result in the fore-end touching the paper. Sand away all contact points and resnug the action screws. Repeat this screw-snugging and sanding process until you have fully tightened the action screws and the sanding paper will still move freely all along the entire length of the fore-end channel.

Remove the barreled-action from the stock.

Photograph 2-61: After we removed most of the excess material using a file we checked the barrel for clearance to the fore-end channel. Here we are using emery cloth to remove some minor high spots from the wood. On a job requiring considerable sanding we would tape-wrap the barrel to protect the bluing against inevitable minor scratches from the abrasive paper's cloth side. If the channel requires considerable work one can use the action screws to incrementally pull the barrel down into the channel as one progressively sands the channel deeper. Note that we are floating the barrel fully, clear back to the recoil lug. A paper-card shim is a good gauge for clearance. For a full discussion, see text and associated photographs.

Remove the tape wrap from the barrel. Finally, refinish the entire interior of the fore-end channel with an appropriate wood sealer. Here, application of a quality wood sealer is particularly important. Having just gone to this trouble to properly float the fore-end, you probably do not want it to warp against the barrel in response to some change in moisture content allowed by a poorly sealed channel! While you are at it, verify proper sealing on the hole for the front sling stud and the associated nut recess.

Action Bedding:

Now we have the stock fitting the shooter and the barrel free-floated. Next we should address bedding the action to the stock. The purpose here is to provide a solid unchanging mount between these two highly dissimilar pieces. On most bolt-action rifles, the barreled-action sits on top of the wood (or synthetic material) with only screw tension to bond these two pieces. A lug located near the front of the action controls recoil. See Photograph #s 2-62/63.

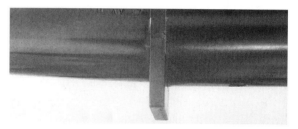

Photograph 2-62: Typical bolt-action rifle recoil lug. This piece interposes barrel and receiver on many rifles. On Mausers and close copies this lug is integral with the receiver, probably a superior arrangement

Photograph 2-63: Original glass bedding at recoil lug on Remington Model-700 (left-hand) bolt-action rifle. We will remove this material and lengthen and deepen this recess. This will provide a good boundary of epoxy, "glass," around the recoil lug. See text.

Many things can render this arrangement far less than perfect: bad fitting or poor contact between the pieces at the intended contact points, the ubiquitous dimensional changes and warpage in the stock, over-tightening or-loosening of the action screws (especially in those designs featuring three screws) and other problems come to mind. The tinker can mitigate almost all of these inadequacies through the combination of proper application of glass bedding and wood sealant.

The natural tendency for wood to change moisture content in response to changes in temperature, atmospheric humidity and atmospheric pressure is extremely high. The amount of moisture any given region of the wood will naturally contain, in any given environment, is directly proportional to the density of that region of wood. The density of any given piece of wood as large as a gun stock is highly variable. Dimensional changes associated with changes in moisture content, therefore, differ from one region of the stock to another. These variations result in warpage. Only the wood's structural strength limits the force that warping wood can apply to the action and barrel! Certainly it can flex an action or push a barrel around.

I have witnessed one gun where barrel-to-fore-end contact on one side caused heating-induced warpage on the stock. When we were shooting at one-hundred (100) yards that heating and warpage pushed each successive shot, in any extended shot-string, fully eight-inches (8") from the last. Of course, as the barrel heated, the barrel also bent farther; it was less able to resist the fore-end's push. There was no evident end to this change in point of impact, that is why I know the fore-end was warping in response to heating. Bullets kept shooting higher and farther to the right with every shot. This tendency seemed limited only by our nerves and ammunition supply. We did fire one string of twenty (20) shots. The last one went many feet over the target — thank goodness for mountainous backstops!

<u>Seal all wood and ensure that it does not touch the action anywhere it should not!</u>

The propensity for warpage, as detailed above, explains the superiority of synthetic or properly laminated epoxy impregnated stocks — those are much less apt to appreciably distort.

There are several areas where different proponents hold considerably different opinions, regarding details of the glass bedding process. Many gunsmiths advocate creating large solid epoxy layers between the top of the stock and the bottom of the action at both the front and rear of the action (around the action screws and recoil lug). Others suggest creating slight (tape thin thickness) clearances around all sides of the recoil lug excepting the back surface while minimizing the area of the pads.

In both regards, my opinion varies. I believe there are two distinct purposes and advantages to glass bedding. First, "glass" (epoxy) provides a rigid purchase against which the action can rest. Second, to some extent, it isolates the action from the wood (which is constantly undergoing differential dimension change owing chiefly to changes in moisture content). Since epoxy is somewhat plastic, this isolation serves to reduce the effect that dimensional changes in the wood can have upon the barreled-action. Finally, if properly applied, epoxy can correctly position the barreled-action in the stock and minimize the potential for movement between these two pieces.

For these reasons, I believe in minimizing the area where epoxy interposes wood and steel. Increasing the area of contact only serves to increase the opportunity for dimensional changes in the wood to transfer to the steel and do something bad, such as flex the action. For the same reason, I believe in creating thick layers anywhere I interpose epoxy between steel and wood. This increases the epoxy's strength; thereby improving its resistance to stresses resulting from dimensional changes in the wood.

Also, I recommend keeping the fit of the recoil lug in the epoxy bed as tight as is feasible (except at the bottom and sides). If this epoxy box has thick enough walls it should adequately resist dimensional changes in the wood. Further, it is difficult to see how this bed of epoxy might reasonably transfer accuracy or zero disrupting forces to the barreled-action by any slight loads it might transfer to the front, back or sides of the recoil lug. It just seems better to closely fit the recoil lug in its recess as a means of rigidly locating the barreled-action in the stock.

The good news is that glass bedding is a very forgiving process. Should you follow the instruction given later and find the results less than satisfying, or should you find these arguments less than convincing and later change your mind regarding how best to do this job, you are free to redo the job and complete it differently! Keep that point in mind.

As an example on the other end of the spectrum, some gunsmiths advocate a system called

Section 2: The Trouble With Stocks, Part I

glass gluing. With this approach, the barreled-action is literally epoxy glued to the stock! The tinker's imagination, and little else, limits the possible variations. However, for most typical rifles I believe the system advocated in this text is a very good choice. See Photograph # 2-64.

Preliminary Preparation of the Action (and Yourself!) For Glass Bedding:

First, I will consider Pillar-bedding, using a Remington Model-700 as a test case. The discussion of glass bedding with this rifle covers all the general areas applicable to almost any bolt-action rifle type or design. First, you need to determine where the action rests in the stock and locate all intentional contact points. Then you need to ensure that any work you perform will not alter the fundamental relationship between the stock and receiver in any unintentional way — the action should remain fully aligned; centered side-to-side; at the same location front-to-rear; at the same height in the stock (it should not raise or lower at the front or rear); and, finally, the action should not rotate from the correct orientation in the stock. Also, your alterations should not remove any areas of necessary contact or create unnecessary new areas of contact — unless you recognize such changes as specifically desirable modifications!

Affix the unloaded gun in a padded vise. If a scope is in place, remove that and store in a safe place. Remove any receiver-mounted sights and sight bases if those might interfere with manipulating the barreled-action or might be subject to damage during handling.

Prepare to separate the barreled-action from the stock: as previously discussed, this ordinarily involves removal of two or three action screws. These screws are typically on the bottom center of the stock. The first is at the back of the trigger guard. The second, where used, is at the rear of the magazine floor-plate. Location of the third screw is at the front of the magazine well, near the juncture of the barrel and the receiver. If the barreled-action does not separate from the stock easily after removal of these screws, check carefully for any additional screws or fixtures that might be attaching it to that stock or restraining it from pulling out of the stock.

Typically, the magazine well simply rests between the floor-plate (or the bottom of the stock) and the receiver. When the tinker removes the barreled-action, this piece might separate and fall out. However, note that some receivers feature a magazine that is secured to the action. Where this is the case, it is sometimes best to separate this piece before proceeding. Also, remove the bolt and any other attachments to the basic barreled-action that might interfere with necessary handling and manipulation or be subject to damage or epoxy infiltration. Chiefly, these include the trigger and safety mechanisms, which you can easily remove on most bolt-action rifles.

(An easy way to keep an action from falling out of a stock is to clamp the barrel in a padded vise, when possible, with the gun upside-down and the barrel horizontal.)

For example, consider Remington's Model-700. Remove the retaining clip that attaches the safety lever. Then drive the trigger-to-action retaining pins out of the action. Be careful not to lose any parts that might come loose as you separate such pieces. Now the trigger assembly and its associated parts will fully separate from the barreled-action. See sub-section on trigger replacement.

On a free-floated barrel, you should secure the front of the action against lowering in the stock or moving from side-to-side as a result of additional inletting preparatory for the glass bedding operation. To accomplish this, wrap exactly enough layers of electrical tape around the barrel near the front of the fore-end channel to allow the tape to just begin to support the barrel when you tighten the action screws normally. On guns where the barrel is not free-floated, you

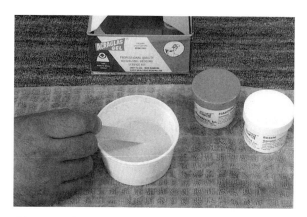

Photograph 2-64: Mixing Brownells' Acraglas Gel is the epitome of simplicity: add equal parts and mix. If desired, one can add die to match wood's color or atomized metal (minute steel or aluminum particles) to strengthen the resulting product. See text and associated photograph captions for a complete discussion.

should apply sufficient layers of electrical tape to each side of the barrel to force it to center in the fore-end channel. However, ensure these layers do not interfere with the barrel resting on the bedding pad in the bottom of the barrel channel.

Poorly centered barrels are quite common. While the original action inletting might initially prevent barrel-to-fore-end centering, you can, and should, use the glass bedding operation to attain proper centering of the barrel in the fore-end channel.

However, before following this approach, verify that the channel in the fore-end is not at fault! Off-center channels are not uncommon. If this channel is badly off-center in the stock, the best approach is to keep the barrel centered in the stock, not in the channel. You can achieve this goal by applying sufficient tape layers to each side of the barrel (more on the side with wide channel clearance resulting from the channel not being centered in the stock) to force the barrel to center in the stock.

Typical designs provide a purchase for the action's tang extension to rest on top of the stock. This purchase often maintains the rotational orientation of the action in the stock. The action screws often serve the same function, especially on round bottomed receivers, such as Remington's Model-700. Here, the screws are often the only thing that retains the rotational orientation of the receiver. See Photograph # 2-65.

The rear action screw, and sometimes inletting at the top of the stock, properly center the rear of the action in the stock. Should you decide to inlet the action deeper at the tang to provide a significantly rigid glass bedding surface there, be careful to avoid upsetting the relationships noted above. Minor inletting at the tang can aid in a solid and square purchase to hold the rear of the action centered and in the proper rotation. However, you should not rely on the tang area for any other support; that is the purpose of proper bedding of the action screws and the recoil lug.

Further, ensure that you provide minor (paper thin is sufficient) clearance around the sides and back of any portion of the tang that is inletted into the stock. This will prevent cracking or splintering of wood in this area as well as prevent undue strain on the action as a result of such incorrect tang-to-stock contact.

Pillar-bedding:
Note: before proceeding with pillar-bedding, understand the implications of this italicized passage. On rifles lacking the floor-plate, such as Remington's ADL, the front pillar cannot extend to the bottom of the stock without damaging the appearance of the stock. Also, the gunsmith has to leave sufficient stock material to support the escutcheon against which the action screw tightens. In this instance, the tinker should tighten the front action screw only lightly until after the epoxy cures! To accommodate this, use wraps of duct tape around the barrel and fore-end to hold the front end of the action properly down as the epoxy cures.

Also note, the associated photographs and captions should clarify any passage not easily understandable in this dissertation. This is one area where a picture truly is worth a thousand words (at least!).

If pillars are not conveniently available for your particular rifle, you can fashion those from the shank of a grade-two bolt of one-half inch (1/2") diameter. Vise the bolt and drill a hole slightly larger than the action screws, centered down the shank of the bolt. This is easiest to accomplish using a drill press. Alternately, you could cut the threaded shank of the bolt off;

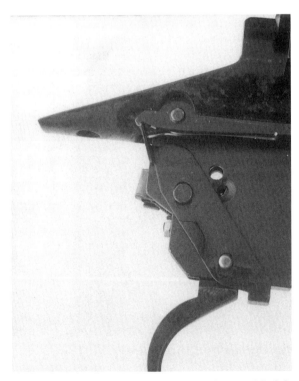

Photograph 2-65: Rear tang on Remington Model-700. Note round bottom on receiver. Action orientation (rotational) in the stock can be compromised during the glass bedding operation. To avoid this, follow the system discussed in the text.

Section 2: The Trouble With Stocks, Part I

center-punch that piece; and chuck it into a vised one-half inch (1/2") drill with the center-punched end showing. With that drill running, it is reasonably easy to drill a properly centered and aligned hole into the bolt shank using a second hand drill fitted with the proper drill bit.

To remove any minor error in hole centering and alignment, if necessary, pass a long hole-fitting bolt (tape wrapped to fit the hole, if necessary) through the drilled bolt shank and snug that smaller bolt in place using a nut. Chuck the protruding shank of that bolt into a hand drill. You can then rapidly true the exterior of the bolt; press it lightly against a flat side of a bench grinder-mounted corundum (aluminum oxide) wheel with both the drill and grinder running. Be sure those tools are turning so the spins add, rather than subtract. If not, simply reverse the drill.

After you have drilled the hole and trued the shank, fashioning the pillar to the proper length and end shape requires a bit of patient work with hand files. However, this presents no significant problem. Similarly you can fashion pillars from aluminum, which has the advantage of corrosion resistance.

Again, before doing any work ensure you have unloaded the rifle. Pillar-bedding involves installing pillars at the front and rear action screw locations. Epoxy rigidly bonds those pillars to the stock. Further, the action screws are smaller than the holes in the pillars. As do all types of "glass" bedding, this process also involves bedding the recoil lug into epoxy where the tinker has removed existing stock material to provide a bed. This process also involves removal of any other stock material, except possibly under the tang, where the existing stock configuration results in contact between the stock and the barreled-action; nothing else should touch. See Photograph # 2-66.

Equally, the magazine floor-plate, where used, should not bind in the stock and should bed only at the action-screw locations. Inletting around this piece should provide sufficient clearance to prevent binding in the wood. If such binding exists, the effects of installation and removal, recoil and dimensional changes in the wood can result in chipped or cracked wood around the floor-plate. Remove any offending wood.

To emphasize: the properly bedded action should touch the stock at the back, front and sides of the recoil lug (although the front and sides are optional), possibly under the tang and at the two pillars but nowhere else. Similarly, the magazine floor-plate and trigger guard assembly should bed against the stock at the action screw locations (pillars) and nowhere else. The action screws serve only to clamp the stock between the combination trigger guard and magazine housing and the receiver. The epoxy or metal pillars resist the clamping force provided by the action screws. This arrangement prevents either the trigger guard assembly or the action from pulling directly against any portion of the stock either at the top or bottom of the receiver.

Either the epoxy pillars or the epoxy that bonds the aluminum pillars to the wood at the action screw locations serve to distribute this load to a greater area of the stock. It also flexes, as necessary, to absorb differential shrinking, swelling or warping in the stock. Finally, the installation has properly centered the action screws in the pillars. This prevents the screw shanks from ever touching the pillars.

Properly done, pillar-bedding results in a barreled-action that is practically immune to problems associated with poor bedding contact between the action and the stock or resulting

Photograph 2-66: Correctly dimensioned pillars in partially assembled action showing relationship of assembly. In use, these pillars are epoxy-bonded to the stock with no part of the stock touching either the barreled-action or the floor-plate assembly. The action screws lock the pillars in place between floor-plate and receiver. This locates the stock to the receiver without wood touching any part of the receiver or floor-plate! The epoxy-bedded recoil lug at the juncture of the barrel and the receiver transfers recoil from the barreled-action to the stock. The action screws are smaller than the holes in the pillars. This prevent transfer of recoil through the pillars. Stock warpage under the receiver can still stress the receiver. However, other dimensional fluctuations of the stock can do little harm, assuming that one has fully free-floated the barrel. See associated photographs and text.

from minor local shrinkage or swelling of the stock. Bedding techniques cannot cure everything. If the stock and action do not meet naturally at any action screw location, tightening the action-screw will bend the action. If, for any reason, the stock warps between the action screw locations it will still flex the action. Sadly mistaken are those who do not believe an ill-fitting stock can flex an action or bend a barrel.

Aluminum pillar-bedding the Model-700 is simple enough. I will assume the gun features a floated barrel and that you have wrapped the barrel near the front of the fore-end barrel channel with vinyl electrical tape to center the barrel in the fore-end channel.

After separating the action from the stock, enlarge both action screw holes to thirty-five sixty-fourths inch (35/64") or nine-sixteenths inch (9/16") diameter (see the following paragraph before deciding which size drill bit to use). This is sufficient clearance to surround typical commercial aluminum pillars with a bonding layer of epoxy, all that is required. A standard high-speed twist drill bit works best for drilling these holes. See Photograph #s 2-67/68.

Begin by drilling a short distance into the bottom of both the front and rear action screw holes in the stock. Turn the stock over and complete the holes by drilling from the top. This extra step will prevent splintering at the ends of the holes. As noted, these holes must be large enough to allow a layer of epoxy resin to surround the pillar on all sides but this layer need not be particularly thick. You should avoid any work that might tend to polish these holes — surface irregularities and porosity in the wood enhance adhesion of the epoxy ("glass"). Consider running a nine-sixteenths inch (9/16") NC tap through the drilled hole, if one is available. In this case, drill the hole with a thirty-five sixty-fourths inch (35/64") drill bit, if available. The threads formed provide substantial mechanical bonding for the epoxy, particularly if you have drilled the holes at thirty-five sixty-fourths inch (35/64"). See Photograph #s 2-69 through 2-72.

Photograph 2-67

Photograph 2-68

Photographs 2-67/68: Left-hand Remington Model-700 bolt-action stock. These views shows bottom of stock at location of rear and front action screw holes, photographs 2-67 & 2-68, respectively. We will enlarge these holes for pillar bedding.

Photograph 2-69: Preparing to drill front action screw hole for pillar bedding. One must pad and support the stock to prevent movement and possible damage. In spite of our best precautions the wood in the divider separating the front action screw (now pillar) hole and the magazine well opening ruptured during the drilling operation. The separated block moved into the magazine well. We epoxy repaired this damage before proceeding. See associated text and photographs.

It is worthwhile to save the shavings from this drilling operation. When using hobby epoxy or regular glass bedding epoxy for other jobs, where rigidity is less important, you can color-match and strengthen the resulting material by mixing in, perhaps, one part of these shavings with one part of the well-mixed epoxy. Where rigidity and strength are critical, as with the following bedding operations, a superior additive is atomized steel or aluminum.

Commercial pillar-bedding pillars feature exterior grooves to enhance adhesion with the epoxy. Also, the manufacturer contours the tops of these pillars to fit the underside of the specific action. However, owing to variations in action screw hole length, you have to cut both pillars to length to match the specific gun. Also, you must

Photograph 2-71: Enlarging the drilled-out rear tang action screw hole on a left-hand Remington Model-700 bolt-action rifle using large, round bastard file. Enlarged hole is necessary for Pillar bedding. The hole should be large enough to allow a reasonable bed of epoxy around the aluminum pillar's circumference.

Photograph 2-70: Remington left-hand Model-700 bolt-action rifle stock with both action screw holes enlarged for pillar bedding.

Photograph 2-72: This added step dramatically improves epoxy-to-wood bonding. This 9/16" NC tap cut shallow threads in the nominally 9/16" diameter hole in the stock. These grooves provide a secure interference fit between epoxy and wood — even if the small-scale surface bonding failed, the pillar could not move without rotating, which it cannot do, owing to its contoured top! For a complete discussion see associated text and photograph captions.

ensure the cut end is flat and square where it fits to the combination trigger guard and floor-plate. See the associated photographs and captions for a complete description of the necessary process. See Photograph # 2-73.

As noted above, you can make pillars. Simply abide with the following guidelines:

First, the pillar should have a centered hole that is somewhat larger in diameter than the action screw

Second, the exterior of the pillar should be slotted, abraded or threaded so as to adhere to the epoxy

Third, the top of the pillar should match the receiver so as to bed solidly on a large area or along linear zones (a shallow V aligned to the axis of the action will work on round-bottomed receivers)

Fourth, both pillars should extend slightly past both the top and bottom of the stock and be flush and square where the floor-plate abuts

Finally, the pillars must be of sufficient diameter and material strength to support the stress imposed by a properly tightened action screw (Copper or PVC tubing will not work!)

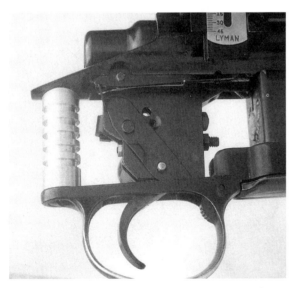

Photograph 2-73: Left-hand Remington Model-700 bolt-action rifle receiver. This view shows rear of receiver with floor plate and pillars in place. One must adjust pillar length before proceeding to glass bedding pillars into the stock. See text. Front pillar is similar and, likewise, one must fit that to the action. Note the annular grooves around this pillar. These provide for solid epoxy bonding and a mechanical interlock. Also note modification to the magazine box. We have soldered a brass washer in place at the rear. This rigidifies the box and provides for a tight fit in the action and the floor plate, a worthwhile improvement. See text.

With the above discussion in mind, you should be able to visualize the intended function of the pillars. Adjust homemade or factory pillars, as necessary, to achieve proper functioning. When you tighten the action screws, the pillars should support the receiver and the combination floor-plate and trigger assembly without any wood-to-metal contact.

The first step is determination of the correct length for the action pillars. The idea is to cut each pillar just slightly longer than the existing distance separating the floor-plate assembly from the receiver when you assemble the rifle normally. The pillars should be, perhaps, fifteen-thousandths (0.015") longer than this distance. For a complete discussion of this process, see the associated photographs and captions #s 2-74 through 2-80.

Photograph 2-74

Photograph 2-75

Left-hand Remington Model-700 bolt-action rifle with dial caliper measuring distance from head of front action screw to the top of magazine port rail (photograph 2-74) and from top of trigger guard opening to top of tang at rear of bolt guides (photograph 2-75) on the assembled rifle. This data is necessary for proper pillar bedding. See text and associated photographs. Caliper indicates just over 1.71", front of action and just over 1.80", rear of action.

Section 2: The Trouble With Stocks, Part I

Photograph 2-76

Photograph 2-77

With stock and magazine housing removed and floor plate assembled to barreled-action with the same screw-head to magazine port rail measurements (about 1.71" at front and about 1.80" at rear) we measure the corresponding gaps between bottom of receiver and top of floor plate, photographs 2-76 & 2-77, respectively. These are a critical measurements. We cut the pillars slightly longer than these distances. See associated text, photographs and captions for a full discussion. Here we measured about 0.735", front, and about 1.23", rear. Our cut lengths are: 0.750", front pillar, and 1.245", rear pillar. This provides 0.015" stock-to-metal clearance.

Photograph 2-78: Cutting pillar to approximately correct length with hack saw. We clamp unused end of pillar in bench vise to facilitate sawing. Next we will polish cut end flat and square to the pillar's axis. See associated photograph.

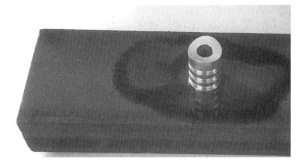

Photograph 2-79: Polishing and squaring cut end of front pillar. We used a coarse stone with a good flat top. See associated photographs and text.

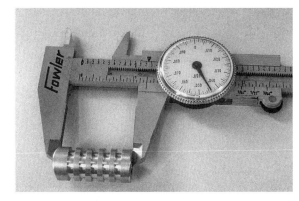

Photograph 2-80: Measuring finished rear pillar. Note that minor length (taken at center of concave face) measures just over 1.245". Correct length for stock and action measurements taken earlier. See associated photographs.

Begin the pillar glass bedding process by filling any holes in the receiver where epoxy might infiltrate. Children's modeling clay or a similar product will do the job. Candle wax works quite well for this. Simply allow the melted wax from a burning candle to drip onto the action at any such hole locations. You can easily trim away excess solidified wax using a fingernail or knife.

Apply a thin film of heavy grease to the action-fitting end of each pillar. This will help prevent epoxy from infiltrating into the top of the pillars. Install a pillar diameter, screw fitting, hard paper washer against the head of each action screw. These washers will act as dams to prevent epoxy from entering the inside of the pillar from the bottom end. Then wrap the shank of the front and rear action screws with sufficient vinyl electrical tape to force those to center in the pillars. Finally, coat the threads of each screw with release agent.

Attach the pillars to the action with the action screws. Tighten the screws moderately but avoid rupturing the paper washer. Make sure you orient the pillars properly where they abut the action.

Apply two layers of vinyl electrical tape both in front of and behind each pillar where it abuts to the receiver. This tape will provide clearance to keep the end of the pillars above the wood, as they should be located. If you want, you can apply two layers of tape along the sides of the pillars to minimize the epoxy clean up chore for where the epoxy will spill over onto the stock adjacent to the pillars. However, with release agent applied to those areas on the stock, the clean-up operation is rather easy. Take your pick.

Apply a generous coating of release agent (available from Brownells) to the action all around both the front and rear action screw holes. The best approach is to spray the entire barreled-action assembly with Brownells' aerosol release agent (Acra-Release). This will facilitate removal of any epoxy agent that happens to find its way where it does not belong, an almost inevitable result! Also, be sure to apply release agent to the entire floor-plate assembly, but especially around the action screw locations. Finally, apply release agent to the stock surfaces adjacent to the pillar holes, where necessary, to keep epoxy from sticking. For this job, you should use a cotton swab saturated with release agent to provide precise application. You do not want to get release agent in the pillar holes!

Clean all exterior surfaces of the pillars using alcohol-saturated cotton swabs. Acetone is a better solvent but ensure adequate ventilation. The pillar exteriors must be immaculately clean so the epoxy can bond; the pillars will become part of the stock. If any release agent might have infiltrated the drilled out action screw holes, clean the interior of the drilled out action screw holes (where the pillars will reside) with alcohol-saturated cotton swabs until those are immaculately clean. A hot air gun or a hair dryer are useful to dry out the holes after cleaning. Again, acetone will work but its superior cleaning action is not necessary here. In any case, if you have dampened the holes at all during cleaning, allow sufficient time for proper drying before proceeding.

Verify that you have fully coated the underside of the receiver near the pillars with release agent. Also verify that you have properly coated the magazine floor-plate with release agent and that you have filled any holes or channels near the action screw holes in both the receiver and the floor-plate with clay or a similar agent to prevent epoxy infiltration. When assembled for epoxy curing, the floor-plate will be at the bottom; non gel-type epoxy will run out, given any opening! Also, apply release agent to the screw heads. (If I sound paranoid about release agent it is only because I understand epoxy!)

Choice of bedding material is wide open. Brownells' gel formula (Acraglas-Gel) is less prone to running, which results in the epoxy getting where it does not belong. This type of glass bedding agent minimizes the potential for infiltration into places epoxy should not be; since this product stays put better, working with it is generally easier. However, the standard formula is more apt to properly fill small voids. Take your pick.

Prepare for the bedding operation by clearing off the area around your bench-mounted vise. Also, get the padding needed to safely mount the stock in the vise and test mount the assembled gun with the bottom up and then with the bottom down, just to get a feel for what will come next. Finally, prepare at least two one-foot long pieces of duct tape and leave those hanging within easy reach of the vise.

On rifles where sufficient barrel protrudes from the fore-end, you can simplify this operation by clamping the barrel between the jaws of a well-padded vise. Vise the barreled-action upside-down with the barrel horizontal. This often allows easier manipulation of the stock and re-assembly of the rifle.

Section 2: The Trouble With Stocks, Part I

Mix sufficient epoxy to bed both action pillars and provide a little excess material, according to instructions. This job should only require, perhaps, one tablespoonful of mix. Add epoxy-strengthening atomized steel or aluminum, as desired.

Mount the stock in a padded vise, with the bottom of the stock at top. Apply epoxy mix into each pillar hole using a small probe (such as a whittled-down popsicle stick). Ensure that you have completely wetted the entire interior of both holes with epoxy and covered the surface in a shallow layer of epoxy. Similarly, coat the entire perimeter of each pillar with a shallow layer of epoxy. Make especially certain you fill any grooves in the pillars flush with the adjacent full-diameter regions.

From below, insert the barreled-action with the epoxy-coated pillars attached, as described above. Carefully align and center the pillars in the holes that are coated with epoxy bedding material. Push the barreled-action fully home in the stock. See Photograph # 2-81.

Position the action under the stock with the pillars lined up with the holes. Insert the action into the stock making every effort to avoid disturbing the epoxy already in the holes. Keep the pillars centered and aligned with the holes. Carefully lift the action while keeping it properly aligned.

To temporarily hold the action in place, tightly wrap one of the prepared duct tape strips around the fore-end and barrel. Wrap the other piece over the bridge of the receiver and around the stock at the magazine well area. Wiggle the action slightly to help the epoxy fill any voids around the pillars or against the wood in the pillar holes. Ensure that you have used sufficient epoxy. Epoxy should fill all voids around the action pillars. Excess epoxy should have welled-up around the bottom end of both pillars. Add epoxy, as necessary, to fill the bottom of the pillar holes to at least flush with the bottom ends of the pillars.

Clean away any excessive epoxy material from around the action screws at the bottom end of the pillars. Ensure the tape wrap is holding the barreled-action tightly in the stock. If not, wrap that assembly with additional duct tape until it is.

Remove the screws and the paper washers. Remove the tape wrap from the action screws and insert those through the floor-plate. Rewrap the action screw shanks with a similar number of layers of vinyl tape. Reapply release agent to the screws.

Make sure the pillars are still properly oriented to the receiver. If the pillar rotates when you remove the screw it will not properly align to the contour of the receiver.

If necessitated by adhesion failure between the duct tape and the sides of the stock (which can happen if the release agent or WD-40 has sufficiently coated the stock in that area), support the action from below to keep it from moving. Cut the duct tape at both sides of the magazine well and remove the piece. Position the floor-plate in the stock. Snug, but do not harshly tighten, the action screws. Rewrap the receiver and stock with several layer of tape. Finally, remove the gun from the vise, turn it over and secure it in the vise with the top of the action up and level.

Allow sufficient time for the epoxy to cure before disassembly. This is easy enough to verify by noting the condition of the unused epoxy in the mixing cup. In this instance, it is only necessary that the epoxy has begun to solidify enough that it will no longer run — it should be in a hard but still plastic state.

Remove the tape and pull the action screws. Then separate the action from the stock. Separate the floor-plate from the stock. Often the tinker will find that he has to use some degree of force to separate these pieces. Should you have this problem, a few well-placed and judicious blows from a plastic hammer will, perhaps, get the job done.

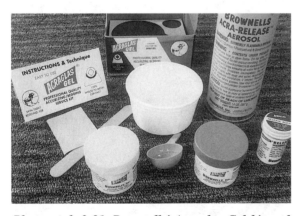

Photograph 2-81: Brownells' Acraglas Gel kit and their Acra-Release aerosol. These products make fast and simple work of action-to-stock glass bedding. Do not skimp on the release agent. Failure to apply this to one-square inch of clean metal can result in a bond that will resist several thousand pounds of force! For practical purposes you cannot separate two pieces thus bonded.

When you have separated these pieces, cut and clean away all the epoxy that has inappropriately interposed the stock and the receiver and the stock and the floor-plate. A Dremel tool fitted with a wire wheel works well. Similarly, remove any epoxy that has migrated onto the outside of the stock or into the trigger guard or magazine housing well inlets. Remove the tape from the screws and the receiver.

Recoil Lug Bedding, When Using Pillar-Bedding:

Now we are ready to move to the second stage of our pillar-bedding operation — recoil lug bedding. In case you are wondering why we do this operation in two steps, I believe it is best to do this stage after the initial pillar-bedding because that approach assures proper stock alignment. If the tinker were to bed both the pillars and the recoil lug in one operation, there would be precious little to keep everything lined up properly. Conversely, with this method the pillars will keep the action properly aligned in the stock while the tinker forms an epoxy bed for the recoil lug.

Cut away the wood from all sides of the recoil lug. Recoil lug-to-wood clearance should be as great as is possible without compromising the integrity of the wood. On the Remington Model-700, side clearance of a full one-eighth inch is certainly feasible; front, rear and bottom clearances approaching one-quarter inch are reasonable. Also, it is certainly worthwhile to undercut this recess to provide an interference fit for the epoxy bed. Once you have obtained adequate lug-to-wood clearance you are ready to glass bed the recoil lug. See Photograph #s 2-82/83.

Secure the stock in a padded vise with the top up and level. Apply a sufficient dam in the stock channel both in front of and behind the recoil lug recess. Again, clay or a similar product works well. Apply release agent liberally to all stock surfaces adjacent to the recoil lug recess. Avoid getting <u>any</u> release agent in the recoil lug recess.

Clean the bottom edge of the recoil lug with alcohol or acetone. Apply two layers of electrical tape to the bottom edge of the recoil lug. Trim those to as close to exactly lug size as is feasible — a new single-edge razor blade does this job nicely.

If you do not want to use the tight fit approach, it will ease disassembly if you apply one layer of cellophane tape to the front and both sides of the recoil lug. Cut these tape pieces to fit

Photograph 2-82: Oblique-view of installed pillar and augured-out recess for recoil lug. This will provide about 1/8" side, front, rear and bottom clearance between recoil lug and wood. We have also scarified and partially removed the epoxy finish on the wood around the recoil lug recess. This action facilitates bonding of excess epoxy, which will well out of the recoil lug recess as we insert the barreled-action. We have applied release agent both to the top and inside of the front pillar and to the front action screw. We also applied release agent to the flat top of the action channel at the sides of the stock, in case epoxy reached that exposed area — it did not.

Photograph 2-83: Top-view of installed pillar and augured out recess for recoil lug. For a complete discussion of this process, see the associated photographs and text.

Section 2: The Trouble With Stocks, Part I

as closely as possible to the edges of the recoil lug. Apply release agent to the barreled-action in all areas adjacent to the recoil lug and, especially, the recoil lug itself. Insert the action screws through the floor-plate then tape wrap both screws so those are a tight fit in the pillars. This will ensure that you have properly centered the action front-to-rear, side-to-side and rotationally when you reassemble the gun. This will force the recoil lug to form a recess that is properly positioned in the epoxy bed. See Photograph # 2-84.

Tape wrap the barrel in front of the recoil lug and the receiver behind the recoil lug. Use only one layer of vinyl electrical tape, continue the tape across and past the pillar. Cut the tape away where the pillar abuts to the receiver. Similarly, apply one layer of vinyl tape over the extreme rear of the tang. These layers will provide epoxy to receiver clearance so that the pillars, and not the recoil lug, are supporting the receiver. See Photograph # 2-85.

Carefully apply release agent to all areas of the barreled-action adjacent to the recoil lug. Similarly, apply a wipe-on agent to the front action screw shank and threads and to the exterior surfaces of the stock adjacent to the recoil lug recess.

Thoroughly mix an appropriate batch of epoxy. In this case, addition of atomized steel or aluminum is a very good idea. According to Brownells' clear instructions on mixing the epoxy, for maximum "glass" strength, use a 50/50 atomized metal to well-mixed epoxy. Use this mix to almost completely fill the recoil lug recess so it is level with the original stock surface.

Use sufficient epoxy mix to completely bed the recoil lug. The recoil lug typically takes up surprisingly little room. Also, cleaning up slight overflows is reasonably easy. Install the barreled-action using care to properly center it front-to-rear and side-to-side to avoid unnecessarily disturbing the epoxy in the recoil lug inlet.

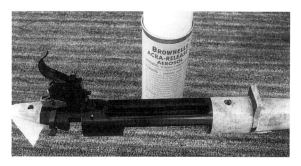

Photograph 2-85: Here we have taken a very critical step in the pillar bedding process. We have already bonded the pillars to the stock. We installed the action over the pillars with a few wraps of masking tape around the action beyond the top of the pillars. This lifted the pillars slightly above the action channel in the stock. We installed the action screws through the floor plate and wrapped one layer of electrical tape around each screw shank to insure the screws centered in the pillars. We installed the floor plate and snugged the screws, making certain the concave end of the pillars aligned with the convex surface of the action.

After that batch of epoxy had solidly set, we disassembled the action. We cleaned off excess epoxy at both ends of the pillars, the stock, the floor plate, the interior of the pillars and the receiver (we had already liberally applied release agent to all surfaces close to the pillar holes and to the bolts.) Finally, we augured out the recoil lug recess to provide sufficient clearance on all sides and under the recoil lug to allow a sufficient bed of epoxy — a fine line between unnecessarily weakening the stock and leaving the epoxy bed weak. See associated photographs and captions.

Here we have masking taped the front, bottom and sides of the recoil lug and wrapped the barrel in front of the recoil lug. We have also wrapped, with one layer of masking tape, the receiver, behind the recoil lug, and the tang. We will next add a second layer to all of these areas except the pillar locations and the front of the recoil lug. This tape provides clearance. After we have epoxy-bedded the recoil lug, the action will rest on the pillars with no contact anywhere else, except at the rear of the recoil lug. See associated photographs, captions and text.

We will liberally apply release agent around the recoil lug areas both on the barreled-action and at the top and inside the front action pillar.

Photograph 2-84: Close-up-view of partially wrapped barreled-action at recoil lug, before recoil lug bedding. A second layer of tape is necessary on the bottom of the recoil lug and on the underside of the barrel everywhere except a radius around the front pillar. This tape provides clearance to keep the action resting on the pillars only. See associated photographs, captions and text.

Install the floor-plate and snug both action screws. See Photograph # 2-86.

After the epoxy has had sufficient time to cure to a rigid state, remove the action screws and separate the action from the stock. Typically, separation might take considerable patience but it should happen without undue force. Again, a few properly delivered taps from a plastic mallet often helps break sticky spots loose.

Clean any excess epoxy from around the recoil lug recess on the stock and any that might have adhered to any part of the action. Also, remove all tape, clay dams, wax fillers and the like. Now come several important steps that many folks often completely overlook. See Photograph # 2-87.

First, the bottom of the recoil lug should not touch the bottom of the recoil lug recess! If so, any swelling or warpage in that part of the stock will almost certainly flex the action and change the gun's zero! That explains our application of two layers of electrical tape to the bottom of the recoil lug before we installed it in the epoxy-filled recess.

When you remove the action, quite often one or both layers of vinyl tape will remain in the hole formed in the epoxy bed for the recoil lug. Use a dental pick or similar instrument to dig out those pieces. Obviously, adhesion of one or both layers of tape with the recoil lug eases this task. Be sure to remove any layer or layers of tape, wherever you might have applied those and wherever those might have adhered.

Second, slightly bevel all edges of the recoil lug (perhaps 0.020" wide but no more). This means bevel both sides and the bottom, both front and rear. This procedure will eliminate stress concentrations at the corners of the epoxy pocket. It will also ease installation and removal of the barreled-action. This simple step can easily double or treble the effective strength of the epoxy pocket!

Third, apply a high-quality, non-hydrocarbon based, lubricant to the recoil lug (molybdenum-disulfide or graphite are the best choices here). This will help prevent the lug from binding with the epoxy pocket in which it sets. Ideally, the recoil lug should be free to adjust in the epoxy bed should the stock warp slightly. Remember, the recoil lug's only job is to transfer recoil from the barreled-action to the stock; it should do nothing else.

Thoroughly clean all surfaces of the stock using alcohol. After this cleaning, it will be necessary to reseal the wood in all areas where anything might have interrupted the wood's seal and where the added epoxy has not covered that interruption. Finally, thoroughly clean the action and recoil lug using a light gun-oil-dampened cloth. This will remove the release agent and other residues and prevent corrosion.

Be sure you have removed the tape wrap

Photograph 2-86: Assembled rifle after we filled recoil lug recess with a bed of epoxy. Note masking tape, used to temporarily hold the floor plate in place until we could get the action screws inserted and tightened into the receiver holes. Again, we installed the action screws through the floor plate and then wrapped one layer of electrical tape around the shank of each screw; this ensured centering of these screws in the pillars and, therefore, centering of the action in the stock. For a complete discussion of the technique, see the associated text, photographs and captions. After the epoxy fully cured, we disassembled the stock from the action and removed the tape. We were lucky this time. The epoxy welled to exactly the contour we prefer — we did not have to remove one iota, that does not happen often!

Photograph 2-87: Finished epoxy bed at recoil lug on left-hand Remington Model-700 bolt-action rifle. Note that excess epoxy welled out of recoil lug recess as we pushed the recoil lug into the hole. Owing to taped-in clearances, this excess epoxy will not touch either receiver or barrel in the assembled rifle. See associated photographs, caption and text. This epoxy layer does, however, support the epoxy in the recoil lug recess. It also stiffens the stock in this area.

Section 2: The Trouble With Stocks, Part I

from the action screws to allow those to float in the pillars. Thoroughly clean the floor-plate and oil it with light gun oil. Remove any remaining tape-wrap from the barrel.

Reassemble the barreled-action and magazine well into the stock and install the floor-plate. If the magazine well does not have a slight amount of vertical clearance when the action screws are snugged, you should trim it, slightly, to provide such clearance — the magazine well should not transfer any stress from the action to the floor-plate.

When you have installed and tightened the action in place it should contact the stock in the following areas: the tang pillar, the front pillar and the action lug. The pillars should make solid contact with the floor-plate assembly. Slight bending of the floor-plate as you tighten the action screws does little harm. Just so long as the floor-plate pulls against the pillars and not the stock.

When you tighten the screws moderately with a properly fitting hand screwdriver the pillars should support the action, clamping the stock rigidly between the floor-plate and the receiver. There should be almost zero stress on the action, the stock or the floor-plate. Similarly, the recoil lug and nothing else should locate the action front-to-rear in the stock. Finally, the recoil lug and tang should align the action both lengthwise in and up and down with the stock.

You should identify and eliminate any other areas of contact between the stock and the action or the floor-plate. As noted above, some gunsmiths advocate providing a large floor of epoxy for the action to rest on, both under the tang and around the recoil lug. That is an option you might want to consider, but try it this way first. If your results are not satisfactory, you can easily add these epoxy floors later. Just follow the same basic procedure described here. Roughen the existing epoxy with a burr on a Dremel tool and add an epoxy layer, as necessary.

Also note, for those working on rifles with long and heavy barrels, adding bedding under the chamber section of the barrel makes sense. On such a rifle the weight of the barrel can be substantial and will significantly bend and stress the receiver. Changing temperature in the receiver will result in equally significant changes in barrel deflection resulting from this stress. Obviously, if you expect to shoot long shot-strings under rapid-fire conditions this same consideration might apply.

Simple Glass Bedding:

Note, many of the procedures discussed here are very similar to the pillar-bedding procedures. Observe the photographs in that sub-section and read it before proceeding here.

This more common glass bedding system involves the same basic process as pillar-bedding but substitutes glass bedding material for the aluminum pillars at the action screw locations. The significant difference is that this method is more difficult to do correctly and it is not as immune to warpage in the stock. Owing to the modest cost of purchasing pillars (or compared to the time involved in making pillars) I highly recommend using commercial aluminum or homemade pillars for pillar bedding, where feasible.

Begin as with aluminum pillar-bedding but bore the action screw holes only about one-quarter inch larger than original hole diameter. Here a single wrap of electrical tape on the entire shank of the action screw will ease removal through the cured epoxy. You will also want to produce a full one-half inch diameter bevel using a one-half inch drill bit at both ends of both holes. This bevel will create a solid epoxy purchase for both the receiver and floor-plate.

(On rifles lacking the floor-plate, such as Remington's ADL, the bottom end of the front action screw hole should be no larger than the boss the action screw tightens against and no additional bevel is possible without damaging the appearance of the stock. In this instance, the tinker must remove the front screw boss before beginning the drilling work. Also, you cannot tighten the front screw until after the epoxy cures! To accommodate this, wrap duct tape around the barrel and fore-end to hold the front end of the action properly down as the epoxy cures.)

Apply one layer of vinyl tape about one-quarter inch (1/4") in front of and behind both action screw holes on the receiver. Apply release agent to the action, the screws and the adjacent areas of the stock. Mix an appropriate batch of epoxy. Insert the screws through the floor-plate and place the floor-plate under the stock. Wrap the shanks of the screws with one layer of vinyl electrical tape. Drip candle wax into the action screw holes in the receiver. Trim any excess wax from around the screw holes. Apply release agent to the stock and receiver but avoid getting any in the newly enlarged action screw holes.

Fix the stock in a padded vise with the receiver channel positioned at the bottom and level. From below, insert the barreled-action in place. Ensure that you have properly positioned the action. Tape the action in place using several wraps of duct tape over the barrel and over the magazine well.

Properly mix a batch of high-strength glass bedding compound and add a fifty percent (50%) charge of atomized metal to provide for the strongest possible finished product. For this job you should mix about two tablespoonfuls.

Fill the action screw holes with epoxy, sufficiently to ensure a solid epoxy column extending fully from top to bottom. On the ADL reinstall the front screw boss. On ADL style actions install the release agent-treated floor-plate assembly. On ADL style guns (those where the stock forms the bottom of the magazine well), install the release agent-treated trigger guard. Install and snug the action screws.

The remainder of the process is essentially identical to pillar-bedding, which see, discussed above.

Stock Checkering:

Stock checkering, contouring and refinishing can all enhance accuracy potential. Stock checkering can improve gun handling properties. A more solid hold can only lead to better shooting. Further, if the shooter can hold the gun solidly with less grip pressure, he or she can usually shoot better, both off-hand or from the bench. Generally, properly applied checkering is beneficial in almost all shooting disciplines. See Photograph # 2-88.

The tools required to do checkering at home are available from Brownells and are modestly priced. The skills required to do a proper job are another matter! The whittler must work with patience and care. Mistakes can be irreparable. If you are not comfortable with these limitations the best course is to have the work done by a competent gunsmith or install a properly-checkered after-market stock.

Cost of an adequate grip and fore-end checkering job is in the one-hundred and fifty dollars ($150) range. This might sound high but, should you do the job yourself, you will likely realize this is more like a genuine bargain.

For utility purposes a coarser checkering pattern is best. Something around eighteen (18) lines to the inch seems about right for most applications. For beauty, you might choose a pattern closer to twenty-two (22) lines to the inch. However, anything finer is apt to lead to problems since typical wood grain often cannot support such fine patterns. See Photograph # 2-89.

The best way to understand what checking should do and how to go about producing a cut checkered pattern on a wood stock is to examine a quality cut checkering pattern on an existing stock. See Photograph # 2-90.

Photograph 2-89: Here we have traced the perimeter of the pattern and a few guide lines for the checkering cross-angle pattern. These lines must be sufficiently permanent and legible. We omitted the crossing scrolls shown on this pattern.

Photograph 2-90: Here we have cut the perimeter and a few of the checkering pattern lines. This step gives the feel for the process. Once you have established the initial straight lines, you generate subsequent lines by using the last line cut as a guide. After completing this step, one uses a different cutter to deepen the grooves to final shape. Similarly, one applies a perimeter pattern. The process is time consuming, requires patience and is fraught with the potential for error.... However, even a sloppy checkering pattern improves handling considerably. For a good-looking job either consider having a professional do the work or expect to spend considerable time doing the job and even more time learning how!

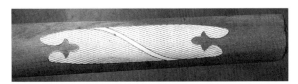

Photograph 2-88: Checkering begins with pattern choice. Here we are observing the appearance of a pattern on the fore-end from an 1895 Marlin. This is not a good type of pattern for a novice to choose. The rounded scrolls (called fleur-de-lis) are difficult to execute properly. Nevertheless, this is a fine pattern for a Marlin fore-end. We decided this was also a good sized pattern for this application. Templates and tools are available from Brownells'. See associated photographs, captions and text.

Section 2: The Trouble With Stocks, Part I

I will not address the details of checkering at greater length here. I will refer those individuals interested in pursuing this art to any of the excellent works dedicated to the hobby, which are available through Brownells, Fajen and other sources. However, the included photographs and captions should provide a fair measure of understanding about what the gunsmithing tinker must do to apply checkering to a piece of wood. Also, I will address custom checkering in *Part II* of this work.

Stock Refinishing:

As has been noted in the proceeding discussion, the quality and type of finish can be a major consideration in the function of a rifle stock. This relates to several issues. First is the question of properly sealing the wood against moisture infiltration or expiration. No finish can completely stop wood hydration and the associated dimensional changes. For that matter, alas, not even the most sophisticated synthetic stocks are immune to moisture induced dimensional changes! The secret is to do everything possible to slow and limit those changes. Common problem areas which often are not properly sealed include the surface under the recoil pad or buttplate, any screw holes and all inletted areas. Ensure that you completely saturate all such areas with a quality finishing oil or an epoxy type sealant.

Another area of concern is the quality of the shaping and sanding applied before the original stock finish. Failure to develop sanding to an appropriate level limits both beauty and finish texture of the stock. Many hardwoods can benefit from sanding to at least 320 grit. In certain instances, highly figured walnut can show scratches from 660 grit sandpaper! See Photograph #s 2-91/92.

Additionally, the overall smoothness and contour of many stocks is less than perfect. Sanding at the existing finish with an unsupported sheet of sandpaper will often reveal high spots on rounded contours. The wood worker can easily remove these contour flaws. This step is worth considering for this reason alone. See Photograph # 2-93.

Photograph 2-92: This quick-setting, clear hobby epoxy and a few drill shavings from the same stock are all we require to fill a hole in the wood. After thoroughly mixing the epoxy, we continued to add wood shavings while mixing vigorously, until the color matched the stock. Our intention is to plug the sling stud hole.

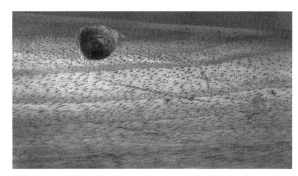

Photograph 2-91: We have removed the sling stud from this Marlin stock. Since we intend this $4^1/_2$ pound .44 Magnum-chambered rifle for handy hand or scabbard carry, addition of a sling is counter-productive. Our intention is to plug this hole with a colored epoxy filler. We will use clear hobby epoxy, mixing in a measure of walnut drill-shavings. This will help match color and add a bit of mottling, which helps hide the repair. To insure solid retention, we opened and roughed the bottom of this hole. See text and associated photographs and captions.

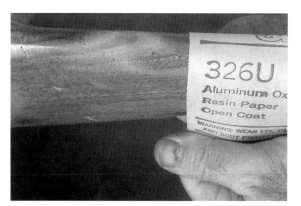

Photograph 2-93: Here we are sanding the polyurethane finish from a Marlin stock. Shown here is the underside of the buttstock. The area to the left of the sand paper at the extreme bottom of the stock shows naked wood. To the right of that and on the near side of the stock is a patch where we have not yet disturbed the original finish. Areas where we have completely sanded away the original finish surround this spot! These, high and low spots in the surface are common on factory stocks. See text and associated photographs.

Should you choose to refinish an existing stock, ensure that you first remove every bit of any non-oil-based finish. Residues of such products will interfere with any new finish you might apply to the stock. On stocks finished with epoxy-based products this removal will require use of chemicals specifically designed to remove such finishes. Brownells offer a product called *Cirtistrip* for specifically this purpose. Brownells also offers several types and grades of polishing compounds and myriad finishing systems. See Photograph # 2-94.

Photograph 2-94

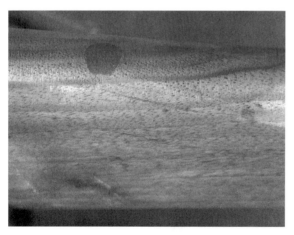

Photograph 2-95

Photographs 2-94/95: We have filled the sling stud hole with a mixture of quick-setting clear hobby epoxy and wood shavings (photograph 2-94). Color will be a good match to the refinished stock. We added wood shavings for that reason. Photograph 2-95: We have sanded the bottom of the stock with 100 grit sandpaper. Note sanding marks and wood-filled epoxy plug in stud mount hole. See text and associated photographs.

Keep the following points in mind. You cannot polish wood too perfectly. You cannot overdo blending or removal of high spots in the stock's contour. Also, often after application of the initial sealing coat or coats, portions of the wood grain will raise and the stock will require additional polishing sanding to retain the finished surface quality desired. Invisible sanding blemishes on the unfinished wood often become clearly visible when the wood worker applies finish to the wood. When stock contour forces cross-grain sanding, always finish-sand at least one step finer than when the sanding strokes follow the grain. (Often referred to as, "With the grain".) With particular hardwoods, such as black walnut, it is reasonable to carry the sanding stages to at least 400 grit — as noted above, some samples of stress-grain walnut show scratches from finer sandpapers. See Photograph # 2-95.

When applying a new finish, do not skimp in coverage or effort. It is impossible to create a too-tight seal on wood! In the future, good service from the rifle will well reward any extra effort. Again, for various reasons, my personal bias is a simple hand-rubbed Tung Oil finish. Not the least of my motivations is that Tung Oil allows easy mitigation of "use marks". Anyone can easily touch up any spots damaged in use and handling. Simply apply the same product over the affected area, as necessary, to match the color and seal the wood. Further, if, after many years of hard use, the owner wishes to refinish a Tung-Oiled piece of wood, he can do the job with a bit of light sanding, as necessary to remove any unwanted scratches, followed by reapplication of Tung Oil. Nothing could be simpler. One final reason I prefer Tung Oil: it provides a truly beautiful and hard finish that is, in my opinion, unsurpassed by any other process. However, when properly applied, the various epoxy and urethane finishes can provide somewhat superior short-term sealing against changes in atmospheric humidity. See Photograph #s 2-96 through 2-104.

Section 2: The Trouble With Stocks, Part I

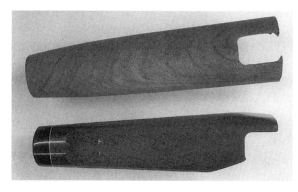

Photograph 2-96: Here, at bottom, you see why we started this job. The factory fore-end had already failed at the back on one side and had cracked farther forward — likely to completely fall off someday! You can see that there is considerable trimming to do to get the Fajen semi-inletted piece shaped up properly. A belt sander and various sanding papers were the only tools required here. The job took about four hours.

Photograph 2-97: I have adapted this hardwood dowel to use as a jig for working on the Fajen fore-end (Remington Pump). Tape-wrap fits fore-end channel, end of dowel drilled to hold the fore-end bolt and dowel clamped in bench-mounted vise.

Photograph 2-98: Fore-end temporarily installed on jigging dowel. This provides a solid working platform — either vised or hand-held.

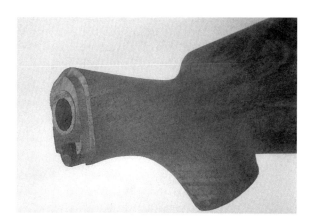

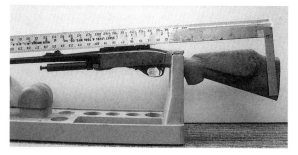

Photograph 2-100: Checking fit of stock for both drop and cast-off. Note the carpenter's square. The inside edge delineates location of stock cut for the desired length (we intend to install a recoil pad so the cut-off is significant).

Photograph 2-101: Receiver-end of new Fajen semi-fancy black walnut buttstock. Note good grain structure in this critical area. This is an important consideration. When one applies checkering, as is common in the tang area on stocks, fancy wood is both wasted and complicates the job. What is more important, fancy-grained wood is seldom as strong as straight-grained wood. Fajen has done an excellent job in this example. Also note, the wood is both slightly larger than the receiver and there is a slight gap between the stock and the receiver at the perimeter — as there should be. Despite proper kiln drying, I expect the stock to continue to shrink, albeit slightly, over the upcoming decades. By leaving it slightly large minor shrinkage will not harm the rifle's appearance.

Photograph 2-99: Perspective-view: Receiver end, semi-fancy Fajen semi-inletted stock for Remington Pump. Minor adjustments here bring a close fit tot he receiver.

Photograph 2-102: Here we have almost finished fitting a Kick-Eez Sorbothane recoil pad. Note that the Sorbothane portion pad is slightly larger at the base, compared to the wood or the pad base. To correct this we will continue to sand to the stock contour, while using a very light touch.

Photograph 2-103: Finished Remington Pump. Note brand-new Fajen buttstock and fore-end. Not readily visible in this view is the Kick-Eez Sorbothane recoil pad. I choose to omit the fore-end and pistol-grip caps. I am a big fan of the simple beauty of wood. Fajen sold these pieces as semi-fancy but you should see the color and fire in this wood. Absolutely beautiful! Cheek piece form is understated and quite functional. By hollowing the buttstock I was able to keep the rifle's weight to within a few ounces of the original configuration, which is increasingly important to my father, whose rifle this is. Having already bagged dozens of elk with this rifle he is now set to kill his next bull with a more beautiful and better-fitting rifle.

Photograph 2-104: Close-up view, Fajen semi-fancy black walnut stock for Remington Pump. Note the fire evident in this grain. This is a beautiful piece of wood and the folks at Fajen showed characteristic care in choosing and cutting this stock — the pretty wood is located in the cheek piece while the less colorful and fancy grain is in the receiver end of the stock, where the wood should be as strong as possible.

Section 3:
The Trouble With Receivers, *Part I*

Receivers can suffer several accuracy deterring problems and other deficits that can reduce the shootability of the gun. On the typical bolt action rifle, the bolt can misalign with the rails in the receiver and therefore close and lock on the cartridge with only one side supporting the case head. This is generally a gunsmith repair item. Another common problem is failure of the locking lugs to fully contact one or more of the bolt lug recesses in the receiver; this leads to asymmetric bolt and receiver reaction to the process of firing a cartridge and a resultant loss of accuracy. Unless this asymmetry is unusually severe, the tinker can easily repair this problem in the home workshop.

Also, factory feed ramp and magazine assemblies sometimes mismatch or do not fit properly. This can lead to difficult bolt cycling, hard magazine loading, rough cartridge chambering and other problems. Often you can correct these problems with a bit of careful filing, grinding, sanding and polishing.

A final common problem is the existence of burs along the guide rails, which can lead to difficult bolt manipulation. You can easily lap away any such burs, as described later in this sub-section.

The Remington Pump Ejection Port:

The Remington pump-action rifle shares some of the aforementioned potential problems and has an additional possible problem; the ejection port is sometimes shorter than the longest useable cartridge, a cartridge that will otherwise function normally through the magazine and action! I will address this Remington-Pump-specific problem first. See Photograph # 3-1.

In the '06 family chamberings, loaded cartridges exceeding SAAMI specified length are often perfectly safe and usable in the Remington Pump. However, sometimes those loads can lead to ejection problems when the shooter attempts to remove an unfired cartridge from the chamber. The bullet tip can hit on the front radius of the ejection port, jamming the gun.

Generally, the tinker can solve this problem by carefully removing material at the front of the ejection port. A Dremel tool equipped with a small (1/4") sanding drum is perhaps the best tool for this job. You can easily ascertain the correct angle at which to hold the sanding drum. Observe the path that the bullet nose on a dummy cartridge sweeps as you slowly pull the pump handle back, allowing the dummy to eject from the chamber. Pull the pump handle only far enough to allow the bullet tip to hang in the ejection port. Note the angle at which the cartridge is sitting in the chamber.

In the ejection port modification step you should hold the Dremel tool so that its shaft is perpendicular to the cartridge centerline

Photograph 3-1: On Remington's pump-action rifle it is sometimes possible to use ammunition handloaded to exceed SAAMI length. In certain instances unfired cartridges of such ammunition might not eject normally. See text and associated photographs and captions for an explanation of how to mitigate this limitation.

assumed by the cartridge at the instant the bullet tip just clears the rifle's ejection port. See Photograph # 3-2.

To determine if this modification is necessary, assemble an over length dummy cartridge, one that just fits inside the clip. Carefully chamber that dummy cartridge. Then slowly open the action until the pump handle stops. If the dummy round does not eject, observe where the bullet tip is hitting at the front of the ejection port — you should remove material at this location and adjacent to it, as necessary. Simply put, you should grind away any offending portion of the front of the ejection port and at the rear of the locking lug recess, but only remove material located inside the ejection port and which prevents the bullet tip from passing when the action is fully open.

It should not be necessary, and is certainly not conducive to the gun's appearance, to remove any material at the exterior of the ejection port. Equally, be careful not to weaken the bolt lug recesses located above and below the ejection port you are reshaping. See Photograph # 3-3.

Removal of the clip facilitates manipulation of the dummy cartridge. By removing the clip and reaching up into the action from the magazine-well opening, you can push the case and bolt back far enough to facilitate removal of the (slightly) too-long cartridge through the ejection port.

Having ascertained where the bullet tip is hitting, carefully grind the interior of the ejection port slightly deeper, following the aforementioned angle. Avoid removal of excessive material, especially since this could weaken the bolt locking boss on the ejection port side of the barrel extension. If you hold the Dremel tool at the proper angle and do not grind too deeply, all the necessary grinding will occur inside the ejection port. Therefore, this work will not detract from the gun's appearance. See Photograph # 3-4.

Grind a little, then recheck the cartridge for ejection. If it clears the action when you open the bolt slowly and fully to the rear by pump-handle

Photograph 3-3: Remington Model-7600 pump-action rifle barrel extension, ejection port relief. Close-up-view showing cut to new angle, location and polishing. See text. A Dremel tool with a small stone is useful for making the initial cut. A jeweler's rouge impregnated felt tip adds the high level of polish shown here. Polishing limits bullet tip drag during ejection of (unfired) cartridges. One can often move this port slightly forward while slightly changing its angle. These changes can facilitate use of slightly longer handloads.

Photograph 3-2: Dremel tool equipped with a jeweler's rouge-impregnated felt tip, used here to polish the ejection port channel at front of a Remington pump-action rifle ejection port. One can slightly lengthen the inside of this port and channel without disturbing the gun's external appearance or weakening the action. Such a modification can allow ejection of slightly longer cartridges, compared to factory configuration.

Section 3: The Trouble With Receivers, Part I

manipulation, you have finished the job. However, you should polish and reblue the affected surfaces. See Photograph # 3-5.

Feed Ramp Work:

Though discussed elsewhere, this important subject deserves considerable attention. When working on a clip, or box magazine, fed action, you should look at polishing the feed ramp that leads from the clip to the chamber. Again, a Dremel tool fitted with a medium or small diameter sanding drum is an ideal tool. Here you should also ensure that the lower end of the ramp extends below the top of any magazine housing so that the bullet tip pushes against a properly shaped and smoothed ramp as the bolt pushes the top cartridge forward and out of the magazine. See Photograph # 3-6.

Load several dummy cartridges in the magazine and slowly manipulate the bolt, observe where the bullet tips impinge on the feed ramp and how the cartridges strip out of the magazine. Repeat this study using dummy cartridges fitted

Photograph 3-5: Remington pump-action rifle ejection port, close-up-view at front of receiver. While we have modified this rifle to properly eject cartridges loaded to the full length the magazine will accept (about 0.050" longer than stock ejection capability) the exterior of this rifle is unaltered. Appearance matters! See text and associated photograph captions for a complete discussion.

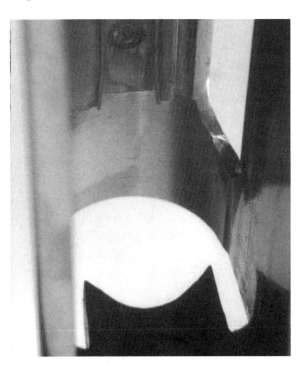

Photograph 3-4: View through bottom of receiver on stripped Remington Model-7600 pump-action rifle. Note ejection port at bottom of photograph. At the front center of this port is a small radiused area on the inside of the receiver. This radius should match the angle of the ejection port cut in the barrel extension, see previous photograph. One should not cut this radius deep enough to alter the outside contour of the ejection port. See text and associated photographs.

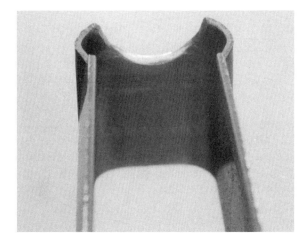

Photograph 3-6: View of top front of Remington Model-700 bolt-action magazine well. Note radiused and polished channel at front center. We contoured this to exactly match the receiver's feed ramp. See associated photographs and captions. If one cuts this face too low bullet tips could, theoretically, jam against the flat portion of the receiver, below the ramp (however magazine design limits that potentiality). Conversely, if one does not cut this area low enough, the bolt will force cartridges out of the magazine at an unnecessarily steep angle. A Dremel tool with a sanding drum and then a jeweler's rouge-impregnated felt wheel are the tools for this job.

with bullets of any type you might use in that gun — just because a round nose bullet will feed and function smoothly does not mean a spitzer bullet will! See Photograph # 3-7.

Polish away any burs, high spots of edges that any bullet catches on and adjust the angle of the ramp as much as is feasible to ensure smooth cartridge feeding with the various types of ammunition. However, be careful not to remove significant material if that work might reduce the strength of the lock-up in the action. Specifically, avoid shortening the locking lug under the barrel at the level of the perimeter of the locking lug cut — shortening the inside edge of the lug harms nothing as long as any portion of that edge remains at full height, see diagram. See Photograph # 3-8.

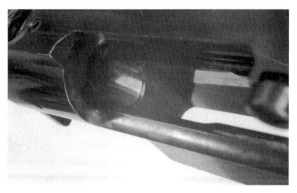

Photograph 3-7: This view shows several features of a modified feed ramp in a left-hand Remington Model-700 bolt-action rifle. Contour at top front of magazine box matches action feed ramp in both height and slope. We have polished both surfaces to a high level. We first sanded out the rough machine marks, then buffed out the sanding marks. A Dremel tool with a sanding drum and then a felt tip impregnated with jeweler's rouge works well for these jobs. Difference in cartridge feeding effort is nothing less than startling.

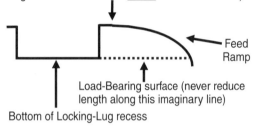

Generally, for safety sake, minimize recontouring in this area. If you are certain that the rifle needs recontouring here, I strongly advise consulting a gunsmith.

Locking Lug Geometry:

Locking lug engagement is another area where it is a simple matter to remedy typical misalignments. Use caution to avoid removing any more material than is necessary to achieve about ninety-five percent (95%) contact on all load-bearing lug surfaces. Also note, this process increases headspace and that can jeopardize the shooter's safety. If in doubt, such as all instances where one lug (or one or more lugs on multiple lug systems) completely fails to contact its recess, consider purchasing a "No-Go" gauge, available from Forster, to ensure that you do not increase the headspace to an unsafe level. If lapping the lugs increases the headspace until the bolt will almost close on the No-Go gauge without using undue force (no one should ever force a bolt closed on any headspace measuring gauge) stop where you are and consider the situ-

Photograph 3-8: Rear-view of magazine well from Remington Model-700 bolt-action rifle. Note soldered area rear bottom of slot joining the two sides. Also note that the slot is not of uniform width, top to bottom. I installed this piece between the receiver and the floor plate (with the stock removed). I then spread the open end until the top snugly fit the receiver-well and the bottom snugly fit the floor plate-well. I then soldered a brass washer over the outside of the magazine-well as shown here. This rigidified the entire assembly. It prevents the magazine-well from shifting position during use.

Section 3: The Trouble With Receivers, Part I

ation. If your lapping operation up to that point has not adequately seated the locking lugs, it is time to consider the services of a professional gunsmith.

A gunsmith can set the barrel back one thread, then rechamber and properly headspace the rifle. Note however, the discussion of lapping the barrel-to-receiver shoulder. Often this operation can shorten headspace by several thousandths of an inch. The dedicated tinker can combine these desirable alterations — the first operation increasing headspace, the second operation decreasing headspace — and end up with zero net change in headspace! See Photograph # 3-9.

Never do anything that might compromise the gun's headspace. As noted in the sub-section on barrel work, in the case of a Savage Bolt-Action rifle that lacks any barrel-mounted sights, you can adjust headspace using only a Forster "GO" gauge. This is about the only exception to this limitation. On almost any other action it is a considerable job to reduce headspace. However, on other bolt guns lacking barrel-mounted sights you can pull the barrel, as noted in the barrel sub-section, remove a few thousandths of an inch of material from the front of the receiver and remount the barrel by turning it back into the receiver further than it had originally been installed. The only harm will be a misalignment of the barrel writing.

Photograph 3-9: Refinished bolt after lapping to remove all high spots from the perimeter and bring almost the entire working surface of the locking lugs into contact with the receiver recesses. Here we show the bolt after rebluing with Brownells' Oxpho-Blue. We believe it is good practice to reblue all reworked areas of any (blued steel) gun before reassembly. Cold bluing minimizes corrosion potential. It also creates a tell-tale that will disclose any undue wear zones that can result from improper functioning or contouring.

Typically, the difference between the Go and the No-Go gauges is six-thousandths of an inch (0.006"). If the bolt locking lugs are almost fully lapped in and the bolt will close on the No-Go gauge, you can file off or lap away six-thousandths of an inch (0.006") of the front of the receiver and calculate the amount the barrel will have to be turned past where it had been to accommodate that six-thousandths of an inch (0.006") extra travel — on a one-inch in twenty-turns (1 in 20) thread that would amount to about one-eighth of one turn of the barrel. Tighten the barrel appropriately. Then lap the lugs just a tad more to ensure adequate headspace.

The problem with this approach, at least if you choose to use a file, is that it requires exquisite attention to detail and great care in the execution of the job to ensure that the front of the receiver remains square to the axis of the barrel threads — lapping is better but could take quite a spell. However, as noted in the sub-section on barrels, you can do this only on guns lacking barrel mounted hardware or extractor recesses. This is the only home-remedy recourse for guns suffering particularly bad locking lug engagement or excessive headspace. I must reiterate this critical point: this method will only work in guns lacking barrel-mounted sights or any other barrel-mounted fixtures.

Generally things are better. A bit of locking lug lapping will only increase headspace a few thousandths of an inch and will result in nearly full simultaneous contact of all locking lugs. Further, as noted, if you lapped the barrel-to-receiver shoulders and the barrel threads, as described in the barrel sub-section, you likely decreased headspace a similar amount in that operation. The point is, these two operations are (usually) complementary regarding resulting headspace alteration.

An easy way to accomplish lug lapping on bolt-action rifles using a spring-loaded ejection plunger (like the Remington) is to chamber a fully lubricated, once-fired case that was fired in that gun (a full length resized case will work but not nearly as well) in the stripped action that has been pulled from the stock and mounted solidly in a padded work vise. Apply silicon carbide lapping compound to the rear surfaces of the locking lugs. (Brownells offers a product dedicated to this task.) Carefully close the bolt, while pushing it forward with sufficient force to fully compress the ejection spring — you want the case head to push flush to the bolt face. Release the forward pressure on the bolt. Rotate the bolt handle, about forty-five degrees (45°) toward the unlocked position, then fully relock the bolt. Repeat this forty-five degree rotation process, as necessary to lap the high spots from the locking lugs. Below I give a detailed account of the process.

Lubricate the fired case over the shoulder, body, neck and head region with high-lubricity gun grease. The idea is to keep the case free in the chamber and in the bolt face. Insert this lubricated case in the chamber with the bolt removed. Strip the cocking assembly, striker and striker spring from the bolt. (Remington bolt disassembly tools are offered by Sinclair, and others.)

Apply a dab of 400 grit lapping compound to the center of the rear surface of each locking lug. Then carefully insert the bolt in a manner to avoid contamination of any other area with the lapping compound. Push the stripped bolt fully forward until it engages the chambered case. Then, while still pushing forward with sufficient force to compress the ejection spring and take up any available headspace on the chambered case, rotate the bolt into the locked position.

Finally, release the forward pressure on the bolt. Then slowly rotate the bolt from the fully locked position, about forty-five degree (45°) toward the unlocked position, then back to the locked position. Repeat this process perhaps twenty (20) times.

Press forward on the bolt to compress the ejector spring. While pressing forward, rotate the bolt to unlock it. Slowly remove the bolt, stopping to retrieve the case before the ejector pushes it free of the gun.

Clean all surfaces thoroughly and ensure that no lapping compound remains in the action or on the bolt — alcohol and a retired tooth brush work well in cleaning the lapping agent from the action recesses. Reassemble the striker into the bolt. Then paint the rear surfaces of the locking lugs on the bolt with a permanent marker (black is best). Reinstall the empty case and insert and lock the bolt, as before, applying sufficient force to fully compress the ejection and striker springs (the gun should be cocked). Relax the forward pressure. Slowly rotate the bolt to the unlocked position. Again, fully remove the bolt from the rifle, pausing to retrieve the empty case.

Observe the pattern on the permanent marker paint on the back surface of the locking lugs. If most of both surfaces show even scratching and removal of the permanent marker ink, lapping has sufficiently mated the lugs to the lug recesses in the receiver. If not (typically one lug will not show significant contact on the marker paint) repeat the above process and keep checking until contact is even and sufficient — always noting the aforementioned possibility of increasing headspace to an unsafe degree.

A similar procedure is possible in the Remington Pump. Here, you must use the action as normally assembled but there is no effective difference except that the early Pumps (Model-760 designation) have myriad locking lugs, while later models have only four.

On bolt action rifles lacking a spring-loaded ejection plunger you must use another method to apply the necessary rearward force to the bolt to provide the lapping action between the rear surface of the bolt lugs and the front face of the receiver locking recesses. One successful method is to simply pull back on the bolt handle. A better method involves the creation of a spring-loaded dummy cartridge. See Photograph # 3-10.

Photograph 3-10: This modified and spring-loaded cartridge casing is useful for lapping action-locking lugs. For use in a gun with a spring-loaded ejector one will achieve best results by removing the ejector assembly before proceeding, see text on ejector plunger removal. This is a resized .280 Remington case with the neck and about 0.050" of the case body removed. This unit will work for a .25-06 Remington, .270 Winchester, .280 Remington, .30-06 Springfield, .35 Whelen or other '06-based wildcat-chambered rifles. Here we used two stiff springs with a connecting dowel — because those are what we had on hand. Hot glue in the case ends retains these springs. Chambering this unit and closing the bolt produces constant bolt thrust. This thrust facilitates lug lapping in the following procedure: Clean and lubricate chamber and bolt face.

Insert this unit into the action in such a manner as to ensure it is locked under the extractor. Apply a dab of 240 grit (finer for finishing) lapping compound to rear surfaces of each locking lug. While applying sufficient pressure to fully push the bolt forward, close and lock the action. Release forward pressure and repeatedly partially cycle the action, sufficiently to rotate the bolt just less than enough to unlock the lugs. After, perhaps, fifty of these partial cycles unlock action, open the bolt and remove this device. Clean all traces of lapping compound from receiver and bolt.

The best method for any action is to use the special spring-loaded tool made for the job and offered by Brownells. Unfortunately, this tool requires pulling the barrel.

This tool screws into the receiver, in place of the barrel. The gunsmith adjusts this device to apply heavy spring pressure to the entire bolt face. This tool keeps the bolt square and true in the receiver while applying sufficient pressure to expedite the lapping operation. See Photograph #s 3-11/12.

A spring-loaded two-piece homemade tool does a splendid job, and without disassembly of the barrel from the action. As an example, consider a .30-06 chambered rifle. To make a tool to lap the lugs, cut a .30-06 case (sideways) into two pieces. Make the cut somewhere near the middle of the case body; use a hacksaw and make a square cut. Then locate a stiff compression spring that will fit inside the case. Cut this spring long enough to hold the two ends of the case apart, perhaps one-half inch (1/2"). A reasonable spring will exert about twenty pounds of force when compressed until the ends of the case touch at the cut line.

Hot glue the spring into the case ends. This results in a homemade tool that will apply constant centered spring force to the bolt when you chamber it and close the action. This tool greatly facilitates lapping of the working surfaces of the locking lugs. Proceed just as with the Remington-style action except that here it might be necessary to remove the extractor before proceeding. Also note, with this tool you can do a superior job of lug lapping, compared to using the spring-loaded ejector; consider removing the spring-loaded ejector for this job, refer to the following sub-section. See Photograph #s 3-13/14.

Ejector Spring Plunger:

On actions featuring a spring-loaded ejection plunger, such as most Remington centerfire guns of modern manufacture, it is sometimes beneficial to reduce the spring pressure on the

Photograph 3-12: Brownells' 600 grit abrasive (lapping) compound is an ideal product for lug lapping, although one can begin this process with 240 grit. Here we have fitted a Remington Model-700 receiver with Brownells' spring-loaded lapping aid (it screws into the barrel receiver threads).

To lap the lugs, we clamp the receiver in a padded vise; apply lapping agent to the rear surface of the bolt's locking lugs and over the perimeter of the front of the bolt; we insert the bolt into the receiver using sufficient force to compress the spring tool enough to allow the locking lugs to clear the receiver recesses (this keeps the lapping agent in place). We release the forward pressure and work the bolt handle up and down about 45°, fifty times (20 times or less if we are using a coarser grit). We will then remove the bolt, clean everything up and examine the rear of the locking lugs. Using a "GO" gauge and cellophane tape we will verify the assembled rifle's headspace. Assuming this initial lapping operation has not increased headspace excessively, we repeat this action, as necessary, until we have fully lapped the entire working surface of both lugs and both lug recesses. See text and associated photograph captions for a complete discussion.

Photograph 3-11: Brownells' lug lapping tool. Use requires separation of barrel from receiver. Interchangeable threaded sleeves are available for most common actions. Small plunger at right is spring-loaded. One screws this device into the receiver, adjusts the bushing so that the spring-loaded plunger pushes against the bolt, then locks the set screw locating this sleeve. Lug lapping then involves only application of a bit of 240 grit lapping agent (finer for finishing) and working of the bolt between fully locked and partially locked, about 45° rotation. Brownells provides more detailed instructions with this unit.

Photograph 3-13

Photograph 3-14

Photographs 3-13/14: This was a real eye opener! I have fired this gun many hundreds of times. I have cycled the action several thousand times. Photograph 3-13 clearly shows failure of this lug to make 100% contact with the corresponding receiver recess. The opposite lug was about 60% mated. This failure to evenly mate and touch across most of the engaging surface is one cause of occasional fliers. It also limits a gun's intrinsic accuracy. In spite of this poor lug engagement precision, this rifle was a good shooter.

Photograph 3-14: The same lug after lapping. Note that we have lapped almost 100% of the rear face of the locking lug. Total material removal was less than 0.001" on each of two surfaces — bolt lug and receiver recesses. Therefore, we increased headspace just less than 0.002". Later work, to the barrel and receiver mating shoulder, allowed the barrel to move back about 0.004". Therefore we decreased total headspace about 0.002". Headspace is a critical issue in any such work. See text for a discussion of this important safety topic. One expects lug lapping to improve intrinsic accuracy. Subsequent testing substantiated our anticipation.

ejector plunger. Older guns with this feature also sometimes have a rounded end on the ejector plunger. It might also be useful to reshape the end of this plunger to a flatter profile. See Photograph # 3-15.

The first step in this operation is to remove the bolt assembly from the gun. Then disassemble the bolt assembly. Finally, disassemble the plunger from the bolt. I have explained bolt removal and disassembly on Remington's Pump-Action Rifle in the sub-section on barrel work. I have described disassembly of Remington's Model-700 and similar bolts in the associated photographs and text. The special Sinclair (or similar) tool is not strictly necessary but it is most helpful.

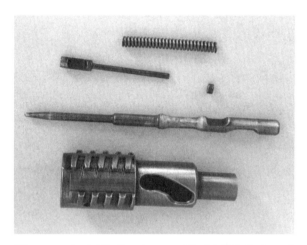

Photograph 3-15: Remington Model-760 bolt and associated parts. Left-to-right: Bolt body —here the multiple locking lugs and one of the camming slots are clearly evident; modified firing pin (lightened); modified ejector rod (flattened front end and tuned length); spacer to limit ejector pin's rearward travel; modified ejector spring (shortened to reduce ejection force.

Note turned down area at middle of the firing pin and cut-out area near rear and opposite factory pin slot. These modifications do not weaken this pin or hinder its functioning. Nevertheless, this work significantly reduces the pin's weight (>10%). This reduces the firing mechanism's lock-time and otherwise improves the gun's accuracy potential. Note location and geometry of these weight-reduction measures. Both features are important to maximizing results. Reduced area in front of factory pin slot must leave a full-diameter ring both at front and rear of turned-down area. Rear slot must leave a full-diameter portion (of the length shown) at rear of firing pin. This cut must be opposite pin slot and must not extend forward past rear of pin slot. Also this slot should not extend deeper than about 40% of the firing pin's diameter.

Section 3: The Trouble With Receivers, Part I

Removing the plunger requires removal of a cross pin. Fix the bolt in a padded vise so you have access to the cross pin that retains this plunger. This pin's location is about one-third of an inch (1/3") from the front of the bolt, toward one side. This pin is about fifty-thousandths of an inch (somewhat under 1/16") in diameter. Also note, on the Remington, at least, this retaining pin is splined on one end. Design suggests removing the pin by driving out of the splined side first. Driving a fifty-thousandths inch diameter (0.050") pin punch in from the correct side will easily dislodge the retaining pin. If the pin does not move with application of light taps from an 8-ounce hammer, most likely, you are trying to drive it the wrong way — try the other side. Continue to tap the punch lightly to dislodge the pin slowly. As the pin comes free, the plunger spring will push the plunger against the punch. The punch will retain the plunger.

Press lightly on the plunger and pull the punch free. You can then remove both plunger and plunger spring. On Remington Rifles, the ejector pin has a shank that runs almost full length down the center of the coil spring that actuates the ejector plunger.

After you have removed this spring, clean the hole thoroughly using an aerosol degreasing agent. Attach a tube spout and insert the tube fully into the ejector plunger hole. Be careful to avoid getting the spray back in your face. A short blast of the aerosol agent will clean this hole right down to the shine!

If the plunger is rounded on the big (working) end, flatten this surface first. Chuck the little end of the plunger in a hand drill. With both the drill and the bench grinder running, you can use a fine corundum wheel to get this job done quite nicely. Orient the drill so that the shank of the plunger is square (normal) to the flat side of the grinding wheel. Slowly advance the ejector pin against the flat side of the corundum wheel until the grinding action has flattened the end of the pin almost to its entire diameter. It is equally easy to polish the ground end. You can accomplish this with a sharpening stone applied to the end of the pin while the hand drill turns the piece. See Photograph # 3-16.

The next step is shortening of the ejector plunger spring. Proceed with caution here. We are trying to achieve a compromise between reliable ejection and minimum disturbance of the cartridge during chambering, along with reduced stress in the action resulting from the ejector spring pushing the chambered cartridge crooked in the chamber.

Typically, you can remove about two complete coils from this spring without suffering any loss of ejection certitude. If you can push the plunger almost flush against the bolt face using only the end of a finger and without suffering undue distress in the process, the spring is probably light enough. If you really want to tinker here, you can install a longer softer spring (lighter spring rate) and compress it more to achieve a more constant ejection force. Such springs are available through Brownells Incorporated. In this manner, you can achieve the same overall ejection authority, albeit with somewhat less action stressing. Certainly a softer, more compressed, spring is easier to fine tune. Experimenting will soon demonstrate the limitations of this approach. For myself, I want the ejector spring slightly stiffer on a hunting rifle, compared to a varmint or target rifle. On a bench rest rifle I would entirely dispense with the ejector spring. See Photograph # 3-17.

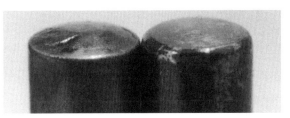

Photograph 3-16: Pictured are stock and modified Remington ejector plunger. I prefer to reduce the radius at the tip to a flat area with only a small rounded perimeter. One can easily accomplish this by chucking the ejector pin in a power drill and grinding the tip flat using the side of a bench grinder while both drill and grinder are running. (Be careful to avoid overheating the pin, if you cannot touch it without burning yourself you are getting it too hot!) A final polish with an appropriate grit corundum paper (400 or finer) while the pin is still in the running drill finishes this job.

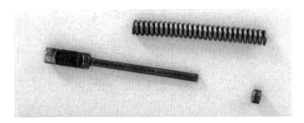

Photograph 3-17: Modified Remington ejector plunger, ejector spring and added plunger depth limiting button. These details can make a big difference in a gun's accuracy and functioning.

Section 4: The Trouble With Triggers, *Part I*

As anyone who has handled <u>typical</u> production rifles of recent manufacture can attest, trigger pull has continued on a downhill trajectory for many decades, (excepting the custom grade rifles commonly available) the last common over-the-counter factory rifles with truly good trigger pulls might very well have been produced before World War II! Things are thoroughly pitiful of late. At least one major manufacturer is running so scared — and, perhaps, rightly so — of unreasonable litigation that they now literally weld the trigger assembly shut in hopes of limiting tampering! Those who find they have such a rifle and are not happy with the atrocious factory trigger pull, might find their best course is to trade rifles. What a shame.

Trigger Adjustments:

However, for those actions designed to allow trigger adjustment, the process is rather simple. Referring to the instructions that came with the rifle (and which are available from the manufacturer for no fee) determine which of the adjustable screws does which job. Typically, you should never adjust sear engagement unless you are absolutely certain that such engagement is excessive. However, you can typically safely reduce trigger spring pressure somewhat and you can install a somewhat softer trigger spring with more compression; this facilitates more precise tuning.

Adjustments often allow limitation of trigger over-travel. However, actual utility of this measure seems questionable and, if overdone, it can render the trigger unreliable. Further, some of the best shooters in the world deliberately <u>add</u> over-travel to a quality trigger.

Referring to the latter point, once the trigger breaks free of the sear it seems unwise to have it hit any rigid stop! A better result is for the trigger to continue freely toward the rear, at least until the bullet clears the bore. For those who yank the trigger this will do little good, since they will likely pull the trigger fast enough to slam it against the inevitable stop long before the bullet exits the rifle. However, for those who properly squeeze a well-tuned trigger this will not be the case. When design or adjustment provides sufficient over-travel, the trigger will break free and continue to slowly move rearward without disrupting the rifle in any significant way. However the choice on over travel is yours.

Should you prefer to limit over-travel, as noted above, do not limit it too critically. That can lead to a sear that drags on the striker, disrupting consistent function; or occasionally fails to release, which can lead to an unintentional discharge — the shooter pulls the trigger and nothing happens, then as he starts to lift the bolt handle or checks the safety to see if it was released . . . KA-BOOM, the gun fires!

I speak from experience here — it was not my gun but a high dollar custom rifle that had not been properly fitted. I squeezed the trigger and nothing happened. I then reached up and touched the safety to verify that it was off . . . KA-BOOM. Happened twice. I thereafter dispensed with ever touching the safety and did not close the bolt until I was ready to shoot.

In my opinion, you should minimize trigger return spring pressure. I define "minimized" as that amount of spring pressure that will reliably return the trigger, ensure that the trigger fully engages the sear and, most importantly, prevent the trigger from disengaging under the stresses of "normal" handling — such as dropping the gun! Obviously, for this latter reason, we have to compromise. Typically, you can set factory triggers to about a 5 pound let-off with consistency and an acceptable margin of safety. You can often set competition after-market replacement trigger assemblies to about 2 pounds let-off.

Various single-set and double-set triggers are also available. You can often adjust the set on set triggers light enough that a strong breeze or a wayward thought can do the job! Finally, several manufacturers offer match-grade triggers that allow adjustment to two-ounces or less.

Though it was not equipped with a set trigger, a revolver I once owned, and abused through use as a quick-draw pistol, finally got to the point that I could, quite literally, blow on the hammer hard enough to drop it from the cocked position — that was something to see. Obviously before the trigger reached that unsafe condition I had long-since retired the gun for any use except informal target shooting.

For many of the traditional applications, these more sensitive triggers make little sense for the average shooter, although a set trigger offering a choice between a more normal trigger pull and a very precise let-off can have its place in a hunting rifle that you also use for varmint or target shooting. Of course, for a specialized varmint or target rifle such a trigger is a natural. However, note the lengthy discussion of this subject in *Part II*.

Trigger pull gauges are available from Brownells Incorporated. You can fashion a functional unit from fishing line, a bent nail and a collection of lead weights. See drawing. Unload the gun and lock it in a vise with the barrel pointing up vertically. Place the bent nail, centered over the trigger, with a length of fishing line attached on either side. Add weights until the trigger releases.

Repeat this test several times to verify consistency. The total weight needed to release the trigger is a sufficiently accurate measure of trigger pull for most purposes. If it is less than 5 pounds on a factory trigger, 2 pounds on a standard after-market trigger, you might be pushing the issue. Also, if repeated tests produce significantly different results, there is either something wrong with the trigger mechanism (dirt or other debris fouling it?) or you are pushing the unit past its ability to function properly — you are trying to set a too-light trigger let-off. Do not do this!

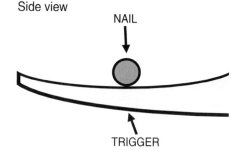

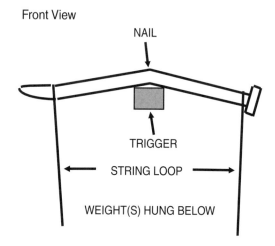

Sear and Hook Polishing:

The next consideration is the quality of the contact surface of the sear and the trigger. If either or both of these surfaces are rough, as is all too commonly the situation, trigger let off will not be smooth or consistent. You can easily correct this problem with a bit of judicious stoning using an adequately fine stone of the proper shape. However, you must use extreme caution here. Specifically, unless you have proof that such a modification is necessary, do not change the geometry of the engaging surfaces of either the sear or the trigger. Further, understand that the geometry of sear engagement is the only thing standing between you and an unintentional discharge of the rifle. If you are not absolutely, positively certain about what you are doing, do not start; this is a job better left to your trusted gunsmith. I cannot over stress this fact. Even if you do have proof that such a modification is necessary, proceed with utmost caution. For this work, a bright, diffuse light and a quality loupe (the Opti-Visor attached with the Opti-Loupe is ideal) are most helpful. If you are the least bit uncomfortable with this operation, please, consult expert advice and assistance.

Section 4: The Trouble With Triggers, Part I

Photograph 4-1

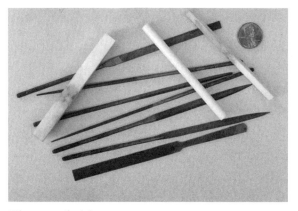

Photograph 4-2

Photographs 4-1/2: Machinist files and fine ceramic stones are most valuable for home gunsmithing. These items, and a plethora of other useful gunsmithing tools, are available from Brownells. Before using these delicate tools, consider investing in a good clamping fixture and a quality loupe. Also, never perform any filing or stoning on any action part unless you fully understand the intended design function of that part and how your modifications will affect that function. Such admonition is particularly pertinent regarding trigger and safety mechanisms. See text and associated photographs.

Assuming you can see the surfaces and that you have identified the roughness that is causing a rough trigger let off, proceed to stone (using only a Hard Arkansas stone of the proper shape) the contact areas of both the sear and the sear hook, watching for any indication that material removal is progressing unevenly. Be absolutely certain that you stone all portions of both surfaces equally. Also note that it is not necessary to remove all the roughness. You only have to remove the tops of the rough spots to completely repair the trigger pull and obtain a smooth let off, as desired. Unless there is a proven problem with the sear or sear catch angle (see the above sub-section and admonitions regarding changing these areas) the <u>only</u> modification the home tinker should make is to polish off any high rough spots from both surfaces — <u>do not change any angles!</u> See Photograph #s 4-1/2.

Trigger Replacement:

Replacement of a trigger with an after-market unit, where available, is typically a very simple matter. For example, on the Remington Model-700 the process for installing the excellent Timney trigger is as described in the following paragraphs. See photograph # 4-3.

Photograph 4-3: Factory trigger in left-hand Remington Model-700 bolt-action rifle. Note attached safety mechanism. Timney, and other replacement triggers, reuse these stock parts. The "C" clip easily slides off the post, facilitating removal of these pieces. Use caution here: The assembled safety lever retains a small detent ball bearing. One can easily lose this piece. See text.

Remove the action from the stock, separate the magazine assembly and remove the bolt. Lock the action upside down in a padded vise and clamp it securely. Remove the safety lever retaining bar from the side of the trigger housing, retained with a "C" clip. Remove the associated lever, pin, washers and detent ball — be careful not to lose anything! Drive the retaining pins, at the front and rear of the top of the factory trigger assembly, out the side opposite the bolt retaining lever. This will free the trigger from the action. Set the old trigger assembly aside. See Photograph #s 4-4/5.

Insert the replacement trigger mechanism into the slot from which you removed the factory trigger. Align the dummy pins in the replacement trigger with the trigger pin holes in the receiver. Insert the front trigger pin in the front hole and lightly tap it through the receiver; this will drive the short dummy pin from the trigger assembly and attach the front of the trigger to the action. Align the rear dummy pin with the rear action trigger mounting hole and install the rear trigger mounting pin, which will drive the dummy pin through the receiver. Assemble the safety lever and other pieces from the old trigger assembly onto the new trigger assembly. The basic process is complete! See Photograph #s 4-4/6.

Photograph 4-5: Factory trigger in left-hand Remington Model-700 bolt-action rifle, sans safety mechanism. See associated photograph showing safety in place. Note detent location where steel ball rests, locating safety lever either in fully-on or fully-off position. See text.

Photograph 4-6: Standard model Timney replacement trigger for left-hand Remington Model-700 bolt-action rifle. One can easily access the adjusting screws. One can adjust trigger pull as lightly as 3-pounds with no problems. If one requires a lighter pull, we suggest installation of a competition trigger, as available from Shilen. That unit allows a 2-ounce let-off. See associated photographs and text.

Photograph 4-4: Remington left-hand Model-700 bolt-action rifle safety and bolt-release mechanisms and associated paraphernalia. Disengagement of the pictured "C" clip from the pictured pin releases these six pieces. On the Remington, one must reuse these parts when installing an after-market trigger. See text.

Section 4: The Trouble With Triggers, Part I

Typically, you might need to do a bit of judicious trimming around the trigger to provide adequate clearance between the trigger and both the stock and trigger guard. However, this is a minor task and completely self-evident — if the trigger lever touches (or almost touches) any portion of either the stock or trigger guard assembly when you assemble the gun the trigger will not work properly or safely! Also watch for interference between either the safety lever or the bolt release actuating lever and the stock. Remove wood, as necessary, to eliminate any such interference. Refinish any area where you trimmed the wood. See Photograph #s 4-7/8/9.

Photograph 4-7: Timney replacement trigger for left-hand Remington Model-700 bolt-action rifle in place before installation of retaining-pins. Note shiny keeper pins, here visible through front and rear mounting holes. As one drives the assembly pins in, those pins drive these stub pins out; installation never compromises the trigger's assembly. One should insert the retaining pins in the side from which one drove those out (the safety-lever side). Install the pins in the same end-for-end orientation as the original installation; one end is often tapered, install that end first. Finally, one should install the rear pin first.

This basic procedure is applicable to most bolt-action rifles where an after-market trigger is available and all such triggers come with installation instructions (some of these instruction sheets are better than others). Unfortunately, after-market triggers are not available for all action types. Where no after-market trigger is available, you will have to modify the existing trigger, as possible and necessary, to achieve an acceptable trigger pull — refer to the above discussion. You can certainly lighten and smooth a two-stage military trigger pull to provide a perfectly serviceable let-off. Study the system, replace or shorten springs to lighten spring pressures where feasible and polish contact and bearing surfaces as necessary. See Photograph #s 4-10 through 4-14.

Remington Pump-Action Rifle Trigger Work:

Unfortunately, on the Remington pump there is no after-market replacement trigger assembly option. Further, there is precious little anyone can do to improve the stock trigger. Because the factory trigger is the major handicap these fine rifles suffer, I will, however, explore several possible minor improvements for that trigger system in some detail.

You can easily remove this trigger assembly from the action. First, remove the clip and cycle the action to ensure the chamber is empty. Leave the action cocked. With a sharp-pointed cartridge, or brass punch, drive the trigger assembly mounting pins, located above and to the front and rear of the trigger guard, out of the receiver. Push the action-lock release lever to release the locking bar. Slide the trigger assembly forward until you can pull it free, through the bottom of

Photograph 4-8: Timney replacement trigger for left-hand Remington Model-700 bolt-action rifle fully installed, view from bolt-release side.

Photograph 4-9: Timney replacement trigger for left-hand Remington Model-700 bolt-action rifle, fully installed, safety side-view.

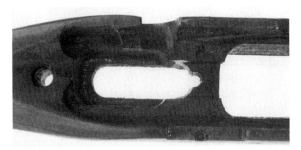

Photograph 4-10: Top-view, left-hand Remington Model-700 bolt action rifle stock. Note relief cuts for Timney trigger (at front of trigger hole) and Lyman receiver-mounted peep sight, bottom right center of photograph. These cuts will vary, depending upon the specific rifle. However, one should make these cuts as small as possible. This will limit degradation of the stock's strength and the rifle's appearance.

Photograph 4-13: Timney replacement trigger in left-hand Remington Model-700 bolt-action rifle. This view shows 0.010" feeler gauge inserted into ground-in clearance between floor plate assembly and trigger-lever on safety side. For safety sake, there must be a bit of side play in the trigger.

Photograph 4-11: Timney replacement trigger in left-hand Remington Model-700 bolt-action rifle. This view shows clearance problem at the safety side of trigger. There is interference between floor-plate assembly and trigger lever. One must correct this problem! For safety sake, the trigger must exhibit a bit of side play. Here it is advisable to remove material from the robust steel trigger rather than from the weak aluminum floor-plate. See text.

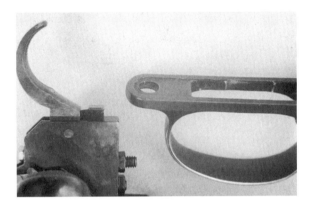

Photograph 4-14: Areas where one might remove material to provide trigger to floor-plate clearance on Remington Model-700 bolt-action rifle, left-hand version shown here. One can make a slight cut on the floor-plate. However, material removal should be no more than a few thousandths of an inch — only to remove any casting burs. One can safely thin the trigger lever, near the base, as necessary to achieve about 0.010" side clearance. If the stock binds with the trigger assembly, safety lever or bolt release lever, remove wood, as necessary to achieve clearance.

Photograph 4-12: Timney replacement trigger in left-hand Remington Model-700 bolt-action rifle. This view shows clearance ground into trigger-lever on safety side. This provides clearance between floor plate assembly and trigger-lever. For safety sake, there must be a bit of side play in the trigger. Here we have removed material from the robust steel trigger-lever rather than from the weak aluminum floor-plate.

Section 4: The Trouble With Triggers, Part I

the action. This latter activity requires a bit of manipulation but you can easily perfect the required technique.

First, just as with the typical bolt-action rifle, it is possible to somewhat reduce the force of the trigger return spring. However, unlike many bolt guns the only good way to do this is to replace the factory spring with a similar, albeit longer and lighter, spring. The uncompressed replacement spring should contain one or two more coil lengths, compared to the uncompressed factory spring. At the same time it should provide less pressure to the trigger — technically, such a spring has a lower spring-rate. Spring assortments are available from Brownells Incorporated. Many hardware stores also stock various diameter compressive coil springs of various spring rates. For the Remington Pump-Action Rifle, proper (critical) internal diameter for this spring is about one-hundred and fifty-five thousandths of an inch (a little larger than 1/8") and outside diameter cannot exceed about two hundred and twenty-five thousandths of an inch (about 7/32"), uncompressed length should be about three-quarters of an inch (3/4"). Look for a spring with about one-half the factory spring stiffness when uncompressed. See Photograph # 4-15.

This is easy to ascertain: place two of the test springs on a flat surface and hot glue a lightweight rigid plate (such as a machinist's scale) to the top end of those. Then hot glue attach the original spring on top of the rigid plate, centered over the two test springs. Place this assembly in a vise and slowly compress the springs. If the test springs begin to compress before the factory spring they are probably too weak. If they have compressed very little when the factory spring reaches full compression, they are probably unnecessarily stiff. If both the original and test springs begin to compress at about the same time, the test springs are probably about the correct stiffness. Here, for safety's sake a slightly too-stiff spring is a vastly superior compromise.

When you have identified a spring of the proper diameter and stiffness, cut it at least one full coil, preferably two full coils, longer than the factory spring; compressing a longer, lighter rate spring to the same overall length results in a more constant spring pressure as you continue to compress the spring. Therefore, when the shooter pulls the trigger the resistance will be more constant.

Install the replacement spring in the trigger assembly. This is just about as simple as removing the original spring; simply slide one end over the sear extension post and compress the other end past the trigger extension, then release it. A small slotted-bit screwdriver with the blade passed between the coils near the free end of the spring works very well for this installation.

The second area for possible improvement is trigger travel. Many older Pumps and some newer models have a great deal of excess play in the trigger. You can easily correct this by installation of a brass cylinder of the proper diameter and thickness around the trigger travel restricter bushing, which also acts as a carrier for the rear trigger assembly attachment pin. See Photograph # 4-16.

Photograph 4-15: This view shows trigger and sear-lever spring on Remington's Model-760 (and descendants) trigger mechanism. Replacement of this spring with a somewhat softer and longer unit can dramatically improve trigger pull. However, use caution here to avoid a too-soft trigger. The sear-lever this spring pushes against is the only thing separating you and an unintentional discharge whenever this rifle is cocked with a chambered cartridge.

Photograph 4-16: Trigger assembly rear mounting locator bushing and custom sleeve. This sleeve limits the trigger's pre-travel — movement before sear disengagement begins. We made this bushing by modifying (thinning) a .30 caliber case neck. Trigger assembly design limits both thickness and width of this bushing. See associated photograph and text.

You can easily fashion such a shim from a cartridge case neck. Those who happen to have an adjustable case neck turning tool can create a series of such shims of various thicknesses. Try progressively thicker bushings until the shim eliminates as much of the trigger creep as possible without preventing proper safety manipulation, which results when the shim is too thick. See Photograph # 4-17.

Proper inside diameter for the shim is about three-hundred and twelve thousandths of an inch (about 5/16"), correct width is one-quarter inch (1/4") and typical thickness is about six-thousandths of an inch (0.006"), or less. This might not seem to be much thickness. However, because of the geometry of these trigger mechanisms, such a shim installed to reduce the excess forward travel of the trigger will often dramatically improve the trigger's subjective feel.

You can make these shims from almost any .30 caliber case. Owing to the thin necks, .30-30 cases work well (.32-20 cases are even better). Outside neck turn to achieve the proper thickness, then run a three-hundred and eleven thousandths of an inch (0.311") diameter expander ball through the case neck. Finally, saw the neck off with a hacksaw; grind it to length; and debur the ground end. Make shims starting at about three-thousandths of an inch (0.003") wall thickness and incrementing, by about one-thousandth inch (0.001") thickness, up to about ten-thousandths of an inch (0.010"). See Photograph #s 4-18/19/20.

Photograph 4-17: Top-view of trigger rebound control pin with sleeve installed. See text. This sleeve limits trigger's forward travel to reduce trigger motion before sear disengagement begins. Proper articulation of the cross-bolt safety normally limits possible thickness of this sleeve — if this sleeve is too thick one cannot engage the safety! However, ensure that this sleeve does not reduce sear engagement. See text.

Photograph 4-19: RCBS case neck turning tool. In use. One can use such a tool to make a .30 caliber bushing for improving the trigger on Remington's pump-action rifle.

Photograph 4-18: Partially turned case neck. With a special case neck turning tool, as available from K&M Services, RCBS or many other sources, one can turn a case neck to any desired thickness although the brass will often fail when one attempts to turn it to less than about 0.005". See associated photographs, captions and text.

Photograph 4-20: Selection of turned case necks, demonstrating that one can easily produce various thickness bushings with these tools.

Section 4: The Trouble With Triggers, Part I

To install the shim, remove the trigger-stop bushing by pushing it out the left side of the assembly only far enough to allow the bushing to slip into the opening, then push the bushing back through the assembly. Begin with the thinnest shim and try the safety. If the safety manipulates normally, try the next thicker shim. Repeat this process until the safety does not set freely. Remove that shim and install the next thinner shim. Finally, verify that shim installation has not compromised sear engagement or safety functioning.

Geometry varies on these assemblies. Some units might allow a slight disengagement of the sear with the safety set in the "on" position. This certainly should not happen and I have never seen it. However, it could happen. In this instance, shimming could result in a reduction of sear engagement, while still allowing the safety to function. This condition, while in itself is intolerable, suggests a problem with the trigger assembly — return it to Remington's Customer Service Department for repair or replacement. In any case, sear engagement should be no less than twenty-five thousandths of an inch (0.025").

I do not recommend any other alteration to the trigger mechanism of these trigger assemblies unless there is something wrong with the unit! In this regard, another area where some Remington Pump-Action Rifles suffer is in the angle of sear engagement. One example of my experience had the sear and sear hook notches cut at such an angle that pulling the trigger visibly rotated the hammer toward the cocked direction. Movement as I manipulated the trigger amounted to about ten-thousandths of an inch (0.010") additional cocking at the big end of the hammer! Obviously this condition is not conducive to a good trigger pull. However, just as with bolt-action rifles, the gunsmith must use extreme caution in modifying any sear or sear hook. Those who do not have the proper tools, a good fixture to hold the trigger assembly, good lighting, a good loupe or other magnifying device and a complete understanding of what they are doing should do nothing!

If the sear engagement surfaces are rough, polish both with a properly shaped stone. I have described the correct basic procedure in the above discussion of bolt-action triggers. However, here you can easily verify a properly contoured sear and trigger geometry.

Mount the trigger assembly in a vise so that you have free access to both trigger and hammer. Place the safety in the off position and place the pad of a finger in front of the hammer (it will hit with sufficient force to injure your fingernail so use caution in this test). Very slowly squeeze the trigger by grasping the rear of the trigger guard and the trigger with the thumb and trigger finger of the other hand. If you do this properly, you should be able to observe the response at the top of the rotating hammer as you slowly move the trigger, until it reaches the point where the sear releases.

If pulling the trigger appreciably rotates the hammer toward the cocked position, sear geometry is less than ideal; ideally the hammer should cock further as the sear disengages but only ever so slightly — perhaps less than one thousandth of one-inch. For this test a dial indicator set up against the back of the hammer is most valuable. Also, the hammer should not uncock at all until the sear does let go. For precise measurement of this characteristic, use a screw clamp to slowly push the trigger.

If the hammer does rotate back noticeably (toward the cocked position) you should consider stoning the sear surface slightly flatter in relation to the hook. See diagram.

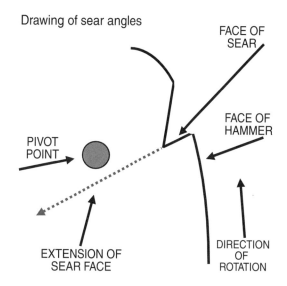

Drawing of sear angles

For safety, design angle of the sear face must tend to pull the sear hook deeper into the sear notch in response to hammer spring tension, as opposed to pushing it off the sear face. The latter condition would create a situation where you were relying upon trigger spring tension to keep the sear engaged, not a safe practice. Geometry is critically important here. On a rotating hammer systems an improperly angled sear can lead to an unsafe condition: a gun that could spontaneously fire without anyone or anything pulling the trigger!

Be careful not to remove too much material or change the sear angle too much. Again, your safety, and that of others, depends on your knowing what you are doing and upon your doing that correctly. If you are not confident in this task or lack the proper stones, seek the help of a qualified gunsmith. Cost for this service should be in the thirty dollar ($30) range.

If you feel especially energetic you can fully disassemble the Pump's trigger mechanism and polish and debur all moving parts. Unfortunately, this seems to offer little improvement in trigger quality. By following the aforementioned guidelines I have been able to achieve safe trigger pulls on most Remington Pumps in the 5 pound range and with little creep. Such a trigger pull is certainly adequate for most hunting applications.

Hammer and Striker Weight Reductions on The Pump:

The tinker can dramatically reduce the lock time of these rifles through lightening of both hammer and firing pin assemblies. Here, unlike typical bolt guns, your only option is removal of material from these pieces. Manufacturers offer lightweight strikers for almost all types of bolt-action high-powered rifles, but, of course, not for the Pump.

On the Remington Pump-Action Rifle you can use a three-sixteenths inch (3/16") carbide drill bit to reduce the weight of the hammer. This is an easy process involving the drilling of three or four holes in the big end of the hammer as shown in the photographs. Since Remington makes this hammer of very hard steel (likely case hardened, as are most hammers) the only good way to drill it is with a carbide drill bit or other hard-surfaced type of drill bit. Fortunately, these drill bits are routinely available from Brownells and other sources. The only concern is that you not overheat the piece while drilling it. See the associated photographs and captions. See Photograph #s 4-21/22.

The advantages of lightening the big end of the hammer are myriad. First, this reduces the action's lock time, the hammer falls faster after the trigger system disengages from the sear. Second, rotation of the hammer disrupts the rifle's aim less. (Newton requires that as the hammer begins to rotate in one direction the rifle must rotate in the other!) Third, given the same spring

Photograph 4-21

Photograph 4-22

Photographs 4-21/22: Modified Remington Model-760 pump-action rifle trigger assembly. (Model-7600 is the same.) This unit is the biggest weakness in these fine rifles, regarding hunting accuracy. In factory trim, trigger pull is highly variable and is seldom better than okay. (In this one man's opinion at least!) Further, no after-market replacement trigger assemblies are available and only marginal improvements of the factory unit are feasible. See associated text and photographs. Note that we have lightened this hammer by drilling three 3/16" holes (as shown in the close-up view, photograph 4-22). This job requires a carbide drill bit owing to the hammer's extreme hardness.

Photograph 4-22: Modified Remington Model-760 pump-action rifle hammer. We have lightened this hammer by drilling three 3/16" holes. Owing to the extreme hardness of the hammer this job requires a carbide drill bit. With careful positioning, it is possible to drill four such holes. However, do not crowd any holes too near any edge or each other. Ideally, the effective rotating mass of this hammer (at the radius of the firing pin contact zone) along with one-half the hammer spring should be exactly equal to the mass of the striker along with one-half the mass of the striker return spring. The latter is an easy thing to measure. The former is definitely not easy to ascertain. One could figure out the geometry and work this out, but it is a lot easier to just drill three holes as shown! However, note, it is best if one combines this alteration with a lightened striker. See associated photographs, captions and text.

Section 4: The Trouble With Triggers, Part I

tension, the lighter hammer will impact the striker at a higher velocity. This results in a higher firing pin velocity. Finally, the effective rotating mass of the lighter hammer will be closer to the weight of the striker; this allows the systems to come closer to the perfect reaction for accurate shooting. Ideally, the hammer should stop when it hits the striker, transferring all of its momentum and energy to the striker, which would then carry that energy to the primer. This ideal result would minimize torque and vibrations.

Similarly you can lighten the firing pin by carefully grinding in the areas highlighted in the photograph and described in the caption. You cannot gain a whole lot here. However, in this instance, a little weight reduction goes a long way. This can significantly reduce lock time and disruption to the rifle resulting from lock-work actuation. See Photograph # 4-23.

Also note that a lighter striker carrying the same energy will disrupt the chambered cartridge less. It will not drive the case into the chamber as deeply. This improves both accuracy and case life!

(Editor: We include this chapter with very mixed emotions. With the vast majority of the modifications described in this book... if our good reader goofs up... things are not going to work as well as they should/could... and it's back to the workbench, hopefully to do it right this time around. But triggers are a different story. Do it wrong, and the gun may start going off at quite unexpected times. Whether this happens in your reloading den, or in the game fields, it is unpleasant and unsettling at best, and painful and/or fatal at worst. Unless you one hundred percent know what you're doing here... this is the very best portion of accurizing to farm-out to a professional gunsmith.)

Photograph 4-23: Lightened firing pin (striker) from Remington Model 760 Pump. Note thinned section near center and slot on bottom at right end. These measures can reduce this pin's weight by about 10% without compromising its strength. These alterations are certainly worthwhile but one must retain certain features of the original pin. Big end must remain full diameter, as shown. Shank must remain sufficiently rigid, as shown. Retaining pin slot, at upper right, must remain same length with solid stops at both ends. Shank must remain full-diameter at step near center.

Section 5: The Trouble With Bolts, *Part I*

There are a few things the gunsmithing tinker can do to improve functioning of the bolt in many, if not all, bolt-action and pump-action rifles. In this section, we will explore several simple tasks and a few difficult operations. As always, if you are not comfortable with any of these tasks, seek a competent gunsmith's assistance.

Action Manipulation Improvement, Pump Action Rifles:

On the various pump-action rifles, actuation of the slide handle performs all the functions necessary to unchamber a cartridge (or spent case), cock the hammer and rechamber a fresh cartridge. One area where both the Remington and Savage rifles can use a bit of attention involves the sliding friction between the bolt carrier and the hammer. In Remington's pump this area also rides over the top cartridge in the magazine. See Photograph #s 5-1/2.

Unlike the Marlin Lever-Action Rifle, on these pump guns the manufacturers have made no accommodation for eliminating friction between the already cocked hammer and the bolt carrier. Likely this is because the operator has tremendous leverage to work these actions, which is not true in the lever-action guns. Regardless, in any rifle, reduction of sliding friction is worthwhile.

In these pump-action rifles modification of the bolt carrier to relieve sliding friction on the hammer, once the action has cocked the hammer,

Photograph 5-2: Barrel and bolt assembly from Model-7600 Remington Pump. Older Model-760 series is slightly different in actual layout. However, both rifles function essentially the same. Here we have partially unlocked action without opening it. Note pin in bolt carrier, near the center of photograph. In front of that pin is front end of the bolt camming slot (a straight portion). This pin runs in that slot to facilitate bolt rotation as one articulates the slide. This slot's back end (hidden here) rolls about 45° around the bolt. Located opposite this pin and slot is a similar, albeit smaller, pin and slot (hidden in this view on the bolt's reverse side). Also evident in this photograph are, left-to-right: firing pin head, bolt-carrier, action bar assembly (wraps over top of bolt-carrier), bolt, barrel extension (On Model-7600 this piece includes locking lug recesses and the visible under lug; on Model-760 series the under lug is a separate piece), barrel under-lug and barrel.

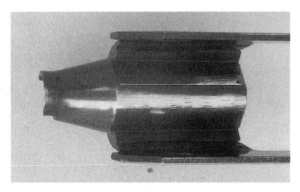

Photograph 5-1: Bottom-view of Remington Model-7600 bolt carrier. (Model-760 is similar.) Note polished areas. Main polished zone along the entire length of the carrier is hammer cocking ramp (left) and then where hammer slides under carrier as one cycles the action fully open (right). Polishing these areas significantly reduces effort required for action manipulation. A jeweler's rouge-impregnated felt wheel on a Dremel tool works well here. See text.

is probably not worthwhile. However, you can certainly reduce this sliding friction through polishing of the offending surfaces. See the applicable sub-section below.

Other areas of friction are easy to recognize on a well-used gun. These will show as areas where frictional contact has worn the bluing off the surface. You should bring any such areas to a high polish. Commonly you can achieve the polish required by application of a Jeweler's rouge-impregnated felt tip on a Dremel tool. In all such operations use restraint and plenty of cold water to avoid overheating the piece you are working.

If the surface is unusually rough, first apply a fine Arkansas sharpening stone, as necessary. It is not necessary to bring these surfaces to a completely smooth polished condition. Simply polish off the high spots. Next, go to work with a Jeweler's rouge-impregnated felt tip on a Dremel tool.

This work will soon render a mirror finish with minimized sliding friction. Finish the job by cold bluing all surfaces that were originally blued. Brownells Oxpho-Blue works well for this refinishing. This procedure can result in a startling reduction in the force required to manipulate the action.

Striker Replacement on Bolt-Action Rifles:

On many bolt-action rifles you can easily reduce lock time by the simple installation of a titanium striker, a stronger firing pin spring or both. On most of these guns the tinker can disassemble the bolt without any special tools — although a bolt disassembly tool certainly simplifies the task on Remington's Model-700. Such a tool is available from Sinclair International. However, striker assembly replacement or modification is a rather difficult operation. Before we look at an example (the Remington Model-700) I need to address an area of safety related to this issue.

Specifically, do not install a "super strength" firing pin spring on a standard striker on any rifle chambered for any cartridge with minimal headspace control, such as the .35 Whelen — this practice can result in case head separations with otherwise normal loads. The problem results from a combination of three factors: a heavy striker assembly, a super duty spring, and limited headspace control on the cartridge case.

In cartridges with limited headspace control, the striker can drive the case into the chamber significantly. In so doing, it sets the shoulder back on the case. In some instances, this can result in a dangerous headspace condition, even though the cartridge was properly headspaced in the gun!

In this situation, when ignition pressure builds in the case, the case walls will expand and lock to the chamber walls after the striker has driven the case forward in the chamber. This leaves the case head hanging free as chamber pressure pushes back on the interior of the case head. Obviously something has to give. In this instance, the case walls near the juncture to the solid web of the case will stretch endwise. This stretching allows the case head to move back until the bolt face's support (resistance to further compression) is adequate to resist the force of chamber pressure pushing back on the inside of the case head. In this situation, the case walls might very well stretch completely in two before the bolt head can provide adequate support to stop the case head's retreat! The result of releasing a large volume of gas at upwards of 60,000 pound of pressure into your rifle's action is something you do not want to experience. Believe me!

Substitution of a lighter striker mitigates this problem. However, if in doubt, a small sacrifice in lock time is certainly worth your piece of mind and safety. Those working with a gun chambered for a cartridge such as the .35 Whelen (where headspace control is modest at best) the .35 Remington or any similar cartridge should use restraint in striker spring substitutions.

Installation of a light-weight striker or aftermarket spring involves disassembly of the bolt, as in normal cleaning, and reassembly with the necessary replacement components. In the middle of these two basic operations comes the problem. Sinclair makes a tool for disassembling the Remington Model-700 series bolt. This handy tool is so useful that it should likely be in every Remington Model-700 shooter's cleaning kit. This tool simplifies striker removal to the point of child's play. See Photograph # 5-3.

This is a good opportunity to ensure that the firing pin hole in the bolt is free of burs and debris. Apply a dab of 220 grit lapping compound to the striker tip and reassemble the bolt. Then insert the bolt in the unloaded action, release the safety, hold the trigger back, lock the bolt and then work the bolt handle up and down between the locked and unlocked position perhaps twenty (20) times. This will work the tip of the striker through the hole in the bolt

Section 5: The Trouble With Bolts, Part I

sufficiently to remove any burs that might exist. If you intend to replace the striker with a titanium unit, do this operation first using the original striker but see the alternate method described below.

If you intend to replace the striker, first remove the old striker assembly from the bolt, then disassemble the striker assembly. On the Remington Model-700 and certain other rifles, this requires a bit of work and either some specialized tools or a bit of ingenuity. The problem here is that the tinker must compress the striker spring to allow the bolt sleeve to move forward to expose the cross pin that retains the assembly.

Holding everything in place while removing the cross pin is difficult, putting the system back together is another matter! One solution is as follows. Vise the large diameter ring at the front end of the striker (the area just in front of the spring) in a solidly mounted bench vise. Do not clamp on the narrow diameter of the striker! Ensure the clamping force is sufficient to hold the assembly rigidly in place. I prepared my vise in this regard by sanding opposed shallow recesses in one end of the jaw using a one-half inch (1/2") sanding drum in the Dremel tool. This creates a solid purchase so the assembly cannot move forward and it limits the potential for the assembly to twist up or down while also limiting the potential for damage to the striker.

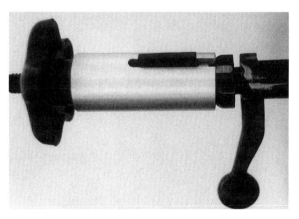

Photograph 5-3: Sinclair International's handy Remington Model-700 bolt disassembly tool. With patience one can do this job using only hand tools. However, it is hardly worth the effort! This tool is too affordable, too handy and too useful. A simple lever (at top center in this photograph) latches over the cocking piece. One then compresses the spring by turning the knob at left. This disengages the cocking piece from the bolt body, facilitating unscrewing of the striker assembly.

With the assembly vised, as noted above, and a set of quality five-inch (5") Vise Grip pliers at hand, you are ready to proceed with disassembly. First, compress the striker spring by pushing the bolt sleeve forward until the sleeve clears the front of the sear unit. Then rotate the bolt sleeve sufficiently to allow it to lock on the front end of the sear unit. Slowly release the bolt sleeve to allow it to move back until it comes to rest.

Now you can adjust the five-inch (5") Vise Grip pliers (this specific tool is perhaps the best available for this task) until they will provide a solid grip on the exposed shank of striker, behind the bolt sleeve. Slightly open the Vise Grip jaw so it will slide along the shank and then use the Vise Grip to force the bolt sleeve slightly away from the sear. Lock the pliers in place. This action contains the unit.

Remove the assembly from the vise and mount the sear end in the vise to facilitate driving the retaining pin free. You can then pull the sear piece clear of the striker. Remount the unit, as it was for spring compression, and apply sufficient force to the pliers to hold the spring tension. Then slowly unlock the pliers just enough to allow the jaws to freely slide on the shank. Then very carefully proceed to allow the pliers to slide off the shank until the striker spring fully relaxes.

Reassembly with a replacement spring requires only reversal of the above process. However, those installing a titanium replacement striker face different problems! Before considering installing a titanium striker make absolutely certain you have the correct tools to do the job without injuring or destroying that very expensive piece! Brownells sells a very affordable tool (about $15) made by Kleinendorst specifically for this task. It takes no genius to figure out the common sense of buying a fifteen dollar ($15) tool to ensure the proper installation of a seventy-five dollar ($75) firing pin!

Once you have the old striker disassembled you can use it as a tool to debur the firing pin hole in the bolt face. Begin by attaching an extension to the stock steel striker (do not use a titanium unit!). For the Remington Model-700 you can fashion a simple extension from a one-half inch (1/2") hardwood dowel. Bore a one-inch (1") deep nine-thirty-seconds inch (9/32") diameter hole centered in one end of a three-inch piece of dowel. Chuck the solid end of the dowel into a one-half inch (1/2") drill and slip the striker into the hole in the dowel. If the striker is not a sufficiently snug fit, simply wrap a layer of duct tape at the juncture.

Apply a dab of 220 grit lapping agent and run the pin fully into the bolt with the drill running on a slow speed. Applying only moderate pressure at the front of the stroke, work the pin slightly back and forth for several seconds to finish the lapping job.

Obviously you can use the same basic tool to hand-lap the hole. Takes a little longer but is certainly effective. In any case, just remember that the only purpose is to remove any possible burs from the firing pin hole in the bolt. Do not overdo this! Specifically, do not force the striker too far through the bolt and thereby enlarge the striker hole in the bolt face.

Clean all grinding compound from the striker (if you intend to reuse it) and the bolt. Check for any burs on the striker shank and polish any such burs away. Then reassemble the striker pieces and the bolt. The striker and striker hole are now positively deburred. This minimizes the potential for binding between the striker and the bolt, even when grit and debris are present (which burs tend to trap).

Polishing Hammer Cocking Surfaces, Remington and Savage Pump-Action Rifles:

As one cycles the action on the Remington and Savage Pump-Action Rifles the bolt carrier cocks the hammer as the action opens. As the bolt carrier passes over the hammer, the contact surface between these two pieces creates continuing friction. Obviously, any burs or roughness at this contact area will translate to increased friction and, therefore, increased effort necessary to cycle the action.

Polishing these contact areas is conceptually simple. On a well-used gun both the hammer and the bolt carrier will show the contact areas as ghost marks. However, since the force between these two pieces is modest and since both are very hard surfaces, simply lapping the areas by manipulation of the action with lapping agent in place is not very effective.

The best course is to disassemble the actions and use a fine Arkansas stone followed by a Jeweler's rouge-impregnated felt attachment in the Dremel tool to polish the entire contacting surface of both hammer and bolt carrier. (A Cratex attachment on the Dremel tool works quite well here.) The improvement in action manipulation can be rather surprising. I believe this is a worthwhile step.

You can also reduce friction by reducing contact area. In this instance, it is possible to slightly reshape the nose of the hammer to a sharp edge. This is particularly useful on the Savage, which has a flat contact surface on the bolt carrier (the Remington carrier is round). However, use caution to avoid altering the area of the hammer that strikes the firing pin.

Polishing the Striker Cocking Ramp (Bolt-Action Rifles):

On typical bolt-action rifles either closing or opening the bolt cams the striker into the cocked position. Most commonly, cocking occurs upon opening. In this discussion we will consider the cocked-upon-opening type of action, such as Remington's bolt-action series, but the concept is the same for any system: polish the cocking ramps. See Photograph # 5-4.

Photograph 5-4: At upper right is the cocking ramp on a Remington left-hand bolt-action bolt. I have polished this ramp using a felt tip impregnated with jeweler's rouge and a Dremel tool. We also polished the hump separating this ramp from the hold-open notch. This simple work, in conjunction with associated work on the cocking piece, reduced maximum bolt opening effort by an astonishing one-third!

Section 5: The Trouble With Bolts, Part I

In these guns it is a simple matter to polish the cocking ramp and the cocking face on the sear housing. Begin by removing the bolt and disassembling the striker mechanism from the bolt.

Locate the bolt in a padded vise positioned so the cocking ramp is visible and fully accessible. You can easily polish this ramp. Use a cone-shaped felt tool mounted on a Dremel tool and treated with jeweler's rouge. Spend sufficient time to bring the entire ramp and the over center lobe (the high spot between the depression where the striker rests with the bolt unlocked, and the cocking ramp) to a high polish. Frequent reapplication of rouge will speed this chore.

The cocking portion of the sear housing is easy to polish using a six-inch (6") long narrow (about 1/2" wide) strip of 660 grit (or finer) corundum (aluminum oxide) paper. Locate the striker assembly in a padded vise with the cocking extension positioned at the top and fully accessible. Run the strip of corundum paper over the rounded nose with the ends about two-inches apart. Work the paper in a sawing motion for several seconds. Examine the end of the cocking extension; it should show a consistent polish along the entire rounded end. If not, repeat the polishing step. When you have polished away all tooling marks with the sanding paper, finish the job with a jeweler's rouge-impregnated felt drum on the Dremel tool. See Photograph # 5-5.

Clean the entire assembly thoroughly (an aerosol degreaser will work well). The best reassembly lubricant might very well be Smooth-Kote® from Sentry Solutions. This is a sophisticated protective dry lubricant with unsurpassed lubrication and corrosion inhibition characteristics. Once properly applied, it lasts indefinitely and will not attract abrasive particles. Lacking that superior product, apply a <u>tiny</u> amount of Moly-Slide™ or a Teflon impregnated gun oil to the threads and the cocking ramp. Lubricate the remainder of the assembly with a dry silicon lubricant (motor-cycle chain lubricant). After normal reassembly you have finished this enhancement. See Photograph #s 5-6/7.

Striker Hole Centering and Repair:

Commonly the striker hole in the bolt face is off-center. Similarly, the striker is often considerably smaller than the hole in the bolt face. The former condition is not conducive to consistent ignition. The latter can lead to pierced primers with otherwise normal loads. Both conditions are correctable. See Photograph # 5-8.

In the case of a significantly off-center striker it is necessary to determine which direction and how far off center the striker hits the primer. You can easily measure this distance by simply observing a fired primer or the ghost ring that is easily visible on the bolt face of any well-used gun; normally a clear outline of the primer shows up as an area surrounding the firing pin hole, this area appears unusually clean and polished. See Photograph #s 5-9/10.

To measure the distance the firing pin is off center, simply measure the distance from the closest edge of the primer cup to the center of the indention in a fired primer. Repeat this measurement from the long side. If these measurements are closer than about ten-thousandths of an inch (0.010"), it is unlikely you can improve upon the centering of the striker. However, if these num-

Photograph 5-5: Partially polished cocking piece end. This hardened-steel piece rides on the cocking ramp in the bolt under rather severe pressure from the striker spring. Polishing this end to a mirror finish significantly reduces cocking effort. Here the job is only about one-half done. However, we have already polished out all machining marks. See associated photograph showing polished cocking ramp.

bers differ by much more than ten-thousandths of an inch (0.010"), you might consider centering the striker.

If you can observe the ghost ring to determine how far off-center the striker hole is, the direction the hole is off-center with relation to the bolt body is also obvious — the hole needs to move toward the widest side of the primer's ghost ring on the bolt face. For those who have to use a fired case to determine the direction the hole needs to move, the task is slightly more convoluted.

In that case, mark a spot on both an empty but primed case and the perimeter of the bolt. Carefully insert the case with the mark on the rim lined up with the mark on the bolt. Point the gun in a safe direction. Close the bolt and fire the cap. (Use caution here. Firing a primer generates considerable noise. Also note, the primer's blast can ignite flammable materials. The primer residues also contain lead, do this test in a well-ventilated area. Finally, you should promptly remove the primer residues from the gun's bore, but certainly before firing the gun with live ammunition — unadulterated primer residues are potentially corrosive and erosive. A better alternative is to do this study at the range using a live round.)

One problem is that the case might not stay aligned in the same rotational orientation while you lock the bolt. To remedy this, consider removing the bolt and hot gluing the case in place, a process that might require removal of the ejector plunger in Remington-style bolts. If you choose this method, use caution to avoid heating the primer significantly. You can understand why it is preferable just to observe the ghost ring! You might also consider marking the bolt face with a thin coating of Prussian Blue (available from Brownells Incorporated) and firing an empty but primed case. This should clearly show the primer's location since the primer will slam back into the Prussian blue on the bolt face with considerable force while the case will not. If none of these alternatives are possible, revert to the hard way.

Remove the fired marked case and note the relationship between the off-center striker and

Photograph 5-6: Here we are using a dental pick to clean debris from a Mauser bolt. For almost any tinker, an Opti-Visor, equipped with the Opti-Loupe (in use here), is, perhaps, the finest vision-enhancing tool on the market! The Opti-Visor and Opti-Loupe greatly facilitate examination of critical surfaces while one functions the part. Try doing that with a hand loupe! The Opti-visor is available with various interchangeable primary lenses. The #3 lens provides significant magnification and a good field-of-view for finish work. The #5 lens is, likely, more valuable for close examination of precision parts. The Opti-Loupe attaches easily and articulates into and out of one's field of view, as needed.

Along with a plethora of other invaluable tools, Brownells stocks the entire line of Opti-Visor products, dental picks and who knows what else!

Photograph 5-7: Almost any lubricant is better than standard hydrocarbon-based products, which attract and retain all manner of dirt and debris. Here we have applied a coating of Smooth-Kote, from Sentry Solutions, to the base pin from a Casull revolver. Clearances in this particular gun are so close that accumulated powder fouling will bind the cylinder, rendering the gun inoperable. Smooth-Kote is a micro-crystalline lubricant. It bonds to the crystal lattice structure and actually discourages fouling accumulation. Further, this product has a very high lubricity, rivaling Teflon. Finally, it provides good protection against corrosion. It is certainly a good choice inside any rifle action.

Section 5: The Trouble With Bolts, Part I

the mark on the bolt and case. A bit of contemplation should reveal which direction the striker is from center. If in doubt, repeat the study using a mark at a different location on the bolt. Repeat the test until you are absolutely certain which direction you need to move the striker hole to center it on the primer.

Once you have ascertained both direction and distance, proceed as described below in the subsection on bushing an oversize hole. Assuming the striker is not off center more than about twenty-five thousandths of an inch (0.025") the following approach will correct the problem. For strikers that are farther off center than this (very rare) you should consider repair via TIG welding or a replacement bolt, neither are jobs I will detail here because both fall strictly under the category of "professional and qualified".

Unless the bolt is case-hardened you can have the bolt face TIG welded, resurface the bolt face, and redrill the striker hole. Depending upon your understanding and technique, the dedicated hobbyist can do all of this successfully and safely or they can create an unsafe gun! Any welding anywhere near the locking lug end of a bolt is an extremely delicate job. I believe most tinkers should leave this to a professional, someone who

Photograph 5-9

Photograph 5-10

Photograph 5-8: Cartridge case fired in Savage Model-170 pump-action rifle. Note three things evident here: First, striker impact is far from centered; second, striker impact is not very robust (shallow indent); third, striker tip is on the large side. With careful work, one can correct all three conditions. See text, photographs and associated captions.

Photographs 5-9/10: Bolt face from Savage Model-170 pump-action rifle. Note ghost ring around striker hole, photograph 5-9. This clearly demonstrates which direction and how far the striker hole would have to move to center the striker on the primer. Correction is possible. Photograph 5-10: Marker ink indicating approximate perimeter of primer in chambered case.

knows exactly what they are doing and can ensure that the welding operation does not damage the bolt's heat treatment.

One method of firing pin centering involves installation of a set screw in the bolt face. Before proceeding with the following alteration ensure that you have an Allen wrench that fits a size 10x32 set screw and will reach completely through the bolt from the rear, the long shank of the Allen wrench must be at least as long as the bolt body! Such wrenches are not generally available and you might have to create your own long version.

To do this fit a grade-8, 10x32 set screw to a straight shank cut from the appropriate size Allen wrench. Attach two nuts to the set screw and lock those together (application of a thread locking agent is a good idea). (Assuming you have a nut driver that will fit the nuts and that has a long enough shank and, finally, that it will fit inside the bolt body, you are ready to go.) In any case, have a wrench that will do the job in hand before beginning this operation.

On Remington and Savage Pump-Action Rifles this alteration is a simple task; both bolt bodies are short enough that a standard Allen wrench will do the job.

While centering and resizing a firing pin hole is a considerable job, the improvement is often well worthwhile. However, do not begin this alteration until you have a wrench that will work and have thought the necessary work out very carefully! Further, as noted above, do not attempt any such repair on any case-hardened rifle bolt. If you cannot file the surface quite easily with a standard file, assume the bolt is case hardened — you cannot drill it with a standard drill bit nor tap it with a standard tap.

For an oversize hole, the simplest correction involves drilling the bolt with a shallow hole, no deeper than necessary to insert a one-quarter inch (1/4") long 10x32 threaded grade-8 set screw into the recoil face of the bolt. The proper drill bit diameter is one-hundred and fifty-nine thousandths of an inch (0.159", # 21 index drill bit). You should also have a set of bottom hole taps in 10x32 thread size. Ensure that you drill the hole squarely to the bolt face. You can achieve this end by setting the bolt body up in a vise on the table of a drill press. Verify it is vertical using a spirit level on two non-opposed sides of the bolt body.

Use of a drill press provides the best results. This also facilitates precise control of hole depth. On some types of bolts, this hole will have to extend entirely through the face of the bolt, this is no problem providing only that the length of the resulting threaded hole is at least one and one-half times the diameter of the 10x32 set screw (about 0.275"). Such a condition will not compromise the strength of the bolt in any way. However, a shorter threaded hole will compromise the ability of the set screw to hold in place in the bolt.

Take measurements to verify that the bolt face will support this length of 10x32 threaded hole before proceeding. This is easily achieved using a long rod of about one-hundred and sixty thousandths of an inch (0.160") diameter. Insert this rod from the rear of the bolt until it bottoms solidly against the taper at the front of the hollow bolt body. Mark the point where this rod aligns with the rear of the bolt body. Measure the portion of the rod that entered the bolt body. Subtract this from the length of the bolt from the rear to the bolt face. If the difference is greater than about two hundred and seventy-five thousandths of an inch (0.275") you can proceed. If not, consider using an 8x32 set screw where a threaded hole of about two hundred and twenty-thousandths of an inch (0.220") depth is sufficient (adjust tools and depths accordingly).

Align and center the rifle bolt under a # 21 drill bit mounted in the chuck of a drill press. Apply cutting oil to the bolt face. Lower the spindle until the drill bit drills just deep enough to create a full diameter bevel in the bolt face. Turn the drill off, then lower the spindle and lock the up travel at this depth (if possible, on your drill press). Note the index reading on the scale. Calculate the reading required to allow two hundred and seventy-five thousandths of an inch (0.275") additional boring depth. If possible, adjust the bottom travel lock to that index reading (to positively prevent excess hole depth).

Reapply cutting oil to the bolt face. Turn the drill on and produce the hole to the additional two hundred and seventy-five thousandths of an inch (0.275") depth. Once you have drilled this hole (an easy task in any non-case-hardened bolt) you can proceed to tap the hole with 10x32 threads. If the hole, thus drilled, proceeds through the entire recoil face and is open and full diameter at the rear, you can use a standard tap.

For tapping a full diameter hole through the bolt face, the best procedure is to leave the bolt body mounted in the drill press as it was for the drilling step. Install the tap in place of the drill

Section 5: The Trouble With Bolts, Part I

bit in the drill chuck, then remove the belt from the drill press.

Apply a quality cutting oil (such as Do-Drill, available from Brownells Incorporated). Lower the spindle and turn it by hand while applying <u>moderate</u> but consistent down pressure to the spindle. To avoid jamming and breaking the tap or fouling the new threads, cut only a third of a turn or less before reversing the rotation, sufficiently to break any cutting burs loose. Repeat this process until the tap proceeds through the entire length of the hole. If the tap jams before reaching one-quarter inch (1/4") into the bolt, remove it and clean the cuttings from the hole.

If the hole bottoms out to a reduced diameter, which is the preferred result, begin as described above using the beginning tap from a three-tap bottoming tap set. Proceed until the tip of the tap abuts the shoulder of the hole. Remove that tap. Then run the intermediate tap into the hole using the same procedure and taking every precaution to align the threads on the intermediate tap to the shallow threads produced by the starting tap — a miscue here can really foul up things! After that tap bottoms out, finish the job with the bottom tap. Again, use due caution to ensure you follow the threads already begun.

If the hole does not proceed completely through the recoil face at full diameter a second drilling operation might be necessary to ensure the existing hole is large enough to accept an Allen wrench that fits the set screw (0.105" across the diagonals) and to accommodate any offset in the firing pin location that will result from this operation. If the existing hole is not at least one-hundred and five-thousandths of an inch (0.105") in diameter at the back of the set screw hole, drill it to that diameter. However, refer to the following paragraph first.

If the firing pin were sixty-five thousandths of an inch (0.065") in diameter at a point about three-tenths of an inch (3/10") from the tip and you intended to relocate the pin ten-thousandths of an inch (0.010") to one side, the hole behind the set screw would have to be eighty-five thousandths of an inch (0.085") in diameter to clear the shank of the firing pin (0.065" pin diameter, 0.010" radial offset resulting in 0.02" clearance from the other side of the hole — the new hole drilled through the bolt face will always center on the original hole!). In that situation, the nominal 0.105" hole drilled to clear the Allen screw would do the job. However, if the pin were seventy-five thousandths of an inch (0.075") in diameter at the three-tenths of an inch (3/10") point and if striker centering required moving the center of the hole fifteen-thousandths of an inch (0.015"), the minimum hole diameter would be one-hundred and five-thousandths of an inch (0.105"). You should always allow a bit of clearance, so, in this example, drill the through hole to about one-hundred and fifteen-thousandths of an inch (0.115).

Should the required hole be larger than about one-hundred and fifteen-thousandths of an inch (0.115") it might make sense to drill the one-eighth inch (1/8" or 0.125") hole full-depth just to simplify matters. Finally, it is time to prepare the Allen screw.

Begin with a set screw that is long enough to allow grinding to an overall length of about three-tenths inch (3/10") and with a flat and full thread diameter face on the end opposite the Allen wrench hole. Then, mount the screw to an Allen wrench using Loctite Product #222, a low-strength thread locking compound. Allow that chemical to set. Gentle heating with a hair dryer will speed the process sufficiently to achieve product set-up in no more than a few minutes.

After the thread locker sets up, use a bench grinder to shorten and square the exposed end of the set screw. Shorten the screw to just slightly longer than three-tenths inch (3/10"). Use restraint and cool the piece often in a water bath to avoid overheating it. If you do overheat the piece, the thread locker will soften, a good test — check the bond after each grinding step. With a gloved hand try to pull the set screw off the Allen wrench; if you can remove it you might have gotten it too hot! If you have overheated it, start with a new one! You do not want to install an ill-tempered set screw!

When you have ground the set screw almost to proper length (3/10"), screw it through two 10x32 hex nuts and loosely lock the nuts together. Mount the assembly in a smooth-jawed vise, clamping across the nuts, and with the exposed end of the set screw protruding slightly through the top nut and accessible above the vise. Finish the end of the set screw by filing it flush and square to the nut surface using a smooth-cut mill file. Remove the Allen wrench by prying against the bent end while the nuts hold the set screw in place in the vise. Remove the set screw from the vise and from the hex nuts.

Insert your long Allen wrench tool through the bolt body from the rear. Push the set screw onto the end of the Allen wrench. Lower the wrench until the set screw touches the bolt face and proceed to turn the set screw into the bolt. With luck, the screw will stop naturally when its face is just flush with the face of the bolt. If you cannot screw the piece sufficiently into the bolt to bring it flush, you can shorten the screw slightly (no more than one thread) to achieve such a condition. Again, ideally, when the screw stops against the end of the end of the threads in the bolt it should be flush with the bolt face. Typically, however, I am seldom that lucky — the screw will enter the bolt to somewhat past flush, and of course, in instances where the hole proceeded full-diameter completely through the bolt face, this result is inevitable.

Once you have properly adjusted this set screw bushing and verified that it will fully enter the hole, as required to achieve flush locating, you are ready to semi-permanently install this bushing. Thoroughly clean and dry the threads on the set screw. Use a heavy duty degreasing compound — the aerosol variety is very handy. Similarly, thoroughly clean the threads in the bolt body. After both pieces are thoroughly dry, liberally apply high-strength thread locking agent (Loctite Product #262 or, better yet, the high temperature version, Product #271) to the threads in the bolt and on the set screw.

Again, insert the Allen wrench through the bolt body from the rear and slip the set screw on the wrench. Then, lower the wrench, while turning it, to thread the screw into the bolt. Continue turning until the filed face of the set screw is just flush with the bolt face, <u>slightly</u> (0.001"-0.002") below flush is okay but <u>this piece must not protrude measurably above the bolt face</u>. With a good light source and a 6x Loupe (available from Brownells) you can observe this relationship quite easily. If in doubt, mount the bolt in a vise and place a one-quarter inch (1/4") wide straight-edge over the set screw. Then turn the screw until you feel the straight-edge lift from the bolt face; then back the screw into the bolt until you feel the straight-edge bottom on the bolt face, perhaps, about one-sixteenth of a turn (<0.002").

If the bolt design permits easy bolt face machining, consider leaving the set screw slightly above flush. This allows exact matching by filing or stoning. In any case, after you have properly positioned the set screw, remove the Allen wrench and place the piece aside to allow the thread locking agent to <u>completely</u> cure, perhaps overnight.

Now you have achieved a bolt face with no striker hole! It might seem as though we are working our way backwards here! However, there are advantages awaiting our attention. When the Loctite has suitably cured you can drill a properly centered hole and adjust that hole and the striker for an <u>exact</u> striker-tip to bolt-hole fit. Of course, you can also properly center the striker by drilling this hole where it needs to be located to center the striker tip in relation to the primer.

Redrilling the Bolt Face:

After the thread locker is fully cured and, if necessary, you have filed the exposed set screw flush with the bolt face, you are ready to mark the bolt to drill the new striker hole — centered and properly sized. The first order is to center-punch the set screw at the proper location for the center of the new hole. This is best achieved using a spring-loaded center-punch. Locate the bolt in a padded vise with the bolt face at top.

Noting that the 10x32 screw is about one-hundred and fifty-six thousandths of an inch (0.156") on the minor diameter and about one-hundred and eighty-eight thousandths of an inch (0.188") on the major diameter, you can quite accurately estimate the distance from center of the set screw to center-punch for the hole. For this discussion, we will assume the striker was initially off center by fifteen-thousandths of an inch (0.015"). Of course, we have also marked the bolt face to indicate the direction the striker needs to move from the center of the old hole, which is also the center of the newly installed set screw.

Since the shiny new polished set screw face is about eighty-six thousandths of an inch (0.086") in average radius (1/4 of ≃ 0.155"+0.187") we need to move the hole just more than one-sixth the distance from the center toward the edge of the set screw in the direction previously noted and marked on the bolt. If we needed to move the hole ten-thousandths of an inch (0.010") we would locate the center-punch just short of one-eighth the distance to the perimeter. Under the constraints of the tools most tinkers will have available, we can hope to do no better than the accuracy such an approach will yield. With care, you should be able to achieve a hole located no more than, perhaps, five-thousandths of an inch (0.005") away from the correct center — not too bad! Similarly, if the original hole is that close to centered, it makes little sense to try to correct its location!

Section 5: The Trouble With Bolts, Part I

After center-punching the set screw with the location for the hole it is necessary to know the diameter of the tip of the firing pin. Here we get a bonus — the ability to exactly fit the firing pin to the bolt face! With a micrometer, measure the extreme tip of the shank of the striker. Choose an index drill bit that is just smaller than this diameter. On the Remington Model-700 the shank under the tip is about seventy-five thousandths of an inch (0.075"), a fairly standard measurement for modern bolt actions. For a seventy-five thousandths of an inch (0.075") striker tip shank diameter the correct index drill bit is a # 49, which will drill a seventy-three thousandths inch (0.073") diameter hole. Obviously, do not attempt this job with a low quality or dull drill bit.

Locate the rifle bolt vertically in a clamp under the drill press spindle, and use a spirit level to verify vertical orientation. Locate the center-punched mark centered under the chucked drill bit in a drill press. Apply cutting oil and carefully drill the hole. Remember, you are drilling a comparatively hard piece of steel with a very small drill bit. Also, it is possible that, as the drill bit proceeds through the rear of the set screw, it might contact along one side of the hex portion of the Allen head of the screw; this situation can drastically stress the drill bit, especially if you advance the spindle too rapidly. Proceed very cautiously to avoid overheating the drill bit or the set screw or breaking the drill bit, especially as it passes out the back of the set screw. See Photograph # 5-11.

To fit the striker to the new hole, you will have to separate the striker from the bolt sleeve, etc. Refer to the sub-section on striker replacement for a thorough discussion of that process.

Fashion a one-half inch (1/2") hardwood dowel that will support and grip to the big end of the striker. You can achieve this by drilling a proper diameter hole in the end of the dowel (9/64") for a Remington Model-700 action; again, see the sub-section on striker replacement. You can lock the firing pin into the dowel using hot glue.

Chuck the dowel in a vised variable speed hand drill or a drill press set at its slowest speed. Apply 220 grit silicon carbide grinding compound to the tip of the striker. Insert the striker into the bolt body until the tip engages the hole in the set screw. Slide the bolt body up over the dowel until the striker enters the drilled end of the dowel. Lower the bolt body slightly to release any pressure on the striker. Turn on the drill (if a hand drill, at a low speed). Raise and lower the bolt body slightly to work the tip of the striker into, and then back out of, the hole in the set screw. Continue this process, adding new lapping compound, as needed, until the tip of the striker protrudes no more than about thirty-five

Photograph 5-11: Bolt face from Savage Model-170 pump-action rifle after modification. Here job is semi-finished. We have installed a 10-32 set screw centered on the bolt's original striker hole. The Allen head of this grade-8 set screw is at the inside. We drilled this screw to properly center the firing pin on a chambered cartridge. Note annular ridge around set screw. Our tapping operation raised this material. We have peened it back slightly to more securely lock the set screw in place. We also applied a high-strength thread locking compound, Loctite Product #271, to the thoroughly cleaned screw threads and in the immaculately degreased hole. Finishing will require filing the screw and elevated ridge carefully until those surfaces are flush with the bolt's unaltered front face. Note that this new striker hole is much smaller than the original, 0.070" versus 0.080". This alteration also required significant firing pin modification and installation of bushings in the bolt body. See text and associated photographs.

thousandths of an inch (0.035") from the bolt face. See Photograph # 5-12.

Remove the striker and thoroughly clean both it and the bolt. The striker will now perfectly fit the hole in the bolt face. It is also well centered in the bolt and it will not drive a case excessively into the chamber. All three are features that contribute to safety and accuracy. At least two of those characteristics are lacking on the average rifle. . . even many of the highest dollar custom jobs! See Photograph # 5-13.

For reassembly of the striker, refer to the aforementioned sub-section on striker replacement.

Photograph 5-13: Fired primer (in unloaded case) after centering a reduced-diameter striker in the bolt on a Savage Model-170 pump-action rifle. See associated "before" photograph. Note that this almost perfectly centered striker impact is much deeper, compared to the "before" impact. Subsequent field tests show a dramatic improvement in dependability.

Photograph 5-12: Partially modified striker from Savage Model-170 pump-action rifle. Note slight radius on tip and reduced shank diameter. As it turned out on this installation, we had to reduce the shank diameter to 0.070" for about 1" of the tip end. We also ended up installing a centering bushing in the bolt's front interior. This keeps both pin and pin return spring centered and prevents binding. Results of all of these efforts were worthwhile. Where this rifle had exhibited a 15% misfire ratio with certain factory ammunition (despite my best efforts to increase hammer tension), it now shows zero misfires with over 300 rounds of mixed vintage tested. Mis-centering, not limited striker energy, was the problem, that problem we have now solved.

Section 6: The Trouble With Box Magazine (Clips), *Part I*

Detachable magazines are a very weak link in any rifle system. I have lost a clip and seen another that was damaged in a most insidious way. It inserted normally and seemed all right as the first cartridge was fed from the clip into the chamber. However, the gun's recoil would dislodge the front of the clip from its proper purchase.

Upon firing the rifle, the clip bounced around in the magazine well and disengaged from the inside front of the magazine well. The front of the clip would then rotate down slightly. When the shooter then tried to chamber another round the bolt would push the bullet's tip directly into the vertical portion of the clip well, just below the feed ramp, very effectively jamming the gun.

Verify that your clips fit and function properly and protect all detachable magazines from damage. Vigilance can pay off here.

Clip Work:

For lack of a better place to mention this I will cover deburring of the typical clip magazine here. Often manufacturers simply cut and stamp these units from sheet steel. Very often the top lip of such a clip will have burs and other imperfections. You should smooth and polish any such roughness out of the interior of the top opening and from the inside of the magazine well.

Look for any hang ups as you load cartridges into the magazine and as you cycle the action to strip rounds from the magazine into the chamber. A bit of careful polishing here can significantly improve magazine and action functioning.

Section 7: The Trouble With Receiver-Mounted Sights, Part I

Commonly, mounts for glass sights (and increasingly electronic aided devices) and peep sights attach to the gun's receiver. In the section on barrel modifications, I touched upon often required work, when improving barrel-mounted sights. Here I will concentrate on receiver-mounted sight and sight bases.

Scope Sight Bases:

Practically every modern rifle is factory prepared for scope sight mounting. Typically, this involves the location of four holes in the receiver. Commonly, two are in front of the magazine and two are behind the magazine. Conceptually, this process is quite straight forward: the person mounting the sight base only has to remove the blanking screws found in these holes, then position and attach the scope base, using the screws supplied with the scope base. See Photograph #s 7-1/2.

Preventing Loose Scope Base Screws:

There are several areas where problems arise. First, scope base mounting screws are notorious for coming loose, and always at the worst possible time, it seems. The tinker can easily correct this problem. Before assembly, thoroughly clean both the screws and the holes using a heavy-duty degreasing agent. Allow the surfaces to dry fully. Apply a dab of medium-strength thread locking agent (Loctite Product #242) to all screws and tighten each reasonably tight with a properly fitting screwdriver. Do not use the high-strength product unless you are certain you will not want or need to remove the base. Given proper application, that product renders the parts sufficiently bonded that

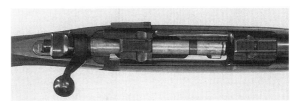

Photograph 7-1

Photograph 7-2

Photographs 7-1/2: Ruger offers a superior invention! Integral receiver scope mounts on their highpower rifles (photograph 7-1). These eliminate an expense and a substantial source of problems. On any given hunting day a staggering number of hunters carry rifles equipped with a loose scope base. That problem is, perhaps, the #1 source of loss of zero in hunting rifles. It cannot happen with a Ruger.

Photograph 7-2: Close-up-view of Ruger's integral scope bases, as shown on this lightweight .30-06 chambered Model-77, are a real boon. These have a double advantage; they cost nothing extra and cannot shoot or carry loose. See associated photograph and caption.

disassembly will almost certainly require the application of heat, as discussed on the sealant's label! See Photograph # 7-3.

You should verify all aspects of scope base installation before the final mounting operation, when the serious shooter should apply a thread locking agent such as Loctite Product #222 or #242 to the mounting screws. One common problem is that the standard installation will render the scope tube sufficiently out of alignment with the barrel that proper elevation adjustment is not possible. If this happens, the gunsmithing hobbyist can either shim one end of the scope base (the front to push bullet impacts down, the back to move impacts up) or he can machine one end of the base, as required, to level the scope to the bore axis. See Photograph #s 7-4/5.

Matching Scope Base-To-Receiver Contact Surface:

As is shown in the associated photographs, you can improve the rigidity of the scope-base installation by improving the fit between scope base and receiver. The basic procedure is quite simple. Place a corundum sheet of moderate-grit (about 320) over the top of the receiver. Pull the sides of the sheet down, cut it to size and tape it in place.

Position the scope base over the receiver and work it back and forth slightly. Check often for progress of mating. When, perhaps, fifty percent (50%) of the bluing is scarred or removed, the job is done.

Application of Loctite Product #609 between the cleaned surfaces will result in a solid bond with a scope base that will not work loose and

Photograph 7-4: Remington Model-700 left-hand bolt-action barreled-action showing 320 grit corundum paper taped across bridge area of receiver. We used this approach to match the underside of the scope mount to the receiver's top. This procedure is imperfect; a fully sanded-to-match scope base would have a slightly larger radius than the receiver (the paper has thickness!). Therefore, if we fully sanded the underside of the scope base to match the paper, the base would rock from side-to-side on the bare receiver — contacting only at the centerline when we tightened the screws. We can avoid this eventuality by sanding only the high spots and then using Loctite Product #609 to mate the base to the receiver. That product fills any minor voids. It cures to a rigid non-shrinking corrosion-preventing layer. We positioned the one-piece base over the receiver, located where it normally sits. Then we slid the base slightly forward and backward until we had polished about 30% of the underside sufficiently to remove most of the bluing. We would use a similar procedure on two-piece bases.

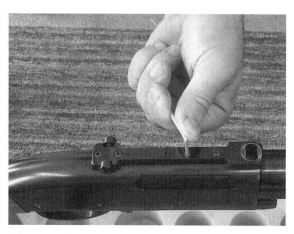

Photograph 7-3: Allen head screws, as provided by Redfield, are much easier to properly tighten without screw head damage. Leupold is now offering Torx® head screws that provide a better-yet purchase. Manufacturers often provide proper tools with systems utilizing such specially headed scope base or ring screws. Here, with the combination of Loctite Product #609 (a mounting agent) applied to degreased surfaces, Loctite Product #222 (a low-strength thread locking agent) applied to degreased screws, which are inserted into degreased holes, and proper screw torqueing, we can be certain that this mount will never spontaneously loosen. These Loctite products also provide corrosion protection for hidden surfaces — no small consideration.

Photograph 7-5: Underside of Redfield one-piece scope base for Remington left-hand bolt-action rifle. Note partial polishing of base-to-receiver mating surfaces. See associated photographs and text for a full explanation of purpose and technique.

Section 7: The Trouble With Receiver-Mounted Sights, Part I

that is rigidly attached. With application of Loctite Product #222 or #242 to the screw threads and screw head the mount is doubly secured. See associated photographs and captions.

Leveling a Scope, Front-To-Rear:

Shims are available through Sinclair International at a very modest price. When the correction requires only a few shims you can often use these without much degradation of the gun's appearance or introducing any other problems. However, a significant thickness of shims to correct for elevation can detract from the appearance of the gun and certainly will require substitution of longer screws to attach that end of the scope base to the receiver. In this situation, it is probably better to thin the other end of the scope base, where possible. See Photograph #s 7-6/7/8.

Usually the tinker can thin one end of a scope base enough to bring the scope on target. As an example, consider a Weaver base on a Remington Pump. Here we have an extruded aluminum scope base that sits over a rounded receiver top. It is possible to thin this base no more than about twenty-five thousandths of an inch (0.025") without compromising the strength of the attachment screw holes in the base. While twenty-five thousandths of an inch might seem an insignificant amount, in this application it actually represents quite a change.

The distance between the centers of the front and rear screw hole pairs on this base is about three-inches (3"). A bit of math will show that lowering the base 0.025" at one of these locations will change the point of impact thirty inches (30") at 100 yards. [3600"=100 yards: (3600"÷3")x0.025"=30"]

This same basic math procedure will work in any example: shoot a 100-yard target to verify how far the bullet's impact is low or high with the scope reticle adjusted near the center of its vertical travel, measure the average distance between the front and rear screw hole pairs, divide that distance by 3600 and multiply that answer by the number of inches the bullets hit above or below the bullseye. This will give the amount of material that you will have to remove

Photograph 7-7

Photograph 7-8

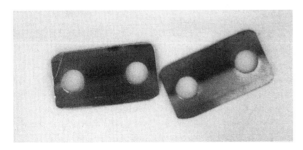

Photograph 7-6: Sinclair International shims, used for scope leveling. Sinclair offers two hole-center patterns. These kits come with shims in a wide selection of thicknesses.

Photographs 7-7/8: Savage Model-170 pump-action rifle with Redfield 6x Widefield scope mounted in Weaver rings on modified Weaver bases (photograph 7-7). Note shims under rear base, at front. This assembly allowed proper eye relief and scope leveling. This rifle easily shoots five-shot groups under 1 MOA with careful handloads and certain types of factory ammunition. Certainly such attention to detail and quality scope mounting is well worthwhile.

Photograph 7-8: Close-up-view of scope base shims under front of rear base, as shown in photograph 7-7.

from one end of the scope base to approximately zero the bullet without adjusting the reticle. Note that other types of scope bases, such as the standard Redfield system, allow much greater adjustment *via* machining.

Returning to the Remington Pump and Weaver scope base example: to thin one end of the base (after verifying which end you need to thin!) mount the base in a padded vise with the bottom up and the scope base parallel to the vise jaws. To facilitate access, clamp the piece as close to the top of the jaws as is feasible.

For further discussion, as an example only, I will assume you have tested the gun with the scope temporarily mounted and the ammunition type you expect to use most often with that rifle. You discover at the range that if you leave the scope elevation turret adjusted near the middle of its travel, the bullet impacts about thirty inches (30") below the bullseye at 100 yards. You decide it would be preferable to have the impact a little closer to center to leave more scope adjustment for possible applications with other bullet types, such as practice loads using lightweight lead bullets at low velocity, which might shoot substantially lower on the target.

Therefore, you want to move bullet impact thirty inches (30") higher on the target at 100 yards while leaving the reticle elevation screw adjustment about centered in the scope, when using your normal loads. In this instance, this means that you need to remove about twenty-five thousandths of an inch (0.025") of material from the front end of the scope base and taper that cut to zero at a point just behind the rearmost scope base screw hole.

Begin this process using a half-round bastard file of a size matched so that the round side of the file has about the same curvature as the top of the receiver. Since the file will never exactly match the top of the receiver, keep in mind that a slightly smaller (more curved) radius is preferable to a slightly larger radius. A too-curved channel will leave both sides of the rail resting upon the top of the receiver, as opposed to only the centerline touching! See Photograph # 7-9.

File the underside of the base, beginning the cut at the front and carefully tapering it toward the rear. Be careful to ensure that the cut surface is flat in the lengthwise sense — the cut surface should follow a straight line from end to end along the channel. When you have completed this cut along this portion of the channel and have thinned the front end to the base by about twenty-five thousandths of an inch (0.025"), you are ready to move on to matching the base to the top of the receiver.

To do this, wrap a full piece of 320 grit wet-or-dry corundum paper over the top of the receiver, then, while pulling this paper tightly in place over the top of the receiver, clamp the action in a padded vise with the rounded top exposed above the jaws. This locks the corundum paper in place, tight over the top of the receiver. Now position the scope base over the receiver and sand the underside of the scope base to match the top of the receiver by sliding it back and forth while pressing down to keep the base solidly aligned to the receiver. Continue sanding

Photograph 7-9: Here we are setting up to thin (lower) one end of a Weaver mount. This mount has a rounded inner surface so we use a half-round file for preliminary filing. We can only remove a small amount of material owing to limitations in screw hole depth (the screw shoulder requires sufficient purchase to resist recoil stresses). In this instance we will remove about 0.015" from the channel's front end. This cut will taper to zero at the location of the furthest screw hole from the front. This modification will provide proper scope leveling on a Remington pump-action rifle, without use of unsightly shims, and without moving the scope's elevation adjustment far from the center position. After this step we tape 240 grit corundum paper over the receiver bridge (paper side toward receiver!) and final-match scope base contour by sanding that against this properly shaped sanding surface. See text and associated photographs for complete discussion.

Section 7: The Trouble With Receiver-Mounted Sights, Part I

until you have eliminated almost all filing marks. If you have performed the initial filing step properly, this sanding step will take no more that a few minutes. See Photograph # 7-10.

Finally, refinish the modified surface using Birchwood Casey's aluminum black, according to their instructions. The refinished appearance will not match the original surface. However, this is a hidden face, the purpose of this step is to inhibit corrosion. See Photograph # 7-11.

A similar approach works on other types of one- or two-piece scope bases. When combined with scope ring lapping, described below, this can provide a precise custom fit. See Photograph #s 7-12/13.

Base Mounting and Attachment Screw Considerations:

When attaching the modified base or when using shims to achieve proper scope leveling, always verify that the scope base mounting screws extend fully through or to the bottom of the scope base holes but that the attachment screws do not extend past the end of the hole, where that result can allow the end of the screw to interfere with any function of the action. For

Photograph 7-10: Partially home-made scope bases (modified Weaver units) for use on Savage Model-170 pump-action rifle — listed Weaver bases did not allow proper eye relief, even with off-set scope rings. We have sanded ends of the bases, as needed to change end heights. This allows scope rings to line up properly. Base shims, shown below, were necessary to sufficiently level scope to allow proper zeroing. Need for shimming is not unusual. Sinclair International provides shim kits specifically for this purpose.

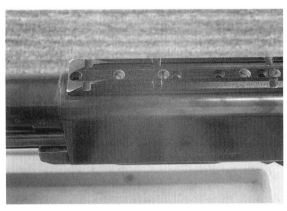

Photograph 7-12: We have highly modified this Weaver Remington Model-760 scope base. Note additional base screw holes, added cross-slots (cut with a small bastard file) and the taper at the front end. We can mount this base in several locations to maintain proper eye relief when using different-length scopes.

Photograph 7-11: Partially home-made scope bases (modified Weaver units) for use on Savage Model-170 pump-action rifle — listed Weaver bases did not allow proper eye relief, even with extended scope rings. Here we have modified both bases to allow scope rings to line up properly. We then reblackened the exposed aluminum using Birchwood Casey's Aluminum Black.

Photograph 7-13: This photograph clearly shows why we cut the taper on the top, front of this base, see associated photograph.

example, a too-long screw here can bind against the bolt body or a locking lug in the receiver race, thereby scarring and binding the bolt during manipulation of the action. See Photograph # 7-14.

You should always check any screw that enters any blind hole to verify that the end of the screw does not impinge the bottom of the hole during normal installation. Any scarring of the finish on the end of the screw is sufficient evidence that the screw is too long. A too-long screw in this situation will certainly fail to properly tighten and retain the scope base but it can also displace the material at the end of the hole, thereby damaging the receiver!

Shorten any screw, as necessary, to avoid these conditions. A bench grinder works well for this but the tinker has to hold the screw carefully to avoid losing his grip on it. This process is both dangerous and can damage the screw threads (needle nose pliers can work here if you are careful). Also, use restraint to avoid overheating the screw in the process, if it gets too hot to hold you are in danger of destroying the screw's temper — no one wants to use a screw that loses its temper!

You should not use too-short screws, resulting either from shim installation or incorrect packaging (which does happen!). Gun stores that sell and install scopes generally stock scope base screws. These are also available in incremental lengths and at a very modest price. Whenever possible, use the correct length screw. If no such screw is available, carefully shorten the next longer screw, as necessary.

When you have verified screw lengths and adjusted the scope base, as necessary, to properly align the scope, you are ready to mount the scope base. Thoroughly clean all screws, the underside of the scope base, every surface of any shims you will use, the top of the receiver and the screws using a heavy duty degreaser. Mount the gun in a padded vise with the top of the receiver exposed. When all the degreased surfaces are fully dry, apply sufficient retaining compound (Loctite Product #609) to fill all voids between the top of the receiver and the bottom of the base. Then apply a medium-strength thread locker (Loctite Product #242) to the screws, both on the threaded shank and on the shouldered head, and the threads in the holes. Carefully position the base over the receiver, lower it and install the screws.

These are high quality screws and with a properly fitting screwdriver you can tighten these sufficiently to damage the threads in the receiver! When the screw feels solidly tight, it is probably tight enough. This is one advantage to using thread locking compound. When using a thread locker, one does not have to rely upon excessive (and potentially damaging) stress in the threads to keep the screws properly tightened.

Adjusting Windage on a Scope Base:
Another common problem with scope bases is windage alignment error. Here the only good solution is to use a Redfield-type base, which allows windage adjustment at the attachment of the rear scope ring base. Mount the scope normally and adjust the scope windage turret to about the middle of its travel. Typically, adjustment of one turn of the windage screws on these bases will move bullet impact about nine inches (9") at 25 yards and thirty-six inches (36") at 100 yards — this is a rather coarse adjustment, but it is usable. See Photograph # 7-15.

(Note that Millet has recently introduced windage adjustment rings that work on Weaver-style bases.)

Set up a large paper target at 25 yards and fire a shot. For example, if bullet impact is twelve inches (12") to the left of the bullseye, adjust the rear of the scope to the right. Loosen the right ring base attachment screw slightly less than one and one-half turns and retighten the left (opposing) screw against the scope ring. Fire a second shot. Note the change in bullet impact.

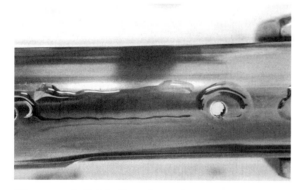

Photograph 7-14: Top-view of Remington Model-7600 pump-action rifle receiver (many other rifle bridges are similar), showing Loctite Product #609 application before scope base mounting. This mounting fixture hardens to fill small gaps. It also creates a considerable bonding force between parts. Application in this and other similar areas reduces loosening potential, eliminates vibration between parts and inhibits corrosion.

From this you can easily calculate which direction and how much you will need to move the screws to center the scope.

Generally, the one-shot zeroing method is a better approach. Set up a 25-yard target. Aim at the bullseye and fire one shot. Position the rifle in a vise or sand bags so it will not move while you adjust the dovetail base screws (or scope adjustments). Align the reticle on the bullet hole. Adjust the base screws (or scope adjustments) until the reticle centers on the aiming point. Done correctly, this will always bring any rifle on paper at 100 yards.

It is not feasible to similarly adjust windage when using Weaver-style bases and rings — unless you use the new Millet rings, as noted above. If windage error is a serious problem, consider using the Redfield-style bases; as available from Redfield, Leupold and Millet. Price is slightly higher but these are truly high quality systems and they do allow significant windage adjustment corrections.

Fitting Rotary Dovetail Rings to the Scope Base:

As supplied from the factory, rotary dovetail rings can be so tight in the base that the enthusiastic gunsmith can easily bend a scope while attempting to turn the ring into the front dovetail in the scope base! The instructions that come with these rings and bases detail the correct way of breaking in these rings and bases. Basically, the process goes as follows: loosely assemble the front ring halves, set that assembly into the front dovetail, insert a one-inch (1") hardwood dowel through the ring, tighten the top of the ring against the dowel; then, while pushing down on the dowel, turn it from side-to-side until the scope ring turns "freely" in the dovetail of the base. In this instance, "freely" means loose enough that you can turn the ring by hand without the aid of a dowel and without application of undue force. Scope tubes are not all that fragile but you should not stress one unduly just to turn a scope ring to align it with the base; certainly, no one should use any valuable scope as a pry bar but I have seen it done! See Photograph # 7-16.

If the aforementioned process will not free the ring dovetail sufficiently, consider lapping with 1200 grit silicon carbide. A little goes a long way here! Do not overdo this step, a too-loose ring, while repairable, is an unnecessary complication.

Should you encounter a too-loose ring in a dovetail mount, the easiest repair involves lightly peening the top of the base around the dovetail opening. Concentrate this action at the front and rear of the front hole. This will allow the front ring to tighten as you turn it to the correct working orientation. This will also ensure the ring is tight in that orientation. Peen using an 8-ounce ball-peen hammer and proceed very slowly. In these dovetail mounts, you measure the difference between a too-tight and a too-loose mount in units of four decimal places!

Lightening Scope Bases and Rings:

In many instances it is possible to significantly lighten scope mounting hardware. This work is primarily beneficial in reducing the stress imposed upon the mounting screws and

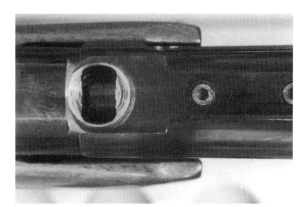

Photograph 7-16: Wear pattern on Redfield dovetail scope base. If base is too tight, one can damage or destroy a scope tube! On a new base or ring, use a hardwood dowel to work the ring. Rotate it first one way, then the other. Continue until the ring is loose enough that you can turn it in the base by hand and without undue force — but no looser.

Photograph 7-15: End of Redfield one-piece scope base partially polished to match receiver top. See associated text.

mounting screw holes. Less stress suggests less change of a screw coming loose or of screw failure. (The one-ounce, or less, reduction in weight does little to lighten the assembled rifle.) See Photograph #s 7-17/18.

Scope Ring Alignment and Fitting:
(Before proceeding with this operation, review the following sub-sections on scope mounting to ensure the rings you have chosen for the task will work!)

Photograph 7-17: Bottom-view of Redfield one-piece base mount from Remington Model-7600 pump-action rifle (other models are similar). Note myriad holes drilled almost through base. Mounting holes are near right end and near left end of narrow shank in areas without these weight-saving holes. Our purpose is to reduce the mount's weight as much as feasible without compromising strength. Here we were able to reduce weight from 1160 grains to 890 grains. Compared to the gun's overall weight, such a reduction might not be significant, but it does significantly reduce stress on the scope base mounting screws — no small consideration.

Photograph 7-18: Customized Redfield base and rings from a Remington Model-700 bolt-action rifle. Note myriad lightening holes in base and ring bottoms. Most of these holes do not proceed through the steel. In this manner, we lightened the rings and base more than one-ounce, and without compromising useful strength one iota. This weight reduction significantly reduces recoil-related stress on the scope-base mounting screws. Millet dovetail rings and bases incorporate considerable skeletonizing, which significantly reduces weight, a worthwhile consideration in one's choice of rings and bases.

Here we have an area that most scope mounters completely overlook. Scope rings seldom, if ever, align particularly well with each other. Either or both rings are often out of alignment with the common axis between them (the direction the scope will take). Also, commonly, the centerlines of the front and rear rings are not at the same windage and elevation. The standard scope mounting procedure relies on flex in the scope tube to accommodate these misalignments! Egad!

This seems like a poor way to treat a scope that might have cost more than the rifle it sits upon. Further, any stress the scope tube endures cannot help but eventually weaken the scope in one way or another. It seems a far better idea to align the rings properly in the first place. Then the scope tube simply sits in the rings with zero lateral stress applied as the gunsmith (whomever that might be) clamps the rings in place.

Sinclair International (and others) offers a simple but handy tool for this operation. This kit consists of a mild steel one-inch (1", or 30mm, as required) dowel equipped with a handle and a tub of coarse grit lapping compound. Use is quite straight forward. See Photograph # 7-19.

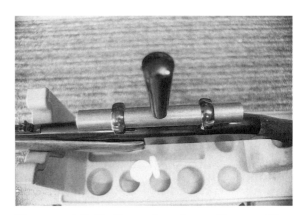

Photograph 7-19: Scope rings do not "just work" as purchased! Here we see Sinclair International's Scope Ring lapping tool ready for use on a Remington pump-action rifle mounted in Midway's Shooter's Vise. Note, open tub of lapping agent (out of focus here). Also note that tool is clean — here we were first aligning Redfield front ring to the scope base's axis. We installed the ring bottoms in the bases and set the tool in those. Then we installed and tightened the ring tops to ensure alignment. We will next remove the ring tops, apply lapping compound to the tool's shank and proceed with lapping. See text and associated photograph.

Section 7: The Trouble With Receiver-Mounted Sights, Part I

Before beginning ring lapping, on those rings where this is feasible, polish the flats between the ring halves. A good flat wet stone will do this job quickly. This affords good reference flats to measure the ring gap, as discussed below.

Secure the gun in a padded vise with the receiver top exposed and level. Mount the ring bases to the scope base and, if necessary, roughly align the front and rear ring to each other (as in the dovetailed mount system). Apply a bit of lapping compound around both ends of the mild steel lapping tool. Set the tool in the rings. Install the ring tops over the tool carefully, to avoid getting lapping agent on the flats. Attach the tops loosely to the bases with all necessary screws.

When you have squarely aligned everything, slightly snug all screws attaching the ring tops to the bases. If necessary, adjust these screws until the ring tops set centered and square over the bottoms. Also, adjust the front and rear screws so the gap is equal width front and rear and the side-to-side screws so the side gaps are equal.

With the ring tops so adjusted, work the lapping tool back and forth endwise while rotating the handle from side-to-side. Soon the tool will loosen as this action quickly removes the high spots from the ring interiors. Slightly and equally snug all ring screws and repeat the lapping process. Remove the ring tops, clean all surfaces and observe the lapping action.

In most instances, two or three cycles of this process will suffice; however, where particularly bad alignment existed you might have to repeat this process many times while recharging the lapping agent and resnugging the screws repeatedly. In any case, do not proceed any farther than necessary to achieve almost complete (95%+) lapping of the entire ring interior surfaces. Through excessive lapping, you could render the rings too loose to properly tighten on the scope tube! However, you could also use this process to open the rings so that proper tightening occurs when the ends' gaps just disappear. . . a splendid touch! See Photograph # 7-20.

After completion of the ring lapping process, reblue or reanodize all lapped surfaces. This will prevent corrosion while minimizing the potential for scarring of the scope tube during assembly and adjustment. See Photograph #s 7-21 through 7-24.

Scope Mounting:

After performing the gyrations noted in the above sub-sections, it remains only to properly mount the scope in the rings. This begins with mounting the gun in a padded vise (Midway's Gun Vise is particularly useful for this operation).

Set the scope in the ring bases and observe all areas of potential interference. The objective bell and the parallax adjustment ring (if present) should clear the barrel and any fixtures, such as the barrel-mounted rear iron sight, by at least one-sixty-fourth inch (1/64") — less clearance can result in vibration-spawned damage to the scope and possibly the iron sight as those pieces bounce around and off each other. The eyepiece and magnification adjustment ring (if present) must clear all portions of the action during all phases of action manipulation and regardless of the rifle scope's magnification setting. If this installation does not achieve proper clearances, use taller scope rings, as necessary. See Photograph #s 7-25/26.

Photograph 7-20: Sinclair International's Scope Ring lapping tool in use on Remington pump-action rifle mounted in Midway's Shooter's Vise. Note, open tub of lapping agent (out of focus here). Also note ghost marks on tool's shank. These marks reflect proper lapping action — while moving the handle from side-to-side push the tool first backward, then forward, fully to the ends of its travel. Begin by snugging both ring tops to provide even side-gaps — tighten only enough to add a small amount of friction to the tool's motion. After sufficient tool manipulation, necessary to lap out all high spots from the ring bores in this setting (as evidenced by easing of the tool's motion), resnug the ring tops and repeat the process. To fully true the ring bores, it is often necessary to reduce the gap between ring bottoms and tops as much as 0.010"! This job can occupy several minutes of lapping. One might have to recharge tool with fresh lapping agent several times.

Begin attachment of the scope to the rings by placing the scope in the attached ring bases. Position the scope about midway front-to-rear along its possible travel. Place the scope ring top halves over the tube. (If you use Weaver style rings, which sometimes snap over the scope tube, wrap a piece of paper over the tube before spanning the ring half over the tube, this will prevent damage to the finish on the scope tube.) Slide the ring tops over the bases and install sufficient screws to secure the scope loosely. During the next operation you will want to move the scope around, so do not snug it sufficiently to prevent easy manipulation.

The next stage is to set the scope for proper eye relief. The <u>only</u> way to correctly set the eye relief on your rifle with your scope to fit you is as follows. Dress in your typical shooting garb. Make certain the gun in unloaded. Assume your typical shooting pose. If you expect to shoot

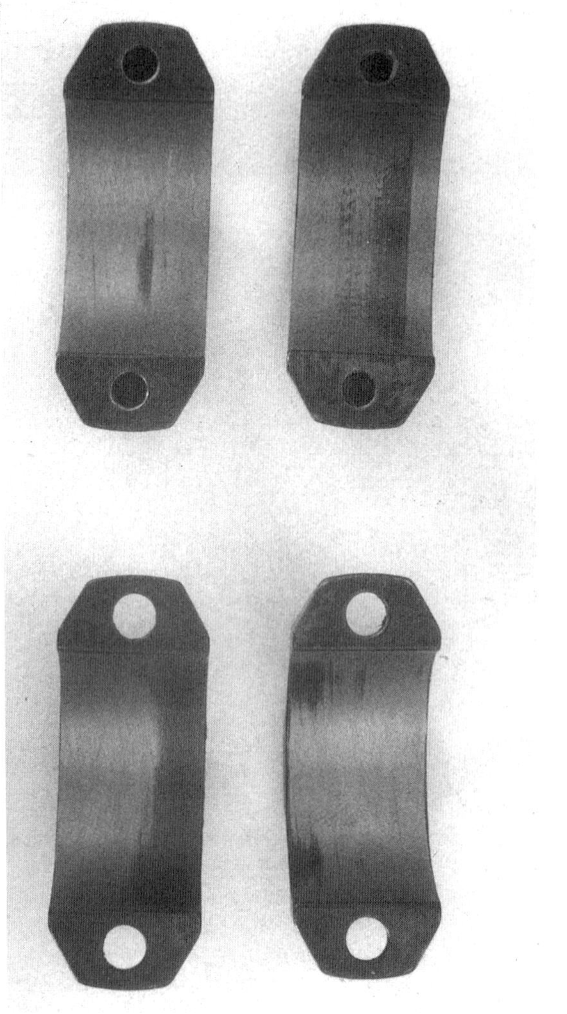

Photograph 7-21: Partially lapped rings. Here we have lapped away about 0.06" of ring gap. We still have not achieved anything approaching 100% simultaneous ring-to-scope-tube contact! One can also see on the ring bases (at bottom) that the inside edges are not lapping as much as the outside edges. This suggests that the one-piece base is flexing on the action — bending up at both ends. Such base and receiver mismatching is <u>very</u> common. This is only one reason ring lapping is so beneficial. Imagine the stress we would place on a scope tube if we did not lap away this misalignment!

Photograph 7-22: Scope rings after lapping bores and polishing flats. Note on the ring base at lower left that we have failed to lap one area (top left of bore). After lapping out a full 0.011" of side-gap I gave up! This 95%+ lapping job is, nevertheless, probably sufficiently complete for our purpose. In lapping the flats we only intend to create a consistent surface to facilitate ring side-gap measurement with a feeler gauge. See text.

Section 7: The Trouble With Receiver-Mounted Sights, Part I

almost exclusively either offhand or with an improvised rest, as with a typical hunting rifle, then do this study offhand. If you expect to shoot from the bench, then do this at the bench.

Close your eyes and bring the rifle into shooting position and your face to rest on the cheek piece as you normally would when shooting. Open your eyes and observe the field of view through the scope.

Let us assume you observe only a partial field of view in the ocular. Carefully, and without moving anything else, use your shooting hand to slide the scope forward. One of two things will happen: either the field of view will enlarge or it will shrink!

If the field of view enlarges, keep sliding the scope forward until the field of view occupies the entire ocular. Then continue sliding the scope forward until the field of view just begins to shrink. Then slide the tube back between one-half inch (1/2") and one-quarter inch (1/4"). On high recoil guns stay with the latter figure, to avoid getting ringed by the scope. This is the correct eye relief setting for that scope, that gun and that shooting pose. However, repeat this process until you are certain you have it right. With this initial setting, the typical shooter can adjust his head to achieve proper eye relief with other shooting poses.

Conversely, if the field of view shrinks when you begin to slide the scope forward, reverse yourself, sliding the scope back. Then follow the above procedure to attain the correct eye relief setting.

Repeat the eyes-closed test several times to ensure you are posing naturally and not practicing old bad habits as you bring yourself and the gun into shooting position. When the eye relief setting is satisfactory, one other scope mounting adjustment remains. To facilitate that process, mark the scope tube by aligning the edge of a one-inch (1") long strip of masking tape at the edge of a scope ring in a convenient location where the edge of tape passes a landmark on the rings. A good location is where the tape crosses the juncture of the base and top of the ring. We will return to this process after addressing the following potential problem.

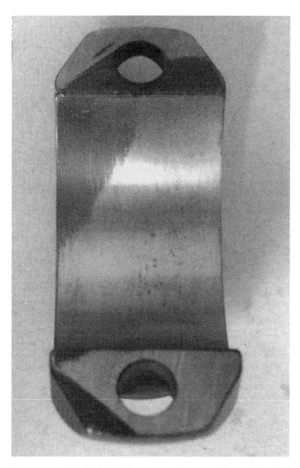

Photograph 7-23: Close-up-view of lapped ring base. Note area at top left of bore. After lapping out a full 0.011" of ring side-gap I gave up! This 95%+ lapping job is, nevertheless, probably sufficient for our purposes. In lapping the flats we only intend to create a consistent surface to facilitate ring side-gap measurement with a feeler gauge.

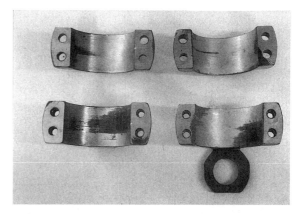

Photograph 7-24: Another set of Redfield dovetail scope rings, partially lapped for alignment. Note weight reducing hole in extension on rear ring bottom. Perspective in this view hides many other weight-reducing holes. Millet dovetail rings and bases incorporate considerable skeletonizing, which significantly reduces weight, a worthwhile consideration.

Unacceptable Eye Relief Limitations:

Often, mechanical limitations will prevent obtaining correct eye relief — either the turret towers or the bell at one end of the scope tube will come up against one or the other of the scope rings. In this situation, the scope mounter can usually achieve a solution by substitution of one or more offset scope rings. These are commonly available from all major manufacturers.

Leveling The Scope Reticle:

Segway Industries offers a wonderful product called the Reticle Leveler. The design and construction of this unit allows it to rest across the scope base and level to that. A rubber band then loosely attaches it to the rifle. The shooter looks through the scope and rotates the scope tube until the reticle lines up with the lines on the Reticle Leveler, which project to either side of the scope tube in his field of view — the essence of simplicity. See Photograph # 7-27.

The following method will work with most types of scopes. (If this approach does not work you will have to resort to sighting through the scope normally, as shown in the associated photographs.) Mount the gun in a padded vise. Stand behind the stock and position your eye until a ghost image of the reticle appears, floating in the ocular. Position your eye until this image centers in the ocular. Then rotate the scope tube until the horizontal reticle is parallel with the lines on the Reticle Leveler. See Photograph #s 7-28/29.

If this method will not work, simply shoulder the rifle and rotate the scope until the horizontal reticle aligns to the lines on the Reticle Leveler. This method has advantages but it is slightly harder to make fine adjustments from this pose.

Final Scope Mounting:

When you have leveled the reticle, as verified by the Reticle Leveler, carefully mark the tape you applied after establishing the correct eye relief. Choose a fixed reference point, such as the top edge of the scope ring base. Then remove the screws retaining the rings tops. While protecting the scope tube (if necessary), remove the ring top halves.

Photograph 7-25

Photograph 7-26

Photographs 7-25/26: Remington Model-7600 pump-action rifle with Bausch & Lomb 2¹/₂-10x Elite 4000 scope mounted in Redfield rings on Redfield base. Photograph 7-25: Note that scope's objective bell is touching the rear sight, a genuine no-no!

Photograph 7-26: Note clearance between scope objective bell and both rear sight and barrel; compare to photograph 7-25. Never allow any portion of any scope to touch anything on the rifle other than the scope rings!

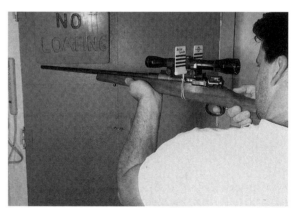

Photograph 7-27: Sighting through scope, to verify reticle alignment, using Segway Products, Reticle Leveler. See text and associated photograph captions for a complete discussion.

Section 7: The Trouble With Receiver-Mounted Sights, Part I

Remove the scope from the ring bases and proceed to clean the following surfaces: channels in the ring bases and ring tops; screws, threads and shoulder of screw head; threads in screw holes; scope tube, where it rests in the rings. Use alcohol (or acetone) and cotton until all pieces are completely clean.

After allowing all pieces to thoroughly dry, apply a thin coat of retaining compound (Loctite Product #609) to the channels in the ring bases. Position the scope over the ring bases and lower it in place. Rotate it until the index mark lines up and slide it endwise to bring the tape against the base.

Install the ring tops (on Weaver rings use a paper shield, if necessary, to avoid damage to the scope tube). Apply a thin coat of retaining compound (Loctite Product #609) to the scope tube where the ring tops will position. Lift the ring tops slightly and slide each into position until the screw holes align. See Photograph # 7-30.

Photograph 7-29: Reticle leveler, in use on Remington pump-action rifle. This view shows poor reticle leveling. With two-piece (Redfield style) rings one has only to adjust the scope tube's orientation until horizontal reticle is parallel to lines on the leveler. With Weaver-style rings (a hook on one side and screws on the other), one must "preload" the reticle with a <u>slight</u> counterclockwise rotation. Preloading with about one-third the turn shown here is typically sufficient to allow the scope to come level as one tightens the scope ring screws.

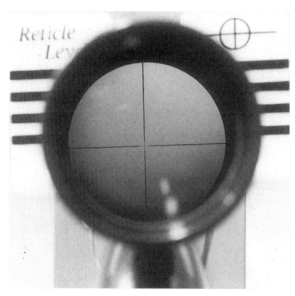

Photograph 7-28: Reticle leveler, in use on Remington Pump. This view shows an acceptably, although not perfectly, leveled reticle. The device rests across scope base. One attaches it with rubber bands mounted over hooks and around bottom of receiver. One merely peers through scope, noting relationship between horizontal reticle and horizontal lines on leveler. With two-piece (Redfield style) rings one has only to adjust the scope tube's orientation until reticle is parallel to lines on the leveler. When one uses Weaver-style rings, one must slightly "preload" the reticle, with a counterclockwise rotation. See following photograph.

Photograph 7-30: Top-view of Remington Model-7600 pump-action rifle receiver with scope base and ring bottoms in place (many other rifles are similar). Here we have applied Loctite Product #609 before scope mounting. This mounting fixture product hardens to fill small gaps and creates a significant bonding force between parts. Application in this and other similar areas reduces loosening potential and eliminates vibration or motion between parts.

Apply a medium-strength thread locking compound (Loctite Product #242) to the threads and shoulder of the screws and begin to install those. If the caps use screws on both sides, snug those carefully until the gap separating the cap and the base is equal along both sides. Proceed to turn the screws until all just touch the caps.

From this point, tighten the screws in exactly one-eighth (1/8) turn increments (always end exactly 1 turn from where you started after each eight cycles). Use the following patterns. If there are two screws on each side of each ring, snug the rear screw on one side, the front screw on the other side, the front screw on the first side and finally the rear screw on the other side. Then switch to the other cap and repeat the above sequence. Repeat these steps until the rings are sufficiently tight. If you properly cleaned everything and used the mounting agent you can tighten the screws sufficiently by applying only modest torque with a properly fitting screwdriver — you can feel the system come up tight, no need to force the issue.

If each ring has only one screw on each side, simply alternate sides and rings until both are tight. If each ring has screws on only one side (Weaver style) the entire process is a bit different.

First, you have to estimate how far the gap between the ring cap and the ring base will close before the rings are properly tightened. This is because tightening the ring caps in place also (almost always) rotates the scope tube! Now, remember, we went to considerable trouble to level the reticle and now (in the final act) we are losing that setting!

Typically the gap will close something less than thirty-thousandths of an inch (0.030") and the scope will rotate as the gap closes on the screw side of the rings' tops. As a first effort (which we hope works), try turning the scope tube until the index mark on the tape is about fifteen-thousandths of an inch (0.015") above the edge of the ring base.

Screw tightening sequence is as follows: snug each screw on one base one-eighth (1/8) turn then snug each screw on the other base one-eighth (1/8) turn. Repeat this until the screws are sufficiently tight (see the discussion above). If the reticle did not end up properly leveled, loosen the screws and adjust the tube accordingly.

Receiver-Mounted & Tang-Mounted Iron Sight Installation:

As is shown in the accompanying photographs, receiver-mounted sight installation commonly requires modification of the gun's stock to provide wood to sight-base clearance. This clearance is critical. Sight-base installations lacking such clearance are almost certain to result in a split stock. There is also the specter of lost accuracy. Always provide several thousandths of an inch clearance between any sight components and the stock. See Photograph # 7-31.

Other problems with iron sight-base installations are similar to problems encountered with scope sight bases: screws that are too long or too short, improper contour between the sight-base and the receiver and failure to treat the screws to protect against loosening. Loctite's Products #222 and #609 are particularly useful here. See Photograph # 7-32.

The associated photographs show several typical installations. Note that I have outlined installation of a right-hand Lyman peep sight on a left-hand Remington Model-700 to allow simultaneous scope and peep sight mounting. Obviously, the mirror image installation is possible and desirable. However, at this time Lyman does not offer a left-hand version of this sight so the task is complicated, slightly.

Photograph 7-31: Lyman receiver-mounted peep sight base for Remington Model-700 bolt-action rifle. View from bottom showing stock mounting screw protrusion, right, compared to modified protrusion, left. We drilled both holes slightly deeper using a square-ended drill bit of proper size. This allowed the supplied screws to reach about two threads further through the base. This allows a more secure mount. However, use a drill press, and caution, to avoid drilling either hole too deeply, thereby weakening the screw head's purchase in the base.

Section 7: The Trouble With Receiver-Mounted Sights, Part I

To achieve a similar installation on a right-hand rifle the tinker will have to include drilling and tapping of two additional holes in the rifle's receiver, one two-tenths inch (0.2") behind each of the existing iron sight receiver mount holes. The proper index drill bit for these holes is a #31 (0.120"). The proper tap is a 6x48, available through Brownells. I would suggest scribing a light line between the existing holes and extending about one-quarter inch (1/4") behind the rear hole. Measure precisely two-tenths inch (0.2") back from the front receiver hole center and mark a hole location with a center punch. Drill that location with the #31 index drill bit. Thread that hole using the 6x48 tap. Cutting oil with molybdenum disulfide added works wonderfully for this (and all tapping operations). Install the sight base using the existing forward hole in the base and the new hole in the receiver. The mating contours on the receiver and base should properly align the base to the receiver. In any case, insure the base is properly aligned. Use a hole center punch to mark a location in the receiver through the rear hole in the sight base. Drill and tap this hole as with the first hole. The remainder of the installation is identical to the left-hand version only in mirror image. See Photograph #s 7-33/34.

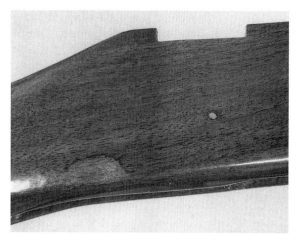

Photograph 7-33: Finished Lyman Receiver-mounted aperture sight-base relief cut in left-hand Remington Model-700 stock.
Note worn area in stock finish just behind this cut at the bottom — this demonstrates why I prefer oil-based finishes. If the manufacturer had used an oil-based finish on this stock I could repair this use-mark to practical invisibility in a matter of seconds. As it is, this mark is part of the package until the epoxy goes! Brownells makes just the product for that, called Certistrip. This stuff wipes on, cleans up with water and simply wipes away the epoxy finish!

Photograph 7-32: Lyman right-hand Remington Model-700 receiver aperture sight base mounted on left-hand rifle. This moves sight assembly slightly rearward (0.2"). Note that mounting holes are not centered front-to-rear in the sight base. This wrong-handed application facilitates use of this aperture sight with a Redfield one-piece base in place. However, clearances are tight. See associated photographs. Note also that the necessary stock relief cut (under the base) is lacking here. Note elevated tang suggesting approximately the amount of stock relief necessary to clear the base. Use caution here: Remove sufficient material to positively prevent this base from touching wood (otherwise the stock is certain to split) but avoid cutting away sufficient wood to cause an unsightly gap between sight base and stock.

Photograph 7-34: Finished Lyman Receiver-mounted aperture sight base relief cut in left-hand Remington Model-700 stock. Stock and barreled-action assembled. Note limited but absolute clearance between sight base and stock. If the base touches anywhere, accuracy will suffer. If the sight base touches wood at the rear, the wood between the sight base and the tang drop will certainly fracture off as a result of recoil-induced stress. Also note that the bottom of both vertical cuts is a slightly radiused transition to the flat bottom of the cut. Also, we have relieved the inside of the stock slightly more from the sight base than at the outside — the sides of the cutout are not parallel to the sight base sides. (Front relief does not show in this perspective.)

Perhaps, one point that I have not stressed sufficiently relates to this particular example. I cannot over stress the value of a backup sighting system on any hunting rifle. The hunter can carry a spare scope in his backpack. Assuming that he has already sighted the scope for the rifle and load and that he can easily change the scopes in the field, this system can provide a handy backup scope in case of a failed or damaged scope. However, the hunter could just as easily wreck the spare scope during carry.

Also, there are plenty of hunting situations where open or aperture sights can come in most handy. For these situations a quality back up iron sight makes plenty of sense. See Photograph #s 7-35/36/37.

Photograph 7-35: Left-hand Remington Model-700 bolt-action rifle with a combination of a Redfield one-piece scope base and a Lyman receiver-mounted peep sight in place! This combination requires use of a modified right-hand Lyman Remington Model-700 sight, slight bolt handle modification, use of medium height rings, and use of a small-diameter aperture (outside size). However, this effort is worthwhile. By simply removing the scope and raising the rear sight to the preset zero-mark, the gun is ready for open-sight use. Certainly, a handy expedient for certain hunting conditions or in the emergency situation of a damaged scope-sight. This assembly just barely fits but one can achieve it. Since Lyman does not offer a mirror-image aperture sight (intended for left-hand rifles) one has to modify this installation through additional hole drilling for application to a right-hand Model-700, see text. As one more added bonus, the scope base supports the aperture assembly against recoil! See associated photographs.

Photograph 7-36: Assembled aperture, here raised slightly higher than it would be in the scope-sighted carry mode. Note failing clearance between bolt handle and aperture. When we lowered the sight to fully clear a mounted scope (in medium height Redfield rings) the bolt handle hit the aperture. We solved this problem by slightly lowering the front of the bolt end of the bolt handle. See associated photographs.

Photograph 7-37: Left-hand Remington Model-700 bolt-action rifle. We have equipped this gun with a Redfield one-piece base and medium height Redfield rings. These rings hold a Bushnell 4x Scope Chief glass. The rifle simultaneously features Lyman's receiver-mounted peep sight, ready to use! One only has to remove the scope and lift the aperture sight (by pressing the elevation release button) to the preset zero to use the open sights, which are high enough to look over the scope base, unobstructed. Clearances are tight, note relief cut in bolt handle, small diameter aperture and that peep aperture just barely clears scope tube. Nevertheless, this system does work. With a larger objective bell and higher rings, clearances are not such a problem.

Section 8: Miscellaneous, Part I

Several items fall outside the scope of this work but, nonetheless, deserve mention. I will address these here primarily through photographs and captions. Many will be revisited in *Parts II & III*.

Rechambering Considerations:

I have skirted the subject of chambering. Included herein I have provided a photographic chronicle of the basic steps that a gunsmith will follow to produce a chamber in a rifle barrel. Note that rechambering might include turning the barrel one thread (or more) deeper into the receiver. This requires appropriate work on the barrel, which I have not demonstrated here.

There are certain rechambering operations that the dedicated tinker might consider tackling at home on some types of rifles. However, after considering the tools, equipment and expertise proper chambering requires, I feel this is a job best left to the professional. See Photograph #s 8-1 through 8-12.

Ammunition Considerations:

In several instances in this text, I have referred to handloaded ammunition. There are several situations where a gun's design or a modification to a gun's action can provide special problems of which the handloader should be cognizant. As noted in the text, handloads can often grow slightly longer in the headspace dimension than typical factory ammunition. If your home gunsmithing operations have changed the gun's headspace you might find your old handloads will no longer chamber properly.

Avoid this problem by using up all old (chamber specific) handloads before performing any work that might shorten your rifle's headspace (or use that ammunition in another rifle where you know it will work safely). On the other side, Redding now offers shell holders designed to allow the handloader to add headspace length to handloaded cartridges. Use of the correct one of these shellholders will allow the handloader to decrease unnecessary handload headspace by up to ten-thousandths of an inch (0.010"). This is an extremely worthwhile improvement, especially since it can improve accuracy, extend case life and add a margin of safety.

Always verify the ammunition in the gun! I am often reminded of a batch of .30-40 Krag ammunition I loaded for a Model-1895 Winchester Rifle. I chose 168 grain HPBT Match bullets and a charge of powder that would provide a useful trajectory for experimenting at longer ranges. The overall length was within typical bounds for that cartridge but the resulting loads would not feed out of the magazine and into the chamber! The sharp jacket tip simply jammed into the front of the magazine well — no amount of force would chamber a cartridge out of the magazine. (For single loading the rounds worked well.)

The point here is that regardless of the work you have done to your fine rifle you cannot assume it will therefore function properly with any given handload (or factory load for that matter). Always verify fit and function of any ammunition <u>before</u> you place yourself in a situation where you have to depend upon it to function properly.

Photograph 8-1: Here our gunsmith has centered the barrel's muzzle in the lathe. A tapered pilot provides a reference for dial-indicator micrometer. The gunsmith similarly centered the barrel's chamber end. Where doing rechambering work this is less critical. Chamber reamers tend to follow an existing chamber and the reamer chuck is designed to float. However, when cutting a new chamber, centering is super-critical.

Photograph 8-2: The only proper method of chambering or rechambering a barrel uses a lathe and proper fixtures. Here our gunsmith has chucked, centered and aligned the barrel, which extends through the lathe's driven head. The gunsmith has mounted the proper reamer in a special JGS reamer holder. Partially hidden on the tool stand is a Brownells' reamer floater, less expensive but also functional. These tools prevent reamer rotation while allowing the reamer to center with the bore's axis — the reamer will float, as necessary, to account for an incorrectly centered barrel. However, in this setup the gunsmith centered the barrel to within 0.0002" at both ends using alignment pilots and a dial-indicator. Here we are rechambering a .30-30 chambered Marlin barrel to .30-30 Ackley Improved. The 10% increase in available muzzle energy is only one of the significant advantages such an alteration affords.

Section 8: Miscellaneous, Part I

Photograph 8-3: Here our gunsmith has set up to rechamber a Marlin Model-336 barrel to .30-30 Ackley Improved. Note oil can, cleaning rod and patches; all are necessary. Cutting oil is critical. The gunsmith must frequently swab all cuttings from the chamber reamer, chamber and bore.

Here we were forced to use a three-jaw chuck. Ideally one would use a four-jaw chuck, which allows proper barrel centering. However, this barrel was too short to allow centering on the muzzle end when using the longer four-jaw chuck. This three-jaw chuck centered the barrel within 0.002" and, since this is a rechambering job, this is certainly sufficient (the reamer will follow the existing chamber).

At left the tail stock holds a JGS-made floating chuck where the gunsmith has affixed the chambering reamer. This assembly prevents the reamer from turning but allows it to center to the bore, even when the bore axis is 0.040" off-center as the barrel turns. See associated photographs and text.

Photograph 8-4: Close-up-view of JGS .30-30 Ackley Improved reamer, chucked in JGS floating reamer holder. This assembly prevents the reamer from turning. However, it allows the reamer to center to the bore, even when the bore axis is 0.040" off-center as the barrel turns. Here the reamer is just beginning to enter the existing chamber on a Marlin-336 barrel. Gunsmith thoroughly lubricates barrel bore and chamber with cutting oil.

Photograph 8-5: Close-up-view of JGS .30-30 Ackley Improved reamer, working in a Marlin-336 barrel. Here reamer is far enough into chamber to begin cutting. Gunsmith generously applies cutting oil to lubricate chamber.

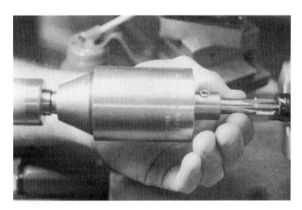

Photograph 8-6: Close-up-view of JGS .30-30 Ackley Improved reamer, working in a Marlin-336 barrel. Here reamer is almost completely into chamber; only about 1/8" left to cut. Gunsmith is advancing tail stock and reamer assembly by hand. He generously lubricates chamber and bore with cutting oil. Here we have stopped the lathe for photographic clarity.

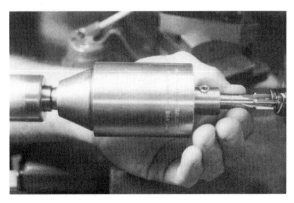

Photograph 8-7: Again, with lathe running. We have almost finished this job.

Photograph 8-8: Job almost done! Here our gunsmith carefully withdraws reamer after finishing chamber reaming. (In this instance, we were able to observe correct chambering headspace based upon reamer rim shoulder just touching existing shoulder at rear of barrel, because this is a rechambering job with a rimmed cartridge.)

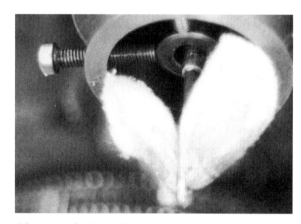

Photograph 8-9: Chip removal is critical in all chambering and crowning work. Here our gunsmith pushes clean patches through the bore from chamber end. Note limited cutting oil and cuttings on this, the third patch.

Photograph 8-10: Cuttings on chambering reamer, after final stage of cutting. The gunsmith should withdraw the reamer often and completely clean both reamer and chamber. Any cuttings left on either surface could result in a scarred chamber! Application of plenty of cutting oil is critical to long tool life and a smooth chamber cut. With a set of reamers costing as much as a typical rifle, tool life is not a small consideration.

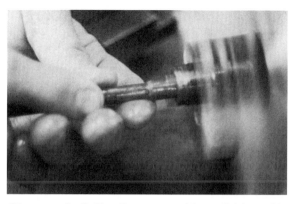

Photograph 8-11: Our gunsmith polishing this newly reamed Marlin-336 .30-30 Ackley Improved chamber. His tool is a slotted hardwood dowel wrapped with 800-grit corundum paper. Lathe is turning at a moderate speed. Fifteen to thirty seconds of this treatment while moving the dowel to-and-fro in the spinning chamber is sufficient to render a beautifully polished chamber.

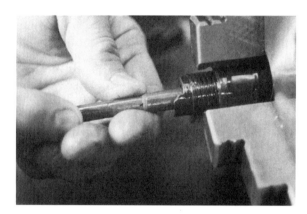

Photograph 8-12: Close-up-view with lathe stopped for photographic clarity. Chamber polishing operation. Note electrical tape around barrel. This protects barrel from cosmetic damage as gunsmith tightens the chuck jaws. Here gunsmith is withdrawing polishing tool from well-oiled chamber. Polishing is not strictly necessary when reamer is sharp, but it is a good idea — a chamber cannot be too smooth!

Parts II & III

Section 9: Acknowledgments and Introduction, *Parts II & III*

My heartfelt appreciation and thanks to all those individuals and companies who have provided considerable additional assistance toward the completion of *Parts II & III* of this book. Specifically, these include: Brownells, Larry Weeks; Colorado West Gunsmithing, my friend, Art Branscomb; DeHart's Custom Gunsmithing (713) 771-3336, Keith DeHart; Harris Engineering, Inc. (bipods), Gerald Harris; JGS Precision Tool Manufacturing, Keith Francis; Kokopelli Products (406) 755-3220, John Werre; Krieger Barrels, John Krieger; Marble's (dovetail front sight inserts); Marlin Firearms Company, Bob Behn; Millet Sights (scopes, rings and bases), Chuck Miller; Randolph Constantine (technical assistance); Nostalgia Enterprises Company (NECO), Roger Johnston; Redfield (scopes, rings and bases), Bob Knopf; Reinhart Fajen, Jerry Foust and Donny Jemes; S. D. Meacham Tool & Hardware Inc. (208) 486-7171, Steve Meacham (technical assistance); Savage Arms, Inc., Ron Coburn and Lynn Johnson; The ROBAR Companies (602) 581-2648, Robbie Barrkman, et al; Williams Gun Sight Co., Inc., Don Campeau; and my wife, Peggy McPherson (editorial assistance and proofreading).

Of course, all those mentioned explicitly at the beginning of *Part I* also contributed to completion of this portion of the manuscript. I would like to express, again, my thanks to those individuals and companies.

Explanation And Purpose Of Accurizing The Factory Rifle, *Part II*:

I should note that there are several subjects that I have covered in some detail in more than one sub-section of this text. Generally, I have tried to include significant information with each sub-section. For this reason, some subjects are covered more than once. However, usually, the emphasis varies, depending upon the subject at hand.

Also, the following introductory text contains an outline of many of the topics in *Part II*. Details of each of these subjects are contained in later sections.

In *Part II*, it is my goal to explore many of the principles and techniques involved in accurizing and improving the functioning of various Lever-Action, Falling-Block and other Single-Shot rifles. Here I will specifically consider the following lever-action rifles: typical tubular-magazine lever-action designs, as exemplified by the various models of both Marlin and Winchester rifles; Savage's unique Model-99 series, both rotary-magazine and removable magazine versions; Browning's BLR (Browning Lever-action Rifle), featuring a removable-magazine; and Winchester's Model-88, also a removable-magazine style.

I will also address several falling-block rifle designs. Explicitly, I will address Ruger's falling-block rifle, as represented by the No. 1. This analysis will indirectly address various other single-shot actions that are conceptually similar. This is a broad class, which includes modern originals, modern replicas and now antique originals; as manufactured by Browning, Winchester, Sharps, C. Sharps, Shiloh Sharps and such custom producers as Steve Meacham. However, I must note that the falling-block is a unique species with myriad accurizing tricks. Gunsmiths have been passing down many of these tidbits for generations. I will make no effort to cover accurizing of the falling-block in minute detail. Those interested in such an undertaking should review, *The Single-Shot Rifle and Gunsmithing Idea Book*, by Frank de Haas. What I will suggest are the general ideas, those modifications with possible application to all such rifles.

I will also touch upon the modern single-shot H&R Ultra and New England Firearms Handi-Rifle, which differ only in the moniker with which they are embossed. In as much as the following are essentially short-stocked, short-barreled rifles, I will also (indirectly) cover the TC/Contender and the various similarly functioning breach-break handguns, and of course, the TC/Contender Carbine.

Many of the areas covered in *Part II* are directly applicable to other single-shot designs such as the Remington Rolling-Block and various British, European and North American single-shot designs of yesteryear. An understanding of the related concepts should go a long way toward allowing the tinker to dramatically improve fit, function and reliability of any single-shot or lever-action repeating rifle. That is my primary goal in *Part II*.

As noted in the introduction to *Part I*, this is a generic tome. Therefore, I cannot make any significant inroads toward particular discussion of every single-shot and lever-action rifle design ever produced. There are simply too many variations on these basic themes. I will, however, try to cover specific areas that are of general interest, and cover those in such a way as to suggest what modifications you might consider for improving your specific rifle.

Practically all (non turn-bolt) single-shot and lever-action repeating rifles share many design characteristics. Perhaps chief among these is the two-piece stocking system. There are exceptions here. Winchester's Model-88 (and the similar Model-100 semi-automatic rifle) carries a one-piece stock. Proper receiver-to-stock bedding is quite unique for those models. I will address that issue separately. Proper receiver-to-stock bedding for other single-shot or lever-action rifles with one-piece stocks will require an understanding of the principles set forth in *Part I* and those expressed in the subsection covering stock-to-receiver bedding for the Winchester Model-88.

In general, however, single-shot and lever-action repeaters feature two-piece stocks. These rifles have separate fore-ends that are attached to the receiver or to the barrel by one, or more, of various methods. Proper receiver, or barrel, bedding of this piece of wood can dramatically improve intrinsic accuracy of these rifles while reducing shifts of zero related to variations in humidity, temperature or how the shooter rests the rifle on the shooting bench before each shot.

Conversely, in all rifles using a two-piece stocking system, buttstock-to-receiver bedding is quite similar (conceptually identical) to that for the Remington or Savage pump-action rifles, as discussed in *Part I*. However, note, the buttstock attachment system on many of the rifles discussed in *Part II* involves only a simple tang bolt. In this system, a bolt connects the upper and lower tangs through the buttstock; tightening that bolt simply clamps the tang extensions onto the interposing portion of the stock — this clamping action does not necessarily form a rigid bond between the buttstock and the receiver that is so desirable from the accuracy standpoint.

Some of these designs incorporate a tapered tang bolt. The design of this system provides for the tang bolt to take up the slack between the corresponding hole in the buttstock and the tang-bolt holes in the receiver. In principle, and if properly fitted, this system will take up the slack between receiver and buttstock and it will provide a relatively tight buttstock-to-receiver bond.

While conceptually ingenious, the tapered tang bolt system is fragile and subject to wear. Aging, that causes shrinkage of the wood, dehydration shrinkage of the stock, or normal wear and tear to the wood in the tang-bolt hole will eventually render this method useless for the intended purpose: solidly abutting the front of the buttstock to the receiver boss. Also, the tapered tang-bolt method cannot take advantage of the tremendous compressive strength of wood in forming a rigid attachment bond between the entire buttstock and the receiver.

The failure of any tang-bolt attachment system to properly bond the buttstock to the receiver is a major cause of inaccuracy in this type of rifle. The chief accuracy influence of this weakness is an unusual propensity for vertical stringing in these rifles. This is of considerable concern to those shooting these rifles from the bench. Minor variations in hold will result in significant vertical stringing.

Conversely, for offhand shooting this is less of a practical concern. In offhand shooting it is much more difficult for the shooter to inadvertently (or even deliberately) vary his hold on the rifle in such a way as to significantly alter the flexure at the joint between the buttstock and the receiver. As a result, in offhand shooting the weak bond between buttstock and receiver will not result in much vertical stringing.

Nevertheless, even for the hunter who never shoots from the bench, solid buttstock-to-receiver attachment is of value for two reasons. First, it does improve the rifle's intrinsic accuracy for offhand or improvised rest shooting, albeit marginally. Second, it reduces the possibility of a broken stock due to mishap. This latter is of no small consequence. Consider that I have seen many broken buttstocks; every one has been a tang-bolt-mounted stock. While I know it must happen, I have never seen a broken buttstock on a rifle that used a through-bolt for buttstock mounting.

The reason a simple tang-bolt buttstock attachment is not conducive to accuracy is related to this weakness. The tang bolt provides a loose fore-to-aft bonding between the buttstock and receiver. This (relatively) loose joint magnifies variations in the shooter's hold and bench technique. With such a rifle, a slight change in pressure between the shooter's cheek and the buttstock can result in a large change in bullet impact (vertical stringing is the most common result). Proper bonding of the buttstock to the receiver can significantly reduce this tendency.

The tinker can achieve the necessary improved bonding quite easily in most such rifles. In *Part II*, I will specify the particulars of this modification in some detail, using the Marlin lever-action rifle as an example. Note that the dedicated tinker can accomplish similar modifications on practically any rifle using a two-piece stocking system — this applied to most single-shot and lever-action designs.

Another area wherein many of these rifles share common features is a general complicity of action function — there are many moving parts. In general, in those rifles featuring a tubular magazine, these articulated parts function to carry a cartridge from the discharge port of the tubular magazine (located in the front of the receiver and under the barrel) and into the opening action and then to properly align that cartridge with the chamber during the closing stroke of the action. Other articulated parts function to lock the action.

This action complexity is not necessarily a negative characteristic; often just the opposite, it results in very good rifle action manipulation characteristics. For a classic example of just how good such a mechanism can be, consider Winchester's Model-71. Typical examples of the Model-71 function with a degree of smoothness and dependability that is simply unmatched by any bolt-action repeater this author has ever seen. As a demonstration of the value of said smoothness and dependability, consider the following facts.

Owing to a relatively high cost of production and the resulting inevitably modest sales, Winchester discontinued the Model-71 in 1955, after only a twenty year production run. Winchester only chambered the Model-71 for what is, by modern "magnum" standards, a rather anemic cartridge, the .348 Winchester. That round launches a 250 grain bullet at about 2200 fps. Nevertheless, despite the modest ballistics of the chambering, in Alaska the Model-71 Winchester rifle is, to this day, the standard against which all serious native hunters judge any other dangerous game rifle used under adverse conditions. As demonstration of that fact, there are thousands of these now well-aged Model-71s in daily use in the frozen north; yet in that region it is essentially impossible to find one for sale at any price! A Model-71 in good condition will bring more money than seems reasonable. The point is, hunters place great value on a mechanism that will reliably chamber a cartridge while affording rapid and easy action manipulation.

Nonetheless, there is a price to pay for this combination of functions; that price is the incorporation of myriad moving parts. However, each place these moving parts rub past each other provides an opportunity for the tinker to improve the function of these rifles, sometimes dramatically. Generally, in any well-used rifle, these friction points are easy to identify: the surfaces betray the contact points, either by wear, burnishing or abrasion of the factory finish. Generally, the simple act of polishing all such contact surfaces to a mirror finish is significantly beneficial toward minimizing action manipulation force, which, I will argue, improves "using" accuracy. If the shooter can work the action faster and with less disruption of his sight picture, he can shoot well-aimed shots faster.

Not all lever-action rifles fit in this category of many moving parts. Obvious exceptions are Winchester's Model-88 and Browning's BLR. The actions of these rifles share more in common with the typical bolt-action rifle than with the classic tubular-magazine lever-action rifle design. Essentially, these are bolt-action rifles with the addition of a sophisticated linkage mechanism that allows proper manipulation of the action, through articulation of a finger-lever. Useful action modifications on these rifles are often more akin to working on a typical bolt-action rifle than to working on a typical tubular-magazine lever-action rifle. For example, bolt modifications are essentially identical to those that are appropriate for a bolt-action rifle.

Another exception is the Savage Model-99. This action features a rear-locking, tilting-bolt mechanism. However, Model-99s feed cartridges from either a rotary-magazine or from a removable box magazine. In function, the Model-99 is very similar to the typical bolt-action rifle. However, the rotary-magazine version has peculiarities that we will address separately.

Winchester's Model-1895 is yet another exception. This rifle incorporates an unusual combination of design features. Lockup is reminiscent of the ubiquitous Winchester Model-94, perhaps Mr. John Moses Browning's most famous invention. However, the magazine on the Model-1895 (another Browning design) is a simple, albeit unusually robust, box affair but with the incorporation of a sophisticated and remotely located follower spring. This design significantly reduces the vertical bulk of the box magazine but it does complicate matters.

Tubular-magazine-fed lever-action rifle mechanisms generally include several springs. These work with detents or ratcheting devices to achieve proper articulation of the action. Often, the prudent reduction of spring tension and bearing surface contact area at friction points within the receiver on these rifles will dramatically reduce the force required to cycle the action. An example is the typical tubular-magazine spring.

Brownells sells a more robust replacement spring for application to several typical tubular-magazine rifles (Winchester Model-94 and Marlin Model-336). For those using such a gun in life-or-death hunting situations, these beefier springs are a good idea — the added security of proper functioning under the worst of conditions more than compensates for the added difficulty involved in loading the magazine against the increased spring tension. (The question of ease of action articulation is another matter....) However, generally, the opposite alteration better serves most casual target shooters and non-dangerous game hunters: reduction of magazine spring tension eases magazine loading while dramatically improving overall ease of action articulation.

There are myriad little accurizing tricks for these various rifles. We will try to cover each of these subjects in sufficient detail to suggest what alterations the tinker should consider and why those alterations might improve his rifle's fit, function, intrinsic accuracy and stability of zero.

While certain gurus have long disparaged the classic lever-action rifle (particularly the tubular-magazine versions) as "simply inaccurate" by design, such proclamations are gross generalizations and are also grossly unfair. Given a good barrel, proper handling of buttstock, fore-end and magazine-tube bedding and general good overall gunsmithing, these rifles are capable of very impressive accuracy — certainly better accuracy than any hunter could ever need.

One reason is obvious. These guns all share an unusually deep and rigidly constructed receiver. However, by the same token, owing to the separate fore-end system, bench testing, to demonstrate the inherent accuracy of these rifles, entails added difficulty.

As noted above, the average shooter will often apply varying amounts of hand, cheek and shoulder pressure to the buttstock for successive shots at a paper target. These variations will cause <u>dramatic</u> vertical stringing — much more so than in a typical bolt-action rifle, with its one-piece stock, which bridges the receiver and carries the varying load between the front and rear rests. Conversely, in terms of accuracy for off-hand and improvised rest shooting (read, real-world-hunting-situations), these two systems are essentially indistinguishable. Nevertheless, stocks attached by a through-bolt are much less prone to breakage. For this reason alone you should consider this alteration.

Understanding the Lever-Action Rifle & Its Limitations:

Unlike the classic turn-bolt rifle, there are tremendous variations in design and functionality among lever-action rifle mechanisms. Before moving on to specific discussions about improving these rifles, I feel compelled to offer the interested reader a little more background on the lever-action rifle with emphasis on its weaknesses and strengths. I wish to address in some detail the various limitations these designs pose to the shooting enthusiast concerned with accuracy. Most of these limitations fall in the following categories: unique stock bedding problems, magazine tube complications, striker (firing pin) limitations, hammer limitations, bolt lockup design and extraction system limitations.

It is important to note that Winchester's Model-88 and Browning's BLR are both front-locking rotary bolt-action rifles. With regard to strength and reloaded cartridge case life, these rifles are indistinguishable from any front-locking bolt-action rifle. However, unlike the classic bolt-action rifle, these designs both lack any camming mechanism that would ease the extraction of a sticky cartridge case from the rifle's chamber. Therefore, unlike a bolt-action rifle, too-hot loads will cause problems with action manipulation. (This observation is not an endorsement of loading at pressure levels that generate sticky extraction, which is certainly not a prudent practice in any rifle.)

Next, note that Savage's Model-99 is a strong rear-locking action that, nevertheless, allows considerable case stretching. In these rifles, case stretching limits case life with top handloads to only a few reloadings: perhaps five (5) total loadings in chamberings using the basic .30-06 case head diameter (.22-250 Remington, .250 Savage, 7-08 Remington, .300 Savage, .308 Winchester) and four (4) total loadings in the larger-bodied .284 Winchester. With those Model-99s chambered for .30-30 Winchester-based cartridges, even when rechambered to Ackley's improved version and loaded to modern pressures, the smaller case head results in dramatically less bolt thrust; case life (with proper headspacing) is ten or more reloadings, just as it is in any front-locking action.

Short case life of the former chamberings results from excessive case stretching. Excessive case stretching implies the need for frequent case trimming when handloading for the Model-99. However, these facts do not reflect any weakness of the Model-99's action; such handloads are perfectly safe in these rifles, as long as the handloader does not try to reuse the cases too many times. Conversely, unlike any other lever-action rifle this author is aware of, Savage's Model-99 does incorporate considerable extraction force. For this reason, this action seems particularly well suited to use as a dangerous game hunting rifle.

Conventional (tubular-magazine) lever-action rifles are rear-locking designs having no mechanism to increase extraction force. These facts suggest that, generally, the handloader must keep chamber pressures close to factory levels and, even so, case life can be somewhat limited.

Nothing noted here is a condemnation of this basic mechanism. (Consider the previous discussion regarding the value of Winchester's Model-71.) In working toward minimizing the negative effects of the limitations of any system, it is important to understand the reasons behind, and consequences of, that system's limitations. Further, it is important to understand that each type of rifle has its limitations. Frankly, no design is perfect!

The Special Stock Bedding Problems Of Rifles With Two-Piece Stocks:

In rifles featuring two-piece stocks, the method and details of attachment and bedding of the fore-end to the receiver can have profound effects upon the rifle's intrinsic accuracy and long-term repeatability (hold of zero). All such rifles share the following characteristic: fore-end attachment is either to the barrel (Savage Model-99 and H&R/Handi-Rifle) or to an extension of the receiver (recent Browning BLRs and the Ruger No. 1). Many such rifles, for example early Browning BLRs, feature a combination of these attachment methods.

Obviously, any system that places wood (or almost any synthetic material) in contact with both the receiver and the barrel offers the potential for the following things to induce stress between the fore-end and the barrel-receiver system: changes in barrel temperature, due to shooting or atmospheric temperature; variation in stock size and shape, due to changes in atmospheric humidity.

Early Browning BLRs were particularly bad actors in this regard. In that design, a receiver extension attaches the fore-end to the rifle. While this is nominally a good idea, those rifles also incorporate a band that surrounds both barrel and fore-end. This combination of attachment systems is an eminently bad idea.

Changes in humidity typically result in dramatic changes in zero in wood-stocked rifles using such a combination fore-end attachment system. Any dimensional change in the fore-end results in a change of stress between barrel and receiver. This change of stress results in strain (bending) in the barrel and at the juncture of the barrel and receiver. In this example, the cure is to properly bed the fore-end to the receiver extension and to eliminate any contact between the fore-end band and the barrel — either discard that abomination or alter it for barrel clearance. The latter method results in a more attractive rifle. (Browning has recently eliminated this barrel band. Good idea!)

Savage's Model-99 fore-end is attached to the rifle through a barrel-mounted hanger and a screw. This dovetailed hanger is located toward the front of the fore-end, directly under the barrel.

The rear of the fore-end is keyed to engage a recess in the receiver. This system is replete with potential problems. First, in many applications, the extreme front end of the fore-end carries the load of tightening the attachment screw — the barrel channel in the fore-end, in front of the attachment screw, tightens against the barrel. Obviously, in this system, barrel bedding pressure is particularly sensitive to dimensional changes in the fore-end, regardless of the reason. The situation is worse than that; minor variations in attachment screw tightening can dramatically alter the rifle's zero. Tightening the screw bends the barrel!

The accuracy enthusiast should alter the attachment system used on the Model-99 and any other rifle using a similar fore-end attachment method. The goal is the creation of an essentially floating barrel channel. The attachment screw should tighten against a metallic boss that is epoxied into the fore-end. That boss should then tighten against the barrel-mounted hanger — preferably through an epoxy bedding layer. This work should include the complete sealing of the rear of the fore-end. Be sure to use an adequate coating of clear epoxy.

The alterations should also incorporate a precise, minimal fore-and-aft clearance between fore-end and receiver. It is also useful to apply a layer of black RTV (Room Temperature Vulcanizing) silicone (as made by *Loctite* and sold under the *Permatex* brand) on the rear surface of the fore-end. While holding the fore-end in place laterally, this layer will deaden the fore-end's connection to the receiver, so that vibrations will not propagate between the two. The fore-end should fit snugly in the key-way in the receiver and against the attachment hanger under the barrel but should not touch the rifle anywhere else.

In my experience, this simple alteration dramatically improves the intrinsic accuracy of these rifles, while eliminating any propensity for wandering zero. As noted, it is advisable to include proper glass bedding at the receiver. A modicum of fore-aft clearance between the fore-end and the receiver is also important. This clearance accommodates the fore-end's long-term dimensional changes resulting from variations in humidity and aging. It also accounts for the barrel's dimensional changes resulting from temperature changes.

Most, but not all, single-shot rifles share a fore-end attachment method that is similar to one of the aforementioned systems. Some designs use something of a combination of these systems. Regardless, all require proper bedding to maximize accuracy potential. For example, (based upon my limited experience) with the Ruger No. 1 rifle, proper bedding of the fore-end makes all the difference between a tack driving rifle that holds its zero year in and year out and one that will not manage 2 minutes of angle (MOA) groups and that shows many MOA wander in its zero. However, as I will note several times in this text, finding the best bedding method for a specific Ruger Single-Shot rifle seems to be a matter of trial and error.

It is fair to say that, in many single-shot rifles, improper fore-end attachment is one of the two major barriers to accuracy! I cannot overstate this. Proper bedding practices are essential to obtaining consistent accuracy with these rifles — just as it is in any other rifle, be they bolt-action sporter or the finest bench-rest target rifle. There is a distinction, however: in a bolt-action rifle, proper bedding is comparatively obvious; in single-shot (and lever-action) rifles, we have to examine the system with a bit of care before we can ascertain what system of bedding is <u>likely</u> to provide the best results. However, just as in the bolt-action rifle system, glass bedding affords simple experimentation! If the accuracy results using one bedding system do not pan out, we can easily try another — no harm done.

For those rifles with a two-piece stocking system equipped with a very nearly straight barrel, there is a worthwhile alternative. In such a rifle it is often possible to glass bed the barrel to the fore-end channel, full length. Again, the goal is to properly key the receiver end of the fore-end to the receiver using epoxy ("glass") bedding material but with proper fore-and-aft clearance included.

Examples from the long-range single-shot target rifle community represent this system quite well; obviously, it works. This system often provides the best accuracy but it will not work in rifles with contoured or highly tapered barrels, especially when using those rifles for firing extended shot strings. Barrel heating results in barrel lengthening. Barrel lengthening induces stress in the barrel and it can also introduce barrel-to-receiver stress through the fore-end bedding. Again, it is easy enough to find out if this system will work on any given rifle. Try it. If this method does not work, simply file out a small clearance in the epoxied fore-end barrel channel and try a different method!

The tubular-magazine repeater is a unique animal. When working with these rifles, the tinker concerned with maximum accuracy must work to solve several significant problems and minimize those problems he cannot solve. The first of these problems that comes to mind is the inevitable vibrations generated in the tubular magazine assembly during the bullet's passage through the barrel. Perhaps surprisingly, there is a simple and effective method of ameliorating the negative effects of these vibrations, which we will detail in the main text.

Next is the problem of the attachment of the tubular magazine and fore-end to the barrel. Systems vary and corrections can differ, depending upon the particular rifle. Generally, the goal is removal of induced stress and minimization of vibrations between tubular magazine and barrel — these alterations are surprisingly simple and dramatically effective at improving shot-to-shot uniformity (accuracy). The theory of fore-end attachment in these rifles shares much in common with the aforementioned Browning and Savage rifles.

Most single-shot and lever-action rifles share some combination of these types of problems associated with fore-end bedding. In each instance, it is critical that the tinker analyze the system and correctly identify the best method of properly attaching the fore-end to the rifle without inducing variable stress to either the barrel or the receiver.

Understanding the Single-Shot Rifle & Its Limitations:

Most single-shot rifles are comparatively strong, front-locking designs — the bolt lockup is comparatively close to the case head. This would suggest that these actions are appropriate for use with ammunition loaded to the limit of modern accepted pressure levels. However, the extractor system on many of these rifles provides limited compounding of primary extraction force. Several designs provide no positive mechanical extraction force. Therefore, while most single-shot actions are eminently strong and are technically suitable for any load that is safe in any rifle, owing to limited extraction capabilities, these designs can be a poor choice for use as dangerous game hunting rifles — any significant resistance between the fired case and the chamber will result in a stuck case, every time. Several common single-shot designs offer even less in the way of extraction force, compared to the classic lever-action rifle! The H&R/Handi-Rifle and the TC/Contender, for example, have a simple spring-loaded plunger that offers precisely zero mechanical extraction force.

This suggests that the handloader and the tinker interested in building a custom rifle should consider the rifle's mechanical extraction system very carefully. Those rifles featuring a simple spring-loaded extractor might not be a good choice for a dangerous game hunting rifle. While these designs are generally simple and dependable, this system simply will not work with loads generating top-end pressures. Any semblance of sticky extraction will result in an inoperable rifle! Several other single-shot designs fall in this class. In this author's opinion, those designs featuring a positive mechanical extractor are a much better choice for a serious hunting rifle.

Most single-shot designs share the two-piece stocking system, with the same weaknesses noted in the discussion covering lever-action rifles. Other potential problems center on the firing pin and hammer arrangement and upon articulation of the breachblock. In the Winchester High-wall, for example, the original, mechanically retracted firing pin is subject to breakage; a replacement firing pin using a spring retractor system is a superior option. This is a common alteration and shops such as Steve Meacham's offer spring-retracted firing pins for gunsmith installation.

On many falling-block rifles the breachblock is a sloppy fit in the receiver. Properly fitted, the breachblock in a falling-block rifle should literally bind in place behind the barrel as the finger-lever reaches full closure. A qualified gunsmith can often achieve this goal by setting the barrel back one thread and fitting the rear face of the barrel to the frame opening and the breachblock. Of course, this alteration also requires rechambering. Unnecessary (excess) headspace is also quite common in practically all rifles chambered for rimmed cartridges. Correction of this deficit follows the same process where possible.

On older falling-block rifles, grossly oversized firing pin holes are quite common. Bushing the breachblock face, as described in *Part I*, is a simple fix but a properly fitting firing pin is often an easier solution here. Finally, lateral movement of the breachblock, resulting from excessive side-to-side clearance, is quite common. If the breachblock does not settle in the same location as the shooter closes the action for each shot, accuracy suffers. The tinker can easily solve this problem by drilling the breachblock and installing Delrin™ or polypropylene pins that act to center the breachblock or hold it against one wall of the receiver. The tinker can sometimes use this method to center the firing pin's impact on the primer (side-to-side).

On a similar note, just as in the common lever-action rifle, the falling-block hammer is often quite heavy and rotates through a relatively long arc. Bolt conditions are problematical. First, the hammer's weight and travel both work to increase lock-time. Second, the same characteristics also work to excessively disturb the rifle's aim before the firing pin hits the primer — for every action there is an equal and opposite reaction. Since the hammer is not balanced around its pivot, when it begins to rotate in one direction the gun must begin to rotate in the opposite direction.

One common gunsmithing solution is to lighten the hammer, use a heavier and redesigned hammer spring and relocate the full-cock notch on the hammer. These changes lessen the hammer's travel without reducing striker energy. Owing to the delicate geometry of the hammer's sear notch, I must advise that the tinker should leave any such alteration to the experienced professional.

A final area of potential alteration on the typical falling-block is in the geometry of the toggle linkage and its relationship to the finger-lever, firing pin and breachblock. Ideally, as the shooter brings the finger-lever to the fully closed position, the toggle linkage should just achieve precise alignment or travel just slightly beyond that point. Providing the links and pins are all in good repair (tight fitting with round pins in round holes), existence, or not, of this proper relationship is easy to ascertain.

This test requires a good dial indicator and a magnetic base. Simply note the upward travel of the breachblock as you close the action. If the breachblock retracts measurably (more than, perhaps, 0.001") as the finger-lever achieves the last measure of its closure, and while you are applying downward (thumb) pressure on the top of the breachblock, the geometry is wrong. We will address the conceptually simple method of altering toggle-link geometry later in the text.

Ruger's No. 1 and No. 3 have an entirely unique lockwork design and offer the tinker a genuine challenge. This author has come to the conclusion that finding the precise tuning that works for any given Ruger single-shot rifle is more a matter of the quirks of that individual rifle than anything else. That is, just because one system of bedding and action tuning worked on one Ruger single-shot rifle does not suggest the same alterations will work on any other Ruger single-shot rifle. My best advice is to keep on tinkering until you find the combination that works for that one particular rifle, and good luck.

As an example, in an effort to reduce lock-time, I once worked long and hard to increase the hammer spring tension on a Ruger No. 1. I succeeded in reducing lock-time by about 20%. I also succeeded in doubling the rifle's best groups! Back to the original hammer spring system….

Explanation And Purpose Of Accurizing The Factory Rifle, *Part III*:

Throughout this text I have covered various items that are probably beyond the talents of the typical home tinker, who has typical home tools available. However, with perseverance and the purchase of a few special tools, which are often available from Brownells or at the local hardware store, many of these jobs can be mastered by the amateur. However, there are some jobs better left to the professional. My purpose in *Part III* is to cover some of those in sufficient detail so that the reader can understand what the gunsmith will be doing on the rifle.

Again, many of the tasks described in *Part I* & *Part II* are nominally gunsmith jobs. For this reason, it is not fair to say that *Part III* is the only section that contains descriptions of professional gunsmithing chores. Whether or not a particular task requires a professional depends upon your skill, patience, and willingness to invest time and money.

In the short text in *Part III*, my goal is to explore in greater detail those things that are almost certainly outside the realm of "Home Tinkering". Specifically, these subjects include: rebarreling, rechambering (as touched upon in *Part I*), custom restocking, custom checkering, refinishing and custom sight installations. I will not claim that all these alterations fall outside the realm of what the talented home gunsmith can accomplish — I have personally accomplished some version of practically every job discussed in *Part III*, and, so far, the results have been "acceptable". Nevertheless, in my opinion, most of us are better off leaving most of these jobs to

Section 9: Acknowledgments and Introduction, Parts II & III

the professional — those persons who have the skill, tools and experience necessary to do the job right. There is a valuable difference between "acceptable" and "exemplary". As much as I enjoy tinkering, I do appreciate exemplary workmanship.

A partial listing of new or distinctly addressed subjects we will explore in *Parts II & III* includes:

    Action Parts Deburring
    Action Type Specific Handloading
        Considerations
    Barrel Rechambering
    Barrel-To-Fore-end Bedding
    Bolt Deburring
    Bolt Lug(s)-To-Receiver Lapping
    Breachblock Centering
    Custom Metal Surface Preparations For
        Finishing
    Custom Restocking (Factory Fitting)
    Custom Stock Checkering
    Custom Stock Refinishing
    Hammer Skeletonizing
    Hot Bluing
    Magazine Tube Bedding
    Plating
    Polymer finishes
    Receiver Deburring
    Receiver-To-Buttstock Bedding
    Receiver-To-Fore-end Bedding
    Special Considerations For Scope
        Positioning & Stock Length
    Striker Modifications
    Surface Treatments
    Toggle Link Adjustments
    Trigger-Spring Adjustment

A partial listing of applicable subjects that were covered in greater detail in *Part I* includes:

    Barrel-To-Receiver Engagement
    Barrel Crowning
    Bore Lapping
    Striker Centering And Striker-Hole Fitting
    Recoil-Pad Attachment
    Kinetic Recoil "Absorber" Device
        Functioning And Installation
    Hydraulic Recoil "Absorber" Functioning And
        Installation
    Cold Bluing
    Cryogenic Treating Of Gun Parts
    Electro-Chemical Barrel Treatments
    Mounting Scopes And Receiver Sight Bases
    Mounting Scopes
    Adjusting Scope-Sight Eye-Relief
    Leveling Scope Reticle
    Spirit-Level Installation

You should review the applicable sub-sections in *Part I* for a more complete discussion of each of these subjects.

For further explanations of my goals in this text, please, refer to the introductory section of *Part I*. That section also includes other explanatory information with useful comments and provides information that is necessary to understanding the text in *Parts II & III*, it is certainly worthwhile reading for those interested in accurizing any rifle.

Section 10: The Trouble With Barrels, *Part II*

Along with barrel problems, as noted in *Part I*, we will address barrel replacement later, in *Part III*. Meanwhile, in this section, we will note that all barrel-related modifications discussed in *Part I* are fully appropriate for consideration in the accurizing of any lever-action or single-shot rifle. Those areas include: proper crowning or recrowning; bore lapping, either by hand or by the NECO fire lapping method; electro-chemical barrel treatments; cryogenic barrel treatment; chamber polishing; barrel-to-receiver contact zone alignment corrections; and barrel-to-receiver attachment thread lapping. For a complete discussion of the corrections involved in each of these areas, refer to *Part I*.

See, also, the lengthy discussion of barrel removal in *Part I*. However, please, note the following critical points. First, on most single-shot and lever-action rifles, it is essential that the tinker completely disassemble the rifle's receiver and magazine components before making any attempt to remove the barrel. Failure to abide by this dictate is likely to result in damage to the tubular magazine, the extractor or the barrel. Also note, never place any strain on any barrel fittings or dovetails — you cannot use these parts for pry points during barrel removal. Any such attempt will almost certainly result in damage to the rifle. See photograph # 10-1.

It seems that barrel removal in these types of rifles might be slightly easier, compared to bolt-action rifles. For what it might be worth, my personal success with barrel removal on non-bolt-action rifles has been a little more encouraging than with bolt-action rifles. This result stems partly from the fact that receivers on these guns generally offer a better purchase (see the following decision). Often, with a bit of patience and the correct (common hand) tools, these barreled-actions are separable in the home workshop.

Barrel Removal, Specific Considerations For Lever-Action & Single-Shot Rifles:

Following the guidelines reviewed in *Part I*, be certain to properly isolate both barrel and receiver from contact with any metallic tool. Note that the box-sided configuration of typical single-shot and lever-action rifles is particularly conducive to the use of clamping-type tools. An 18" adjustable wrench (such as the ubiquitous Crescent™ wrench) is a handy asset. Either pad the receiver with a quality reinforced tape, such as electrician's glass fiber tape, or insert hard plastic or rubber pads between the wrench jaws and the receiver. Vise the barrel in properly constructed wood blocks (see *Part I*). Then wrench on the receiver, being sure to turn on the receiver in the correct direction to loosen the barrel threads (practically all barrel threads are right-handed). Then, while applying torque, use a hard plastic mallet to hammer on either the wrench or, preferably, an exposed and rigid surface of the

Photograph 10-1: You cannot use barrel hangers, such as this Marlin dovetailed fore-end attachment, for pry points during barrel removal. Avoid applying any stress to dovetail- or screw-attached barrel fixtures. Failure to abide by this bit of common sense is apt to result in damaged or destroyed parts.

receiver — directly over the threads is an effective area to apply this shock. See photograph #s 10-2/3.

However, note, be absolutely certain that you do not wrench or hammer against any thin or unsupported area of the receiver. Generally, it is best to install the wrench only at the receiver's extreme forward end, which is almost always amongst the most rigid of areas on these types of receivers. Also note, the following will help prevent damage to the receiver: use of a bigger wrench, with its longer jaws; tightest feasible adjustment of the wrench jaws (which spreads the torque across a larger area on the receiver).

Damage from improper technique, wrenching location or tools is likely to manifest as bending along the receiver's sides or marring of its finish. Obviously, you want to avoid that at all cost. Also, as noted in *Part I*, application of penetrating oil will help break loose over-tightened or corroded barrel-to-receiver threads.

Lapping Barrel-to-Receiver Abutment Shoulder & Barrel Threads, Lever-Action & Single-Shot Rifles:

(For a general discussion and photographs of these processes, refer to the appropriate sub-sections of *Part I*.)

There is nothing unique about this process, when applied to this type of rifle. However, ensure that your lapping operations do not allow the rear face of the barrel to move toward the back of the receiver sufficiently to upset either of the following: headspacing, which is the proper (and necessary) clearance between the bolt (or breachblock) face and the barrel's rear face (on rimmed case chamberings); and barrel-to-receiver indexing (after properly tightening the barrel into the receiver). See photograph #s 1-41/42.

Bolt clearance is particularly critical in falling-block style actions. Many of these, particularly those produced with utmost precision, are built with essentially zero clearance between the rear of the barrel and the front face of the falling-block. Custom gunsmiths often deliberately dimension these rifles to achieve an interference fit, so that when the finger-lever is fully closed it wedges the falling-block (breachblock) between the rear face of the barrel and the rear face of breachblock raceway in the receiver.

Obviously, under these circumstances, any alteration that allows the barrel to move further into the receiver can interfere with proper functioning of such a well-fitted mechanism. In many

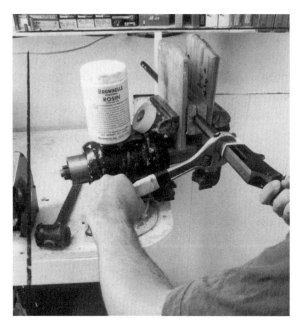

Photograph 10-2: This photograph shows a good setup for removing the barrel from a lever-action rifle. Note that the receiver, fore-end and magazine assembly are removed before attempting to remove the barrel. Refer to the related section in Part I for detailed suggestions.

Photograph 10-3: If direct torque will not get the job done, application of shock loading will often do the trick. Here a nylon mallet is used for this purpose (it worked). The fiberglass reinforced tape prevents a properly fitted wrench from marring the rifle's finish. Another option is to apply torque, as shown in photograph 10-2, and simultaneously hammer on the receiver over the barrel threads. Penetrating oil applied to the barrel threads can help dramatically.

Section 10: The Trouble With Barrels, Part II

instances, a slight facing of the rear of the barrel, which you can accomplish using a high quality, flat-faced sharpening stone (available through Brownells), can correct this problem. However, be cautious here; it is critical to maintain complete contact between the front of the breachblock and the rear face of the barrel. The latter should always be at right angles to the axis of the bore.

However, note that this is a situation where your gunsmith might improve a stock falling-block rifle. He can design the aforementioned tight lockup into almost any falling-block action by performing the following work: recutting the barrel's abutment face forward sufficiently to allow the barrel to turn into the receiver one additional turn, rechambering the barrel, shortening the rear face of the barrel and re-cutting the extractor slot, etc. We will address this process in more detail in *Part III*.

Unless this should prove necessary, in order to achieve proper barrel tightening torque, never remove more material at the contact zone between the barrel's shoulder and the receiver's face than is necessary to achieve full simultaneous perimeter contact at that joint. In any case, never remove sufficient material to prevent proper barrel tightening while maintaining proper barrel-to-receiver alignment. You will find detailed coverage of these subjects in the corresponding sub-sections of *Part I*. Also, before considering barrel removal, refer to *Part I* and ensure that you understand the importance of index marks on the barrel and receiver. These provide for proper barrel alignment upon reinstallation. This is critical on any barreled-action where the barrel has any location-critical features. Examples include: dovetails, extractor slots, markings, other cuts and attachments. See photograph # 10-4.

Be sure to apply an adequate doping of a cold bluing agent. Since the threads and abutment surfaces are normally hidden, it is important to do everything feasible to limit corrosion on these surfaces.

There really is nothing unique about perfecting barrel attachment in these types of rifles. Simply abide by the dictates of performing this alteration, as pointed out in *Part I*. However, on rifles with tubular magazines it is highly advisable to use a well-distributed dab of low-strength thread locking agent (Loctite #222) on the barrel's properly cleaned threads before screwing that into the properly cleaned threads of the receiver. Of course, do not reassemble with thread locker until you have finished all alterations that might require, or benefit from, separation of barrel and receiver. See photograph # 10-5.

Photograph 10-4: This photograph clearly shows why barrel indexing is critical in lever-action and falling-block rifles. This barrel has a hood and extractor slot, both must line up with the receiver properly or the rifle will not function. If you look closely at the upper portion of this extractor ramp, you should be able to see that the extractor has been riding up this ramp (and away from the cartridge rim) when the bolt was closed. Generally, this is counter to accuracy. See the text.

Photograph 10-5: Here I am ready to assemble the barrel and receiver. Moderate application of Loctite's low-strength (product #222) thread locker is a very good idea. This type of rifle generates considerable barrel torquing. I do not want to have to excessively tighten the barrel into the receiver; Loctite #222 will keep the barrel in place without the need for excessive torquing.

The thread locking agent is a particularly good idea on this type of rifle. The tubular magazine and fore-end assembly increases potential barrel torquing and shooting related vibrations. These factors can combine to loosen a barrel that is sufficiently tightened so that it would never spontaneously loosen on a bolt-action rifle. This added insurance is worthwhile. However, avoid using more than a few drops of any thread locker and use only the lowest strength agent — at some future date, you might want to again separate the barrel and receiver....

Too-Tight Or Imprecise Barrel Threads, Lever-Action & Single-Shot Rifles:

Imperfect barrel threads are quite common on these rifles. Marlin uses forty-one thousandths of an inch (0.041") wide square barrel threads. These threads typically do not make full contact along the length of the corresponding threads in the receiver. However, note that spotty thread-to-thread contact is the rule, rather than the exception, regardless of thread type. Although this condition is rare on the Marlin, other rifles occasionally have a too-tight fit between the threads of the barrel and those in the receiver. Lapping is beneficial in achieving uniform load bearing along the length of the threads and eliminating any constrictive interference fit. Refer to *Part I* for a complete discussion of how to eliminate problems here and achieve the desirable result of proper mating on these threads.

Mitigation Of Excessive Barrel-To-Receiver Torque, Lever-Action & Single-Shot Rifles:

As with any other gun, factory barrel installations on lever-action and single-shot rifles are quite often tighter than necessary; very often the factories tighten these barrels beyond all reason. Such over-tightening can be extremely detrimental to accuracy. Commonly, rifles with over-tightened barrels evidence significant vertical stringing as the gun heats during extended firing. You will find detailed coverage of the steps necessary to mitigate this problem in *Part I*. Also refer to the above discussion about the added justification for using a thread-locking agent when final assembling a tubular-magazine, lever-action rifle. See photograph # 1-57.

Barrel Installation, Lever-Action & Single-Shot Rifles:

Before reassembling the barrel make sure you have performed all anticipated modifications to the rifle where having the barrel removed might possibly be beneficial. See especially *Section 11* and the subsequent discussion of polishing the feed ramp in the receiver.

Refer to *Part I* for a complete discussion of lapping the barrel and receiver abutment faces and barrel threads to achieve proper interference fit. Note that on the Marlin, with its steeply pitched threads, only a slight rotation of the barrel after contact on the abutment surface is necessary to achieve proper tightening. For these rifles if the witness marks are no more than twenty-thousandths of an inch (0.020") apart, at first abutment contact, the interference fit at witness mark alignment is certainly sufficient. On rifles with more typical thread pitch, fifty-thousandths of an inch (0.050") offset in witness marks, at the instant the abutting faces make contact, provides fully adequate interference fit — sufficient to normally prevent spontaneous barrel loosening.

After completing all lapping and fitting operations, consider using a cold bluing agent to refinish all lapped surfaces both in the receiver and on the barrel. This step is well worthwhile as it limits the potential for corrosion in these normally hidden areas. Refer to *Part I* for a discussion of products and procedures. See photograph # 1-24.

Before reassembling the barrel to the receiver, thoroughly clean all contaminants from all pieces involved in the work. Either alcohol or carburetor cleaner is a good choice for removing oil-based compounds. A final wash with a diluted ammonia solution is a good final step and will remove all traces of oils. As noted above, you might consider application of a small dab of a low-strength thread-locking agent (Loctite Product #222) to the clean cold blued threads. This will sufficiently bond the barrel against inadvertent loosening. Regardless of your decision in that regard, you should also use a retaining agent (Loctite Product #609) between the barrel and receiver mating shoulders. See photograph # 1-58.

As noted elsewhere, these products serve many useful purposes. Both prevent infiltration of corrosive agents while sealing the mated surfaces against climatic evils; fill inevitable voids; bond the surfaces against vibration; aid in preventing unintentional barrel loosening; and lubricate the surfaces to substantially facilitate reassembly without metal-to-metal galling. For those who choose not to use a thread-locking

Section 10: The Trouble With Barrels, Part II

agent, Brownells offers a product called *Brownells Barrel Assembly Paste*. This product is designed to prevent galling and help achieve increased barrel tightening at any given level of applied torque. Any molybdenum-disulfide-impregnated grease will provide the same benefit.

Please note, do not use graphite or solutions containing graphite in any such application. As compared to molybdenum-disulfide, which is a good electrical insulator, graphite is highly conductive. Wherever and whenever two dissimilar metals are in electrically conductive contact, that conductivity will result in electrochemical (galvanic) corrosion — we scientists call such an arrangement a dry-cell battery! Very few pieces of steel are identical. (For this reason, any lubricant containing graphite seems a poor choice for use on almost any metallic parts!)

Headspace Considerations, Lever-Action & Single-Shot Rifles:

Owing to various barrel dovetail cuts, the extractor slot, and similar recesses in the rear face of the barrel, found on most of these rifles, you have to install the barrel to the same orientation as the factory installation. Therefore, there is little chance of altering the rifle's headspace by lapping the threads or adjusting the barrel-to-receiver contact shoulder to reduce the torque required to install the barrel so that the index marks line up properly. See photograph # 10-4.

Nevertheless, if the barrel had previously been tightened to a very high torque and you have reduced the interference by lapping the contact shoulder and the threads, it is possible that headspace might be reduced sufficiently to cause a problem with certain handloads.

For example, consider bottlenecked cartridge handloads that headspace to the case shoulder. The handloader can size such ammunition to properly fit the rifle's chamber through adjustment of the full-length sizing die or use of an extra thick shell holder (as available through Redding, in the *Competition* shellholder set). This deliberate cartridge headspace alteration, combined with the resulting minor (albeit potentially consequential) rifle headspace alteration is unlikely to cause a problem. However, in rare instances, it could.

The reason for this problem is that tightening a barrel extra-tight crushes and swells the front end of the receiver and that portion of the barrel in front of the abutment shoulder. At the same time such barrel tightening stretches the threaded portion of the barrel. Lapping of the abutment shoulders and threads results in a reduction of this interference fit. This alteration can allow the rear face of the barrel to move slightly further into the action when the barrel is tightened to the same orientation. Whether or not this happens depends upon which of these two pieces (barrel or receiver) was originally deformed the most, where that piece was deformed, and upon how much material the lapping process removed from each piece.

Whether headspace will increase or decrease is not necessarily something we can predict. Usually, any resulting difference in headspace is minuscule but with particularly close-fitting ammunition the change might be sufficient to prevent proper cartridge chambering.

Should you encounter this problem, factory ammunition and standard handloads will almost certainly still function correctly. Further, by simply readjusting the sizing die or using a one-step shorter Redding Competition shell holder to move the case shoulder back two thousandths of an inch (0.002") your custom-fitted handloads will still work fine.

Reassembly is straight forward. First, clean all surfaces with a good degreasing agent. After cold bluing all lapped surfaces (on bluable alloys), again clean all surfaces with alcohol to remove every trace of the bluing agent. Then apply a drop, or two, of Loctite #222 to the threads on the barrel and spread that along the entire length of the threads by using a fine paint brush. Also, spread a drop of Loctite #609 over the abutment face at the front of the receiver. See photographs # 10-5 & # 1-58.

Lock the receiver in a padded vise with the threads pointing up. (Remember to remove the bolt to prevent damage to the barrel or extractor.) Then carefully thread the barrel into the receiver until it is finger tight — the abutment faces should now touch everywhere around the perimeter. Remove the receiver from the vise. Clamp the barrel in the wood barrel clamp, using rosin and sufficient vising force to hold the barrel against the subsequent tightening torque. (If you have properly fitted the barrel to the receiver this torque is quite modest.) Hand tighten the receiver until the witness marks line up correctly.

If hand tightening is inadequate to achieve this goal, try the following. While twisting on the receiver with one hand, rap on the receiver's bottom front edge with a hard plastic mallet. If you have properly adjusted the barrel and receiver, through lapping at the abutment face and on the threads, this latter method should be sufficient to achieve proper tightening with little effort. This is opposite what is shown in photograph # 10-3 for loosening the barrel.

Remember, the thread locker and mounting agents will begin to cure the instant you begin the assembly. With properly cleaned surfaces you might not have more than one or two minutes to work.

After allowing sufficient time for complete curing of any thread locking or retaining agents used, perhaps one day or longer, a thorough application of a quality penetrating rust preventive is a very good idea. There is no better product available for this purpose than TSI-301, available through NECO. See photograph # 1-59.

Section 11: The Trouble With Bolts, *Part II*

For various reasons, I will cover these items a little differently than I did in *Part I*. For a complete understanding of these issues, please refer to the related discussion in *Part I*.

Extractors And Other Bolt Extensions, Lever-Action & Single-Shot Rifles:

Like most modern rifles, the extractor design on all lever-action rifles allows the nose of the extractor to snap over the rim of a chambered cartridge, when necessary. Since such an extractor necessarily extends considerably past the front of the case rim, the rear face of the barrel must include a corresponding slot to accommodate the extractor's nose when the bolt is fully closed. Typically this slot begins at the rearmost extension of the barrel and extends forward along the outside of the barrel but at an angle to the bore axis — the barrel gets thicker and the slot gets shallower toward the muzzle. Usually, at the extreme rear of the barrel this slot reaches to almost full depth of the side of the chamber. See illustration and photograph # 11-1.

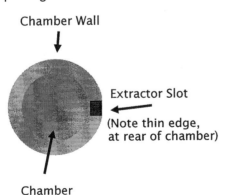

Rear Opening of Chamber

There are sometimes (often) other similar slots cut into the rear of the barrel. Typically, extensions of the bolt enter into one or more such slots. For example, on the Savage Model-99 a tab at the top of the bolt enters a matching slot in the perimeter of the barrel. The purpose of this forward bolt extension is to capture the head of the cartridge during chambering. This piece prevents the cartridge's escape through the top of the action as the bolt strips the round from the magazine or lifts it from the cartridge carrier — at the beginning of the cartridge chambering process. (Once the bullet has entered the chamber sufficiently, the cartridge is trapped between bolt and chamber and this tab is no longer functionally necessary.) Other similar extensions on various lever-action rifle designs have similar purposes. See photographs that show such an extension on the Savage Model-99 bolt. See photograph # 11-2.

Generally, all that these extensions and corresponding slots require is a good polishing along all friction surfaces. Refer to *Part I* for a complete discussion of how to identify friction points and how to polish those. See photograph # 1-70.

It is often useful to radius the forward ends of such bolt extensions to prevent any slight mis-

Photograph 11-1: Often the tinker will find that barrel threads are not properly mated to the corresponding receiver threads. A bit of lapping with #240 grit will soon bring the entire barrel thread into contact with the entire receiver thread. For the accuracy enthusiast, this is a desirable goal.

alignment between bolt and barrel (which might naturally occur while closing the bolt) from resulting in the bolt extension jamming into the rear face of the barrel. When replacing the barrel, it is also possible, and quite desirable, to cut the corresponding slot in the barrel to precisely match the width of the bolt extension pin. Such precision fitting facilitates precise bolt-to-barrel alignment. For example, on the Model-99 this approach is quite useful since the bolt can otherwise settle with a surprising degree of latitude with regard to where the front of the bolt rests side-to-side in the action. However, note, such precise fitting requires a combination of precise barrel tightening and properly radiused ends on both slots and pins. See photograph showing close-up of Model-99 bolt extension in the receiver ring with bolt closed and barrel removed. See photograph # 11-3.

Returning to the extractor: here we have a genuine quandary. First, we want to polish the forward inside edge of the extractor to a mirror finish; this facilitates the extractor's nose smoothly slipping over the case rim, when necessary. There are several obvious benefits, with reduction in action manipulation force and elimination of damage to case rims being the most obvious. Second, we would like to adjust the extractor so that it aids rather than diminishes accuracy. This aspect is a little more complicated to explain and understand.

The quandary is that what would seem to be the obvious fix is often the wrong fix. That is, modifying the extractor so that it does not touch the chambered cartridge is probably a mistake. However, this result probably depends upon the particular rifle. Let us consider, first, the typical Marlin lever-action rifle. In these guns, there are normally no springs or plungers pushing against the chambered cartridge. As the bolt closes, the extractor clearance ramp in the barrel normally lifts the extractor away from the case head. See illustration. This characteristic might seem to be quite desirable. However, that is not necessarily true. The reason behind this counter-intuitive fact relates to chambering tolerances. All factory ammunition and all full-length resized handloads are somewhat smaller in diameter near the case head than the corresponding portion of the rifle's chamber. If this were not the situation, it would be difficult or impossible to chamber the cartridge. See photograph #s 11-4/5.

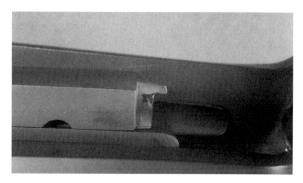

Photograph 11-2: Notice the tab, which extends from the top of the bolt. This is a cartridge guide: as the finger-lever closes the bolt, the bolt strips the cartridge from the magazine; this tab captures the case rim and prevents the rear end of the case from escaping the action — out the top of the receiver. Once the bolt has pushed the case sufficiently into the chamber, this bolt extension is no longer functionally necessary. However, by careful barrel fitting it is possible to incorporate this tab as a bolt alignment mechanism.

Photograph 11-3: The tab on the top front of Model-99 bolt reaches through the receiver ring and engages a slot in the back of the barrel. For this reason the barrel must be properly indexed. The extractor (which is barely visible in this photograph) also intrudes and aligns to a slot in the barrel. By properly fitting the tab to the slot in the barrel you can provide precise and repeatable bolt alignment, an important accuracy asset.

Section 11: The Trouble With Bolts, Part II

Diagrams Showing Extractor pulled away from cartridge
(Note that the head of the cartridge is centered in chamber but lying against bottom of chamber)

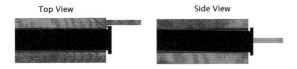

Diagrams showing extractor pushing against cartridge rim
(Note that the extractor holds the base of cartridge against opposite side of chamber)

When the extractor always holds the case head against the opposite side of the chamber, shot-to-shot chambering alignment is <u>probably</u> more consistent.

When you chamber such a (slightly undersize) cartridge, unless something else is pushing on it, it tends to lie in the bottom of the chamber (gravity works). The trouble is, this is not a particularly precise means of aligning cartridges in a rifle's chamber: one round might lie in the bottom of the chamber while the next might hang up, jammed between the front of the bolt and the shoulder in the chamber. In this situation, the case head might stay located against the top, side or any other portion of the chamber's rear opening. Such round-to-round variations in the location of the chambered case head result in poor shot-to-shot uniformity — what shooters call inaccuracy.

A design or mechanism that forced the heads of all chambered cartridges to stay against the same side of the chamber would improve accuracy. On many of these rifles, the extractor can serve as a built-in means of achieving this desirable goal. Simply modify the extractor clearance groove in the rifle's barrel so that it does not push the extractor away from the case head as the finger-lever brings the bolt to the fully closed position. By so doing, you will have created a situation where the spring-loaded extractor pushes the heads of all chambered cartridges against the opposite side of the chamber. That will improve accuracy because all chambered cartridges will be misaligned in the same manner — consistency is the benchmark of accuracy. See photographs #s 1-71/72/73.

Conversely, Winchester lever-action rifles all feature a spring-loaded plunger in the bolt face. This plunger almost certainly provides for consistent case head-to-chamber alignment. Therefore, it is unlikely that alteration of the

Photograph 11-4: This Model-1894 Marlin extractor (far side of bolt in this view) is quite rough. Proper polishing will improve the rifle's functioning. Our focus here, however, is to note that this spring can act as a cartridge aligner in the chamber.

Photograph 11-5: To allow the extractor spring to hold the head of the cartridge against the other wall of the chamber (the back side in this view) the extractor cannot touch this clearance ramp when a cartridge is chambered and the bolt is closed. Modification to this ramp or the extractor (or both) will usually achieve this goal quite easily. Before altering any such ramp, review the following text, drawings and photographs concerning the geometry of the chamber and solid web of the case head....

extractor clearance ramp would be of any particular benefit in Winchester lever-action rifles. However, since this modification might help and since this modification can also increase the purchase of the extractor on the case rim, I suggest it anyway. See photograph # 11-6.

Other lever-action repeaters and single-shot rifles have various methods and mechanisms. A careful analysis of the particular action will suggest what alterations are likely to be helpful and which of those might be most beneficial in any given rifle.

One final point about extractors. Be certain that any alteration you perform does not inappropriately change the relationship between the hooking face of the extractor and the chambered case rim. Ideally, you should slightly undercut this face of the extractor (perhaps 0.005" from the outside edge to the inside edge) and include sharp-topped grooves and ridges running from side-to-side across the hook. The undercut serves to apply all extraction force to the inner edge of the case rim. With this arrangement, as the extractor bends, under the force of extraction, it resists rolling over the case rim. In situations where sticky extraction might occur, this geometry is particularly important. See illustration.

You can incorporate these sharp-edged serrations using a carbide-tipped scribe (available through Brownells). You can produce a very similar effect by using a smooth double-cut three cornered file, as when you are filing to slightly increase the undercut angle. Under harsh extraction forces, the resulting sharp-edged ridges tend to cut into the case rim, thereby providing additional purchase for the extractor. Such grooves need only be deep enough to feel. The beneficial surface roughness they impart comes from the innate small-scale disruptions the scribing imparts to the extractor's working face. See illustration.

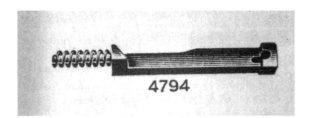

Photograph 11-6: Winchester lever-action rifles use a unique ejector. This line-drawing is from the 1916 Winchester catalogue. Replacing the original ejector spring with a somewhat weaker coil can slightly ease action manipulation.

It should be obvious that polishing the working face of the extractor is a genuine no-no.

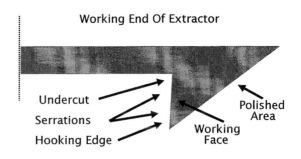

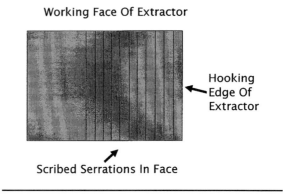

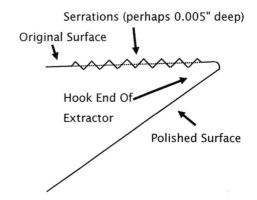

Altering Barrel Clearance Slots, Lever-Action & Single-Shot Rifles:

Before attempting any such alteration, consider the geometry of the slot with regard to the chambered cartridge case. Never make any alterations to any such slot that might weaken the chamber if that cut is farther forward than the front of the solid portion of the case head (the web). For practical purposes, that solid portion of the case head extends a minimum of one-

Section 11: The Trouble With Bolts, Part II

hundred and fifty-thousandths of an inch (0.150") in front of the bolt face. Specifically, ensure that you do not thin any portion of the chamber that is more than one-hundred and fifty-thousandths of an inch (0.150") in front of the bolt face. See illustration and photograph # 11-7.

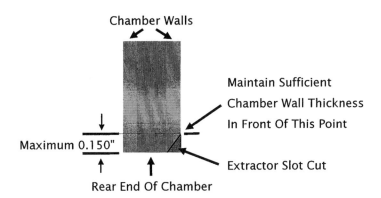

Photograph 11-7: Do not thin any chamber at a position that is in front of the solid web of the case head. This "solid" portion of the case head extends at least 150/1000" in front of the bolt face. Normally the case does not press against the barrel at all in this solid case web zone.

Section 12: The Trouble With Sights, *Part II*

I have attempted to thoroughly cover the general principles of this subject in *Part I*. Refer to that text for a complete discussion and photographs. Here I will cover unique aspects, that are particularly germane to single-shot rifles.

The following discussion is adapted to adding a telescopic sight base. However, note that the particulars are germane to any barrel installation that requires drilling and tapping a hole. For example, adding a different metallic sight to the barrel. Adding such a sight to the receiver is different because you can usually safely drill the necessary hole completely through the receiver, which dramatically simplifies matters.

Adding Barrel-Mounted Sights, Lever-Action & Single-Shot Rifles:

Here, as elsewhere, I have to advise against modifying any original part of any antique rifle. The collector's value of these rifles is just too great. If you have such a rifle and want to modify it to allow attachment of a scope, begin by replacing the barrel — put the original in storage. Someday the unaltered rifle could well be worth more money than you could ever imagine.

Barrel-mounted metallic sights are typical of lever-action rifles. Proper telescopic sight installation on most single-shot rifles requires scope sight base attachment to the barrel shank. The former subject, was addressed in detail in *Part I*. I will give the latter special consideration in this sub-section. See photograph #s 1-78 through 1-89.

Some have adapted telescopic sights to single-shot actions by attaching a rear scope sight base to the receiver and a front scope sight base to the barrel. For myriad reasons, not the least of which is the weakening of the receiver ring resulting from the holes needed to attach the rear scope base, attachment of the rear base to the receiver ring is a genuinely bad idea. It is far superior to attach both sight bases to the barrel. In some applications it might be necessary to use an offset rear scope sight ring to maintain proper eye relief but this is no problem as almost all major telescopic sight ring manufacturers provide offset rings.

Ruger incorporates a quarter-rib telescopic sight base on some of their falling-block (No. 1) rifles. This is a useful method and similar aftermarket ribs are available for attaching telescopic sights to other single-shot rifles. See Brownell's catalogue.

Should you decide to adapt a telescopic sight base, or bases, to any barrel, keep in mind that proper hole location is critical and that a too deep hole will ruin the barrel and possibly result in a dangerous situation. Generally, drilling such holes requires special tools: centering hole punches, square-ended drill bits, bottoming taps. (All are either available from Brownells or easily fashioned in the home workshop). See photograph # 12-1. This job also requires some skill and patience. It is probably best to use a quality drill press and drill press vise (to provide for

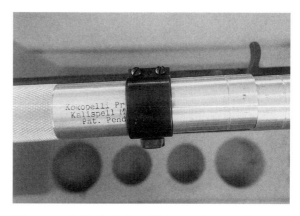

Photograph 12-1: Kokopelli Products scope bars are quite useful. Here you can clearly see the misalignment of these scope rings. The front bar has a more useful feature for this job. See photograph 12-2.

precise hole depths). I have to advise that this is a job for only the qualified and careful tinker; all others should hire a professional to do this delicate and critical work.

Should you have the skills, equipment and desire to do this job yourself, consider the profile of the barrel. If it includes a chamber swell, located behind a graceful contoured section that leads to a straight-tapered section located in front of the chamber, you might choose to install a cantilevered beam that attaches over the chamber. This system leaves the forward end of the telescopic sight base unsupported where it extends forward, over the smaller portion of the barrel. In this situation, you should install three or more screws into the portion of the base that rests over the chamber.

This method provides for proper telescopic sight base-to-bore alignment and often gives much greater metal thickness under the screw holes. On many rifles this extra thickness is necessary to retain sufficient barrel strength. Drilling holes into a barrel is always a critical operation — drill too deeply and the rifle's safety is compromised. Conversely, if the hole is not drilled deep enough, the attachment might not be sufficiently robust for the task at hand. The following guidelines should be helpful.

Generally, drill and tap the holes to a depth that equals about one and one-half times the diameter of the attaching screw, but in no case drill the hole deeper than about one-half the thickness of the chamber or barrel or so as to leave a solid wall of steel equal in thickness to at least two-thirds the screw shank diameter.

Attachment screws for most telescopic sight bases use a 6x48 thread. These screw shanks are about one-hundred and thirty-five thousandths of an inch (0.135") in diameter. For this size screw, the optimum hole depth is about two-tenths inch

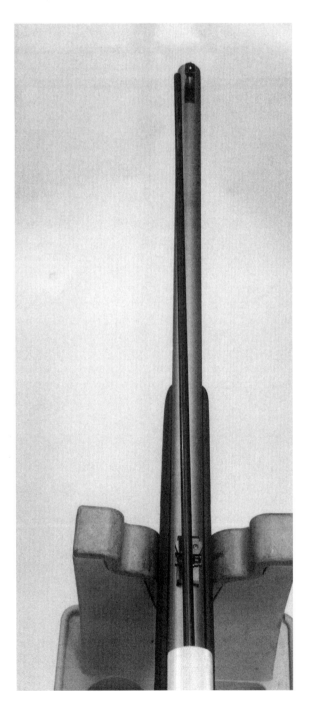

Photograph 12-2: Here I have installed the front Kokopelli Scope Bar into both rings and mounted the rings on a mounted scope base. I then inserted a cleaning rod into the hole in the front of the Scope Bar. Note that the front of the cleaning rod is not aligned over the center of the barrel. This is clear evidence that the scope base holes on this rifle are not properly aligned to the barrel. By positioning this fixture (scope bar, rings and bases) over an undrilled receiver or barrel you can properly align the bases to the barrel. You then need only to scribe the necessary screw hole locations. Better, you could temporarily attach the bases to the barrel in this correct orientation. To do this, clean and degrease the top of the rifle and the bottom of the bases, then apply Loctite #609 to the contact area. Align and attach this assembly in place using heavy rubber bands. Allow several hours for the mounting agent to cure. Then remove the scope rings from the bases. The bases will be bonded sufficiently to allow hole marking, drilling and tapping — if you are cautious. See the text for a discussion of critical safety concerns before drilling into the wall of any barrel or receiver.

Section 12: The Trouble With Sights, Part II

(0.2"). However, you should leave no less than ninety-thousandths of an inch (0.090") of solid chamber or barrel wall under the bottom of the hole. Leaving less material between the bottom of the hole and the chamber or barrel is apt to result in a swelled spot under the screw! (For holes at the muzzle end of a barrel it is acceptable to leave less barrel wall thickness since, by the time the bullet reaches the muzzle, chamber pressure is much lower than it is when the bullet is near the chamber.)

Contrary to intuition, a deeper hole using a longer screw will add little to the strength of the attachment. If the steel of the hole and the screw were of equal hardness and strength, a threaded hole of a depth equal to one and one-half times the screw's diameter would provide sufficient purchase to pull the screw in two before the threads striped. However, the barrel is never anywhere nearly as strong as the screws used in this application, so this rule would seem not to apply.

The reason this "one and one-half times" rule does, nonetheless, apply relates to deformation of the threads in the hole resulting from the stress associated with tightening the screw. In a deeper threaded hole, the combination of thread deformation and thread binding results in so much friction that it becomes impossible to gain any significant attachment force just by using a deeper threaded hole in combination with a longer screw.

Conversely, a shallower hole is apt to provide insufficient attachment strength. If possible, try to get the hole to a minimum of one-hundred and seventy-five thousandths of an inch (0.175") depth for a 6x48 screw. See illustration. If that is not possible, install more, smaller screws for the mounting. Brownells sells a variety of smaller screws and the appropriate taps.

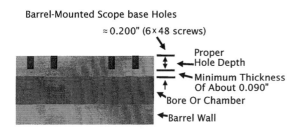

It is useful to paint the top surface of the rear end of the barrel with machinist's paint (Dykem, available through Brownells) or some similar substance — the red version provides better visibility on most steels. With this paint in place, lay a straight edge along the barrel. Center it along the length of the top of the barrel. If the rifle has sights, use those to align the straight edge to the bore axis. Then scribe a light mark in this "paint" to indicate the proper centerline for the scope sight base attachment holes. See photograph #s 12-1/2.

With a mark so scribed, proceed to find the proper hole locations, as follows. Loosely mount the scope sight you intend to use in the rings you will use. Adjust the relationship of the rings and the scope sight so that neither ring touches the turret or either of the telescopic sight bells (the swelled ends of the scope tube). It is best if you center the rings between the turret and the telescopic sight bells. This method provides clearance to allow further fine tuning; should you later decide you need to move the riflescope slightly forward or backward in the rings to achieve proper eye relief or action clearance, you can do so. Attach the riflescope to the scope sight base(s). (Hereafter, I will follow this discussion assuming you are using two-piece bases; this procedure varies only in detail for mounting a one-piece base.)

Next, hold the rifle at your shoulder as you normally would for shooting. Set the riflescope, with rings and bases attached, on the barrel. For obvious reasons, this is a job best accomplished with the aid of a helper. However, you can use heavy rubber bands to temporarily attach the telescopic sight assembly to the barrel. While maintaining a natural shooting pose, slide the riflescope fore and aft on the barrel until you obtain the proper sight picture. Then scribe the Dykem or paint to indicate this, proper, fore and aft positioning of the sight bases.

Now, if you have the correct tools and skills (see above), you can proceed to prepare the barrel for sight base attachment. Remove the sight bases from the riflescope and place those over the barrel, properly centered and aligned over the scribed centerline mark. Tape the sight bases in place with several tight wraps of electrical tape but avoid getting the tape over the attachment holes.

With the proper hole-center punch (it will just fit the small diameter of the hole in the sight base), mark one attachment hole location. With the gun properly affixed in a vising fixture, insert the hole-center punch and strike it a sharp blow with an 8-ounce ball-peen hammer. (Midway offers a very good fixture for this purpose, they call this handy tool the *Shooter's Vise*.) See photograph # 12-3.

It is possible to mark all holes at the beginning of this process. However, you can often achieve a more precise hole alignment by marking one attachment hole for each base, drilling and tapping that hole and then attaching the base with that one screw before marking, drilling and tapping the second hole. The choice of method is yours. However, note, it is very difficult to properly align the bases to each other in order to drill both holes for each base at the same time. The method described here provides for much better alignment.

With the initial holes thus located, remove the bases and vise the barrel under the drill press. Carefully locate the barrel so that the drill press spindle naturally centers the proper size index drill bit (#31 or #32 for a #6 screw), squarely over the locating dimple that you developed with the hole-center punch. It is critical that you set the drill press to limit hole depth, as noted in the above illustration, and in the preceding text. (Note, the #31 drill bit will allow easier tapping, the #32 drill bit will form <u>slightly</u> stronger threads — the difference cannot amount to more than about 5%, but stronger is stronger.)

After drilling the initial hole so that it reaches the full necessary depth, but no deeper, at the very center of the hole (which is deeper than the sides, owing to the tapered point on a standard twist drill bit), substitute a two-size smaller index drill bit (#33 or #34 for a #6 screw) modified and with an essentially square cutting end. With such a drill bit it is easy to finish the hole with a square bottom, which provides more depth for threads, without unnecessarily weakening the barrel. To take advantage of this increased potential threading depth, you will have to have a bottoming tap of the correct size and thread pitch (typically 6x48).

I have formed such "square ended" drill bits myself using a bench grinder. Simply reduce the point angle until it is almost square to the shank of the drill bit. Then, resharpen the point as you normally would — cut the leading edge of each flute at an angle that is slightly greater than ninety degrees (90°) to the axis of the drill bit.

Drill with this modified drill bit to achieve a nearly square bottom on the hole without deepening it. See illustration. Then proceed to tap the hole using a quality tapping oil and the proper tap. In this instance, the correct tap to begin with is the "plug", not the "taper". In shallow, blank-ended holes the taper tap will not grab hold and cut significant threads before bottoming in the hole.

Perhaps the easiest method of tapping such holes is to proceed as follows: after drilling the hole and without removing the barrel from the drill press vise, or moving the drill press table, remove the drill bit from the drill press, install the plug tap of the proper size and thread pitch in the drill chuck; remove the belt from the drive; then turn the chuck by hand while applying moderate down pressure to the spindle. You can feel the tap grab hold as it begins to cut threads. After this, the tap will tend to advance the spindle downward as you continue to tap the hole deeper. However, use caution and do not force the weak threads that form at the beginning of this process

Photograph 12-3: Hole-Center Punches (as are available from Brownells) are invaluable for properly positioning holes under pre-drill attachments. All you have to do is properly position the piece (such as a telescopic sight base) over the work, then insert the correct punch and give it a sharp rap with a small hammer. This will produce a properly positioned dimple that is properly shaped to center a drill bit.

Section 12: The Trouble With Sights, Part II

to hold the chuck down against the spindle's spring tension. Use the spindle crank to keep the chuck pushing down just slightly on the tap.

With a proper bottom hole tapping kit you will have three taps. As noted, usually, in shallow holes you should start with the medium tapered (plug) tap. Advance that tap, in steps, until it lightly bottoms. Never turn any standard tap past the point where cuttings begin to add resistance to the tapping action. If you feel the resistance increase, you have gone too far! Before that happens, back the tap out sufficiently to shear off the cuttings inside the hole. When necessary, remove the tap and clear the cuttings from the tap and out of the hole. An aerosol cleaning product (such as carburetor cleaner) fitted with a small extension nozzle is ideal for this chore. Also, be very careful not to tap so deeply that the point of the tap pushes against the end of the hole. This can result in either the shallow threads stripping or in the end of the hole being pushed forward, which will create a bulge inside the chamber or barrel! Finally, to avoid tap breakage and to prolong tap life, always use a quality cutting oil and plenty of it — cutting oil is a lot cheaper than a tap. Note, the addition of molybdenum disulfide to tapping oil will dramatically reduce friction and the risk of tap breakage.

Also, it is highly advisable to use only carbon steel taps for such delicate work. When a tap made from high speed steel shears in a new hole in which you are forming threads, you will find that removing the broken off portion tap is reminiscent of major dental work *sans* laughing gas or any other pain killer. Conversely, broken ends of carbon steel taps are easy to shatter using a small punch and a light hammer. The pieces will just fall out of the hole. You can then resharpen the broken tap or use a new one to finish the job; little harm done.

After completing this operation with the plug tap, repeat these steps using the bottoming tap — be careful that it finds and follows the same threads! After this tap hits the bottom of the hole, consider modifying a similar tap by grinding all the taper from the end. Then use this square-ended tap to cut the last thread fully to the bottom of the hole. This will give the attachment screw that much more steel against which to pull. In shallow holes this is no small consideration.

Also, consider fitting a too long screw to properly fit the hole with the base in place. By carefully grinding a too-long screw down to length (without overheating it), you can have full threads reaching fully into the hole. Again, in shallow holes the advantage of one forty-eighth of an inch (1/48") more threads is no small matter!

Before proceeding to properly fit the attachment screws, refer to the following section. If you later change the thickness of either sight base, you will have to refit the attachment screws for that base.

To fit such a screw, choose a too long sight base attachment screw. Begin by grinding the end flat. Then insert this screw in the tapped hole in the barrel and thread it in until it stops. Measure the distance from the screw head to the barrel (the hole gauge on a dial caliper is the correct tool for taking this measurement). Remove that screw. Place the proper sight base over the hole and install a similar but too-short screw. Turn that screw until the head snugs against the sight base. Measure the distance from the screw head to the barrel.

Getting this measurement will require measuring several things and doing some math. Depending upon the sight base configuration, you might measure the height of the top of the base from the top of the barrel, then measure the height of the top of the attachment screw from the top of the sight base. (For example, if the sight base was 0.1625" above the barrel and the screw head was 0.015" below the top of the sight base, the screw head would be 0.150" above the barrel.)

The difference in these two measurements represents the amount of screw shank you should remove from the too-long screw. For example, if the head of the bottomed too-long screw was two-hundred thousandths of an inch (0.200") from the barrel and the too-short screw head was one-hundred and fifty-thousandths of an inch (0.150") from the barrel, you need to shorten the too-long screw by fifty-thousandths of an inch (0.050") to begin the precise fitting stage.

Measure the too-long screw and then shorten it by the difference of the amounts measured in the above test. Then screw this pre-fitted screw into the hole until it bottoms solidly in the hole but do not force it. Note the orientation of the screw head. Remove the screw.

Set the sight base over the hole and install the pre-fitted attachment screw. Tighten the screw as before (do not force it). Note the orientation of the screw head. If this is unchanged from when the screw was installed without the sight base in place, remove the screw and grind about five-thousandths of an inch (0.005") from the end of the screw shank. Install the screw and turn it until it is snug. IF the screw head is still in the same orientation, repeat this test-and-shorten process one more time. Eventually the screw head will tighten solidly against the sight base instead of in the screw shank tightening against the bottom of the screw hole in the barrel. This condition will be evidenced by the screw slot coming to rest in a new orientation when the screw is tightened. To reiterate: your goal is to make certain the screw head is bottoming against the base, rather than the screw shank bottoming against the end of the screw hole in the barrel. The approximately five-thousandths of an inch (0.005") clearance between the end of the screw shank and the bottom of the hole will give you room to properly torque the screw without the screw shank pushing against the end of the hole.

Fitting each attachment screw the same way will provide the maximum possible attachment strength. However, there is one disadvantage to this system. Unless you have managed to drill each hole to almost precisely the same depth, this method will create a situation where it is critical to use each screw only in the hole to which it was fitted. Keep this in mind if you happen to disassemble the bases in the future.

When you have finished this work, thoroughly clean all cuttings and oil from the hole or holes. As noted, an aerosol carburetor cleaner with a nozzle installed in the spray valve works best for cleaning out small closed ended (blank) holes.

As noted above, after drilling and tapping one hole for each base, you can temporarily attach the sight bases to the barrel using a screw of the proper length, see the above discussion of fitting screws to blank holes. Snug the attachment screws sufficiently to lock the sight bases in place on the barrel.

If necessary, properly align the sight bases to center the other hole over the scribed centerline mark in the Dykem. You can accomplish this most easily and accurately by attaching the telescopic sight rings and then the riflescope in place over the bases — when you snug the rings over the riflescope tube, that tube will align the bases with each other. Proceed to mark the other holes with the hole-center punch. Finish this job by drilling and tapping the remaining telescopic sight base holes, following the method described above.

Adding Attachment Screws To Barrel-Mounted Sight Bases, Lever-Action & Single-Shot Rifles:

At this point you might consider adding additional telescopic sight base attachment screws. This is particularly desirable in those instances where a thin barrel prevents using holes of the desirable depth (0.200"), which is quite common. With all existing holes properly cleaned out and the base(s) attached snugly to the proper positions on the barrel you can proceed to add screws.

It is worth noting that by staggering the position of a third screw in each sight base you can permanently identify each sight base's proper position as to front or rear location and as to front-to-rear orientation. Since the bases are not identical, even if you have not fitted those to the gun, this is a very worthwhile consideration.

On many two-piece sight bases there is insufficient room to center an additional attachment screw hole between the existing front and rear screw holes. Also, note that on many sight bases you cannot add a third screw at all, owing to inadequate room. Finally, on Weaver-style sight bases any added base attachment screw must not interfere with the cross-bolt on the telescopic sight ring — a shallow-headed screw can fit directly under the cross bolt. However, on most one-piece sight bases, and some two-piece sight bases, there will be sufficient room to add one additional attachment screw near one or both ends of the sight base.

Since the force of recoil tends to result in the telescopic sight pulling up on the rear of the sight base, it makes sense to add any additional screws nearer the rear of each sight base, or toward the rear of a one-piece sight base. If you deem this addition feasible and desirable, proceed as follows.

Adding additional screws to telescopic sight bases involves the drilling of a two-diameter hole in the sight base; the larger portion of this hole (located on the top side of the base) forms the countersink for the head of the attachment screw. First, locate the centerline of the sight base and drill punch a location where the added attachment screw will do the most good and will not interfere with attachment of the riflescope sight ring. Do not place this hole any closer than necessary to the existing adjacent attachment screw.

It is best to begin this drilling by counter sinking the larger hole to a depth that allows the entire beveled point of the drill bit to enter past the flat surface of the sight base. If you can,

Section 12: The Trouble With Sights, Part II

mount this sight base in a padded drill press vise, or lacking that, if you can clamp the base onto a drill press platform, you can easily gauge the proper depth for the countersink in this new hole. Simply gauge the drill travel using one of the existing screw attachment holes in the sight base. Lacking that, use trial and error to get the hole just deep enough to allow the attachment screw head to enter past flush. However, to determine that depth, you will first have to bore a screw shank diameter hole through the sight base, using the appropriate (smaller) drill bit.

The correct drill bits (when using Weaver 6x48 screws): for the countersink, index # 5 but a seven thirty-seconds inch (7/32") fractional drill bit will suffice; for the screw body hole, index #27 is correct. Remember, for the blank hole in the barrel use index #31 or #32.

After you have finished the countersunk hole through the base, reattach the base firmly to the barrel using both existing screw locations. Hole-center punch the barrel at the new hole's location. As with the original holes, make certain you have adequately located this hole by the application of a deep punch mark so that the drill bit will not wander. Proceed to drill and tap this hole as you did the original holes.

Telescopic Sight Alignment Considerations For Barrel Mounted Sight Bases, Lever-Action & Single-Shot Rifles:

On many falling-block and other single-shot rifle actions the original barrel is a straight taper, either round or hexagonal in form. Since most of these barrels are chambered for rather low velocity cartridges, it is often beneficial to simply attach the telescopic sight base(s) to the barrel with no modification to accommodate for the fact that the front sight base is closer to the axis of the bore than the rear base. This method places the riflescope at a slight angle to the bore axis. However, owing to the rainbow-like trajectory of blackpowder era cartridges, this condition often allows for proper riflescope zeroing at intermediate ranges without using up a large amount of the riflescope's internal elevation adjustment.

If this method proves to provide too much riflescope-to-barrel tilt, try splitting the difference. Measure the barrel diameter both under the rear base and under the front base. Subtract the latter measurement from the former measurement and divide the difference by four, e.g., 1.000" (rear diameter), 0.960" (front diameter), difference 0.040", difference divided by four 0.010". In this example (as a first effort), you would file and polish 0.010" from the bottom side of the rear base.

If you find such an alteration is necessary, it is extremely important to lap the scope sight rings to achieve proper alignment after the alteration. Shortening one base is certain to introduce additional sight ring misalignment. (I have yet to see a perfect set of rings and bases, and even if I had I would not have known those pieces were perfect since manufacturers are yet to build the perfect receiver or barrel.)

See the appropriate discussion of scope ring lapping in *Part I*. It is simply foolish to clamp an expensive telescopic sight into a set of rings without properly aligning those first — scope tube damage is inevitable.

If you are attaching a one-piece base or a quarter-rib telescopic sight mount system, be certain to immaculately clean both the barrel under the sight base and the underside of the base (use alcohol followed by dilute ammonia). Then apply ample Loctite #609 between the barrel and base before securing those parts. Here it is particularly important to minimize vibrations and potential for movement. Even with two-piece bases it is advisable to coat the barrel faces of the clean bases with Loctite #609 before attaching those to the barrel.

Consider temporarily attaching the base(s) with the #609 in place but without tightening the screws. Let gravity hold the base against the barrel and use the screw only to get the proper alignment. After the #609 has fully cured, remove the screws, clean off the threads and clean out the holes. Then apply ample Loctite #222 or #242 to fully coat the threads. Not only does the thread locker keep the screws from coming loose but it also strengthens the bond — the weaker threads in the barrel will resist more stress if you use Loctite! See photograph #s 7-3/4.

This method allows the Loctite #609 (mounting agent) to take up any slack in the barrel-to-base joint. After the #609 cures, installing and tightening the sight base attachment screws will not stress the barrel by forcing the sight base and barrel into contact at the screw locations.

I cannot overstate the importance of using these products in these and similar applications. Loose sight base attachment screws are quite common. This leads not only to accuracy problems but also to the potential for attachment screw hole stripage in the barrel, a disastrous condition. While oversize taps and screws are available from Brownells, such is a problem best avoided.

Dovetailed Barrel Attachments, Lever-Action & Single-Shot Rifles:

Along with the common barrel-mounted fixed-sights found on other types of rifles, many single-shot and lever-action rifles have one or more additional dovetail slots in the underside of the barrel for fore-end and tubular magazine attachment purposes. I attempted to cover barrel-mounted sight alterations and other considerations quite thoroughly in *Part I* and in the previous sub-sections. Refer to those sub-sections for appropriate discussions of those topics.

If your plans include rebluing of the barrel, it is most advisable to silver solder the corresponding fore-end and magazine tube hangers, properly centered, in the dovetail slots in the barrel. Brownells offers a high-strength, low-temperature solder called Hi-Force 44™ that is perfect for this application. See photograph # 10-3.

Hi-Force 44 flows at modest four-hundred and seventy-five degree Fahrenheit (475°F) and provides a surprising 28,000 psi bonding strength (many times greater than any epoxy or anaerobic bonding agent). You can achieve a superior hold by using Brownells Hi-Temp Hi-Force™ solder. This product flows at six-hundred and fifty degrees Fahrenheit (650°F) and provides a very impressive 38,000 psi bond.

If properly applied, neither product will in any way harm a heat treated barrel. However, Hi-Temp Hi-Force contains cadmium. For this reason, do not use this solder without proper and adequate ventilation or if you cannot control the temperature to less than seven-hundred and forty degree Fahrenheit (740°F) — higher temperatures liberate dangerous quantities of toxic fumes. Employ extreme caution.

Proper soldering includes properly debluing and cleaning of the working surface of the dovetail and that portion of the piece that mates to the dovetail. Using a cotton swab, apply a dab of dilute hydrochloric (Muriatic) acid. This acid is sold as a pH-balancing agent for swimming pools. Small quantities are also available from most pharmacies. Dilute one part of this product with ten-parts water by adding the acid to the water. Since the acid solution will strip the bluing and allow the solder to adhere, apply acid only to the areas you intend to solder. Use extreme caution to avoid getting the acid on anything else, including yourself. Always wear safety goggles when working with acid. Lacking hydrochloric acid, you can achieve the same result using white vinegar, However, this acetic acid solution will take several hours to fully remove the bluing. Heating the barrel by using a portable hair dryer can considerably speed this action.

Once you have cleaned and deblued the surfaces, preheat the barrel as much as is feasible using a hair dryer. If one is available, use an oven to heat the barrel to not more than four-hundred degrees Fahrenheit (400°F), interpose an opaque barrier between any heating element and the barrel to avoid overheating the barrel through radiant heating.

Locate the barrel on a wood table with wood blocks near the one-third points along the barrel's length but keep these blocks well clear of the dovetails. Lightly clamp the barrel in place with the dovetails aligned to the top. Alternatively, rest the barrel in wood blocks with "V" notches. Then use a propane torch to heat the dovetail cut area until # 4 Comet flux (available from Brownells) flows over the surface. Do not apply too much flux; it should only wet the dovetail area. Given enough time and heating, Comet flux will remove the bluing and allow the solder to wet the steel. Then melt a small dab of solder onto the middle of the dovetail. Continue to heat the area until the solder flows over the fluxed surface and wets all surfaces of the dovetail. Add sufficient solder, as necessary, to fully wet the entire area of the dovetail, both the bottom and the undercut sides. Finish this "tinning" (solder wetting) operation by using a clean and fine wire brush to remove all the excess solder. Leave only a shiny solder film on the surface.

Omitting the unnecessary preheating step, repeat the solder wetting process with the barrel hanger. Be sure to completely solder wet all surfaces of the hanger that abut to surfaces in the dovetail on the barrel.

For the next critical step you will need to have and use small pliers, a welder's leather glove and a small brass punch and hammer. Position the hanger in a small pair of pliers so that you can align it against the dovetail. While both pieces are still hot enough to keep the solder liquid, as evidenced by the shiny surface, align the hanger to the right side of the dovetail and tap it into place. It might be necessary to apply additional heat. Tap until the hanger moves to the center of the barrel. Finish this job by applying a very tiny amount of flux along the joint, if necessary (a toothpick works well), then heat the hanger until the flux flows between the surfaces. Move the flame to the far side of the hanger and continue to apply heat while touching the solder wire at the joint of the hanger and the barrel on the near side (opposite the flame). Soon, the solder should flow into and fill the joint. Use a damp cotton rag to wipe away any excess solder from the surface. This finishes the job. Allow the piece to air cool until it comes to room temperature.

Silver soldering such hangers to the barrel is beneficial for two reasons. First, it positively prevents movement and dramatically (by several times) strengthens the bond between barrel and hanger. On high-recoil rifles (such as the Marlin Model-1895, .45-70 Government) this is a major consideration. Second, the heating and mechanical bonding involved in the soldering operation and process helps to eliminate stress between the hanger and barrel! The solder bond acts to carry the joint and the heating relieves the stresses imposed by inserting the hanger in the (normally slightly smaller) dovetail slot. This effect could improve the rifle's intrinsic accuracy and should reduce any tendency for zero wander as the barrel heats during extended shot strings.

If you do not plan to reblue the barrel and you do not wish to apply solder, the following steps are a minimum toward improving any dovetail attachment system. Properly clean and degrease the hanger and the dovetail slot (finish this cleaning with a dilute ammonia solution followed by distilled water). After all surfaces have dried, apply Loctite product #609 (mounting agent) and insert the hanger from the right side until you have it properly centered over the barrel. Use of #609 can, perhaps, double the bonding between hanger and barrel. For modest recoil guns, this method is most certainly sufficiently strong.

Screw Attached Front Sight Bases, Lever-Action & Single-Shot Rifles:

Many rifles, such as Marlin's Model-336 and new Model-1894, use screw-attached front sight assemblies. These particular sights are certainly acceptable for hunting use. However, improvement is possible in several areas; most significant are dependability and visibility. The first big step any serious shooter should consider is a matter of improving the sight's dependability. See *Part I* for a complete discussion of these improvements. See photograph # 12-4.

Also, consider that it is a simple matter to silver solder the front sight base to the barrel. See the discussion of silver soldering dovetail attachments in the previous sub-section.

Barrel-Mounted Rear Sight Modifications, Lever-Action & Single-Shot Rifles:

Tang- or receiver-mounted metallic sights offer an increased sight radius. For this reason, I highly recommend considering installation of a tang- or receiver-mounted rear sight, to replace the existing barrel-mounted sight. However, the existing sights are worth looking at with an eye toward improvement. See *Part I* for discussions of both processes. See photograph #s 12-5 through 12-11.

Photograph 12-4: This (typical) barrel-mounted front sight demonstrates two major weaknesses. First, what is to keep the screws from coming loose? Second, what is to insure that the dovetail will hold the insert? Do not bet your hunt or your life on either of these flimsy systems. Silver soldering is a good option here. However, application of Loctite #609 (a mounting agent) and Loctite #222 (a thread locker) will essentially solve all such problems. Here the base has already been bonded to the barrel with #609. Note the oil-free area under the base. Complete degreasing is essential for maximum adhesion of these types of chemicals. A few drops of #609 in the dovetail before the sight is driven back home will insure that it will never move on its own account.

Photograph 12-5: This photograph shows the modification necessary to attach the new Lyman tang-mounted aperture sight to a Marlin lever-action rifle. The tools needed include: a proper hole-center punch, the correct drill bit and the right sized tap (complete instructions are included with the sight). This tang is ready to accept the intermediate base (necessary to prevent illegal damage to the federally mandated serial number).

Photograph 12-6: Application of Loctite #609 (a mounting agent) will ensure a solid bond between the intermediate base and the tang.

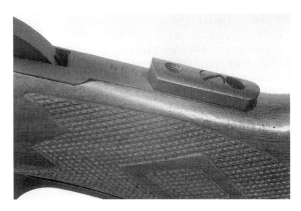

Photograph 12-7: The intermediate base is initially attached by only one screw.

Photograph 12-8: Installation of the sight finishes the job. The rear sight screw replaces the standard tang screw; the front base screw reaches only through the tang.

Photograph 12-9: The Lyman tang sight in the working position.

Section 12: The Trouble With Sights, Part II

Photograph 12-10: The Lyman tang sight in the carry position.

Photograph 12-11: Here a modified Lyman receiver-mounted aperture sight is installed on a Marlin Model-1894. Note the unused exposed screw hole. Both attachment holes are hidden under the vertical riser. This sight was built for an entirely different rifle (a bolt-action .22 Rimfire, I believe). Nevertheless, after a bit of modification, it functions quite well on this rifle.

Section 13: The Trouble With Lever-Action and Single-Shot Rifle Stocks, Part II

We will visit this subject again in *Section 15*, where we go into greater detail on the accuracy related aspects. For a better understanding of the principals involved, I suggest that you familiarize yourself with both sub-sections.

For related photographs and a general discussion of the principles of proper fit and function of a rifle stock, see *Part I*. Here we will address those aspects that are unique to lever-action and the various single-shot types of rifles.

Glass Bedding Winchester's Model-88 & Other One-Piece Stocked Lever-Action & Single-Shot Rifles:

Winchester's innovative, if ill-fated, Model-88 and a few, more-or-less, obscure single-shot rifles carry one-piece stocks. The bedding process for these rifles is similar to that used in the typical bolt-action rifle but requires special considerations. Before moving on to the discussion of two-piece stock bedding, I will address proper bedding of the somewhat unique Model-88, as an example and in particular. Those owning any single-shot rifle (even a muzzle-loader!) with a one-piece stock should review this information and that given in *Part I*. An understanding of the goals of glass bedding with a one-piece stock (minimizing the potential for the stock to transfer stress to the receiver, as pointed out in *Part I*), should allow anyone with any rifle having a one-piece stock to determine the best method of glass bedding that barreled-action.

The stock-to-barreled-action attachment used on the Model-88 is reminiscent of the time-honored hooked-breech system, as found on many muzzle-loading rifles of days gone by. The rear of the receiver hooks into a separate piece that is attached to the stock with a through-bolt. Hereafter, I will call this piece on the Model-88 the rear action boss. See photograph # 13-1.

On the Model-88 the barrel rests in the fore-end channel. A screw located several inches forward of the barrel's chamber section attaches the fore-end to the barrel through a dovetailed hanger. This screw tightens against a boss in the fore-end by screwing vertically into the hanger that is attached to the barrel. See photograph # 13-2.

The section of the barrel located directly in front of the receiver is double radiused. This barrel section forms a smooth transition from the

Photograph 13-1: The rear action boss and through-bolt from the Winchester Model-88 lever-action rifle. This boss works just as the time-honored hooked breach system found on the famous Hawken style rifle (and many other long guns of yore). In this application the through-bolt positively bonds the boss to the stock. Nevertheless, proper rear action boss bedding in reinforced epoxy will dramatically improve the receiver-to-barreled-action bedding system.

full diameter portion, at the barrel-to-receiver shoulder, to the straight-taper section. This double-radius zone is functional in proper bedding on these rifles. See photograph # 13-3.

There is also a lower receiver extension. This piece is located at the bottom front of the receiver, just behind the barrel and forward of the magazine well. This piece enters a lateral dovetail in the lower receiver rails. This unit carries the magazine latch. The sloping front face of this extension forms the primary front receiver-to-stock bedding surface. As you tighten the attachment screw that enters the barrel hanger through the fore-end, the sloping surface on the lower receiver extension forces the barreled-action back in the stock, until the receiver comes to bear against the rear action boss. See photograph # 13-4.

If everything is properly proportioned, this produces a rigid bond between the rear action boss and the receiver. This tight bonding is critical in preventing front-to-rear play of the barreled-action in the stock. Without this tight bond, consistency is an accident, rather than the rule. Remember, consistency is the benchmark of accuracy.

Similarly, when you hook the rear of the receiver into the rear action boss and rotate the front of the barreled-action down into the stock, the double-radiused portion of the barrel comes to rest against a slightly radiused shoulder in the stock. Proper fit at this location also works to force the barreled-action to mate tightly against the rear action boss (as you tighten the barrel hanger attachment screw in the fore-end). It is critical that both bedding points (at this barrel radius and at the lower receiver extension) are properly positioned so that the barrel will pull completely down into the barrel channel in the fore-end, and do so without stressing the barrel — which would bend if subjected to such stress. See photograph # 13-3.

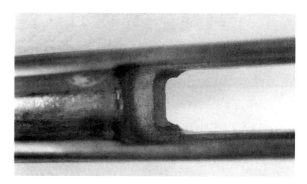

Photograph 13-3: This bottom view at the front of the receiver opening on the Winchester Model-88 stock shows the bedding area (the flat angled portion at center and toward the top of the stock), which mates to the front of the lower receiver extension. Located between that area and the barrel channel you will note a cornered recess that leads into the small radiused zone, which is adjacent to the barrel channel. When bedding this stock, you should fill all of these areas with steel-reinforced bedding material.

Photograph 13-2: On the Winchester Model-88 (like several other lever-action and single-shot rifles) the fore-end is attached to the barrel by a simple screw that protrudes through the fore-end and engages a barrel-attached hanger. Typically the hanger is dovetailed to the barrel, as it is on the Model-88. Note that on the Model-88 the barrel is fully bedded in the fore-end barrel channel — at least in factory trim....

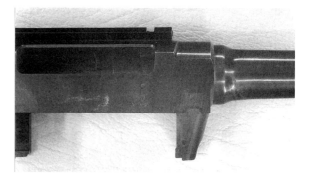

Photograph 13-4: This view shows the corresponding surfaces on the barreled-action (see photograph 13-3). Your goal is to glass bed the lower front receiver hanger and the rear barrel swell to the stock. At the same time you want the bedding material to force the receiver solidly into abutment against the rear action boss. Achieving this goal takes careful planning, some tinkering and proper execution of the bedding process. See the text for a complete rundown of the necessary steps.

Section 13: The Trouble With Lever-Action and Single-Shot Rifle Stocks, Part II

Unfortunately, this critical fit is the only thing that works to form a rigid and solid bonding between the receiver and the rear action boss. Therefore, to prevent a loose front-to-rear bonding between receiver and stock, certain stock dimensions are critical. First, the rear boss must be properly aligned to the receiver and it must also be properly bedded to the stock. Second, the relief radius in the stock, where the barrel radius fits, must fit the barrel radius and it must also be at the correct location. Finally, the front of the stock opening, where the lower front receiver extension rests, must be properly positioned and shaped. See photograph #s 13-3/4.

There does not appear to be any simple method whereby it would be reasonably easy to modify this attachment system to eliminate these problems — critical dimensions and weak fore-and-aft bonding of receiver and stock. However, a gunsmith with a milling machine could solve the front-to-rear bedding concern and at the same time eliminate the need to maintain critical inletting dimensions.

This proposed solution would require building a replacement piece to substitute for the stamped steel part that bridges the rear of the receiver. This replacement would extend behind the receiver and include a threaded hole that lined up with the through-bolt, which nominally connects the rear action boss to the stock.

By altering the rear action boss, to allow for clearance of this receiver extension and to allow for a longer through-bolt to pass through the unit, it would be possible to tighten the barreled-action directly to the stock, by tightening the through-bolt. With the interposed rear action boss properly glass bedded to the stock and aligned to both the stock and the receiver, receiver-to-stock bonding would be perfect — superior even to the best bolt-action bedding! Tightening the through-bolt would do all the work. It would then only remain to provide proper clearance for the remainder of the barreled-action and to properly attach the fore-end screw without stressing the barreled-action. In this case, the fore-end attachment screw would act only to keep the barrel from pulling too far away from the stock. (The following discussion gives a general idea of how to achieve that goal.)

Obviously, the above described alteration is rather complex and I suggest leaving it to a gunsmith. However, you could do this work using a welder and hand tools . . . if you have the skill and the patience. However, before altering the rear action boss, keep in mind that this piece is fitted to the individual receiver and is essentially irreplaceable — if you foul it up you will have a very tough job in building a replacement!

If you opt to stay with the original bedding system, you will note that correct barreled-action bedding depends upon the wood in the receiver area not changing in size or shape. The only good news here is that the stock along the sides of the receiver is formed of relatively thin panels, this reduces the potential for the stock to warp. Further, if the stock does warp, it cannot place significant strain on the receiver. See photograph # 13-5.

Your goal is to glass bed the rear action boss to the stock in such a manner as to produce a solid bed of epoxy between that piece and the stock. At the same time, you should work to

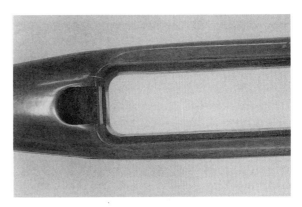

Photograph 13-5: This view shows the top, rear receiver opening in the Winchester Model-88 stock. Note the recess for the short tang on the rear action boss. You can also see the hole where the through-bolt (which attaches the rear action boss to the stock) reaches through the buttstock and into the receiver well. Proper barreled-action-to-receiver bedding requires that you install bedding material into the spaces between the wood and the back and sides of the rear action boss. However, note that there are several surfaces here that are rounded and are, therefore, neither normal (square) to nor parallel to the axis of the stock. You must not allow bedding agent to form a solid layer between the rear action boss and the stock in any of these zones. That would almost certainly (eventually) result in a cracked stock. The bedding agent would transmit the rearward recoil stresses to the angled wood surfaces and those would convert the rearward stresses to a spreading (tensional) force — wood has essentially zero tensional strength. Before installing bedding material, clean and roughen the rearward surfaces of this opening. Equally important, apply release agent to the proximal exposed surfaces of the stock.

make both the fit and front-to-rear bonding between the receiver and the rear action boss as nearly perfect as is possible. Finally, attaching the barreled-action into the stock, by tightening the attachment screw in the fore-end, should not place any undue stress upon either the barreled-action or the stock.

The very nature of this system suggests that simultaneously achieving all these goals is bound to be a little difficult. Before performing any alterations, note that the original bedding relies upon a relatively heavy epoxy wood finish inside the stock's receiver and barrel cutouts. Also note that the barrel is more-or-less fully bedded, full length in the fore-end barrel channel.

The first step in glass bedding these rifles is to ensure that the rear action boss is properly aligned to the receiver and that it is properly glass bedded in the stock. You can achieve these goals quite easily by installing a pad of bedding epoxy between the rear action boss and the stock and then forcing the barreled-action to push back solidly against the rear action boss as you tighten the fore-end attachment screw and to stay in that condition as the bedding agent cures. Tightening the fore-end attachment screw pulls the barreled-action home and, simultaneously, aligns the rear action boss to the receiver. Proceed with this work as follows.

After removing the barreled-action (by removing the fore-end attachment screw), remove the through-bolt to free the rear action boss and remove that piece. Degrease and roughen all steel-to-wood bedding surfaces in the stock. Alcohol, wire brushes and steel wool are good tools for this chore. Be doubly certain that all such surfaces are clean and adequately roughened to provide for good adhesion between the glass bedding epoxy and the existing stock surface. However, avoid grinding through the existing waterproofing finish. That result would serve no purpose and could compromise the factory "waterproofing" seal on the wood. However, if the surface of this finish is compromised, remove any oil-soaked wood.

When you have readied the stock for application of the epoxy bed behind the rear action boss, apply a six-inch piece of vinyl electrical tape into the stock. This tape should begin somewhat behind the fore-end attachment screw hole, pass back along the bottom of the barrel channel, then run down through the front end of the magazine opening and back out along the underside of the fore-end. See photograph # 13-6.

Next comes preparation of the rear action boss. Begin by degreasing all exterior surfaces. Then apply a layer of masking tape to all radiused surfaces and to the outside edges of all surfaces that are at an angle to the axis of the stock — you should not apply tape to any surfaces that are parallel or perpendicular to the bore axis. The photograph shows the areas of the rear action boss that you should cover with tape. Be sure to get a layer of tape over the radius at the top rear of the pseudo tang portion. Failure to apply tape to these surfaces is apt to, eventually, result in a split stock. See photograph # 13-7.

After applying this tape, apply glass bedding release agent to the entire rear action boss, to the threaded end of the through-bolt and to the stock on all exterior surfaces that are adjacent to the rear action boss. Be careful not to get any release agent on any interior stock surfaces.

It is easy to apply the release agent to the rear action boss using Brownells aerosol version of this product. To apply release agent to the exterior of the stock, use a cotton swab — either spray the aerosol version onto the swab (hold the swab against the nozzle and press the valve lightly) or dip the swab into the liquid version.

Mix about a tablespoon of glass bedding agent. I prefer the gel-type bedding agent for this application. Since the edges of this bedding will be visible in the finished rifle, consider adding a minute dab of brown colorant (as available from Brownells). Keep adding the colorant until the bedding agent is approximately the same color as the finished wood. Caution: a little of this colorant goes a long, long way. See photograph # 13-8.

Photograph 13-6: This view shows a layer of vinyl electrician's tape applied through the opening at the front of the receiver-well on this Winchester Model-88 stock. Application of this single layer of tape is critical to achieve correct rear action boss bedding. This tape provides alignment and clearances to provide for proper barrel floating in the subsequent stages of the bedding operation.

Section 13: The Trouble With Lever-Action and Single-Shot Rifle Stocks, Part II   205

Photograph 13-7: Pictured is the Winchester Model-88 rear action boss. At the top in this view is the tang extension. Note that all rounded or angled surfaces of this piece that are adjacent to rounded stock surfaces in the assembled rifle are covered with one layer of masking tape. Equally important, all other surfaces are bare. This taped piece must be thoroughly coated with release agent before installation into the epoxy bed in the stock.

Photograph 13-8: Since surfaces of the bedding agent will be visible in the assembled rifle, you might want to die it to match the wood color. To do this, mix a small dab (and I do mean small) of this product into the gel-type bedding agent.

Using a small screwdriver, or similar tool, paint a thin layer of this mix to cover the entire rear interior surface of the stock opening. A thin layer is all that you need to apply in most areas; undue excess will cause problems. However, you will note that a portion of the rear action boss adjacent to the through-bolt is significantly relieved so that a large air space will occur between the rear action boss and the stock. Apply sufficient bedding agent to fill this area. Be sure to get a thin layer of bedding agent on all inside surfaces of the pseudo-tang relief cut in the stock and along that portion of the stock where the rear action boss extends forward in the stock — where the machined sides of the rear action boss rest. Save a small portion of the bedding mix as a test sample.

Tentatively install the rear action boss. Slide it back in the stock until you have it properly positioned top-to-bottom and the piece begins to press against the epoxy bed. Install the through-bolt and turn that into the rear action boss until it just begins to snug the boss against the epoxy bed — do not tighten the bolt during this initial portion of this particular bedding operation.

Using a release agent saturated cotton swab, paint the area of the stock inside the action channel adjacent to the front of the rear action boss (epoxy is apt to squeeze out into this area as the receiver pushes the rear action boss back). Also, apply release agent to the rear surfaces of the (assembled) receiver.

Install the barreled-action into the stock in the normal manner. Note that the tape layer in the barrel channel and at the front of the magazine opening will prevent the barreled-action from falling fully into the stock.

Using your hand, apply clamping pressure to pull the rear of the barrel fully down into the barrel channel. While holding this pressure, tap the end of the buttstock sharply with a plastic mallet. Slightly tighten (just barely snug) the fore-end attachment screw into the barrel hanger. When the screw is snug, tap the top of the barrel-receiver joint with a plastic mallet to insure that the barrel comes to rest fully into the bottom of the barrel channel in the fore-end. If necessary, re-snug the fore-end screw.

Allow the bedding agent to cure to a solid consistency, as noted by examination of the test sample you saved. This will normally be six- to twelve-hours after the mix was first formed. After the bedding agent has cured to a consistency where it is difficult or impossible to dent it with your fingernail, tighten the through-bolt.

Remove the fore-end screw and separate the barreled-action from the stock. Remove the vinyl tape and clean all epoxy bedding agent from inside the receiver channel in the stock, the front of the rear action boss and the rear of the receiver. Then use a single-edge razor blade, or similar tool, to carefully trim all epoxy from the joint of the rear action boss and the stock. Lay the blade nearly flat to the stock and cut toward the boss but use caution to avoid scarring either the steel or the wood. See photograph # 13-9.

After you have cleaned all excess and extraneous epoxy bedding agent away from the perimeter of the rear action boss, loosen the through-bolt about one full turn. Then, without removing the screwdriver from the through-bolt slot, tap on the handle end of the screwdriver with a plastic mallet. This will break the rear action boss free from the epoxy bed in the stock.

Remove the through-bolt and pull the rear action boss from the stock. Remove all masking tape, from the stock or the rear action boss (depending upon where it stuck). Clean the bedding agent from the threaded portion of the through-bolt. Re-install the rear action boss and the through-bolt. Tighten the through-bolt sufficiently to prevent its loosening.

If you did this job correctly the receiver will mate squarely to the rear action boss and the stock will rigidly support the rear action boss. This is the critical first step in bedding these rifles. See photograph # 13-10.

The next step is to bed the front receiver lower extension, barrel radius and the barrel hanger to the stock. Begin by placing one layer of vinyl electrical tape in the barrel channel between the barrel hanger and the magazine well opening. Leave the front end of the tape about one-half inch from the screw hole. Leave the rear end of this tape about one-half inch in front of the radiused portion of the fore-end barrel channel. Place a second short strip of tape in the bottom of the barrel channel, beginning about one-half inch in front of the screw hole. These pieces of tape will provide the proper vertical positioning of the front end of the barreled-action so that the rear of the receiver will squarely engage the rear action boss. Also, when the barrel screw is snugged it will not unduly bend the barrel or the receiver.

Apply release agent to the barrel hanger, the underside and sides of the barrel and to the lower-front portion of the receiver. Using the cotton swab method, apply release agent to the outside surfaces of the stock adjacent to the barrel channel and the front of the magazine well opening. Thoroughly coat the fore-end screw with release agent.

Before proceeding, consider your options. You can glass bed the barrel at any or all the fol-

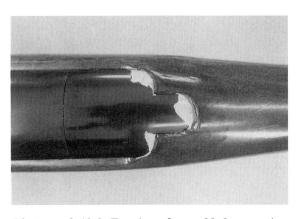

Photograph 13-9: Top view of assembled rear action boss and receiver. Note the extruded bedding agent and the masking tape. The tang extension beds on top of a layer of Brownells gel-type glass bed. The sides of the extension and the main body of the boss also bed against this material. Note that the hidden back surfaces of the boss also bed against epoxy. This forms a super-solid recoil surface. Tightening of the through-bolt, after the bedding agent has fully cured, will bond the rear action boss and the stock into an extremely rigid pair. Note the proper alignment of the top rear of the receiver and the top front of the rear action boss. This critical alignment requires attention to detail and a multi-step bedding operation.

Photograph 13-10: This bottom view of the rear of the Winchester Model-88 receiver opening in the stock shows extruded epoxy, masked off corners, and the solid abutment between the receiver and the rear action boss. Refer to photograph 13-9.

lowing areas: at the front of the magazine well opening, along the barrel channel behind the barrel hanger, around the barrel hanger, in the barrel channel in front of the barrel hanger. Of these locations, it is only necessary to bed the barrel at the front of the magazine well opening and in the area around the barrel hanger. The former is necessary to properly bond the barreled-action to the rear action boss. The latter is necessary to prevent variations in barrel screw tightening from bending the barrel.

The choice of barrel bedding in the front and rear portions of the fore-end barrel channel is wide open. If you want to experiment with variations in bedding, begin by omitting these areas, as described here, then add bedding in one or both of those areas in a separate bedding session and compare accuracy results.

If, after doing so, you find that you achieved the best overall accuracy when only the front of the magazine well and the fore-end screw areas were bedded, you will have to rasp adequate barrel clearance in the fore-end barrel channel and re-bed around the fore-end screw. This is not really all that much work. It is probably worth the effort just to know what system works best with that rifle. Your goal is, after all, accuracy.

One likely disadvantage of full barrel bedding is that this increases the potential for the gun to exhibit wandering zero in response to long-term changes in atmospheric humidity or to short-term changes in temperature (shooting related barrel heating). Without testing both systems, I suspect the following method is superior, as it is most apt to minimize those undesirable consequences.

For filling the area at the front of the magazine well cutout, mix a sufficient batch of epoxy bedding agent. Again the gel-type product works best. In this instance, it is useful to add about two-parts atomized steel to three-parts mixed bedding agent. See photograph # 13-11.

Note that the, as-inletted, stock does not fit the front of the receiver in this area. Only spots touch. The goal is to fill the recessed areas to provide a large zone of solid receiver-to-bedding-agent contact. Be sure to apply sufficient bedding agent to achieve this goal. Remember to leave a small amount of bedding agent as a test sample. See photograph # 13-3.

Equally, apply a bed of epoxy in the area around the fore-end screw. Before assembly, be sure you apply a proper coating of release agent to both the hanger and the area around the hanger on the barrel. Also, ensure that you have adequately coated release agent on the screw threads and shank.

Securely mount the stock, positioned vertically in a well-padded vise. While keeping the barreled-action pushed toward the rear of the stock, install it into the opening. Be careful not to dislodge the bedding agent from the area of the stock adjacent to the front of the magazine well opening, or from around the screw hole. Snug, but do not tighten, the fore-end screw.

In order to ensure the barreled-action is snug against the rear action boss, tap on the end of the barrel with a plastic mallet while tightening the fore-end screw. When the bedding agent has cured to a rigid consistency (as demonstrated by the test sample), remove the fore-end screw. Remove the barreled-action from the stock.

Observe the added bedding agent's distribution. If the initial bedding effort did not fill the barrel radius relief cut in the stock, mix another batch of bedding agent and repeat this process (be sure to clean the release agent from the epoxy surface where you intend to add material). Assuming the bedding agent is properly filling

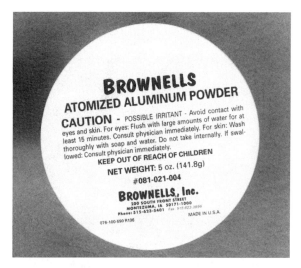

Photograph 13-11: Brownells atomized aluminum is considerably less expensive than their atomized stainless steel. However, the aluminum product does not provide quite as much rigidity and strength in the bedding material. However, it is certainly much better than adding nothing. Either of these materials can be added to standard bedding materials in anything up to a one-to-one (volume) ratio. I recommend adding two-parts atomized metal to three-parts mixed bedding agent. It takes a bit of effort to fully blend the metal into the epoxy.

the relieved areas in the front of the magazine well cutout, proceed to clean off any excess bedding agent.

Your goal is to have the agent only support the front of the receiver and the rearmost portion of the barrel. Cut away any bedding agent that has infiltrated into the magazine well, the outside of the stock or significantly forward under the barrel. Also, cut away any bedding agent that has migrated significantly up either side of the barrel channel or more than about one half inch in front of or behind the fore-end attachment screw hole. Remove the pieces of tape.

One final step is necessary to minimize bedding stresses. Remove the fore-end screw from the stock and drill the hole through the epoxy bedding pillar using a fractional drill bit that is one size bigger than the screw shank. Similarly, drill a hole in the epoxy bed from the inside of the barrel channel and following the screw hole. This hole should be large enough to prevent the fore-end hanger from binding in the epoxy bed. Also, use a sharp well-pointed knife to cut away a thin layer of the epoxy from the front and rear tapered surfaces of the hole where the tapered sides of the hanger rested as the epoxy cured. The photographs show the necessary alterations. See photograph #s 13-12/13.

Finally, carefully file the head of the screw a few-thousandths of an inch smaller in diameter. You can achieve this easily by chucking the screw shank in a vised electric drill and proceeding as follows. With the drill running, apply a bastard-cut file to the flats at the side of the screw head. This will rapidly reduce the screw head sufficiently to provide the necessary clearance — a few-thousandths of an inch is adequate.

These alterations allow the barrel and screw to move end-to-end or side-to-side in the screw hole without creating stresses between the barrel and the stock. For the same reason, apply a coating of graphite or molybdenum-disulfide powder to all bedding surfaces in the stock.

Completely degrease the screw and the screw hole. An application of Loctite product #222 to the screw will allow you to only lightly snug the screw without worrying about it coming loose. This can be very helpful with accuracy.

Install the barreled-action in the stock. Make certain it is fully down in the barrel channel. Just barely snug the fore-end screw (remember to use Loctite #222 on the threads). This finishes the bedding job. However, note the discussion in the sub-section on bedding two-piece fore-ends with straight tapered barrels. On the Model-88 the

Photograph 13-12: The second step in bedding the Winchester Model-88 (adding bedding agent at the front of the receiver) is not reviewed in a photograph. See the text for an explanation of that step. Here we see the results of the third step, which you can combine in the same stage with the second step. This bed of Brownells metal-reinforced gel-type bedding agent fills the barrel hanger cutout in the barrel channel. Note that the screw shank and the hanger flats will bind in this epoxy pillar. You must fix this problem, as described in the text and shown in photograph 13-13.

Photograph 13-13: Refer to the text and photograph 13-12. Here I have trimmed the epoxy from the flats of the barrel hanger recess to allow the hanger lug to move fore and aft in the stock. Next I will drill the screw hole slightly larger, to allow the screw shank to move with the hanger. Finally, I will turn the head of the screw slightly smaller, to allow it to travel endwise. These steps are important aspects of minimizing stress on the barreled action. Inclusion of a good coating of graphite or molybdenum-disulfide on all bedding surfaces is also a useful technique in this regard.

Section 13: The Trouble With Lever-Action and Single-Shot Rifle Stocks, Part II   209

fully-bedded-barrel method might, possibly, prove more accurate. Only experimentation will tell the tale.

Fore-end Bedding (Non Tubular Magazine), Two-Piece Stocked Rifles With Sculptured Barrels:

(Read the above sub-section that covers dovetail barrel attachments, and consider the potential advantages of silver soldering the fore-end hanger in its dovetail slot.)

For specific unique details of bedding straight-taper barreled guns, see the subsequent sub-section titled, *Fore-end Bedding (Non Tubular Magazine), Two-Piece Stocked Rifles With Straight-Tapered Barrels*. However, please, familiarize yourself with this sub-section for an understanding of concepts and specific details.

For bedding of fore-ends on tubular-magazine rifles, see the sub-section that covers bedding fore-ends on tubular-magazine rifles. Again, several concepts noted in this sub-section are germane.

I will address desirable fore-end modifications for Browning's BLR (and any similar systems), separately.

As noted in the introductory sub-sections of *Part II*, along with questions of proper fit and finish, two-piece stocking systems pose several unique problems for the shooting enthusiast who is concerned with maximum rifle accuracy. In this regard, we will address possible alterations and corrections for the fore-end first.

I will consider the Savage Model-99, as an example, throughout this and the related following sub-sections. On all modern versions of these rifles, a screw that is located about six and one-half inches (6½") forward of the receiver connects the fore-end to the barrel. That screw enters a threaded hanger, which fits into a dovetail slot in the barrel. A keyed rearward extension of the fore-end locates the wood laterally and vertically into the receiver and around the barrel. Tightening the attachment screw pulls the extreme front end of the fore-end against the barrel.

The forward two- to three-inches of the fore-end's barrel channel (which is in front of the attachment screw's location) transfers the tightening load to the barrel. Since the fore-end's barrel channel normally touches the barrel only at the forward end, the tighter you turn the fore-end attachment screw the more bending stress the fore-end applies to the barrel. See photograph # 13-14.

Further, the fore-end is sometimes a snug fit, fore and aft, between the receiver and the hanger and screw assembly, sometimes it is not. This depends upon the particular rifle's fit and whether the fore-end has shrunk appreciably — a condition that is quite common on older guns.

There are several single-shot rifles that share a very similar attachment system for the fore-end. With consideration of dimensional variations and minor differences in structural details, the following discussions are appropriate to all such rifles.

It should be obvious that this attachment method, as described, will place a significant bending moment upon the barrel whenever you tighten the attachment screw sufficiently to form a solid bond between the fore-end to the barrel. This bending stress is carried by the fore-end between the bedded forward end and the keyed rear end. Tightening the fore-end attachment screw pulls the barrel and fore-end together at the hanger, which necessarily bends the barrel. Tightening the screw tighter will bend the barrel more. Also, barrel heating and subsequent fore-end heating will alter the strain (bending) of the barrel. Finally, changes in humidity and aging of the wood will alter the force the fore-end will transfer to the barrel.

Clearly, such a system is less than ideal. My limited experience suggests that the following described simple alterations, which result in a semi-free-floating fore-end will often cut group

Photograph 13-14: At right is the front end of this (typical) Savage Model-99 fore-end. Note the rounded surface in the barrel channel there. Behind that is the attachment screw hole. Note that the screw hole does not abut against the barrel or the barrel hanger. Also note that the only other place where the fore-end touches the rifle is at the receiver. This design results in the following situation: when the tinker tightens the fore-end attachment screw, the barrel bends down into the barrel channel at the attachment screw location. How much the barrel bends depends only upon how tightly the nimrod torques the attachment screw and upon how strong the fore-end is! An eminently bad design.

sizes in half on these rifles and will eliminate zero wander. As with all glass-bedding operations, if this system does not work on your particular rifle, the good news is that you can easily alter it to a different system by adding epoxy ("glass") along the fore-end channel until you find a combination that does work.

As noted, I alter Savage Model-99 style fore-ends to float everywhere along the barrel channel except at the attachment hanger location and at the rear, which is fixed only laterally (it is free to move fore and aft).

I ensure that the fore-end has sufficient clearance, fore and aft, between the receiver and the barrel hanger (perhaps 0.010"). This prevents any subsequent dimensional changes in the wood or heating in the barrel from binding the fore-end between the hanger and the receiver. I then glass bed the rear of the fore-end into the receiver to eliminate any lateral clearance without eliminating the fore and aft clearance.

I also glass bed a steel pillar block into the fore-end. This pillar supports the fore-end hanger's threaded screw boss extension and locates the attachment screw both laterally and vertically in the fore-end.

This area (around the attachment screw pillar) is epoxy bedded so that the hanger precisely fits in the pillar and the screw tightens the boss against the hanger (through an interposing layer of epoxy bedding material). Bedding agent also locates the shank of the screw.

For various reasons, I skeletonize the fore-end and apply RTV silicone to the rear face and along the barrel channel. I will address each of these alterations in detail in the following related sub-sections.

Skeletonizing Fore-ends, Lever-Action (Non Tubular Magazine) & Single-Shot Rifles:

An additional touch worth considering, since this can be of surprising accuracy value, is skeletonizing the fore-end (hollowing to remove wood from the interior). This step is beneficial for two reasons. First, it can dramatically reduce recoil stress on the fore-end hanger and attachment screw. Through skeletonizing I have reduced the weight of the original fore-end on a Savage Model-99F (featherweight) from about six and one-half (6$^1/_2$) ounces to about three and three-quarters (3$^3/_4$) ounces. This alteration is equivalent to making the attachment screw and hanger forty-three percent (43%) stronger! It is likely that reducing the weight of the fore-end will also reduce any negative effects the fore-end might have on the gun's accuracy. See photograph #s 13-15/16/17.

The second advantage of skeletonizing results from the fact that it reduces the fore-end's rigidity — for any given stress load, the fore-end will flex more. A more flexible fore-end will transfer less bending stress to the barrel. This is beneficial, especially when the fore-end is not properly bedded or if it should ever warp. Not that that ever happens!

The subject of wood and warpage reminds me of a famous question asked to a group of students by a famous firearms instructor for the Soviet KGB. Here I will paraphrase slightly.

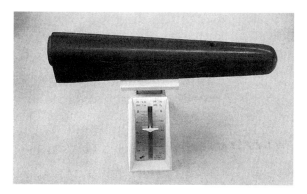

Photograph 13-15: This fore-end is from a Savage Model-99F (featherweight). Here I have performed only the first step in skeletonizing — drilling of a longitudinal hole from the receiver end (see the text). I believe that hole removed at least 3/4 of an ounce of wood. That suggests the original weight was about 6$^3/_4$ ounces. (I did not think to weigh this piece before starting.)

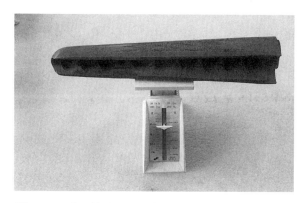

Photograph 13-16: Further skeletonizing (notice the holes along the bottom of the barrel channel) removed an additional 2 ounces of wood. Fore-end weight is now 4$^1/_2$ ounces.

Section 13: The Trouble With Lever-Action and Single-Shot Rifle Stocks, Part II

Instructor, inquisitively: *Is it gun?*
Student, exasperatedly: *Yes.*
Instructor, rhetorically: *Is it safe?*
Student: pauses
Instructor, sarcastically: *No!*

I adapt that thus:
Is it wood, *(yes?)*,
Will it warp, *YES!*

If you make no other fore-end alterations, consider skeletonizing. If you do skeletonize the fore-end, or the buttstock, be sure to properly seal all freshly exposed wood surfaces.

In the following paragraphs I will detail several of these alterations. For rifles other than the Model-99F (a rotary magazine version of the Savage lever-action rifle) certain measurements and tool sizes will likely vary. However, if you keep this goal in mind, *removal of wood without significantly weakening the fore-end and without altering its installed appearance*, you can easily determine the necessary sizings and spacings for skeletonizing any piece of any stock.

Since I believe this step is so valuable, I will begin the discussion of specific fore-end modification with this sub-section covering weight and rigidity reduction measures. This process is quite simple and involves nothing more complicated than the correct use of a few drill bits (twist, auger and blade) of the proper size, a few sharp blades in an X-acto (or similar) knife, and, perhaps, a small rotary sanding drum or rasp in a moto tool (Dremel). Given plenty of time, the dedicated whittler could accomplish these alterations using nothing but a pocket knife!

You should first decide your priorities. The fundamental decision revolves around whether you will lighten the fore-end as much as is feasible, while maintaining sufficient strength, or whether you will maintain as much strength as is feasible, while reducing the fore-end's weight as much as possible. See photograph #s 13-18/19.

This is not just a matter of semantics. The difference of about one ounce of typical walnut can amount to a huge difference in the fore-end's strength and fracture resistance. The included photographs compare the results of one method of achieving a much lighter fore-end, without sacrificing very much strength, with the

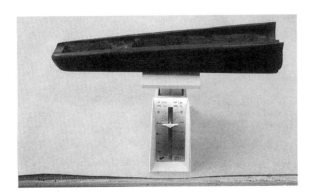

Photograph 13-17: Through additional skeletonizing (note removal of partitions in bottom of barrel channel), I have reduced the weight to 4 ounces. Ultimately, I did a bit more whittling to bring the walls of the channel to a uniform thickness of about 3/10" and thereby managed to get the final weight to about 3³/₄ ounces — a whopping 45% reduction in weight. This results in a similar reduction in fore-end hanger and attachment screw stress. This modification also reduces the fore-end's rigidity; a more flexible fore-end cannot transfer as much stress to the barreled-action system.

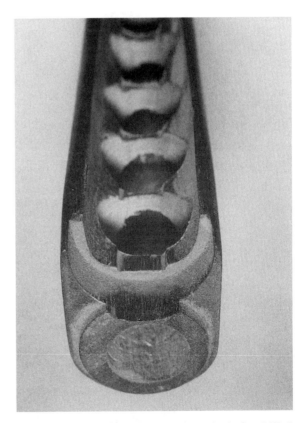

Photograph 13-18: This view shows the holes drilled to produce the "Robust Skeletonized" version of the fore-end. The longitudinal hole extends from the receiver key to about 1/2" from the barrel hanger boss. All holes are sized to leave a 3/10" wall thickness at all points in the fore-end.

results of making a "light as possible" fore-end, which is still sufficiently robust for practically any hunting use. Take your pick; the one-ounce difference and a slight reduction in rigidity suggest the latter as a better choice for most applications. However, since the additional advantages of the lightest feasible version are slight, the cautious soul might very well opt for the more robust version.

After you have decided what amount of skeletonizing you intend to achieve, affix the fore-end in a well-padded vise, clamp only along the lower edge of the forward end. Position the fore-end to locate the barrel channel at the top and with the underside of the fore-end level.

Photograph 13-19: This view shows the (almost) finished "Fully Skeletonized" version of the fore-end. The entire barrel channel excepting the front, rear and hanger location is hollowed and the fore-end walls are thinned to about 3/10".

For peace of mind in the later hole drilling operations, verify that the fore-end's underside is level (a torpedo level works well here). With the fore-end thus located in a vise, it is easier to adjust the hole boring drill bit to keep it running at the correct orientation in the wood. You can easily observe the drill bit's left-to-right alignment as you are drilling the hole. You can periodically check that the drill bit is progressing horizontally by stopping the drilling and checking the drill bit's shank with the level. Be sure not to let the drill hang on the drill bit while checking the level and be certain you keep the drill bit's shaft centered in the hole. Also, it is a good idea to periodically withdraw the drill bit and visually inspect the hole to ensure that it is staying in the center of the bulk of the fore-end and is not getting too close to the bottom of the fore-end. Alternatively, you can enlist a willing accomplice to watch from the side of the drill bit and to provide coaching as to whether you need to hold the drill higher or lower.

With blade-type drill bits you can easily alter the hole's axis as you proceed with the drilling, in order to keep the hole centered. This is an advantage of these affordable drill bits. However, this specific characteristic also allows blade drill bits to wander from the intended line, quite easily. In any case, use caution to ensure that you do not drill too close to any of the external surfaces of the fore-end. Assuming the fore-end is made of good wood, a remaining outside surface wood thickness of three-tenths inch (0.3") is certainly adequate. A remaining thickness that is less than two-tenths inch (0.2") is probably insufficient to provide the requisite fore-end strength.

Regardless of your precise methods, your goal is to bore a hole of the proper diameter, starting at the rear of the fore-end and angling toward the front, so that the exterior wood remains approximately equally thick everywhere under the fore-end's rounded bottom perimeter. Hole size and depth will vary, depending upon the dimensions of the particular fore-end.

On a typical Model-99F fore-end, the correct hole diameter for this initial drilling is thirteen-sixteenths (13/16"). Of course, a smaller drill bit will do but it will also provide less benefit. I prefer to use an auger drill bit since those tend to follow a truer course while drilling. Further, like the blade type drill bit, it is easy to extend an auger drill bit to achieve greater hole depths, when necessary. The second best choice is an extra long (jobber) twist-steel drill bit.

Section 13: The Trouble With Lever-Action and Single-Shot Rifle Stocks, Part II

Locate and punch a sufficiently deep starting hole, centered on the fore-end's round extension — that is the portion of the fore-end designed to key into the front of the receiver on the Model-99. Applying a good deep hole center is less critical when using an auger-style drill bit. Owing to the vagaries of wood grain, both twist steel drill bits and blade type drill bits have a tendency to wander as you begin drilling a new hole. A deeper hole-center mitigates this problem.

Keep the drill bit following the profile of the bottom of the fore-end. For the Model-99F, drill the hole no more than three and one-half inches (3½") deep. Then substitute an eleven-sixteenths (11/16") drill bit and continue the hole until the extreme front end of the hole reaches a total depth of just over six inches (no deeper than 6.2") from the rear face of the fore-end. Use caution to avoid getting closer than about three-tenths inch (0.3") to the center of the attachment hole.

This is an important aspect. If you do not leave sufficient wood to support the attachment screw, the fore-end could fail under the stresses of recoil. If you are using a blade or auger drill bit, you must take into account the guide extension of the drill bit. In any case, be careful not to weaken or destroy the critical attachment screw boss area of the fore-end. See photograph # 13-20.

With this initial hole completed, center punch a location just about eight-tenths inch (0.8") behind the center of the attachment hole location and centered in the bottom of the barrel channel. Using due caution, since the drill bit might catch on undrilled areas as it enters into the axial hole (the one you just completed), use an eleven-sixteenths inch (11/16") twist steel drill bit to drill a hole through the barrel channel to intersect the axial hole. Advance slowly and stop drilling when the point of the drill bit enters the heart of the channel of the axial hole. See photograph # 13-20.

Locate a second hole-center about one-inch behind the center of the first vertical hole (this will leave a wood partition of about three-tenths inch (0.3") minimum width in the bottom of the barrel channel). If available, substitute a three-quarters inch (3/4") twist steel drill bit. Drill this second hole, as you did the first.

Locate a third hole about one and one-tenth inch (1.1") behind the second hole center. Substitute a thirteen-sixteenths inch (13/16") drill bit. Drill this hole as the last two. Locate and drill a fourth and a fifth hole, each spaced an additional one and one-tenth inch (1.1") behind the next hole forward. Be sure the rearmost hole does not extend closer than about one-half inch to the extreme rear of the fore-end. That would unnecessarily weaken the rear of the fore-end. You want to leave a strong perimeter there. If necessary, use a smaller drill bit for this rearmost hole.

As with the axial hole, these holes, if properly centered and drilled, will not thin any exterior surface of the fore-end to less than about three-tenths inch (0.3") and they will not alter the fore-end's appearance when it is installed — all these holes are invisible from the "outside". These are your goals, regardless of the particular dimension of the fore-end upon which you are working. Obviously, the drill bit sizes and hole locations will vary if the fore-end's dimensions vary.

For the Model-99F, locate additional hole centers at the following positions (centered in the bottom of the barrel channel): 0.7", 1.5" & 2.3" from the extreme front of the fore-end. Use an eleven-sixteenths inch (11/16") twist drill to produce holes to the following maximum depths (as measured from the bottom of the barrel channel to the extreme deepest portion of the hole: foremost, 0.45"; middle, 0.52"; rearmost, 0.60". See the above comments for considerations when working with differently dimensioned fore-ends and in no case allow the tip of the drill

Photograph 13-20: View looking down into the modified barrel channel on the Savage Model-99F fore-end. Note the skeletonizing holes in front of and behind the fore-end attachment hole. Also note that the attachment hole is already drilled out to accept the steel-reinforced pillar. After all skeletonizing and pillar operations are finished I will fully seal the interior surfaces

bit to come closer than about one-quarter of an inch (1/4") to the bottom of the fore-end. See photograph # 13-21.

For the "Robust Skeletonizing" version, this job is complete. Such an alteration typically removes several ounces of wood. It also substantially reduces the flexural rigidity of the fore-end, while leaving the fore-end sufficiently strong to withstand any foreseeable rough handling. If you break a fore-end that is modified in this manner, you will almost certainly have worse problems about which to worry!

Finish all interior surfaces with a generous coating of wood finishing epoxy or sufficient oil-based finish to substantially seal the wood. Set the fore-end aside and allow the wood finishing agent to properly cure. Then apply bedding agent and black RTV silicone to the fore-end, as described later in this sub-section.

To fully skeletonize the fore-end, simply whittle away at the partitions formed between the vertical drill holes and along the sides of the channel interior. Do not remove the rearmost partition — the one between the rear hole and the back of the fore-end. Keep removing small wood shavings until you achieve a reasonably uniform wall thickness along the sides of the fore-end. Where necessary, continue to whittle out more wood to bring the wall thickness down to about three-tenths inch (0.3"). See photograph # 13-22.

With attention to detail, this additional alteration can remove, perhaps, one more ounce of wood. It does little to alter the flexural rigidity of the fore-end but it does somewhat weaken this piece. As with the robust version, finish this job by properly sealing all newly exposed wood.

One ounce does not sound like much weight reduction for the effort required. However, consider this: on my Model-99F, the difference was from about five ounces to about four ounces. That means the lighter version will place 20% less recoil stress on the fore-end attachment mechanism. Further, one ounce is one ounce. On a featherweight hunting rifle every ounce matters.

Providing Fore And Aft Fore-end Clearance, Barrel-Mounted Fore-end, Two-Piece Stocked Rifles:

Begin by verifying that the fore-end-to-receiver joint has fore and aft clearance. Apply several layers of masking tape to the perimeter of the front of the receiver under the barrel — this is the area that surrounds the rear of the fore-end. Trim the tape so that it does not intrude inside the flat perimeter area of the receiver (this will be important in the lateral glass bedding step).

Assemble the fore-end to the receiver. If the fore-end attachment screw freely enters the barrel hanger, the system has sufficient fore and aft clearance. If not, carve on the perimeter relief of the fore-end until you provide such clearance.

Next, proceed to epoxy bed the rear of the fore-end to provide a tight lateral fit between the receiver's perimeter key-way and the fore-end. Leave the layers of masking tape in place on the front receiver perimeter.

Mix a small batch of gel-type bedding agent. Since this material will be visible on the finished rifle, add a dab of brown colorant to match the hue of the fore-end.

Photograph 13-21: View at front of "Robust Skeletonized" Savage Model-99F fore-end. Note the wide solid web across the front of the fore-end in the bottom of the barrel channel. Also note the modest divider between the holes. In the "Fully Skeletonized" version this latter web is removed and the sides of the channel are hollowed out to create a uniform wall thickness in the hollow channel.

Photograph 13-22: Top view of finished, "Fully Skeletonized" Savage Model-99F fore-end. Note the hollow channels, the solid dividers at the front, rear and center-front locations. The center-front divider carries the epoxy bedded steel fore-end pillar at the fore-end hanger location.

Section 13: The Trouble With Lever-Action and Single-Shot Rifle Stocks, Part II

Ensure that the portion of the fore-end that enters into the alignment perimeter at the front of the receiver is clean. If necessary, use alcohol or carburetor cleaner to clean any oil from the wood. First dry off any excess solvent, then use a portable hair dryer to heat the wood and evaporate the remaining solvent. See photograph # 13-23.

Apply the bedding agent to the keying portion of the fore-end (the relieved perimeter that you just cleaned). Be sure to get a sufficient coating to adequately cover the surfaces that extend back inside the receiver and the flat that aligns to the front of the receiver at the perimeter. Do not apply bedding agent anywhere else at this time. Retain a test sample of the epoxy to monitor its condition as it cures.

Apply release agent to the front of the receiver, to the underside of the barrel that is adjacent to the receiver and to the flats and adjacent outside surfaces of the fore-end. Apply several layers of vinyl electrical tape around the barrel about two inches in front of the barrel hanger. Install the fore-end to the rifle. Install the attachment screw and tighten it until it just begins to snug the fore-end against the tape wrap.

After the bedding agent cures so that the test sample is hard, yet pliable (about six hours), use a single-edge razor blade or an X-acto knife to cut the excess epoxy from the perimeter of the fore-end-to-receiver joint. Be careful to avoid scarring either the wood or the steel.

Disassemble the fore-end from the rifle. Clean off any bedding agent that has migrated where it should not be. Remove the clearance tape but leave the tape wrap on the barrel.

The finishing touch here is to seal the entire rear end of the fore-end with a quick-setting finishing epoxy or other wood sealing finish. Be sure to clean off all traces of the release agent first. Again, alcohol is a good solvent for this task.

After the finish has cured, apply a sufficient coating of Loctite's Black RTV silicone (sold under the *Permatex* banner) to the entire keyed area at the rear of the receiver. Then reapply release agent to the entire front of the receiver and to the back of the barrel. Install the fore-end and allow the RTV at least 24 hours to cure.

Trim away any RTV that has extruded beyond the surface of the fore-end or receiver. Remove the fore-end and trim out any RTV that infiltrated between the barrel and fore-end.

The purpose of the RTV is to deaden the contact between the fore-end and the receiver. Some shooters would argue against this approach. As with other bedding measures, it is easy to test both methods. However, if you do not apply the RTV bed before completing the fore-end bedding operation you will have to install temporary tape layers on the back of the fore-end when bedding the fore-end attachment screw hole.

Pillar Bedding Fore-end Attachment Screw, Barrel-Mounted Fore-end, Two-Piece Stocked Rifles:

We will follow the steps necessary for this alteration using the fore-end for the same Model-99F as an example. Excepting possible variations in fore-end height and screw size, there will be few differences when working with other fore-ends that are attached with a barrel hanger.

To properly bed the fore-end, you should install a steel pillar between the attachment

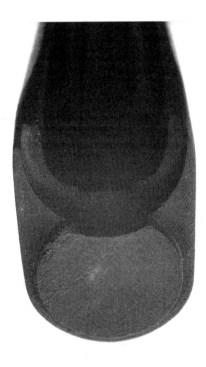

Photograph 13-23: Pictured is an unaltered Savage Model-99F fore-end. Note the protruding (rounded) portion of the proximal end. This extension keys into a round recess in the front of the receiver. Proper bedding here will provide for precise lateral location of the fore-end without any fore and aft contact. See the text for a complete discussion of how to achieve this accuracy-enhancing goal.

screw boss (located at the bottom of the fore-end attachment screw hole) and the barrel channel. This is a straight forward project. Items you will need include a few twist steel drill bits (15/32", 5/16" & 7/32"), a three-quarters inch (3/4") long piece of seven-sixteenths inch (7/16"), grade-2 (or grade-5) threaded bolt shank and a small amount of glass bedding epoxy.

Start by positioning the fore-end in a well-padded vise with the barrel channel located at the top and approximately level. Snug the vise sufficiently to hold the fore-end but avoid clamping excessively, especially on the "Fully Skeletonized" version!

Using a standard fifteen thirty-seconds inch (15/32") twist-steel drill bit, carefully drill the attachment screw hole through (from the barrel channel side). Drill this hole deep enough so the point of the drill bit just touches the screw boss, at the center of the hole. This will create a fifteen thirty-seconds inch (15/32") diameter hole that is about three-quarters inch (3/4") deep. Clean out the chips and set the fore-end aside.

Position a three-quarter inch (3/4") long section of seven-sixteenths inch (7/16") threaded bolt shank, either grade-2 or grade-5, in the vise. A drill press vise is a better method here — the idea is to drill a properly centered hole, end to end, through this piece. Clamp sufficiently to hold this piece for drilling. In this instance, damaged threads are beneficial; after installation this damage will positively prevent the piece from turning in the bedding agent! See photograph # 13-24.

Carefully mark the bolt's center with a deep center punch indent. Apply cutting oil and carefully drill a seven thirty-seconds inch (7/32") diameter hole, end to end, through the bolt shank. This is another operation where a confederate is most helpful. You can watch the vertical orientation of the drill in one plane while your helper watches in the other vertical plane (at a right angle to the one you can see). Since this amounts to a very deep hole for such a small drill bit, periodically withdraw the drill, to clear the cuttings, and reapply cutting oil. With care, you should be able to keep the hole sufficiently centered for this task. If not, try again! Bolts are cheap and you want this hole centered to within one-thirty-second inch (1/32") throughout the length of the bolt shank.

When you have a properly centered hole, drilled completely through the bolt section, substitute a five-sixteenths inch (5/16") drill bit.

Again, being careful to keep the hole axial to the bolt, drill with the larger drill bit to a maximum depth of about one-half inch (1/2"). Avoid drilling deeper, since that would weaken this piece.

Verify that this larger hole is of sufficient depth and diameter to allow the barrel hanger to fully enter. Simply position the piece over the hanger and ensure that it will freely slide over the hanger until the end of the bolt touches the dovetail flats of the hanger. Clean the oil from this piece.

Temporarily install the new pillar in the hole in the fore-end and ensure that the top is approximately flush with the bottom radius of the barrel channel. If not, grind the upper end sufficiently to achieve that relationship. This pillar should not touch the barrel or hanger; you want room for an interposing layer of bedding material. In any case, ensure that the top of the pillar is square to its shank. See photograph # 13-25.

Use a proper solvent to thoroughly degrease the pillar and that section of the fore-end. Pay particular attention to the area of the original attachment screw ferrule, which will often have accumulated considerable oily detritus. (Allow

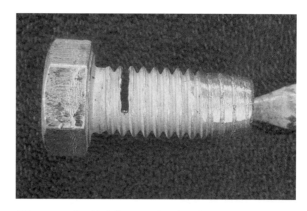

Photograph 13-24: Here is the threaded bolt that will become the fore-end attachment pillar on my Savage Model-99F. Note the tapered end, the hacksaw cut (that nearly separates the head from the shank) and the punch in the tapered end (signifying that the longitudinal hole has already been completed). Conversion of this piece into a proper pillar in the rifle requires drilling a two-diameter hole, endwise, through the shank and cutting the shank to the proper length. Similarly, the stock must be drilled to accept this piece. See the associated text and photographs. However, note, I did not follow my advice in this installation. The text description is a better plan than the (experimental) one shown in these photographs!

sufficient time for the solvent to fully evaporate from the wood, consider applying hot air, before applying the bedding agent.)

Mix up a small batch of gel-type epoxy bedding material (as available from Brownells). Optionally, consider adding about two-parts atomized steel or aluminum to three-parts gel mix. This will significantly strengthen the bedding material. Wipe the bedding material mix inside the re-drilled fore-end attachment screw hole in the fore-end to achieve a complete wetting of the wood. Similarly, coat the exterior threads of the pillar; use sufficient elbow grease to ensure the bedding agent fully fills the threads on the pillar's exterior. Make sure you have applied sufficient bedding agent to completely fill the voids that will form between this bolt section and the fore-end. See photograph # 13-26.

Locate the pillar so the large end of the interior hole is at the top. Insert the pillar into the fore-end. If necessary, apply a modicum of additional epoxy bedding material around the attachment screw hole in the bottom of the fore-end channel. Be sure there is enough bedding material here to cover the barrel channel and fill any voids immediately adjacent to the pillar and to fill the area between the inside of the pillar and the barrel hanger.

This bedding layer does not have to extend more than about one-quarter inch (1/4") from the pillar. If excess bedding agent has entered the screw hole during this installation, drive that out using a section of three-sixteenths inch (3/16") dowel and paper towels.

Be sure to save a test sample of the bedding agent, for monitoring. This sample will indicate the condition of the bedding agent in the fore-end. This is needed information during the disassembly and cleanup stages.

Apply release agent to the barrel hanger, the fore-end attachment screw and the barrel around the barrel hanger. Install the fore-end on the barrel. Install the fore-end attachment screw. Turn this screw sufficiently to bring the fore-end into contact with the tape wrap at the front of the barrel channel but do not tighten it any further.

Allow the bedding agent sufficient time to cure to a semi-rigid consistency — you should still be able to dent the test sample with your fingernail. Remove the fore-end attachment screw and pull the fore-end free from the barrel.

Clean bedding agent from the screw and out of the screw hole in the hanger. Also trim away any bedding agent that has migrated more than about one-quarter inch from the pillar. To provide attachment screw clearance, run a three-sixteenths inch (3/16") drill bit through the fore-end attachment screw hole. Trim off any burrs of bedding agent. Remove the vinyl tape wrap from the barrel.

Reinstall the fore-end and slightly tighten the attachment screw. Allow the bedding agent at least 24 hours to cure. Before making the final attachment, review the following sub-section. If you choose to apply the RTV bed, defer final assembly with Loctite until that step is completed.

If you choose to omit the RTV bedding step, proceed as follows. Remove the attachment

Photograph 13-25: Here I have glass-bedded the pillar bolt into the modified Savage Model-99F fore-end. My goal was to center the pillar in this manner and then use the pre-sawed cut as a break off point, after the epoxy had cured. This seemed to work well but there is a better method — refer to the text for a description. See photograph 13-24.

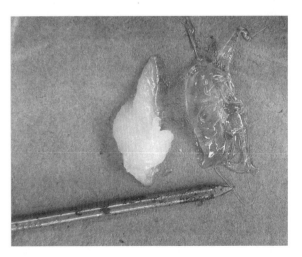

Photograph 13-26: This is a sufficient batch of gel-type bedding agent for bedding the fore-end pillar. For maximum strength in this critical joint, add two-parts atomized steel to three-parts of this mix.

screw. Thoroughly degrease the screw and the hanger threads. Apply Loctite #222 and install the screw. Tighten it to solidly attach the fore-end to the barrel. The job is finished.

RTV Silicone Barrel Channel Bedding, Barrel-Mounted Fore-ends, Two-Piece Stocked Rifles:

Optionally, I can recommend laying a bead of silicone down the barrel channel. Assuming the fore-end is bedded at the receiver and at the fore-end attachment hanger (as described in the previous sub-sections), this RTV layer can aid in preventing resonation of vibrations between the fore-end and barrel. Further, it will not produce or allow significant stressing between the fore-end and the barrel. See photograph # 13-27.

If you have skeletonized the fore-end, the RTV bedding should only interpose between the barrel and fore-end along the top of the sides of the fore-end. On a stock fore-end you can apply the RTV bedding material to completely fill the space between the fore-end and the barrel.

Begin by degreasing the entire barrel channel of the fore-end. Alcohol works well for this. Allow the solvent sufficient time to dry.

Use a cotton swab to paint the entire outside of the fore-end that is adjacent to the barrel channel with release agent. Also, similarly paint the bedding agent in the bottom of the barrel channel around the pillar. Then hold the fore-end by inserting a small dowel through the pillar and spray the entire outside of the fore-end with release agent, be careful to avoid getting the release agent inside the barrel channel. In any case, make sure you get release agent everywhere on the outside for the fore-end. Then apply release agent to the front of the receiver and the entire rear 12" of the barrel. As a last step here, douse the entire attachment screw.

This thorough coating of Brownells Release agent is absolutely necessary to facilitate future fore-end disassembly. You will discover that the RTV will still stick to the barrel, despite this application! However, with a bit of patience, it will come loose. Without the application of release agent the adhesion is tremendously strong — you would almost certainly have to destroy the fore-end to remove it!

The easiest way to finish this job is to install the barreled-action in a vise of some sort, upside down and about level (Midway's Shooter's Vise is an ideal tool). Since RTV will be squeezing out of the contact zones, you do not want to have to handle the rifle! Touching or smearing the RTV is apt to cause it to stick to the areas that you smeared it across, despite the release agent coating!

Apply black RTV silicone (as available from Loctite in a squeeze tube) into the barrel channel. On the skeletonized version, apply a bead along both sides, near the top of the barrel channel. In this instance, only a fine bead of RTV is necessary, it only needs to fill the slam gap and extend about one-half inch down the sides of the barrel channel.

On the unskeletonized version of the fore-end, apply a heavy bead along the bottom of the barrel channel. Here you want to use sufficient

Photograph 13-27: On two-piece stocked rifles (including tubular magazine models), black RTV (Room Temperature Vulcanizing) silicone is the magic elixir for bedding the fore-end to the barrel and receiver. However, be doubly certain to apply a good thick coating of release agent to the barrel and receiver — failure to do this will almost positively guarantee that you will not be able to separate the fore-end from the barreled-action without destroying one or the other! This product does exactly what the name implies — it vulcanizes, bonding with tremendous tenacity and strength.

Section 13: The Trouble With Lever-Action and Single-Shot Rifle Stocks, Part II

RTV to completely fill the barrel channel. However, leave a one-inch gap between the silicone bead and the barrel hanger. Also, the barrel channel in front of the barrel hanger will require only a modest bead to fill it — the clearance is only that provided by the layer of tape used during the pillar bedding operation. Spread these beads to cover the entire surface of the barrel channel with a sufficiently thick layer to fill the gap between the assembled fore-end and the barrel.

Place aside a dollop of RTV to test for curing. You will need a piece that is about one-half inch (1/2") thick.

With the release agent and the RTV in place, you are prepared to install the fore-end. Begin by tipping the fore-end so that the rear keyed portion enters the receiver first, while the front is several inches from the barrel. Then, while holding the fore-end fully back against the receiver, slowly push it up against the barrel. If you have used sufficient RTV, the product should extrude from between the barrel and the fore-end along the entire barrel channel. Be careful to avoid touching and smearing the RTV. Install the fore-end attachment screw.

Periodically (over the next few minutes) slowly snug the attachment screw, perhaps a quarter-turn at a time. You want to keep tightening the screw until the fore-end pillar just begins to contact the barrel. However, you do not want to flex the fore-end or barrel in the process. It is necessary to proceed slowly. This allows the viscous RTV sufficient time to fill voids and move out of the way, where necessary.

Invert the rifle in the vise and allow the RTV sufficient time to cure to a soft rubbery consistency, about six to twelve hours. At this time the RTV is still "green", it has not developed its full strength.

Use a single-edge razor blade or an X-acto knife (or similar tool) to carefully trim away the RTV that has extruded from between the fore-end and the receiver. If you applied release agent properly, the RTV will not stick too tenaciously to the exposed wood or metal surfaces. You should not have any trouble cutting and peeling the extruded RTV away from the barrel and fore-end.

For best results lay the blade at about a fifteen degree (15°) angle to the edge of the wood. The goal is to cut the RTV layer off flush at the wood side but deeper at the barrel side. This will hide the RTV better and will also reduce the possibility of damage to the RTV during handling or disassembly. See the illustration.

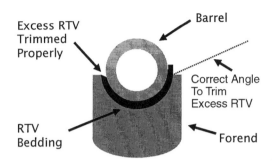

Idealized Cross Section View Of RTV Bedded Forend

Allow the RTV at least 24 hours to cure. Test the dollop to verify that it is cured to a tough and solid consistency, throughout. Remove the fore-end and clean out any RTV that infiltrated into the pillar bedding area. Also clean out any excess RTV from between the back end of the fore-end and the front of the receiver. You do not want a large flat area filled with RTV here. Only the original perimeter of RTV (installed earlier) should touch the receiver. On the skeletonized version, trim out the excess RTV that will have entered into the hollowed out areas of the fore-end. This completes the bedding operation.

Clean off any RTV from the barrel, receiver, hanger and attachment screw. Degrease the hanger threads and the screw threads. Apply Loctite #222 to the attachment screw. Install the fore-end, install the attachment screw and tighten the screw sufficiently to bond the fore-end pillar solidly to the barrel.

With this system of bedding, tightening the attachment screw only serves to bond the hanger to the epoxy bed in the pillar. Variations in temperature and humidity should not alter this relationship or result in the fore-end significantly stressing the receiver or the barrel. Finally, the RTV bed should act as a vibration damper and as an isolator to minimize the consequences of variations in shooter hold or benchrest technique.

Fore-end Bedding (Non Tubular Magazine), Two-Piece Stocked Rifles With Straight-Tapered Barrels:

Read the above sub-section covering, dovetail barrel attachments, and consider the potential advantages of silver soldering the fore-end hanger in its dovetail slot. Also note the above sub-sections on fore-end-to-receiver bedding, fore-end pillar bedding and fore-end skeletonizing as applied to rifles with two-piece stocks and sculptured barrels.

Older Savage Model-99 rifles, most original Winchester falling-block rifles and many other single-shot rifles feature either round or hexagonal barrels that have no enlarged chamber section. These barrels are "straight", with a very slight taper. It is often possible to improve accuracy and consistency of rifles equipped with such a barrel by fully glass bedding the fore-end along the entire barrel channel.

As noted elsewhere, one of the better features of epoxy bedding is that it facilitates tinkering. If the method described hereafter does not provide appropriate accuracy with a solid zero, try the RTV isolating method described in the preceding sub-section, which covers fore-end bedding with sculptured barrels. Any such subsequent modification would only require a bit of rasping in the channel to provide relief combined with the subsequent addition of an RTV bed.

The method proposed hereafter, full glass bedding along the barrel channel, is not applicable to rifles featuring barrels with chamber swells or rapidly tapered sections under the fore-end. The reason this method will not work on such rifles relates to both fore-end and barrel dimensional stability.

If you try to use the full-barrel glass bedding method with a sculptured or highly tapered barrel, barrel heating (resulting either from shooting or just from a large change in atmospheric temperature) and significant changes in long-term atmospheric humidity (which will alter the fore-end's dimensions) will both result in the generation of huge stresses between the barrel and the fore-end. Barrel expansion (heating) or fore-end shrinkage (dehydration or aging), will probably produce the worst affect.

Nevertheless, you can certainly try this bedding method on a sculptured barrel. However, results are not apt to be impressive. Keep in mind that this system might seem to work fine until you take your prize rifle on a hunt in a different clime!

Regardless of the rifle, always ensure that you have dimensioned the fore-end to allow a small amount (perhaps 0.010") of fore and aft play between the mounting screw and the receiver. As described in the previous sub-section titled, *Providing Fore And Aft Fore-end Clearance, Barrel-Mounted Fore-end, Two-Piece Stocked Rifles*, a bed of RTV interposed between the rear of the fore-end and the front of the receiver is a very good idea here. The RTV will accommodate small dimensional changes without introducing monumental stresses to the barrel or receiver.

Prepare the fore-end attachment screw hole just as was described in the sub-section titled, *Pillar Bedding Fore-end Attachment Screw, Barrel-Mounted Fore-end, Two-Piece Stocked Rifles*. The idea is to provide a reinforced steel pillar that will interpose the screw head and the barrel hanger. While elimination of the column of wood between the screw head and the hanger is the basic advantage, it is also advisable to keep a shallow layer of reinforced bedding material interposing the steel pillar and the barrel.

The next step is to rasp out any unsound or oil-soaked wood from the barrel channel (oil is the enemy of epoxy). If such wood extends to the top of the sides of the channel, you can certainly leave it in place for the sake of appearance. However, remember that it is best to remove any oil-soaked wood, where feasible. Where this is not possible, use carburetor cleaner to leach out the oil. Several dousings followed by drying with a paper towel and a portable hair dryer should do the trick. You can see when the wood is free of excess oil, as it will look dry and whitened.

Next you can consider skeletonizing the fore-end as I covered in the sub-section titled, *Skeletonizing Fore-ends, Lever-Action (Non Tubular Magazine) & Single-Shot Rifles*. In this application, skeletonizing adds the same benefits as were previously noted. However, you can choose to fill the skeletonized areas with bedding material. This provides an unusually rigid and warpage-resistant fore-end. You can even include an aluminum longitudinal beam. However, owing to the typically limited strength of the fore-end attachment hanger and screw, I would advise against any such approach for use on any rifle generating serious recoil (epoxy bedding agent is quite heavy).

Assuming you have RTV bedded the rear of the fore-end into the receiver and provided the steel pillar for the fore-end attachment screw you are ready to glass bed the barrel channel. Note the location of the extreme front end of the fore-end on the barrel. Apply two or three layers of vinyl electrical tape around the barrel at this location. This tape should fully seal off the barrel channel here.

Apply a clay dam at the rear of the barrel channel. Install sufficient modeling clay (or

Section 13: The Trouble With Lever-Action and Single-Shot Rifle Stocks, Part II

some similar substance) to fill the rearmost one-half inch of the barrel channel, to prevent the epoxy bedding agent from infiltrating here.

Mix a sufficient batch of gel-type bedding agent to fill the barrel channel. If desired include dye to match the wood color. Better for accuracy, include two-parts atomized steel to three-parts bedding agent. This latter approach will strengthen the bedding material and bring its coefficient of thermal expansion closer to that of the barrel, which is a very desirable goal.

Thoroughly coat the front of the receiver, the rear 12" of the barrel, the fore-end hanger and the fore-end attachment screw with release agent. Then use a small brush or a cotton swab to apply release agent to all outside surfaces of the fore-end that are adjacent to the barrel channel.

Apply sufficient bedding agent into the barrel channel to fill the gap between the barrel and fore-end when the rifle is assembled. Be sure to save a small test sample of bedding agent. Mount the barreled-action in a vise. Leave the rear of the barrel accessible and positioned at the bottom.

Install the fore-end by tilting it to allow the rear portion to enter the receiver first. Then, while holding the fore-end against the receiver, rotate it until it begins to come into contact with the barrel. Install the attachment screw and slowly snug it until the fore-end just begins to touch the tape wrap at the front of the barrel channel.

Allow the bedding agent to cure until the test sample is semi-rigid, typically about four to six hours (you should be able to dent the test sample with your fingernail). Trim away the extruded bedding agent from the contact of the fore-end and barrel. See the related illustration in the previous sub-section covering RTV bedding.

Remove the fore-end attachment screw. Then separate the fore-end and clean out the clay dams and any bedding agent that has infiltrated where it should not be. Trim off any burrs of bedding agent. Clean off and degrease the attachment screw. Similarly, clean out and degrease the threads in the fore-end hanger. Remove the tape wrap from the barrel. One last time, apply release agent to the underside of the barrel.

Install the fore-end. Thread the attachment screw in place and tighten it until it pulls the fore-end solidly against the epoxy bed. Allow the bedding agent at least 24 hours to cure.

Remove the fore-end and clean off all of the release agent from the steel and bedding surfaces. Apply a uniformly thin coating of molybdenum-disulfide (or graphite) to the entire bedded barrel channel, the receiver end and the hanger recess area. Apply Loctite #222 to the fore-end attachment screw. Install the fore-end and tighten the screw to bring the fore-end into solid abutment to the barrel. This job is now (finally) finished.

Alternative Fore-end Bedding Schemes, Two-Piece Stocked Rifles:

After reviewing the previous sub-sections, consider the following options. You might want to try one of these alternative methods.

For the fully glass bedded fore-end channel, a combination approach, where the fore-end is partially skeletonized (the "Robust Skeletonizing" method described earlier in this text) and the remaining barrel contact surfaces are epoxy bedded is particularly desirable. Simply follow the directions noted in the sub-section of RTV bedding but substitute gel-type bedding epoxy for the RTV and install a layer between all barrel channel surfaces and the barrel. Be certain to apply ample release agent to the barrel surfaces and remember that you can tinker with the details of any bedding plan.

With the latter thought in mind, you might consider experimentally epoxy bedding the rear face of the fore-end to solidly abut the receiver. Such bedding could add a particularly solid bond if there was a method of pulling the fore-end against the receiver. Browning's BLR affords just such a system. We will cover that system in detail later. On those rifles the fore-end slips over an extension of the receiver. The attachment-screw threads into that extension from the front of the fore-end. Tightening that screw pulls the fore-end against the receiver. These rifles might very well benefit from an epoxy bed between the fore-end and the receiver.

Some single-shot rifles (such as the Ruger No. 1) have an angled fore-end attachment screw. Here many gunsmiths note a similar advantage for bedding the rear face of the fore-end to the receiver.

This consideration also suggests a more complicated bedding alteration involving modification of the fore-end hanger, to provide just such an attachment system. Since this would involve milling out a custom hanger or, at the least, cutting and welding the existing hanger, this work gets closer to the professional end of things. I will not detail this modification here. If you understand the goal, which is to pull the fore-end solidly against the receiver, you should be able to figure out how to do this work. Specifically, the goal is to design an attachment system that forces the attachment screw to pull the fore-end back, against the receiver, as it tightens it up, against the barrel.

With an attachment screw that angles from front-to-back at about thirty degrees (30°) from the vertical, and with proper handling of the epoxy bedding, this desirable goal (simultaneous bedding at the receiver and barrel channel) is rather easy to achieve. This can be dramatically beneficial on rifles with particularly light barrels or less rigid receivers. Excepting that the screw enters a hanger that is an extension of the receiver, this is the system used on Ruger's falling-block rifles. However, as noted, usually, it is best to leave the fore-end floating on the Ruger and other rifles using similar receiver-mounted fore-end hanger attachment systems.

Keep in mind that a system allowing complete separation of the fore-end and the barrel is usually superior to any system that attaches the fore-end to the barrel. Therefore, before considering altering a barrel-attached fore-end hanger, consider attaching a fore-end hanger to the receiver. On several rifle types this conversion is highly feasible.

Bedding Fore-end, Browning BLR and Ruger No. 1 & #3 Rifles:

(Note that you should handle any rifle combining a two-piece stock with a receiver extension, designed to connect the fore-end to the receiver, in essentially the same manner as that discussed in this sub-section.)

Early BLRs featured a combination receiver extension and barrel band fore-end attachment. Later models omit the bastardizing barrel band and rely exclusively on the receiver extension to support the fore-end. In all such rifles the goals are the same, solid fore-end-to-receiver attachment with limitation of shooter- or rest-related stress transfer from the fore-end to the receiver. On early models of the BLR there is one minor complication. You should also modify the barrel band to allow it to completely clear the barrel during normal use.

Barrel Band Clearance, Browning BLR (Early Models):

(Rifles made after about 1996 have no fore-end/barrel band.)

Let us dispose of the barrel band problem first. Disposing with the barrel band itself is a very good idea but that simple approach to the problem leaves an unsightly fore-end. You could choose to fit a newer (unbanded) fore-end to the rifle. This alternative is probably a lot easier, if more expensive, compared to the following method. Also, in my opinion, the barrel band does add a certain visual appeal (nostalgic charm?).

If you choose to keep the barrel band, remove it from the rifle (remove the cross bolt and slide the band forward). Insert the big end of the band in a well-padded vise. Apply clamping pressure only against the front and rear face of any such band, do not clamp across the opening. Tighten the vise sufficiently to hold the band in place. Be sure to leave the barrel banding zone extended well above the top of the vise.

Measure the inside diameter of the barrel opening in the barrel band at a convenient location. Note this dimension for comparison during the enlarging process. Use a large diameter round file to file on the inside of the barrel spanning portion of the barrel band. You will need to remove a uniform layer of about ten-thousandths of an inch (0.010") thickness. Be careful to avoid filing the band thin in one spot or marring its exterior. When you have completed this filing operation you will want to polish the file marks from the interior, which will also increase the barrel clearance.

Obtain a 9" long section of five-eighths inch (5/8") hardwood dowel. Drill a thirteen-sixty-fourths inch (13/64") hole about 1" deep straight into one end of the dowel. Tap the resulting hole with a standard thread (20 tpi) one-quarter inch tap. Cut a three inch (3") piece of one-quarter inch all-thread and thread that into the dowel. Using a hacksaw, cut a one and one-half inch (1½") long slot, centered and along the axis of the other end of the dowel.

Cut a long strip of 150 grit sandpaper about one and one-half inch (1½") wide. Hold the dowel with the end opposite the bolt facing toward you. Insert the end of the sandpaper strip into the slot, from top-to-bottom and with the abrasive side on the left. Align the paper square to the dowel. Tightly wrap the paper, clockwise and rough side out, around the dowel until it forms a roll that is just about equal to the barrel diameter at the location of the barrel band. Tear off the excess portion of the sandpaper. To keep the wrap in place, apply masking tape over one end of the roll — several wraps of tape are a good idea.

Section 13: The Trouble With Lever-Action and Single-Shot Rifle Stocks, Part II

Chuck this hole-sanding tool into an electric drill (using the one-quarter inch bolt). Hold the sandpaper tightly wrapped and insert this tool into the barrel channel in the vised barrel band. With the drill running in the "forward" direction, proceed to sand the barrel channel portion of the barrel band. Make an effort to keep the tool square to the band and try to keep applying pressure over the entire barrel spanning surface of the barrel band. Your goal is to eliminate all file marks while removing a uniform thickness of material from the entire barrel spanning portion of the band.

Periodically, remeasure the barrel channel. Proceed until total material removal has reached at least fifteen-thousandths of an inch (0.015"). Reinstall the band on the fore-end and run a paper shim between the fore-end-to-barrel band and the barrel and through the barrel-to-fore-end channel to insure adequate clearance at all points (see the following sub-section). If necessary, continue sanding until you achieve such clearance (adequate clearance here is about the thickness of a playing card).

Full Floating Barrel, Fore-end Mounted On Receiver Hanger, Lever-Action (Non Tubular Magazine) & Single-Shot Rifles:

See the related photographs and discussion in *Part I*, the sub-sections covering fore-end-to-barrel floating with Remington and Savage pump-action rifles. The following discussion applies to all Browning BLRs (and other rifles using similar fore-end attachment systems). However, for those (older models) which also have a barrel band, the first step is to free float the barrel band from the barrel — as noted in the previous sub-section.

It is important to ensure that the barrel channel clears the barrel along its entire length. If necessary, rasp away any high spots in the barrel channel until there is sufficient clearance to slip a playing card between the fore-end and the barrel channel with the fore-end normally installed. The card should not bind at any point. (On those models featuring a separate barrel-to-fore-end band, remove the barrel band before performing this test.) The best tool for increasing the barrel-to-fore-end clearance is probably a half-round file although a large round file will work. Be careful to avoid damaging the finish of any external surfaces.

Once you have achieved sufficient barrel-to-fore-end clearance, seal any freshly exposed wood surfaces. I suggest using a quick-drying wood finishing epoxy here. Do not build this finish to sufficient depth that you eliminate the critical barrel-to-fore-end clearance you just achieved.

Finally, clean, degrease and roughen the rear end of the fore-end — 150 grit sandpaper does a good job for the latter operation. Also, ensure that the receiver extension channel is clean, well degreased and roughened with 150 grit sandpaper.

Apply a good coating of glass bedding release agent to the front of the receiver, the receiver extension, the underside of the fore-end area of the barrel, the receiver attachment bolt, the extreme front end of the attachment bolt hole in the fore-end (the area of the fore-end under the head of the attachment bolt), the outside rear of the fore-end that is near the rear face of the receiver, and the rearmost portion of the fore-end barrel channel.

Mix a sufficient batch of gel-type bedding epoxy. Add colorant to match the bedding agent to the wood, as necessary.

Using an appropriately sized wood dowel, apply bedding agent inside the receiver extension hole through the fore-end. Use sufficient material to eliminate any clearance between the hole through the fore-end and the receiver extension. Coat the rear face of the fore-end with sufficient bedding agent to fill all voids between fore-end and receiver. Apply a tinker's dam (a plug made of modeling clay) to any holes in the receiver, to prevent bedding agent infiltration, as necessary. Save a test sample of the bedding agent.

Locate the rifle in a well-padded vise. Install the fore-end onto the receiver extension. Make sure you keep the fore-end rotated so that the barrel-channel-to-barrel clearance is precisely equal on both sides of the fore-end — insert sufficient paper shims along the sides of the barrel to lock the fore-end in this orientation.

Lightly snug the attachment screw. Only tighten the screw sufficiently to begin to bring the fore-end into contact with the receiver. It is acceptable to turn the screw until the bedding agent begins to squeeze from between the receiver and the fore-end. However, avoid tightening this screw. Once the first spot of wood contacts the receiver, the screw is already too tight! The problem is: you want to leave a bedding layer of epoxy material interposing the fore-end and the receiver. Otherwise, the bedding material cannot properly isolate these two pieces. If you were to continue to tighten the fore-end after the initial wood-to-receiver contact, the fore-end would necessarily bend the receiver extension to bring other areas of the fore-end into contact with the receiver. That condition will place a strain on the receiver, that will result in a loss of accuracy and will likely lead to a wandering zero. Since this is precisely the situation you are attempting to prevent, by interposing a layer of epoxy between the wood and the steel, the need to avoid over tightening the hanger at this time should be obvious.

When the bedding agent reaches a semi-rigid plastic state, as noted on the test sample (about four to six hours), it is easy to cut away any excess material that has extruded from between the receiver and the fore-end. Use a sharp single-edge razor blade and caution, to avoid damaging either the wood or the steel. Remove the attachment screw and clean away any bedding agent from the threads and shank. Run a hole-fitting drill bit into the attachment screw hole and cut out any bedding agent in the forward end of the hole. Then clean any bedding agent out of the end of the receiver extension.

When the bedding agent has cured sufficiently so that it is difficult to indent a sample with your fingernail (about twelve hours), remove the fore-end. This could very well require a great deal of force. Clamp the receiver in a well-padded bench vise. Pull on the fore-end while twisting, first clockwise then counter-clockwise, wiggling the fore-end from side to side and then wiggling it up and down. If you were careful in applying the release agent, the fore-end will eventually come loose without the application of excessive force…eventually. Clean out any bedding agent that infiltrated the barrel channel. Remove the clay plugs and other extraneous material, as necessary.

This completes the proper glass bedding of the BLR fore-end. Reinstall the wood and snug the attachment screw tightly. Ensure that the barrel channel still has sufficient clearance. If so equipped, reinstall the barrel band. Ensure that this piece still has sufficient barrel clearance.

Bedding Fore-ends & Magazines, Tubular-Magazine Lever-Action Rifles:

You will find a discussion of the proper method of disassembly and the suggested modifications for the typical tubular magazine in the sub-section covering *lever-action receiver (action) modifications* and the subsequent pertinent sub-sections located later in *Part II*. Also, before beginning with these modifications, please, read the entire applicable following sub-sections through the sub-section covering *reassembly of tubular magazine & fore-end*. If necessary, reread all these sub-sections. This work is not difficult or even complicated, just convoluted.

Before removing the magazine tube and fore-end assembly, note the orientation of all parts. The screw heads on the bands usually go on the loading gate side of the rifle. Also, mark the barrel side of the magazine tube band with a piece of tape or by some other temporary method.

Finally, before bedding the fore-end and tubular magazine, refer to *Section 14*. If you intend to alter the tubular magazine system in any way, it is best to apply those alterations before performing these bedding steps.

For reasons that will become obvious, I will combine the magazine and fore-end attachment discussions into one sub-section; there really is not any other good way to handle this, the two are a complete system and proper bedding always involves modifications to both pieces. I will proceed with this text using a Marlin Model-336 as the example. However, most tubular-magazine rifles are sufficiently similar to warrant essentially the same alterations and barrel attachment bedding steps.

Note that there are two common systems for fore-end attachment. First is the combination barrel and fore-end band. In this system, a band rests over the top of the barrel, near the front end of the fore-end. The remainder of the band is a tight fit over the fore-end. See photograph #s 13-28/29.

A screw enters a hole in the fore-end and passes between corresponding alignment slots in the barrel and magazine tube. The configuration of the fore-end and this screw hole (with screw installed) prevents the band from moving on the fore-end. The aligning slots in the barrel and magazine tube prevent the screw from moving either forward or back on the rifle. This system can also lock the tubular magazine in place. In turn the tubular magazine prevents the barrel band (and therefore the fore-end) from rotating around the barrel. Therefore, both barrel band and fore-end are properly oriented on and fixed to the rifle.

The second method of fore-end attachment involves a fore-end cap. In this assemblage, a

Section 13: The Trouble With Lever-Action and Single-Shot Rifle Stocks, Part II

stamped steel cap fits snugly over the front end of the fore-end. Screws enter each side of this cap and attach to a hanger that is mounted in a dovetail slot in the barrel. This cap captures the fore-end and the screws (which enter from both sides), locating the fore-end cap to the barrel. Typically, the cap also captures the magazine tube, locking it in place against the barrel but not front to rear on the rifle. However, some tubular-magazine rifles use a half-magazine, which the fore-end completely hides. In those rifles, besides locating and containing the fore-end, the fore-end cap hides the front of the magazine tube and prevents its forward movement. See photograph # 13-30.

Both the band and cap methods of fore-end attachment are functional. Neither method seems to have any clear accuracy advantage.

Similarly, tubular magazine attachment follows two main methods. First is the barrel band. This is a piece resembling a figure eight with the interior side-to-side connection cut away. The top half surrounds most of the barrel; the lower half surrounds most of the magazine tube. Usually, a screw passes through the band from side to side. This screw slips between the barrel and magazine tube by passing through aligned slots in those two pieces, which also provide clearance for the screw shank. The band secures the magazine tube to the barrel. The screw shank prevents the band from moving endwise or rotating around the barrel. Equally, it prevents the magazine tube from moving forward, backward, turning in the band or rotating around the barrel

Photograph 13-29: View of Marlin Model-336 fore-end hanger. This is the typical band system, as used by most Marlin and Winchester rifles. Note the RTV between the barrel and magazine tube (gray used for photographic purposes). See the text for an explanation of the use of this product in this application.

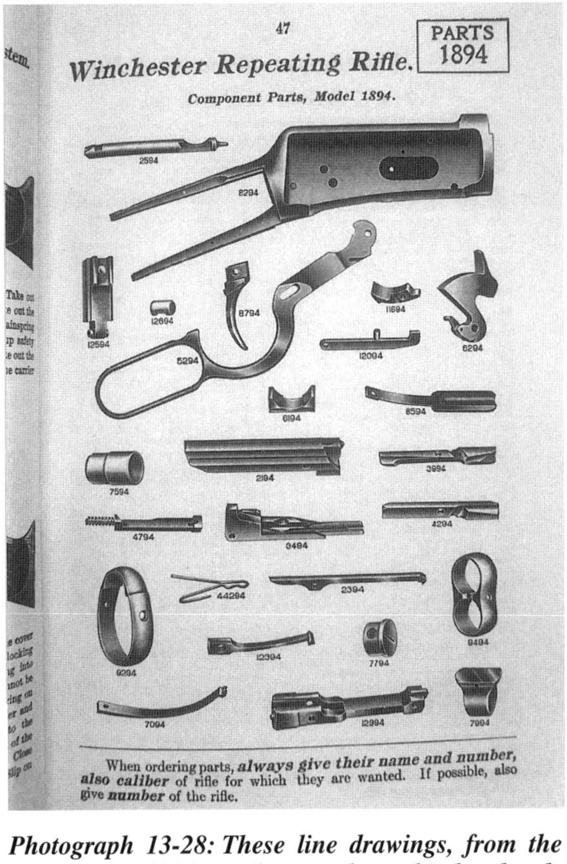

Photograph 13-30: Customized Marlin Model-1894. Note shortened barrel (16 1/4"), reversed and shortened barrel hanger (prevents hood from pulling off the front, owing to recoil!), ROBAR's NP3 (electroless nickel with PTFE) plated barrel-to-fore-end band, fore-end hanger and screws. In this view the proper gap between the barrel and tubular-magazine is quite evident in the area between the fore-end and the front band. In the original photograph this accuracy-enhancing gap was just visible in front of this band. Note that Loctite #222 will not bond to NP3!, try Loctite #271.

Photograph 13-28: These line drawings, from the Winchester 1916 catalogue, show the band-style fore-end and magazine-tube hangers (9294 & 9494), as used on the Model-1894.

(the receiver would also prevent the tube from moving backward).

The second common magazine tube attachment system uses a dovetailed stud attachment. Rifles like Marlin's new Model-1895 have a shorter (three-quarter length) magazine and use this magazine attachment method. Typically, a stud is affixed to the underside of the barrel in a milled dovetail slot. This stud fits through a hole in one side of and near the front end of the magazine tube. The magazine tube cap is inserted into the end of the magazine tube and the hanger stud also enters a hole in this cap. A screw enters through a corresponding hole in the opposite side of the magazine tube then through the cap and threads into the hanger stud.

The stud affixes the magazine to the barrel and the screw locks both magazine cap and magazine tube in place on the stud. As noted, Marlin's new Model-1895 uses this system. Assuming the dovetail and hanger are sufficiently robust and tightly bonded, this system seems adequate. In this particular application, this system might be superior to the barrel band from the accuracy standpoint. It is almost certainly superior from the strength standpoint. All high-recoil tubular-magazine rifles either do or should use this system.

Earlier we discussed silver soldering of dovetailed hangers. If your rifle uses dovetail hangers and you have not already silver soldered those in place, consider that option. At the very least, remove the hangers, thoroughly clean and degrease the slots and the hangers, apply Loctite #609 and reassemble.

Magazine & Attachment Hardware Modifications, Tubular-Magazine Lever-Action Rifles:

The next step is to insure that there is no unwarranted contact between the assembled magazine tube and the barrel. On a used rifle the existence of any such contact is easy to determine. Simply observe wear spots on the bluing on either the magazine tube or the barrel. Polished, steel-colored or rusty areas are a sure sign of such contact.

While you are at it here, plan to polish the interior contours of the magazine tube band(s) and the barrel contour of the fore-end band or fore-end cap to eliminate point contacts under those pieces. The idea is to provide for contact over a large area, as opposed to point loads. This is a very simple process and we will discuss it now; we will return to the task of providing clearance between the magazine tube and the barrel. See photograph #s 13-31 through 13-34.

Photograph 13-31: View of Marlin fore-end band. Note the gray areas near the upper right side in this view. These are the spots where this band had been touching the barrel, the only spots! I polished this loop so that a broader area would touch the barrel. See the text and photograph 13-32.

Photograph 13-32: See photograph 13-31. Barely visible in this photograph is the wear point on this Marlin Model-336, where the fore-end band is touching the barrel in one small area. Polishing on the interior of the band can help spread out the contact zone and will probably improve accuracy. See text.

Section 13: The Trouble With Lever-Action and Single-Shot Rifle Stocks, Part II

First, if the gun uses a fore-end cap, observe the barrel sides for evidence of contact with the uppermost interior edges of the fore-end cap. Then look at the inside edges of the cap where it could touch the barrel. Carefully clamp the cap in a well-padded vise. Use a smooth-cut half-round file to slightly widen and smooth the opening at the top of the cap. Normally, there is no need to remove more than about ten-thousandths of an inch (0.010") of material from each side. Use a coarse Cratex wheel in a moto-tool to polish the filed surfaces. Finish by cold bluing the filed surfaces.

For working on the bands, build a sanding dowel (as described in the text on barrel band alteration, found in the prior sub-section covering *Browning BLR, barrel band clearance*). Clamp the band in a well-padded vise. Keep the end you wish to polish well exposed. (Do not polish the fore-end side of the fore-end band.) Install the dowel in a drill and proceed to polish the channel(s) in the band(s) until all inside surfaces are shiny — do not remove any more metal than is necessary. Repeat the polishing process on both interior loops of the magazine tube band. Remember, your goal here is to modify the bands so that most of the interior surface touches the barrel or magazine tube, not to provide clearance between the band and the barrel or tube. The latter result is counter productive. To function properly, these bands have to clamp around the barrel and magazine tube.

When you have properly polished both bands, apply a good cold bluing agent to all polished surfaces. Also, clean all sanding debris from the bolt holes and all surfaces.

Moving back to the tubular magazine, there are three places this highly flexible tube is likely to touch the barrel. Moving from the front, these locations are: at the extreme front end and near the forward magazine tube band or hanger; at the fore-end band or hanger location; at the extreme rear (inside the corresponding recess in the receiver). You should remove steel from each of these areas (and any others where contact occurs), to the extent feasible in order to prevent barrel-to-magazine-tube contact.

Starting at the front, it is simple enough to file on the tube to form a small flat area along the zone where contact has occurred or might occur. With the Marlin Model-336 example, often the entire portion of the magazine tube in front of the front band touches the underside of the barrel. Grind or file a flat, along the barrel side of the magazine tube in front of the front band. Taper this flat from just deep enough to reach through the bluing in the area adjacent to the band, to, perhaps, one-half the thickness of the tube wall at the extreme front end. As long as you file only on the topside and do not file completely through the side of the tube, you cannot hurt anything. Better to ensure clearance than to be too circumspect here. For visual appeal add a radius to the flat area, if you so desire. Polish and reblue the modified area.

Temporarily reassemble the rifle and look for clearance in the filed area, as exemplified by light passing between barrel and tube. If you note contact, remove the tube and file slightly deeper, where necessary. Continue this process until the tube does not touch the barrel. Clearance equal to several layers of standard stationery is sufficient here.

Photograph 13-33: See photographs 13-31/32. In this view of the barrel (adjacent to the tubular-magazine band on a Marlin Model-336) the wear from the rough interior of the band that connects the barrel to the tubular magazine is quite evident. Note front sight, which must be removed to remove barrel band. See text.

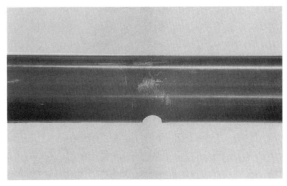

Photograph 13-34: See photograph 13-33. Same view after front sight removal.

Similarly, file the barrel-side of the tube anywhere else it touches the barrel. Of course this is not possible at the attachment points between the magazine tube and a barrel hanger(s), as is used on Marlin's new Model-1895. Also, do not thin the tube too much on either side of the barrel band's screw-clearance slot; that alteration could compromise the screw's ability to retain the tube against the considerable forces of recoil. See photograph # 13-35.

Finally, and perhaps most importantly, verify that the tube has end-to-end clearance between the locating slots (or hanger) and the receiver. Quite often the magazine tube just fits between the tapered step in the receiver recess and the barrel attachment points. For several reasons this situation is potentially detrimental to accuracy — vibrations, stress transfer, etc.

This condition is quite simple to correct. A bench grinder is the best tool but a file will suffice. Grind a forty-five degree (45°) bevel on the outside of the rear end of the tube. Extend this bevel to about one-half the thickness of the magazine tube on the receiver end of the tube. Also polish the outside of the rear one-quarter of an inch of the tube, as necessary to provide for radial clearance between the tube and the recess in the receiver. Apply a cold bluing agent to the affected surfaces. This simple fix will usually provide sufficient end clearance for the tube. See the illustration and photograph #s 13-36/37.

Receiver End Of Magazine Tube Modification

Original   Modified.

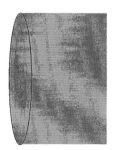
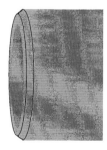

Note Bevel on end of modified magazine tube.

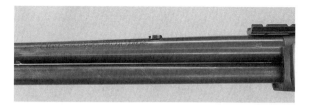

Photograph 13-35: Marlin Model-336 with fore-end removed. Here the proper gap between the tubular-magazine and barrel is quite evident. However, with the fore-end and fore-end-band in place, these two tubes are pulled closer together. Do not trust this view, check the barrel and the magazine tube for signs of rubbing contact — the bluing will be worn off any places that do touch during normal assembly. See text.

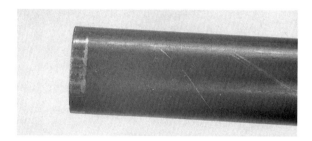

Photograph 13-36: Receiver end of magazine tube from Marlin Model-336. Note the shiny band near the end and the spiral scars on the bluing. The worn bluing on the end suggests this tube is a tight fit in the receiver. For best accuracy, I will sand this section down until it is a loose fit in the receiver port and then bed the tube into RTV silicone. This will help isolate the tube from the receiver. The spiral wear marks are the result of two problems. First, I removed the tubular magazine without pulling the front sight (which is necessary to remove the front band from the barrel) — I had to slide the tube through the band. Second, the front band had a rough interior. See text and photograph 13-37.

Photograph 13-37: Receiver end of Marlin Model-336 magazine tube, after sanding down for clearance. Before reinstalling I will also grind a bevel on the outside end. See text, sketch and photograph 13-36.

Section 13: The Trouble With Lever-Action and Single-Shot Rifle Stocks, Part II

Fore-end Attachment, Tubular-Magazine Lever-Action Rifles:

To achieve proper barrel-to-fore-end clearance, use a half-round file to remove sufficient material to achieve adequate clearance to allow a playing card to pass between the barrel and the installed fore-end. When you have accomplished these steps, address the necessary bedding modifications at the ends of the fore-end.

Apply one or two layers of masking tape on the flats of the perimeter of the front end of the receiver. Then, use a file to remove sufficient wood from the front and rear contact surfaces of the fore-end to provide clearance so that when you install the fore-end normally it will shift fore and aft, just slightly. Remove the fore-end but leave the tape on the receiver in place.

Apply a varnish or epoxy-type sealing agent to the fore-end channel to seal all newly exposed surfaces against moisture. For ease of handling, allow this coating to cure sufficiently before proceeding. This sealant is an important step so do not overlook it; also, do not assume the factory has properly sealed the interior surfaces of the fore-end....

Apply release agent to the receiver, the fore-end portion of the barrel, the fore-end cap (especially the inside surface) and the fore-end hanger or barrel-to-fore-end band and attachment screws. Mix a sufficient batch of epoxy bedding agent to completely coat the surface of the fore-end at the rear and along any contact areas under the fore-end cap. Reinstall the fore-end and allow the epoxy to cure.

After the bedding agent has reached a plastic state, trim away any that has extruded from between the fore-end and receiver and from under the fore-end cap, as necessary. With a bit of care you can do this job using a single-edge razor blade or an X-acto knife and without marring the steel or the wood.

Disassemble the fore-end. Remove the masking tape from the receiver. Reapply release agent to the front of the receiver.

Tubular-Magazine & Fore-end Reassembly, Lever-Action Rifles:

Note, on rifles using a magazine-tube barrel band, removal of the front sight will facilitate ease of reassembly. Typically, the front sights on these rifles are either dovetailed directly to the barrel or onto a sight base, which is attached to the barrel with screws. Regardless of sight attachment method, remove the entire front sight assembly before proceeding.

At this point the process gets a little convoluted. First, you need to understand what you are trying to accomplish. I can best describe this concept as follows: reduce the magnitude of vibrations or mitigate the deleterious effects of those vibrations. The best way to accomplish those goals is to interpose a layer of black RTV silicone between the barrel and the magazine tube as well as between the rear of the fore-end and the front of the receiver and between the sides of the fore-end and the barrel. On rifles with banded attachments, it is also useful to include a thin film of RTV on all inside surfaces of the bands where those touch (or might touch) steel.

This list represents a plethora of things that you have to do correctly to achieve the best possible results. Therefore, it might be helpful to further explain the goals before continuing with detailed instructions. Those goals include interposing a layer of RTV silicone between the magazine tube and the barrel, between the fore-end and the barrel, between the barrel band(s) and the barrel and between the fore-end cap and the fore-end; and to also provide for release agent between all of these parts, which is necessary to facilitate future disassembly.

Properly accomplishing these goals can be a bit messy and a bit of a handful. It is best to vise the barreled-action, bottom side up, to provide clear access to the bottom of the barrel without having to hold the gun or worry about it shifting around as you proceed with the reassembly.

To facilitate the necessary subsequent disassembly, carefully follow these instructions. Tape off the top one-quarter inch of both sides of the barrel channel in the fore-end. Also, tape off the area that will be under the barrel band. Finally, tape the rear one-half inch of the outside of the magazine tube.

Apply release agent to all exposed surfaces of the fore-end. Apply release agent to the front end of the receiver, especially inside the magazine tube recess, and on the receiver's sides, near the front end; inside the rear end of the magazine tube; to the underside and sides of the barrel, full length of the magazine tube; to all surfaces of the barrel band, fore-end bands or barrel-mounted hangers; to all screws and to all surfaces of the fore-end plug.

Equally, degrease the following areas: top surface of magazine tube, full length; sides of magazine tube, in the area that rests under the fore-end, and in the area that is under any magazine-to-barrel band; those areas of the barrel under the barrel bands; the rear face of the fore-end.

Remove the tape from the area under the fore-end band, if used, and the top of both sides of the fore-end channel. Then remove the tape from the rear of the magazine tube.

Now comes the fun part. Apply a modest bead of RTV along the top of the magazine tube, but only in the area that will be under the fore-end. Then, with the tube in the proper orientation, slide the fore-end over the magazine tube until the tube extends slightly from the back of the fore-end (with care you should be able to do this without smearing the RTV. Apply a thin bead of RTV to the rear one-quarter inch of the outside of the magazine tube (the entire area that enters the recess in the receiver). Apply a sufficient RTV layer to the entire rear end of the fore-end. Clamp the magazine tube in a padded vise with the tube level — tighten the vise only sufficiently to hold the tube in place (the tube is very easy to crush).

Unless a small bead of black RTV interposing the barrel and exposed portion of the magazine tube will offend you, proceed as follows, otherwise, omit this step. Install the nozzle on the RTV tube and snip the end to allow production of a thin bead. Apply such a thin bead of RTV along the top edge of the magazine tube from the front end back to the heavier bead that you already applied. Allow these RTV beads to set for a spell, perhaps 10 minutes, to allow the RTV to develop some strength and a light skin. See photograph # 13-38.

Lay a small bead of RTV along the upper surfaces of the fore-end at either side of the barrel channel. Do not apply an excess of RTV but insure you have applied sufficient RTV to form a solid layer between the fore-end and the barrel. See photograph # 13-39.

Remove the fore-end and magazine tube from the clamp. Install the rifle in a padded clamp with the barrel exposed, level and with the bottom side at the top. If possible, in one fluid motion, install the fore-end and magazine tube in place (under) the barrel. Keep the forward end of the magazine tube and the fore-end away from the barrel until the rear of the magazine tube and the fore-end have both entered into their respective recesses in the receiver.

Be certain you have the magazine tube properly oriented (so the slots line up) and fully installed into the receiver. Equally, make sure you have the fore-end fully engaged into the front of the receiver but do not force it back (you do not want to squeeze out the beneficial bedding layer of RTV). Apply a thin layer of RTV around the magazine tube and barrel in all areas that will be under attachment bands.

Install all attaching hardware but omit the magazine spring and cartridge follower. Snugly tighten the attachment screw(s). Allow the RTV at least 24 hours to cure. Use an X-acto knife, or similar tool, to trim away any excess RTV that has extruded from the barrel channel and between the fore-end and receiver.

Remove the magazine plug and front band screw to facilitate installation of the cartridge follower and magazine spring. However, before proceeding, run a close-fitting dowel through the tube to ensure that no RTV is inside the tube anywhere. Likely areas where RTV might have infiltrated the tube's interior are: the band screw slots

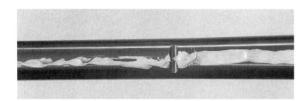

Photograph 13-38: Gray RTV silicone (instead of black, for photographic clarity) applied to bottom of Marlin Model-336 barrel. See text for an explanation of the purpose and procedure involved in introducing a layer of RTV between the barrel and the magazine tube. Note, on some rifles it is easier to install this product onto the magazine tube (as explained in the text). Note also that the bead is wider behind the fore-end hanger location; it will be hidden by the fore-end, so a more robust bead is in order.

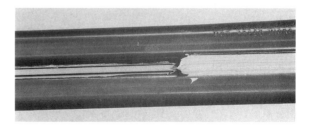

Photograph 13-39: Gray RTV (see photograph 13-38) installed between barrel and magazine tube on Marlin Model-336. Note thick bead in area that will be hidden under fore-end. See text for explanation and purpose.

Section 13: The Trouble With Lever-Action and Single-Shot Rifle Stocks, Part II 231

and the joint of the magazine tube and the receiver. It will be reasonably easy to break any extraneous RTV loose from inside the tube using a close-fitting hardwood dowel. Make sure you have cleaned all such RTV out of the magazine tube and receiver. Then reassemble the magazine to verify correct functioning.

Properly done, this bedding system provides all the desired benefits. It is most assuredly worthwhile. However, note, if you have no intention of ever removing the magazine assembly or fore-end, consider omitting the release agent and truly bonding these pieces together and to the barrel and receiver. This approach will certainly strengthen the bond and possibly provide superior accuracy but it will even more certainly almost guarantee destruction of either the fore-end or the magazine tube, or both, in any subsequent disassembly attempt.

Disassemble the magazine tube and fore-end. Clean up any RTV that might have extruded into voids in the fore-end. Reassemble the rifle. Clean and degrease all associated screws and screw holes. Apply Loctite #222 to the screw threads.

Reassemble the fore-end and magazine tube assemblies. Snug the screws only slightly. When reattaching the front sight refer to the appropriate sub-section in *Part I* to ensure you do a proper job.

As noted at the beginning of the sub-section covering *magazine tube and attachment hardware modifications*, since this process is worthwhile, do not let the convoluted description given here discourage you or foil your efforts. Reread these sub-sections, as necessary, to understand the process and then proceed. It is worth the effort. You can expect these steps to dramatically improve the accuracy of your classic tubular-magazine lever-action repeater.

Buttstock Attachment, Two-Piece Stocked Lever-Action & Single-Shot Rifles:

Before considering buttstock modifications, refer to the sub-section covering *stock removal* in *Part I*. The discussion of stock removal on the Remington Pump found there covers the basic requirements and is applicable to any two-piece stocked rifle using a through-bolt. On those stocks connected with a tang bolt, it is only necessary to remove that one bolt. However, for most stock modifications, as discussed in the sub-sections referenced in *Part I*, you will have to remove the buttplate or pad.

On those rifles featuring a through-bolt in the buttstock (for example, the Browning BLR), refer to the sub-section in *Part I* on buttstock bedding for the Remington Pump. For all practical purposes, all such buttstocks require essentially identical modifications to ensure perfect buttstock-to-receiver bedding.

On all rifles featuring a tang-bolt connection for the buttstock, the best approach is to install an auxiliary through-bolt connection system. This modification allows you to properly tighten the buttstock against the receiver, forming a tighter and much more rigid bond. This alteration also strengthens the buttstock. Bedding of the buttstock is identical to that described for the Remington Pump in *Part I*, refer to that sub-section. However, note, be certain that bedding epoxy does not interpose the stock along any angled surfaces anywhere behind the extreme front end of the stock. Many of these rifles have several such surfaces. With improper bedding, any one of those can become a load bearing surface. This condition can lead to a cracked stock and will almost certainly reduce the potential rigidity of the buttstock-to-receiver joint.

Adapting A Through-Bolt To A Tang-Bolt-Mounted Buttstock, Two-Piece Stocked Lever-Action & Single-Shot Rifles:

Before proceeding with this sub-section, see the discussion in *Part I* on proper bedding of a two-piece buttstock to the receiver. A proper epoxy bed is critical before proceeding with this work. See photograph # 13-40 and #s 2-45 through 2-48.

Excepting the Remington Model-8, every rifle I can think of that features a two-piece stock and uses a tang-bolt attachment for the buttstock, affords a very simple means of adding a through-bolt that anchors (indirectly) to the tang bolt. This is a very desirable method of achieving a through-bolt attachment system on such rifles. In addition to providing the necessary anchor for the through-bolt, tightening against an anchor supported by the tang bolt flexes that bolt, which clamps the tangs tighter against their respective bedding surfaces of the buttstock. However, for the same reason, it is preferable to use only hardened steel tang bolts in rifles with this alteration. Otherwise, serious tightening of the through-bolt, which is very desirable, results in an equally seriously bent tang bolt, which is not very desirable and leads to a serious case of the disassembly blues. I strongly advise obtaining and modifying a one-quarter inch (1/4") grade-8 bolt to replace the existing tang bolt before performing this alteration; lacking that, avoid tightening the through-bolt more than just somewhat snug, which is still a whole lot better than nothing. See photograph # 13-41.

Modifications For Adapting Tang-Mounted To Through-Bolt-Mounted Buttstock, Two-Piece Stocked Rifles:

The basic process involves the following alterations and fabrications. First, drill a hole through the stock from about the center of the web separating the top and lower tang and angling toward the center of the rear end of the stock. Since most stocks have factory drilled weight-reduction holes in the butt end, it is desirable to aim the new hole to intersect near the bottom center of an existing hole, where feasible. The included photographs clearly demonstrate the steps involved.

Begin by clamping the buttstock in a well-padded vise. Note the angle of the line from a point centered between the upper and lower tang relief cuts and the center of the bottom of an existing hole in the buttstock or the center (top to bottom) of the rear face of the buttstock, on those stocks that have no skeletonizing holes. Clamp the buttstock in the vise with this imaginary line as close to level as is feasible. I have had success by placing a wooden rule along the side of the stock, aligned to this imaginary line, then taping the rule in place on the side of the stock. It is then a simple matter to set a torpedo level on the edge of the rule. It is then possible to adjust the stock to get this drill hole marker essentially level, which facilitates proper drill bit alignment to keep the hole following the desired path along the desired drill line.

For this job, a long-shanked auger drill bit of five-sixteenths inch (5/16") diameter is just about the ideal tool. Position this drill bit to start drilling at the center of the divider between the tang relief cuts, hold the drill to keep the drill bit aligned with the stock, side to side. On the Marlin, the stock's tang extensions, located on either side of the drill bit, are a good visual clue of proper lateral alignment. See photograph # 13-42.

If you can get a helper to watch the drill bit's alignment from the side, it is a simple matter to drill the hole adequately aligned along the desired path. Lacking that, drill only until the main body of the auger drill bit begins to drill into the wood. Stop there. Set the torpedo level on the top edge of the protruding drill bit. Adjust

Photograph 13-41: Proper buttstock-to-receiver bedding is a critical first step in improving the buttstock attachment system on any two-piece stocked rifle. Shown here is only the first step in converting a Marlin Model-336 from a tang-bolt mounted buttstock to a through-bolt mounted buttstock. The bedding agent used here is Brownells gel-type with brown colorant added so that it will match the wood — unless the wood is almost black, use only a dab of colorant. Note the tape that shows at the upper center of the tang. This was attached over the radius on the tang to provide clearance between the tang and the stock — so the buttstock beds only against flat surfaces. See text.

Photograph 13-40: When you repeatedly see groups like this, the rifle might very well have a bedding problem. In this case, the likely culprit is a loose buttstock-to-receiver attachment. See the text for methods of correcting this problem on two-piece stocked rifles that use a tang-bolt buttstock-attachment system.

Section 13: The Trouble With Lever-Action and Single-Shot Rifle Stocks, Part II

the drill's height until the bubble indicates the drill bit is level. If you then lean against the back end of the drill you can position it with your body so that as you drill the hole deeper you can simply lean forward, thereby advancing the drill bit without substantially changing its horizontal alignment. If you do this carefully, you can drill a 9" deep hole without the far end of the drill bit diverging more than, perhaps, one-quarter of one-inch (up and down) from the desired path. You should be able to do substantially better with the side-to-side accuracy. I have often done much better. See photograph #s 13-43/44.

If this work makes you nervous, try practicing on a block of pine 2x4 (that does not have any knots) until you are confident that you can do this job in the stock. Remember, a helper who understands what you are doing can be most valuable.

Do not try to drill this hole more than about 9" deep. If the stock has a factory hole in the butt end, your 9" hole should certainly intersect that hole. If the stock has no such hole, stop drilling this pilot hole at about 9" depth and proceed as follows.

Measure the thickness of the center of the buttstock at a point about four inches in front of the rear end. Choose a blade type drill bit that is about one-half inch smaller in diameter than the stock's width at that point.

Insert a one-quarter inch dowel in the new hole you just drilled, to get an idea where that hole ends. With a bit of tinkering you should be able to visualize almost exactly where the hole ends, both side-to-side and top-to-bottom in the buttstock. For example, insert the dowel to the bottom of the hole, mark the dowel to indicate that depth and note its angle compared to the straight edge attached to the stock.

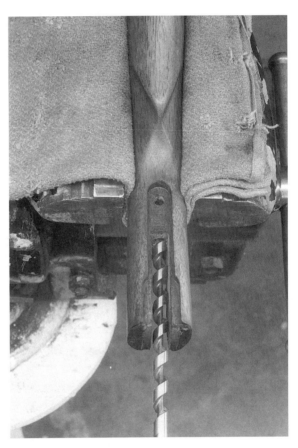

Photograph 13-43: Preparing a Marlin lever-action buttstock to accept a through-bolt. This view (from the top) shows how the forward panels will help align the proper size drill bit — used for drilling the initial hole. See text and photograph 13-44.

Photograph 13-42: In the world of tang-bolt mounted rifles, the Remington Model-8 is unusual. The tang mounting screw inserts through the lower tang, is a 12x40 thread screw, and has a tapered seat. Also, owing to receiver extension that houses the action spring, modifying this rifle to accept a through-bolt is somewhat more difficult, compared to the typical lever-action or single-shot rifle.

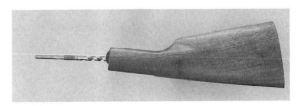

Photograph 13-44: In this view the auger bit is inserted about six inches into the end-to-end hole through the buttstock. This top-to-bottom angle is about right, the other end of the hole will be about one-inch above the bottom buttplate screw hole. Drill this hole only about 9" deep. See text and photograph 13-43.

Remove the dowel, position it alongside the stock at the same angle and to the same depth. Use a grease pencil to mark the side of the stock at the position of the end of the dowel. Extend a line from that point, parallel to the hole you drilled and toward the rear end of the stock. Mark this location with the grease pencil. These marks indicate your starting point and target for the new hole you will drill into the rear end of the buttstock.

Relocate the stock in the vise, with the butt end exposed for drilling. Center punch a good deep hole that is centered, side to side, adjacent to the mark at the back of the side of the stock. Start the drill bit and drill toward the forward mark. Again, a helper is the best course. Lacking that, you can use the bubble-level method noted above. Either way, it should be no problem to correctly intersect the first hole so that the bottom of this new hole is very nearly centered over the through-bolt hole — the hole you drilled from the tang end of the buttstock. However, use caution in drilling this second hole to keep it as nearly centered as you possibly can between the sides of the stock.

Next, install a long-shanked nine-sixteenths inch (9/16") blade or twist-steel drill bit in the drill. Carefully drill along the five-sixteenths inch (5/16") hole, beginning at the butt end of the stock. Proceed until the larger drill bit drills about one-quarter inch past the tang bolt hole. Use due caution to prevent the nine-sixteenths inch (9/16") drill bit from wandering too far from the intended path, which is parallel to the original (5/16") hole.

The bottom of the larger hole in the butt end of the stock forms a seat where a washer on the through-bolt will rest. For structural reasons it is preferable if you use a through-bolt that is as long as is feasible. However, there is very little benefit in having the through-bolt extend closer than to within about four inches from the butt end of the stock. See photograph # 13-45.

At this point the stock is ready to accept a through-bolt. However, you will want to properly seal all the fresh surfaces and you might also want to do a bit of additional skeletonizing while the drill bits are handy. If you do remove additional wood, just try to keep the dividers between any drill holes no less than about one-eight inch (1/8") thick and try to keep the interior surface of any hole at least one-quarter inch (1/4") from the surface of the stock. It is okay if two holes intersect at a point forward in the stock, as long as those holes are not too large in diameter and are not too nearly parallel. One additional caution, be sure none of the holes compromise either the seat that the through-bolt will pull against or any of the screw holes in the stock. Such as holes used for butt pad screws or the sling stud. The last necessary alteration of the buttstock involves drilling the tang bolt hole at least two fractional drill bit sizes larger than the diameter of the tang bolt you will use, which will usually be a one quarter inch shank. Therefore, you should drill the tang bolt hole in the stock to nine thirty-seconds inch (9/32") diameter.

For sealing the newly exposed wood, and any surfaces that were not properly sealed at the factory, which is quite common, I prefer to apply a good coating of Tung oil. I use at least three applications. However, an aerosol epoxy wood finish is a very good option for this application. You can easily spray this product directly into the holes and quite easily achieve a full water-proofing coating of the normally hidden wood surfaces. Whatever method you use, be certain to

Photograph 13-45: Enlarged hole in butt end of stock will form the seat for the washer on the through-bolt. The through-bolt enters the hole that reaches through the stock. See photographs 13-44/45 and see the associated text.

Section 13: The Trouble With Lever-Action and Single-Shot Rifle Stocks, Part II

accomplish a good seal. You have created a tremendous amount of surface area that can transmit a considerable amount of water vapor into or out of the wood in a hurry. That situation will cause dimensional changes in the wood.

Building A Through-bolt For Adapting Tang-Mounted To Through-Bolt-Mounted Buttstock, Two-Piece Stocked Rifles:

While the stock finish is curing, you can begin construction of the through-bolt and anchor. This system is quite simple. It involves a quarter-inch diameter bolt of the correct length, a quarter inch fender (oversize) washer (to fit in the hole in the butt end of the stock) and an extra-long quarter-inch nut with a transverse hole near one end (for the tang bolt to pass through). See photograph # 13-46.

Hardware stores often stock long nuts, which are designed to connect two pieces of all-thread. If you can locate such a pre-made nut, all the better. All you will have to do is drill a transverse one-quarter inch diameter hole, centered, side to side, and about seven-sixteenths inch (7/16") from one end. This is a simple task and I will leave it to you. However, note, since the tang bolt will almost certainly not pass squarely through this hole, you should wobble the drill to produce a hole that is elongated along the long axis of the nut. If you produce a hole that allows the angle of the drill bit to vary by plus-or-minus fifteen degrees (+/–15°) the nut will work fine.

If you cannot locate such a nut or would like to have a stronger anchor for this application, you can easily make your own. Obtain a section of grade-5, seven-sixteenths inch (7/16") bolt shank that is about one-inch (1") long. If necessary, grind one end square to the shank. Mark the center of the square end with a good, deep drill punch indent.

Locate this piece in a bench-mounted vise or a drill press vise. Drill a thirteen sixty-fourths inch (13/64") hole at least five-eighths inch (5/8") deep that is centered on and parallel to the axis of the bolt shank. Use plenty of cutting oil and clear the cuttings from the drill bit flutes often. When this hole is complete, tap it to full depth using a quarter-inch twenty threads-per-inch (tpi) tap ($^1/_4$ x 20, to match the threads on the through-bolt). Use proper thread cutting technique and plenty of cutting oil.

Note, Brownells stocks a $^1/_4$ x40 tap and a matching die. If you are producing your bolt and nut, consider the significant advantage of using this thread. You will need a #2 index drill bit to produce the correct hole size in the nut (0.221"). This thread will dramatically improve the feel when you tighten the through-bolt. However, it will also provide twice the end thrust on the stock at any given through-bolt torque. Use caution to avoid destroying the nut or the tang bolt.

When you have finished this step, relocate the piece and produce a deep drill punch mark seven-sixteenths inch (7/16") from the closed end of this new nut. Drill a transverse one-quarter inch (1/4") hole through the center of the bolt shank at that location. See the above discussion of producing a slot to allow the tang bolt to pass through at an angle. See photograph # 13-47.

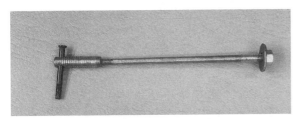

Photograph 13-46: Homemade through-bolt and through-bolt nut. Note the tang screw that is inserted through the nut (to show the transverse hole). This shows how the through-bolt system works. The tang bolt captures the nut. Tightening the through-bolt pulls the nut back, the nut pulls the tang bolt back, the tang bolt pulls the tangs back. Conversely, the hex nut on the through-bolt pushes the washer forward, the washer (which is seated on a shoulder in the stock) pushes the stock forward. When tightened, the bolt is stretched and the stock is compressed. This forms a very solid receiver-to-buttstock bond.

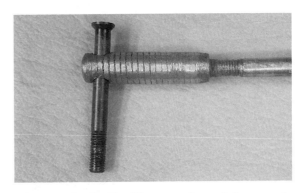

Photograph 13-47: Close-up view of homemade through-bolt nut. Note that hole for tang bolt is elongated so that bolt does not have to pass through nut at a right angle. Also note that this particular bolt is the extended tang bolt supplied with the Lyman tang-mounted aperture sight system for the Marlin Model-336.

Assemble the bolt, washer and nut. Thread the bolt about five-sixteenths inch (5/16") into the nut. Install the assembly in the stock and observe the location of the hole in the nut, compared to the tang-bolt hole. Also note whether or not the bolt head is resting on the washer. If the transverse hole in the nut does not reach the tang-bolt hole, use a longer bolt, or slightly deepen the through-bolt washer seat in the buttstock. If the head of the bolt is not resting on the washer, or is not very close to doing so, shorten the bolt sufficiently to achieve that goal.

Properly fitted, the through-bolt should thread freely about seven-sixteenths of an inch (7/16") into the nut as it tightens the stock to the receiver. That will allow a full-strength connection between the nut and bolt and provide sufficient latitude to accommodate slight errors in measurement, etc.

Building A Modified Tang Bolt For Adapting Tang-Mounted To Through-Bolt-Mounted Buttstock, Two-Piece Stocked Rifles:

On the Marlin lever-action rifle the original tang bolt is a 12x32 threaded piece that is not particularly hard. You can improve the through-bolt attachment system by replacing this factory bolt with a one-quarter inch grade-8 bolt. You will either have to turn down and thread the end of this bolt, to fit the threaded hole in the rifle's lower tang, or modify the rifle's lower tang to accept a one-quarter inch (1/4") bolt.

If you use such a bolt you will also have to enlarge the bolt hole in the upper tang from the existing 0.230" diameter to about 0.245" diameter. The best tool for this is the letter drill bit "D" but a standard one-quarter inch (1/4") fractional drill bit will do. Perhaps surprisingly, on the Marlin, it is not necessary to modify the bolt head recess in the upper tang.

To produce the modified tang bolt you will need to obtain a two and one-half inch (2½") long grade-8 hex-head bolt. Normally, such a bolt will have an unthreaded shank portion that is about one and one-half inches (1½") long. If not, choose a longer bolt, you need that one and one-half inches of unthreaded bolt shank.

Chuck the threaded end of the bolt into a vise-mounted electric drill or a drill press. Then run the drill and lightly file the shank of the bolt, to remove any plating, scale or blemishes. Then use four-ought steel wool (0000), or 320 grit sandpaper, to polish the shank of the bolt. Generally, this work will reduce the shank to 0.245" diameter, or slightly smaller. Do not file the bolt shank any smaller than necessary to clean it up.

The next step is to grind the head of the bolt round and to about 0.305" in diameter. At this diameter the replacement bolt head will just fit into the existing upper tang bolt head recess. The easiest way to grind down the hex head is to chuck the threaded portion of the bolt into a high speed electric drill (minimum 1100 rpm), then use a bench-mounted grinder in conjunction with the running drill. Here a fine water mist from a spray bottle will be needed to prevent overheating the bolt. Keep it cool!

To keep the head of the bolt centered over the shank of the bolt, it is important to run the drill at its top speed and to have the bolt turning the same direction as the grinder (the working side of the bolt is turning up and the grinder wheel is turning down). Carefully grind the bolt head, first round and then smaller. Periodically check for centering between the modified bolt head and the bolt shank. If necessary, stop the drill, then turn the bolt manually to grind on the wide side, as necessary to narrow it. It is critical that the bolt head is centered over the bolt shank.

The last grinding step is to thin the modified bolt head to match the thickness and top profile of the original tang bolt head. Keep the bolt in the electric drill. With both drill and grinder running, you can remove enough of the top of the modified bolt head and shape it to a slight convex surface in a few seconds. Use a mist of water to keep it cool. Often, you can leave the replacement bolt head somewhat thicker than the original (perhaps 0.050"), which might be a good idea. However, any undue excess thickness will result in the replacement bolt head extending above the top of the upper tang.

To polish the ground surfaces, vise the drill. Lock it on and wrap 320 grit sandpaper over the modified bolt head to remove the grinding marks. Then run the sandpaper over the top of the bolt head to polish that area. Finish polishing using four-ought steel wool. Wrap a large wad over the head of the turning bolt and grip it tightly. In a few seconds the bolt head will have a sufficiently polished surface to match the other bolts on the rifle.

Remove the bolt from the drill and mount it in a padded vise. Use a hacksaw to cut a slot, centered across the head of the bolt to about two-thirds the thickness of the bolt head. Keep this slot both centered on the bolt head and square to

Section 13: The Trouble With Lever-Action and Single-Shot Rifle Stocks, Part II

the shank of the bolt. Finish this screwdriver slot with a flat jeweler's file of the proper thickness (about 0.040"). Chuck the bolt in the electric drill and use four-ought steel wool to polish off the burrs formed by the hacksaw and file. Apply cold bluing agent to the polished portions of the bolt.

This completes the head and shank of the bolt. Now you have a decision to make. You can either turn down and thread the end of the modified bolt shank, to fit the threads in the rifle's lower tang (10x32 on the Marlin), or you can drill out the lower tang and rethread that to match full-diameter threads on the modified bolt.

The former approach is a little less disturbing, since you will not have to modify the rifle. The latter is slightly easier, since you will not have to turn down the bolt shank so drastically.

Brownells offer 10x32 dies and both taps and dies in various one-quarter inch (1/4") thread pitches. If you opt for the full-diameter conversion, I strongly recommend using the super-fine machinists thread, $1/4$x40. This thread will provide the strongest possible attachment between bolt and tang.

If you opt to turn down the shank of the bolt for threading to 10x32, begin by marking the bolt shank at a point one and one-quarter of an inch (1$1/2$") from the bottom of the bolt head. The easiest way to do this is to paint that portion of the bolt shank with a permanent marker, then scribe a line through the paint.

Chuck the threaded end of the bolt in a vised drill. The scribed mark should be at least three-quarters inch (3/4") from the drill chuck. Run the drill and use a small bastard-cut file to reduce that three-quarter inch portion of the bolt shank down to 0.210" diameter. Leave a radius at the juncture of the full-diameter shank and this turned-down portion. Apply a taper to the last quarter-inch of bolt, that portion adjacent to the drill chuck, and turn the shank to 0.185" diameter adjacent to the drill chuck. This tapered portion will help line up the threading die, which will help you form threads that are square to the axis of the bolt. Use a hacksaw to cut through the bolt next to the drill chuck.

Carefully file or grind the cut end of the bolt to a rounded profile. Securely mount this bolt in a padded vise. Apply a quality molybdenum-disulfide impregnated cutting oil and carefully thread the turned down portion of the shank with the 10x32 die. Run the threads fully against the transition radius (where the shank changes to full diameter).

Saw the bolt to a shank length of precisely one and one-half inch (1$1/2$"). File the end and sand the cut to remove any burrs. Apply cold bluing to this new tang bolt and to the hole in the upper tang.

If you choose to use the full-diameter bolt, the job is easier. Begin by marking a point on the bolt shank that is one and one-half inch (1$1/2$") from the underside of the bolt head. Apply a permanent marker to the area and scribe a line through that paint.

Chuck the end of the bolt in a vised drill but leave about one-half inch (1/2") of the bolt shank between the chuck and the scribed line. Run the drill and apply a slight taper to the portion of the bolt below the scribed mark, bring the shank down to about 0.215" diameter at a point that is about one-quarter inch below the scribe mark.

Cut the bolt off at the small end of the taper. Carefully file or grind the cut end to a rounded profile. Securely mount this bolt in a padded vise. Apply a quality molybdenum-disulfide impregnated cutting oil and carefully thread the turned down portion of the shank with the $1/4$x40 die (preferred, though any 1/4" thread will do).

Saw the bolt to a shank length of precisely one and one-half inch (1$1/2$"). File the cut end of the shank and sand the cut to remove any burrs.

Drill the lower tang hole to the proper diameter for threading to match the new bolt. In the $1/4$x40 example, the correct index drill bit is the #2 (0.221"). Coarser threads require smaller holes — match the hole to the thread pitch. Proper tap drill sizes are listed in Brownells catalogue, and often with (or on) the tap.

Chuck the correct drill bit into an electric drill and run it through the upper tang, to align it correctly, then drill through the 10x32 threaded hole in the lower tang.

Apply a quality molybdenum-disulfide impregnated cutting oil to the tap. Run it through the upper tang and carefully tap threads into the enlarged lower tang-bolt hole. Apply cold bluing to the new tang bolt, the hole in the upper tang and the threaded hole in the lower tang.

Assembly of the stock using this modified attachment system, is as follows: lubricate the tang surfaces of the stock with graphite or molybdenum-disulfide. Do not use oil — remember these surfaces are sealed and trued with epoxy and oil is the enemy of epoxy. Assemble the bolt, washer and nut (turn the bolt only about three threads into the nut); insert that assembly into the stock; assemble the stock to the receiver; if necessary turn and slide the through-bolt nut to align the slot to the tang hole (either by turning the bolt or by using a small screwdriver to reach through the tang-bolt hole and manipulate the nut), install the tang bolt and tighten it somewhat snug (do not try to tighten it as much as possible but do tighten it until you can feel the receiver tangs begin to squeeze against the stock), tighten the through-bolt until the stock pulls solidly against the receiver at the forward abutment surfaces (if you installed the one-quarter inch (1/4") hardened steel tang bolt you can tighten the through-bolt very tight. If you did not use a hardened steel tang bolt do not tighten the through-bolt very tight (a typical 10-year-old child should be able to loosen it using only a standard screwdriver handle). In the latter instance, to ensure the stock pulls forward solidly, you might want to rap on the rear face of the buttstock using a plastic mallet, then recheck the through-bolt to ensure "snugness".

If your particular rifle does not accommodate such a system, the above discussion should help you understand how you might come up with some different arrangement that will work. For example, I have considered adapting a spacer block between the tangs and running the through-bolt directly into that. Such a system would allow use of a high-strength through-bolt and truly serious tightening, which is certainly desirable. However, that system would require more precise hole drilling. It would also require removal of considerable additional wood, extending the side panels perhaps one inch further back along the stock. Finally, it would be a matter of fitting to combine that method with a means of tightening the tangs against the stock to provide additional rigidity. Therefore, despite the vastly increased difficulty involved, likely the result would not actually prove to be any better than the system I have heretofore detailed in this sub-section.

Special Considerations For Shooter Fit & Functional Handling, Lever-Action & Falling-Block Rifles:

Please refer to the general discussion and photographs covering this subject in *Part I*; specifically, the sub-sections on stock modifications. Note that all the observations made therein are appropriate to lever-action and single-shot rifles. There are, however, two points I would like to address in detail in this sub-section.

First, unlike what is typical in bolt-action rifles, the factories routinely equip lever-action and single-shot rifles with barrel-mounted open sights — in many instances a telescopic sight is either inappropriate or unfeasible. Tang- or receiver-mounted aperture sights are also quite popular on these rifles. Regardless of the particular metallic sights used, you need to adjust the stock fit to take maximum advantage of these, normally, lower-mounted sights. Follow the directions given in *Part I*, as to determining the correct buttstock-to-shooter fit just as you would for a scoped rifle — fundamentally, if you are not automatically looking through the sights when you bring the rifle to bear, the stock does not fit you properly. For hunting rifles this one fact is, perhaps, more important than any particular aspect of the rifle's intrinsic accuracy.

Equally, when mounting a telescopic sight on any rifle with an exposed hammer, telescopic sight positioning and height can be an issue simply because the mounting has to provide for clearance between the scope's ocular and the rifle's hammer. For the same reason, on most single-shot actions, you have to mount the telescopic sight properly to provide adequate clearance for inserting cartridges and extracting empties. Hammer access and chambering access can dictate mounting the telescopic sight higher than would otherwise be desirable. Clearance for power-ring adjustment and other considerations can also necessitate mounting the telescopic sight either forward or back, compared to what might be the most natural mounting location. Any of these can result in the need to raise the cheek piece or alter the stock length. Keep these points in mind when designing the stock — it would be a shame to build a perfect fitting stock, then change sights and discover that the rifle no longer fits!

Another buttstock consideration, which is almost unique to lever-action and falling-block rifles results from the fact that action manipulation requires the shooter to move his trigger finger hand forward as he manipulates the finger-lever to operate the rifle's action. Certain lever-action models require a rather large arc of the finger-lever to achieve action manipulation. On these rifles, it is entirely possible to build a buttstock that feels perfectly comfortable with the rifle at the ready, but which makes it difficult or impossible to work the action without moving the rifle — remember, you have to move your hand several inches forward to work the finger-lever.

Section 13: The Trouble With Lever-Action and Single-Shot Rifle Stocks, Part II

For this reason, it is often desirable to cut the stock for lever-action rifles to give a butt-to-trigger measurement (length of pull) that is one- to two-inches shorter than it would be for any other type of rifle action. For the same reason, even on short-throw lever-action and falling-block rifles, you should consider cutting the stock on the short side, rather than on the long side of your length-of-pull comfort zone. Doing so can significantly ease action manipulation with the rifle at the ready. This is one instance where a too-short stock is a far better choice than a too-long stock. See photograph # 13-48.

In general, when you are standing and holding the rifle in a normal offhand shooting pose, while attired in your hunting garb, if you cannot fully manipulate the finger-lever without straining, the stock is too long. This is a very common condition for lever-action rifles. Further, many gunsmiths and tinkers fail to consider the matter fully. They add a recoil pad without shortening the stock, only to discover that the rifle is no longer properly functional — as the saying goes... "been there, done that!".

The following concepts and the details of the associated modifications are covered in so-titled sub-sections in *Part I*: *Shortening a Buttstock; Lengthening a Buttstock; Adjusting Cheek Piece Height (Drop at Comb); Inertial Recoil Mitigation Devices (Mercury Recoil Suppressers); The Counter-Coil Hydraulic Recoil Absorber; Installation of Recoil Pads; Adjusting Cheek Piece Fit (Drop at Comb); Strengthening Buttstock-To-Receiver Attachment, Remington or Savage Pump-Action Rifles* (portions are applicable to any two-piece stocked rifle)*; Stock Checkering; Stock Refinishing*. The lever-action and falling-block rifles really do not present any special problems in these areas — at least none that I did not address in *Part I*.

However, please note the above discussion concerning the special needs of these types of rifles, owing particularly to: hammer-to-telescopic sight clearance, scope-to-cartridge clearance and finger-lever manipulation concerns. Also note that the tang system used in buttstock attachment on many of these rifles makes it very difficult to alter the stock's drop. It is probably better to simply purchase a custom semi-inletted stock with a raised cheek piece — as are available through Reinhart-Fajen. Finishing one of those is not a difficult matter at all and it affords the opportunity to install fancy wood that properly fits both the shooter to the gun.

Photograph 13-48: Shortening of a factory stock is often necessary. When installing a recoil pad on a lever-action rifle this is particularly important because a rifle that seems to fit properly for offhand shooting might not fit correctly after all. See the text for an explanation of this critical concept.

Section 14: The Trouble With Lever-Action & Single-Shot Receivers, Part II

For a general discussion and photographs of the types of problems that any receiver can have, refer to *Section 3* of *Part I*. In this sub-section we will address specific concerns in any of several lever-action and single-shot rifles. A thorough understanding of principles expressed in *Section 3* of *Part I* and this sub-section should go a long way toward helping you determine what modifications might be beneficial in any similar action. As noted before, we simply cannot offer a complete discussion that is specific to every type of rifle that fits in these categories.

Traditional Chamberings & The Possible Use Of Pistol Primers For Handloads, Lever-Action (And Antique Single-Shot) Rifles:

My experience is sufficient to suggest that those rifles chambered for low- to moderate-pressure cartridges can benefit from the combination of a lighter hammer spring and use of pistol primers. This includes all the traditional lever-action chamberings or originally black-powder loaded rifle cartridges used in these rifles, numbers such as the .218 Bee, .219 Zipper, .22 Savage High Power, .25-20 WCF, .25-35 WCF, .30-30 WCF, .32-20 WCF, .32 Winchester Special, .38-55 WCF, .444 Marlin and .45-70 Springfield come to mind. However, if the pistol primers you try show cratering, try other brands. If cratering persists, consider bushing the firing pin hole in the bolt, as described in *Part I*. See photograph #s 14-1/2.

Do not use pistol primers in full-pressure loads used in modern high-pressure cartridges chambered in these rifles. This short list includes only the .307, .356 and .375 Winchester. In such an application, pierced primers are likely. A pierced primer could release sufficient gas and particulate matter to pose a hazard to the shooter or bystanders. Another likely result of that inappropriate application is blanked primers. In a blanked primer, the pierced portion comes free of the primer cup and enters the firing pin raceway in the bolt. That problem can lead to a jammed firing pin — which equates to the gun going "click" instead of "boom"; refer to the elk hunter story described later (in the sub-section on the cross-bolt "safety" used on newer Marlin and Winchester lever-action Rifles…).

Receiver Modifications & Function Testing Dummy Cartridges, Lever-Action Rifles:

Commonly, there are several areas where it is feasible to improve the rifle's functioning and intrinsic accuracy through minor modifications. In the strict sense of what a receiver is, some of the areas covered in this sub-section might not seem to fit here. However, I will argue that every part of any rifle that acts to feed cartridges is part of the action. Therefore, you will find discussions about clips and tubular magazine parts included in this sub-section.

After making any modification to any part of the rifle's action, you should test the system for functionality. The only safe way to do this in the workshop is with functional dummy cartridges.

I strongly recommend assembling a full complement of dummy cartridges, a sufficient number to fully load the rifle's magazine and chamber. Resize a sufficient batch of cases. One at a time, clamp the cases at the case head in a well-padded vise. Drill through the primer pockets with a drill bit that is slightly larger than primer size (7/32" for large primered cases, 3/16" for small primered cases). Insert bullets to normal overall length and crimp normally. Degrease these tools and paint each one with a bright spray paint — if you know your dummies are red and you insert a brass-colored case when you intend to insert only dummies, you should also notice the dangerous error!

These dummies are an invaluable asset. After any action modification that could in any way alter action functioning, use these *faux* cartridges to verify that the action functions properly. It is simply not safe to use live ammunition for functionality testing.

Receiver Modifications, Tubular-Magazine Lever-Action Rifles:

We will follow this discussion as if we were working on a Marlin Model-336. Where there are significant differences in the work needed on various other Marlin lever-action models or in the various tubular-magazine fed Winchester lever-actions I will attempt to note those points.

Magazine Removal, Tubular-Magazine Lever-Action Rifle:

Use caution in disassembling the magazine; the magazine spring can eject with considerable force. For most such rifles, disassembly of the

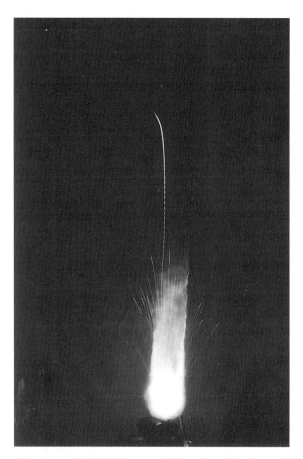

Photograph 14-1: No, my fellow handloaders, all primers are not created equal. This CCI-250 is quite typical of large rifle primers. The ignition energy it produces is far greater than most rifle cartridges require for consistent ballistics. Use of a milder primer can often improve the accuracy of smaller, low-pressure rifle cartridges.

Photograph 14-2: The CCI-300 is a standard Large Pistol primer. Compared to the CCI-250, the CCI-300 produces much less energy. For this reason, it is apt to disturb the bullet less and therefore result in better ballistic uniformity in certain rifle cartridge applications. This primer is also much easier to properly ignite, which can improve ballistic uniformity in loads chambered in rifles with moderate firing pin energy. See the text for a more rigorous description of possible applications. Never use any primer in any handload unless it is specifically called for by the data producer.

Section 14: The Trouble With Lever-Action & Single-Shot Receivers, Part II

magazine tube requires removing several screws. The first screw secures the plug at the front of the tube and screws in from the bottom. The second screw passes sideways through the front barrel band, which secures the magazine tube to the barrel.

Then there are one or more screws securing the fore-end to the barrel, either through a band or a cap. On some systems it is also necessary to remove these screws.

Some rifles, such as the Marlin 1895, lack a separate barrel band. On these, removal of one screw at the front of the magazine tube and the two screws at the front of the fore-end will allow disassembly of the magazine tube. Regardless of the particulars, remove whatever screws are necessary to allow the magazine plug, magazine spring and cartridge follower to be removed from the front of the tube. At this stage, it is not necessary to separate the magazine tube from the rifle. However, you might consider skeletonizing the magazine tube, which I will discuss in a later sub-section. Reducing the weight of the magazine tube will reduce the stress on the magazine tube hangers and might reduce the vibrations the magazine tube can transfer to the barrel. For these reasons any weight reduction step is worth considering.

If you intend to skeletonize the magazine tube, remove the fore-end attachment screw or screws. On rifles with a fore-end band there is one screw that passes sideways through this band. On rifles with a fore-end cap there are two screws, one from each side. Removal of the applicable screws will allow separation of the fore-end band or cap. That allows separation of the fore-end and magazine tube from the rifle.

Cartridge Follower Modifications, Tubular-Magazine Lever-Action Rifles:

Consider the cartridge follower in the tubular magazine. In most Marlin lever-action rifles, this piece is a rather robust chunk of steel. Since this follower only functions to transfer the modest magazine spring pressure to the cartridges, its construction seems unnecessarily heavy for its design purpose. For this reason and because the cartridge follower acts as a sliding hammer in the magazine tube during recoil, you might want to consider lightening this part.

When the bullet begins to accelerate through the barrel, the gun accelerates in the opposite direction. At first, the rifle pulls back, away from the cartridges in the magazine. This action thereby compresses the magazine tube spring. Then, as the rifle stops accelerating backward, the spring decompresses and thereby accelerates the follower and the cartridges contained in the tubular magazine toward the rear of the gun. Shortly thereafter, the cartridges slam against the cartridge lifter in the receiver. Obviously, the lighter the cartridge follower, the less violent this hammering will be.

For this reason, and because it seems reasonable that reducing the weight in the magazine might improve intrinsic accuracy, I advocate reducing the weight of the follower as much as is feasible. Note that on most newer Winchester 94s this part is already a very light steel stamping, there is little to gain here.

Compared to the ubiquitous Marlin Model-336, other models of Marlins have different size magazine tubes. For example (so that it will accommodate the fatter bodied .45-70 cartridges), the Model-1895 Marlin has a larger magazine tube. Other models have smaller tubes to accommodate such cartridges as the .32-20 and .357 Magnum. Therefore, I will not specify sizes in the following discussion. However, these modifications are rather generic, so determining the correct sizes for the associated tools should pose no problem. The basic idea is to skeletonize the follower (and other parts) without compromising the part's fit or function.

There are several basic modifications, each quite simple to understand. The illustration should make the goal quite clear.

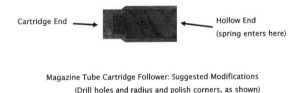

These simple modifications, involving nothing more complicated than drilling a few holes and rounding some edges, can reduce the weight of the typical Marlin follower by as much as 40%, and without weakening it appreciably or reducing its functionality. As a matter of fact, radiusing and polishing the external corners will significantly improve the follower's functioning.

Be certain to polish any drill burrs from both the outside and inside surfaces. Such burrs can interfere with proper functioning. Worse, if those break off and enter the action, jamming could result. Finish this work by applying a good cold bluing agent to the entire follower; this part, which is normally hidden, could rust badly if it is not properly blued.

Assemble the rifle. Fill the magazine and chamber with the functional dummies. Cycle the action to work the entire magazine through the action. Note any unusual functioning either during magazine loading or action cycling. The most likely problem would be a burr on the follower catching on something in the tubular magazine. If necessary, pull the follower from the magazine tube and polish off any offending burrs.

Magazine Tube Skeletonizing, Tubular-Magazine Lever-Action Rifles:

Skeletonizing the magazine tube is also a useful improvement. This work involves: drilling of holes of the proper size and in the proper locations, deburring around those holes (both inside and outside the tube), and rebluing. Be sure to use a sharp drill bit to avoid crushing the thin-walled magazine tube. If possible, consider sizing a hardwood dowel to just fit inside the tube. Install that dowel before proceeding with the drilling operation to prevent crushing of the tube.

Begin by noting the portion of the magazine tube that protrudes in front of the fore-end; for cosmetic reasons, and to limit the opportunity for debris to enter the action, do not drill any holes in this exposed portion of the tube. Measure the outside diameter of the tube. The correct diameter for the skeletonizing holes is approximately two-thirds to three-fourths the outside diameter of the tube. The photograph shows a reasonable hole spacing. However, it is feasible to space the holes closer than is shown in this picture. Just make sure you space the holes sufficiently apart to provide adequate strength in the dividers between the holes.

Also note that it is important not to drill a hole on the side opposite the loading gate and too near the back end of the tube. Drilling a hole in this location can result in jamming during magazine tube loading. The nose of the cartridge you are inserting into the magazine tube, through the loading gate, can catch on the edge of the hole — as the round first enters the magazine tube it is not aligned with the tube. To avoid this problem, simply locate the rearmost hole on that side of the tube at least one cartridge length forward of the rear of the tube. See photograph #s 14-3/4.

It is, perhaps, easiest to drill these holes in two rows at right angles to each other. You might

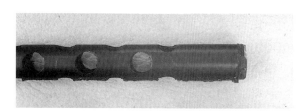

Photograph 14-3: This skeletonized magazine tube from a Marlin Model-1894 (.44 Magnum) shows several accuracy enhancing features. The weight reducing holes also reduce the tube's rigidity, which is probably beneficial. The evident RTV silicone forms a vibration-damping layer between the tube and the barrel and between the tube and the receiver (note end of tube). This tube also has a bevel at the magazine end. This bevel provides fore and aft clearance so the tube will not bind in the receiver. The rearmost transverse skeletonizing hole is located sufficiently forward to prevent the nose of the cartridge that is entering the loading gate from jamming into the opening. By the time the cartridge is inserted sufficiently so that the bullet nose reaches the perforated portion of the tube, the round is fully into the tube and is unlikely to tip.

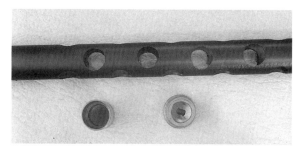

Photograph 14-4: These three-parts are all easily lightened. The magazine tube can be perforated with considerably more holes if those are spaced closer together. <u>Note that the portion of the tube that reaches beyond the fore-end is not perforated.</u> Besides being unsightly, this would allow infiltration of all manner of debris. The drilled holes must be fully deburred. The cartridge follower, lower left, can be drilled with transverse holes and otherwise considerably lightened — see the associated sketch. It is important to round all edges, to provide for smooth functioning. The magazine cap, lower right, can be lightened considerably by drilling into the hidden end with a properly chosen drill bit. Do not drill too deeply here. See the text.

choose to align one row with the vertical axis of the magazine tube and the other with the tube's horizontal axis. However, it might be better to rotate each row forty-five degrees (45°). This would reduce the tendency of the case rims or bullet noses to drag on the holes.

I found that a padded vise on the drill press table worked quite well for aligning the tube as I drilled the holes. Before beginning the drilling, I scribed a line along the top and one side of the area of the tube that rests under the fore-end. I then marked the tube where I wanted each hole and drill-punched each location. I then inserted the tube in the loosely clamped padded drill press vise, aligned the endmost center-punched hole location with the drill bit and drilled through both sides of the tube. By advancing the tube in steps and drilling new holes I was able to complete the task in very short order.

Deburring the holes was a little more complicated. Smoothing the outside of the tube was easy, that required only a bit of work with a file and sandpaper. For the inside, I wrapped a slotted dowel in 150 grit sandpaper and used an electric drill to polish out all the burrs. This step is quite critical, you cannot afford to leave anything that might snag the rim of a cartridge or the follower.

I finished this job by cold bluing the entire worked area, inside and outside. Total weight reduction can amount to about 20% of the unaltered tube's weight, which, by itself is no small consideration — this reduces the recoil forces the magazine attachment system must withstand. Further, since this work will also render the tube more flexible, and therefore less likely to bind on the barrel or hangers, it seems worthwhile. It might even reduce shot-related vibrations in the system.

Reassemble the rifle. Fill the magazine with the dummy cartridges. Notice any hanging that might occur between either the cartridge follower or the cartridges and the magazine tube. Cycle the finger-lever to work the entire complement of dummy rounds through the rifle and verify that the action cycles normally. If necessary disassemble the tubular magazine and remove the burrs you missed the first time through.

Magazine Cap Modification, Tubular-Magazine Lever-Action Rifles:

On the Marlin, the magazine tube cap often contains considerable unnecessary steel. This added weight places more strain on the magazine tube attachment system. It is quite simple to dramatically reduce the weight of this piece.

You will note that the rear of this part is solid steel and extends significantly into the magazine tube. Mark the center of the rear face with a drill punch. Choose a drill bit that is about one-eighth inch smaller in diameter, compared to this rear extension.

Locate the cap solidly in a well-padded vise. Proceed to drill into the center of the rearward extension of the magazine tube cap. Be careful to keep the drill bit parallel to the sides of the cap. Drill the hole until the center of the drill bit just breaks through into the transverse hole, near the front end of the cap. This is the hole that the magazine tube screw enters. Do not drill any further. This simple step can significantly reduce the weight of this hanging part and is, therefore, well worthwhile. See photograph # 14-5.

Reducing Magazine Spring Tension, Tubular-Magazine Lever-Action Rifles:

(If you are considering using this rifle for hunting dangerous game, refer to the following sub-section.)

The next thing to consider is the tubular-magazine spring. Typically, these springs are quite robust. I believe that reducing the spring tension is a worthwhile modification for most shooters, especially those who use these rifles for hunting non-dangerous game or simply "plinking". Lessening spring tension eases loading of the magazine and, moreover, it reduces the effort necessary to manipulate the action.

Photograph 14-5: Close-up view of magazine tube cap from a Marlin Model-1894. Note the hole drilled into the normally hidden end. The attachment screw hole is just breached in the center, the threads of that hole are visible in the bottom of this skeletonizing hole. Do not drill this hole any deeper.

Here is my "sophisticated" method for reducing magazine spring tension. Remove the magazine plug and allow the spring to naturally extend to full length, then ensure the cartridge follower and the other end of the spring are fully inserted to the receiver end of the magazine tube. Measure the amount of spring extending from the magazine tube. Cut the exposed spring at the point that is one coil toward the spring's free end from the mid-point of the exposed portion of the spring.

For example, say that 12" of spring is exposed. Also, that in this relaxed state, the spring has one coil per inch of spring length. In this instance, I would remove 5" of spring [(12"/2)–1"=5"].

After clipping the spring, fashion the new end to match the factory-formed end you have removed. This is quite easy to accomplish using a pair of needle nose pliers. It is only necessary that the free end does not bind in the magazine tube during installation. However, it is also convenient to make the spring symmetrical; if you do that, it will not matter which end you insert into the magazine tube first. Also, for obvious reasons, I advocate rounding the sharp edges of the cut end of any spring. Reassemble the magazine and ensure that it functions properly using the functional dummies.

Load the magazine full of dummy rounds and work the finger-lever slowly to cycle each round through the rifle. Reload the magazine with the dummies and work the finger-lever as fast as you can to cycle each round. Put one dummy in the magazine, point the barrel straight down and open the finger-lever. The follower should push the cartridge fully into the action. If not, you have cut the magazine spring too short — which suggests you did not follow the advice given!

On rifles used solely for plinking, I have often cut the magazine spring very short, fully aware that doing so eases magazine loading and improves action manipulation but that it can also significantly compromise functionality. For a serious hunting rifle such liberties are ill-advised.

Increasing Magazine Spring Tension, Tubular-Magazine Lever-Action Rifles:

If you are planing to use this rifle for hunting dangerous game, consider one of the stronger replacement springs, as offered by Brownells.

Note that these springs do increase the difficulty of loading the magazine and cycling the action. However, in a life-or-death situation, the added functional security offered by the stronger spring might be a critical consideration, at least to some hunters.

If you do consider installation of a stronger magazine spring, follow the same test of manipulation with functional dummies. Do not assume that just because you installed a stronger spring everything has to be okay!

As a counter-example, Marlin lever-action rifles have a ratcheting mechanism on the cartridge carrier, if the spring tension on the cartridge follower is sufficiently high, it might be possible to bind the carrier so tightly that the ratchet would trip and the carrier would not lift! This would be especially likely with a full magazine when using a stronger-than-factory spring. Use the dummy cartridge to verify that this does not happen.

Also, keep in mind that you can compromise between the tension of the factory spring and the tension of the heavier Brownells' spring by clipping a few coils from the latter. My theory would be that if the original spring worked all of the time, using a slightly stronger (10%?) replacement spring might make more sense than using a much stronger (50%?) replacement spring.

There is certainly no law that says you cannot have two magazine springs for the rifle, a light spring dedicated to plinking use and a robust spring for serious hunting work. However, note that you should accuracy and zero test the rifle with the hunting spring; it might not shoot to the same point of impact with each of the two springs. I do not want to even get into the accuracy consequences of a tubular magazine that contains a varying number of live rounds — one less for each subsequent shot. . . . However, rest assured, it is reasonably predictable that each subsequent shot will shoot to a slightly different zero. Refer to the following sub-section.

Accuracy Testing, Tubular-Magazine Lever-Action Rifles:

Generally, these rifles will not shoot as small a group when a string of shots are fired from the magazine as when an equal number of shots are fired by single-loading. The reason relates to changing gun mass, change in balance and differences in barrel vibrations. Often, each shot, beginning with a full magazine, will tend to shoot to a slightly different point on the target. I will refer to this effect as the "shot number variation" syndrome.

Section 14: The Trouble With Lever-Action & Single-Shot Receivers, Part II

Any modification to any part of the tubular magazine system can affect the rifle's accuracy when target strings are fired from the magazine. Some alterations can reduce shot number variation, others can increase shot number variation. Obviously, it is worthwhile to look for alterations that reduce shot number variation.

You might consider firing five full magazines of ammunition to make separate five-shot targets for each shot number. That is, each sequential shot from each full magazine should be fired at a dedicated bullseye. For example, with the typical Marlin Model-336 you would make seven groups, one group for each of the six rounds in the magazine and one for the round in the chamber with a full magazine.

To clarify: load the chamber and fill the magazine once — this is set one (S1). Fire the first shot from S1 (S1-1) at bullseye "A", the second shot from S1 (S1-2) at bullseye "B", the third shot from S1 (S1-3) at bullseye "C", etc. Load the chamber and fill the magazine a second time — this is set two (S2). Fire the first shot from S2 (S2-1) at bullseye "A", the second shot from S2 (S2-2) at bullseye "B" etc. Repeat this until you have fired five shots at each of the seven bullseyes. The tally would be like this: bullseye "A", shots S1-1, S2-1, S3-1, S4-1, S5-1; bullseye "B", shots S1-2, S2-2, S3-2, S4-2, S5-2, etc.

Then locate the approximate center of each of these groups. Most likely, you will find that each group is centered slightly differently, compared to your aiming bullseye for each group.

Alterations of the magazine spring (and the other modifications we have or will address in these sub-sections) can work to increase or decrease these variations. Your goal is to decrease the differences. With careful tuning you can achieve this goal. For example, on a fully-skeletonized Marlin 1894 chambered in .44 Magnum, these weight saving alterations worked to essentially eliminate shot-to-shot variations, at least with heavy cast bullet loads. This rifle demonstrates very little shot number variation with such loads.

This metallic-sighted rifle will routinely put all nine shots, beginning with a full magazine and a fully loaded chamber, into a group that is less than one and one-half inches (1½") at fifty yards. Since I would not use it on game beyond one-hundred and fifty yards, this accuracy is certainly sufficient. This rifle demonstrates what can be achieved with a bit of tinkering.

Your results will most likely vary. You will have to do some testing to see what alteration reduces shot number variation. The good news is that it is relatively inexpensive to replace any altered part, should that alteration prove to have increased shot number variation.

General Considerations Of Moving Parts & The Modern Cross-Bolt Safety, Tubular-Magazine Lever-Action Rifles:

Inside the receiver there are several articulated parts. In the Marlin you will find the following: finger-lever, finger-lever detent, loading gate, cartridge carrier, carrier ratchet (or pawl), locking lug, ejector, bolt, hammer, hammer strut, trigger, trigger sear, trigger interlock, firing pin (two pieces), extractor, and several springs. Newer models include a damnable cross-bolt safety — owing to liability concerns, I will not suggest any modifications for this confounded mechanism. See photograph # 14-6.

However, I will note that this piece can be a real problem for those who grew up using traditional lever-action rifles. The problem follows from these two facts: the shooter cannot see, or easily feel, the safety button when the rifle is at battery; when the trigger is pulled with the safety "on", the hammer falls with an audible click that sounds almost exactly like the fall of the hammer on a dud cartridge or an empty chamber!

Photograph 14-6: Lower-left, in this picture, is the newfangled cross-bolt safety on a Marlin Model-336. Winchester has incorporated a similar device on their lever-action rifles. See the text for an explanation of a significant problem that this mechanism poses to the hunter. Note the line of contact over the point of this hammer. This suggests that the bolt and hammer are properly fitted and polished for minimum friction and the easiest possible action manipulation.

One can easily cycle through several cartridges as that fine spike bull elk peacefully moves to "safety". Here is how this goes: novice hunter sees small legal bull elk; hunter works action to chamber cartridge; forgetting "safety" is "on", hunter takes careful aim at stationary broadside small trophy bull elk; hunter carefully squeezes trigger, sights indicated perfect hold and hunter knows the nice sized trophy bull elk is his; the rifle goes "click"!; big trophy bull elk hears rifle go "click" and looks toward hunter; frantic hunter assumes a dud cartridge and cycles action as fast as possible; ever-growing trophy bull elk sees hunter's motions and prepares to exit the scene, *post haste*; hunter (now developing the first symptoms of a serious case of buck fever) tries to take aim at world-class trophy bull elk, but finds gun has developed world-class wobble; hunter finally gets sights to settle down a bit, just as monster bull elk launches into full run; hunter manages the perfect lead on world's biggest bull elk ever, and (miraculously) carefully squeezes trigger just when sights are where they should be; gun goes "click", hunter watches what he is now convinced must have been the biggest bull elk in the history of the universe disappear into timber and "safety". Hunter begins to shake and weep uncontrollably. Sitting down to calm himself, he notices rifle's "safety" is "on". Hunter realizes that "safety" worked perfectly ... for the elk! Hunter cusses all lawyers. Hunter takes up golf.

Excepting the interesting phenomenon of the "ever growing elk that got away" effect, this scenario almost happened to a friend of mine. However, he did have time for a third try, and he did finally remember the safety, and he somehow managed to maintain his cool (admirably) and he therefore did kill his first bull elk. No world-class trophy but a regulation four-point model, his first elk. I suspect that if my friend had not had time for a third try he would very likely remember that elk as the biggest bull that ever walked the face of the earth. Since he is not quite the type, I doubt, however, that he would have taken up golf! Nevertheless, you can bet lock, stock and barrel my friend has some very interesting and colorful things to say about the cross-bolt safety on his lever-action rifle.

Winchester's New Transfer-Bar Safety System, Lever-Action Rifles:

Note, owing to a sophisticated and extremely functional transfer bar safety mechanism, it is not feasible to alter the hammer system on newer Winchester lever-action rifles in any way. Since this is a rebounding hammer safety system, proper functioning of the passive safety mechanism, as well as proper primer ignition, rely upon the existence of a proper and delicate balance between the component masses and spring tensions used in this system.

While this mechanism is exemplary for its safety innovations, it is a nightmare for action manipulation. It, necessarily, delays initial hammer cocking until the finger-lever has opened past the point where good mechanical advantage exists. Therefore, even with the best polishing of all friction surfaces, it is impossible to reduce the effort required to cycle the action on these rifles below what I would call, ridiculously difficult. Perhaps you can comfortably cycle the action on a new Winchester Model-1894 without removing the rifle from your shoulder, I certainly cannot.

Nevertheless, the only modification I can recommend for the trigger and hammer system on these models is a thorough polishing of frictional contact points. Make no other alterations of any kind, please.

Hammer & Firing Pin Modifications, Tubular-Magazine Lever-Action Rifles:

Returning to the receiver, most of the modifications I will discuss here involve the simple processes of polishing friction surfaces. However, here I will also cover modifications to the hammer and firing pin that are potentially particularly beneficial in reducing lock-time, improving reliability and improving the rifle's intrinsic accuracy.

There is an ideal relationship between the weight of the hammer and the weight of the firing pin. If these two pieces were properly matched, when the hammer hit the firing pin, the hammer would stop rotating and the firing pin would take on all the momentum and energy the hammer had been carrying at the moment of contact. If the hammer were traveling in a straight line when it hit the firing pin, this would seem to make it quite simple to modify the hammer and firing pin to provide maximum ignition energy, the correct mass relationship would be when the two pieces were equal in weight.

However, the hammer is not moving linearly but is rotating; therefore, the rotational inertia of the hammer is the characteristic that should match the linear inertia of the firing pin. Owing to its complex mass distribution (shape), calculating the rotational inertia for the hammer is very difficult. Further, it so happens that the hammer spring's mass also enters into the picture. It is, therefore, quite difficult, and certainly beyond our ability here to describe or calculate the correct hammer and firing pin mass for any particular lever-action rifle in either an exact or an explicit way.

Worse, most traditional lever-action rifles have a two-piece firing pin. These rifles incorporate a small interposing transfer safety pin that interlocks with the bolt to prevent the rifle's firing if the locking lug is not fully engaged in the bolt recess — an extremely worthwhile safety feature. On such (two-piece) firing pin systems, calculation of the ideal hammer and main firing pin weight relationship would be too complicated to even consider here (as a matter of fact, that calculation is essentially impossible!).

Despite these limitations, we can note that reducing the mass of both the hammer and the firing pin will reduce the rifle's lock-time and the resulting disturbance to the rifle during the hammer's fall. Weight reduction of the hammer involves drilling holes in appropriate places to reduce its mass without compromising its fit, function or strength. Since most hammers are surface hardened, you will have to obtain carbide drill bits to proceed with any of these modifications.

Special safety note: whenever drilling with a carbide drill bit, follow the instructions included with the drill bit; do not try to cut too fast and always wear safety goggles to avoid getting sharp steel shards on or in your eyes! Also note, tungsten carbide is very hard and tough but it is brittle as glass; if you push too hard, you <u>will</u> shatter the drill bit. Also note, do not use cutting oil; carbide is very susceptible to thermal shock. The presence of oil can increase the potential for the fragile carbide to shatter. Proceed slowly to avoid heating the hammer. Drill a little, then remove the drill bit from the work and allow it to cool naturally. Spray water onto the hammer to keep it as cool as is feasible — do not get water on the carbide drill bit.

The included idealized illustrations and photographs (*Part I*, Remington Pump Hammer Modifications) show typical areas where it is safe to reduce the hammer's mass through drilling.

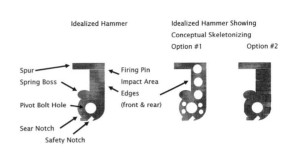

Option No. 1 Notes: Drill holes sideways through the hammer, as indicated in conceptual drawing No. 1. Avoid drilling holes close to the following areas: hammer spring boss, sear notch, safety notch, firing pin impact area, any front or rear surface or the hammer pivot hole.

Option #2 Notes: Drill holes on the hammer extension from the rear of the hammer, as indicated in conceptual drawing #2. Such holes should not penetrate fully through the far (front) surface, as indicated. These holes should not be larger in diameter than two-thirds the hammer's width (side-to-side at each hole's location).

General Note: There is no reason you cannot combine these techniques to achieve maximum mass reduction while maintaining sufficient hammer integrity.

Important Concepts: The value of removing a unit of mass is proportional to the square of the distance that mass is from the hammer's pivot point. Obviously, removing one unit of mass near the hammer spur does a lot more good than removing one unit of mass near the pivot. If the hammer's center of balance was at the pivot point, its rotation would not result in a torque on the rifle. (The spring's push against the rifle would be essentially linear.) Therefore, removing material on the side opposite the hammer spur does reduce lock-time but at the expense of an increase in torque on the rifle. Consequently, it is not particularly desirable to remove material from that area of the hammer.

Firing pin mass reduction is quite simple. On a Marlin you can remove the firing pin from the bolt by driving out two roll pins; one retains the safety firing pin, the other retains the main firing pin. With removal of the main firing pin from the bolt body a flat spring will also come free. Note this spring's location and orientation during this disassembly. (This small flat spring actuates the safety firing pin.)

Note that the main firing pin has a flat side where it passes through the finger-lever slot in the bolt, this flat area provides clearance for the finger-lever and is also cut so that the finger-lever bolt boss positively retracts the firing pin as the finger-lever unlocks and opens the action. There is also a flat side for clearance for the retaining roll pin. This elongated flat also provides the requisite firing pin travel and limits that travel. Finally, at the rear top of the pin there is a third flat area, which has a transverse notch at the front end. This area provides clearance for the firing pin safety spring. The notch at the end of this flat retains that spring to the main firing pin. Do not alter the firing pin in, or immediately adjacent to, these areas. See photograph # 14-7.

To lighten this (or any similar) firing pin, chuck it into an electric drill. Insert only a sufficient portion of the pin's cylindrical end to facilitate the pin's alignment to and proper hold in the drill chuck. Clamp the electric drill in a bench vise so that the firing pin is accessible. When you are ready to begin the work, lock the drill in the "on" position (using the trigger-lock mechanism). Set the speed adjustment so the drill is turning at a moderate speed. Set the direction so the top side of the firing pin is turning toward you. Use a coarse-cut round file that is of about the same diameter as the firing pin to remove most of the excess material.

While holding the big end of the file toward you, push the file over the top of the firing pin to produce rounded grooves in the cylindrical portion of the firing pin. These grooves should only be applied in the areas between the flat-sided portion of the firing pins. Be sure to leave a full-diameter section of firing pin adjacent to each of the factory flats on the pin and to not alter the pin along the flat sections. Finally, leave a full-diameter ring between each of these grooves. These features are necessary to limit the firing pin's flexure (bending) — bending can lead to breakage. See the illustration.

File these grooves to a depth of about one-third the firing pin's diameter — the thinnest portion at the middle of each groove should be about one-third of the original diameter of the firing pin. Begin producing these grooves in that portion of the cylindrical shank that is furthest from the drill.

Application of penetrating oil on the file will help keep it free of chips. Apply modest pressure to the file. As noted above, push it away from you (small end foremost) over the top of the firing pin as the pin's top surface turns toward you. This process will complete the necessary grooves within a few minutes. Again, be careful not make the grooves too deep.

After finishing this filing operation, wrap 150 grit, wet-or-dry corundum paper over a dowel of the proper diameter. With the drill running, sand the grooves free of all filing marks. This step will reduce any stresses imposed during filing and will also reduce the chance for stress fractures related to sharp grooves in the surface of the steel. You might choose to go one step further and polish all grooves to about three-hundred twenty (320) grit; this is a good idea but is less valuable than the initial sanding to (about) 150 grit. The illustration and photograph show the desired goal.

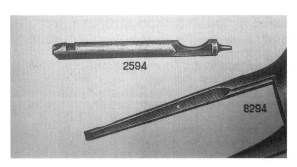

Photograph 14-7: This line drawing from the 1916 Winchester catalogue clearly identifies the firing pin for the Model-1894 Winchester rifle. It is possible and desirable to lighten this pin. See the text and sketches for an explanation of the purpose and procedure.

It is neither feasible nor desirable to alter the safety interlock firing pin in any way.

The last step in firing pin and hammer modification is to use a medium-grit Cratex polishing wheel to remove any burrs or high spots from around any holes you drilled in the hammer. This chamfering is beneficial for handling, action smoothness and stress mitigation — sharp edges are prone to stress concentrations, therefore rounded edges are stronger.

Section 14: The Trouble With Lever-Action & Single-Shot Receivers, Part II

To finish the hammer work, polish the surface where the bolt rides over it during the cocking operation. I take this surface to a mirror finish using the finest Cratex wheel followed by a felt wheel impregnated with jeweler's rouge. Since the hammer is made from hardened steel, it is easy to polish its surface to a very bright finish and that finish will stand up to the rigors of long hard use. There is no such thing as too much polishing on this high-load friction surface.

Alterations to hammer and firing pin on other lever-action rifles are similar. Always make certain that you do not weaken any stress areas or remove any functional portion of either the firing pin or the hammer when making such alterations.

Modifications Of Hammer Spring Tension, Tubular-Magazine Lever-Action Rifles:

Before considering any hammer spring alteration, complete any hammer and firing pin alterations. Refer to the previous sub-sections.

On Marlin and older Winchester lever-action rifles that you use solely for informal target practice ("plinking"), you might consider reducing the hammer spring tension. However, as noted above, on the new transfer-bar safety equipped Winchester lever-action rifles, no such alteration is feasible: do not alter the trigger or hammer system on those guns in any way.

On some older rifles, hammer actuation comes through a leaf spring. The only correct way to reduce hammer spring tension on these rifles is to thin the spring along its edges. Be certain to maintain a proper taper. A properly tapered leaf spring bends everywhere, and progressively, along its length as the working end is pushed — the farther from the dead end (the fixed, or attachment, end) you look, the farther the spring bends. The rate of progressive bending is constant.

For example, when you cock the hammer on a rifle with a properly designed leaf spring, the spring's deflection everywhere along its length is in direct proportion to the square of the distance between that point and the anchor point (at least this relationship is true to a first approximation). At the one-fourth point (from the anchor), the spring will move one-sixteenth as far as it does at hammer; at the one-half point, one-fourth as far, etc.

This (proper) ratio of deflection indicates two things: first, every portion of the spring is equally stressed, everywhere along its length (it will last as long as possible); second, for the amount of spring tension involved, the spring is delivering the most energy possible combined with the shortest possible lock-time. These are both desirable goals.

You can achieve these goals by adjusting the thickness and often the width of the spring. Obviously, the spring's cross sectional area should taper smoothly from the anchored end to the working end. By careful observation during hammer cocking, you can determine if any portion of a leaf spring is not bending properly. You should thin or narrow those areas that do not bend sufficiently. However, note that any such work will reduce total hammer energy and increase lock-time, so do not make any such alteration unless the system can tolerate that result — such adjustments are only valuable as a means of properly reducing hammer spring tension. See the following discussion covering ignition energy.

Coil springs, as are found on most modern rifles, are much easier to deal with: simply shorten the spring slightly. However, use caution here; these springs are typically of the high spring rate, low preload variety. This means that a slight reduction in the spring's length results in a large reduction in the hammer's energy. It is very easy to go too far here. Reducing hammer energy too much results in an unreliable rifle.

Reducing hammer spring tension also increases lock-time, which is a big argument against this approach. However, this alteration also reduces the torque resulting from the hammer's rotation and the vibrations induced by the hammer's impact with the firing pin and bolt. Therefore, despite the increased lock-time, hammer spring tension reductions often improve working accuracy. Obviously, this modification involves something of a compromise. Owing to the general improvement in action manipulation smoothness, I prefer to reduce hammer spring tension as much as is feasible without significantly compromising ignition dependability.

If you anticipate this alteration, I can only suggest buying several nominally identical replacement springs and doing some tinkering. For example, with two replacement springs in hand, place one aside as the "final assembly" spring. Use the other as a sacrificial "test" spring. (Save the original spring for a rainy day, like a hunt in Alaska....) The idea is to sequentially shorten the test spring until it is demonstrably too short to provide reliable ignition and then shorten the final assembly spring appropriately less.

Shortening these springs is, perhaps, easiest to achieve by grinding one end shorter using a bench-mounted grinding wheel and plenty of water. Do not allow the spring to heat sufficiently for the surface to discolor. That will kill the spring's temper and ruin any portion of the spring that gets so hot. The best bet is to keep the end of the spring immersed in a water mist while you grind the end away. Go slowly here.

You will also need dummy cases loaded only with a primer and, optionally, tissue paper to deaden the report. I prefer to trim off the case neck and shoulder from several cases (at least three), this eases insertion of tissue and clearly identifies these cases as test blanks.

Begin by shortening the test spring slightly. Grind off, perhaps, one-half of one coil. Reinstall the spring and spring retainer back into the unloaded rifle — it is neither necessary nor desirable to reinstall the buttstock.

Cock the hammer. Use a grease pencil to mark the upper tang to indicate where the end of the hammer spur rests. Then measure the spacing between the top of the tang to the underside of the hammer spur (a dial caliper works well for this). On a Marlin this is about one-tenth inch (0.1"). Lower the hammer fully against the bolt. Then measure the distance from the grease pencil mark on the tang to the end of the hammer spur. On the Marlin this is just less than one and one-half inch (about 1.45"). This suggests a linear travel of the end of the spur of about one and thirty-five one-hundredths inch (1.35"). The goal is to produce a jig that will limit the hammer's energy during the subsequent hammer ignition energy test. I prefer a test energy no greater than 90% of the hammer's normal, full-cock energy. If this (90%) energy will routinely fire a primer, I am confident that the 100% energy delivered by the fully cocked hammer will always do the job. The best way to achieve a consistent reduced energy test is to interpose a spacer that prevents the hammer from reaching its full-cock notch.

For the Marlin, make a small wooden spacer that is one-quarter inch (1/4") thick. A section of one-quarter inch hardwood dowel works splendidly for this spacer. For each primer test, insert this piece between the hammer spur and the tang, as depicted in the illustration.

The dowel will keep the hammer from moving the last 0.15" of its normal travel (0.25"x0.10", the cocked hammer normally rests 0.1" from the tang). The hammer will then only fall 1.20" compared to 1.35" (the normal fill-cocked drop) — 89% as far.

Marlin Hammer Spur (typical) With Test Jig Attached

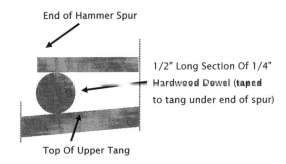

Note that with this jig in place it will be impossible to fully open the action. Therefore, on some rifles you will have to remove the jig to chamber and to remove each test case — this depends upon the particular action type and upon how short you made the test blanks.

Also note that primers are very loud devices; wear hearing protection. Also, to muffle the substantial report, stuff a good wad of tissue paper into each test blank.

Note that primer byproducts are toxic and there is also a hazard of fire, especially when using the tissue wadding. Take the appropriate precautions.

Finally, be sure to properly clean the rifle's chamber and barrel after finishing this test, primer residues are very bad actors under these circumstances and you must positively verify that you leave no tissue paper in the barrel!

Test the hammer's energy in the following manner: prime three of the special (shortened) test cases with rifle primers; in turn, chamber each primed-only test case; install the jig under the hammer spur, as depicted; point the rifle in a safe direction; while holding the trigger back, cock the hammer until the hammer spur hits the spacer; slip your thumb back over the rear end of the hammer spur, allowing the hammer to fall unobstructed (but keep the trigger fully pulled).

If the result of this protocol is consistently popped primers, the spring is probably sufficiently strong. In that instance, shorten the test spring one more stage, perhaps one-quarter of one coil, and repeat this test.

Continue this shortening and testing procedure until you get one or more misfires in three test blanks. Then, simply shorten the "final-assembly" spring to a length equal to the test spring at the shortest test length where reliable 100% primer pops occurred at the 90% hammer energy level.

For example, say that after you have ground one and one-half coils from the sacrificial hammer spring, in quarter-coil steps, you get one misfire from the three test primers in this test. Then you should shorten the "using" spring one and one-quarter coils.

Assuming the two springs were actually equal in strength and that you did the test carefully and as described here, there would be an exceedingly small chance that you would ever get misfires with the "using" spring and the same brand and lot of primers. Therefore, by carefully following this regimen, you should be able to reduce hammer spring tension without significantly compromising reliable ignition.

However, as alluded, there is one caveat: not all primers require the same firing pin energy for reliable ignition. Different primer brands, production lots and types (Magnum, Standard, Benchrest or Military Specification) often have significant differences in threshold ignition energy. For this reason, the above procedure is subject to producing a gun that will not necessarily reliably fire with <u>any</u> ammunition brand or (in handloads) <u>any</u> primer type you might use. I am aware of no good way around this problem excepting either testing all likely primers (egad!), or sticking to the test primer type for use in all serious working ammunition.

For example, I recently discovered that a Model-336 Marlin I had modified in this manner would not reliably fire ammunition loaded with some very old (not even available since about 1975) Alcan primers I once loaded. This rifle has produced completely reliable ignition when using every other brand of primer. Nevertheless, this is the sort of limitation that can result from tinkering with hammer spring tension — in an effort to try to absolutely minimize hammer related torque and vibrations while improving action manipulation. As with so many things, hammer spring tension is a compromise.

Further, I should note that reducing hammer spring tension will almost certainly reduce the ballistic uniformity of any given ammunition. This is another trade-off. Reduced ballistic uniformity will certainly increase the load's vertical stringing. However, since shooters seldom use conventional lever-action rifles against truly long-range targets, this seems a minor concern.

In any case, whether this alteration will improve accuracy for you in your rifle is a question to settle at the range. It is a simple matter to fire groups with each of the two springs (original and modified) in place. Were I hunting dangerous game with such a rifle, I think I would install the original full-strength spring before departing into the wilderness. In that situation, I will gladly sacrifice the last modicum of accuracy or ease of action manipulation, for a bit of peace of mind — any day.

Deburring The Hammer And Hammer Spring Strut, Tubular-Magazine Lever-Action Rifles:

Once you have the hammer spring tension where you want it, it is also worthwhile to look for burrs or other obvious friction points on the hammer spring strut. Polish any such areas to a mirror finish; the medium Cratex wheel on a moto (Dremel) tool works very well for this sort of polishing.

Then use the same tool to polish any grinding burrs from the shortened end of the hammer spring. Make sure the hammer strut slips freely through this spring. Usually, you should install the end you ground next to the hammer.

I also note the sides of the hammer; any shiny or scratched areas there suggest burrs in the receiver channel. Polish those out using the same Cratex wheel. Generally, a simple radiusing at the entrance to this channel will remove all such friction points. However, it is a good idea to paint the sides of the hammer with a permanent marker, Dykem or the like, reassemble the gun and work the action several times, letting the hammer fall on the empty chamber. (By first letting the hammer down fully by hand you can push the firing pin forward and thereby eliminate the hammer-damaging shock such dry-firing would otherwise cause.) See photograph # 14-8.

If the paint on the sides of the hammer shows fresh marring, pull the hammer out and polish the inside edges of the channel until you have removed the offending high spots or burrs. This work completes the recommended modifications to the hammer system.

Trigger & Interlocking Trigger-Safety Modifications, Marlin & Winchester Lever-Action Rifles:

Moving to the trigger, there is only one alteration that seems advisable and worthwhile. You might choose to <u>slightly</u> lighten the trigger spring's tension. At the same time, on traditional lever-action rifles it is possible to slightly reduce the spring tension on the trigger interlock safety (this is the piece that interposes the trigger and the frame, preventing the trigger from releasing the sear latch, before the shooter has fully closed the finger-lever — and locked the action). Use extreme caution in both of these alterations: your safety, and that of others, depends upon your cautious approach to any modifications entertained here. If in any doubt... have a professional do the work.

Since custom springs are not readily available and because the spring that tensions the trigger and the trigger safety interlock, on modern version of these rifles, is a rather complex wire spring form, it is not feasible to fundamentally alter the spring or to fashion a new one from a lower spring tension material. How then to modify this spring's tension?

The only viable method I have found involves reducing the preload on the existing spring arms. You can accomplish this by simply over-bending the spring arm(s). However, use caution. As with the hammer spring, this spring is of the high spring rate, low preload variety; a slight alteration of the spring's untensioned geometry results in a large difference in the pressure it applies when in use.

Proceed by trial and error. If you get the tension too light, it is simple enough to bend the spring back. However, if you have gone back and forth several times, you should consider replacing the spring. Factory replacement springs are dirt cheap and readily available.

I like to bring the interlocking safety tension down to a point where it does not appreciably add to the trigger spring tension as the trigger pushes against the interlocking safety tab. Test this by fully closing the finger-lever (with an empty chamber), hold the hammer fully back against the hammer spring and pull the trigger through its full travel. You should be able to feel a slight increase in trigger tension as the trigger encounters the safety interlock. The spring should just apply any tension when the safety tab is in the interlock position (whenever you have not fully closed the finger-lever). However, if you make this modification it is increasingly important that you deburr the safety interlock and then keep the area reasonably free of grit and debris. The lighter this spring tension the less "grunge" it will take to render this useful safety device inoperable.

Correct minimum tensioning for the trigger spring is more difficult to explain. I can tell you that on each of three Marlin rifles I have on hand I have modified the trigger spring to achieve the following no-load spring tension (finger-lever closed, hammer held back, trigger just begins to move against spring): about 8 ounces. With no other modification, this adjustment usually gives a trigger pull of about 4 pounds. On Winchesters and other rifles the proper no-load trigger spring tension might vary considerably. Also, on the new transfer-bar passive-safety Winchesters, do not attempt to reduce trigger pull below about 5 pounds. Do not attempt to reduce trigger pull let-off below about 4 pounds on any hunting rifle or any rifle with a standard single trigger system. Again, safety is a paramount consideration. See photograph # 14-9.

Excepting polishing the friction surfaces of the interlocking trigger safety mechanism, I have never found any other trigger, sear or hammer sear notch modification either necessary or desirable on any traditional lever-action rifle. If you believe such modifications might be neces-

Photograph 14-8: The areas on the side of this Marlin lever-action rifle's hammer clearly identify places where it is rubbing in the receiver channel as it drops. To improve consistency and reduce spurious vibrations, polish these surfaces and remove the offending burs in the receiver. See the text.

Section 14: The Trouble With Lever-Action & Single-Shot Receivers, Part II

sary, refer to the related sub-section in *Part I* (where I explained correct sear and sear notch geometry). If in doubt, pay a professional!

As a final step, reblue all surfaces of the hammer, trigger and trigger interlock, as necessary, to restore the original finish. This corrosion-limiting step is certainly worthwhile, especially on these visible and critical mechanisms.

Bolt Modifications, Tubular-Magazine Lever-Action Rifle:

Next we will consider bolt modifications. Here there are several basic types: various Marlin models use either the superior round bolt or the traditional square bolt; Winchester bolts are somewhat more complex in design and are always rectangular in basic plan. Regardless of these differences, the basic goal is to polish and deburr all friction surfaces. Again, the Cratex abrasive wheels are the tool of choice.

There are several areas where polishing can significantly reduce friction during action manipulations. It is also useful to slightly alter the cocking ramp on the bolt so that the hammer rides along a line on the bolt, instead of a surface — less contact area, less friction. See photograph # 14-10.

To modify the cocking ramp, remove the bolt from the rifle. On the Marlin this requires only the removal of the finger-lever pivot screw — open the bolt slightly and slide the finger-lever from the bottom of the action. The bolt then slides out of the back of the receiver. Note that the ejector will also come free of the receiver.

Affix the bolt in a padded vise with the underside up and accessible. Using a smooth single-cut file, <u>slightly</u> bevel each side of the cocking ramp until only the very middle (side-to-side) remains untouched by the file. Use caution here to avoid removing too much material, the hammer's failure to cock during action manipulation is the ultimate result of that mistake. I repeat, file at a slight angle to create a bevel on both sides along the length of the bolt-mounted cocking ramp but do so without touching the center of said ramp — when the filed surfaces <u>almost</u> meet along the front-to-rear centerline of the original surface of this raised portion of the bolt, quit filing. See photograph #s 14-11/12.

When you have done this, use a coarse Cratex wheel to polish the center of the cocking ramp, the filed surfaces and the back end of the bolt, where it pushes against the hammer as you open the bolt. Polish until you have removed all file or tooling marks. Then polish the entire center portion of the ramp with the medium, then the fine Cratex wheels. It is desirable to bring this area to a mirror finish with a jeweler's rouge impregnated felt wheel. Again, you cannot polish these surfaces too well — the shinier the better.

Next, look for any exterior surfaces of the bolt showing significant surface marring, wear or abrasion. If these exist, try to identify the responsible areas in the receiver. If possible, use an appropriate Cratex tool and polish the offending

Photograph 14-10: Here I am in the early stages of modifying the bolt cocking ramp on a Marlin Model-336. I have painted the hammer's cocking surfaces using a permanent marker (firing pin impact zone, the radiused area leading to the flat in front of the spur and the flat in front of the spur). I then cycled the action several times. Note that the bolt has only touched about the middle one-third of the radius area of the hammer. A modicum of additional forming could slightly reduce cocking friction by narrowing the portion of the bolt that rubs over the hammer during action opening (with the hammer uncocked). However, the indicated condition is sufficient for my needs. See the text for a full discussion.

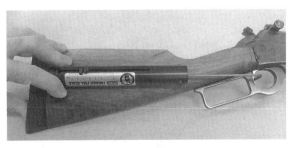

Photograph 14-9: The recording RCBS Deluxe Trigger Pull Scale is an invaluable asset. Note that this highly customized Marlin Model-1894 .44 Magnum chambered rifle has a trigger let-off of $3^{1}/_{4}$ pounds. However, I cannot recommend that anyone try to reduce the trigger pull on any lever-action rifle below about 4 pounds, about 5 pounds on the new transfer-bar safety equipped Winchesters.

surface until you have removed the burr. At the same time, slightly round off any sharp edges. You can polish the bolt but this destroys the attractive factory finish (found on the Marlin round bolt). If you do polish the bolt, consider polishing the entire exterior to the same mirror appearance. However, use caution to avoid removing any more metal than is absolutely necessary. That will increase tolerances, which is generally counter to the goal of improving intrinsic accuracy. It is only necessary to polish the tops of the high spots.

At the same time, note that there is little benefit in polishing the bolt if you do not polish the bolt raceway to eliminate burrs and provide for a glass-smooth surface in which the bolt can work. However, polishing inside the raceway is difficult and requires considerable patience and the use of several specially-shaped polishing wheels. Considering that these steps will inevitably increase the amount of clearance in the bolt-to-receiver fit, I can recommend neither, unless combined with a plating process to reduce clearance and tighten up the action. We will cover one such, most desirable, plating process, in *Part III*.

On the Marlin, there is a channel along the normally hidden side of the bolt where the extractor runs. Polishing this channel (and the corresponding surfaces of the extractor) can dramatically reduce friction in the action. Be careful not to widen this channel. Owing to its narrow dimensions, this channel is not easy to get into with any standard power polishing tools. However, it is quite easy to polish using the proper flat jeweler's file. For a finishing touch, wrap a piece of 600- or 800-grit corundum paper over the narrow edge of a thinner file. This makes a fine sanding block. In a few minutes you can bring the entire working length of the channel to a mirror finish. See photograph # 14-13.

We have covered the extractor elsewhere. However, note that you should polish the leading edge of the extractor, which (when necessary) snaps over a chambered cartridge, to a mirror finish. Cratex wheels and a jeweler's rouge impregnated felt wheel are in order. See photograph # 14-14.

Photograph 14-11: Marlin Model-336 bolt. This view shows the rear bottom of the bolt. The cocking ramp is the surface that is painted. Note the narrow line of contact between the bolt and the hammer, as indicated by the thin burnished line near the centerline of the bolt. See photograph 14-12 and text.

Photograph 14-13: Marlin Model-336 bolt. Note the longitudinal slot. Polishing this slot can dramatically reduce action manipulation force. Note the thin film of black material in this slot. This is NECO's Moly slide, painted on with a cotton swab. This 60% molybdenum-disulfide synthetic based lubricant can dramatically reduce sliding friction.

Photograph 14-12: Marlin Model-336 hammer. Note the thin shiny line centered on the radius. This indicates a minimal friction surface that results from a properly shaped cocking ramp on the bolt. See photograph 14-11.

Photograph 14-14: Marlin Model-336 Extractor. Note the polished surface at the right side. The step on the left side in this view catches the cartridge rim and extracts the case. The rounded and flat portions run in the slot in the bolt, see photograph 14-13. Polishing these surfaces and the sides of this piece dramatically improves action manipulation.

Section 14: The Trouble With Lever-Action & Single-Shot Receivers, Part II

You should also polish the bottom edge of the bolt's recoil face (that portion that rests against the chambered cartridge) until the tops of the high spots develop a high luster finish. This will ease the centering of the cartridge during chambering.

Last, observe the extensions on the front of the bolt. Make certain that none of these touch the barrel. If necessary, file each such surface sufficiently shorter to prevent it from touching the barrel when you force the bolt fully forward against a chambered cartridge. However, do not remove more material than is absolutely necessary; doing so can compromise the rifle's function. Correctly done, this alteration (by preventing the bolt from touching the barrel) prevents the hammer's fall from setting up wild vibrations in the barrel — the bolt cannot carry the hammers impact directly to the barrel. This one alteration can dramatically improve accuracy in these rifles. See photograph # 11-4.

Cartridge Carrier & Finger-Lever Modifications, Marlin & Winchester Lever-Action Rifles:

Polish then cold blue any surfaces on the finger-lever that show wear or abrasion. Polish the working end of the finger-lever detent. See photograph # 14-17. Consider possibly installing a slightly weaker detent spring. However the detent spring should be robust enough to keep the finger-lever closed under any handling situation. See photograph #s 14-15/16/17.

The cartridge carrier has two main functions. First it blocks the magazine tube to prevent the next-in-line cartridge from inappropriately entering into the receiver. Second, it lifts and regulates the "working" cartridge so the bullet end is aligned with the rifle's chamber before the bolt pushes the cartridge home. It also cradles and contains the "working" cartridge until the bolt pushes it sufficiently into the chamber so that the cartridge is trapped between the barrel and the bolt.

Examine all surfaces of the carrier. You should look for areas where action manipulation has worn brass from the cartridge cases (as evidenced by brass staining on the piece) and for places where the carrier slides past other action parts (as evidenced by burnishing on the carrier or other action parts). Pay particular attention to the carrier's front end, where it slides over the head of the next-in-line cartridge. For example, the front of the Marlin carrier moves past the head of the next-in-line cartridge twice as the finger-lever closes the action. First, as the carrier lifts to align the working cartridge to the chamber. Second, as the bolt pushes the working cartridge home, it also pushes the carrier back down, behind the next-in-line round. Be sure to polish any high spots and tool marks off the front end of the carrier to minimize friction between it and the head of the next-in-line cartridge. See photograph # 14-18.

Polish any other friction surfaces to remove any tooling marks or burrs. On the Marlin there is a spring-loaded pawl on the inside edge of the action, near the back of the carrier. This part interlocks with the finger-lever to lift the carrier as the finger-lever begins to move back during action closing. During action opening, the finger-lever

Photographs 14-15/16: These photographs show wear points on the sides of the Marlin finger-lever. For ease of action manipulation, polish all such areas. Be sure to reblue the polished surfaces to minimize the potential for corrosion

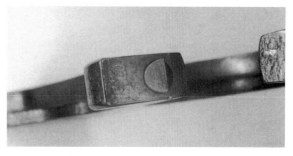

Photograph 14-17: Centered in this view of a Marlin finger-lever, is the detent that holds the action closed. Polishing the working face of this plunger and slightly reducing spring tension can improve action manipulation. However, be careful not to install too weak a spring — the finger-lever should never spontaneously open.

pushes the working end of this pawl aside, against the spring. Usage does a good job of marking the contact zones between this pawl and the finger-lever on any well-seasoned rifle. It is somewhat beneficial to polish these surfaces. However, use caution to avoid removing excess material and be especially careful not to round the carrier pawl latching surface on the front of the finger-lever extension. See photograph # 14-19.

Loading Gate Modifications, Marlin & Winchester Lever-Action Rifles:

I suggest polishing the front end of the outside surface and the entire front end of the loading gate, where it is radiused. I have also modified the interior at the extreme front end by increasing the bevel to produce an almost sharp front edge. This modification can reduce the propensity for the rim of the last-inserted cartridge to hang up on the loading gate. However, this is a trial and error proposition. You have to remove the loading gate, examine the inside front edge for tell-tale signs of where the rim is catching (as is often evidenced by brass staining), round that area and polish the new surface, reinstall and try again.

This process can take several iterations and considerable patience. If you choose to work on this part (as an effort to fix a rifle that has a bad tendency of catching the last-inserted round's rim on the loading gate), proceed slowly with any metal removal — it is hard to reapply steel.

This short list just about covers what is feasible and desirable to do inside the action of traditional lever-action rifles. As noted earlier in this text, many of these alterations are germane to any exposed-hammer lever-action rifle, some also apply to the Savage Model-99, Winchester Model-88 and Browning BLR.

Ejector Modifications, Marlin Lever-Action Rifles:

Occasionally, I see a Marlin lever-action rifle that has an ejector with an entirely too-strong spring. Such a spring can add tremendously to the force required to manipulate the action. It is, however, a simple matter to reduce this spring tension to a more reasonable level. See photograph # 14-14.

This is another of those trial and error processes. Pull the bolt (which requires only the removal of the finger-lever, which requires only removal of the finger-lever pivot bolt). The ejector will then come free from the action.

Insert a small nail (4 penny or smaller) or an equally small drill bit between the leaf spring and the ejector, as near to the fixed end of the spring as is convenient. With the nail held in place, bend the free end of the leaf spring until it touches the ejector. Reinstall the ejector and bolt and measure the ejector spring force in the following manner.

Clamp the rifle with the ejection port up and that face of the receiver approximately level. Install the ejector and start the bolt into the action sufficiently to hold the ejector in place. Stand a two inch (2") long section of three-eighths inch (3/8") dowel on the end of the ejector. Sit an empty bullet box on the end of the dowel. Add weigh into the box. When the weight is sufficient to begin to compress the ejector spring, stop adding weight. (The ejector spring's design causes it to apply increasing force as the bolt pushes the ejector closer to its fully depressed position).

If you want to get fancy you can grind a shallow taper on the end of the dowel and thread that to five-sixteenths inch (5/16") fine thread. Drill a hole in the bottom center of a plastic bullet box

Photograph 14-18: As the action cycles, the forward end of the cartridge carrier slides past the head of the next-in-line cartridge in the tubular magazine. Reduce this friction source by polishing the nose of the carrier. It is useful to also polish any other places on this piece (or anywhere in the action) where cartridge brass is evident. See text.

Photograph 14-19: At top, just left of center, is the working nose of the cartridge carrier ratchet (Marlin). When the finger-lever opens, it slides past and pushes this spring-loaded pawl into the carrier. Polish this and any other friction surface. See text.

and thread that to fit the dowel. Then thread the dowel into this hole.

However you go about measuring the spring's force, the ejector should compress when you have about 2 pounds of weight on it. (A dietary portion scale is ideal for weighing the bullets and box or you can just add up the bullet weight in grains and divide by 7000 (the weight of the box and dowel are insignificant).

If the ejector spring is significantly heavier than this, remove the ejector and repeat the spring bending step using a slightly smaller nail. Continue checking until you have the tension right.

Ejector Modifications, Winchester Lever-Action Rifles:

Similarly, on the Winchester rifle you might choose to slightly reduce the spring tension on the ejector, which is a plunger in the bolt face. Use caution here; the ejector should sharply eject the dummy round. Further, on typical Winchester lever-action rifles, lightening this spring does little to smooth or ease action manipulation.

As an approximation, this plunger should require a minimum of about four (4) pounds to push it fully flush in the bolt. In this application it is probably feasible to substitute a weaker spring installed with more compression. Such a replacement spring will achieve a more uniform force on the ejector. See photograph # 11-6.

Locking Lug Modifications (Replacement), Marlin Lever-Action Rifles:

Examine the locking lug (all Marlins and most Winchesters) or lugs (the Model-1892 Winchester). Locate and polish off any burrs. Do not alter the lug's dimensions; only polish sufficiently to remove burrs.

This work requires almost complete disassembly of the receiver. On the Marlin, you do not have to remove the loading gate or the cartridge carrier. However, you do have to remove the finger-lever and the lower receiver. Begin by removing the buttstock (pull the tang bolt and separate the buttstock from the barreled-action). Then remove the hammer spring (slide the spring retainer out the side of the tang). Remove the hammer screw, the screw at the bottom front of the lower tang and the screw on the left side of the receiver, centered over the finger-lever pivot screw. Since this simplifies matters, you might as well also separate the finger-lever and the lower tang.

Owing to the geometry of the Marlin bolt and locking lug, it is quite easy to replace the factory lug with a custom-fitted lug and thereby reduce headspace to properly fit chamber and cartridge rim dimensions. Owing to the typically gross headspace excesses found in practically all rimmed cartridge lever-action rifles this alteration is a very good idea. However, for obvious reasons, Marlin will not sell this lug to anyone who is not a qualified gunsmith. Also, this modification requires the use of some sort of jig. The angle of the working face of the locking lug is critical to the action's lockup strength. Equally, cutting too much from that surface will exacerbate, rather than mitigate, the headspace problem.

Any gunsmith with a milling machine should be able to do this work quite easily. Since I did the work using only hand tools and thereby reduced actual headspace on my Marlin Model-336 from 0.012" (with Norma Cases) to <0.001" with the same cases, I will describe the process I followed. (I chose to fit the action to work properly with Norma cases because those have the thickest rims of .30-30 Winchester cases I have measured.)

The Marlin repair shop can supply (any qualified gunsmith) with an otherwise fully finished but slab-sided locking lug — this piece requires only fitting with the angled face. Marlin makes two versions of this lug. These versions accommodate the long- and short-action rifles. Be certain to obtain the correct lug.

In order to "tight" headspace a Marlin lever-action rifle, proceed as follows. Begin by finding a sample case with the thickest rim of those you expect to use in the rifle. I have noted that among rimmed cases Norma's brass typically has thicker rims; rims that are much closer to SAAMI maximum specification, compared to any other brand. Having found this thickest rimmed case you expect to ever use, add one layer of cellophane tape across the case head of the <u>unprimed</u> and fully sized case. Trim the edges of the tape so that those do not extend past the case head.

For target applications you can omit this cellophane tape layer on the case head. However, keep in mind that by doing so you could very well run into the odd case that will not chamber and allow the bolt to fully close. However, it is no trouble to pull the locking lug and remove a few-thousandths of an inch of material from the locking face. Should you later discover you have the rifle's headspace set up too tight, simply do so.

Observe the factory lug; you will note a beveled surface on the top front side. This is the locking (working) face, which slides into the corresponding recess in the bolt. The opposite side of the lug, in turn, rests against the rails in the receiver. Note that the unfinished lug lacks this beveled face. Your task is to create a corresponding beveled face on the new lug but not to make that face as large as it was on the factory lug. This results in the face of the new lug being further from the back side of the lug. Consequently, the new lug is effectively thicker. This thicker lug serves to force the bolt further forward when the finger-lever pushes it home as the action locks. Accordingly, the thicker locking lug reduces headspace. See photograph # 14-20.

Note, that the extensions on the front of the bolt might be longer than the case rim is thick. In this situation, it would be impossible to move the bolt sufficiently forward to achieve tight headspacing. Also, this condition is anathema to accuracy since it places the bolt in direct contact with the barrel and thereby makes a perfect hammer and bell system — the falling hammer will indirectly hit the barrel and thereby cause wild vibrations. If you do nothing else, fix this condition as described in the following paragraphs.

Mark the front of the bolt extensions. Prussian Blue is ideal for this job. Insert the sample case and insert the bolt fully forward in the receiver. Force it forward as far as you can by hand, then rotate it back and forth as much as possible. Remove the bolt and observe the bolt extensions and the back of the barrel for any evidence of contact between those surfaces. Any Prussian Blue on the barrel is sufficient evidence.

If you note such contact, file the high spots down several-thousandths of an inch. Repeat this test until no contact occurs. Obviously, the inclusion of the test case, chambered in front of the bolt, is critical, otherwise there is nothing to stop the bolt's forward travel excepting the extensions, which you are attempting to gauge just shorter than the case rim is thick.

After completing this test (and any required modifications), proceed to fit the replacement locking lug. If you are very cautious, you can do most of the beveling required on the replacement locking lug using a bench-mounted grinder. Bring the recoil (working) face of the lug, at the proper angle for the bevel, to bear against a clean straight side of a fine corundum wheel. Proceed slowly and do not overheat this critical piece. Use a spray bottle to apply water to cool the locking lug during the grinding operation. In any case, do not allow the locking lug to heat to the point where you cannot hold it bare fingered.

Be careful so that you grind the face at as close to the correct angle as you can. If in doubt, stop and proceed by hand. That takes longer but you cannot afford error here.

When, by using the power grinder, you have produced a beveled face that is at approximately the same angle and, perhaps one-half the size of the beveled area on the original locking lug, stop and set up your jig. Affix a quality whetstone with a good flat face in a padded vise (a 6" long Norton corundum medium-by-fine stone works well). Tighten the jaws only sufficiently to lock the stone in place. Thin rubber pads on the jaws are the best means of holding a whetstone without damaging it. By the way, Brownells sells such jaw pads and the proper whetstone.

Insert the shank portion of a seven sixty-fourths inch (7/64") drill bit aligned to the juncture of the protrusion at the lower front of the locking lug and the front face of the lug. See the illustration.

Photograph 14-20: Left is a locking lug from a factory Marlin lever-action rifle. Right is the semi-finished equivalent. See the text for a discussion of correcting headspace through proper fitting of a replacement locking lug.

Section 14: The Trouble With Lever-Action & Single-Shot Receivers, Part II

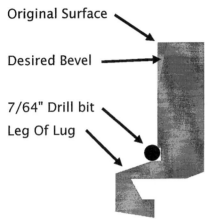

Marlin Locking Lug & Jig
(idealized sketch, side view)

- Original Surface
- Desired Bevel
- 7/64" Drill bit
- Leg Of Lug

Set this assembly over the edge of the stone and slide it back and forth while keeping the drill bit in place, near the edge of the stone. Avoid pushing the lug hard against the side of the stone, that will form a channel in the leg of the lug where you do not want to weaken it. Also, use plenty of quality cutting oil.

Periodically check the beveled surface on the lug. When you have this surface fully matched to the stone's surface (your stoning efforts have removed all grinding marks), check the lug in the rifle for fit, as described below.

Locate the receiver in a suitable clamp with the bottom up and accessible. Insert the headspace dummy, the one with the thick rim and the layer of cellophane tape. Insert the bolt fully until the extractor snaps over the case rim. On round-bolt Marlins, ensure that you have the bolt properly oriented in the receiver (the easiest way to do this is to install the extractor before installing the bolt). Drop the lug into the lug raceway (correct orientation is with the beveled end inserted first and the bevel facing the barrel). Force the lug fully into the bolt's locking lug recess and hold it there. Use a dial indicator to measure the distance from the bottom of the receiver to some flat reference point on the locking lug. You should be able to use the hole gauge on the caliper to easily get a good measurement.

Replace the custom locking lug with the original locking lug and repeat this measurement. Remember that the lug is pushing against the flat spring that holds the safety firing pin down, so you will have to push the lug into its receiver raceway to keep that safety spring compressed — to simplify this test, press the safety pin up and forward to lock that piece in place, this effort will eliminate the spring tension problem. (If you handle the bolt carefully the safety pin will stay forward, where it stays locked in the up position and will, therefore, not push against the locking lug.)

Note the difference between the replacement locking lug measurement and the original locking lug measurement — receiver bottom to locking lug flat. This will give you an idea of how close to the correct "depth" the bevel is. Remember, owing to the geometry, removing one-thousandth of an inch (0.001") of material from the beveled surface on the locking lug will result in about eight-thousandths of an inch (0.008") more locking lug travel. Record the original locking lug measurement as a working reference.

Paint the beveled face of the replacement locking lug with Dykem, or a common permanent marker. Again run the locking lug into the bolt's lug recess as far as you can by hand, then use a brass punch and a small hammer to tap it lightly into the recess until it binds. To remove the locking lug, install the finger-lever in the bolt slot, hook the locking lug catch in the locking lug and pry up on the finger-lever while holding it forward. The locking lug should come loose quite easily, if not, persevere and be a little gentler with the tapping next time!

Observe the painted surface. A rectangular portion (square bolt models) or rounded portion (round bolt models) of the beveled area should be wiped free of paint. This area represents the locking surface that should abut to the corresponding surface in the bolt. Compare this area to the corresponding area on the original locking lug, which — on a well-used rifle — will betray the locking surface by burnishing in that area. If the paint is only bruised across one edge or at one corner, you will have to adjust your stoning technique to cut that high side or corner deeper until you have achieved the necessary simultaneous contact across the entire locking surface. If you were careful in your original grinding and in the subsequent stoning, this adjustment should be, at most, minor. See photograph # 14-21.

Continue the work on the stone, periodically repeating the depth into the receiver measurement with the replacement locking lug. When the replacement locking lug begins to get close to entering the raceway in the receiver as far as the original locking lug, within, perhaps ten-thousandths of an inch (0.010"), again do the

Dykem test to insure the beveled surface is at the correct angle to achieve full simultaneous contact with the corresponding area on the bolt's locking surface. If not, adjust your stoning angle and technique accordingly. On some guns it might prove necessary to use a slightly smaller or larger drill bit for the alignment jig. In that case, an index drill bit set would be indispensable.

When the new locking lug freely enters to nearly the same depth as the original lug (to within perhaps 0.005"), change to the fine stone surface and finish the beveled area to a fine polish. Continue polishing until the replacement lug just fully enters the bolt recess until the locking lug's top surfaces contacts the bolt. The rifle's headspace adjustment is now perfect.

As noted before, you can omit the clearance tape on the case head, if so desired, to create truly tight headspacing. The disadvantages of that approach include the occasional thick rimmed case that will not fully chamber and the problem that a bit of grime could render otherwise functional rounds unchamberable. Since I try to keep my guns and ammunition a little cleaner than that, you can guess how I headspaced my Marlins.

Special Receiver Considerations, Winchester Model-88 Lever-Action Rifles:

This rifle is somewhat unique with its internal hammer and interconnected trigger system — these particular parts share a single actuating coil spring. There are rumors that Winchester went through a plethora of design modifications (16?) in a protracted effort to solve a little problem with the Model-88 — spontaneous firing. There might be some truth to these rumors.

This author saw one of these rifles fire while being carried, slung over a hunter's shoulder with the barrel pointed (safely?) in the air — thank goodness. He did have the safety set to the "on safe" position, he did not jar or touch the trigger and he did not jostle the rifle or bang it against anything. While that hunter was walking on smooth ground the gun just fired. I am also aware of two other Model-88s that fired under similar circumstances.

For this reason, you should be doubly cautious about any Model-88 — particularly the earliest versions. Certainly, be careful before doing any work that might affect the trigger, hammer or hammer interlocking safety systems on these rifles. Generally, polishing internal action parts to eliminate friction points, as evidenced by wear marks, is okay. However, do not touch the trigger or the hammer in any areas of the complicated interlocking sear engagement surfaces.

Also, note that the forward portion of the finger-lever on this rifle carries several pieces that will spontaneously disassemble when you remove the pin that holds the finger-lever in the frame (the finger-lever pivot pin). Removal of the trigger pivot pin results in a similar but more complicated profusion of loose parts. See photograph # 14-22.

Photograph 14-21: This view of the Marlin lever-action locking lug shows the recoil face at top. Note the burnished surface near the center at either side of the cut out section. This burnished area is the portion that enters the recess on the bolt and takes the stress of the bolt's back thrust when the gun fires.

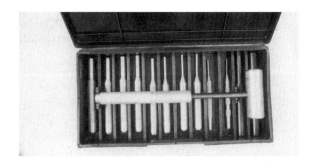

Photograph 14-22: A set of brass punches and a small brass hammer are invaluable in any work that involves driving pins. This handy set, produced by John Masen, is available from Brownells at a modest price.

Section 14: The Trouble With Lever-Action & Single-Shot Receivers, Part II

I have found that the correct procedure for reassembling these mechanisms, without using a specially designed jig, is too complicated to even try to explain! While I could do this, it was no mean task. In addition to nearly unlimited patience, you will have to have, at the very least, tapered pins and one stub pin. You will need the tapered pins to align the hammer and the trigger system parts. You will need the stub pin to hold the hammer in place while you insert the through pin that connects the finger-lever to the receiver (while you simultaneously hold the finger-lever in place). These ancillary tools dramatically ease (nay, make possible) the reassembly process.

Even so, lacking proper jigs, these tasks require more strength, patience and manual dexterity than I like to expend. If you are short on any of these commodities, do not touch this mechanism. If you do decide to open it up, be aware that there is a small coil spring under the sear interlock, which pivots on the trigger pivot pin. It would be easy to overlook this little coil spring. . . . after working for an hour to get the rifle assembled, it is no fun to again disassemble the rifle just to insert this puny but essential coil spring. (If this sounds like the voice of experience, there might be a reason!)

Finger-Lever Lock Modification, Winchester Model-88 Lever-Action Rifles:

Beginning at the rear of the receiver, it is tempting to try to reduce the spring tension on the finger-lever lock mechanism. Doing so would reduce the pressure needed to unlock the action and would, therefore, reduce the effort necessary to begin to rotate the finger-lever to open the action. However, this spring also functions with one of the safety interlock mechanisms in the action. Reducing this spring tension, even slightly, is apt to result in the rifle's refusal to fire! Therefore, this alteration is haphazard, at best. I strongly suggest against it. See photograph # 14-23.

A better solution is to polish the interlocking surfaces of the hook on the finger-lever and the corresponding latch in the receiver. You can accomplish this easily by using a Cratex polishing wheel in the Dremel tool. Be careful not to alter the geometry of these surfaces. Polishing the high spots can dramatically reduce the effort required to unlock the finger-lever and is certainly worthwhile. Remember to apply a cold bluing agent to the polished areas. This will minimize the potential for corrosion on these normally hidden surfaces.

Action Linkage Polishing, Winchester Model-88 Lever-Action Rifles:

Generally, there is no drastic need to do any polishing inside the receiver. However, by removing the hammer pivot pin it is possible to remove the finger-lever assembly from the bottom of the receiver. If you do so, be certain to observe the geometry of the toggle links and where each came from — there are four ways to install each link, only one will work! Before any disassembly, mark each toggle link plate to indicate which side it goes on and what edge is at front, top and outside. Note that the beveled side of these links faces the <u>outside</u> of the receiver (this surface provides necessary clearance for the bolt-connector linkage rods. See photograph #s 14-24 through 14-28.

With the action disassembled, observe all friction points, as evidenced by wear in the bluing. Polish all such surfaces with a fine Cratex wheel mounted in the Dremel tool. Similarly, polish the exterior surfaces of the finger-lever, where the toggle links run. If desired, you can also polish the corresponding interior surfaces of the lower receiver extensions. For this work, a

Photograph 14-23: At the left in this view is the finger-lever latch on the Winchester Model-88 rifle. Polishing the latching surfaces in this area is very helpful in easing and smoothing the unlocking of the finger-lever. The actuating coil spring (just visible here) cannot be modified because this system is also part of the safety interlock on the rifle. See the text.

properly sized wood block wrapped in 600 grit (or finer) corundum paper is the proper tool. As with all such polishing, remove only the high spots — there is no benefit to polishing the entire area, but there are disadvantages, such as increased play.

Hammer Weight Reduction & Polishing, Winchester Model-88 Lever-Action Rifles:

Since the Model-88 features an extremely light firing pin, it is generally desirable to lighten the hammer. The idea is to reduce the mass of the hammer to allow it to rotate faster and with less disturbance to the rifle. It is best to reduce the mass in that portion of the hammer that is furthest from the pivot.

A simple version of this alteration is extremely easy to perform on the Model-88. Note in the photographs that a portion of the hammer between the pivot and the firing pin striking area extends toward the spring. This is the spot that is shaped like an outside corner on a box. It is easy to remove this corner once you have separated the hammer and trigger. If the trigger is locked to the hammer, simply com-

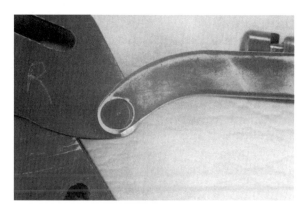

Photograph 14-26: Close-up view of Winchester Model-88 toggle link. Note the wear surfaces on the finger-lever extension (lower left) and near the pivot pin on the toggle link (left center). Also note the scribed "R" on the connecting link (left). This "R" indicates the outside of the right link. See text and photograph 14-28.

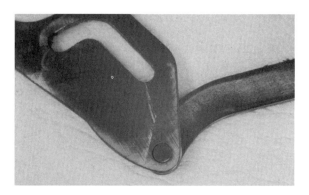

Photograph 14-27: Winchester Model-88, inside left toggle and connecting links. Note the wear pattern and tooling marks on these pieces. See photograph 14-28.

Photograph 14-24: Winchester Model-88 action parts. This view shows the bolt, toggle links and finger-lever in approximately the same orientation as when the rifle is assembled and the bolt is locked.

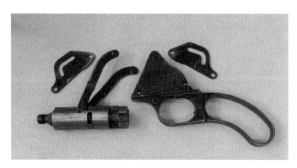

Photograph 14-25: Winchester's Model-88 action parts. This view shows friction surfaces on the toggle links and finger-lever. Polishing these friction surfaces can slightly improve the functioning of these rifles. See text and photograph 14-28.

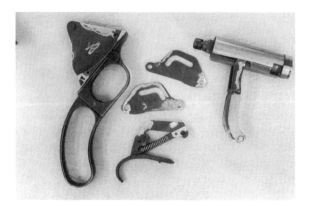

Photograph 14-28: Winchester Model-88 action parts. Note polishing on these friction surfaces. Here it is only necessary to polish the high spots. See photographs 14-24/28 and the associated text.

press the spring by pressing the two pieces together between your hands and allow the sear to rotate out of the hammer. This will free the pieces. You will note that the combination hammer and trigger spring runs on a two-piece guide rod. Also, note that the small end of this rod pivots on a pin in the hammer. This pin will slide out to release the rod. To avoid losing any parts, completely disassemble the hammer before beginning the grinding.

Use a standard bench-mounted grinder with a three-quarters inch (3/4") wide wheel. Apply plenty of misted water to the hammer during the grinding operation to prevent its over-heating. Also, be extra careful not to touch the grinding stone to the sear surfaces or the area near the hammer spring boss. Remove steel until the shank of the hammer has parallel sides, as shown in the photographs. This requires removal of the entire outside corner portion and results in a significant reduction in lock-time. See photograph #s 14-29/30.

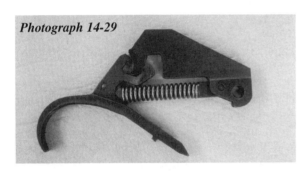

Photograph 14-29

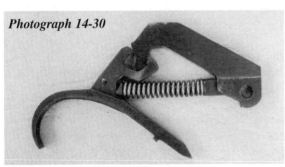

Photograph 14-30

Photographs 14-29/30: Winchester Model-88 trigger and hammer assembly. This includes the trigger, hammer, trigger/hammer spring, a two-piece spring strut and the spring strut pivot pin. In photograph 14-29 the hammer is in stock form. In photograph 14-30 it is shown after alteration to reduce mass. This alteration reduces the gun's lock time and can result in greater firing pin energy (the hammer will fall faster and will be closer in weight to the firing pin). See the associated text.

Alternatively, you can also reduce the hammer's mass through hole drilling, as described in the sub-section on lightening the hammer on the Remington pump-action rifle, *Part I*. Be careful not to weaken the hammer in any critical areas — hammer to firing pin impact face, sear surface and hammer spring boss.

Again, this is a hardened steel piece. Drilling will require carbide drill bits. As with any hardened steel part, be careful not to overheat the hammer during any drilling or grinding operations.

Considering the comparatively minuscule mass of the firing pin in these rifles, it seems that it would be very difficult to over-lighten the hammer. Nevertheless, if you were to carry the above techniques to the extreme, such a result might be possible. My advice is to simply remove the outside corner area, as described above and shown in the photographs, and make no other alterations.

Note the nose of the hammer, where the bolt rides over the hammer as the finger-lever opens the action. This is a serious friction point. It is also a machined surface. Using a Dremel tool, polish this area with a Cratex wheel followed by a jeweler's rouge impregnated felt wheel. This will produce a very slick mirror finish. Apply a similar finish to the corresponding surface on the firing pin extension. This alteration alone can dramatically reduce the force required to work the finger-lever. See photograph #s 14-31/32.

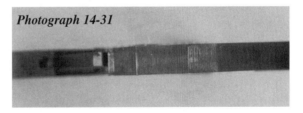

Photograph 14-31

Photograph 14-32

Photographs 14-31/32: Winchester Model-88 hammer cocking and firing pin impact surface. Photograph 14-30 shows the unaltered hammer. Note the minor wear near the center of the picture and the crossing tooling marks in this region. Photograph 14-31 shows the same part after polishing. This minor work eases bolt manipulation. See the associated text.

Magazine Release Spring, Winchester Model-88 Lever-Action Rifles:

The final modification I would suggest involves the magazine release spring. The factory spring seems a bit on the stiff side for my tastes. Your rifle might be fine and you might prefer a truly robust spring here. After all, a lost magazine will bring no joy to Mudville. However, install the magazine and, while wearing gloves, on a cold day, try to remove it. If you find the latch is difficult to release, you might want to reduce the spring tension.

As with other similar modifications, it is likely best to replace this stock spring with a similar diameter spring made of smaller wire and cut to the same length or slightly longer. (A longer spring will deliver a more consistent spring tension as you rotate the latch to release the magazine.) However, if you are careful, you can probably achieve an acceptable result by simply shortening the factory spring, albeit slightly — no more than one coil. See photograph # 14-33.

No other unique modifications are necessary or desirable in the Model-88's action. Before reassembly, clean all parts. Using a cotton swab, apply a sufficient amount of cold bluing agent to render all polished surfaces thoroughly blued. Remove all traces of the bluing agent. Using a cotton swab, apply a minute film of NECO's Moly-slide (or some other molybdenum-disulfide based lubricant) to all friction surfaces and pivot points. Reassemble the action. Check the action for proper functioning. Reinstall barreled-action in the stock.

Now, I will note that in the last paragraph I made these operations sound very easy. However, note the opening paragraphs of this sub-section. Reassembly of the Model-88 action requires tapered pins, stub pins, patience, strength and manual dexterity. Be doubly certain that you do not lose any parts or inadvertently leave out any parts!

Review the sub-sections on feed ramp polishing and ejection port modifications for the Remington pump. Similar modifications are also beneficial in the Model-88. Generally, Winchester did a very good job of building Model-88 magazines. For this reason, these require little, if any, work. However, it is always beneficial to slightly bevel sharp edges and polish off burrs that might interfere with proper magazine functioning — cartridge loading, cartridge feeding, magazine insertion and magazine removal.

Special Receiver Considerations, Browning Lever-Action Rifle (BLR):

This rifle is an interesting development, perhaps especially so now that it is available chambered for full-length cartridges. The BLR has a traditional exposed hammer (with a half-cock, folding-hammer safety feature). It also uses a thoroughly modern removable box magazine. The bolt is a rotary front-locking unit that is fully capable for chambering to any standard modern high-pressure cartridge.

A sophisticated gear mechanism transfers and converts the rotary motion of the articulated finger-lever to a linear motion of the rifle's bolt. The finger-lever carries the trigger system, which features an interlocking mechanism that makes it impossible for the trigger to release the sear unless the finger-lever is fully closed (and the bolt head is, therefore, fully locked).

Following is a laundry list of this rifle's deficits. First, this action has no means of significantly multiplying primary extraction force (too-hot handloads are apt to result in a stuck case). The rotary hammer is less than the ideal accuracy arrangement. Hammer spring tension reduction, as described in the sub-section on Marlin rifles, is not particularly feasible. Owing to the folding hammer feature and what is evidently a modest factory hammer energy setting, I cannot recommend any alteration. The firing pin seems to be quite heavy (lightening, as described in the sub-section on Marlin rifles, can be quite beneficial). The trigger guard and finger-lever openings are both entirely too small; using this rifle for hunting, while wearing a glove on the trigger finger hand, is essentially impossible. Early models featured a barrel band

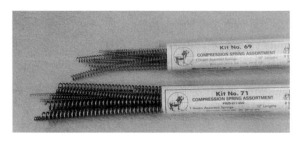

Photograph 14-33: Brownells offers these handy spring kits. Many extra-light and extra-heavy springs for gunsmithing applications are found in each tube. I have mentioned myriad potential applications throughout this text.

on the fore-end, this piece contributed to wandering zero in those rifles (we have covered repair of that problem elsewhere).

Action disassembly requires attention to detail; there are several critical parts that the incautious tinker could lose, quite easily. Worse, correct action lockup depends upon proper timing of the gears — proceed with caution and only after studying the relationship of the closed action quite carefully. It is very easy to assemble the mechanism incorrectly, a potentially dangerous circumstance.

I recommend only the following described modifications.

Magazine Deburring, Browning Lever-Action Rifle (BLR):

First, disassemble the clip magazine and polish any burrs or sharp edges. Deburring and a slight rounding of the inside top edge of the magazine box are beneficial steps.

While you are at it, observe the exterior of the magazine and ensure that it does not have any burrs or sharp edges that could bind in the receiver opening. Observe the receiver opening for the same sort of problems. Polish any such areas to achieve smooth rounded surfaces.

Feed Ramp Polishing, Browning Lever-Action Rifle (BLR):

Polish and contour the feed ramp, as described under the sub-section in *Part I*, where I covered this process as it applies to the Remington Pump. The necessary work is quite similar here. Also, note that it might be beneficial to polish and modify the ejection port, as described in the sub-section on the Remington pump.

Firing Pin Weight Reduction, Browning Lever-Action Rifle (BLR):

To remove the firing pin, open the finger-lever fully and support the bolt on a wood block. Drive the firing pin retaining pin far enough through the bolt to free the firing pin and its spring. Remove the firing pin. Lighten the cylindrical shank as described in the discussion covering lightening the Marlin firing pin, above. Remove the firing pin retaining pin from the bolt. Reassemble the firing pin into the bolt and install the retaining pin from the top. Note the slight taper on one end of this pin. Insert that end into the top of the bolt. Before driving the retaining pin home, make certain that you properly align the firing pin to allow the retaining pin to pass.

Decreasing the firing pin return spring tension will slightly increase firing pin energy. As long as the spring is somewhat compressed and forcefully retracts the firing pin when the hammer is cocked, it is heavy enough to do its job. Consider replacing the original spring with a weaker and longer unit (lower spring rate with greater pre-load).

Finger-Lever Modifications, Browning Lever-Action Rifle (BLR):

I strongly recommend that you consider having a gunsmith cut, weld and refinish the finger-lever to bring both the trigger guard opening and the finger-lever opening to usable dimensions. Why Browning designed the finger-lever for this rifle with such petite openings is an enduring mystery. That they insist on continuing to do so is something else entirely. If you hunt in cold, wet climes, where gloves are necessary, I cannot recommend this rifle unless you have truly small hands — that is, not unless you have the finger-lever modified.

If you happen to be a competent welder or know someone who is, and if a TIG or MIG wire feed welding machine is available, you can do this alteration yourself. The only significant precaution is that you should use a good heat sink to prevent overheating the gear area of the finger-lever and you should keep the pieces cool enough to prevent warpage.

The basic method requires removal of the finger-lever from the action, followed by these steps. Fully disassemble the finger-lever. Cut through the main body at the vertical centerline of the trigger guard and finger-lever openings. Add an appropriate amount of steel (use at least 70,000 psi low-carbon welding rod) between the cut surfaces. Weld the two pieces back together. Contour the new surfaces to match the original. Reblue.

You might also want to extend the length of the finger-lever opening. To do this, remove the rear of the finger-lever by cutting through from top to bottom near the extreme back end. Then, as before, add a bit of material, weld the pieces back together, grind to contour and refinish to match the original contour and finish. This is a considerable amount of work but it is not really all that difficult. If I were to buy a BLR, I would most certainly have to make this change. Besides being practically impossible to use with a gloved hand, the finger-levers on these rifles do not even look "right" in stock trim.

Proper fore-end and buttstock bedding are also important but are covered elsewhere.

Special Receiver Considerations, Savage Model-99 Lever-Action Rifles:

Savage produced the Model-99 in prodigious quantities in both removable box magazine and fixed rotary-magazine versions. Savage also used two safety configurations and many other variations, some of which warrant separate discussions. We will begin with basic receiver work that is applicable to all models.

I have to mention that Savage's Model-99 is the only lever-action rifle that I know of which features a completely in-line firing pin system. Compared to the almost ubiquitous (in lever-action rifles) rotating hammer, this is a vastly superior system, shared with practically every bolt-action rifle. Unlike the common lever-action rotating hammer system, the firing pin on the Model-99 imparts no rotational torque to the rifle. This characteristic suggests superior accuracy potential. The Model-99's firing pin is also comparatively light and travels a very, very short distance. This contributes to a very short lock-time (shorter than many quality modern bolt action rifles!), which also contributes to accuracy.

Feed Ramp Polishing, Savage Model-99 Lever-Action Rifles:

To work on the receiver, remove the buttstock by removing the buttplate and the through-bolt. The buttstock will then slip off, exposing the receiver's heart for inspection.

The first thing to look at is the feed ramp, which is located in the receiver, just below the barrel. This area is often comparatively rough and deserves a good polish. However, even with the barrel removed and the receiver fully stripped, you will find that it is very difficult to get polishing tools into this area (especially on the rotary magazine versions of this rifle). This access problem can make polishing very difficult. At least in my experience, on the rotary-magazine version of this rifle, the tinker can see what he needs to do but he will find it very difficult to get any tool in there to do the needed work. I suspect that a small diameter Cratex polishing "bullet" on a long shaft is the best bet. I went through about fifteen different Dremel attachments before finding anything that would do any good. I should have fashioned a longer shank for use with the Cratex abrasives, and that is what I suggest. However you go about achieving it, a good polish here is very beneficial to smooth action manipulation during cartridge chambering. See photograph #s 14-34/35.

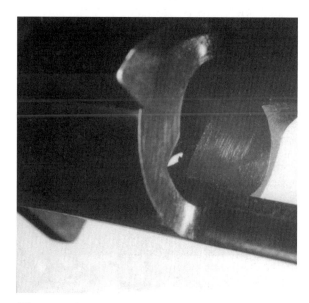

Photograph 14-34

Photograph 14-35

***Photographs 14-34/35:** These photographs of a Remington Model-700 feed ramp show the difference that a little polishing can make. Photograph 14-34 shows a typical ramp before polishing. Photograph 14-35 shows the results of a few minutes work with the proper tool.*

Section 14: The Trouble With Lever-Action & Single-Shot Receivers, Part II

Finger-Lever Modifications, Savage Model-99 Lever-Action Rifles:

There are several minor alterations and detail work that you might consider performing on the finger-lever system on this rifle. However, do not consider any such work until you have carefully studied the rifle and fully understand it workings.

Finger-Lever Bolt Boss Modification, Savage Model-99 Lever-Action Rifles:

You will note that the finger-lever extension has a boss that runs in a milled slot in the bolt. When you close the finger-lever this boss manipulates the bolt, first pushing it forward and then lifting it into its locked position. See photograph #s 14-36/37/38.

On older rifles, you might discover that the effects of long use (wear and tear) have resulted in this boss not raising the back of the bolt fully into the receiver lug when you fully close the finger-lever. Rifles in this condition present a sloppy fit between the bolt and the receiver. This can result in a rifle with somewhat excessive headspace. Further, this condition does nothing to improve the rifle's intrinsic accuracy.

Bolt removal on the Model-99 is quite simple. With the buttstock removed, fully open the finger-lever. You will notice a small tab inside at the left rear of the lower tang, against which the lower left rear of the bolt comes to rest. Remove the screw affixing that tab to the receiver. Remove the tab. See photograph # 14-39.

This will allow the bolt to move further back in the receiver. When you move the bolt fully to the rear of the receiver you will note that it is then free to rotate out of the receiver. You can accomplish this by twisting the bottom rear of the bolt

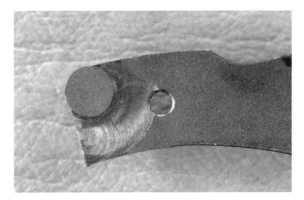

Photograph 14-37

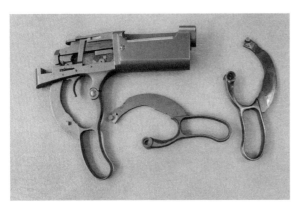

Photograph 14-36: Savage Model-99F (rotary magazine, lever-action), action parts. This shot shows the open receiver with only the barrel removed. This particular Model-99 was treated to ROBAR's superlative electroless nickel with Teflon™, which ROBAR calls NP3 (Nickel with Polytetrafluoroethylene). Application of this product results in what is essentially a welded-on surface that contains microscopic particles of Teflon, throughout. This surface is incredibly tough, unusually slick and essentially immune to corrosion. There is, however, one little problem with NP3 — it is so slick that low-strength thread lockers will not bond! At right is the original finger-lever, in the middle is a partially fitted finger-lever (note the shiny spot near the bolt boss, left side, and the marking where steel removal would lighten the unit without compromising its functional strength). See the associated text and photographs for a complete discussion of the many alterations involved in the conversion of this receiver to a super custom unit.

Photograph 14-38

Photographs 14-37/38: Savage Model-99 finger-lever bolt boss and bolt boss channel. Photograph 14-37 shows a close-up of the finger-lever boss. This piece runs in the slot in the bolt, shown in photograph 14-38. See text for important considerations in perfecting these parts.

out the left side of the action, then pulling the bolt body back and free of the receiver.

Note that (at least on rotary-magazine models) removing the bolt also frees the cartridge guide and the cartridge guide actuating spring. These parts are normally located in a slot in the upper left side of the action, above the magazine well. See photograph # 14-40.

To separate the finger-lever from the receiver, remove the finger-lever pivot and pivot-retaining screw. Turn the screw, counterclockwise, to remove it. Use a small pin punch to reach through the pivot from the screw side. Then tap on the punch with a small hammer to drive it free of the receiver. This action frees the finger-lever.

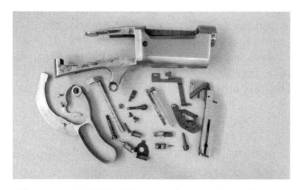

Photograph 14-39: Like most lever-action rifles, the Savage Model-99 has myriad action parts. Omitted from this photograph are the rotary magazine with its actuation spring, the magazine cap with its retainer and several action springs. Note the weight-reducing grooves in the firing pin and the matte finish. The former serves to reduce lock time and improve striker energy. The latter is a world-class finish for several reasons, as discussed in the text and associated photographs.

Photograph 14-40: At the center back of this picture of a partially opened Savage Model-99F (a rotary magazine model) is the cartridge retainer.

However, you have to place the safety in the proper position and orient the finger-lever correctly to make room for the bolt boss pin on the finger-lever extension to pass through the lower tang. See photograph # 14-41.

Savage Arms will provide any qualified gunsmith with a replacement finger-lever (in the rough). You can easily fashion this part to move the bolt boss slightly further from the pivot point, compared to the stock finger-lever, and thereby achieve correct lockup on the bolt. However, this fabrication involves considerable work and requires considerable skill. I have done this job using only hand tools, sandpaper and a moto tool (Dremel) with sanding drums and Cratex attachments.

With this experience behind me, I cannot recommend this work to the faint at heart! I would expect a gunsmith to charge not less than $150 for the same work. As I said, this is a tough job. See photograph # 14-36.

However, Savage Arms might agree to do the finishing after you or your gunsmith have properly fitted the finger-lever bolt boss to the bolt boss channel and thereby correctly adjusted the rifle's headspacing. Since Savage has tooling and jigs, finger-lever finishing is a much less onerous task for the factory and they might do this work for a modest fee — this is worth checking into.

The goal is to fashion a finger-lever with the bolt boss pin sized and positioned so that it fits the bolt boss raceway in the bolt with little play and so it will force the bolt all the way to the top

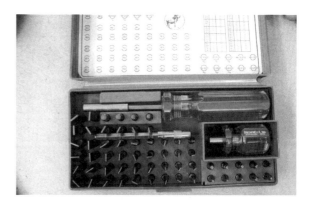

Photograph 14-41: This Brownells screwdriver kit is the ideal accessory for working on any gun. Having the correct bits and a handy place to keep those, properly sorted, is key to having and using the correct screwdriver for the job at hand. Using the correct fitting tool will help eliminate scarred screw heads.

Section 14: The Trouble With Lever-Action & Single-Shot Receivers, Part II

of the receiver as the finger-lever comes fully closed. This combination minimizes headspace, increases lockup strength and reduces play in the action during manipulation.

Note that on some rifles the front of the lower bolt extension, in front of the bolt boss raceway, might hit the rear carrier for the rotary-magazine before the bolt moves fully to its maximum upward travel. If this condition should occur on your rifle, it is a simple matter to grind away the offending steel from the bolt extension. However, it is better to pull the magazine carrier and trim that piece, as necessary to achieve the requisite clearance. See the following discussion of rotary-magazine removal. (After you remove the magazine, all you have to do to pull the rear carrier is remove the cross bolt from the receiver.) Note where the bolt extension was hitting the carrier and grind that area of the carrier to provide sufficient bolt-to-carrier clearance. As a final touch, you should cold blue the area that you modified.

Also note, on some rifles, altering the finger-lever to raise the rear of the bolt further into the locking lug recess in the receiver might cause other problems. Chiefly these are: interference between the forward bolt extension (the tab at the top front of the bolt) and the barrel, interference between the bolt face and the feed ramp, sufficient alteration of headspace to cause chambering problems with certain handloads (it is very unlikely this work could cause problems with factory ammunition, but in extreme instances, it could), loss of contact between the main body of the locking lug and the locking lug recess in the receiver.

A slight shortening of the bolt face extensions is easy to achieve with a bit of judicious filing. Simply paint the front of the extensions with a permanent marker and fully close the bolt. If closing the action mars the painted surface, file off a few-thousandths of an inch of the end of the extension and repeat the test. Continue this incremental process, as necessary.

Interference between the lower front of the bolt and the feed ramp is equally easy to correct. Use the same paint, test, file and fit system. Remove material from the bolt, as necessary until it does not hit the feed ramp or any other part of the receiver.

The change-of-headspace problem would most likely occur only where the handloader had deliberately not been sizing the cases completely, as he might in an effort to reduce headspace.

Therefore, you can easily address this potentiality by resizing the cases more fully. Unless there was something wrong with the rifle's headspace or the factory-set bolt lockup, it should not be possible for this work to shorten the headspace sufficiently to cause problems with factory ammunition.

Separation of the bolt's locking surface from the receiver's locking lug recess (resulting from the bolt moving forward as the rear of the bolt lifts fully to the top) compromises headspace control. This potential condition is easy to test for before altering anything. Pull the buttstock and close the finger-lever fully on an empty chamber. Pull the trigger to unlock the firing pin. While pushing the top of the front of the bolt back, reach inside the receiver with a small prying tool and lift the rear of the bolt. If the bolt's locking lug surface moves forward and away from the receiver's locking lug boss as the bolt moves to the top of the receiver, there is a potential problem.

This condition is easy to correct by slightly increasing the radius along the lower edge of the receiver lug recess. However, this is a job where you have to proceed by trial and <u>not</u> error.

Paint the locking lug recess in the receiver. Be sure to paint both the locking surface and the radius leading to it — below it in the receiver. Prussian Blue works well here.

Install the bolt and push it fully forward in the receiver — with the finger-lever removed. While continuing to push the bolt forward, rotate the rear of the bolt fully to the top of the receiver. Then, while holding the back of the bolt fully toward the top of the receiver, push the bolt back, against the locking surface. Finally, push the bolt back forward and push the rear of the bolt back down into the receiver. Remove the bolt from the action.

The mismatch that results in the bolt pushing forward as it raises fully into the locking position should be revealed by the existence of the blue die on the radius in the bolt just under the vertical locking surface.

Use a small half-round jeweler's file to carefully remove a few-thousandths of an inch from the receiver radius at that contact zone. Wipe the die from the bolt, reapply a thin coating to the locking surface and radius of the receiver, as necessary. Repeat this fitting test and filing operation until the entire locking surface of the bolt comes against the receiver when you have lifted the bolt fully into place and pushed the bolt back against the locking surface in the receiver.

To test for this condition, do the following test: insert the bolt in the Prussian Blue painted receiver (as described above). Push the bolt forward between the tangs. Hold the bolt forward, then raise the rear of the bolt as high as it will go. Then, while holding the rear of the bolt solidly at the top of the receiver, push the bolt back. Then, again, push it forward. While holding it forward, push it down and out of the receiver. If you have done this test correctly and the locking surface of the bolt is reasonably covered with Prussian Blue, you can rest assured the lockup is correct.

Finish this job by thoroughly polishing the filed radius area. Use the Cratex polishing wheels, as necessary, to remove all filing and tooling marks.

Do not do this work unless you also replace the stock finger-lever with a custom-fit replacement finger-lever — as described above.

Ideally, this work will allow you to get the maximum possible lockup strength while binding the rear of the bolt in the receiver. This combination provides the maximum action rigidity, shot-to-shot uniformity and action strength that is possible in this rifle. These alterations require much work and the tinker must proceed with due caution. However the results can be most rewarding.

Finger-Lever Trigger Interlock Modification, Savage Model-99 Lever-Action Rifles:

The second Model-99 alteration I will address is a conversion you might want to consider if you own a Model-99 produced after 1954 — if so, it will have a tang-mounted safety. When Savage incorporated the vastly superior tang-mounted safety, they also modified the finger-lever to prevent the time-honored "slip-closed-uncocked" method of carry.... A bit of background and explanation is in order.

Owing to the prejudice of experienced riflemen of that era, with regard to the safety of carrying any gun with the "hammer" cocked, Savage incorporated a method of closing the finger-lever without cocking the internal firing pin — all that is required is pulling and holding the trigger back as the finger-lever gets to a certain point and until the closing finger-lever pushes the trigger back forward. Since the original Savage design used an inertial firing pin (as have all subsequent models), it is perfectly safe to carry the rifle with a loaded chamber and the firing pin uncocked.

The trigger and finger-lever also have an interlock that prevents pulling the trigger (to release the firing pin) unless the finger-lever is fully closed and the action is therefore locked or the finger-lever is open and the hammer spring is relaxed. All Savage lever-action rifles after the earliest production runs also featured a visible and tactile means of determining if the firing pin was cocked (the original 1895 model had only a visual cocking indicator).

Therefore, the hunter could conveniently chamber a round and close the action without cocking the firing pin, the inertial firing pin made it essentially impossible for the rifle to generate an unintentional discharge — one would have to drop the rifle, muzzle-first, onto a very hard surface and from a prodigious height; it is hard to imagine how that unlikely combination could cause subsequent injury or harm to anyone.

Cocking the gun with a chambered round requires only opening the finger-lever slightly and then reclosing it without pulling the trigger. The average hunter can do that just about as fast and silently as he can push a safety to the "off-safe" position.

For reasons that I cannot imagine, the newer Savage system deliberately eliminated this time-honored, close-without-cocking feature. Note that the Model-99's trigger mechanism does have an interlock that makes it impossible for the firing pin to fall unless something pulls the trigger or some rather robust part fails. For the trigger to pull with the safety on would also require the failure of a very robust piece of steel. Having examined this trigger system, I will attest that this is among the best and safest I have ever seen on any gun that does not contain a positive striker block.

However, that is precisely the heart of my complaint with the new Savage Model-99 design.... If the firing pin was cocked and the rear end of the firing pin or the shank of the firing pin failed, anywhere behind the front firing pin spring carrier, the firing pin would fall. If the rifle held a chambered round, it would fire. While I have never heard of such a failure happening, this is most assuredly possible. I am a firm believer in the philosophical tenant that anything not specifically forbidden is mandatory. Therefore, I believe it is better to carry a gun uncocked. That way, I can carry it with a chambered round and still get it ready to fire before I can get it to my shoulder.

Section 14: The Trouble With Lever-Action & Single-Shot Receivers, Part II 273

How to go about doing this on newer Model-99s? This modification requires only the proper shortening of the trigger interlock ramp on the inside of the finger-lever extension (the part that carries the bolt boss, refer to the previous subsection). The photographs show the proper modification quite clearly. The following points are critical: do not excessively shorten the interlock, do not move the front surface of the interlock back at all, the leading edge of the interlock ramp must be steep enough to prevent uncocking the firing pin when the firing pin spring has already stored sufficient energy to overcome the firing pin retractor spring's tension. These considerations entail many critical details to watch out for and keep track of.

I will offer a number for the distance that you should expect to shorten the trigger interlock section to on a typical Model-99. However, note that the only way to do this perfectly is to go by trial and not error — if you get this interlock too short, you might create a dangerous condition. Shorten this section some, reassemble the receiver, try to close the finger-lever without the gun cocking — simply pull the trigger just before the firing pin latch engages the firing pin, which you can watch happening as you close the finger-lever (when you have removed the buttstock). If the trigger will not move when the finger-lever is at that point in its arc, you will have to grind the interlocking section slightly shorter and try again. If the trigger will move, but not far enough to release the firing pin latch, you are getting close. When the trigger will just barely move far enough to release the latch, just as the firing pin extension starts to pull forward on the firing pin latch, you have the ramp perfect.

You should grind the ramp on the front of the finger-lever arm that leads from the trigger-free to trigger-locked-forward portions at the angle shown in the pictures. If you make this ramp too steep the finger-lever can bind on the ramp when you continue to hold it back while closing the action, after unlocking the latch to close the action without cocked the firing pin. If you make this ramp too shallow, you could get a situation where you could accidentally release the firing pin latch after the striker spring had stored sufficient energy to possibly fire the round — by pulling the trigger at the wrong position in the finger-lever's travel. Since this would happen when the action was unlocked, the results would certainly be devastating — at the very least. Obviously, avoid that condition at all cost. As noted, the same result would occur if you moved the leading edge of the interlock portion of the ramp too far back.

The only good tool for grinding the finger-lever to incorporate this slipped-closed modification is a one-quarter inch (1/4") sanding drum on a Dremel tool. One-quarter inch is the correct radius for the leading edge of the modified ramp. (These finger-levers are typically case hardened, so filing is not possible and there is no way to get to this surface with a bench grinder.)

Cut the area behind the interlock ramp only deep enough to allow the trigger to rotate far enough to release the firing pin latch. You can check this by moving the finger-lever until the newly cut portion is under the trigger's interlock extension. Pull the trigger and note if you can then manually rotate the firing pin latch forward. If not, remove more material from the proper area of the front of the finger-lever extension. Note, you can do all of this work with the receiver assembled; however, be careful where the sanding drum gets so that you do not sand areas you do not intend to sand; also note that after finishing the fitting you will have to do a complete disassembly and thoroughly clean all parts to get the sanding grit out of the action. See photograph #s 14-42/43.

On my rifle, I found that an alteration moving the beginning of the ramp (that area where the finger-lever extension begins to widen) to five-hundred and seventy-five thousandths of an inch (0.575") from the closest edge of the trigger release cut (which is the square notch in the front of the finger-lever extension, next to the finger-lever loop), was perfect. Finish this job by polishing the newly ground surface to a mirror finish. A small Dremel tool mounted Cratex wheel is the right tool for this polishing work.

Polishing Bolt Surfaces, Savage Model-99 Lever-Action Rifles:

Observe that the Model-99's bolt runs in raceways, trapped between the receiver's upper and lower tangs. It is certainly worthwhile to polish all surfaces inside the receiver where the bolt makes contact as it slides back and forth. This is slightly difficult but by assembling 600 grit corundum paper over small hardwood blocks, that you have cut in long rectangles of the proper proportions, you should be able to polish the top surfaces on all high spots with just a few minutes effort. This is all that is necessary. The goal is to polish only the spots where the bolt can touch.

Polish the corresponding friction surfaces on the bolt. On any used rifle these will be easy to identify through the surface marring. Chiefly, these areas are along the bottom and outside the rearmost extension of the bolt and along the top and side of the portion of the bolt immediately in front of the locking lug (along the flat top of the bolt). These areas are readily accessible with a Cratex wheel mounted in a moto-tool (Dremel). Note, however, that the top of the bolt on all newer Model-99s has a fancy machine-turned finish, polishing here will destroy this touch of class. For this reason, it is much better to polish the hidden area inside the receiver, along the top raceway. See photograph # 14-44.

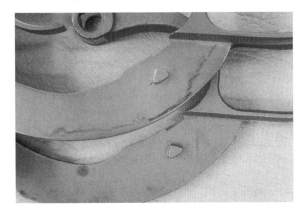

Photograph 14-42

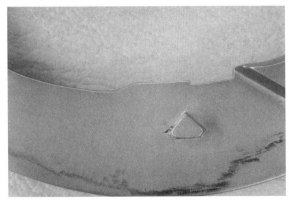

Photograph 14-43

Photographs 14-42/43: Savage Model-99 finger-levers. Shown at the top of photograph 14-42 is the modified finger-lever that allows closing the action without cocking the firing pin; at bottom is the original finger-lever, for comparison. Photograph 14-43 shows a close-up view of trigger interlocking section of the altered finger-lever. See the text for important safety considerations before attempting any such alteration.

Next, look for any other friction points, such as where the bolt runs past the cartridge guide (on the rotary-magazine models). Polish these friction points using the same tool.

Polish the high spots from the front lower face of the bolt — that area below the firing pin hole on the face of the bolt. This will facilitate the case head sliding up on the bolt during cartridge chambering. This work will thereby eliminate grabbing and catching. Be careful not to remove more than a slight amount of material — do not try to polish out all the tooling marks, which could dangerously alter headspace. Polish only the tops of the high spots.

The last area you need to polish is a little tougher to get into with polishing tools. This is the slot where the finger-lever bolt boss pin runs. You will note that this is a square-bottomed somewhat narrow slot that has a wider area near its closed end. If you clean all detritus and grease from this slot you should be able to see where the finger-lever boss has been rubbing in the slot during action manipulation. The best tool I have found for polishing inside this slot is a Cratex cone-shaped (bullet) polishing tip. As this tip wears away, it will polish along the adjacent side of the bottom of the channel simultaneously as it polishes the side of the slot. Moving to the other side of the slot finishes polishing the bottom of the channel. In that portion of the slot where the bolt boss rests when you have fully closed the finger-lever, make no effort to polish the surface to a mirror finish — that would indirectly increase headspace. It is, however, okay to polish the rest of the slot quite thoroughly.

Photograph 14-44: View of left side of Savage Model-99 receiver with bolt partially opened. Note wear marks on side of bolt. To ease action manipulation you should polish these, and other, friction surfaces. See associated text.

Section 14: The Trouble With Lever-Action & Single-Shot Receivers, Part II

Properly Fitting Bolt To Receiver, Savage Model-99 Lever-Action Rifles:

The final modification related to smooth functioning of the bolt involves the receiver. Install the bolt in the bare receiver. Then, while moving the bolt back and forth in the receiver, note the vertical play between the bolt and the upper and lower tangs. If this vertical travel is excessive (more than, perhaps, 0.025"), you might consider one of the following modifications.

The first option involves the simple expedient of bending the upper and lower tangs together. However, before even considering this alteration, read and understand this entire subsection. If you do not understand it, do not attempt this alteration. If you do this work improperly you could damage, or destroy, the receiver.

However, if you use a properly-padded vise, this alteration can be done quite safely. You must ensure that you do not apply clamping force to the area behind the tang safety on the upper tang — that rearmost extension of the upper tang is weakened by the safety raceway cuts and will simply bend down at those cuts if you apply clamping pressure too far back on the upper tang. Obviously, this is not where you want to bend the upper tang.

Your goal is to <u>very</u> <u>slightly</u> bend the upper tang so that the gap between the upper and lower tangs is not too wide, you want the bolt to just fit between the tangs with minimal clearance. The necessary bending should occur at a point near the upper tang's juncture with the receiver's solid sides. Again, it will only take a slight bending here to tighten the tangs to properly fit on the bolt as it moves through the raceways between the tangs.

Before making the decision to bend the tangs closer together (to tighten the bolt raceway in the receiver), note the relationship between the upper and lower tangs and the following pieces: the safety slide and the buttstock. (The safety slide is that piece, located on the right side of the tangs, which locks the trigger and finger-lever when the safety tab on the upper tang is set to the "S" position.)

If there is not sufficient vertical travel in the safety slide to accommodate the requisite reduction of the distance between upper and lower tang, you will have to slightly modify the slide. Note the vertical play in the slide by observing the relationship of the front portion of its lever end and the slot in the lower tang that that portion of the safety slide runs in during safety manipulation. If, after all, this modification of the safety slide proves necessary, it is quite simple. However, approach this alteration with caution. The fact is, the gun's dimensions and clearances should accommodate a proper tang-to-bolt raceway clearance without any alteration to the safety slide. If you think you need to alter this piece, perhaps you have made a mistake in some measurement.

To disassemble the tang-mounted safety parts you have to drive out a pin from the lower tang. There is also a spring in the lower tang, which provides on-off resistance on the safety. Before proceeding to disassemble the safety, note the orientation of this spring.

In any case, you can wait to alter the safety slide until you have bent the tangs together and then reassembled the safety parts. If it does, after all, prove necessary to alter the safety slide, that modification is quite simple to achieve. All this requires is a slight shortening of the front portion of lower guide extension of the safety slide, where that piece runs in the slot in the lower tang. Shorten this only enough to provide necessary clearance. The photograph shows the area where this piece could, theoretically, bind. See photograph # 14-45.

The second consideration is buttstock-to-receiver fit. If these pieces happen to match very closely, and if you intend to keep the existing buttstock, without refinishing it, you might want

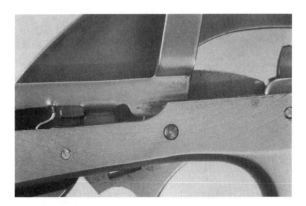

Photograph 14-45: View of right side of Savage Model-99 receiver, just above the trigger. Note the wire spring visible near the left side. This spring tensions the safety slide both for and aft. The lower front of this sliding piece enters a groove in the lower tang (just above the trigger pivot pin). Note the Moly-Slide lubricant showing at that point. See the text for a discussion of possible modifications in this area.

to leave the tangs alone (refer to the following alternative fix method). However, if you only need to tweak the tangs slightly to properly tighten the raceway-to-bolt clearance, this work might not hurt the appearance of the tang-to-buttstock fit. (The last Model-99 I worked on had such a poor buttstock-to-receiver tang fit that this alteration made no difference.)

If you intend to alter the tang spacing, proceed as follows. Remove the bolt, finger-lever and safety mechanisms from the receiver. Ensure that your bench-mounted vise has well-padded jaws and that the pads are up to the task of bending steel without failing. As an added precaution against marring of the tang surfaces, consider applying several layers of glass-reinforced electrician's tape onto the top side of the upper tang and over the finger-lever pivot on the lower tang. Install the finger-lever pivot-pin and screw into the appropriate hole in the lower tang.

The correct clamping force will be applied between the finger-lever pivot point and at a point opposite that on the upper tang. That is, you should apply the clamping force at right-angles to the bore axis. The force on the finger-lever pivot point might be sufficient to deform that portion of the lower tang by smashing the finger-lever pivot hole somewhat shut. This is why you should install the pivot pin and the pivot pin screw — to reinforce that portion of the lower tang. (Note that barrel removal dramatically simplifies this work because that reduces the torque in the vise; however, barrel removal is not necessary.)

There are three basic methods in approaching this task. First, you can proceed by trial and error, which dictates caution to avoid bending the tangs too close together — bending the tangs back apart, to provide necessary clearance, is a world-class pain. Second, you can produce a gauging block from hardwood; this is a much better approach. It involves only making a piece that will act as a guide to show when you have clamped the tangs some predetermined amount closer together. Since the tangs will spring before they bend, this process also involves a bit of trial and error, but it is much less prone to error.

For a starter gauge, try a block that is equal to the existing opening minus twice the clearance between the bolt and the tangs. Clamp until the tangs touch that block, remove the clamping force and recheck the bolt fit. If necessary, remove about twenty-thousandths of an inch (0.020") from the block and repeat the clamping process. Continue, in small increments until the unclamped tangs are a proper fit on the bolt.

However, if you will use a bit of caution, the following method is slightly easier. The caution is in order for two reasons. First, the following method requires you to stop tightening the vise before you have gone too far. Second, you will have to hold the receiver steady in the vise (especially critical if you have not removed the barrel), while adjusting the vise and measuring the distance between the established reference marks — this would seem to require about four hands. Obviously, this is one of those situations where a helper is most valuable. The advantage of this method is that you can easily determine the spring-back of the tangs so that you should be able to get the right adjustment accomplished in no more than three tries, assuming only that you maintain the same orientation and location of the clamping force.

To apply this method, proceed as follows. With no clamping force applied, measure the distance between marked reference points near the end of the upper tang and to a point on the lower tang opposite that spot. A dial caliper is the correct tool here. Tighten the vise until you have reduced that distance by about twice the amount of clearance you measured between the bolt and the tangs. Relieve the clamping force and remeasure. Note the difference from the original measurement, if any. If necessary, clamp tighter in small increments until the unclamped distance is correct. Note, you should be able to feel when the force is sufficient to cause the tangs to begin to permanently bend closer together. Proceed slowly. Again, it is a lot easier to approach the correct point slowly than it is to bend the tangs back apart. See photograph # 14-46.

Adding A Positioning Plunger To The Bolt, Savage Model-99 Lever-Action Rifles:

As an alternative to bending the tangs closer together, or as an adjunct that will remove the bolt's play inside the receiver, consider adding a spring-loaded plunger to the bolt. The included photographs show this alteration quite clearly. The plunger I used came from a new-model Ruger Single-Action revolver. This system (spring and plunger) is the cylinder hand tensioner in the Ruger. These parts are available from Ruger at a modest cost.

File a flat side on the plunger, near the upper end of the shank. Leave only a small portion of the spring end at full diameter (the spring end

Section 14: The Trouble With Lever-Action & Single-Shot Receivers, Part II

has a turned-down section over which the spring slips). The flat section (slot) should be only deep enough to facilitate the retaining pin. The flat should be long enough to allow the plunger to enter its hole until it is flush to the bolt body while allowing it to extend sufficiently from the bolt body to take up the slack in the raceways. For example, if the vertical play between the bolt and the tangs is fifty-thousandths of an inch (0.050") and the retaining pin is fifty-thousandths of an inch (0.050") in diameter, you will need a slot that is about one-tenth of an inch (0.1") long. You can produce such a slot using a jeweler's file. The slot should be no deeper than about one-third the plunger's diameter.

Locate a point toward the rear of the lower face of the bolt extension. The bolt extension is that portion of the bolt behind the finger-lever boss raceway, which runs in the lower tang raceway on the left side of the receiver and normally abuts the bolt retaining tab mounted on the lower tang. See photographs #s 14-47/48. Correct positioning for the plunger hole is as follows: 0.350" from the rear face of the bolt extension and centered, side to side. Drill punch the bottom of the rear bolt extension at this location.

Note the relationship of this spot and the finger-lever bolt boss raceway in the bolt. To prevent drilling into that raceway, drill the plunger hole at an angle, pointing slightly toward the rear of the bolt extension.

Measure the diameter of the plunger and choose the index drill that is just larger in diameter. Proceed to drill the plunger hole until that hole is just sufficiently deep to allow the spring and plunger to fully enter when you fully compress the plunger spring. This hole depth will provide the maximum spring tension on the plunger.

Remove the plunger and hold it alongside the bolt, aligned with the new hole. Position the plunger's head flush to the bottom of the bolt. Note the correct location for retaining pin hole. You can apply a magnet to the bolt body and that will keep the plunger in position so you can manipulate it to determine where to drill the retaining pin hole and where the center of that hole should be.

Photograph 14-47

Photograph 14-48

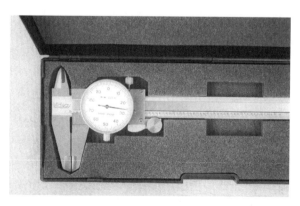

Photograph 14-46: Midway offers this eminently affordable and functional six-inch (6") range dial caliper that is accurate to one one-thousandth of an inch (0.001"). This precision tool comes in its own padded storage case and has all the features for which the home tinker could ask. An important consideration is that, unlike similar fancier and costlier electronic units, there is no battery to go dead.

Photographs 14-47/48: These photographs show a Savage Model-99 bolt that I have altered to include a spring-loaded plunger in the bottom of the lower rear extension. This plunger keeps the bolt lifted so that it does not rattle around in the action during bolt opening and closing. See the text for a complete explanation of this job.

With the retaining pin in the correct position the plunger will push into the hole until it is flush, without binding on the retaining pin. Further, the retaining pin will allow the plunger to extend the requisite amount from the bolt (0.050", in our example) necessary to push the bolt to the top of the raceway between the tangs. I should point out here that you should not try to build a plunger that will take up more than about fifty-thousandths of an inch (0.050") of play — if too much of the plunger is sticking out from the bolt, it is apt to bind in the hole.

A 4-penny nail shank works fine for the retaining cross pin. Remember to offset this hole appropriately from the centerline of the plunger hole and to account for the following factors: the diameter of the retaining pin, the slot on the plunger and for the angle of the plunger hole. Drill punch a location and produce the hole using an index drill bit that is one size smaller in diameter, compared to the cross pin (4-penny nail) diameter.

Install the plunger with the flat aligned to the retaining pin hole. Insert the shank of the index drill bit that you used to drill the retaining-pin hole. If the drill bit binds on the plunger as you try to install it through the hole, or as you work the plunger up and down, you will need to deepen the slot on the plunger. Also note whether the plunger will, in fact, enter fully flush to the bolt without binding and whether it will protrude sufficiently from the bolt to accommodate the clearance between the bolt and the tangs. If not, adjust the slot accordingly — either make it slightly deeper or longer, as needed. See photograph # 14-47.

When all is well, thoroughly clean the holes and the plunger and spring assembly. Cuttings in the plunger hole will cause no end of troubles. Insert a dab of a molybdenum-disulfide impregnated synthetic grease (such as Moly-Slide, available from NECO) in the plunger hole. Insert the plunger in the hole to spread the lubricant, then invert the plunger and spring assembly and install that fully into the hole and insert the drill bit used to drill the cross pin hole.

Prepare the cross pin as follows. Grind the pointy end of a 4-penny finishing nail to a slight taper. Starting from the outside of the bolt (the side that runs against the left rail in the lower tang), use this modified nail to push the drill bit through the hole (this method will keep the plunger in place during installation of the final retaining pin. Use a small hammer to drive the nail through the hole until it protrudes sufficiently through the bolt. It should be a tight fit in the hole on both sides of the plunger. Verify that the plunger still works freely and properly, as described above.

Apply electrician's vinyl tape over the plunger to keep that area clean of sanding debris. Use a cut-off wheel in the Dremel tool to cut the protruding end of the nail flush to the sides of the bolt extension. If necessary, install a one-quarter inch sanding drum to grind the retaining pin fully flush with both sides of the bolt. You will harm nothing by grinding a bit of extra material away here. Conversely, leaving this retaining pin protruding any on the outside of the bolt extension will definitely cause problems — it will hang up on the sides of the bolt raceway in the lower tang.

This plunger will keep the bolt from wobbling in the receiver. It will also reduce friction to a minimum. This might seem like a great deal of work for a little benefit to some tinkers, but to me it seems worthwhile.

Box Magazine Work, Savage Model-99 Lever-Action Rifles:

The clip magazine versions of the Model-99 are very similar, regarding valuable modifications, to the various other clip-fed rifles types. Refer to the appropriate sub-section in *Part I*, and the earlier sub-sections covering the Browning BLR and Winchester 88, for general discussions of appropriate and useful modifications.

Rotary Magazine Work, Savage Model-99 Lever-Action Rifles:

The rotary-magazine Versions of the Model-99 and the Model-99's forerunner, the Model-1895, carry a unique mechanism. On these rifles a spring-loaded rotary brass or aluminum spool located in the bottom of the receiver controls, locates and feeds cartridges. Most versions feature a cartridge counter window located on the left panel of the receiver, the number that shows through this window indicates how many rounds remain in the magazine.

Model-99 rotary-magazine capacity is as follows: five rounds in .22 Savage High Power (Imp), .22-250 Remington, .243 Winchester, .25-35 WCF, .250-3000 Savage, 7mm Waters, 7mm-08 Remington, .30-30 WCF, .300 Savage, .308 Winchester, .303 Savage, .358 Winchester, .38-55 WCF; four rounds in .284 Winchester cham-

Section 14: The Trouble With Lever-Action & Single-Shot Receivers, Part II

bered rifles. This magazine system positively protects the bullets from recoil damage in the magazine. A feature that is most valuable and almost unique among repeating hunting rifles.

As noted in the sub-section on bolt modifications, these rifles have a cartridge retainer guide on the left side of the receiver. This spring-loaded mechanism allows magazine loading but prevents the loaded rounds from coming free of the action while the bolt is open. There is little to do to this piece that is of much value. However, two simple alterations come to mind.

First, polish all friction points where the bolt slides past this piece. This work is simple enough to accomplish, since all such points are readily visible as marred places on the outside surface. Second, you might consider skeletonizing this piece by drilling shallow holes into the back side, as is shown in photograph # 14-49. This serves to improve functioning and reduce friction on the action during rapid manipulation — the mass-reduction resulting from drilling these shallow holes allows this piece to respond faster to the spring that pushes it out as the finger-lever brings the bolt to its fully-open position. Similarly, the lightened piece produces less resistance to rapid bolt closing. During rapid bolt manipulation this latter effect might be noticeable.

Since replacement parts for the rotary-magazine versions of this rifle are difficult or impossible to obtain, proceed with due caution. Protect against drilling too far through this piece. Use a drill press and take careful measurements to prevent this part-destroying eventuality.

You might consider removing the spool and polishing the inside of the receiver in the spool

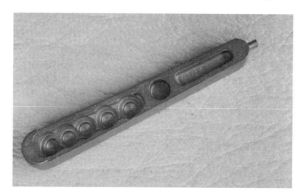

Photograph 14-49: These shallow skeletonizing holes in this Savage Model-99F cartridge retainer (a rotary magazine model) do not remove much weight but they are easily drilled and offer some advantage. See the text for precautions.

raceway to remove any burrs. A large dowel wrapped in 600 grit corundum paper and adapted to a drill would be a good tool for this operation. As is usually the case, there is no real benefit to polishing the interior to a mirror finish, only remove the burrs and high spots.

While you are at it, you could also polish away any burrs on the spool itself. However, unless you have reason to suspect the spool needs polishing, it seems this work would be of limited value. The rotary-magazines of the Model-99s I have seen all functioned flawlessly as shipped. That is one of the noted characteristics of these rifles, flawless functioning.

Before attempting to remove the rotary-magazine spool, carefully note the amount of spring tension on the spool. This information will be helpful when you reassemble the system. There are several ways to preload the spool spring. Only one of these is as the factory intended. Factory preload on the rotary magazine spool spring usually provides just the right spool tension to allow the shooter to easily load the magazine and to properly feed the loaded rounds during action cycling.

To remove the spool, remove the fore-end and note the internal spring clip in the hole located under the barrel at the front of the receiver. Note also the forward extension of the piece this clip is holding in place — the rotary magazine tensioner. Before installing the fore-end, said extension should always be positioned at top center, aligned under the barrel. If not, the fore-end will not slip back into the receiver.

While holding that tab in place, reach into the receiver with a small screwdriver, hook the spring clip and twist it free from its slot. Pull the spring clip from the receiver. Carefully allow the spool cap to rotate clockwise to fully relax the preload on the spool spring. Note how far the cap turned as the spring relaxed. As noted previously, this information will be a useful reference when you reassemble the spool into the rifle.

Carefully slide the spool cap from the receiver. Often you will have to use a bit of force. One method of providing this force is to reach inside the receiver with an appropriate tool and pry against the spool, pushing it forward. However, be careful! — the spool is fragile, do not apply much force here. If the magazine tensioner binds hard, try wiggling it by manipulating the tab. If this still will not work, use a long pin punch to reach through the rear of the disassembled receiver. Place the end of that punch against the rear of the spool, which protrudes through the rear spool guide, and tap on the punch with a small hammer.

When the cap comes free, the spool spring and the spool should also come free. Examine the relationship of these parts and note how the ends of the spring are hooked onto the spool and into the cap. Wear marks will disclose the factory installation point for the looped spring end that hooks on the rotary magazine tensioner — there are four possible settings. Use a permanent marker to further label this point.

Polish the receiver interior and spool, as necessary, to achieve smooth functioning and to remove any burrs that might catch on cartridges. Check the functioning with the decommissioned dummy cartridges you prepared. When all is well, reassemble the magazine spool assembly into the receiver.

Reassembly is easily accomplished in the following manner. Clamp the receiver in a padded vise with the barrel pointed straight down and the bottom of the receiver toward you and accessible.

Assemble the spool, spool spring and rotary magazine tensioner with the spring ends properly located. Note that you can add or decrease to rotary spool spring tension by adjusting the location of the looped end of the spring one position (one quarter turn) from the original setting. If you feel the original setting was too tight or too loose, give this a try.

Hold this loose assembly, spool up, and carefully feed it up, into the receiver. There is only one rotational position where it will bind with anything. If necessary, rotate the assembly slightly, until it freely enters the receiver. Be careful not to let these pieces separate, which will unlatch the spring, from either the spool or the cap. If that happens, you will have to start this process over.

When the spool gets almost all the way home, you will need to reach inside the receiver and jiggle the pin on the rear end of the spool until it enters the corresponding hole on the rear spool guide. A fashioned paper clip is just about the ideal tool here. When the rear spool guide enters the rear guide, slide the assembly fully in place. Turn the cap (counterclockwise) to fully rotate the spool in the receiver until the single extended cartridge divider comes to rest against the cartridge guide, which is located on the right side of the receiver, under the ejection port. Then continue to turn the cap until you have applied the proper preload to the spool spring — the tab on the rotary magazine tensioner will be directly under the barrel. Install the spring clip. Be sure to leave the cap in the proper orientation — if the tab is not centered under the barrel, the fore-end will not install properly.

Section 15: More Troubles With Two-Piece Stocks, Single-Shot Rifles, Part II

My friend, Steve Meacham, is a very modest person. While he reviewed *Section 15* and also provided a great deal of the information I have reiterated in *Section 16*, he would never claim to be an expert. I would hold otherwise. By my favorite definition of a true expert: *One who knows enough to know what he does not know*, Mr. Meacham fits the bill quite well.

Meacham manufactures reproduction Winchester falling-block rifles. He uses the best modern steels and produces the receiver parts with a combination of CNC (Computer Numerically Controlled) and EDM (Electrical Discharge Machining) techniques. He holds the parts he produces to standards of fit and finish that would have made any of the old-time gunsmiths shake their heads in awe and wonder. For example, the breachblock on a Meacham rifle fits the opening in the receiver. There is no slop in the receiver on an *S. D. Meacham Tool & Hardware Inc.* rifle.

The point here is, as a competitive single-shot rifleman and a producer of world-class reproductions, Steve Meacham knows the falling-block action inside and out. What follows is a compilation of his comments to me regarding what areas the serious tinker or gunsmith should address in order to make one of these rifles shoot at its ultimate accuracy potential. (While Mr. Meacham has reviewed this text, please understand the following: any errors are mine, not his!)

Another friend, Roger Johnston (NECO), reviewed the preliminary version of this text and made several critical observations. As an experienced single-shot rifle competitor, Roger's concerns are certainly worth reviewing. I have tried to adequately address many of his concerns throughout the subsequent sub-sections. Roger's major comment was that finding an accurate load for a traditional single-shot rifle is essentially a handloading proposition. I have touched upon that issue in the following sub-section on handloading considerations.

Replacement Stocks For Single-Shot Rifles:

As I will address in the following sub-section, proper stocking and stock bedding is a critical accuracy concern in two-piece stocked rifles. Proper stock design and bedding is perhaps more critical to the "using accuracy" of one of these rifles than any other mechanical feature or characteristic!

Reinhart Fajen® Inc.[1] offers a line of truly top quality replacement wood stocks adapted for most popular single-shot rifles. Fajen offers buttstocks that are properly designed for telescopic sight mounted rifles and fore-ends that are designed for use with a sandbag (wide flat bottom). Installation of this style fore-end, to replace the original rounded-bottom fore-end, typically affords a dramatic accuracy improve-

---

[1] Editor: Regrettably, the Fajen company has gone out of business since this was written.

ment, owing to the rifle's increased stability on the bags used for shooting off a bench. See photograph # 15-1.

Fajen offers the home tinker both semi-inletted wood to work with and custom factory installations. Consider these options carefully ... a good stock is a joy to hold and behold.

Stocking Concerns, Falling-Block (And Other Single-Shot) Rifles:

Mr. Johnston notes that different types of single-shot rifles show sensitivity to different stocking variables. For example, the Ruger No. 1 does not seem to be particularly sensitive to buttstock bedding but is extremely sensitive to fore-end bedding — possibly because the fore-end houses the hammer spring? Conversely, the Miller single-shot rifle is almost insensitive to fore-end bedding but is quite sensitive to buttstock bedding. Generally, each type of two-pieced stocked rifle will be more sensitive to the particulars of either the buttstock-to-receiver bedding or the fore-end-to-receiver bedding. However, some rifles will be particularly sensitive to both.

Without knowing the characteristics of any given rifle, my argument would be that proper wood-to-receiver bedding of both the buttstock and the fore-end are worthwhile goals in any attempt to maximize the rifle's accuracy. Since (as I have pointed out throughout this text) tinkering with bedding is so simple, I strongly suggest trying various bedding methods. With a bit of perseverance, you are bound to find the perfect combination. In the following text I have offered several guidelines and options.

The big difference in the accuracy potential of practically any single-shot rifle and the typical bolt-action rifle stems from the stocking system. Where the bolt-action rifle usually has a one-piece stock, which bridges the receiver and thereby carries the load from the rear support to the front support (be those sandbags or the shooter's hands), the typical single-shot rifle uses a two-piece stock, this design forces the receiver to bridge the gap, so to speak — it has to carry the entire load.

In the bolt-action rifle, slight changes in how the shooter holds the gun result in slight stress changes in the stock. With a stock-to-receiver connection that is properly bedded, these slight stress variations in the stock do not result in significant differences in the amount or type of stress transferred to the barreled-action. Since any rifle's accuracy reflects how consistently the barreled-action responds to the firing of a cartridge, stocking rigidity is a critical accuracy issue. Still, even in the best bolt-action rifle, large variations in bench technique will result in noticeable changes in zero. This is precisely why many Benchrest competitors shoot their rifles in an essentially free recoiling mode. The less they touch the gun, the less influence they will have on the rifle and the more consistently their shots will fall.

It is important to note that most competitive events featuring single-shot rifles require cartridges of sufficient recoil as to prevent the use of the free-recoil bench technique. The shooter has to lock himself to the rifle. This makes it even more critical to properly bed the wood to the receiver.

As with the bolt-action rifle, in a two-piece stocked rifle, any variation in shooter hold or bench technique (where the sandbag rests are located under the rifle, etc.) will necessarily result in a large variation in the rifle's dynamic mass and mass distribution. As the bullet accelerates through the barrel the gun reacts by accelerating in the opposite direction — we call this recoil.

Since the gun's effective center of mass falls along a line that is below the centerline of the bore, the gun will rotate as it recoils. The muzzle end of the barrel moves up and the butt end of the buttstock moves down. Depending upon how the

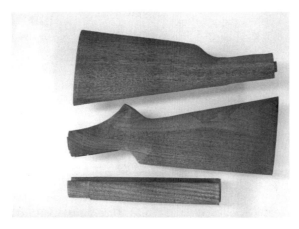

Photograph 15-1: Reinhart Fajen® Inc., offers a wide variety of replacement wood stocks for many applications. Besides straight-grain stocks with standard profiles, as pictured here, they can deliver top quality highly figured stocks in special configurations. See the text for a complete discussion of restocking.

Section 15: More Troubles With Two-Piece Stocks, Single-Shot Rifles, Part II

shooter positions his shoulder behind the stock, the muzzle also moves to one side and the buttstock moves to the opposite. The torque imparted to the bullet by the rifling will result in a tendency for the rifle to lay over to one side — the gun will rotate opposite to the direction of bullet's spin. Finally, recoil forces interacting with the shooter and gun rests can also push the entire gun sideways, or up, or both.

The magnitude of each of these effects is dependent upon the shooter's physiology and how he holds the gun — that is, how he alters the rifle's intrinsic mass. The interaction of the rests also affects the gun's response to firing a shot. As noted, these variations occur regardless of the stocking system used. However, there are other effects that produce vastly different consequences, when comparing two-piece and one-piece stocking systems.

As noted, in the one-piece stocking system, the stock bridges the load between the front and rear rests. The properly bedded one-piece stock isolates the barreled-action from any direct stress that is applied to the stock. Conversely, the two-piece stocking system transfers all (100%) of the stresses generated at the forestock and buttstock rests, or at the shooter's holding points, through the receiver.

A two-piece stocked rifle's receiver has to act as a bridge. This characteristic results in two problems. First, no attachment system can entirely eliminate the potential for differential stress when attaching wood to steel. Second, no receiver is perfectly rigid. Regardless of how solid a piece of steel might seem, it always bends under stress. There is no such thing as a threshold, any stress results in some strain (bending). Under low stress load conditions this relationship is precisely linear — double the load, double the bending.

Anything that bends the receiver will necessarily alter the barrel's alignment to the receiver. Further, the stress in the receiver will necessarily result in a change in the way the system vibrates as the bullet passes through and then clears the barrel. Both effects (alignment and vibration) will alter the bullet's ballistic flight.

Apart from choosing a rifle with a more rigid receiver and developing a good (consistent) bench shooting technique, there is little the tinker can do about flex in the receiver. Conversely, there is a lot the tinker can do about minimizing differential stress at the wood-to-steel joint.

The subjects of properly bedding two-piece stocks were well covered in the sections on the lever-action and pump-action rifles. However, note that some single-shot rifles, such as the Ballard and the Martini, have a factory-installed through-bolt. A properly designed through-bolt allows you to tighten the stock-to-receiver joint very, very tightly. This is precisely how the stock-to-receiver joint should be assembled!

With the stock properly tightened to the receiver with a through-bolt, the metal-to-wood joint cannot move as a result of vibrations. Without damaging something, the tighter you can get a through-bolt, the better. The tensioned through-bolt also acts like a spring. If it is tight enough, it will prevent the buttstock from bouncing free of the receiver in response to the vibrations generated during the bullet's passage through the bore. If the two pieces cannot separate, they cannot vibrate independently from the one another. Independent vibrations will result in all sorts of inconsistencies ... and inconsistencies are the enemy of accuracy.

The through-bolt design also maximizes the bonding of buttstock and receiver so that linear variations in the shooter's hold result in linear variations in stress in the system.

Conversely, in systems where the buttstock is loosely attached to the receiver, slight variations in pressure on the cheek piece, or at the tang, typically result in additional bending at the buttstock-to-receiver joint with little added stress in the receiver. The easiest way to visualize this situation is to imagine a rifle with a loose tang bolt. In this case, applying more pressure on the cheek piece bends the through-bolt more (until the buttstock begins to touch the receiver). Additional through-bolt bending does not transfer much additional stress to the receiver.

Such a system would seem to somewhat isolate the receiver from slight variations in the shooter's hold. Therefore, this might seem like a good thing. However, like so many things that might seem to be a good idea, this is not.

Consider what happens during recoil in a rifle with a loose buttstock-to-receiver joint. As the cartridge fires, the bullet begins to accelerate forward through the barrel. Therefore, the barreled-action begins to accelerate backward. For the sake of this discussion, assume there is a ten-thousandths of an inch (0.010") gap between the receiver and the buttstock when the bullet starts moving through the barrel. Until the barreled-action moves back ten-thousandths of an inch (0.010"), the only thing that can happen at the buttstock-to-receiver joint is a slight alteration in any bending stress on the through-bolt.

At the instant the receiver has moved ten-thousandths of an inch (0.010"), which will always happen before the bullet leaves the barrel, everything changes — the receiver hits the buttstock. Three important things happen.

First, the receiver-to-buttstock impact sets up vibrations in the barreled-action — the steel has just received a rather stout blow from a large wooden mallet. The faster the receiver is moving when it hits the buttstock the more violent the resulting vibrations will be.

For minute gaps between buttstock and receiver (as are typical in loose buttstock-to-receiver joints), impact velocity is essentially linearly related to the gap — twice the gap, twice the impact velocity.

Obviously, different buttstock-to-receiver gaps will impart vibrations of different magnitudes. On a loose buttstock-to-receiver joint, there is nothing to keep the buttstock-to-receiver gap the same from one shot to the next.

Second, the receiver transfers some of its recoil velocity to the buttstock — how much recoil velocity it transfers depends upon the effective mass of the buttstock, which depends upon how the shooter and rear bag interact with the stock. To see how this can affect accuracy, consider the following paragraphs.

Third, the buttstock imparts a torque (rotation force) to the receiver. The magnitude and direction of this torque depends upon precisely where along the buttstock-to-receiver joint the impact occurs. Pool players will see the relationship instantly; hitting the cue ball off center imparts a spin. The rate of that spin depends upon the weight and velocity (momentum) of the cue stick and how far off center the cue stick hits the cue ball.

For the sake of this discussion you only need to realize that an impact that occurs higher along the buttstock-to-receiver joint will impart <u>less</u> torque to the receiver! Why less? Because the top of this joint is closer to the rifle's longitudinal center of mass. A longitudinal impact at the longitudinal center of mass would impart no torque. (In pool, a centered impact on the cue ball imparts no spin in the pool ball.) Referring to the previous paragraph, an increase in the effective mass of the buttstock will increase any imparted torque resulting from an off-axis impact.

Now it only remains for us to realize that the torque imparted to the receiver will necessarily result in a bending of the barreled action. As the receiver rotates (typically) downward, the barrel initially stays pointed where it was. Then, as the stress wave (traveling at about 20,000 fps) travels up the barrel, the barrel will bend. When this wave reaches the front of the barrel, the muzzle will begin to move up. This sets up a vertical vibration at the rifle's muzzle. This vibration will begin to die down immediately but it will not die down significantly before the bullet exits the bore.

I should also note that there is nothing to say the receiver-to-buttstock impact zone has to be centered (side-to-side) behind the bore axis! Typically it is not. The magnitude and pattern of the resulting barrel vibrations will depend upon the details of the buttstock-to-receiver interaction. These interactions (and the resulting vibrations) are not likely to be the same from one shot to the next.

It is to be hoped that I have run this subject into the ground. My goal in this lengthy discussion was to try to explain why you cannot expect a rifle with a loose buttstock-to-receiver joint to deliver consistent accuracy.

In such a rifle, slight alterations in hold result in large vertical (and sometimes horizontal) stringing. This is not hypothetical; generations of target shooters and specific shooting tests have well demonstrated this effect.

Bedding The Buttstock To The Receiver, Two-Piece Stocked Single-Shot Rifles:

As noted elsewhere, in order for any tang-bolt attachment system to work properly, just as with the through-bolt, you will have to glass bed all surfaces of the stock that abut to the receiver and those that are parallel to the sides and flats of the tangs. Equally, be certain that none of the surfaces of the wood or tangs that run at any other angle touch each other. Typically, the tangs have rounded surfaces at the rear. Angled surfaces also occur along the inside edges and where the sides of the tangs step down and narrow. Apply tape on these areas during the bedding operation to positively preclude stock-to-tang contact at these locations.

Also note that some tangs are not parallel to each other. In these rifles, tightening of the tang bolt can squeeze the tangs together and force the stock to pull back from the receiver — precisely what you do not want to have happen. On all two-piece stock systems incorporating a tang bolt that clamps the tangs together, be certain to include a sufficient epoxy bed along the wood surfaces that are under the tangs so that clamping the tangs will not result in significant bending of the tangs.

If neither a through-bolt nor this tapered tang bolt modification is desirable or feasible, at the very least, glass bed all surfaces of the buttstock and provide reliefs so that tightening the tang bolt does not pull the stock away from the receiver and so that all recoil is taken up at the flats on the front end of the stock. This epoxy bedding layer will strengthen the buttstock, extend the life of the joint and seal out moisture and cleaning solvents.

Adding A Through-bolt, Falling-Block (And Other Single-Shot) Rifles:

If a through-bolt modification is possible, it is best to design this bolt to pull on both the upper and lower tang as you tighten it. It is also desirable to use the longest through-bolt that is feasible. Doing so puts most of the buttstock wood under compressive stress and the bolt under tension. This makes the strongest attachment system possible. See photograph # 15-2.

For a complete discussion and photographs of this process, refer to the sub-section on adding a through-bolt to a two-piece stocked lever-action (Marlin) rifle.

If a through-bolt alteration is not feasible, refer to the following sub-section for a description of how to replace the existing straight tang bolt with a tapered tang bolt. This alteration, while not as good as a through-bolt, will dramatically improve the rifle's accuracy potential.

Adding A Tapered Tang Bolt, Falling-Block (And Other Single-Shot) & Lever-Action Rifles:

Before making any alterations to the existing (original) stock, consider the rifle's collector's value. On any antique rifle you should obtain a replacement stock — save the unaltered original for future restoration of the valuable rifle.

Technically, any threaded and headed object smaller than one-quarter inch (1/4") in diameter is referred to as a screw. Nevertheless, throughout this discussion I will refer to the original *Tang Screw* (which is almost always smaller than 1/4" in diameter) as a *Tang Bolt*. This is done for the sake of clarity — this piece does not screw into the stock and the replacement piece is based upon a one-quarter inch, or larger, bolt.

Stevens and Hepburn single-shot rifles, among others, used a simple non-tapered tang bolt to attach the buttstock. Some other tang-mounted buttstocks use a tapered tang bolt, which is certainly a useful and more sophisticated system. However, after a few years use and aging, most tapered tang-bolt attachments are worn out so that the tapered bolt does no good.

Regardless of the make or model of rifle, if it has a two-piece stock and the buttstock does not attach with a through-bolt, try to figure out a good way to incorporate a through-bolt. The resulting improvement in shot-to-shot consistency (accuracy) can be quite dramatic. Refer to the previous sub-section and the applicable sub-sections on lever-action rifles for a discussion of how to incorporate a through-bolt, if possible.

If the incorporation of a through-bolt is neither feasible nor desirable, consider converting the rifle to use a tapered-shank tang bolt instead of the existing straight-shanked tang bolt.

If you combine a tapered tang bolt with a tang bolt hole in the stock that you have lined with steel-reinforced-epoxy, and if you form the proper taper and clearance in that hole, you can produce a joining system that is very, very good at bonding the buttstock solidly to the receiver. Unlike the through-bolt, this system will not tension the entire buttstock so it does little, if anything, toward strengthening the buttstock. Nevertheless, this is a worthwhile alteration. In the following paragraphs I describe one method of incorporating a tapered tang bolt.

Photograph 15-2: Like most modern rifle makers, Dakota Arms uses a through-bolt on their marvelous single-shot actions. This design also incorporates an automatic cocking hammer and one of the best safety systems on any rifle — the safety blocks the hammer's fall, when the safety is applied, even a mechanical failure in the hammer system cannot result in the rifle firing!

I will follow this discussion as if the rifle had a tang bolt that threads into the lower tang, as most do. If the tang bolt on the rifle you are working on threads into the upper tang, reverse upper and lower (in this discussion), as necessary — you should not change the bolt's orientation. Note that tang bolts usually have a standard slotted fillister head. Also note that for the sake of clarity I will continue this discussion as if I were modifying a rifle that originally had a No. 12 tang bolt (screw).

Before beginning, verify that the tang bolt hole in the lower tang has standard threads or that you can get a die that will cut those threads on a bolt — 12x28 and 12x32 bolts are common but many guns use either a bastard thread, unique to that gun or model, or a special machinist's thread that you cannot easily get taps and dies for.

Note, Winchester uses a special thread profile. Although, at a glance, it looks the same as the standard fractional inch thread profile, it is different. Usually, you can use a tap or die of the same size and thread pitch to form a threaded hole or a bolt that will function with the corresponding Winchester threaded part. Nevertheless, these threads are not the same.

Tang Work For Adapting A Tapered Tang Bolt When A Correct Bolt-Threading Die Is Not Available, Falling-Block (And Other Single-Shot) & Lever-Action Rifles:

If this existing tang bolt is not a size and thread that you can get a die for (see Brownells), this alteration is somewhat complicated. For example, assume you have a rifle with a 12x40 tang bolt. Rifles commonly use this bolt size and thread but you cannot find a die to cut these threads unless you go to a specialty machine shop supply house (such as MSC, Industrial Supply Company, 1-800-645-7270). What to do? Either order a die from such a house or modify the lower tang to accept a (larger) standard thread.

Again, before proceeding, consider the potential collector's value of the rifle. If this is a concern, make no permanent alterations. Better to get replacement pieces, put the original parts in storage and do any work on those replacement parts.

However, if the rifle you have has no collector value consider the following alteration. This involves adapting a substantially larger tang bolt. This will necessitate several rifle alterations, as described next.

(If you can get a die to cut threads on a replacement tang bolt to fit the existing thread in the lower tang, refer to the following subsection.)

In this example, we have to drill the lower (threaded) tang hole just large enough to clean out the existing threads and allow tapping that hole to the next size larger standard bolt size, usually one-quarter inch (1/4"). When you have a choice of thread pitch, the extra fine ("machinist") thread is always the best choice. Finer threads are easier to cut and provide more attachment strength. Such taps and dies are often available by special order from hardware stores and Brownells carries a wide selection. They offer the superfine-machinist-thread $^1/_4$x40 taps and dies. Since these taps and dies are readily available, that would be the thread to use here. To drill the correct hole diameter for tapping to $^1/_4$x40 threads, you will need a #2 index drill bit (0.221").

Be careful in drilling this hole in the lower tang. You want to keep this hole and these threads square to the existing tang bolt holes. The best way to ensure this is to drill through the existing upper tang bolt hole with the #2 index drill bit. Then continue drilling through (and enlarging) the existing lower tang-bolt hole. Since you will later need to enlarge the existing hole in the upper tang, any slight error in drilling through that hole will harm nothing. By drilling through the existing hole in the upper tang first, you will be able to properly align the new hole in the lower tang with the hole in the upper tang.

In this instance, a good next step is to drill through the upper tang hole with the "B" letter drill bit (0.238"). The $^1/_4$x40 tap will cut shallow threads in this hole. Start the $^1/_4$x40 tap from the top and thread it through the upper tang. As noted, it will form shallow threads and will, therefore, be properly centered in and aligned with the hole through the upper tang.

The threaded portion of the $^1/_4$x40 tap should be long enough that the tap will begin to thread the hole in the lower tang before it comes loose from the upper tang. Thereby you will achieve essentially perfect alignment between these holes!

After completing these preliminary tang modifications, locate a five-sixteenths inch (5/16"), grade-8, hex-head or socket head cap bolt. You will need a bolt that has an unthreaded shank portion that is at least as long as the original tang bolt — usually about one and one-half inches ($1^1/_2$"). This bolt will require extensive

Section 15: More Troubles With Two-Piece Stocks, Single-Shot Rifles, Part II

modifications. Also, you will have to modify the upper tang to accept the bolt head and shaft.

If you are using a hex-head bolt, you will later modify it to a fillister head that is three-eighths inch (3/8") in diameter. If you are using the socket head cap screw, you will later grind the head down to three-eighths inch (3/8") diameter and shorten it to about one-quarter inch (1/4") high with a rounded top. Note that the socket head bolt will <u>necessarily</u> protrude slightly from the top of the tang — if you make the bolt head short enough so that it will not protrude from the tang, it will probably not have a sufficient socket depth to allow proper tightening. Despite this cosmetic flaw (the socket head protruding above the top of the tang) the socket head provides a vastly superior method of tightening and is, therefore, certainly worth considering.

The next step is to modify the bolt head recess in the upper tang, as needed, to fit the oversize bolt head. In this example, you will need to produce a flat-bottomed hole that is three-eighths inch (3/8") in diameter and centered over the existing hole in the upper tang. Use extreme caution to avoid drilling too deep and, thereby, weakening the tang.

Mount the receiver in a well-padded vise in a position that provides good access to the upper tang. A drill press vise is ideal. Locate the existing upper tang-bolt hole squarely centered under a standard (pointed) three-eighths inch (3/8") twist drill bit. With the drill turning at about 1100 rpm, carefully advance the drill bit until the center of the drill bit <u>just</u> touches at the perimeter of the original bolt shank hole through the upper tang. (If the original tang hole had a tapered bottom you will have finished the necessary modification to the upper tang.)

For a fillister bolt head recess you will have to produce a flat bottomed recess in the tang. Black & Decker sells twist steel drill bits with a small point in the middle and flats at the outside edges of the point. These drill bits will produce perfect flat-bottomed, shouldered bolt head recesses. However, you cannot normally use these drill bits to enlarge an existing hole . . . they will not properly self-center in an existing hole. However, with the initial bevel cut by the standard pointed drill bit, these special Black & Decker drill bits might work, but only if you can lock the receiver in a padded drill press vise so the end of the drill bit is precisely positioned and square to the existing hole. Even then, advance this special drill bit very, very carefully.

Lacking that, you can do it the old-fashioned way, modify a three-eighths inch (3/8") twist steel drill bit to create a flat-ended drill bit. You can do this easily with a bench grinder. Use plenty of water to keep the drill bit cool. Hold the drill bit square to the side of the grinding wheel. Then grind off the entire tapered end of the drill bit while spinning it slowly between your fingers. Then use a file to produce a slight undercut on each flute, so the forward edge will cut into the steel.

Complete the sides of the bolt head recess in the upper tang-bolt hole using the fancy Black & Decker bit or this modified (flat-ended) drill bit. Again, be doubly careful to avoid drilling too deeply into the tang — be very careful to drill no deeper than the bottom of the original bolt head recess.

The final work needed on the receiver is to enlarge the upper tang-bolt hole to five-sixteenths inch (5/16"). Although this is simple enough, make every effort to drill the hole squarely through the tang. At best, you will only have a one-thirty-second inch (1/32") wide shoulder (at the bottom of the bolt head recess) for the modified bolt head to pull against, you do not want to damage, and thereby weaken, that narrow shoulder!

Tang Work For Adapting A Tapered Tang Bolt When A Correct Bolt-Threading Die <u>Is</u> Available, Falling-Block (And Other Single-Shot) & Lever-Action Rifles:

A typical example would be when you have chosen a one-quarter inch bolt to replace an original 12x32 bolt. Head diameter on a standard fillister head No. 12 bolt is about 0.295". However (usually), the recess in the upper tang will accept a bolt head of about 0.310" without any alteration.

Head diameter of a one-quarter inch (1/4") socket head cap screw is about 0.365". It is possible to reduce the outside diameter of a socket head one-quarter inch (1/4") bolt to about 0.305" diameter without destroying the socket head. Similarly, you can grind down the hex head on a one-quarter inch (1/4") bolt to 0.305" diameter. This alteration will leave sufficient seating area in the bottom of the existing bolt head recess.

Therefore, if you can modify and use a one-quarter inch (1/4") bolt, the only tang modification you will have to make is to drill the upper tang-bolt hole to about 0.242" (letter drill bit "D").

Making A Tapered Tang Bolt, Falling-Block (And Other Single-Shot) & Lever-Action Rifles:

In this description, I will assume you are using a one-quarter inch (1/4") bolt and have the correct die to create threads that match the existing threads in the rifle's lower tang. Sizing and details will be slightly different if you are working with a five-sixteenths inch (5/16") bolt, where you had to drill and tap the tangs to accept a larger bolt.

Cut the shank of the grade-8 bolt to about one-quarter inch longer than the original bolt's shank. Chuck the bolt head in an electric drill. Normally, the hex head will align the bolt to the drill — when the drill turns, the bolt shank will not wobble. This condition is important for the subsequent grinding steps. If necessary, remove, reinstall and retighten the bolt until the shank is true to the axis of the drill's chuck — when the drill turns, the bolt shaft does not wobble.

Mark the portion of the shaft that corresponds to the part that will be located between the tangs (usually about 1¼"), include that part of the bolt shank that will pass through the upper tang in the assembled rifle. You will have to grind this portion down so that it tapers. Begin this taper directly under the bolt's hex head, where you should leave the shaft at the existing diameter (typically, 0.245" on the nominal 1/4" bolt).

Mark a point that will be about one-eighth inch (1/8") from the top of the lower tang when the finished bolt is assembled into the rifle. The bolt diameter at that point should be the same as the threaded portion of the original tang bolt, about 0.210". This thirty-five thousandths of an inch (0.035") taper provides the entire functioning of the tapered tang bolt — get it right! This tapered section should have straight, smooth sides — there should be no change in taper rate.

Reduce the remaining portion of the end of the shaft to about five-thousandths of an inch (0.005") larger than the major diameter of the threads on the original bolt. This will vary slightly, depending upon the thread pitch. Measure the diameter of the threaded portion of the existing tang bolt and grind down the end of the replacement bolt accordingly.

Then, to facilitate cutting threads that are square to the bolt's axis, grind the last one-quarter inch of the shank to form a slight taper. See diagram.

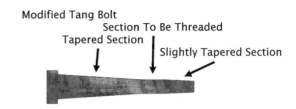

To form these tapers, begin with the bench grinder. With the drill set to run in reverse, hold it on the right side of a bench grinder wheel to bring the bolt shank into contact with the grinding surface.

With both the drill and grinder running, you should be able to grind the shank to approximately the proper size and shape in a few minutes. To avoid overheating this heat-treated steel, use a hand-pumped spray bottle to douse the bolt with water. Do not allow the bolt to overheat but be cautious to avoid getting water in the drill or grinder motor — avoid electrical shock.

Take periodic measurements at the end of the taper using a dial caliper. When you have reduced the shaft to within about five-thousandths of an inch (0.005") of the desired size, stop grinding. Mount the drill in a vise and apply the trigger lock to keep it running. Then true both the tapered and the future threaded portions of the shank using a standard bastard file. Take measurements and continue filing until the shank meets the sizes described above.

Finish this work by polishing the tapered shank using progressively finer grades of corundum paper. Polish to at least 320 grit, though 600 grit is better. Remember, you want the surface of the tapered shank to be as smooth as possible. Be careful to avoid creating steps or changes in the taper rate.

Reverse the modified bolt in the drill, insert the future threaded portion in the chuck. Verify that the bolt is square to the drill — it should not wobble when the drill turns. Using the drill and the grinder, proceed to grind the head round and to the proper diameter to fit the bolt head recess in the upper tang (just under 0.310" for this example, using a 1/4" bolt shank).

If you used a socket head cap screw, grind the head to one-quarter inch (1/4") thick. Then grind the top into a truncated dome shape. If you used a hex head bolt, grind and profile the head of the bolt to match the thickness and shape of the original tang-bolt head — usually you can leave the replacement bolt head somewhat thicker than the original, just as long as it fits about flush in the tang-bolt recess.

Use the running drill to polish the ground surfaces of the head with 320 grit sandpaper followed by four-ought (0000) steel wool. This finishes the head of the socket head cap screw. On the modified hex head bolt you will need to cut a screwdriver slot.

Solidly mount the bolt in a padded vise. Use a hacksaw fitted with a high-quality 32 tpi blade to cut a square screwdriver slot in the bolt head. Saw to a depth of about two-thirds (2/3) the thickness of the bolt head. Then use a flat jeweler's file of the correct thickness (0.040") to produce a square-bottomed, straight-sided slot that is equal in depth across the bolt head. Brownells sells files made specifically for producing screwdriver slots in bolt heads. To finish the bolt head, polish off any burrs using four-ought steel wool.

Insert the bolt head into a drill chuck and use the drill and grinder to produce a slight taper on the last one-quarter inch of the end of the bolt. This will facilitate threading die alignment. This little touch makes it much easier to cut threads that are properly squared to the bolt shank.

Locate the modified bolt in a padded vise with the untapered shank portion accessible. Use the die that matches the threads in the lower tang to cut threads on the appropriate portion of the tapered bolt.

You can also mount the bolt in the chuck on a drill press and rest the die holder on the drill press table. Then lower the spindle to bring the bolt into contact with the threading die and turning the drill press spindle by hand. Given a slight taper on the end of a properly sized work piece, this method will generate perfectly aligned threads.

Threading of grade-8 steel requires patience, a good sharp die and plenty of cutting oil — adding molybdenum-disulfide to almost any cutting oil dramatically reduces friction during thread cutting. Despite the difficulty involved in threading grade-8 steel, this can be done. The advantages of using a grade-8 bolt suggests the additional effort is well worthwhile.

Produce the necessary threads on the straight portion of the modified bolt. Be careful to produce the threads square to the shank. If you produced the slight taper on the extended (waste) end of the shank, this task is much easier to accomplish correctly.

On rifles where the threaded end of the tang bolt enters a blind hole, you will have to remove this excess one-quarter inch of bolt shank before continuing. On rifles with an open-ended threaded tang-bolt hole, leave this extension as an alignment guide — remove it later, after you have completed the fitting steps.

Apply cold bluing to all freshly cut surfaces on the tangs and the replacement bolt. After the bluing agent has acted, clean it off and apply a protective and lubricating coating of molybdenum-disulfide impregnated grease to the underside of the bolt head, the bolt head recess in the upper tang and the threads in the lower tang.

Modifying The Buttstock For A Tapered Tang Bolt, Falling-Block (And Other Single-Shot) & Lever-Action Rifles:

Before expending a lot of energy modifying the existing buttstock, ensure that it is worth it. If it is not a good, solid piece of wood that properly fits you, the sighting system and the rifle, consider replacing it with a piece of high-quality wood, as is available through Fajen. Also, consider the collector's value of the original stock on any antique — do not alter any such wood. The rule is, do not alter any original antique part. Get a replacement and put the original in storage.

To modify the stock for use with the tapered bolt, begin with a buttstock that is properly glass bedded at the receiver contact zones, as described elsewhere in this text. Drill through the tang attachment bolt hole. Use the largest drill bit that will not scar the exterior of the buttstock in the areas outside the tang channels. It is quite convenient if you can choose a drill bit size that will allow you to tap a partially-threaded hole through the tang hole after drilling that hole oversize. Such threads are a great adjunct to the epoxy's natural adhesion. If you can get such threads cut to any significant depth in the wood, the epoxy plug will never move.

Next you will need to perform a critical alteration of this enlarged hole. Locate or make a wood chisel that is long enough to reach at least half way through the tang-bolt hole in the stock — usually about three-quarters inch (3/4"). If possible, use a chisel that is just as wide as the oversize hole you drilled.

Use this chisel to carve out the front side of the hole to form a square side facing away from the butt of the stock. See the associated diagram. Without this modification, it is possible to split the stock by over-tightening the modified (tapered) tang bolt. Conversely, with this modification, the glass bedding plug directs the tightening stress against the strength of the wood and does not introduce a direct spreading force — it is much less likely to split the buttstock.

If feasible, taper the square side of this hole so that it is wider at the bottom of the stock (at the thread end of the modified screw) — this will help prevent the plug from moving toward the top of the hole as you tighten the tang bolt.

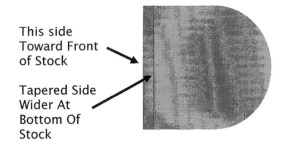

Bottom View of Modified Tang Bolt Hole In Stock

This side Toward Front of Stock

Tapered Side Wider At Bottom Of Stock

Glass Bedding The Buttstock For A Tapered Tang Bolt, Falling-Block (And Other Single-Shot) & Lever-Action Rifles:

If the sides of this hole have any openings through into the tang recesses in the stock, seal those holes with a dab of modeling clay or tape applied at the other end of the holes. Unless a hole is a necessary recess for an action part, do not prevent the epoxy bedding agent from filling it — epoxy entering any such holes can dramatically strengthen the bond between the epoxy plug and the stock and will generally strengthen the tang portion of the buttstock.

Mix a sufficient batch of gel-type epoxy bedding agent to fill the drilled, threaded and chiseled out tang-bolt hole through the buttstock. Add two-parts atomized steel (available from Brownells) to three-parts mixed bedding agent. Stir this mix sufficiently to fully homogenize the steel into the epoxy mix.

Temporarily apply tape over the ends of the modified tang-bolt hole in the stock. Then apply masking tape over the entire exterior surface of the tangs on the stock. Cut away the tape where it covers the tang channels. Very liberally spray bedding release agent over and into the entire tang area of the stock. Equally apply release agent to the entire tang area of the receiver. Also, thoroughly coat the modified tang bolt and a similarly sized nail with release agent.

Remove the tape that covers the modified tang-bolt hole in the stock. <u>Fill</u> that hole with the steel reinforced bedding agent mix. Ensure that the agent completely fills out into the hole, so that it presses into the irregularities (and threads, if you made those) in the hole. The success and value of this job depends upon the epoxy mix <u>fully</u> filling this hole. Save a test sample of epoxy to monitor its curing progress.

With the hole filled, drive the release agent treated nail through the center of the epoxy. Do not wiggle this makeshift tool around in the bedding agent. Just form a hole that is big enough to allow the modified tang bolt to pass through, reasonably unobstructed.

Mount the receiver in a padded vise with the tangs pointed up and accessible. Immediately assemble the stock to the rifle. Press the stock fully down (forward) on the tangs and tap the butt end of the buttstock with a plastic mallet to ensure that you have it solidly seated against the receiver. Remember, this method applies only to stocks that were properly glass bedded and clearanced to begin with.

Install the modified tang bolt. Turn it into the lower tang until only about one-half the thickness of the bolt head extends from the upper tang. <u>Do not tighten this bolt at this time</u> — that will destroy the value of this work. Equally, do not fiddle with the excess bedding agent that is produced from the tang-to-stock openings during this installation. However, do apply an additional coating of release agent to both ends of the bolt and to the visible areas of the tang near the bolt holes — any areas where the assembly process might have disturbed the release agent.

Check the test sample periodically, when the epoxy has cured to a rubbery consistency (about 4 hours), remove the tang bolt and clean it free of any epoxy that might have adhered to the bolt or torn loose and filled the threads.

Wait until the epoxy has cured to a hard plastic consistency (about 6 hours). Then remove the stock. This can require application of quite a bit of force so be careful not to bend or bust something. The secret is to keep pulling, twisting and wiggling the end of the stock slightly. Eventually it will come free.

With the stock removed, clean all extraneous epoxy from the tangs and the tang openings in the stock. This is an easy job if you properly applied release agent to all affected surfaces and

Section 15: More Troubles With Two-Piece Stocks, Single-Shot Rifles, Part II

if you included the atomized steel in this batch of bedding agent — the resulting steel color makes it easy to differentiate this bedding agent from any previous (unreinforced) glass bedding material. Be doubly certain that none of this bedding agent remains in the back end of the tang relief channels in the buttstock. Carefully whittle out a <u>slightly</u> convex cavity in both the top and bottom ends of the epoxy bedding plug. A one-half inch (1/2") twist steel drill bit will do this job quite well. Spin the drill bit between your fingers and apply just enough pressure to cut a shallow recess in each end of the plug. You should center this relief pocket on the tapered bolt hole.

This small cavity will ensure that the tangs do not bind against this plug before pulling solidly against the wood in the channels. Also, it will keep any slight deformations of the epoxy from pushing against the tangs.

Drill the small end of the epoxy plug with a drill bit that is, perhaps, five-thousandths of an inch (0.005") larger than the threads on the modified bolt. This will provide the necessary clearance for the bolt to enter further through the plug as you fully tighten it in the final assembly.

Then use a small round file to rasp out the rear (buttplate) side of the tapered hole in the epoxy plug. Be careful to avoid any filing on the front (receiver) side of this precisely formed hole. File away at least ten-thousandths of an inch (0.010") of the bedding material to provide fore-and-aft clearance full length (top to bottom) of this hole. The sides of the hole should be parallel and the back surface should be smoothly radiused.

Thoroughly degrease the pieces that you sprayed with release agent. Verify that the front of the tapered hole in the epoxy plug is smooth. Apply a thorough coating of graphite or molybdenum-disulfide into the hole and to all normally hidden surfaces of the tangs that will touch the buttstock. Remove the tape from the stock. Allow the epoxy to cure for at least two additional days. More time cannot hurt; less time can destroy the critical dimensions of the epoxy plug. The epoxy should be very, very hard before you complete the final assembly.

When the bedding agent has fully cured, assemble the buttstock and insert the modified tang bolt. Note that, as you tighten the bolt, it will come up against the epoxy on the front (receiver) side of the plug and begin to pull the stock toward the receiver before it ever begins to pull the tangs together. This is as it should be. Be sure to use a properly fitting screwdriver bit and to hold the screwdriver square to the bolt. Tighten the bolt as tight as you feel comfortable in doing.

Where necessary, note how much of the other end of the tang bolt sticks out past the bottom of the lower tang. Mark the juncture of the protruding bolt with the lower tang. Remove the bolt and eliminate that excess by grinding to this mark.

Remember, you originally formed this bolt about one-quarter inch longer than needed. Be careful not to overheat the tang bolt while grinding to remove the excess at the end of the shank. Polish the ground end and cold blue that area.

Final Fitting Of Glass Bedding For Tapered Tang-Bolt, Falling-Block (And Other Single-Shot) & Lever-Action Rifles:

Reinstall the tang bolt and tighten it. If it will not tighten sufficiently to squeeze the tangs against the wood, cut waxed card paper spacers (playing cards or waxed paper) to fit in the bottom of the tang channels. Add sufficient paper layers to provide for simultaneous tang bolt to epoxy plug tightening and tang-to-tang channel tightening.

Usually, this is not necessary. However, the goal is to apply a large end-force on the stock, necessary to bond the buttstock to the receiver, and then to clamp the tangs against the tang channels in the buttstock. This combination provides the maximum rigidity possible with this type of connection. Use shims, as necessary, to achieve this goal.

Note that if you used paper shims between the tangs, you can remove some of those at any later time, if necessary, to accommodate wear or shrinkage that might loosen the fit between the front of the epoxy plug and the tapered tang bolt.

Fore-end Glass Bedding, Falling-Block (And Other Single-Shot) Rifles:

For a complete discussion of this work, refer to the earlier sub-sections covering fore-end bedding on lever-action and single-shot rifles.

Remember, your overall goal is to minimize flexure between the buttstock and the receiver and between the fore-end and receiver. On rifles with straight taper barrels, consider full glass bedding along the length of the barrel channel but be sure to include a slight space between the rear of the fore-end and the front of the receiver.

Consider filling that void with black RTV silicone (available in a squeeze tube under the *Permatex* banner and sold in most automotive parts stores). Your goal is to prevent any point contact between the fore-end wood and the receiver steel. Such contact can result in cracked wood or point stress loads when the fore-end warps (I keep waiting to see a piece of wood that will not, eventually, warp).

However, note that some experienced shooters suggest that the RTV bedding system is not necessarily a good idea in single-shot rifles with fully bedded barrels. Again, as with epoxy bedding, it is easy to experiment. If the RTV bed improves accuracy, use it!

Fore-end Attachment Systems, Falling-Block (And Other Single-Shot) & Lever-Action Rifles:

What might seem to be the best system is a fore-end hanger, which fully floats the barrel and supports the fore-end at the receiver only. Examples include the Ruger No. 1 and the Miller. In those systems, a layer of glass bedding between the receiver and the fore-end and under the fore-end hanger screw are all that are required to provide an ideal fore-end attachment.

This system minimizes the potential for fore-end warpage to stress the barrel. However, it cannot mitigate the problem of variations in shooter hold or bench technique. You still have to be consistent to avoid stressing (and bending) the receiver differently on each shot, which will definitely alter each bullet's impact point.

As with the rotary-magazine Savage Model-99, there might be some single-shot action designs where it would be possible to adapt a fore-end hanger to the receiver (as noted, several are factory equipped with such a system). If you believe this is feasible, discuss the matter with your gunsmith and proceed. Review the discussion covering proper fore-end bedding in the Browning BLR.

Section 16: The Trouble With Single-Shot Rifle Receivers, *Part II*

As noted at the beginning of *Section 15*, Steve Meacham provided much to the technical information allowing me to write this section. While Mr. Meacham has reviewed this material, please note that any errors are mine, not his.

I should also note at the outset that you should probably leave almost all the work mentioned in this section to the professional. If you do not have the skills or equipment necessary to do this work correctly, please hire an expert. (Why take a chance on destroying a valuable and irreplaceable rifle?) Further, if you have an antique rifle, please, do not alter any of the original parts. Replacement parts are available or can be fabricated. By procuring a replacement part to modify (as needed), you can keep the original part in its original condition, which will preserve the (often substantial) collector's value of the gun.

Also note, before doing any mechanical work on any antique single-shot rifle you should realize that these guns were built for use with ammunition that is no longer available — black powder loads using lead bullets. You should never fire any of these rifles using jacketed bullet ammunition, as that will rapidly destroy the barrel.

Finding the most accurate load is a major handloading undertaking. In search of that goal you will have to test various cast bullet designs and weights and use different bullet alloys. Equally, you will have to test several powders and primers. Until you have done all of that, no amount of mechanical tinkering will allow you to bring out the rifle's true accuracy potential. I will address this subject in slightly more detail later, in the sub-section titled *Ammunition & Handloading Considerations, Single-Shot & Related Rifles*.

Just like the lever-action, the single-shot rifle is a new world for many gunsmiths. Many of the potential problems are entirely different from those facing the tinker or the professional working on a bolt-action rifle. As one example, consider the relationship between the breachblock and the rear face of the barrel: in a bolt-action rifle this is a non-critical fit, five-thousandths of an inch (0.005") bolt-to-barrel gap is just as good, and no better than, ten-thousandths of an inch (0.010") bolt-to-barrel gap; on a falling-block (and most other single-shot rifles) proper breachblock-to-barrel fit is <u>critical</u> to accuracy, five-ten-thousandths of an inch (0.0005") gap is not functionally the same as ten-ten-thousandths of an inch (0.0010") gap!

Loose Linkage, Single-Shot Rifles:

Before attempting any other alterations or fittings, carefully inspect all linkage pieces. Ensure that all pins and their corresponding holes are in good repair. Look for cracked or broken parts. As necessary, repair these parts to produce round pins and round holes that precisely fit those pins. These parts should fit. Not <u>almost</u> fit, but <u>precisely</u> fit. For example, in the falling-block, the breachblock-to-pin joint should be a friction fit, the link-to-pin joint should be a sliding fit. Any slack in any connection will result in excess play (slop) in the action's linkage. Also, any such misfit is an opportunity for wear-inducing grit to infiltrate between the working surfaces. Further, when a pin does not properly fit a hole, the stresses transmitted through the two are concentrated along a line, rather than along a surface, that characteristic will dramatically increase wear. In any case, these are gunsmith repairs.

You can use a magnetically attached dial indicator to check for linkage wear in most single-shot actions. Look for play between the breachblock and the finger-lever at any portion of the finger-lever's travel.

Hardened and heat-treated steel pins can last through generations of hard use: if those pins are round and properly fitted into round holes in properly hardened steel. With such proper fit, it is possible to achieve an unusually long action life and a delicate lockup in the action. This delicate lockup is critical to accuracy.

Loose Fitting Breachblock, Single-Shot Rifles:

Potential movement between the "locked" breachblock and the receiver is a big source of vertical stringing in these rifles. The classic example is the falling-block. A breachblock that can move laterally in the receiver or rotate around any axis, will generate vertical stringing. This shot-to-shot stringing results from differences in precisely where the breachblock comes to rest as the shooter closes the action for successive shots and from the fact that a loose breachblock will move as the hammer falls and as the cartridge fires.

Firing pin energy is another issue. A movable breachblock typically results in the hammer delivering less energy to the firing pin — it is moving the breachblock, too. Also, shot-to-shot uniformity of firing pin energy is apt to vary — depending upon how much the breachblock moves. It should be rather obvious that the magnitude and type of barrel vibrations will depend upon where the breachblock happens to be resting at the instant before the hammer strikes.

Centering the Breachblock, Single-Shot Rifles:

Short of building or buying a breachblock that precisely fits the opening in the receiver (e.g. S. D. Meacham Tool & Hardware Inc. offers replacement breachblocks that can be welded up and properly fitted), the next best thing is to fix the breachblock to prevent its unwanted movement. One common method of repair is to drill holes in the appropriate places in the breachblock and insert tight-fitting plugs made from a tough and durable plastic. Delrin is the most common choice; this product is durable, rigid and essentially immune to chemical solvents. It is used by many competitive shooters in older rifles, with good success.

Before considering installation of any such plug, verify that you have fixed any other problems in the action. It is also critical that you understand what you are doing. Do not make any holes that could compromise the strength of the breachblock or its functioning. Keep the pin holes as shallow as feasible to do the job (0.020"). Also, do not alter any antique breachblock — get a replacement and do the work on that, store the valuable original.

See the discussion below. Also, note where the firing pin hits the primer. If possible, move the breachblock sideways to center the firing pin's impact on the primer. Finally, if possible, correct front-to-rear play in the breachblock by adjusting the headspace on the ammunition — on shouldered cartridges move the shoulder forward (of course, this is a handloading-only option).

On essentially straight-sided, rimmed cartridges this alteration is not possible. In this instance, install plugs to hold the closed breachblock toward the rear of the receiver opening and obtain cases with the thickest rims you can find. You can also seat the bullet against the rifling (with proper precautions), but this is not the best course of action.

However, consider installation of brass shims on one or both sides and the front face of the breachblock. These can be installed with a bonding epoxy and then filed and polished to form a near perfect fit between the breachblock and the receiver. This work does not harm the original breachblock in any way.

If you get a replacement breachblock and have access to a TIG or MIG wire feed welder and can use it properly, or if you have a trusted welder, consider welding up the sides and front face of the replacement breachblock and then surface grinding it to precisely fit the receiver. You can hand file and polish the breachblock to fit but this is seriously touchy work. See the discussion of fitting a replacement locking lug in a Marlin lever-action rifle.

This job is not really all that difficult. However, be sure to use a high strength (minimum 70,000 psi tensile), low-carbon welding rod and do not do any welding on any modern rifle or any rifle that is chambered for or will ever use a high-pressure cartridge — anything over about 40,000 CUP, which is .30-30 Winchester class chamber pressure.

Again, before considering any breachblock alteration, consider the collector's value of the rifle in question. It is best to obtain a replacement breachblock and keep the original in unaltered condition.

Section 16: The Trouble With Single-Shot Rifle Receivers, Part II

On actions where the breachblock moves forward during the locking operation (Ballard, Browning, Martini, Stevens, Winchester, etc.), adjust the modified breachblock so that when it comes up, fully into battery, it wedges against the rear face of the barrel. With proper fitting, this system can completely eliminate fore and aft play in the locked breachblock.

However, such precise fitting requires careful headspacing of the cases. Cases with thicker rims than the cases the rifle was headspaced to fit can jam the action — the breachblock might bend the case rim, if you force it closed. Close fitting necessitates paying closer attention to details. Master machinist and single-shot competitor Roger Johnston (NECO) suggests keeping about one-thousandth of an inch (0.001") breachblock-to-barrel clearance, just to avoid problems.

Toggle Link Timing, Single-Shot Rifles:

Once you or your gunsmith have repaired the toggle link pins, toggle link and properly fitted the breachblock to the receiver opening, it is time to look at the toggle linkage timing. See photograph #s 16-1/2.

Given only one special tool, this timing is easy to observe. Attach a magnetic base for a dial indicator to the receiver. Position the dial indicator to record the upward movement of the breachblock. Slowly close the finger-lever; you will note that the breachblock moves up rapidly at first, then moves progressively more slowly as it approaches the top of its travel.

If, as the finger-lever comes to rest against the lower tang, the breachblock stops and then moves down appreciably. The toggle-link timing is wrong. This condition is not only common in well-used rifles, it is how the factories originally

Photograph 16-1

Photograph 16-2

Photographs 16-1/2: This interesting page, from the Winchester 1916 catalogue, shows a line drawing of the action of the Winchester single-shot rifle. Close-up view shows delicate timing between firing pin, toggle link, breachblock and hammer.

fitted these actions on most antique falling-block rifles and how most manufacturers still fit modern versions. Trust me here, this is not how John Moses Browning intended it. Such sloppy assembly measures are a result of the dictates of sloppy manufacturing, nothing more. However, this is not an indictment of any manufacturer: to keep the rifle affordable many have chosen to use less critical fitting, this requires allowing the linkage to swing somewhat further past alignment than is ideal.

Correctly, the linkage should just barely rotate past the straight alignment point (where the breachblock achieves its uppermost travel) as the finger-lever comes to rest against the tang. While it would be functionally acceptable if the linkage were just at perfect alignment, for safety sake linkage travel slightly beyond the point of perfect alignment is a better method of fitting.

Assuming a tight fitting breachblock and properly fitting pins in the toggle links, it is easy to determine this point of proper alignment. Fully close the finger-lever. Apply slight finger pressure to the top of the breachblock. Then slowly open the finger-lever while watching the dial indicator. When the dial indicator first shows that the breachblock has reached the highest point in its travel, you have the linkage properly aligned.

Perhaps surprisingly, it is usually a relatively simple matter to adjust the toggle linkage timing. This requires only heating and bending of the finger-lever — by the proper amount and in the proper place, and, possibly a bit of alteration to the firing pin cam on the toggle link. Each system differs and the proper method of correcting the linkage timing is different for almost every model of rifle that uses a falling block.

For several reasons, correcting the toggle-link timing is a task best left to the professional. Not the least of these reasons is the simple matter that the requisite heating will destroy the metal finish and possibly its hardness. Proper refinishing will require a gunsmith's services anyway. Then there is the troublesome firing pin retractor problem.

Hammer Modifications, Single-Shot Rifles:

The next likely improvement involves lightening the hammer. As was noted elsewhere, this alteration is valuable on almost all rifles featuring rotating hammers. About the only rifle that comes to mind where this is not particularly feasible is the Remington Rolling block. On that rifle the hammer is part of the action's lockup. For this reason, the gunsmith would have to be very careful in lightening the hammer — to avoid weakening the action. This certainly can be done but you have to know where you can remove steel without weakening the lockup.

Conversely, *Moulds Limited* makes a commercial replacement hammer for the Ruger No. 1. This hammer has a shorter fall and reduced mass. Installation of this hammer can dramatically improve that rifle's accuracy. This hammer is available through Brownells.

On the Sharps, Trapdoor and falling-block rifles, gunsmithing experts often drill holes to lighten the hammer, relocate the full cock notch to reduce its rotation, and replace the hammer spring in order to reduce lock-time without compromising hammer energy. A light hammer falling through a short arc and hitting the firing pin at a higher velocity is always the goal. These changes will improve accuracy since the lighter hammer that falls faster will disturb the gun less and, at the same time, improve consistency of primer ignition.

However, I cannot suggest any sear work for the amateur. Here you are working with the safe functioning of the rifle. With an improperly positioned or shaped hammer sear notch, the hammer might not stay cocked, even without anything touching the trigger! See photograph # 16-3.

Note that relocation of the hammer sear notch requires the use of a different hammer spring. The hammer does not rotate as far between the cocked and down positions. Therefore, cocking the hammer does not bend the hammer spring as far. Therefore, the spring will not do as much work in rotating the hammer — the hammer will not develop as much energy.

Also realize that there is a direct relationship between hammer spring tension and trigger pull. Increasing hammer spring tension will necessarily increase trigger pull.

Firing Pin Centering, Single-Shot Rifles:

After repairing the breachblock, the linkage and the timing, make certain the firing pin properly centers on the primer. Load a dummy case with primer only. File a mark on the case rim. Insert the case with the mark at top dead center in the chamber. Close the action and fire the primer. Do this in a well-ventilated area, where the spark generated will not start a fire. Primers are loud, so protect your ears by wearing hearing protection.

Section 16: The Trouble With Single-Shot Rifle Receivers, Part II

Observe where the firing pin hits the primer relative to the center and to the mark that was at top dead center of the chambered case. If the center of the firing pin's impact is more than about fifteen-thousandths of an inch (0.015") from the center of the primer, you should consider the accuracy benefits of centering the firing pin.

Where this is possible, correct a side-to-side off-center impact by centering the breachblock (adjust the locating pins or shims along the sides of the breachblock, see the earlier sub-section). For firing pin impacts that are vertically off center, install a different length toggle link to raise or lower the breachblock, as needed. Your gunsmith can help you with making a new toggle link of the proper length.

It is also possible to install a bushing in a replacement breachblock (again, on any antique, save the valuable original). See the sub-section on pump-action rifles and bushing the firing pin hole in the breachblock. The same breachblock bushing method discussed there is perfectly applicable here except that, in this instance, you will want to drill the new firing pin hole through the bushing deliberately off-center, as needed to center the firing pin. You also want to install a bushing that is larger than the body diameter of the firing pin. Leave a shoulder to support the bushing. Most likely, this is a gunsmith repair job.

Firing Pin Protrusion, Single-Shot Rifles:

You should adjust firing pin protrusion to fifty-five thousandths of an inch (0.055"), with the hammer fully forward. This is easy to measure by inserting a bore-fitting hardwood dowel into the barrel with the action closed and the hammer uncocked. Cut the dowel so that about three inches protrudes from the muzzle. Measure the protrusion using the depth gauge on a dial indicator. Then cock the hammer and repeat the measurement.

However, be absolutely, positively certain that the firing pin's protrusion from the breachblock face is zero (or less) whenever the action is opened or the hammer is cocked. It is quite common to find falling-block rifles that have had improperly proportioned replacement firing pins installed. Often, the tip of such firing pins can rest against the primer, even when the hammer is cocked or the action is not fully closed. This is potentially very dangerous. Theoretically, with such a firing pin condition, closing the breachblock over a sensitive primer could fire the round!

Testing for firing pin protrusion is quite easy. Insert the hardwood dowel (with polished and square ends) into the unloaded rifle with the hammer cocked. Then use a light hammer to tap on the end of the dowel. Remove the dowel and examine the inserted end. If there is any dimple in the polished surface, the firing pin is too long. Repair, as necessary.

Testing for mechanical firing pin retraction is equally simple. Install the unloaded rifle in a padded vise — action fully closed, hammer fully down. Then insert the dowel, fully against the breachblock. Use the hole gauge on the dial

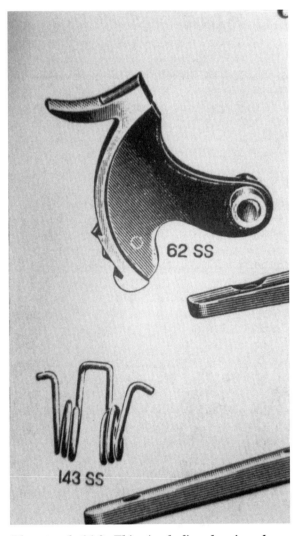

Photograph 16-3: This simple line drawing shows the Winchester falling-block hammer and hammer spring. No picture or drawing can do justice to the delicate geometry of a hammer sear notch. Never perform any work on any hammer that might alter the safe functioning of the sear notch and, therefore, the rifle.

caliper to measure the distance the dowel protrudes from the muzzle.

Let us say we measure 3.055". Remember, we cut the dowel to protrude 3.000" from the barrel, with the hammer cocked. For this example, we will assume the rifle has a properly fitted firing pin that protrudes precisely 0.000" with the hammer cocked and 0.055" with the hammer fully down — 3.000" + 0.055" = 3.055".

Then, while pushing slightly in on the dowel, slowly begin to open the finger-lever while watching the breachblock. First, the finger-lever should move slightly (perhaps 1/4" at the back end) before the dowel begins to move — this signifies correct clearance between the toggle link cam and the firing pin. Also, you should feel the dowel move back into the barrel before you see the breachblock move appreciably down in the receiver. The dowel should stop moving before the breachblock begins to drop significantly. If not, the mechanical firing pin retractor cam on the toggle link is not correctly fitted to the firing pin.

Other Firing Pin Concerns, Falling-Block (And Other Single-Shot) Rifles:

S. D. Meacham Tool & Hardware Inc. also offers spring-retracted firing pins in the Mann-Neidner style to replace Winchester's elegant but breakage-prone original, mechanically retracted, version. Many original falling-block rifles were converted to similar firing pins decades ago. For various reasons, which I will touch upon later, this conversion is a good idea, albeit not simple.

As an aside, Mr. Meacham notes that many a tinker or professional gunsmith has made a replacement firing pin for a falling-block rifle. In an effort to increase firing pin life, quite often, gunsmiths have made replacement firing pins that are entirely too hard. This is a troublesome mistake. The problem is, a too-hard firing pin will break without warning. It is much better to have a too-soft firing pin!

A softer firing pin will evidence wear before it fails. With such a firing pin the rifleman is not surprised in the middle of a competitive match (or a once-in-a-lifetime hunt) with a broken firing pin. Since a broken firing pin either renders the falling-block rifle non-functional or at least destroys its accuracy potential, this is no small consideration. Any tough high-strength steel will make a perfectly useful firing pin.

The correct steel to use is technically described as a steel with low notch sensitivity (high fatigue strength). I will address this issue further later. In any case, after hardening the firing pin it should be drawn back to a hardness of approximately 25-30 Rc (Rockwell "C" scale).

Owing to improper fit, falling-block (and certain other single-shot) rifle firing pins are prone to failure. It is easy to fashion replacement firing pins from any quality steel. The trouble is, many tinkers and gunsmiths believe the solution to rapid firing pin failure is to harden the replacement firing pin. Many such pins are very hard indeed. This is, however, precisely the wrong solution. Owing to the shocks associated with the hammer's blow and the primer's percussion, such hardened pins are subject to breakage without warning.

For this reason, it is much better to fashion a firing pin from a tough steel that is not too hard. Though often used, drill rod is precisely the wrong choice. Of the common steels, 8620 is hard to beat, 4140 or 4340 are, perhaps, better choices but only if you draw those back (after hardening) to 30 on the Rockwell "C" scale, or softer. This requires heating to about twelve-hundred degrees Fahrenheit (1200°F). Such a firing pin will give plenty of warning (as evidenced by wear) before it fails. Conversely, a harder firing pin will not show any wear; it will simply break.

Many a target-shooting competitor has learned the disadvantage of a too hard firing pin the hard way . . . typically this happens just before the last shot of the match when the shooter has just made the beginning of a winning group. . . . Murphy strikes again.

Often, the design of replacement firing pins for Falling-Block Winchester rifles is incorrect. Make certain the retractor cam of the firing pin does not touch the toggle link when the hammer is fully down. There should be some clearance, but only just a little clearance, between the action link and the firing pin's retraction cam. Refer to the previous discussion of checking for improper firing pin protrusion.

Excess clearance between the toggle link cam and the firing pin boss will result in a situation where the breachblock begins to move down before the toggle link retracts the firing pin from the primer, firing pin breakage will result. Similarly, the firing pin hitting the toggle link, instead of the shoulder in the breachblock, will create a large lateral stress that will soon cause fatigue and breakage. See photograph # 16-4.

Section 16: The Trouble With Single-Shot Rifle Receivers, Part II

Photograph 16-4: Close-up view of cam-retracted firing pin on Winchester falling-block rifle. The rifle's safe functioning, and the firing pin's long life depend upon proper and delicate fitting of this simple piece of steel. See the text for a complete discussion.

Section 17:
The (Lack Of!) Trouble With The New England Firearms Handi-Rifle (H&R Ultra), *Part II*

This interesting single-shot rifle offers surprising accuracy in a very modest package. This rifle's accuracy potential belies its very affordable price. Further, the tinker need only do a few special things to bring the best out of one of these rifles. Of course, you should review the applicable generic discussions covering muzzle crowning, bore lapping and buttstock adjustments. Consider incorporating any of those alterations, where that seems useful. See photograph # 17-1.

Fore-end Attachment, Handi-Rifle:

The Handi-Rifle fore-end is attached to the rifle with a screw that enters a welded-on barrel hanger. This screw has a large beveled head. This bevel centers the screw against the outside end of an oversize hole through the fore-end. On the unaltered rifle, tightening this screw pulls the fore-end against the lower contour of the barrel. See photograph #s 17-2/3.

This system is certainly adequate, as evidenced by the astounding accuracy produced by typical examples of these rifles. However, I prefer to modify this system so that the attachment screw passes through an epoxy pillar and the fore-end rests on an O-ring that surrounds the attachment screw hanger stud. These alterations should help minimize the effects of variations in fore-end pressure or placement of the front sandbag when shooting from the rest.

A plastic pivot at the rear of the fore-end supports and locates the wood on the receiver. Two small screws attach this piece to the rear of the fore-end.

You might consider including an epoxy bedding layer between the fore-end and this plastic cap. This step might provide a more solid and more consistent purchase for the rear of the fore-end. Added consistency is always beneficial.

You will need to modify the fore-end so the new epoxy pillar cannot move in any direction.

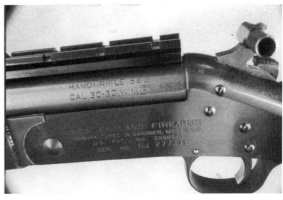

Photograph 17-1: The New England Firearms Handi-Rifle (and the equivalent H&R Ultra) are a marvel of modern engineering. Price is in the bargain basement; performance is in the clouds. These rifles function and shoot better than most hardened riflemen will believe. One acquaintance tells of a tough old Texas rancher, a multi-millionaire, who chose this rifle as his Alaska and Canada hunting companion on world-class safaris. If that were not surprising enough, he fitted his .30-06 Springfield chambered Handi-Rifle (about a $200 gun) with a top-of-the-line Schmidt & Bender hunting riflescope. (For those who do not know, Schmidt & Bender is to riflescopes what Rolls-Royce is to automobiles.)

The enlarged recess in the barrel channel will certainly prevent the pillar from pulling through the outside of the fore-end. However, on the unaltered fore-end, only the epoxy's adhesion to the wood would prevent the epoxy pillar from moving toward the barrel.

You can easily address and correct this latter concern. Use a fine-thread seven-sixteenths inch (7/16") tap to produce threads in the existing hole. These threads will solidly affix the epoxy pillar in place. It cannot rotate and if it cannot rotate it cannot move in the (now) threaded hole! See photograph # 17-4.

The final necessary alteration is to produce clearance between the hanger and the hole. If you omit this step the epoxy bedding pillar will be extremely weak and fragile since only a very thin-walled section of epoxy will connect the top and bottom ends.

To prevent this weakness, enlarge the barrel channel side of the existing hole. Use a twist steel drill bit of one-half inch diameter to enlarge the existing hole. Drill into this hole one-quarter of an inch (from the barrel channel side).

Mix a tablespoonful batch of gel-type glass bedding agent. Reinforce this with two-parts atomized steel added to each three-parts epoxy mix.

Note the location of the front of the fore-end on the barrel. Wrap one layer of vinyl electrical tape over the barrel at this location. Similarly, wrap one layer of tape over the barrel just in front of the chamber swell.

Apply release agent to the fore-end hanger and the barrel in that area. Also apply release agent to the attachment screw. Use release agent to paint the outside of the fore-end in the area around the hanger screw hole. Similarly, in the area around the fore-end hanger relief hole, paint inside the barrel channel with release agent — do not get release agent into the fore-end attachment stud relief pocket. Properly thread a two-inch long piece of one-quarter inch hardwood dowel (one-quarter inch coarse threads). Screw that dowel stub into the hanger.

Fill the hanger recess with the steel reinforced epoxy bedding agent. Make sure that you wet all the surfaces and drive the epoxy mix into the threads. Add sufficient epoxy to insure that it will fill the entire recess. See photograph #s 17-5/6.

Photograph 17-2: Close-up view of the welded-on fore-end hanger on the Handi-rifle barrel. Note the O-ring slipped over the shank of the hanger. This little item can be worth a considerable accuracy improvement. See the text and associated photographs.

Photograph 17-3: The H&R Handi-Rifle fore-end is quite simple in design and function. It is equally simple to modify for maximum accuracy potential.

Photograph 17-4: This technique, tapping the hole, is useful for any situation where you intend to install an epoxy plug in a round hole in wood. The thread gives the epoxy a large interlocking bonding surface. A similar modification is useful on the Handi-Rifle fore-end. See the text.

Section 17: The (Lack Of!) Trouble With The N.E. Firearms Handi-Rifle, Part II

Clamp the barreled-action, upside down, in a solidly affixed vise. Install the fore-end over the receiver pivot and onto the barrel. Unscrew and remove the dowel. Install the attachment screw. Then, while pushing back on the fore-end, tighten the attachment screw until the fore-end touches the tape wraps on the barrel, at the front and rear. Invert the rifle and fix it in the vise — barrel level with fore-end down and leveled from side to side.

Allow the epoxy sufficient time to cure to a rubbery consistency (several hours). Then remove the fore-end and clean the epoxy from inside the barrel channel (leave it in the hanger recess). Clean epoxy from the hanger threads and from the attachment screw.

Verify that the hanger recess is filled with epoxy. If not, degrease the epoxy surface, mix another batch and try again.

Photograph 17-5

Photograph 17-6

Photographs 17-5/6: The H&R Handi-Rifle fore-end before epoxy bedding the fore-end hanger screw, photograph 17-5, and after applying the reinforced epoxy pillar, photograph 17-6. Note the O-ring seat in the epoxy bed. See the text for a rundown on the correct procedure.

Addition of an O-ring is a useful final touch here. Locate an O-ring that just fits around the hanger. A good size for this O-ring is as follows: inside diameter, 0.3625"; outside diameter, 0.5625".

Use a one-half inch twist drill bit to slightly chamfer the hanger side of the still semi-plastic epoxy pillar. Remove only enough epoxy to <u>almost</u> make room for the O-ring between the barrel hanger and the epoxy pillar. Add a second layer of tape to both taped locations on the barrel. Your goal is to make the O-ring a squeeze-tight fit between the hanger and the pillar. If you do this correctly, no other part of the fore-end will touch the barrel. See photograph # 17-3.

If you do this work when the epoxy is still just slightly plastic, you can then mold the pillar to form a fitted pocket around the O-ring. After removing almost enough bedding agent to allow the fore-end to easily come up to touch the vinyl tape wraps on the barrel, attach the fore-end and tighten the screw sufficiently to compress the O-ring.

You should be able to feel when the hanger touches the pillar and when the fore-end touches the tape. Do not continue to tighten the fore-end hanger screw after the fore-end touches the tape wraps on the barrel.

Remove the fore-end and observe the pillar where the O-ring was seated. This should be a smooth impression of the O-ring. If not, try again. If so, remove the O-ring and the tape wraps. Reassemble the fore-end and tighten the screw until the fore-end touches the barrel.

After allowing the epoxy bedding agent sufficient time to cure to a solid state, remove the fore-end, reinstall the O-ring and reassemble the fore-end to the rifle. The job is done.

This modification solves several problems. First, it removes the necessity to ensure that you always tighten the fore-end attachment screw to the same torque. Second, it reduces the effects of variations in front rest pressure and placement. Finally, it helps to kill vibrations that might otherwise propagate between the fore-end and the barrel.

When you have finished this chore you can consider adding an epoxy bed between the rear fore-end hanger and the fore-end. This is simple enough.

Separate the plastic pivot by removing the two wood screws. Apply a thin coating of gel-type bedding agent to the rear face of the fore-end and into the screw head pockets in the plastic pivot. Reattach the plastic pivot, but only slightly snug the screws. Do not tighten these screws — you want the hanger to center and position itself correctly through the tightening of the hanger attachment screw. The epoxy around the pivot attachment screw heads will form a purchase for these screws that is solid and properly centered. See photograph # 17-7.

Mount the fore-end and snugly tighten the hanger screw. Excepting the possible need to clean away excess bedding agent that extruded from between the fore-end and the plastic fore-end pivot, this completes the suggested fore-end modifications. However, refer to the sub-section on skeletonizing fore-ends.

Trigger Work, Handi-Rifle:

The trigger system on these rifles incorporates a transfer bar. The hammer spring also tensions the action lock release lever. You might consider lightening the hammer or <u>slightly</u> reducing the trigger spring tension. However, these alterations require disassembly of the mechanism, which requires driving the serrated pivot pins from the receiver. This also requires a delicate touch in reassembly — the parts are inside the closed receiver.

If you were to pull the trigger and hammer mechanism apart, it would be useful to polish the sear engagement surfaces. In this case, you should only polish the tops of the high spots. For this work, use only a jeweler's rouge impregnated felt wheel on a moto-tool (Dremel). Since I have discussed similar work in several other places in this text and I do not feel that this is a necessary alteration on the Handi-Rifle, I will not discuss it separately here.

Marrying The Trigger Sear To The Hammer Sear Notch, Handi-Rifle (And Other Exposed-Hammer) Rifles:

The several Handi-Rifles I have seen did not need any significant action work. All that I did to obtain near world-class trigger pulls on these rifles was to perform the classic "marrying" process.

To do this, follow the instruction given here. Make certain the rifle is empty. Better yet, separate the barrel from the receiver. Cock the hammer. Then push the hammer spur against the trigger sear. Apply about twenty pounds force. You can do this with your thumb without experiencing any undue discomfort; if it hurts, you are pushing too hard — you might manage to destroy something!

While holding about twenty pounds of pressure against the hammer spur, slowly pull the trigger to release the hammer. Repeat this process about ten times. This should burnish the rough edges from the sear and sear latch surfaces — this will result in wear to the contact surface that is somewhat similar to that provided by long-term usage. Since the hammer and trigger surfaces are hardened, this will not damage the parts unless you apply entirely too much thumb pressure to the hammer spur.

On my .30-30 Winchester chambered Handi-Rifle, this simple process reduced the trigger pull from a crisp three and one-half pounds ($3^{1}/_{2}$#) to a super crisp two and three-quarters pounds ($2^{3}/_{4}$#). This particular rifle has one of the finest factory triggers I have ever seen — bar none. I have not seen any Handi-Rifle with a truly poor trigger pull.

Buttstock-To-Receiver Glass Bedding, Handi-Rifle:

As is shown in the associated photographs (#s 17-8/9), the rear face of the Handi-Rifle receiver is sculptured and includes interior openings. A through-bolt attaches the buttstock.

To increase the rigidity of this system, I suggest several alterations. First, consider applying a good thick layer of bedding agent that is rein-

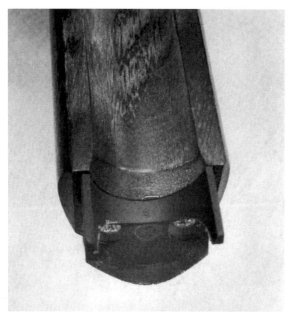

Photograph 17-7: This plastic fore-end cap on the Handi-Rifle is easily epoxy-bedded to the fore-end. This might be worthwhile. See the related text.

Section 17: The (Lack Of!) Trouble With The N.E. Firearms Handi-Rifle, Part II

forced with atomized steel between the wood and receiver.

Use a black dry erase marker to paint the front of the buttstock, where it extends beyond the sides and top and bottom of the receiver. Then clamp the receiver in a well-padded vise with the barrel pointing to the sky. The buttstock should hang, just about straight down. Remove the butt pad (requires removal of two screws). Loosen the through-bolt (requires a 9/16" socket on a long extension and a ratchet).

With the through-bolt loosened sufficiently to let the buttstock hang free, note if the stock hangs centered on the through-bolt or if it lies against one side. If necessary, adjust the receiver until the stock balances on the through-bolt — this will be important during reassembly.

Remove the buttstock. Note where the perimeter of the receiver rests on the assembled buttstock, as evidenced by the dry erase marker. Drill shallow and evenly spaced three-sixteenths inch (3/16") diameter holes just inside this perimeter and across the entire portion of the stock that is inside this border. Finish this work by sanding to roughen the existing finish on the unaltered front of the buttstock inside the bordering holes. See photograph # 17-8.

Apply release agent to the rear of the receiver, the outside of the front of the stock in the narrow front perimeter outside the border of holes (where the dry-erase marker is or was), and to the threaded end of the through-bolt.

Mix a tablespoonful of gel-type bedding agent. Add two-parts atomized steel to three-parts epoxy bedding mix and thoroughly blend in the steel. Apply a sufficient layer of this mix to the front of the buttstock to fill all the holes you drilled and to coat the surface with a layer about one-sixteenth on one inch thick. Then paint this material into the front one-half inch of the through-bolt hole.

Rest the through-bolt on a short nine-sixteenths inch (9/16") socket attached to a long extension. Insert the through-bolt into the hole in the buttstock. If necessary, clean the epoxy from the threads on the end of the bolt and repaint the end of the bolt with release agent.

Use the socket extension to hold the through-bolt fully inserted. Carefully lift the buttstock toward the receiver until the through-bolt touches the threaded hole in the receiver. Be careful to keep the buttstock rotated correctly on the receiver. The sculpturing on these surfaces will do this job when the two pieces are close enough together. However, you do not want to bring the two pieces together when they are out of alignment. That would scrape the epoxy from where you want it.

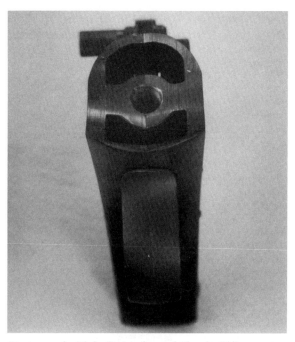

Photograph 17-8: Rear view of Handi-Rifle receiver. Note the centered through-bolt connection and the hollow portions of the receiver. The latter are likely locations for reinforced bedding agent to form interlocking pillars. See the associated text.

Photograph 17-9: Side view of Handi-Rifle at the receiver-to-buttstock joint. Note the double-sculpturing at the joint — all four corners are extended. This allows the buttstock to interlock quite rigidly. Tightening the robust through-bolt bonds the stock in all directions — it cannot move up or down, left or right, forward or back or twist clockwise or counterclockwise! Nevertheless, adding an epoxy bed at this joint will improve the rigidity of the buttstock-to-receiver joint. See the text for a complete discussion.

Thread the through-bolt into the receiver. As you turn the through-bolt, epoxy will squeeze out from the perimeter of the buttstock-to-receiver contact zone. Turn the socket extension, by hand, until the buttstock just barely begins to touch the receiver. It is better to leave a slight wood-to-steel gap than to have any wood-to-steel contact.

Your goal is to leave a layer of epoxy between the wood and the receiver. As long as the epoxy bedding layer is of equal thickness around the perimeter (so the stock's alignment is unchanged), the thicker this epoxy layer, the better. Note that you could use this system to easily make minor adjustments to the drop on these stocks.

Such an alteration would only require bending the stock the needed amount before adjusting the through-bolt sufficiently to bring one side of the buttstock into contact with the receiver — while holding the needed alignment, snug the through-bolt until the top, or bottom, edge of the receiver touches the stock (this depends upon whether you are increasing or decreasing the stock's drop). Fix the stock in place and allow the epoxy to cure sufficiently to hold the angle. With a few clamps and weights, this is easy to arrange.

Allow the epoxy about six hours to cure to a plastic state. Trim the excess epoxy from the perimeter of the receiver-to-buttstock joint. Separate the buttstock and clean the epoxy from the through-bolt.

Allow the epoxy about two days to fully cure. Reassemble and solidly tighten the through-bolt.

Through-bolt Modification, Handi-Rifle:

Next, you might consider installation of a longer through-bolt. To do this, obtain a 10" fine thread three-eighths inch (3/8") bolt and matching nut. Since this is an unusual bolt length, you might have to use a piece of all-thread, which is available at automotive parts houses. Grade-5 is sufficient in either case.

You will also need to fashion a washer that just fits the seven-eighths inch (7/8") diameter hole in the stock. Finally, you will need one ounce of 20-minute epoxy, as available from Brownells, and an 11" long section of three-eighths inch (3/8") hardwood dowel.

Slightly taper both ends of the three-eighths inch (3/8") hardwood dowel. Then apply about one-half inch of three-eighths inch (3/8") fine threads to each end. Thoroughly coat the dowel with release agent (apply this product several times over a period of several minutes, until the release agent fully saturates and coats the wood's surface). Grind the perimeter of a three-eighths inch (3/8") fender washer until it just fits into the seven-eighths inch (7/8") hole in the rear of the stock. Paint this washer with release agent. Also, thoroughly coat the nut and a short nine-sixteenths inch (9/16") socket.

Mount the receiver in a well-padded vise with the stock pointing toward the ceiling. Adjust the receiver in the vise until the through-bolt is approximately vertical. Snug the vise, to lock the receiver in place.

Separate the buttstock from the receiver. This requires removing two #2 Phillips head screws from the recoil pad and then removing the through-bolt (you will need a 9/16" socket and a long socket extension).

Screw the hardwood dowel into the receiver about one-half inch. Apply a tape wrap on the dowel at a point about two inches from the receiver. Apply sufficient tape so that the buttstock will just slip over the wrapped portion of the dowel. Install the buttstock over the dowel (which is vertically orientated, if you have the rifle vised correctly).

Note the time. In a two-ounce measuring cup, thoroughly mix the entire contents of a one-ounce kit of Brownells 20-minute epoxy. Add almost an equal portion of atomized steel — the cup should be almost full. Stir this mix until the steel is completely and uniformly distributed into the epoxy. Again, note the time and observe how many minutes you have to work before the epoxy will begin to cure significantly — assume no more than 15 minutes from the time you first began to mix it.

Pour about two-thirds of the steel-reinforced epoxy mix into the seven-eighths inch (7/8") diameter hole in the back of the buttstock (which you have assembled over the vertically oriented dowel installed in the vised receiver). Allow the mix sufficient time to fill the bottom of the hole and surround the dowel. Add sufficient mix to fill the hole to within about one-half inch of the top end of the dowel.

Note the time, and wait about five minutes to allow any trapped bubbles to surface. However, keep the 15 minute working time limit in mind. As necessary, add more epoxy mix.

When you have filled the hole about one-quarter inch below the top end of the dowel, insert the washer. Use a one-half inch dowel to carefully push the washer into the hole. Keep the washer flat in the hole — if you sized the washer properly, this will push any excess epoxy in front of the washer. Use the nine-sixteenths inch (9/16") socket to slip the washer over the end of the three-eighths inch (3/8") dowel and force it fully down, against the epoxy. Install the nut and turn it until it holds the washer solidly against the epoxy.

Allow the epoxy to cure to a rubbery consistency. Remove the nut and pull the stock free from the receiver — wiggle and pull, wiggle and pull, repeat until the buttstock comes loose. If the dowel breaks you can easily drill it out after the epoxy fully cures. Unscrew the dowel from the receiver and clean up the excess epoxy, as necessary. Allow the epoxy to cure for at least one full day, then assemble the stock using the 10" through-bolt.

This alteration represents considerable work but it can provide a significantly superior buttstock-to-receiver bond. Tightening the lengthened through-bolt places almost the entire buttstock in compression. Through the compression of wood and the tensioning of steel, this forms a very rigid system. This rigidifies the stock.

Section 18: Miscellaneous Considerations, Single-Shot (And Other) Rifles, Part II

Throughout this text I have scattered jewels of tinkering that can improve the average hunting rifle. In this short sub-section, I will cover several topics that are more appropriate to application on long-range target rifles, particularly the single-shot variety. Many of these modifications are strictly gunsmith items but I will cover the basic concept of the required work in this sub-section.

General Principles of Weight Reduction, Lever-Action & Single-Shot Rifles:

Many rifles provide ample opportunity for the home tinker to reduce the gun's weight. We have covered several of these areas in the preceding text. Generally, it is possible to remove wood from the stock, or stocks, and it is often possible to remove steel from various action parts. Be careful with any alterations to the receiver. Make certain any such work does not reduce the strength of the action, particularly in the locking lugs. Also, make certain that any such alterations do not result in a significant reduction in the action's rigidity. See photograph # 18-1.

With these limitations in mind, it is still possible to dramatically reduce the weight of many rifles. As an example, consider the Model-1894 Marlin chambered in .44 Magnum. By the judicious application of skeletonizing techniques, combined with barrel shortening, I have reduced the weight of my wife's 44 Magnum chambered 1894 Marlin from about seven pounds to four and three-quarter pounds. This despite adding a thick Pachmayr Decelerator recoil pad and a receiver-mounted aperture sight! See photograph # 18-2.

These alterations have not in any way reduced that rifle's integrity, functionality or accuracy. Recently, I fired an eleven-shot fifty-yard group, using open sights and Black Hills' cast-lead 320 grain loading (muzzle velocity in that rifle, 1300 fps), that group was essentially one hole.

The rifle is a pleasure to carry and is fully capable of taking any species on this continent, given only the proper ammunition and that the hunter restricts his shots to appropriate ranges — perhaps 150 yards, maximum. While the original Marlin rifle was equally capable in the latter regards, it was not nearly so fun to carry.

Note that in rifles chambered for pistol cartridges or similar rifle rounds, shortening the barrel to sixteen inches (the minimum legal length) will not significantly alter ballistics.

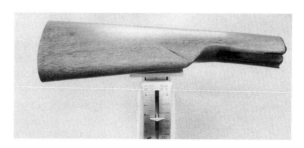

Photograph 18-1: This skeletonized Marlin buttstock weighs in at just under nine ounces (9 oz.). Factory buttstocks often weigh closer to one-pound (16 oz.). This sort of weight reduction can dramatically alter the rifle's handling qualities. See the text for hints on how to put your rifle on a weight reduction program.

(Please leave a slight edge to protect yourself from the Ruby Ridge syndrome; cut no rifle barrel shorter than about 16¼", for shotgun barrels no shorter than 18¼".)

For example, top-end ammunition loaded with the slowest feasible powder in the .44 Magnum (Winchester-296/H110, which is the same powder), will only be about 20 fps slower in a 16" barrel, compared to a 20" barrel. The ballistic difference is hardly worth considering. With such cartridges, barrels longer than about 20" will not generally deliver a measurable increase in muzzle velocity, even with top loads using relatively large charges of slow burning powders. With milder loads, using faster powder, longer barrels often reduce muzzle velocity! Bore friction is the culprit, eventually the chamber pressure is insufficient to overcome the resistance. My point is, in that .44 Magnum chambered rifle I was not sacrificing a significant amount of velocity by shortening the barrel almost four inches.

I also skeletonized the following areas: buttstock, tangs, lower receiver, finger-lever, bolt, locking lug, cartridge carrier, upper receiver, magazine tube, magazine follower, magazine end cap, receiver sight base. In performing these alterations, I drilled over 150 holes in these various parts. Hole sizes and locations were carefully chosen in order to avoid weakening any critical part at all or significantly weakening any structural portion of the rifle. See photograph # 18-3.

Only a few of the holes are visible when the action is open and none are particularly evident when the action is closed. To the casual observer the rifle looks very similar to any other carbine. However, those who have handled this rifle invariably fall in love with it for its handling, shooting and functional qualities. The thick Pachmayr Decelerator recoil pad and the Williams receiver-mounted aperture sight add dramatically to this rifle's appeal.

Ammunition & Handloading Considerations, Single-Shot & Related Rifles:

As noted elsewhere in this text, certain rifles and certain cartridges can benefit from special handloading considerations. My intention in these sub-sections is to reiterate many of those considerations into one specific portion of the text. At the expense of some repetition, I can

Photograph 18-3: This view of a highly-skeletonized Marlin buttstock shows several interesting points. First, note the shoulder (visible in the lower of the large holes). I have modified this buttstock for use with a through-bolt (see text). Also note that both recoil pad attachment screw holes have been drilled out and refilled with wood-reinforced epoxy. This dramatically improves the holding power of the stock on these screws.

Photograph 18-2: Williams offers well fitted and finished receiver-mounted aperture sights that are constructed of high-strength aluminum and, therefore, add almost nothing to the weight of the rifle (compared to the original barrel-mounted rear sight). Note also, the ROBAR electroless Nickel/Teflon (NP3) finish on the hammer, bolt and screws of this rifle.

thereby simplify the reader's task of finding this important information.

Ammunition & Handloading Considerations, Antique Single-Shot Rifles:

As I previously noted, all antique single-shot rifles were designed to shoot accurately with ammunition using lead bullets and black powder. For this reason, any effort to bring out the accuracy potential of any such rifle will have to include bullet casting and handloading.

If you are unwilling to undertake those chores, do not expect to see any such rifle produce impressive accuracy — regardless of how well it is mechanically tuned. However, note that those who have gone to the trouble to test various bullet diameters, designs, weights and hardnesses, and who have tested various powders and charge weights have often found combinations that would produce astounding accuracy.

One last point here: generally, the steel used in the barrels of these rifles will not tolerate extensive use with jacketed bullets; in many instances the rifling was cut to work only with cast bullets; very rarely does the groove diameter of these rifles match the diameter of the jacketed bullets used in modern factory ammunition. The former fact suggests that using jacketed bullets is foolish. These latter facts lead to gross inaccuracy. My best advice (and that of many experts) is to never fire any jacketed-bullet ammunition in any antique rifle. Even if that ammunition did manage to shoot reasonably well it would rapidly destroy the irreplaceable barrel — within a few hundred shots, perhaps. Conversely, when used with the correct cast bullet loading, these barrels can last many tens of thousands of rounds!

The first order of business is to slug the rifle's bore to determine correct bullet diameter. Use a bore-fitting hardwood dowel and a plastic mallet to drive a lubricated oversize pure lead ball through the (clean) barrel. Measure the maximum diameter of the slug. You should order a mould designed to cast bullets that are about one- thousandth to one and one-half thousandths of an inch (0.001"x0.0015") larger than the slug.

To develop the most accurate load you will almost certainly have to test several likely bullet designs. Cast bullet moulds are available from many sources. For a starter load, find a design that closely matches the original bullet used in that cartridge. The old Lyman reloading manuals are a good source for that information. Another likely source is any bullet mould manufacturer — most keep records of customer reports.

The next order is to determine the correct bullet hardness. Here the bullet caster has to work with both alloy and hardening techniques. Oven hardening and tempering is probably the only way to ensure that all the bullets from one casting batch are of the same hardness. You have to match bullet hardness to the load's peak chamber pressure.

If the bullet is too hard, it will not properly obturate and upset to seal the bore and drive the lubricant from the grease groove against the barrel. Leading is certain to result from use of too-hard bullets.

If recovered bullets show gas cutting along the heel portion of the bullet shank, the bullet is likely too hard. There are four distinct ways to correct for this problem: use a softer alloy (less antimony or more lead), oven temper the bullet, increase the powder charge (where safe), use a faster burning powder (where safe).

If the bullet is too soft, it is liable to strip in the rifling and upset excessively. This will result in inaccuracy and probably barrel leading.

If recovered bullets show signs of stripage in the rifling — usually evidenced by a smearing at the front of the bullet shank — the bullet is likely too soft. There are four distinct ways to correct this: use a harder alloy (more antimony or less lead), oven harden the bullet, decrease the powder charge (where safe), use a slower burning powder (where safe).

Most of these subjects are covered in sufficient detail in *Metallic Cartridge Reloading, 3rd Edition*. For detailed information, refer to that source. My goal in this sub-section is to try to impress on the tinker the fact that realizing the accuracy potential of these rifles requires dedicated handloading. If you are not willing to handload or hire professional handloading done, there is little chance of making one of these rifles shoot impressive groups. Conversely, with proper loads, many of these rifles can shoot tiny little groups.

Ammunition & Handloading Considerations, All Types Of Rifles:

Before specifically covering handloading issues I should mention something that many otherwise serious shooters do not seem to realize: the type of factory ammunition used can have a dramatic influence on the accuracy of the rifle.

When a bullet travels down a barrel, the barrel vibrates wildly. The end of the barrel will typically vibrate in such a way that it will trace out a figure-eight or some other complicated path. Imagine the simplest case, where the end of the barrel vibrates up and down or side to side in an essentially straight line. It is easy to see that the muzzle is pointing in different directions as the barrel vibrates. Further, in any given increment of time the muzzle is changing where it is pointing the most when it is moving the fastest. It is moving the fastest when it is near the middle of its path (precisely at the center, as a matter of fact). Conversely, when it is near the end of its path, and changing directions, the end of the barrel moves the slowest. It never completely stops in any real-world situation because it is never vibrating along a completely straight line — there is always some loop in the muzzle's path.

Since no two bullets will ever pass through the barrel in precisely the same amount of time, the secret of finding accurate ammunition is to discover loadings that launch the bullet when the barrel is near the end of its arc, where the muzzle is slowing and changing directions. These loads are apt to produce each bullet from the barrel when the muzzle is pointing more nearly in the same direction, compared to loads where the bullets come out as the end of the barrel is moving through the center of its arc. See illustration.

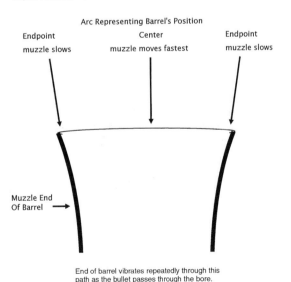

Idealized Arc Representing Path Of End Of Barrel During Bullet's Passage (Highly Exaggerated)

End of barrel vibrates repeatedly through this path as the bullet passes through the bore.

For this reason, often, a rifle will do much better with one bullet weight or even with one weight and one specific brand of ammunition. This is not necessarily a reflection that said ammunition is particularly superior; rather, that type just works better in that rifle — often because the bullets happen to exit the bore when the muzzle is near the end of its arc.

However, for various reasons (different powder, etc.), the next production lot of that ammunition might produce a slightly different velocity (which relates to barrel time). It, therefore, might not shoot as well in that rifle.

Handloaders can tune their ammunition to the particular rifle. It is very common for the most accurate load to be a combination that uses a particular bullet weight loaded with some specific powder to generate some specific velocity. It is a happy combination when the bullet one hopes to use produces its best accuracy when launched at a velocity that is generated by something that is close to the maximum safe load.

Such fortuitous combinations are not so rare as you might suspect. In the first place, all other things being equal, the muzzle will spend more time located near the end of the arc, rather than in the middle of the arc — it is moving slower near the endpoints. However, all other things are not equal, some rifles will have a misfortunate harmonic vibration condition that will reduce the time the barrel spends near the end of the arc. Sometimes slightly shortening the barrel will solve this problem.

Another thing that increases the handloader's potential for finding a fortuitous combination has to do with powder choice. The handloader can usually test several different powders that have a similar burning rate. Perhaps surprisingly, when loads use a different powder to launch the same bullet to the same velocity, barrel time will usually be significantly different! For this reason it is likely that one useful powder will give the needed barrel time to produce the best accuracy in any given rifle. That is one of the reasons many of us handload.

However, handloaders tend to get into a rut. Often, they will make wild and unfounded assumptions. A good example of this problem centers upon primer choice. The first point I want to make here concerns the use of Magnum primers. Use of a hotter (Magnum) primer is not necessarily always a good idea. Moreover, not all rifle loads benefit from use of rifle primers! I will return to this point later.

An obvious counter-example to the use of Magnum primers concerns chamber pressure.

Section 18: Miscellaneous Considerations, Single-Shot (And Other) Rifles, Part II

Substituting a Magnum primer for a standard primer often increases chamber pressure 20%, sometimes a lot more! That, my friends, represents the difference between perfectly normal loads and proof-pressure test loads.

Even if we leave the question of chamber pressure aside, Magnum Rifle primers are often a poor choice. For many chamberings, ammunition loaded with standard primers usually generates better accuracy. Generally, if you are loading for a cartridge that uses less than about 70 grains of smokeless powder, use standard primers — unless the data specifically calls for Magnum Rifle primers. Equally, a standard Large Rifle primer will usually do the best job in any standard cartridge and loading using nearly a full case of powder. This includes most loads using less than about 90 grains of powder, with a powder that is faster burning than IMR4064. However, if you are loading a large case and using slower powders or in combinations where the powder occupies substantially less than 95% of the available powder space, you should probably use only the hottest Magnum Rifle primers.

On the other side, many cartridges that are nominally rifle chamberings can benefit from reloading with pistol primers. Generally, in low- to moderate-pressure numbers, so long as the combination of chamber pressure and the fit between the firing pin and bolt do not lead to cratered or pierced primers, pistol primers are worth trying. Likely candidates include the following: .22 Hornet, .218 Bee, .219 Zipper, .22 Savage High Power (.22 Imp), .25-20 WCF (.25-20 Winchester), .25-35 WCF (.25-35 Winchester), 7mm Waters, .30-30 Winchester, .32 Winchester Special, .38-55 WCF (.38-55 Winchester), .40-65 WCF (.40-65 Winchester), .45-70 Government, .50-70 Government. These, and similar chamberings, will often produce more consistent ballistics when loaded with any standard Large Pistol primer.

There are two reasons these milder primers can produce superior ballistics. First, the light hammer fall provided by many of these rifles cannot properly and consistently ignite any rifle primer (pistol primers are dramatically easier to ignite properly). Second, most rifle primers are entirely too hot for these applications (standard pistol primers are generally much milder). The rifle primer often moves the bullet before the powder ignites and that situation increases variability.

However, if the load combination results in a substantial unused powder space, stick to rifle primers. Also, do not use pistol primers in any such loads for use in truly cold climes. Determining the best primer for any given load requires testing and experimentation. Also, as noted elsewhere, watch for excessively cratered or pierced primers. If this occurs, do not use pistol primers until you repair the loose fitting firing pin.

Despite anything said here, never use any primer without first verifying that application. Either refer to modern published data or call the technical information department at the powder manufacturer.

Another subject I should reiterate here is bullet pull, which is a function of case neck tension and crimping. In hunting ammunition, a solid bond between the bullet and the case neck is an essential characteristic. This condition will help prevent bullets from moving into or out of the cases during handling or as a result of recoil forces in the rifle. In ammunition used in tubular-magazine rifles, the addition of a solid crimp is a valuable aid in limiting the potential for a bullet to be driven back into the case as a result of the substantial recoil battering that can occur in the magazine of these rifles.

However, when loading ammunition for use in a tubular magazine rifle, I prefer to use a powder and bullet combination that provides for a substantially compressed powder charge, especially if that ammunition will be used for hunting. If the bullet is already significantly compressing the powder charge, it is unlikely that magazine battering or chambering forces will push the bullet further into the case. It is generally possible to find a powder that will produce good accuracy and ballistics at a safe pressure level when so compressed. Classic examples include IMR4064 in the .30-30 Winchester and VARGET in the .45-70 Government.

Note that you cannot rely upon a crimp to lock the bullet in the case. If bullet-to-case-neck tension is insufficient, no crimp will properly hold the bullet in place every time. For loads used in hunting, I suggest reducing the diameter of the expander ball in the full-length sizing die to no greater than bullet diameter minus three-thousandths of an inch (0.003"). Generally, if the seating operation does not damage the bullet or deform the case, more neck tension is always better.

Handloads in obsolete rifle cartridges used in single-shot rifles often include cast lead bullets.

These and many other accuracy handloads are often assembled so that the bullet is driven well into the rifling as the bolt (or breachblock) is closed. Generally, this practice is fraught with potential hazards. The two most obvious are the stuck bullet and unpredictable chamber pressure results.

In the first case, the shooter decides not to fire the shot, then opens the action and withdraws the case, only to find that the bullet is no longer in the case but is stuck in the barrel — real handy, and guess where the powder charge is?

In the second instance, the handloader believes that seating the bullet out of the case so that it jams into the rifling will not raise chamber pressure significantly — often that is true. Equally often, this action will skyrocket pressures. Examples of this include varmint loadings using slow powders and soft bullets and any load using any solid copper or brass bullet or any similarly designed bullet. Those and other combinations can turn a perfectly normal load into a potential disaster. Obviously, if you intend to load ammunition to seat bullets against the rifling, seek expert advice and exercise extreme caution.

This is not a handloading text so I have limited my ammunition comments to subjects that seem particularly germane to certain rifle applications. Those interested in exploring these subjects (and many others) in greater detail should refer to the highly acclaimed reloading manual, *Metallic Cartridge Reloading, 3rd Edition*, available through DBI Books (now Krause) and, I must confess, written by this author.

Rimmed & Rimless Cartridges, Single-Shot Rifles:

It is difficult to effectively convert the extractor systems used in many single-shot rifle actions to work correctly with rimless cartridges. Further, many single-shot chamberings are either cylindrical or straight tapered rimmed cartridges. On such cartridges it is impossible to hold the cartridge's headspace except through the rim. There is a class of chamberings that are an exception to this rule, the rimless pistol cartridges, which headspace on the case mouth. Since those cartridges are not well suited to single-shot rifles, we will ignore those here.

Modifications that allow use of belted and rimless cases in traditional single-shot rifles do exist. An obvious example is the Ruger No. 1.

However, these extractor systems are significantly complicated and the fact remains, rimmed cartridges are always a better choice in these rifles.

The trouble is, over the years, manufacturers have played fast and loose with both rim thickness and chambering headspace on many of these low-pressure cartridges and guns. As a result, excessive headspace is the rule, rather than the exception.

The reason we have gotten away with this situation is more a function of the low pressures normally used in these cartridges than anything else. Similar grossly loose headspace on modern high-pressure cartridges would result in catastrophe.

Another point worth noting is that few shooters have very high expectations for accuracy with a ".30-30" type rifle. Therefore, there has been little incentive for manufacturers to improve accuracy through proper fitting.

On bottlenecked versions of rimmed cartridge, such as the .30-30 Winchester, it is a simple handloading matter to move headspace control to the case shoulder. This is, in fact, what most accuracy-minded handloaders do. Handloaders have three options to achieve this desirable goal. First, they can simply adjust the full-length sizing die to leave the shoulder sufficiently forward to take up the slack — a poor method, owing to inconsistencies. Second, they can use Redding's Competition shell holders to achieve the same goal with more precision. Third, they can use custom full-length sizing dies that are cut to practically match the rifle's chamber — with only a modicum of clearance, to allow easy chambering of the resized case.

Those shooting straight-taper cartridges such as the .32-20 Winchester, .32-40 Winchester, .38-55 Winchester, .40-65 Winchester, .44 Magnum, .444 Marlin, .45-70 Government and .50-70 Government have no such option. These numbers, and many more, have to headspace on the case rim. Here the handloader could locate and use only thicker-rimmed cases, but no such cases that are readily available can account for the excess headspace built into the typical rifle. See photograph # 18-4.

The only permanent solution is to have the barrel set back one thread; then rechambered to allow proper headspacing with typical cases. In this instance, there are apt to be occasional thicker rimmed cases that will not chamber. This is a small price to pay for proper headspacing, which dramatically increases both accuracy and case life.

Section 18: Miscellaneous Considerations, Single-Shot (And Other) Rifles, Part II

Note, the Marlin lever-action rifle is an exception, proper headspace is easily achieved through proper fitting of a replacement locking lug. This work was described earlier in this text.

The process of setting a barrel back is as follows. First, pull the barrel from the receiver; this task might require special tools. Then cut the receiver mating shoulder on the barrel, moving it forward sufficiently to allow the barrel to turn into the receiver precisely one additional turn. Next, either form a relief cut at the front of the threads on the barrel, or in the corresponding threads in the receiver, or thread the new portion of the turned-down barrel shank to thread into the receiver. Then trim the rear face of the barrel to allow proper bolt clearance. Finally, rechamber the barrel to provide "proper" headspace and recut any barrel slots such as the extractor cut.

Here, "proper" headspace provides sufficient rim clearance so that most cases will chamber or so that a specific batch of a specific type of case will chamber. Many serious target shooters have headspace cut so critically that they have to custom trim the front of each rim to achieve a precise rim thickness for use in that rifle. Turning the front of the rims has the advantage that it trues the rim thickness around the entire perimeter.

Each of the alterations noted in the above paragraph is an opportunity for your gunsmith to improve your rifle — refer to the related subsections in *Part I* of this text. For this reason alone, you might well consider having your rimmed-case chambered rifle properly headspaced.

An alternative solution is to have your gunsmith make you a special die that will form thicker sections on the case rim. Some handloaders have used this method with some success. However, it seems a poor choice, at least to this perfectionist.

I must also note that case rims are often terribly inconsistent. It is not uncommon to find rimmed cases where rim thickness varies by fully two-thousandths of an inch (0.002") on any given case from one side to the other! Case-to-case rim thickness variations of three-thousandths of an inch (0.003") in samples from the same production lot are typical. Variations between lots and brands can be even more startling. Norma seems to do a better job of keeping rim thickness uniform on individual cases, consistent from one case to the next and closer to the SAAMI maximum limit. When those are available, I always choose Norma brand cases when precision handloading (enough said).

Installation And Functioning Of Set Triggers, Target & Hunting Rifles:

The set trigger comes in several varieties. Almost all are adjustable. A commonly available unit for falling-block single-shot rifle is the double-set. In this system, the shooter can choose to "set" the main (front) trigger for a very light trigger release by pulling the rear trigger to cock a mechanism. Conversely, he can use the front trigger as a standard trigger by simply omitting the cocking action of the rear trigger. Other systems include the single-set — pushing the single trigger forward sets the intermediate, or trip, hammer. See photograph #s 18-5/6/7.

Typically, after the mechanism is "set", a very light touch to the main trigger (often measured in ounces, sometimes in fractions of an ounce) releases a spring-loaded intermediate "trip" hammer (technically the knock-off). This piece then strikes the main sear and trips that free from the hammer.

Photograph 18-4: Here are three examples of rimmed cartridges that have to headspace on the rim — there is no shoulder or other feature to provide headspacing. Left-to-right: .45-70 Government (circa, 1873), .40-65 Winchester (circa, 1887), .40-65 Falin (circa, 1994). The latter is a straight-tapered .444 Marlin case with a long straight neck. Excepting the smaller rim and slightly shorter case body, this cartridge duplicates the .40-70 Ballard (circa, 1881).

The mechanical price of using a set trigger is that three things have to happen before the sear releases the hammer. First, the trigger has to move; second, the trip hammer has to move; finally, the sear latch has to move.

The net result is that, compared to a single (standard) trigger, the set trigger system introduces more vibrations into the rifle and also significantly increases lock-time. Lock-time is the delay between the trigger's movement and the firing pin's impact on the primer.

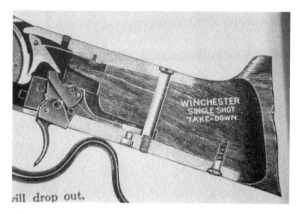

Photograph 18-5

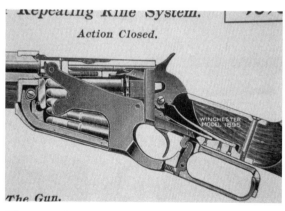

Photograph 18-6

Photographs 18-5/6/7: These photographs are taken from pages of the Winchester 1916 catalogue. The trigger on the Winchester falling-block rifle is quite intricate, as shown in photograph 18-5. Even the trigger on the Model-1895 Winchester involves several intricately interacting pieces, as you can discern from photograph 18-6 — the trigger pushes on the sear and that rotates to disengage the hammer sear notch. However, compared to these mechanisms, the set trigger is in an entirely different class. Photograph 18-7 shows only two of the three basic types of set triggers.

However, it is essentially impossible to design a truly safe non-set trigger that will duplicate the delicate release provided by the best set trigger systems. The trade off is a crisp and delicate trigger release compared to a system that provides a faster lock-time and produces fewer rifle vibrations and, often, vibrations of reduced magnitude.

Competitive single-shot target shooters, in those disciplines that allow use of set triggers, have their choice. The result is that shooters using set triggers win the vast majority of blackpowder and similar competitions. Evidently the advantages of a crisp trigger outweigh the aforementioned disadvantages — at least for most target shooters.

However, note that some successful competitors do their best shooting with conventional triggers. Further, in the benchrest game, where competitors fire the smallest groups produced in any target discipline, all competitors use conventional, albeit very high quality, triggers.

There is good evidence to suggest that which trigger a particular shooter does best with is more a matter of experience than anything else. Perhaps the reason set triggers win most black-

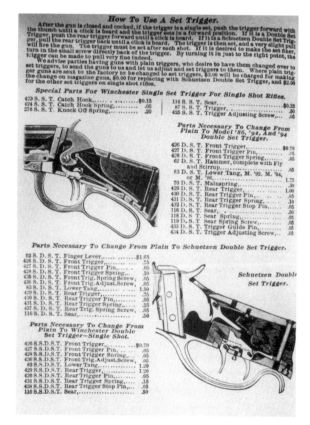

Photograph 18-7

powder competitions is that most competitors have learned to target shoot using that seemingly superior trigger system. By the time the typical shooter gains sufficient experience to realize the set trigger's disadvantages, he is ingrained into using it. He automatically compensates for the increased lock-time before touching off his shots. Since these two trigger systems have distinct lock-times it would be very difficult, indeed, for any shooter to switch back and forth without repeatedly suffering through a significant learning curve. This is exactly what is reported.

On the other hand, it is just possible that the advantage of a reduction in the stress between the trigger finger and the trigger, when using a set trigger, outweighs the disadvantages related to increased rifle vibrations and lock-time. The lighter trigger pull results in the rifleman disturbing the gun less in the act of applying pressure to the trigger, in the instant before the hammer falls. Also, since he does not have to pull as hard on the trigger to fire the rifle, there will be less disturbance between himself and the rifle when the trigger does release. (Esoteric? Perhaps.... Real? For sure!)

Note that many novices do have trouble using a set trigger because they try to adjust the set trigger too fine and are, therefore, unable to control the let-off timing. Most shooters should adjust the set trigger for a few pound let-off and then adjust it finer as they gain skill at trigger control.

In any case, you should not assume that a set trigger is automatically a superior accuracy choice. It seems that most early-stage (novice) target shooters can do better work when using a rifle equipped with a properly adjusted set trigger. I suspect that that observation merely reflects those shooters' inexperience at trigger control. The evidence from the target community suggests that a practiced rifleman should be able to use a rifle that is equipped with a standard trigger to produce better accuracy than he could with the same rifle equipped with a set trigger — refer to my earlier comments on the benchrest game.

This suggests that most of us would be better served to practice more and spend less. Keep these facts in mind before making the expensive decision to have a gunsmith install a set trigger on your prized rifle.

One other important consideration is safety. When using a gun equipped with a set trigger, never, never "set" the trigger until you are absolutely ready to fire. Properly adjusted, these triggers are so delicate that it is difficult to imagine any hunting situation where it would be fully appropriate or particularly advantageous for a novice to use this feature.

Nevertheless, a set trigger is an elegant touch and most of us can do better offhand shooting with a rifle so equipped. If you decide to have your gunsmith install such a trigger, expect to pay a good price. First, the trigger system itself is a necessarily delicate and precise instrument built with quality parts. Second, proper fitting can entail quite a bit of precision work and significant alterations to the rifle.

Brownells stocks a wide variety of set triggers adapted to many different rifle actions. Formerly, Winchester offered set triggers as a factory option on many of their rifle lines. Custom gunsmiths have widely copied these trigger systems, with varying degrees of quality, precision and success. Note that S. D. Meacham Tool & Hardware Inc. sells complete assemblies and conversion kits for gunsmith installation on the falling-block rifle.

If you do opt for a set trigger, be sure not to adjust the set trigger too fine. Very few shooters can handle the finest settings that are possible. Literally, the pulse of your heartbeat in your trigger finger can fire the rifle before you realize you have touched the trigger! Clearly, such a setting is too fine. As noted, begin by setting it coarse, then, as you increase in skill, adjust it finer.

To give an idea of just how fine a practiced shooter can set and use the best of these triggers, consider that some top competitors cut the trigger portion of the original main trigger off and install a fine piece of piano wire as a substitute trigger. Because this delicate wire only touches a small portion of the trigger finger, an equal force on this "wire" trigger results in a greater sensation on the shooter's finger. For this reason, this fine flexible wire gives the skilled shooter a better feel of the trigger and, therefore, more precise control. However, learning such precise trigger control requires more practice than most shooters can afford.

Metallic Sights, Traditional Target Rifles:

Aperture sights, both front and rear, with the addition of a spirit (bubble) level, can provide surprisingly precise sighting accuracy. As has long been demonstrated in the NRA Highpower target game and, historically, in many other forms of long-range competitions. Surprisingly, it is possible to hit a target that you cannot actually see!

However, the sighting systems used on such rifles by such riflemen are no ordinary metallic sights. Typically, the front sight is an aperture surrounded by a hood. The size of the aperture in this sight is precisely matched to the apparent size of the target bullseye (at the range the competitor is shooting) to provide for a black circle in a white ring. Equally, the rear aperture is adjustable and matched to the lighting conditions and the shooter's eyes to provide for a ring in ring sighting picture. The barrel-mounted bubble level is particularly critical for long-range shooting; minor canting of the rifle can move the shot many inches off the intended target.

These sighting systems are precision instruments, designed to provide for precise adjustments with essentially zero play (technically called backlash), one click will move the sight picture a specific distance at a specific range. Each click will move the sights the same distance. Changing directions on the adjustment will reverse the movement. There is no play in the sights at any given setting. It is no wonder a set of such sights costs more than a typical varmint hunting rifle and target riflescope combined!

On single-shot rifles, keep in mind that installation of a receiver-mounted rear aperture sight requires hand-fitting. First, many of these rifles were hand contoured on the top of the receiver — there was no standard contour, whatever it took to get a pleasing shape from the rough forging was what was used. For this reason, it is often necessary to fit a receiver sight to the receiver so that it will set approximately vertical. Accordingly, manufacturers design most sight bases to touch the receiver only along the side edges. This provides for solid mounting and simple adjustment through filing on one edge of the sight base.

You can easily file one edge to tip the sight, as necessary. Note that on the Trapdoor Springfield the vernier rear sight was deliberately canted about one and seven-tenths degrees (1.7°) from true vertical. The designer incorporated this cant so that elevation adjustments would automatically compensate for long-range bullet drift. With the sub-sonic bullets used, this was the best compromise to keep the bullet as close to the point of aim as possible across the calibrated range. In order for the rifleman to use this system effectively, he has to hold the rifle true to the vertical.

Since most shooters have a serious tendency to cant a rifle, the installation and proper use of a spirit bubble level is critical for long-range accuracy. This is true with any rifle using any sighting system. See photograph # 18-8.

Target Shooting, Traditional (High Recoil) Target Rifles:

Traditional benchrest rifle rests and holds do not work with heavy recoiling blackpowder rifles. Most successful target competitors using such rifles hold the fore-end tightly, rest their cheek solidly on the stock (when possible) and stay in position ("on the gun") appreciably after it fires.

This last point is critical; in these rifles, the bullet is in the barrel for a good long time. Owing to the relatively high mass of the bullet and powder charge, the rifle moves a substantial distance before the bullet leaves the muzzle. This combination of long barrel time and high recoil velocity work together to make it critical that the shooter does not alter his hold until after he realizes the gun has fired.

Believe it or not, it is possible to alter the bullet's impact by many inches (almost all is vertical) by simply pulling your head away from the cheek piece the instant you realize the gun has fired. I repeat, this is not theory. I have proved this effect and so have many other shooters — much to our mutual chagrin.

Photograph 18-8: Bill Falin, chief ballistician for Accurate Arms Company, demonstrates truly long-range target shooting with a traditional rifle. This is a C. Sharps reproduction chambered in .40-65 Falin. Note the hooded front sight with spirit bubble level. At this range, canting the rifle a few degrees will introduce many feet of sighting error. Also note that the long-range rear aperture sight is almost fully extended. Here we were lobbing 420 grain pointed lead bullets across 7/8 mile. Time of flight was over 5 seconds! And yes, we could hit anything. In one string of sixteen shots the author put five bullets inside a ten foot circle. This, despite having to hold as much as twenty feet left or right, as the swirling breeze (less than 5 mph, usually) changed. Mr. Falin's superior coaching allowed me to concentrate on the sight picture as he watched the wind conditions through a spotting scope.

Section 19: Gunsmith Specific Alterations, Part III

Throughout this text I have alluded to and discussed many alterations that are better done by a professional gunsmith. In this sub-section, I will address several that should *only* be done by a *professional*. An amateur that has the proper equipment and skills to correctly do these chores is rightly a professional amateur or an amateur professional.

Barrel Replacement:

Very few manufacturers equip their run-of-the-mill rifles with top quality barrels — although there are exceptions (all in the upper end custom rifles). This has always been the situation; a matter of basic economics. Few shooters are willing to spend several hundred additional dollars just for the privilege of getting a rifle with a premium barrel factory installed. However, there are a few who are willing to pay the requisite price for any accuracy advantage. This has always been the situation.

Currently, the best conventional barrels (as equipped on the typical hunting rifle) are capable of shooting about one-half inch groups at one-hundred yards. Replacement of such a "stock" barrel with one of the better custom barrels will often cut group sizes in half — but you cannot count on that. The best barrels and loads can do substantially better still!

In days gone by, the magnitude of these differences were similar. However, I should point out that the best rifleman in the world seventy-odd years ago would have bowed in reverence to any rifle and load that would routinely put five shots into a one-inch group at one-hundred yards (about 1 MOA, Minute Of Angle). As recently as thirty years ago, it was the rare factory rifle and load that would consistently manage one and one-half (1½) MOA.

Today, we can do much better. Those willing to invest in a top-quality barrel, an adequate telescopic sight and to develop proper handloads can expect any good rifle to make very tiny groups. However, the key here is the proverbial weak link. If you are shooting a factory rifle with a $20 barrel, you cannot expect to produce groups comparable to what the same rifle, when equipped with a $300 barrel, would manage. Is that any surprise? Also note, the production of a superior barrel requires superior material, tooling, skill and considerable hand labor. These factors well justify the increased price.

In this text, I have pointed out myriad tricks intended to allow you to modify your factory rifle to produce its best groups. I have mentioned but not dwelled upon the fact that different rifles will perform best with different factory loads or specific handloads. However, that characteristic should be obvious. Something I have not explicitly noted is that no amount of tinkering or load development can make any gun consistently shoot better than its intrinsic accuracy level — when it occasionally does, that group is the result of a happy accident.

If you have done all the tricks in rifle modifications and load development and the accuracy you are getting still does not satisfy you, your only recourse (with that rifle) is to start replacing parts. I have formerly discussed installation of a better trigger. However, a bad trigger is very seldom a fundamental limitation upon any gun's accuracy potential. Conversely, a bad barrel most assuredly is.

The barrel is the one thing that likely stands between your properly-tuned rifle and the production of truly tiny groups. Further, in many calibers, well-used rifles have "shot-out" barrels. As little as a few hundred rounds can crater the average barrel in some of the superduper chamberings (.220 Swift, .264 Winchester Magnum, etc.). For any of these reasons, you might want to consider the installation of a replacement barrel.

Factory replacement barrels are generally a bargain and will often shoot adequately well. However, accuracy is our primary interest here; that fact suggests opting for a premium-quality barrel.

Installation of a new barrel is not as simple as it might seem. First, someone has to decide upon the length and contour of the barrel. Since it is your rifle, the best person to make this decision is you. There are many considerations here.

Regarding the ballistic characteristics of barrels, generally: longer barrels provide additional velocity; shorter barrels provide superior intrinsic accuracy (ounce for ounce, shorter barrels are stiffer and the muzzle will vibrate through a shorter arc); heavier barrels provide better intrinsic accuracy (reduced ambient temperature sensitivity, slower heating, faster cooling, less vibration).

Then there is the option of fluting the barrel. Given specific weight and length limits, fluting can provide a stiffer barrel that cools faster. Fluting currently costs about $100. Many target and varmint shooters consider this alteration a bargain. It could certainly have application in a lightweight hunting rifle as well. See photograph # 19-1.

After settling upon barrel length and contour, you have to decide upon the manufacturer. Here I can only note that the best barrels are all reflected by the highest prices. However, note that certain shooting publications (such as *Precision Shooting* magazine) report the equipment used by the most successful competitors in various competitions. Such information, advice of a trusted gunsmith, and comments from competitive shooters are good guides in choosing your barrel maker. See photograph # 19-2.

After you have chosen a barrel maker and contour (usually your gunsmith will adjust the barrel's final length to your request), you still have to decide upon rifling rate (twist) and, in some instances, upon the quality level for which you want to pay and the type of steel you want (stainless or chrome-moly). Even after deciding all those things, you still have other important decisions to make.

First, how will you chamber your new highly precise barrel? If you do not chamber to SAAMI (Sporting Arms and Ammunition Manufacturers' Institute, Inc.) specifications for

Photograph 19-1: Here gunsmith Skip Otto is deburring the freshly cut flutes on a customer's barrel. This is the first step in polishing the flutes. Fluting has many potential advantages. It can change the harmonics of the barrel, it will increase the barrel's relative stiffness, and it increases the barrel's cooling rate. (Skip's Machine, telephone number: (970) 245-5417.)

Photograph 19-2: This Krieger barrel is representative of the world-class barrels that are now available from several top manufacturers. Quality comes at a price. If you want top accuracy, expect to pay several hundred dollars for this tube, which is at the heart of your rifle's accuracy potential.

Section 19: Gunsmith Specific Alterations, Part III

a standard cartridge, or if you choose to chamber for any wildcat round, you will have to specify some or all the chambering specifications. Reamer manufactures (such as JGS) can provide reamers in any feasible configuration.

Rather than follow standard SAAMI specifications when chambering a custom rifle, gunsmiths often deliberately alter such things as throat diameter and length. Generally, gunsmiths intend these alterations to provide a chamber that will deliver improved accuracy potential. It makes little sense to chamber a high dollar barrel with an unnecessarily loose chamber.

Second, you have to decide who will do the chambering work? If you do not have a trusted gunsmith, finding one can be a nightmare. Often, the best gunsmiths in any given area are also the busiest; you can wait months to have a barrel installed. When making such an important decision, never forget, anyone can nail up a gunsmithing shingle.

As an overall example of the decisions involved in rebarreling a rifle, I will catalogue my recent experiences in the process of developing of a custom, switch-barrel rifle chambered for four wildcat cartridges. In retrospect, it seems unlikely I could have encountered any significant additional difficulties or decisions. This, my first outing, has to be viewed as trial by fire!

I have a rotary-magazine Model-99 Savage that was factory chambered in .284 Winchester. I decided that, as a project, I would create a switch-barrel rifle based upon that action. My goals included barrels chambered for each of the following applications: a long-range target and varmint rifle; a lightweight elk hunting rifle; a medium-weight, medium-bore hunting rifle; a large-bore, big and dangerous game rifle.

Owing to the rotary-magazine in this rifle, I chose to develop four wildcat chamberings, each based upon the same case body — an improved version of the .284 Winchester. For other reasons, I choose the following calibers for these wildcats: 6mm (long range target and varmint); 7mm (light-weight, intermediate-range mountain hunting); 0.338" (medium-range, North American hunting); 0.375" (short-range, heavy-cover, large and dangerous game hunting). See photograph #s 19-3/4/5/6.

Obviously, I could have chosen other calibers — 6.5mm, .30 caliber and .416 caliber come to mind. Those chosen reflect personal decisions made after considerable pondering. Many things entered into these decisions, examples included: characteristics of the parent case (capacity, etc.), characteristics of the bullets available in each caliber; personal tastes. For example, I would have preferred to use the quarter-bore as the smallest member; however, the best target bullets in the world are now made in 6mm.

As another example of a path not taken, consider the very attractive candidate for the big bore version, a .416 caliber. I considered this option long and hard. However, the lightest premium bullets now offered in this caliber are close to 300 grains in weight. Such bullets are rather long and would occupy a considerable

Photograph 19-3: In this setup, a ball end mill is aligned over the rotary magazine spool from a .284 Winchester chambered Savage Model-99F rifle. I am converting this rifle to a switch-barrel multi-purpose custom gun. One of the chamberings is the .375-284 Mac (an improved and necked-up .284 Winchester). This chambering requires additional clearance at the front of the spool. My friend, Randolph Constantine, agreed to do this work so that I could get photographs for this text. Note that Mr. Constantine does not do general gunsmithing, please do not call him on such matters — he is too busy as a competitive NRA Highpower competitor.

portion of the available powder space, which reduces ballistic potential. The parent case (.284 Winchester) would provide a relatively short neck to hold such a bullet in place and there would likely be a considerable loss of cases in the process of converting case necks from 0.284" to 0.416". Then there is the issue of case shoulder area and headspace control. While, most likely, my improved version of the case would provide ample headspace control in .416 caliber, I was more comfortable with the generous shoulder the .375 caliber version affords. Finally, recoil would be a real concern with top loads launching 300 grains bullets at close to 2400 fps from a 10-pound rifle.

Nevertheless, should I someday manage a trip to Africa, I might want to have a .416 barrel made. The good news is, that is no problem. All this will require is a new barrel, a chambering reamer, loading dies and a bit of gunsmithing.

Having settled upon four basic cartridges, I had to design the reamers. With the indispensable assistance of Keith Francis at JGS Precision Tool, I was eventually able to do so.

Our initial discussion demonstrated that we shared a love for the .284 Winchester case, which is, indeed, a very good moderate-capacity cartridge case. However, we agreed that the SAAMI-specification body taper is entirely too great. We designed the new case using Mr. Ackley's long-established standard body taper for rifle cartridge cases. This change increased the chamber diameter at the juncture of the shoulder and case body from 0.475" to 0.490". Besides providing a surprising 4% increase in usable capacity (about 2.4 grains of typical powder), this modification also reduces bolt thrust and eases case extraction with top loads. More importantly, it dramatically increases headspace control with the .375 caliber version (an increase of almost 20%).

Photograph 19-4: Here a mocked-up .375-284 Mac rests in the spool before any alteration. Note that the case neck rests against the corresponding recess on the spool. The case body is not fully down in the spool recess. This results in the bullet shank and case mouth extending too far from the centerline of the spool — this cartridge will not function through the unaltered magazine.

Photograph 19-5: Here Mr. Constantine has used the ball end mill to modify the first cartridge recess in the spool. Note that the case neck and bullet are resting closer to the centerline of the spool, the case body now rests on the spool. By properly positioning the work piece, using the correct cutter and correctly manipulating the table, this alteration is easily achieved.

Photograph 19-6: Here Mr. Constantine has completed the cuts on the first two positions in the spool. Note the paint highlighting the trimmed areas on the first position. This alteration in no way harms the spool, it will still function perfectly for any smaller-necked version of this cartridge. Note that this magazine system positively prevents bullet tip damage due to recoil — the case shoulder cannot move forward.

Section 19: Gunsmith Specific Alterations, Part III

Next, we designed the chambering reamers to provide a slightly smaller diameter for the rear of the chamber, 0.498" compared to the SAAMI nominal 0.500" for the .284 Winchester. This minor alteration provides for better case centering and will still provide for chambering of any SAAMI specification case. This is a small touch but it is certainly worthwhile.

For several reasons, I chose to leave the shoulder angle unchanged. First, at thirty-five degrees (35°), the .284 Winchester case shoulder is just about perfect. Second, altering the shoulder would have required significant modifications in the complicated rotary-magazine. Third, this allows factory cases to provide proper headspacing without any shoulder alterations. Finally, altering the shoulder would have necessitated use of a custom headspacing gauge — much less expensive this way. When wildcatting with other cartridges and for use in more typical rifles, it is common to alter the placement and angle of the existing case shoulder. Happily, in this design, I was able to bypass these decisions.

Since I intend to use only handloaded ammunition in all four versions, I chose to make up sample cases and turn the necks to the maximum possible uniform thickness. Fortunately, the .284 Winchester has a thick case neck, so my turned necks are still quite robust, even in the .375 caliber version.

If the neck expanding is handled properly, the necks shorten while expanding. Some of the material forming the neck length is converted to material that increases the neck diameter. Therefore, neck wall thickness is not reduced as much as you might suspect. Surprisingly, the 0.375" necks are only about two-thousandths of an inch (0.002") thinner than the original 0.284" necks.

My decision to use only turned case necks in my handloads made it possible for me to specify a comparatively tight chamber neck for each of the four cartridges. Where normally I might have opted for chamber necks that were six-thousandths of an inch (0.006") larger in diameter than the nominal SAAMI cartridge case neck, here I could make this accuracy-compromising tolerance much smaller. In the target 6mm chamber, I choose a chamber neck that would provide no more than 0.001" radial clearance to the case neck on the loaded cartridge; in the 7mm, about 0.0015"; in the 0.338" version, about 0.002"; in the 0.375" version, about 0.0025". These numbers reflect the anticipated uses and the necessary tradeoff between accuracy potential and functionality of each version. I have no real fear of a charging ground squirrel at a quarter mile … on the other hand, a charging grizzly bear at a quarter of one-hundred yards might tend to heighten my awareness, so to speak.

I also chose to design the chamber to allow for no more than 0.005" case stretching. Most SAAMI chambers will allow for much more case stretching before case-neck-to-chamber interference occurs. Since I will handload all these cartridges and I trim cases after each firing, this is not a concern. For this reason, I can keep the chamber neck clearance much shorter and that improves accuracy potential.

Mr. Francis pointed out that the SAAMI specification throat (or leade) design for the .284 Winchester is simply atrocious. In a SAAMI specification .284 Winchester chamber, the bullet enters a funnel shaped leade that begins an astounding six-thousandths of an inch (0.006") larger in diameter than the bullet shank! It is a small miracle that any factory .284 Winchester chambered rifle can shoot with any degree of accuracy.

Mr. Francis has designed an alternative leade that allows for factory .284 Winchester ammunition to fire safely in the chamber but eliminates this obscene clearance. Of course, I went with this expert's design. In each of these four wildcat chamberings, we designed the leade with accuracy in mind. Therefore the amount of freebore was an issue.

Here I provided sample bullets to JGS, this is necessary. The bullets I sent were those that I hoped to use in my handloads for each cartridge. JGS measured those bullets under an optical comparator and thereby determined the length of freebore needed to provide the bullet-to-rifling jump I wanted to use with each particular bullet in each bore size.

With the limited cartridge overall length, as dictated by the magazine in this rifle, leade freebore is critical. If the reamer were to cut the chamber with a typical amount of freebore, cartridges with bullets seated to provide the most accurate bullet-to-rifling jump (typically 0.020" to 0.070") would neither fit in nor feed from the rifle's magazine.

I also converted several cases to each of the calibers and trimmed those only sufficiently to provide a square case neck. Since the parent case has a comparatively short case neck, I wanted to leave as much neck length as possible … or so I thought.

However, Mr. Francis did the measurements, and it turned out that if I left the 6mm version of the case neck as long as possible, the bullet I wanted to use would have nearly a one-tenth inch (0.065") jump before it touched the rifling, even if the leade had zero length beyond the case mouth — that is, if the leade began entering into the rifling at the end of the case neck portion of the chamber! This one knocked me for a loop. Obviously, I did not want to have that sort of bullet jump with a target load.

Then, after some reflection, I realized that target and varmint chamberings often feature very short case necks on purpose. Further, the 6mm bullets will require very little neck tension since the rifle will weigh more than 11 pounds and recoil will be minimal. After considering these facts, I simply redesigned the case with a fifty-thousandths of an inch (0.050") shorter neck. This shortening, combined with the forty-thousandths of an inch (0.040") overall length tolerance I had originally included in the design means that, if I find this approach necessary to achieve maximum accuracy, I can seat the design bullets against the rifling in the new chamber. Even as the throat begins to wear, I can seat the bullets out further to keep the shank touching the rifling (if that proves to provide the best accuracy) without losing the ability to feed rounds from the magazine. All is well, after all.

Then I had to tell the folks at JGS what diameter I wanted for the neck portion of each chamber. This depended upon bullet diameter, case neck thickness (of the turned necks) and desired case neck clearance.

Now that I had settled upon the chambering dimensions, no mean task, I was still not done with the reamer design stage! I also had to specify for a special resizing roughing reamer so that I could rough cut the chambers with the same reamer that would later be used by RCBS to make full-length resizing dies! But, I was *still* not done. I had to then decide upon what reamer system to use regarding cost versus value.

Since all four versions of the cartridge use the same case body, I had a choice. I could get one basic resizing reamer and one basic finishing reamer, then add necker/throater reamers to finish the chambers in the three larger barrels. However, this method is not ideal from the accuracy perspective since it requires proper centering of the necker/throater reamer in an established chamber. Further, this would require either careful measurements with a dummy cartridge or separate gauges to allow the gunsmith to measure when the necker/throater has cut the chamber neck to the proper depth.

Alternatively, I could choose the more expensive but superior method of cutting one basic resizing reamer and four complete finishing reamers. This latter option, was my choice. Since I planned to invest well over $1000 in world-class barrels with a similar amount in gunsmithing costs, I simply could not justify saving a few hundred dollars in reamer costs at the expense of increasing the work for the gunsmith, while taking a chance on compromising the quality of the finished product.

Then there was one more little item, the headspace gauge. The good news here is that this chamber is designed to use standard .284 Winchester headspacing gauges, which are much less expensive than a custom wildcat gauge, all I have to do is order the standard factory gauge.

Now that I have given you a rundown of just how complicated it can be to order a custom reamer, I should point out that it will almost certainly be easier for you to order a chambering reamer. At the simplest, your gunsmith will already own the reamer you need. That happy situation will dramatically reduce your costs and also eliminate the need to make any chamber or reamer design decisions.

I should also note that reamers are a precision tool. Expect to spend several hundred dollars if you plan to purchase a custom reamer of any kind. However, note that most established gunsmiths often have many of the more common SAAMI specification and custom reamers in stock.

For example, perhaps you want to build a .223 Remington chambered varmint rifle. Many gunsmiths will have a reduced- or tight-neck reamer on hand. Normally, you can even use factory ammunition in a rifle chambered with the reduced-neck reamer. Pressure might be slightly higher and some military or surplus ammunition might not chamber or fire safely (so you cannot use it) but this is a small price to pay for the significant added accuracy such a chamber can provide. For the dedicated handloader a custom (tight-neck) chamber is the only way to go.

Having ordered reamers, I then chose my barrel maker. For me this was really no choice at all. Krieger Barrels stood out for myriad reasons. First, I know Mr. Krieger and have found him to be a kindred spirit. He believes in what he is doing and is not afraid to experiment. When he

Section 19: Gunsmith Specific Alterations, Part III

learned that I was proceeding with a series of lever-action rifle projects, to try to ascertain just how accurate such a rifle can be, he was thrilled to be involved. Then there is the little matter of steel used.

Happily, Mr. Krieger likes 4140 chrome-moly steel and so do I. I could have chosen stainless but then how would that look on a traditional lever-action rifle? Also, Krieger Barrels now offers as a factory option cryogenic barrel treatment. They report an obvious improvement in machinability when they pretreat the barrel blanks. I ordered my barrels with before-and-after cryo treating — you simply cannot have too much of a good thing. Finally, just before beginning this project, I got a call from Mr. Roger Johnston, at NECO. He called just to tell me of his elation after observing a cut-rifled barrel with his bore-scope. He reported that this was the first cut-rifled barrel he had ever seen that he would consider using on one of his target rifles. The maker? Krieger, of course. As I said, no decision at all.

Nevertheless, let me emphasize that there are plenty of other quality barrel makers out there. Review the published results from the various target competitions. Then make your own, measured decision.

I then told the fine folks at Krieger what contours I wanted for each barrel. Again . . . trouble. To keep the rifle's weight up around 10 pounds, *sans* sights, I wanted the 0.375" barrel to be as heavy as is feasible in a hunting contour. Since I envision this barrel as ending up at 21" long, this meant that I needed what is called a 5A contour to provide as much weight as possible. However, owing to the limited diameter at the receiver on this rifle, such a barrel would have looked deformed — something between a straight taper and a contoured form. The machinist at Krieger called and said, "I have it ground to your specifications and it looks like a mistake, we hate to ship an ugly barrel!". I hated to ask them to. . . as the man says, "Life is too short to hunt with an ugly rifle."

So, this required another revision. I decided to opt for a somewhat lighter barrel contour and, if necessary, include provisions for adding weight to the buttstock (especially for bench testing purposes). A small price to pay for a classy looking barrel, which it is.

Finally, I had the barrels and the reamers on order. Now it remained only to find a gunsmith. I hoped to find one who was interested in the project. I did, but that fell apart for reasons beyond his or my control.

I have now coerced a friend, Mr. Randolph Constantine, who has the proper tools, equipment and skills to help me finish this project. However, please, do not call him, he is not in the gunsmithing business. This was my only good option since the nearest gunsmith is now a long way from here and I will want to take pictures of the processes as the work proceeds. I hope you will have less trouble in this regard.

The gunsmithing process of rebarreling includes everything discussed in rechambering, as explained in the following sub-section. Also included can be the processes of drilling and tapping holes, cutting dovetail slots for sight bases or other fixtures and silver soldering attachments in place. While each of these jobs is possible using only more common hand tools, these are chores best left to the professional (especially where the barrel might be quite thin).

Any rebarreling operation includes crowning. When working with a high quality barrel, typically the gunsmith will offer either a flat target crown or a recessed target crown. The choice depends on what kind of use the rifle is apt to see. On a strictly target rifle, the flat target crown is the best, most accurate option. For a hunting rifle, which runs the risk of having the end of the barrel banged against anything, the recessed crown is a much better choice. The slight reduction in intrinsic accuracy is well compensated by the reduced risk of accuracy-destroying muzzle damage adjacent to the bore.

Barrel finishes include options of surface texture and protective coating chemistry. Those options you can discuss with your gunsmith. I am partial to a satin blued finish. This minimizes glare, provides superior resistance to wear-through and is just plain attractive — to my eye.

Alternately, consider the superior electroless plating and baked on finishes as provided by The ROBAR Companies, Phoenix, AZ. Electroless nickel or their NP3 (micro-Teflon impregnated electroless nickel) finishes are both durable and attractive. NP3 does present one minor problem for the gunsmith or home tinker. It is so slick that treated screws will not adhere to low-strength thread locking agent! Try Loctite #271.

Their ROGUARD is a baked on black polymer finish over parkerizing that provides a slick tough finish that beats any conventional bluing process in terms of durability and corrosion protection. These types of finishes are applicable to any metal gun part and are certainly worthy of consideration. We will visit this subject in greater detail in the sub-section on finishes.

Cutting dovetails and drilling and threading screw holes are both jobs that are theoretically possible without any sophisticated tools or equipment. However, to do these jobs right, the gunsmith will use a vertical mill and several special cutters and bits. Before any dovetails or screw holes are drilled the barrel has to be threaded, chambered, headspaced and installed to determine the correct indexing for the attachments.

Typically, dovetail slots are formed by first using a carbide cutter to produce a transverse slot of the proper depth (usually 0.100") across the barrel at the correct location. Then a special dovetail cutter is used to produce the undercut sides. Finally, the barrel is moved slightly endwise to lengthen the dovetail sufficiently to allow the necessary piece to enter with only a modest interference fit.

Similarly, the gunsmith will use the vertical mill to drill and tap any blank holes on the barrel. Here the process is very similar to how you would do it with a drill press. Only the drill bits (cutters) used will vary.

Now I want to move on to the discussion of rechambering, as this covers all the remaining areas involved in rebarreling a rifle.

Barrel Rechambering, Both Wildcats & SAAMI Specification Cartridges:

Any new barrel chambering or old barrel rechambering operation requires essentially the same steps. The gunsmith will sometimes alter the sequence slightly but the necessary steps are the same.

The gunsmith has to form square ends on the correctly contoured and cut-to-length barrel. As noted in the previous sub-section, the gunsmith also has to produce any threaded holes or dovetails required for barrel attached fixtures. Sometimes the barrel will have one or more flats milled out for clearance. The gunsmith will also crown the muzzle. The gunsmith has to turn down and thread the chamber end of the barrel, so it will properly fit the receiver. It also must have a concentric and square shoulder where the barrel abuts to the receiver. The gunsmith must form a chamber that is properly centered on the bore axis, is of the proper dimensions, has an adequately polished surface finish and is correctly aligned to the bore axis. Finally, the rear face of the barrel must include any necessary bolt relief cuts or other special machining, as required by the particular gun. Also, on many barrels the finish applied is of some importance. I will cover finishes later in *Part III*. See photograph # 19-7.

Typically, the gunsmith will chuck the barrel into the jaws of a lathe. It is best if he uses a four-jaw chuck. Unlike the typical three-jaw chuck, which tightens all jaws simultaneously (just like a common Jacob's chuck on an electric drill), the four-jaw chuck requires tightening of each jaw independently. For this reason, the four-jaw chuck also allows the gunsmith to precisely center one end of the barrel in the lathe.

For our example, we will consider a setup where the barrel passes through the head stock of the lathe. In this case, the gunsmith will place a bore guide (as available from JGS Precision Tool Mfg.) in each end of the barrel. The barrel's muzzle end passes through the head stock of the lathe with the big (chamber) end exposed inside the rails of the lathe.

He will affix the chamber end in the chuck by tightening the jaws. This serves to center the chamber end of the barrel on the lathe's axis of rotation and to lock it to the rotation of the head stock. The barrel's muzzle end will be affixed at the other end of the head stock with a special "spider" device. This piece serves only to center the barrel's muzzle end to the lathe's rotation axis.

The bore guides are precise tools that enter the bore of the barrel. Owing to precise fit, these

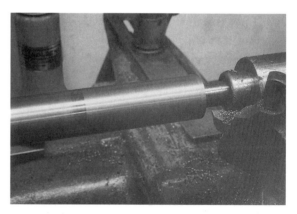

Photograph 19-7: Here Mr. Constantine has turned the final few inches of the barrel to proper diameter, the lathe is now set to produce a square end on the barrel. However, in this application, that is not necessary. The chamber end, shown here, will require extensive modifications for application on a Marlin Model-1895 rifle.

Section 19: Gunsmith Specific Alterations, Part III

center on and align to the bore axis. By affixing dial indicators to magnetic bases attached to the headwork of the lathe, it is possible to use these guides to center the bore axis of the barrel very precisely to the rotation axis of the lathe.

This centering and alignment is an essential first step in forming a square shoulder and properly centered threads on the chamber end of the barrel. Depending upon the type of tool used to hold the reamer, this critical alignment is more-or-less essential to achieving a properly centered and aligned chamber. However, regardless of the precise system used, it is impossible to have the barrel too accurately centered in the lathe. Precision pays.

Once the barrel is properly affixed in the lathe, the gunsmith will usually produce the receiver threads first. This involves the following steps. First, he will face off the chamber end of the barrel, to insure that it is "perfectly" square to the bore. Second, he will turn-down a section of barrel at the chamber end. He will make this equal in diameter to the outside of the needed threads. He will make the length equal to the needed thread length. He might also include a relief chamfer at the shoulder end of this section. He would reduce this chamfer to slightly smaller than the small diameter of the receiver threads. See photograph # 19-8.

Finally, he would produce threads of the proper pitch (threads per inch or per millimeter), shape, width and depth, onto the turned-down shank. He will finish the threading with a final polish using a smooth cut file to remove the "fuzz" (tiny burrs) followed by a thorough sanding with 800 grit sandpaper. Usually, the gunsmith will thread the receiver onto the barrel to verify that all is well with the threads. See photograph # 19-9.

If the barrel requires extractor cuts or other attachment, he might choose to make marks for those at this time. To do so, he will have to assume some specific amount of preloading during barrel tightening. Note that my opinion is that no barrel should be any tighter than is necessary to prevent it from coming loose on its own

Photograph 19-9: Here Mr. Constantine has finished the threads and turned the inside diameter of the portion that will become the partial hood, as shown on the original Marlin Model-1895 barrel, left. There is still a long way to go at this point. A partial list: indexing the barrel to the receiver, cutting away the extraneous hood and shaping the remaining portion, cutting the extractor slot, chambering with correct headspace, forming a flat side on the bottom (to accommodate the tubular magazine), cutting and fitting three dovetails (front sight, fore-end hanger and magazine tube hanger).

Photograph 19-8: Here Mr. Constantine has made two passes in the production of the square threads on this Krieger barrel that is destined for installation on a Marlin Model-1895, .45-70 Government chambered rifle. He has already turned the correct length of the end of the barrel to the correct major diameter for the barrel threads. Note the Dykem paint used for photographic clarity. Here we are using a modified cutter from Brownells. It was made to cut ten pitch threads, Marlin uses twelve pitch. Therefore, we had to thin the blade about 9/1000".

or pushing away from the receiver during the stress of firing. A quick calculation suggests that a preload of only about one-thousandth of an inch (0.001") on the abutment shoulder is certainly sufficient to prevent those problems.

Once the threads are properly formed, the next step is to cut the chamber. Here things get a little tense. You have an expensive barrel with considerable gunsmithing time already invested. If the chamber is cut off-center or too deep into the barrel . . . trouble.

One method of providing for a centered reamer is to use the self-centering reamer holder, as offered by Brownells. Opinions vary wildly. Some argue that if the barrel is properly centered in the lathe, the only correct method is to properly center the reamer and lock it in place. Generally, you will just have to trust your gunsmith here. See photograph # 19-10.

Whatever method he uses will involve locking the reamer against rotation and providing a means of pushing it into the chamber. During this cutting operation the gunsmith will use plenty of oil and he should clean the chamber and reamer of cuttings quite often. He should cut a spell, then pull the reamer and run several clean cotton swabs from the muzzle end and out the chamber end before continuing.

When the chamber gets close to the proper depth, he will have to start taking measurements for headspace. There are myriad good methods. One involves measuring the distance from the receiver's barrel shoulder to the bolt face and using that to back calculate the correct distance for the "GO" gauge to protrude from the chamber. The GO gauge indicates the minimum depth that the chamber can be cut to and still provide chambering for any SAAMI cartridge. Often, the gunsmith will get the chamber close with this gauging method and will then assemble the rifle and see if the bolt will close on the GO gauge. If not, an experienced gunsmith can usually tell how much deeper he will need to cut the chamber. If he has set things up right in the lathe he can do this entire operation without removing the barrel from the head stock or the reamer from the tail stock.

When the chamber is properly cut, the barrel is turned, end-for-end in the lathe. It is again properly centered. If necessary, the muzzle end is cut off to achieve the desired length. Finally, the crown is produced. Any additional work, such as milling dovetails or drilling and tapping holes is then done, as necessary, to complete the metalwork. See photograph #s 19-11 through 19-15.

Availability Of Custom Wood & Synthetic Stocks, For All Rifles:

In several places throughout this text, I have discussed modifications to the factory wood. Here I want to point out that several custom stocking options are available. There are two main choices for those working with typical

Photograph 19-10: This is one method of chambering. Here the gunsmith (at McBros Rifle Company) is using a steady rest to center the barrel. Note the reamer and cuttings. There are several methods of aligning the barrel and reamer, your gunsmith will probably have a favorite. All methods share one tenet: they require skillful setup and operation to produce superior results.

Photograph 19-11: Cutting a dovetail slot requires several steps. Here Mr. Constantine has set up the end mill and is leveling the barrel in the vise. We are preparing to cut the initial channel side-to-side across the barrel (front sight installation). This square-ended cutter is set to just touch the top of the barrel as we move the table back. We will make several passes until we have formed a groove that is 1/10" deep.

Section 19: Gunsmith Specific Alterations, Part III

Photograph 19-12: Here Mr. Constantine has made several passes across the barrel. Note the lead strap used to isolate the barrel from the vise jaws. The chamber end of the barrel is similarly supported. This prevents marring of the barrel's surface while allowing sufficient tightening in the vise to produce enough friction to lock the barrel solidly in place.

Photograph 19-13: Here we have finished the preliminary, square-sided slot across the barrel. Note the Dykem paint. This was used to make it easier to determine when the cutter had just touched the barrel. Knowing the table's vertical positioning when the cutter first touched, as it crossed over the top of the barrel, allowed Mr. Constantine to index the calibrated vertical adjustment wheel — one revolution produces the desired 1/10" inch lift of the table.

Photograph 19-14: After replacing the square-ended cutter with this standard sight-base dovetail cutter (there are several types and sizes of dovetail cutters), Mr. Constantine adjusted the table to the correct height. Then, with the application of plenty of cutting oil, he slowly advanced the cutter through the, just-finished, slot (by moving the table back). Since the cutter was working on a large and interrupted surface and because this barrel is 4140 steel, he had to advance the work very slowly to avoid chattering.

Photograph 19-15: Closer view of the almost finished dovetail. All that remains is to lengthen the slot — that is, make it longer endwise in the barrel. The standard cutter is not designed to cut the slot at full width — not all dovetail fixtures are built with precisely the same base dimensions; making the cutter too thin allows the machinist to precisely fit the slot to the fixture.

bolt-action rifles — wood or synthetic. Those working with non-bolt-action rifles are usually limited to custom wood stocks although there are a few manufacturers offering synthetic stocks for the more popular of these rifles — the Winchester, Model-94, for example. Companies such as Ramline and McMillan come to mind. See photograph #s 19-16/17.

The low-end synthetic stocks and some wood stocks are sold as essentially drop-in installations. However, owing to wide variations in receiver dimensions and the problem of caliber-dependent barrel diameters, drop-in stocks are not necessarily a good idea. Finding such a stock that properly fits a particular rifle is slightly haphazard. Conversely, consider the semi-inletted or custom-fitted stocks, as offered by McMillan.

McMillan and most other high-end synthetic stock manufacturers produce stocks only for bolt-action rifles. Consider the products and services McMillan Fiberglass Stocks, Inc. offers. Simply send them a barreled-action from almost any bolt-action rifle and specify which stock type, stock weight, weight distribution, drop, length of pull, finish and recoil pad you want installed. Within reasonable limits, they will "custom" fit and glass bed your barreled-action to one of their premium synthetic stocks, which come in myriad configurations.

If you want a featherweight camouflaged stock for a mountain rifle, they can provide that.

Photograph 19-16: These McMillan fiberglass stocks are at ROBAR for fitting and finishing. ROBAR is in the process of applying their proprietary backed-on polymer. These stocks and this finish represent the culmination of the art of perfecting the synthetic stock.

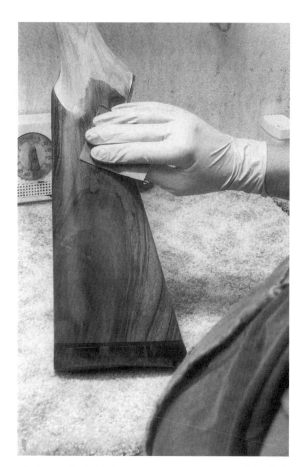

Photograph 19-17: Here an employee of Dakota Arms has applied the first coating of an oil-based finish to this fine piece of walnut. The finished product will assemble onto someone's custom ordered and highly prized hunting rifle. This author never ceases to be amazed by the beauty in the grain structure of fine wood. However, this is only one aspect of a custom stock. As with the synthetic stocks, the custom wood stock (as available through Fajen) allows the shooter to precisely fit his rifle to his body, shooting style and special needs.

Section 19: Gunsmith Specific Alterations, Part III

Their lightest stock is a good many ounces lighter than the lightest conventional wood stock. It is also much, much stronger than the strongest wood stock. If that were not enough, it will also reduce felt recoil because the butt portion of the stock compresses during recoil, acting like a sophisticated shock absorber!

Conversely, if you want a 25# stock that is painted bright red-and-white tartan (or almost any other color or pattern) to put under your long-range varmint special, McMillan can do that, too. If your stocking needs are a little unusual, McMillan can probably satisfy your desires. Options in their standard line include: thumbhole, Fibergrain® (a beautiful replica wood grain), checkered, patterned, adjustable cheek pieces and butt attachments. Also note, other custom synthetic stock manufacturers offer similar services.

Reinhart Fajen[2], on the other hand, specializes in conventional and laminated wood stocks. They are now offering a cartridge trap in the lower rear of the butt and several stock designs in highly skeletonized thumbhole configurations. Another interesting innovation from Fajen is the ventilated fore-end channel. This barrel cooling adaptation is no small consideration for the varmint hunter.

Like McMillan, Fajen can provide many custom alterations on the basic theme. If you will deliver your warm body and the rifle you want to install a custom stock on to their facilities, they will take measurements and precisely fit the rifle to you! That, my friends, is no small thing. I have tried to point out in other places in this text the value of a properly fitting rifle. That, I cannot over-emphasize.

A properly fitting rifle can add dramatically to your ability to get on target fast and place a shot where you want it to go. If you want a rifle that fits like a glove, I can offer no better solution than to have the experts at Fajen measure you and your gun, to produce a stock that is precisely correct for you.

In the same manner, any qualified gunsmith can take a semi-inletted Fajen stock (of the proper design) and fit it to your rifle and to you. In addition to all of the standard items — drop at heal, drop at comb, length of pull, cheek piece configuration, etc. — this custom fitting involves several other issues: type of finish applied; where sling or bipod attachments are located; pattern, size and coverage of checkering; type of recoil pad installed. Further, particularly important for those with special physiological needs, a custom-fit wood stock can include alterations of the butt location left-to-right and adjustments of the butt, to rotate its vertical axis to that of the action. Within reasonable limits, there is no end to the touches that can be applied. If it makes the gun easier for you to mount and shoot, it might very well be worthwhile.

I cannot over-emphasize the value of proper fit; consider this tale of woe. Several years ago, the last time I hunted deer in Colorado, I lost the chance to take a very good mule deer buck. Why? Because the padded strap on the back pack I was wearing got in the way. I could not mount the too-long-in-the-buttstock rifle and see through the scope. By the time I got the back pack off, the fast moving buck was out of reasonable range.

I had mounted a recoil pad on that rifle without shortening the stock. When I was wearing normal attire it worked fine. However, with the combination of a heavy coat and that padded strap, it was hopeless. I learned a valuable lesson. Just because you <u>can</u> use it does not suggest that it fits properly. Take the time to assure yourself that the stock on your rifle fits you properly. One final word here, as noted in the lever-action sub-sections, a too-short stock is much less of a handicap than a too-long stock.

Metal Surface Refinishing:

Here there are precisely two alternatives: home remedies and professional finishes (which include both chemical alterations and plating processes). First, consider the home remedies. Cold bluing for steel, anodizing for aluminum and blacking for brass come to mind. Birchwood Casey and Brownells sell several products for these applications. In my opinion, these are all useful products but they are products that are best restricted for use in repairing scars on similarly finished pieces, rather than finishing entire parts.

I would not say that it is impossible to achieve a good finish using these products. With the brass black you can usually do an acceptable job. However, my experience with the aluminum anodizing products suggest that achieving a high-quality finish is very, very difficult. Similarly, the cold bluing products are tough to work with when covering large areas of any typical steel.

---

[2] Editor: Regrettably, the Fajen company has gone out of business since this was written.

Another problem for the home application of chemical finishes is that the surface preparation of the steel is critical to the finish achieved. The gunsmith will have the tools necessary to prepare the entire surface to a sufficiently consistent texture so that the finished surface will look the same everywhere.

My gunsmith, Art Branscomb, recently finished a barrel for me. First, he bead-blasted my thirty-year-old barrel using 240 grit aluminum oxide. Then he power-brushed it using a soft wire wheel. He then finished it in a standard caustic hot blue. The lettering on the barrel is as sharp as the day it was stamped, the finish looks as if it is a mile deep and the sheen is simply perfect for installation on a receiver that is finished with a matte gray electroless nickel/Teflon surface (ROBAR's NP3).

I could never have done that job at home. This is a typical example. If you want a beautiful finish, you will have to have an expert apply it.

Besides the traditional bluing, there are several quite useful, attractive and highly functional finishes on the market today. For plating, I have to recommend the electroless processes. Companies such as ROBAR (Phoenix, AZ) can apply any of several finishes to steel or aluminum. Further, ROBAR offers an extremely durable baked-on polymer finish for metal parts and a matching low-temperature polymer finish for synthetic stocks. They can also fully camouflage the rifle so that you will have trouble seeing where the wood or fiberglass ends and the barreled-action begins. See photograph #s 19-18/19/20.

Photograph 19-18: Custom metal finishing is no small-time operation. In this view we can see only part of the main room at The ROBAR Companies, Inc. In this area, customer's guns are torn down, individual parts are identified with the job number, and minor repairs are made. After the plating or coating operations are completed, those parts are then reassembled and preliminary tested here. Other operations done in this area include machine engraving. At the other end of this room (behind the camera) is the heavy equipment (lathes, mills and grinders) needed in any custom gun manufacturing plant. ROBAR has two other rooms of similar size and complexity. The point is, custom metal finishing requires much special equipment. If you want a superior job of plating done, hire a professional metal finisher to do it. Conversely, for simple surface treatments, such as bluing, a gunsmith only has to have a few pieces of special equipment.

Photograph 19-19: Here an employee at The ROBAR Companies, Inc. prepares a small part for electroless nickel plating. ROBAR can vary the surface texture of the finished part by using different media in the sand blasting machine (and by applying other techniques, such as buffing or wire brushing, etc.). "Sand" blasting and an acid bath are always included in part preparation because electroless plating relies, among other things, upon having an immaculately clean working surface on the substrate.

When used on steel, the polymer finishes are applied over a parkerized finish so that the inevitable interruptions in the polymer finish do not significantly compromise corrosion resistance. Further, their polymer finish, known as ROGUARD, provides a dramatic reduction in friction for moving parts. See photograph # 19-21.

However, I prefer the electroless-nickel options ROBAR offers. First is the standard nickel finish. This can be applied over any type of surface texture on either steel or aluminum. For those with a Remington BDL rifle, this is a particularly attractive and effective method of solving the (very commonly seen) ugly, scarred floorplate syndrome. Have ROBAR apply their electroless nickel to both the floorplate and the bolt. The parts will match perfectly. The hard nickel will last for a long, long time and if it does wear through or become scarred, the blemish will be difficult to see against the aluminum or steel background. Further, it is easily repaired by another trip to ROBAR.

ROBAR's NP3 is an exciting electroless plating that incorporates microscopic spheroids of Polytetrafluoroethylene (PTFE, brand name Teflon™) that are encapsulated in a nickel matrix. Like any properly applied electroless metallic plating, this surface is essentially welded to the substrate. It cannot peel away from the steel. This surface is very slick, <u>extremely</u> corrosion resistant and has a beautiful matte gray color. If applied over a bead-blasted and power-brushed surface, it provides a most attractive finish that will last many times longer than any blued finish. (Note that low-strength thread locking agents will not adhere to NP3, try Loctite #271.) See photograph #s 19-22 through 19-26.

Any one of these ROBAR finishes (ROGUARD, baked-on polymer; Electroless Nickel; Electroless Nickel with PTFE) will provide a degree of corrosion protection that is unmatched by any conventional finish. I can highly recommend any one of these for any rifle that is likely to see use under very adverse conditions or for those who live in the most humid areas of the country or where salty air is a problem.

Photograph 19-20: It does not look like much but this room is the heart of The ROBAR Companies, Inc. operations. Here, in these dozens of vats, metal preparation and plating is carried out with any of several processes. What you do not see is quite critical here ... there are no electrodes involved. Electroless plating relies upon delicate control of pH and temperature to drive the plating process. The difference in this process and electrically driven plating is akin to the difference between latex paint <u>on</u> the surface of wood and oil finish <u>in</u> the surface of wood. Technically, electroless plating results in a surface that is essentially welded to the substrate, it cannot peel or chip away.

Photograph 19-21: A comparison of ROBAR's ROGUARD baked-on polymer finish (top) with a traditional, albeit well done, chemical bluing (bottom). The ROGUARD is applied over a parkerized surface — even when this surprisingly tough polymer is compromised, the surface is still protected from corrosion. This surface is longer lasting than any blued surface could ever be and provides a pleasing matte surface that is slick and easy to clean. Nevertheless, no polymer finish can compare to the richness of a well-executed blued steel finish, as applied by my friend Art Branscomb.

One thing I have not mentioned in this regard is lubrication. Each of these plated-on surfaces is sufficiently slick that is it strictly unnecessary to lubricate plated parts with anything for any reason! While lubrication might further reduce part-to-part friction, it will also increase abrasion potential, since it gives grit a chance to stick. For a serious hunting rifle, a clean dry action is always the best bet. With application of these platings, you can keep your action parts clean and dry without any concern about corrosion, undue friction or contact galling. Who could ask for anything more? See photograph # 19-27.

Photograph 19-22: This Marlin Model-1895 (.45-70 Government) has been modified by the addition of a receiver-mounted aperture sight and special metal finishing. The receiver, finger-lever, barrel and magazine tube are finished with ROBAR's super-durable and protective, baked-on polymer finish (ROGUARD). The loading gate, screws and almost all other steel parts are finished with ROBAR's electroless NP3 process (nickel that is micro-impregnated with Teflon™). Note that screws treated with NP3 require application of a high-strength thread locker (Loctite #271) — low-strength products will not adhere.

Photograph 19-24: An excellent application for ROBAR's NP3 electroless plating (see associated text and photographs). This Remington Model-700 has been treated to NP3 on the floorplate and bolt assemblies. Note that the aluminum and steel surfaces are now indistinguishable. This solves the "worn through the finish" uglies on the Remington floorplate. At the same time the appearance of these action parts match. As a bonus, the bolt is 30% easier to cycle and lubricant is not needed!

Photograph 19-23: My wife's highly customized Model-1894 Marlin (.44 Magnum) has been treated to NP3 (see photograph 19-22 and text) on the internal action part, screws, finger-lever and barrel attachments. This extra durable finish eliminates the need to lubricate anything and produces a much slicker working action. This rifle weighs $4\,^3/_4$ pounds, complete with a thick Pachmayr Decelerator recoil pad and the Williams receiver-mounted aperture sight. Despite its light weight, this rifle will produce one-hole 50-yard groups using almost any good ammunition. It is particularly happy with heavy cast bullet loads or Speer's 270 grain Gold Dot loading.

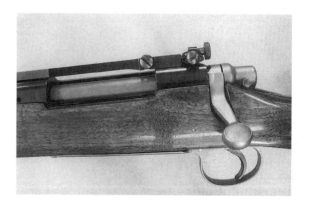

Photograph 19-25: Different view of the rifle shown in photograph 19-24. Note the pleasing matte finish on the bolt body and other parts. This rifle is now the slickest working Remington I have ever handled. If the NP3 finish should ever wear through, on either the bolt or the floorplate, that fact will not be obvious and ROBAR can readily refinish the worn part anyway! See text.

Section 19: Gunsmith Specific Alterations, Part III

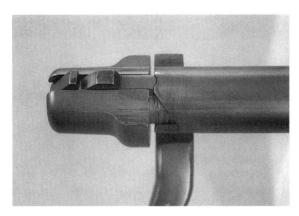

Photograph 19-26: Here is a close-up view of the cocking ramp on the Remington Model-700 bolt that has been electroless plated with NP3 (see text). Application of this tough and durable plating dramatically reduced cocking force on this already highly polished rifle.

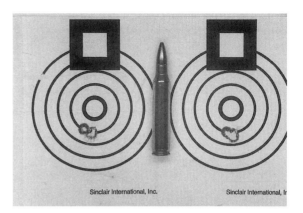

Photograph 19-27: These five-shot, 100-yard groups, fired by Dr. Richard Maretzo (President of Precision Shooting Inc.) demonstrate what a well-tuned rifle can do. In this instance, the ammunition was Black Hills remanufactured, .223 Remington using molybdenum-disulfide plated bullets. Black Hills Ammunition has a license agreement with NECO for use of the incomparable NECO-Coat™ plating process.